# THE WILEY SERIES IN RISK AND INSURANCE

Oscar N. Serbein, Editor
Stanford University, Stanford, California

ELLIOTT and VAUGHAN
Fundamentals of Risk and Insurance

HESTER and TOBIN
Risk Aversion and Portfolio Choice
(Cowles Commission Monograph No. 19)

SEAL
Stochastic Theory of a Risk Business
(Published in the Wiley Series in Probability and Mathematical Statistics)

# FUNDAMENTALS
# OF RISK
# AND INSURANCE

# FUNDAMENTALS

# OF RISK

# AND INSURANCE

the late
CURTIS M. ELLIOTT
Department of Economics
University of Nebraska

EMMETT J. VAUGHAN
Department of Business Administration
University of Iowa

JOHN WILEY & SONS, INC.
New York    London    Sydney    Toronto

Library of Congress Catalog Card Number: 70-37437
ISBN 0-471-90350-7

Printed in the United States of America.

10 9 8 7 6 5 4

The writing of any book is a difficult task. Writing a book on the subject of insurance is particularly troublesome, for the field of insurance is marked by constant change, and it is often difficult to know when the book is finished. To my direct beneficiary, Connie, who told me when this book was finished, and to my contingent beneficiaries, Therese, Emmett Jr., Timothy, Mary Susan, Joan, Tom, and Michael, who brought me to the point where I agreed with her, this book is dedicated.

# Preface

This text is designed for use in a college level survey of the area of risk and insurance. As an introduction to the subject, it is intended for students who have had little or no prior education in insurance. It may serve as the basis for more advanced texts for those students who intend to specialize in the field of insurance, and at the same time it constitutes a self-contained survey of the field for those who do not intend to do further work in the area.

The intent from the beginning has been to create a text that is consumer-oriented. The main emphasis is on the insurance product and the use of insurance within the risk management framework. The traditional fields of life insurance, health insurance, property and liability insurance, and social insurance are treated in terms of their relationship to the wide range of insurable risks to which the individual and the business firm are exposed. Although many texts in use in colleges today intentionally avoid detailed analysis of insurance contracts, several of the chapters in this book concentrate on the analysis of specific policy provisions, because in our estimation we can best emphasize the relationships and principles involved in insurance by studying their application in selected insurance contracts.

We have attempted to compose what we consider to be a logical sequence of subject matter. The book is divided into three major sections. In the first section we examine the concept of risk, the nature of the insurance device, the principles of risk management, and we provide a general overview of the insurance industry and the manner in which it operates.

The second section deals with the traditional fields of life and health insurance as solutions to the risks connected with the loss of income. The social security system is also discussed in this section to permit a discussion of social security benefits in income protection planning.

The final section of the book deals with the risks connected with the ownership of property and legal liability. Here the book departs somewhat from the traditional organization in which the various property and liability fields are studied line by line. In an attempt to focus on the consumer, we have divided the property and liability coverages according to buying units. Those coverages applicable to the individual or family are treated in separate chapters from those designed for the business firm. This approach follows the multiple-line trend in the industry, and will also permit instructors who may prefer to do so to concentrate on the coverages for the individual and give only slight treatment to the commercial coverages.

Many persons have rendered valuable assistance in the preparation of this book. Richard C. Allgood, CPCU, worked closely with Dr. Elliott in editing early drafts of the manuscript. My colleague at the University of Iowa, Professor Michael L. Murray offered valuable suggestions and helped to clarify many of the concepts herein. Special thanks goes to Professor Oscar N. Serbein, whose editorial effort went far beyond the call of duty. His many comments and suggestions have helped to eliminate errors that would otherwise have existed. Finally, a special thanks to the secretaries of the College of Business Administration at the University of Iowa, who performed the tedious task of typing and retyping the manuscript.

Plato wrote that "the beginning is the most important part of the work." This book was begun by Dr. Curtis M. Elliott several years before his death. At the time of his death, he had completed substantial portions of the manuscript. Completing the work so well begun by Dr. Elliott has been a satisfying experience. "Doc" Elliott was my teacher in the field of insurance. He was also my friend. Insofar as I am a product of his teaching, this book is, in a very direct sense, his work. However, I alone am responsible for the contents of the book, including all errors and omissions.

Iowa City, Iowa                                                    EMMETT J. VAUGHAN
February 1972

# Contents

# Appendices                                                   617

# Section I

# RISK
# AND
# INSURANCE

# 1 The Conceptual Framework

*"When I use a word," Humpty Dumpty said, in a rather scornful tone, "it means just what I choose it to mean—neither more nor less."*

*"The question is," said Alice, "whether you can make words mean so many different things."*

*"The question is," said Humpty Dumpty, "which is to be master, that's all."*
—Lewis Carroll, *Through the Looking Glass*

Every field of knowledge has its own specialized terminology, and terms which have very simple meanings in everyday usage often take on different and complicated connotations when applied in a specialized field. In this chapter we will examine a number of basic concepts used in the study of insurance. In particular, we will concern ourselves with the concept of risk, for risk is the basic problem with which insurance deals.

## THE CONCEPT OF RISK

It would seem on the surface that the term "risk" is a simple enough notion. When someone states that there is risk in a given situation, the listener understands what is meant: that in the given situation there is uncertainty about the outcome, and that the possibility exists that the outcome will be unfavorable. This loose intuitive notion of risk, which implies a lack of knowledge

**3**

about the future and the possibility of some adverse outcome, is satisfactory for conversational usage, but for our purpose a somewhat more rigid definition is desirable.

Economists, statisticians, decision theorists, and insurance theorists have long discussed the concepts of "risk" and "uncertainty" in an attempt to find a definition of risk that might be useful for analysis in each field of investigation. At the present time, they have not been able to agree on a definition that can be used in each field with the same facility; nor does it appear likely that they will do so in the near future. A definition of risk that is suitable for the economist or statistician may very well be worthless as an analytic tool for the insurance theorist. The fact that each group treats a different body of subject matter requires the use of different concepts, and although the statistician, the decision theorist, and the insurance theorist all use the term "risk," they may each mean something entirely different.

Insurance is still in its infancy as a body of theory. As a result, we find many contradictory definitions of risk throughout the literature dealing with this phenomenon from an insurance point of view. One reason for these contradictions is the fact that insurance theorists have attempted to borrow the definitions of risk used in other fields. Surprising as it may seem, insurance text writers have not been able to agree on a definition of risk.

To compound the problem, the term risk is used by people in the insurance business to mean either a peril insured against (e.g., fire is a *risk* to which most property is exposed), or a person or property protected by insurance (e.g., many insurance companies feel that young drivers are not good *risks*). From time to time in this text we may use the term risk in one of the two ways insurance practitioners use it, but for the most part the term risk will be used in the abstract to indicate a situation where an exposure to loss exists.

## CURRENT DEFINITIONS OF RISK

If we were to survey the best-known insurance text books used in colleges and universities today, we would find a general lack of agreement concerning the definition of risk. In general, we would find the term defined in one of the following ways:

1. Risk is the chance of loss.
2. Risk is the possibility of loss.
3. Risk is uncertainty.
4. Risk is the dispersion of actual from expected results.
5. Risk is the probability of any outcome different from the one expected.

Now, if each definition means approximately the same thing, then there is no real problem. If, on the other hand, each has a different connotation, we must come to a decision as to which is preferable, and which, if any, is suitable for our purposes.

### Risk Is the Chance of Loss

Many writers define risk as the "chance of loss." What exactly is meant by this term? Webster defines "chance" in two ways: as "a possibility or likelihood of something happening" and as ". . . a degree of probability." One defect in the definition of risk as the "chance of loss" is that we cannot always be certain which of these two meanings is intended. Chance of loss may be used to indicate a state where there is an exposure to or a possibility of loss. This meaning seems to square with our intuitive notion of risk. On the other hand, "chance of loss" is often used to indicate a degree of probability in a given situation, and many writers reject the definition of risk as the "chance of loss" because of the possible connotation of probability.

When used to indicate a degree of probability, the "chance of loss" is most frequently expressed as a percentage or a fraction. In this context the chance of loss is simply the probability of loss. If I agree to pay you $1 if you cut a red card from a normal deck, the chance of loss is 1/2 or 0.5. If the wager is that you will cut a spade, my chance of loss is 1/4 and your chance of loss is 3/4. If you are willing to wager that you can cut the ace of spades, my chance of loss is 1/52, while your chance of loss is 51/52.

Those writers who reject the definition of risk as "the chance of loss" insist that a distinction must be made between risk and the "chance of loss." They argue that if "risk" and "chance of loss" mean the same thing, the degree of risk and the degree of probability should always be the same. Yet when the chance of loss (defined as the probability of loss) is 100%, the loss is certain and there is no risk. Risk always has the implication that the outcome is somehow in question. When the chance of loss (again defined as a probability) is either 100% or zero, the degree of risk is zero.

In spite of the fuzziness and the possible dual meaning of the term "chance of loss," many writers find this definition perfectly acceptable. The definition is logically consistent as long as we specify that it is Webster's "possibility or likelihood of something happening" and not "a degree of probability" that is meant by "chance of loss."

### Risk Is the Possibility of Loss

Another way of defining risk is to say that it is simply the possibility of loss. This is merely a variation of the "chance of loss" definition which seeks to avoid the ambiguity inherent in that definition. Note that when we define risk as the possibility of loss, no attention is given to the probability as long as it is not zero or one. The term "possibility" means that the probability of the event is between zero and one, and the very notion of risk implies that the outcome is in question. This definition probably comes the closest to the notion of risk used in everyday conversation. However, it is a rather loose definition, and does not lend itself to quantitative analysis.

### Risk Is Uncertainty

There seems to be general agreement that risk and uncertainty are somehow related. Some writers have carried this relationship to its ultimate degree and maintain that risk *is* uncertainty. Unfortunately, like the term "chance of loss," the term "uncertainty" is ambiguous; it has several possible meanings, and it is not always immediately obvious which of these is intended.

The first scholarly treatment of the area of risk in relation to insurance was *The Economic Theory of Risk and Insurance* by Alan H. Willett, originally published in 1901. Willett recognized that risk is commonly used in an ambiguous manner and sought to construct a somewhat more rigid definition. As the passage below indicates, he arrived at the conclusion that the uncertainties of the world are an illusion based on man's imperfect knowledge.

> We are told by the philosophers that all the activities of the universe are obedient to law. Nowhere have they left any opportunity for the intrusion of chance. Events which appear to take place in a purely accidental way are just as much determined as those whose occurrence can be accurately foretold. The appearance of accident is due entirely to human limitations. It is because we do not know all the previous conditions or all the laws governing them that a particular phenomenon appears to us to occur by chance. In this sense then, chance is purely subjective; it is merely an appearance resulting from the imperfection of man's knowledge and not a part of the course of external nature.
>
> . . . The word risk, as it is employed in common speech, is by no means free from ambiguity. It is sometimes used in a subjective sense to denote the act of taking a chance, but more commonly and preferably in an objective sense to denote some condition of the external world. To avoid ambiguity its use in the following pages will be confined to this latter sense.
>
> . . . it seems necessary to define risk with reference to the degree of uncertainty about the occurrence of a loss, and not with reference to the degree of probability that it will occur. Risk in this sense is the objective correlative of the subjective uncertainty. It is the uncertainty considered as embodied in the course of events in the external world, of which the subjective uncertainty is a more or less faithful interpretation.[1]

[1] Alan H. Willett, *The Economic Theory of Risk and Insurance* (Philadelphia: University of Pennsylvania Press, 1951), pp. 3, 5, 6.

These passages provide an example of the first of several meanings of "uncertainty." Here it is used in the sense of objectified uncertainty or indeterminancy as it appears to be embodied in the real world. We say "as it appears to be embodied . . ." because uncertainty does not exist in nature, but is merely an illusion created by man's imperfect knowledge. The weather report reads: "Rain is probable tomorrow." The word "probable" denotes uncertainty, but who or what is it that is uncertain? Is it nature that is in a state of vacillation, not being able to make up its mind, or is it the weatherman? Given such and such conditions, rain tomorrow is certain. Given other conditions, it is impossible. There is nothing doubtful or uncertain in nature, and we must attribute the uncertainty in the statement that "rain is probable tomorrow" to the imperfection of the weatherman's knowledge.

Events that appear to take place on a random basis are just as much determined as those that we know to be determined, but because of our lack of knowledge, we cannot predict their occurrence. However, the fact that these events are determined is really of little consequence if our best efforts do not permit us to predict the outcome. Objectified uncertainty exists when it appears to us that an event may or may not happen; in this sense it is contrasted with objectified certainty (where the probability of the event is one) and with impossibility (where the probability of the event is zero). Thus we may speak of an event that is certain to occur (no risk), an event that is impossible (no risk), or an uncertain event (risk may exist). If we define risk as "uncertainty," meaning this apparent indeterminancy, it would seem that there is little difference between this definition and the definition of risk as the "possibility of loss."

The second possible meaning of "uncertainty," which is somewhat related to the first, is that which has a psychological connotation and refers to a state of mind characterized by doubt or by a conscious lack of knowledge about the outcome of an event. We will call this "subjective uncertainty" to contrast it with the "objectified uncertainty" discussed above. In many instances where insurance writers have used uncertainty as their definition of risk, they have referred to this psychological phenomenon:

> For our purposes, we shall define risk as uncertainty of loss. As such it is a psychological phenomenon that is meaningful only in terms of human reactions and experiences.[2]

Advocates of this position maintain that there is a relationship between our subjective feelings or belief and objective reality, or that there is a close cor-

[2] Herbert S. Denenberg, Robert D. Eilers, G. Wright Hoffman, Chester A. Kline, Joseph J. Melone, and H. Wayne Snider, *Risk and Insurance* (Englewood Cliffs, N.J.: Prentice-Hall, 1964), p. 4.

respondence between the facts and our awareness of them. In this they follow Willett and his statement that subjective uncertainty is a "more or less faithful interpretation" of the uncertainty embodied in the course of events in the external world.

Subjective uncertainty, then, is the individual's evaluation of the objective risk situation. It is a psychological factor in the true sense of the term. It is based on the knowledge and attitudes of the person viewing the situation, and different subjective uncertainties are possible for different individuals under identical circumstances of the external world. According to the subjective uncertainty definition of risk, risk fluctuates with the state of mind of the individual subject to that risk. To illustrate: Two individuals may be exposed to the same possibility of loss, and yet one may be unaware of the existence of the possibility. For the individual who does not recognize the existence of the possibility, there is no subjective uncertainty and therefore no risk. According to this definition, there is no risk for a small child playing with an electrical outlet, for the possibility of an unfavorable outcome is not perceived. On the other hand, according to this definition, if the individual is uncertain about the outcome of a given situation and feels that the outcome may be unfavorable, risk exists for him, regardless of the actual probability of loss. Those who define risk as "subjective uncertainty" would maintain that Columbus "risked" falling off the edge of the world because there was subjective uncertainty about the outcome. While common usage does not necessarily make a definition preferable, it would seem that in seeking a definition we should attempt to find one that does not run contrary to the intuitive concept of the term. It seems rather uncomfortable to state that risk must be perceived in order to exist, or that a loss exposure that is not perceived does not involve risk.

A contribution of major significance in the area of risk theory as it relates to insurance was provided by Irving Pfeffer in his *Insurance and Economic Theory*, for Pfeffer draws a distinction between risk and uncertainty. According to Pfeffer, "uncertainty is a state of mind relative to a specific fact situation." On the other hand:

> Risk is a combination of hazards and is measured by probability. Uncertainty is measured by degree of belief. Risk is a state of the real world; uncertainty is a state of mind.[3]

Pfeffer's contention that risk is a state of the real world and uncertainty is a state of mind seems to coincide with the intuitive concept of risk. More than any other writer, Pfeffer focused on the contradiction inherent in defining risk as uncertainty.

---

[3] Irving Pfeffer, *Insurance and Economic Theory* (Homewood, Ill.: Richard D. Irwin, 1956), p. 42.

A final meaning of uncertainty is that used in decision theory, based on Frank Knight's distinction between measurable and unmeasurable uncertainties. Knight points out that the outcomes of some types of events are calculable, while those of other types of events are not. If there are sufficient statistical data available, we should be able to calculate the statistical probability of the occurrence of an event. Since our predictions will not always be completely accurate, there will be uncertainty surrounding the prediction, and Knight calls this uncertainty "risk." Knight makes his distinction between risk and uncertainty in the following passage:

> To preserve the distinction . . . between the measurable uncertainty and the unmeasurable one, we may use the term "risk" to designate the former and the term "uncertainty" for the latter.[4]

In decision theory, uncertainty is a condition where the decision maker is unable to assign any objective probabilities to the possible outcome of the event. In this sense, uncertainty is to be contrasted with certainty, where the decision maker can assign a probability of either zero or one, and with the decision theorist's notion of risk, in which the decision maker assumes that he can assign a probability to the outcome somewhere between zero and one. This is precisely the same as Knight's distinction between measurable and unmeasurable uncertainties. It is very unlikely that this is the meaning intended by insurance theorists who speak of risk as uncertainty, for here risk and uncertainty are exact opposites.

While the decision theorist's definition of risk has not found much favor among insurance writers, both the "objectified uncertainty" and "subjective uncertainty" definitions are widely used. They have found acceptance primarily because they lend themselves to quantitative analysis. If we define risk as uncertainty, we can measure risk through the statistical tools designed to measure the dispersion of actual from expected results. Pfeffer's criticism of the definition of risk as uncertainty seems to override this advantage.

### Risk Is the Dispersion of Actual from Expected Results

Statisticians have long defined risk as the degree of dispersion of values around a central position or mean, and since the operation of the insurance mechanism is based on the theory of probability, it is not surprising that many insurance writers have adopted the statistician's definition of uncertainty.

The insurance company makes predictions about losses that are expected to occur and charges a premium based on this prediction. For the insurance

---

[4] Frank H. Knight, *Risk, Uncertainty, and Profit* (Boston and New York: Houghton Mifflin, 1921), p. 233.

company, then, the risk is that its prediction will not be accurate. To illustrate with a simple example, let us assume that the insurer in question insures 100,000 houses, and that on the basis of past experience it is estimated that 1 out of every 1000 houses will burn. On the basis of the 100,000 houses, we might predict that 100 houses will burn, but it is highly unlikely that 100 and only 100 houses will burn. The actual experience will undoubtedly deviate from the expectation, and insofar as this deviation is adverse, the insurance company faces risk. Therefore, the insurance company makes a prediction not only with respect to the number of houses that should burn, but also estimates the range of error. Let us say that the insurance company predicts that there will be 100 losses, and that the range of possible deviation will be $\pm 10$. Some number of houses between 90 and 110 will burn, and the possibility that some number more than 100 will burn is the insurer's risk. Students who have studied statistics will note that when one of the standard measures of dispersion (such as the standard deviation) is used, risk is measurable, and we can say that more risk or less risk exists in a given situation, depending on the standard deviation.

The definition of risk as the dispersion of actual from expected results is actually a version of the "risk is uncertainty" definition, where the relative dispersion is an expression of the statistical uncertainty inherent in predictions. Unfortunately, the notion of relative dispersion of actual from expected results places the emphasis in an aggregate content. The relative dispersion notion is based upon actuarial risk theory and is concerned primarily with the variability of the insurer's experience. It has little relevance for the individual.

### Risk Is the Probability of any Outcome Different from the One Expected

Another variation of the concept of risk as a dispersion maintains that risk is an objective probability that the actual outcome of an event will differ significantly from the expected outcome.[5] By objective probability it is meant that the probability is not a degree of subjective belief, but rather a relative frequency based upon the best scientific knowledge available. The key point in this definition is that risk is not the probability of a single occurrence or loss, but the probability of some outcome different from that expected. For example, we know from actuarial tables that the death rate at age 21 is

---

[5] This definition is the result of the separate and collective thinking of a number of individuals. The definition as presented here was formalized by George L. Head. See "An Alternative to Defining Risk as Uncertainty," *The Journal of Risk and Insurance* XXXIV (June 1967). Head credits the original inspiration of his article to a publication by David Houston ["Risk, Insurance and Sampling," *The Journal of Risk and Insurance* XXXI (December 1965)] and to discussions in one of J. Robert Ferrari's classes at the Wharton School of Finance and Commerce, University of Pennsylvania.

1.83 per 1000. With this low probability of death, the 21 year old does not expect death, and the risk of death is that the actual results will differ from what is expected. In the case of a large number of exposures, risk is measured by that portion of the objective probability distribution of outcomes which is beyond the bounds of the decision maker's expectations.

### Selecting a Definition

There is no indication at this point that insurance theorists will be able to agree on any of the above definitions in the immediate future. Each has found numerous adherents, and each has certain qualities that make it preferable for some purposes. Even though we cannot agree on a universal definition, examination of those given above indicates that there are certain elements that must be present in whatever definition is used.

1. The outcome must be in question. The idea of fortuitousness is inherent in each definition. When risk is said to exist, there must always be at least two possible outcomes. If we know in advance what the outcome will be, there is no risk. For example, investment in a capital asset involves a realization that the asset is subject to physical depreciation and that its value will decline. Here the outcome is certain and there is no risk involved.
2. At least one possible outcome is undesirable. This may be a loss in the generally accepted sense where something in the possession of the individual is lost, or it may be a gain that is less than the amount of gain that was possible.[6]

### Our Definition of Risk

For our purposes, two definitions discussed above will be used, but in a slightly modified form, hopefully providing a precise, yet intuitively acceptable notion of risk. We define risk as the possibility of an adverse deviation from a desired outcome that is expected or hoped for. Since an "adverse deviation from a desired outcome" may be viewed as a loss, we may also define risk as a possibility of loss. This is quite similar to the definition of risk as "the probability of any outcome different from that which is expected." The major differences are the substitution of "possibility" for "probability"[7] and the introduction of the notion of an *adverse* deviation from a *desired* outcome that is expected or *hoped for*. If you own a house,

[6]For example, the investor who fails to take advantage of an opportunity "loses" the gain he might have made. The investor faced with the choice between two stocks may be said to lose if he chooses the one that increases in value less than the alternative.

[7]When we say that an event is possible, we mean that it has a probability between 0 and 1. We may or may not know or be able to determine the probability.

you hope it will not burn. When you make a wager, you hope the outcome will be favorable. The fact that the outcome in either event may be something other than what you hope for constitutes a possibility of loss or risk.

Note that this definition is not subjective. Risk is a state of the external environment. The possibility of loss must exist, even though the individual exposed to the possibility of loss may not be aware of it. If the individual believes that there is a possibility of loss where none exists, there is only imagined risk, and not risk in the sense of a state of the real world. Finally, there is no requirement that the possibility of loss must be measurable, but only that it must exist.

In its broadest context, this definition includes any situation where there is a possibility of an unfavorable outcome. For example, the student who does not study faces the possibility of receiving an "F" for the course. Few would deny that there are some risks that do not involve money. However, since our purpose here is to relate risk to insurance, we will focus on a special type of risk—that which involves the possibility of financial loss. We define "financial loss" as a decline in or disappearance of value due to a contingency. This means that if the loss of value is intended or if it is certain, it is not a loss within the context of our definition.

### The Degree of Risk

As if the problem of agreeing upon a definition of "risk" were not enough, we are faced with the equally perplexing one of agreeing on what we mean by the "degree of risk." Precisely what is meant when we say that one alternative involves "more risk" or "less risk" than another?

For those who define risk as uncertainty, the answer is relatively simple. The greater the uncertainty, the greater the risk. Those who define risk as uncertainty maintain that risk is greatest when there are two possible outcomes, each of which is equally likely to occur. In other words, they maintain that uncertainty (risk) is at its highest point in the individual case when the probability of loss is 0.5.

Suppose we take the fascinating game of Russian Roulette to examine this position. If I hand you a revolver in which I have placed three cartridges, leaving three of the chambers in the cylinder empty, the chance of loss is 3/6 or 1/2. To those who define risk as uncertainty, this represents the point of greatest risk. Accordingly, if I place one more bullet in the cylinder, the degree of risk declines. Thus, there would be less risk when there are four bullets in the cylinder than when there are three, and less risk when there are five than when there are four. This position seems to run contrary to the logical notion of the degree of risk.

It would seem that the most commonly accepted meaning of "degree of risk" is related to the likelihood of occurrence. We intuitively consider those events with a high probability of loss to be "riskier" than those with a low probability. In our example of the game of Russian Roulette, it seems more accurate (or at least less confusing) to state that adding the fourth bullet increases rather than decreases the risk. Adding the fifth bullet increases the risk even more. This intuitive notion of the degree of risk is consistent with our definition of risk. If risk is defined as the possibility of an adverse deviation from a desired outcome that is expected or hoped for, the degree of risk is measured by the *probability* of such an adverse deviation.

For the individual, the higher the probability of loss, the greater the risk, for the greater the probability of loss, the greater the probability of a deviation from what is hoped for. In the case of the individual, the hope is that no loss will occur, so the probability of a deviation from what is hoped for (which is the measure of risk) varies directly with the probability that a loss will occur. Adding the fourth and fifth bullets increases the probability of a deviation from the hoped-for outcome. If a sixth bullet is added, the player can no longer expect or even hope that the outcome will be favorable. The sixth bullet makes the outcome certain, eliminating risk. If the probability of loss is 1, there is no hope of a favorable outcome and therefore no probability of an outcome other than that which is expected. When the probability of loss is 0, there is no possibility of an outcome other than that which is expected and therefore no risk.

In the case of aggregate exposures, the expectation is that the number of losses predicted will occur. In this instance, the degree of risk is the mathematical measure which expresses the probability of a deviation from the expected result that is likely to occur. This concept will be treated in greater detail in Chapter 2.

At times we use the terms "more risk" and "less risk" to indicate a measure of the possible size of the loss. Many people would say that there is more risk involved in a possible loss of $1000 than in a possible loss of $1, even though the probability of loss is the same in both cases. It would seem that we should make some allowance in the measurement of risk for the financial impact of the loss. Certainly both the probability and the amount of the potential loss contribute to the impact with which risk is felt. Given two situations, one involving a $1000 exposure and the other a $1 exposure, and assuming the same probability in each case, it seems appropriate to state that there is a greater risk in the case of the possible loss of $1000. This is consistent with our definition of risk, since the loss of $1000 is a greater deviation from what is hoped for (i.e., no loss) than is the loss of $1. On the other hand, given two situations where the amount exposed is the same (say $1000), there is more risk in the situation with the greater probability of loss.

While it may be difficult to relate the size of the potential loss and the probability of that loss in the measurement of risk, the concept of "expected value" may be used to relate these two facets of a given risk situation. The expected value of a loss in a given situation is the probability of that loss multiplied by the amount of the potential loss. If the amount at risk is $10 and the probability of loss is 0.10, the expected value of the loss is $1. If the amount at risk is $100 and the probability is 0.01, the expected value is also $1. This is a very useful concept, as we shall see later.

## RISK DISTINGUISHED FROM PERIL AND HAZARD

It is not uncommon for the terms "peril" and "hazard" to be used interchangeably with each other and with "risk." However, to be precise, it is important to distinguish these terms. A *peril* is a cause of a loss. We speak of the peril of "fire" or "windstorm," or "hail" or "theft." Each of these is the cause of the loss that occurs. A *hazard*, on the other hand, is a condition that may create or increase the chance of a loss arising from a given peril. It is possible for something to be both a peril and a hazard. For instance, sickness is a peril causing economic loss, but it is also a hazard that increases the chance of loss from the peril of premature death. Hazards are normally classified into three categories:

1. *Physical hazards* consist of those physical properties that increase the chance of loss from the various perils. Examples of physical hazards that increase the possibility of loss from the peril of fire are the type of construction, the location of the property, and the occupancy of the building.
2. *Moral hazard* refers to the increase in the probability of loss which results from evil tendencies in the character of the insured person. More simply, it is the dishonest tendencies on the part of an insured that may induce him to attempt to defraud the insurance company. A dishonest person may intentionally cause a loss in the hope of collecting from the insurance company, or he may exaggerate the amount of a loss in an attempt to collect more than the amount to which he is entitled.
3. *Morale hazard*, not to be confused with moral hazard, results from a careless attitude on the part of insured persons toward the occurrence of losses. The purchase of insurance may create a morale hazard, since the realization that the insurance company will bear the loss may lead the insured to exercise less care than if he were forced to bear the loss himself.

## CLASSIFICATIONS OF RISK

Risks may be classified in many ways; there are certain distinctions that are particularly important for our purposes. We have already noted the division proposed by Knight between measurable and unmeasurable uncertainties. In addition, certain other distinctions have been made.

### Financial and Nonfinancial Risks

In its broadest context, the term risk includes all situations where there is an exposure to adversity. In some cases this adversity involves financial loss, while in others it does not. There is some element of risk in every aspect of human endeavor, and many of these risks have no (or only incidental) financial consequences. Even a blind date involves an element of risk. In this text we are concerned with those risks which involve a financial loss.

### Static and Dynamic Risks

A second important distinction is between static and dynamic risks.[8] Dynamic risks are those risks which result from changes in the economy. Changes in the price level, consumer tastes, income and output, and technology may cause financial loss to members of the economy. These dynamic risks normally benefit society over the long run, since they are the result of adjustments to misallocation of resources. Although these dynamic risks may affect a large number of individuals, they are generally considered less predictable than static risks, since they do not occur with any degree of regularity.

Static risks involve those losses which would occur even if there were no changes in the economy. If we could hold consumer tastes, output and income, and the level of technology constant, some individuals would still suffer financial loss. These losses would result from sources other than the changes in the economy, such as the perils of nature and the dishonesty of other individuals. Static risks, unlike dynamic risks, are not a source of gain to society. Static losses involve either the destruction of the asset or a change in its possession as a result of dishonesty or human failure. Static losses tend to appear with a degree of regularity over time, and as a result are generally predictable.

### Fundamental and Particular Risks

The distinction between fundamental and particular risks is based on the differences in origin and consequences of the losses.[9] Fundamental risks are those which involve losses that are impersonal in origin and consequence. They are group risks, caused for the most part by economic, social, and

---

[8] The dynamic–static distinction was made by Willett. See Alan H. Willett, *The Economic Theory of Risk and Insurance* (Philadelphia: University of Pennsylvania Press, 1951), pp. 14–19.

[9] The distinction between fundamental and particular risks is based on C. A. Kulp's discussion of risk (which he referred to as "hazard"). See C. A. Kulp, *Casualty Insurance*, 3rd ed. (New York: Ronald Press, 1956), pp. 3, 4.

political phenomena, although they may also result from physical occurrences. They affect large segments of or even the entire population. Particular risks involve losses which arise out of individual events and which are felt by individuals rather than by the entire group. Unemployment, war, inflation, earthquakes, and floods are all fundamental risks. The burning of a house or the robbery of a bank are particular risks.

Since fundamental risks are caused by conditions which are more or less beyond the control of the individuals who suffer the losses and since they are not the fault of anyone in particular, it is held that society rather than the individual has a responsibility to deal with them. Although some fundamental risks are dealt with through private insurance,[10] it is inappropriate for dealing with most fundamental risks, and some form of social insurance or other transfer program may be necessary. Unemployment and occupational disabilities are fundamental risks treated through social insurance. Flood damage or earthquakes make a district a disaster area eligible for federal funds.

Particular risks are considered to be the individual's own responsibility and are not considered appropriate subjects for social action by society as a whole. They are dealt with by the individual through the use of insurance, loss prevention, or some other technique.

### Pure and Speculative Risks

One of the most useful distinctions is that between pure risk and speculative risk.[11] The term "pure risk" is used to designate those situations which involve only the chance of loss or no loss. "Speculative risk," like pure risk, involves a situation where there is a possibility of loss, and also a possibility of gain. One of the best examples of pure risk is the possibility of loss surrounding the ownership of property. When a person buys a house, he immediately faces the possibility that something may happen to damage or destroy the house. The possible outcomes are loss or no loss. Gambling is a good example of a speculative risk. In a gambling situation, risk is deliberately created in the hope of gain. If a student wagers $10 on the outcome of Saturday's game, he faces the possibility of loss, but this is accompanied by the possibility of gain. The entrepreneur or capitalist faces speculative

---

[10] For example, earthquake insurance is available from private insurers in most parts of the country, and flood insurance is frequently included in all risk contracts covering moveable personal property. Flood insurance on real property is available through private insurers only on a limited basis.

[11] Although the distinction between pure and speculative risk had been introduced earlier, Albert H. Mowbray formalized the distinction. See Albert H. Mowbray and Ralph H. Blanchard, *Insurance, Its Theory and Practice in the United States*, 5th ed. (New York: McGraw-Hill, 1961), pp. 6, 7.

risk in his quest for profit. The investment made may be lost if the product produced is not accepted by the market at a price sufficient to cover costs, but this risk is accepted in return for the possibility of profit.

The distinction between pure and speculative risks is an important one, because normally only pure risks are insurable. Insurance is not concerned with the protection of individuals against those losses arising out of speculative risks. Speculative risk is voluntarily accepted because of its two-dimensional nature, which includes the possibility of gain. Not all pure risks are insurable, and a further distinction between insurable and uninsurable pure risks may also be made. A discussion of this distinction will be delayed until Chapter 2.

## CLASSIFICATIONS OF PURE RISK

While it would be impossible in this book to list all the risks that an individual or business faces, we can briefly outline the nature of the various risks that we face. Here we are concerned with pure risks, which for the most part are also static risks. Pure risks that exist for individuals or businesses can be classified under one of the following:

1. *Personal risks* involve the possibility of the loss of income or assets as a result of the loss of income earning ability: the risks of (a) premature death; (b) dependent old age; (c) sickness or disability; and (d) unemployment.
2. *Property risks* involve the possibility of loss of property, the use of that property, or income from the property: the risks of (a) direct physical loss of or damage to property; (b) loss of use of the property or income from the property; and (c) additional expenses occasioned by the loss of the property.
3. *Liability risks* involve the possibility of loss of present assets or future income as a result of damages assessed or legal liability arising out of either intentional or unintentional torts or invasion of the rights of others.

## THE BURDEN OF RISK

Whether we define risk as the possibility of loss, uncertainty concerning loss, or the probability that the actual result will differ from what is expected, the greatest burden in connection with risk is that some losses will actually occur. When a house burns, or money is stolen, or a wage earner dies, there is a financial loss. When someone is negligent and that negligence results in injury to a person or damage to property, there is a financial loss.

These losses are the primary burden of risk and the primary reason that individuals attempt to avoid risk or alleviate its impact.

In addition to the losses themselves, there are other detrimental aspects of risk which exist apart from the cost of the losses. The uncertainty as to whether the loss will occur requires the prudent individual to prepare for the occurrence of the loss that may take place. In the absence of insurance, one way this could be done would be to accumulate a reserve fund to meet the losses if they do occur.[12] If such a reserve fund is accumulated, there is an opportunity cost involved, for the reserve fund must be available at the time of the loss and must therefore be held in a highly liquid state. The return on such funds will presumably be less than if they were put to alternate uses. If each property owner accumulates his own fund, the amount of funds held in such reserves will be greater than if the funds are accumulated collectively. Furthermore, the existence of risk may have a deterrent effect on economic growth and capital accumulation. Progress in the economy is determined to a large extent by the rate of capital accumulation, but the investment of capital involves risk that is distasteful. This disutility will not be incurred voluntarily unless something is to be gained by so doing. Investors as a class will incur the risks of a new undertaking only if the return on the investment is sufficiently high to compensate for both the dynamic and static risks. The cost of capital is higher in those situations where the risk is greater, and the consumer must pay the higher cost of the goods and services or they will not be forthcoming.

Finally, the uncertainty connected with risk usually produces a feeling of frustration and mental unrest. This is particularly true in the case of pure risk. Speculative risk is attractive to many individuals. The gambler obviously enjoys the uncertainty connected with wagering more than he enjoys the certainty of not gambling—otherwise he would not gamble. But here it is the possibility of gain or profit, which exists only in the speculative risk category, that is attractive. In the case of pure risk, where there is no compensating chance of gain, risk is distasteful.

The individual is exposed to risks of many kinds. Some of these are recognized by those who are exposed to them, while others go unrecognized. When risk is perceived, uncertainty exists as a special form of disutility. Most people hope that misfortunes will not occur in their lives, and that their present state of well-being will continue. While they hope that no misfortune will occur, men are nevertheless likely to worry about these possible misfortunes. This worry, which results in a lesser feeling of well-being is an additional burden of risk.

---

[12]One great danger of this approach is the possibility that a loss may occur before a sufficient fund has been accumulated.

## METHODS OF HANDLING RISK

There is no escape from the presence of risk, and mankind must accordingly seek ways of dealing with it. The existence of risk is a source of discomfort to most people, and the uncertainty which accompanies risk is a cause of anxiety and worry. Since risk is distasteful and unpleasant, man's rational nature leads him to attempt to do something about it. Basically, man deals with risk in five ways. Risk is avoided, assumed, transferred, shared, and reduced.

### Risk May Be Avoided

Risk is avoided when the individual refuses to accept the risk even for an instant. This is accomplished by merely not becoming involved in the action that gives rise to risk. If you do not desire to face the risk of losing your savings in a hazardous venture, then pick one where there is less risk. If you want to avoid the risks associated with the ownership of property, do not purchase the property, but lease or rent it instead.

The avoidance of risk is a method of dealing with risk, but it is a negative rather than a positive technique. For this reason it is an unsatisfactory approach to dealing with risk. If risk avoidance were utilized extensively, the individual and society would suffer as a consequence.

### Risk May Be Assumed

Risk assumption is perhaps the most common method of dealing with risk. As noted previously, the individual faces an almost unlimited array of risks; in most cases he does nothing about them. When the individual does not take positive action to avoid, reduce, or transfer the risk, he assumes the possibility of the loss involved in that risk. This risk assumption may be involuntary or voluntary. Voluntary risk assumption is characterized by the recognition that the risk exists, and a tacit agreement to assume the possibility of loss involved. The decision to assume the risk voluntarily is made because there are no more attractive alternatives. A risk may be assumed because it is too insignificant to warrant action (e.g., the breaking of a shoestring) or because the possibility is too remote (e.g., being kicked by a yak). Or, the loss involved may be both severe and with a high probability, but there may be no alternative. Involuntary risk assumption takes place when the individual exposed to risk does not recognize the existence of that risk. In these cases the person so exposed assumes the financial consequences of the possible loss without realizing he does so.

Risk assumption is a legitimate manner of dealing with risk; in many cases it is the best way. Each person must make a decision as to which risks he will assume and which he will seek to avoid or transfer on the basis of his margin for contingencies or his ability to stand the loss. A loss that might be a financial disaster for one individual or family might easily be assumed by another. As a general rule, the risks that should be assumed are those which involve relatively small certain losses.

### Risk May Be Transferred

Risk may be transferred from one individual to another who is more willing to bear the risk. An excellent example of the transfer of risk is the process of hedging, a method of risk transfer accomplished by buying and selling for future delivery, whereby dealers and processors protect themselves against a declining or increasing market price between the time they buy a product and the time they sell it. It involves simultaneous purchase or sale for immediate delivery and purchase or sale for future delivery, such as the sale of futures in the wheat market at the same time that a purchase is made in the spot market. For example, a miller might buy 1000 bushels of wheat at $1 per bushel with the hope of selling the flour made from this wheat at the equivalent of $1.10 per bushel. However, since it will take a month before the wheat is processed and ready for sale, the miller faces a risk in connection with the possibility of a decline in the price of flour between the time processing is begun and the time the flour is ready for sale. The miller may protect himself by selling 1000 bushels of wheat futures (i.e., 1000 bushels to be delivered in one month) at the futures price (for simplicity, say $1) when he purchases the 1000 bushels he intends to process. When he has processed the wheat and is ready to sell it as flour, he will buy spot wheat (i.e., wheat for immediate delivery) in order to meet the obligation which he incurred in selling the wheat futures. Now, if the price of flour has dropped from $1.10 to $0.90, the miller will lose $0.20 per bushel on the wheat he has processed into flour, but he will make a profit of $0.20 on the wheat futures. The 1000 bushels of wheat he sold a month ago, which he must now deliver, can be purchased for $0.80. On the other hand, if the price of flour has increased from $1.10 to $1.20, the gain he makes on the price change will be offset by a loss in the futures transaction.[13] In this way, hedging protects the miller from a drop in the price of flour, but he also forgoes the possibility of a gain from a price increase.

Additionally, risk may be transferred or shifted through contracts. A hold-

---

[13] The underlying assumption is that the price of wheat and flour will move in the same direction and by approximately the same amount. While this may not always be exactly true, the operation of the system approximates the underlying assumption. Hedging operations are made possible by speculators who buy and sell futures contracts in the hope of making a profit as a result of a change in price. The speculator attempts to predict the prices months in advance of delivery and buys and sells on the basis of these estimates. It is the speculator's willingness to buy and sell futures that makes possible the hedging process, and it is to the speculator that the miller transfers his risk.

harmless agreement, in which one individual assumes the possibility of loss of another person, is an example of such a transfer. Insurance is also a means of shifting or transferring risk. In consideration of a specific payment (the premium) by one party, the second party agrees in a contract to indemnify the first party up to a certain limit for the specified loss which may or may not occur.

### Risk May Be Shared

The distribution of risk is accomplished in a number of ways in our society. One outstanding example of a device through which risk is shared is the corporation. Under this form of business, the investment of a large number of persons is pooled. As we shall see, insurance is another device designed to deal with risk through sharing. One basic characteristic of the insurance device is the sharing of risk by the members of the group.

### Risk May Be Reduced

Risk may be reduced in two ways. The first is through loss prevention and control. There is almost no source of loss where some efforts are not made to keep the loss from occurring. Safety programs and loss prevention measures such as medical care, fire departments, night watchmen, sprinkler systems, and burglar alarms are all examples of attempts to deal with risk by preventing the loss or reducing the chance that it will occur. Some techniques are designed to prevent the occurrence of the loss, while others, such as sprinkler systems, are designed to control the severity of the loss if it does occur. From one point of view, loss prevention is the most desirable means of dealing with risk. If the possibility of loss could be completely eliminated, risk would also be eliminated. From a second point of view, loss prevention is seen to be an inadequate approach to dealing with risk. No matter how hard we may try, it is impossible to prevent all losses. In addition, in some cases the loss prevention may cost more than the cost of the losses.

In addition to reduction of risk through loss prevention activities, risk can be reduced in the aggregate through the use of the law of large numbers. Through the combination of a large number of exposure units, a reasonable estimate of the cost of the losses can be made. On the basis of this estimate, it is possible for an organization such as an insurance company to assume the possibility of loss of each exposure, and yet not face the same possibility of loss itself. In Chapter 2 we will see how this is done.

### Questions for Discussion and Review

**1.** Two 9-year-old boys are watching a television replay of the first Liston–Clay fight on "Great Fights of the Century." Since the fight took place before they were old enough to remember the outcome, neither knows who won, and they bet on the outcome. Tom bets on Clay and Tim bets on Liston. Does risk exist in this situation? For Tim? For Tom?

**2.** The distinction between "pure risk" and "speculative risk" is important because only pure risks are normally insurable. Why is the distinction between "fundamental risk" and "particular risk" important?

**3.** If risk is distasteful, how do you account for the existence of gambling, a pastime in which the participants indicate that they obviously prefer the risk involved to the security of not gambling?

**4.** Discuss the detrimental aspects associated with pure risk from (a) the point of view of the individual, (b) the point of view of society as a whole.

**5.** Mike says, "The possibility that my house may burn is a pure risk for me, but if I purchase insurance, it is a speculative risk for the insurance company." Do you agree?

### Suggestions for Additional Reading

Athearn, J. L. *Risk and Insurance*, 2nd ed. New York: Appleton-Century-Crofts, 1969, Chap. 1.

Bickelhaupt, D. L. and Magee, J. H. *General Insurance*, 8th ed. Homewood, Ill.: Richard D. Irwin, 1970, Chaps. 1, 2.

Denenberg, H. S., Eilers, R. D., Hoffman, G. W., Kline, C. A., Melone, J. J., and Snider, H. W. *Risk and Insurance*. Englewood Cliffs, N.J.: Prentice-Hall, 1964, Chaps. 1–5.

Greene, M. R. *Risk and Insurance*, 2nd ed. Cincinnati, Ohio: Southwestern, 1968, Chap. 1.

Hammond, J. D. (ed.) *Essays in the Theory of Risk and Insurance*. Glenview, Ill.: Scott, Foresman, 1968.

Head, G. L. "An Alternative to Defining Risk as Uncertainty." *The Journal of Risk and Insurance* **XXXIV** (June 1967).

Houston, D. B. "Risk, Insurance, and Sampling." *The Journal of Risk and Insurance* **XXXI** (4) (Dec. 1964).

Knight, F. H. *Risk, Uncertainty and Profit*. Boston and New York: Houghton Mifflin, 1921.

Kulp, C. A. and Hall, J. *Casualty Insurance*, 4th ed. New York: Ronald Press, 1968, Chap. 1.

Mowbray, A. H., Blanchard, R. H., and Williams, C. A., Jr. *Insurance*, 6th ed. New York: McGraw-Hill, 1969, Chap. 1.

Pfeffer, I. *Insurance and Economic Theory*. Homewood, Ill.: Richard D. Irwin, 1956.

Willett, A. *The Economic Theory of Risk and Insurance*. Philadelphia: University of Pennsylvania Press, 1951.

Williams, C. A., Jr. and Heins, R. M. *Risk Management and Insurance,* 2nd ed. New York: McGraw-Hill, 1971, Chap. 3.

Wood, Oliver, G., Jr. "Evolution of the Concept of Risk." *The Journal of Risk and Insurance* **XXXI** (1) (March 1964).

# 2 The Insurance Device

*Bear ye one another's burdens*
*— New Testament,* Gal. 6:2

## THE NATURE AND FUNCTIONS OF INSURANCE

### Risk Sharing and Risk Transfer

As we have seen, there are a number of ways of dealing with risk. In this book we are primarily concerned with the most formal of the various approaches —insurance. Insurance is a complicated and intricate mechanism, and it is consequently difficult to define. However, in its simplest aspect, it has two fundamental characteristics:

1. Transferring or shifting risk from one individual to a group.
2. Sharing losses, on some equitable basis by all members of the group.

To illustrate the way the insurance mechanism works, let us assume that there are 1000 dwellings in a given community and, for the purpose of simplicity, that the value of each dwelling is $10,000. Each owner faces the risk that his house may be set on fire. If a fire should occur, a financial loss of up to $10,000 could result. Some houses will undoubtedly burn, but the probability that all will is remote. Now let us assume that the owners of these dwellings enter into an agreement to share the cost of losses as they occur, so that no single individual will be forced to bear an entire loss of $10,000. Whenever a house burns, each of the 1000 owners contributes his proportionate share of the amount of the loss. If the house is a total loss, each of the 1000 owners will pay $10 and the owner of the destroyed house will be indemnified for his $10,000 loss. Those who suffer losses are indemnified by those who do not. Those who do not suffer losses are willing to pay those unfortunate members of the group who do because by doing so they help to eliminate the possibility that they themselves might suffer a $10,000 loss. Through the agreement to share the losses the economic burden of these losses is spread throughout the group. This is essentially the way insurance works, for what we have described is a pure assessment mutual insurance operation.

There are some difficulties which might arise in connection with the operation of such a plan, the most obvious is the possibility that some members of the group might refuse to pay their assessment at the time of a loss. This problem can be overcome by requiring payment in advance. To require payment in advance for the losses that may take place, it will be necessary to have some idea as to the amount of those losses. This may be calculated on the basis of past experience. Let us now assume that on the basis of past experience we are able to predict with reasonable accuracy that two of the 1000 houses will burn. We could charge each member of the group $20, making a total of $20,000. In addition to the cost of the losses, there would no doubt be some expenses in the operation of the program. Also there is a possibility that our predictions might not be entirely accurate. We might therefore, charge each member of the group $40 instead of $20, thereby providing for the payment of expenses and also providing a cushion against deviations from our expectations.

Each of the 1000 homowners will incur a small certain cost of $40 in exchange for a promise of indemnification in the amount of $10,000 if his house burns down. This $40 premium is in effect the individual's share of the total losses and expenses of the group.

### Insurance Defined from the Viewpoint of the Individual

On the basis of its function as described above, we may define insurance from the point of view of the individual as follows:

> From an individual point of view, insurance is an economic device whereby the individual substitutes a small certain cost (the premium) for a large uncertain financial loss (the contingency insured against) which would exist if it were not for the insurance contract.

The primary function of insurance is the creation of the counterpart of risk, which is security. Insurance does not decrease the uncertainty for the individual as to whether or not the event will occur, nor does it alter the probability of occurrence, but it does reduce the probability of financial loss connected with the occurrence of the event. In other words, insurance reduces the probability of financial loss and the uncertainty regarding the economic burden of losses. From the individual's point of view, the purchase of an adequate amount of insurance on his house eliminates the uncertainty regarding a financial loss in the event that the house should burn down.

Many persons consider an insurance contract to be a waste of money unless a loss occurs and indemnity is received. Some even feel that if they have not had a loss during the policy term, their premium should be returned. Both viewpoints constitute the essence of ignorance. Relative to the first, we already know that the insurance contract provides a valuable feature in the freedom from the burden of uncertainty. Even if a loss does not occur during the policy term, the insured has received something for his premium: the promise of indemnification if a loss had occurred. With respect to the second, one must appreciate the fact that the operation of the insurance principle is based upon the contributions of the many paying the losses of the unfortunate few. If the premiums were returned to the many who did not have losses, there would be no funds available to pay for the losses of the few who did. Basically, then, the insurance device is a method of loss distribution. What would be a devastating loss to an individual is spread in an equitable manner to all members of the group, and it is on this basis that insurance can exist.

### Risk Reduction through Pooling

In addition to the elimination of risk at the level of the individual through transfer, the insurance mechanism involves a reduction of risk (and the uncertainty related to risk) for the economy as a whole. As we shall see, the risk the insurance company faces is not merely a summation of the risks transferred to it by individuals, for the insurance company is able to do something that the individual cannot do, and that is to predict within rather narrow limits the amount of losses that will actually occur. Insofar as its predictions are completely accurate, the insurance company faces no possibility of loss, for it will collect each individual's share of the total losses and expenses of operation and use these funds to pay the losses and expenses as they occur. If the predictions are not accurate, the premiums the insurer has charged may be inadequate. The accuracy of the insurer's predictions are based on the law of large numbers. By combining a sufficiently large number of homogeneous exposure units, the insurer is able to make predictions for the group as a whole. This is accomplished through the theory of probability.

### Probability Theory and the Law of Large Numbers

Probability theory is that body of knowledge concerned with measuring the likelihood that something will happen and making predictions on the basis of this likelihood. It deals with random events and is based on the premise that while the occurrence of some events appears to be a matter of chance, these events actually occur with regularity over a large number of trials. The likelihood of an event is assigned a numerical value between 0 and 1, with events that are impossible assigned a value of 0 and events that are certain to occur assigned a value of 1. Events that may or may not happen are assigned a value between 0 and 1, with higher values assigned to those events estimated to have a greater likelihood or "probability" of occurring.

At this point, it may be useful to distinguish between two interpretations of probability:

1. *The relative frequency interpretation.* The probability assigned to an event signifies the relative frequency of the occurrence of the event that would be expected given a large number of separate independent trials. In this interpretation, only events which may be repeated for a "long run" may be governed by probabilities.
2. *The subjective interpretation.* The probability of an event is measured by the degree of belief in the likelihood of occurrence of the given event. For example, the coach of a football team may state that his team has a 70% chance of winning the conference title, a student may state that he has a fifty-fifty chance of getting a "B" in a course, or the weatherman may state that there is a 90% chance of rain.

Both these interpretations are used in the insurance industry, but for the moment let us concentrate on the relative frequency interpretation.

**Determining the probability of an event.** In order to obtain an estimate of the probability of an event in the relative frequency interpretation, one of two methods can be employed. The first is to examine the underlying conditions that cause the event to occur. For example, if we say that the probability of getting a "head" when tossing a coin is 0.5 or 1/2, we have assumed or determined that the coin is perfectly balanced and that there is no interference on the part of the "tosser." If we ignore the absurd suggestion that the coin might land on its edge, there are only two possible outcomes, and these are equally likely. Therefore, we know that the probability is 0.5. In the same manner, we know that the probability of rolling a six with a single die is 1/6 or that the probability of drawing the ace of spades from a complete and well-shuffled deck is 1/52. These probabilities are deducible or obvious from the nature of the event. Because they are determined before an experiment in this manner (i.e., on the basis of causality), they are called *a priori* probabilities.

These *a priori* probabilities are not of great significance for us except insofar as they can be used to illustrate the operation of the law of large numbers. Even though we know that the probability of flipping a head is 0.5, we also know that we cannot use this knowledge to predict whether a given flip will result in a head or a tail. We know that the probability has little meaning for a single trial. Given a sufficient number of flips, however, we would expect the result to approach one-half heads and one-half tails. We feel that this is true even though we may not have the inclination to test it. This common-sense notion that the probability is meaningful only over a large number of trials is an intuitive recognition of the law of large numbers, which in its simplest form states:

> The observed frequency of an event more nearly approaches the underlying probability of the population as the number of trials approaches infinity.

In other words, for the probability to work itself out, a large number of flips or tosses are necessary. The greater the number of trials or flips, the more nearly the observed result will approach the underlying probability of 0.5.

Clearly, this *a priori* method of determining the probability of an event is the preferred method, but except in the most elementary situations, determining causality is not practical. Therefore, another approach is employed. When we do not know the underlying probability of an event and cannot deduce it from the nature of the event, we can estimate it on the basis of past experience. Suppose that we are told that the probability that a 21-year-old male will die before reaching age 22 is 0.00183. What does this mean? It means that someone has examined mortality statistics and discovered that, in the past, 183 men out of every 100,000 alive at age 21 have died before reaching age 22. It also means that, barring changes in the causes of these deaths, we can expect approximately the same proportion of 21 year olds to die in the future.

Here, the probability is interpreted as the relative frequency resulting from a long series of trials or observations, and it is estimated after observation of the past rather than from the nature of the event as in the case of *a priori* probabilities. These probabilities, computed after a study of past experience, are called *a posteriori* or empirical probabilities. They differ from *a priori* probabilities, such as those involved in flipping a coin, in the method by which they are determined, but not in their interpretation. In addition, while the probability computed prior to the flipping of a coin can be considered to be exact, those computed on the basis of past experience are only estimates of the true probability.

The law of large numbers, which tells us that *a priori* estimates are meaningful only over a large number of trials, is the basis for the *a posteriori* estimates. Since the observed frequency of an event approaches the underlying probability of the population as the number of trials increases, we can obtain a notion of the underlying probability by observing events that have occurred.

After observation of the proportion of the time that the various outcomes have occurred over a long period of time under essentially the same conditions, we construct an index of the relative frequency of the occurrence of each possible outcome. This index of the relative frequency of each of all possible outcomes is called a probability distribution, and the probability assigned to the event is the average rate at which the outcome is expected to occur.

In making probability estimates on the basis of past experience or historical data, we make use of the techniques of statistical inference, which is to say that we make inferences about the population based on sample data. It is not usually possible to examine the entire population, and we must therefore be content with a sample. We take a sample in order to draw a conclusion about some measure of the population (referred to as a parameter) based on a sample value (called a sample statistic). In attempting to estimate the probability of an event, the parameter of the population in which we are interested is the mean or average frequency of occurrence, and we attempt to estimate this value on the basis of our sample. Because only partial information is available, there is the possibility that our estimate of the mean of the population (the probability) will be in error.

We know that the observed frequency of an event will approach the underlying probability as the number of trials increases. It therefore follows that the greater the number of trials examined, the better will be our estimate of the probability. The larger the sample upon which our estimate of the probability is based, the more closely our estimate should approximate the true probability.

Unfortunately, it is seldom possible to take as large a sample as we would like. In such instances, we make an estimate (called a point estimate) of the mean of the population based on the mean of the sample, and then estimate the probability that the mean of the population falls within a certain range of this point estimate. Put somewhat differently, we estimate the population mean on the basis of the sample, and then we allow a margin for error. The extent of the margin for error will depend on the concentration of the values that make up the mean and the size of the sample. The greater the dispersion of the individual values from the mean (i.e., the greater the variation in data upon which the sample mean is based), the less certain we can be that our point estimate approximates the true mean of the population.

To illustrate this principle,[1] let us assume that an insurance company

---

[1]This example is not intended as an illustration of the way insurance companies actually compute rates. As a matter of fact, industry rate-making practices bear little resemblance to the process described above. The example merely serves to illustrate how the law of large numbers is the basis for the insurance mechanism.

which has insured 1000 houses each year for the past 5 years examines its records and finds the following losses:

| Year | Houses that burn |
|--------|:----------------:|
| First | 7 |
| Second | 11 |
| Third | 10 |
| Fourth | 9 |
| Fifth | 13 |

Over the 5-year period, a total of 50 houses have burned, or an average of 10 houses per year. Since the number of houses insured each year was 1000, we estimate the chance of loss to be 1/100 or 0.01. In so doing, we are simply saying "The average number of losses in our sample was 10 houses per 1000. If the mean of our sample approximates the mean of the entire population (all houses), the probability of loss is 0.01, and we predict that 10 houses will burn the sixth year if 1000 houses are again insured." But we cannot be certain that we are correct in our estimate of the probability. The mean of our sample (our estimate of the probability) may not be the same as the mean of the universe (the true probability). The confidence we can place in our estimate of the probability will vary with the dispersion or variation in the values that make up the mean of the sample. Compare this second set of losses with the above data:

| Year | Houses that burn |
|--------|:----------------:|
| First | 16 |
| Second | 4 |
| Third | 10 |
| Fourth | 12 |
| Fifth | 8 |

The total number of losses over the 5-year period is again 50, and the average or mean losses per year is again 10. However, there is a much greater variation in the number of losses from year to year. Even though the mean is the same in both groups, we would expect the mean of the first set of data to correspond more closely with the mean of the population. The greater the variation in the data upon which our estimate of the probability is based, the greater is likely to be the variation between our estimate of the probability and the true probability. Since there is a relationship between the variation in the values that make up the sample mean and the likelihood that the sample mean approximates the population mean, it is useful to be able to measure the variation in these values.

**Measures of dispersion and the probability estimate.** Statisticians have developed a number of measures of the dispersion in a group of values. For example, in the case of the first set of losses (7, 11, 10, 9, 13), the number of losses in any given year varied from 7 to 13; in the second set of losses (16, 4, 10, 12, 8), the number of losses varied from 4 to 16. This variation from the smallest number to the largest number is called the "range," which is the simplest of the measures of dispersion. Another measure is the "variance," which is computed by squaring the annual deviations of the values from the mean and then taking an average of these squared differences. For example, the variance of the two sets of losses would be computed as follows:

| Year | Average losses | Actual losses | Difference | Difference squared |
|------|---------|--------|------------|----------|
| First | 10 | 7 | 3 | 9 |
| Second | 10 | 11 | 1 | 1 |
| Third | 10 | 10 | 0 | 0 |
| Fourth | 10 | 9 | 1 | 1 |
| Fifth | 10 | 13 | 3 | 9 |
| | | | | 20 |

$$\frac{\text{Summation of differences squared}}{\text{Number of years}} = \frac{20}{5} = 4$$

| Year | Average losses | Actual losses | Difference | Difference squared |
|------|---------|--------|------------|----------|
| First | 10 | 16 | 6 | 36 |
| Second | 10 | 4 | 6 | 36 |
| Third | 10 | 10 | 0 | 0 |
| Fourth | 10 | 12 | 2 | 4 |
| Fifth | 10 | 8 | 2 | 4 |
| | | | | 80 |

$$\frac{\text{Summation of differences squared}}{\text{Number of years}} = \frac{80}{5} = 16$$

The variance of the first set of losses is 4, and that of the second set is 16. The larger variance of the second set is simply an indication of the greater variation in the data that compose the mean.

The square root of the variance is called "the standard deviation," which is the most widely used and perhaps the most useful of all measures of dispersion. Since the variance of the first group of losses above is 4, the standard deviation of that group is 2. In the case of the second set, where the variance is 16, the standard deviation is 4. Like the variance, the standard deviation is simply a number that measures the concentration of the values about their mean. The smaller the standard deviation relative to the mean, the less the dispersion and the more uniform the values. To return to the question of the accuracy of our point estimate of the probability based on the sample mean, the standard deviation is particularly useful in making estimates concerning the probable accuracy of this point estimate.

In a normal distribution, 68.27% of the cases will fall within the range of the mean plus or minus one standard deviation. The mean plus or minus two standard deviations will describe the range within which 95.45% of the cases will lie, and the range of three standard deviations above and below the mean will include 99.73% of the values in the distribution. Using the sample mean as our point estimate of the probability, we can estimate the probability that the mean of the population is within a certain range of the sample mean, provided that we know the standard deviation of the distribution. In the case of the first set of losses, where the number of houses burning in the past was 7, 11, 10, 9, and 13, and the standard deviation was calculated to be 2, there is a 68.27% probability that the true mean is some value between 8 and 12 (i.e., $10 \pm 2$),[2] a 95.45% probability that the true mean is between 6 and 14 ($10 \pm 2 \times 2$), and a 99.73% probability that the true mean is between 4 and

---

[2]Technically, the measure above is the standard deviation of the sample mean, but it is interpreted as the standard deviation of the sampling distribution of means, called the standard error of the mean. A sampling distribution of means is the distribution that would result if a very large number of samples were taken from any population. If these are taken, the means of the samples will approximate a normal probability distribution (i.e., a distribution where the values are distributed symmetrically in a bell shape, trailing off in either direction from the mean, which is located in the center). This means simply that if we could take a very large number of samples, and then compute the average of the averages of those samples, we could obtain a good approximation of the mean of the population from which the samples were taken. It is impractical to estimate the standard error of the mean for the distribution of sample means, because the distribution of sample means (i.e., the distribution which would result if a very large number of samples were taken) is a hypothetical distribution which is assumed rather than actually constructed. The standard deviation of the sampling distribution of means is estimated on the basis of one sample and is used to describe the dispersion of the hypothetical distribution of sample means. What we are actually saying here is that if a large number of samples were taken, 68.27% of the means of those samples would fall between 8 and 12.

16 (10 $\pm$ 3 $\times$ 2). In the case of the second set of data, where the values were more dispersed and the standard deviation was calculated to be 4, there is a 68.27% probability that the true mean is between 6 and 14, a 95.45% probability that the true mean is between 2 and 18, and a 99.73% probability that the true mean is between 0 and 22.

Exactly what does all this mean? It means that there is uncertainty inherent in our predictions. During the past five years the average number of losses per 1000 dwellings has been 10, and on the basis of our estimate of the probability, we might predict 10 losses if 1000 houses are insured the sixth year, but we cannot be certain that our estimate of the probability is correct. As a matter of fact, in the case of our first sample, our computations indicate that at best we can be 99% certain only that the true probability lies somewhere in the range of 4 to 16 losses per 1000 houses. The number of houses that may be expected to burn next year, other things being equal, is some number between 4 and 16. This means that actual results may be expected to deviate by as much as 6 from the predicted 10. This represents a possible deviation of 60% (6/10) from the expected value.[3]

Other things being equal, the larger our sample, the more closely we will expect the mean of the sample to coincide with the mean of the population and the smaller will be the margin we must allow for error. This is reflected by the fact (which can be demonstrated mathematically) that the standard deviation of a distribution is inversely proportional to the square root of the number of items in the sample. For example, let us assume that we are able to increase the number of houses in our sample from 1000 to 100,000 per year, and that we observe a 100-fold increase in losses.[4] The number of losses observed per year will increase from 10 to 1000. The standard deviation will also have increased, but, and this is the critical point, it will not have increased proportionately, for the standard deviation increases only by the square root of the increase in the size of the sample. Observed losses increase 100-fold with a 100-fold increase in exposures, but the standard deviation will increase only 10-fold. Thus the standard deviation which is calculated to be 2 at the 1000 exposure level will increase to only 20 at the level of 100,000 houses. The new mean is 1000 and the mean plus or minus three standard deviations is now 1000 $\pm$ 60 and not 1000 $\pm$ 600. This means that

---

[3] This measure of uncertainty is somewhat related to the traditional statistical concept of the coefficient of variation, which is the standard deviation divided by the mean. The coefficient of variation at the 1000 exposure level in this example is 2/10 (20%).

[4] It is entirely possible that this larger sample might indicate a different number of losses per 1000 houses than the smaller sample, simply because our estimate based on the sample of 1000 was a poorer estimate of the true probability than that based on a sample of 100,000. For the purpose of simplification, we have assumed that the number of observed losses per 1000 does not change.

we may be 99% confident that the mean of the population (the underlying probability) lies somewhere between 940 and 1060. We can predict 1000 losses next year if 100,000 houses are insured, and, we can feel 99% confident that the actual number of losses will fall somewhere between 940 and 1060. This represents a potential deviation of only 6% (60/1000) from the expected value. The area of uncertainty has decreased, because the size of the sample has increased. Note that in our example, neither the probability nor our estimate of it has changed. The number of losses expected per 1000 houses is the same, but we are more confident that our estimate approximates the true probability.

### Dual Application of the Law of Large Numbers

One additional point should probably be made. Even when we have estimated the probability on the basis of the sample of 100,000 houses per year, we cannot expect the narrower range of possible deviation if our estimate is applied to 1000 houses. As we have seen, even in the case of *a priori* probabilities where the probability is known, it must be applied to a large number of trials if we expect actual results to approximate the true probability. Therefore, in the case of empirical probabilities, the requirement of a large number has dual application:

1. In order to estimate the underlying probability accurately, the insurance company must have a sufficiently large sample. The larger the sample, the more accurate will be the estimate of the probability.
2. Once the estimate of the probability has been made, it must be applied to a sufficiently large number of exposure units to permit the underlying probability to work itself out.

In this sense, to the insurance company, the law of large numbers means that the larger the number of cases examined in the sampling process, the better the chance of making a good estimate of the probability; the larger the number of exposure units to which the estimate is applied, the better the chance that actual experience will approximate a *good* estimate of the probability.

In making predictions on the basis of historical data, the insurance company implicitly says "If things continue to happen in the future as they have happened in the past, and if our estimate of what has happened in the past is accurate, this is what we may expect. . . ." But things may not happen in the future as they have in the past. As a matter of fact, it is likely that the probability involved is constantly changing. In addition, we may not have a good estimate of the probability. All this means that things may not turn out as expected. Since the insurance company bases its rates on its expectations of future losses, it must be concerned with the extent to which actual experience is likely to deviate from predicted results. For the insurance company, risk (or the possibility of financial loss) is measured by the potential deviation of actual from predicted results, and the accuracy of prediction is enhanced when the predictions are based on and are applied to a large number of exposure units. If the insurance company's actuaries could be absolutely certain that their predictions would be 100% accurate, there would be no possibility of loss for the insurance company, because premium income would always be sufficient to pay losses and expenses. Insofar as actual events may differ from predictions, risk exists for the insurer. To the extent that accuracy in prediction is attained, risk is reduced.

### Insurance Defined from the Viewpoint of Society

In addition to eliminating risk for the individual through transfer, the insurance device reduces the aggregate amount of risk in the economy by substituting certain costs for uncertain losses. These costs are assessed on the basis of the predictions made through the use of the law of large numbers. We may now formulate a second definition of insurance:

> From a social point of view, insurance is an economic device for reducing and eliminating risk through the process of combining a sufficient number of homogeneous exposures into a group in order to make the losses predictable for the group as a whole.

Insurance does not prevent losses,[5] nor does it reduce the cost of losses to the economy as a whole. As a matter of fact, it may very well have the opposite effect of causing losses and increasing the cost of losses for the economy as a whole. The existence of insurance encourages some losses for the purpose of defrauding the insurer, and, in addition, people are less careful and may exert less effort to prevent losses than they might if it were not for the existence of insurance contracts. In addition, the economy incurs certain additional costs in the operation of the insurance mechanism. Not only must the cost of the losses be borne, but the expense of distributing the losses on some equitable basis adds to this cost.

### The Economic Contribution of Insurance

Property that is destroyed by an insured contingency is not replaced through the existence of an insurance contract. True, the funds from the insurance

---

[5] This statement is not intended to disparage the loss-prevention activities of insurance companies. In many forms of property and casualty insurance, attempts to reduce loss are perhaps the most important feature of all, but these loss-prevention activities are not essentially a part of the operation of the insurance principle. Insurance could exist without them, and they could and do exist without insurance. Insurance in and of itself does not favorably alter the probability of loss.

company may be used to replace the property, but when a house or building burns, society has lost a want-satisfying good. Insurance as an economic device finds its justification in the certainty about the financial burden of losses it creates and in its function of spreading the losses that occur. In providing a mechanism through which losses can be shared and uncertainty can be reduced, insurance brings peace of mind to the members of society and makes costs more certain.

Insurance also provides for a more optimal utilization of capital. Without the possibility of insurance, individuals and businesses would be obligated to maintain relatively large reserve funds to meet the risks that they must assume. These funds would be in the form of idle cash, or would be invested in safe, liquid, and low-interest-bearing securities. This would be an inefficient use of capital. When the risk is transferred to the professional risk bearer, the deviations from expected results are minimized. As a consequence, insurers are obligated to keep much smaller reserves than would be the case if insurance did not exist. The released funds are then available for investment in more productive pursuits, and this results in a much greater productivity of capital.

### Insurance and Gambling

Perhaps we should make one final distinction regarding the nature of insurance. It is often claimed that insurance is a form of gambling. "You bet that you will die and the insurance company bets that you won't" or "I bet the insurance company $20 against $10,000 that my house will burn." The fallacy of these statements should be obvious. In the case of a wager, no chance of loss, and hence no risk, exists previous to the wager. In the case of insurance, the chance of loss exists whether or not there is an insurance contract in effect. In other words, the basic distinction between insurance and gambling is that gambling creates a risk, while insurance provides for the transfer of existent risk.

### Elements of an Insurable Risk

While it is theoretically possible to insure all possibilities of loss, some are not insurable at a reasonable price. For practical reasons, insurers are not willing to accept all the risks that others may wish to transfer to them. In order to be considered a proper subject for insurance, there are certain characteristics that should be present. The four prerequisites listed below represent the "ideal" elements of an insurable risk. Although it is desirable that the risk have these characteristics, it is possible for certain risks which do not have them to be insured.

1. *There must be a sufficiently large number of homogeneous exposure units to make the losses reasonably predictable.*   Insurance, as we have seen,

is based on the operation of the law of large numbers. Unless we are able to calculate the probability of loss, we cannot have a financially sound program.[6]

2. *The loss produced by the risk must be definite.*  It must be a type of loss that is relatively difficult to counterfeit, and it must be capable of financial measurement. In other words, we must be able to tell when a loss has taken place, and we must be able to set some value on the extent of the loss.

3. *The loss must be fortuitious or accidental.*  The loss must be the result of a contingency, i.e., it must be something that may or may not happen. It must not be something that is certain to happen. If the insurance company knows that an event in the future is certain to happen, it also knows that it must collect a premium equal to the certain loss that it must pay, plus an additional amount for the expenses of administering the operation. Depreciation, which is a certainty, cannot be insured; it is dealt with through a sinking fund. Furthermore, the loss should be beyond the control of the insured. The law of large numbers is useful in making predictions only if we can reasonably assume that future occurrences will approximate past experience. Since we assume that past experience was a result of chance occurrences, the predictions concerning the future will be valid only if future occurrences are also a result of chance.

4. *The loss must not be catastrophic.*  It must be unlikely to produce loss to the majority of the exposure units at the same time. The insurance principle is based on a notion of sharing losses, and inherent in this idea is the assumption that only a small percentage of the group will suffer loss at any one time. Damage which results from enemy attack would be catastrophic in nature. There are additional perils, such as floods, which, while they would not affect everyone in the society, would effect those who had purchased insurance. The principle of randomness in selection is closely related to the requirement that the loss must not be catastrophic.

### Randomness

The future experience of the group to which we apply our predictions will approximate the experience of the group upon which the predictions are

[6] The reader is no doubt aware of the much publicized instances in which Lloyd's writes insurance on the physical attributes of a rising starlet, or insures against loss from some unique event. Technically speaking, these transactions are not true insurance; although they involve transfer of the risk, there is no reduction of risk through combination. The underwriters at Lloyd's are able to engage in such practices because they substitute mass underwriting (where a single risk is spread among many insurers) for the mass of exposures and because the premiums charged for such coverages are heavily loaded.

based only if both groups have approximately the same characteristics. There must be a proportion of good and bad risks in the group equal to the proportion of good and bad risks of the group upon which the prediction is made. Yet, human nature acts to interfere with the randomness necessary to permit the random composition of the current group. The losses that are predicted are based on the average experience of the old group, but there are always some individuals who are, and who realize that they are, worse than average risks. Since the chance of loss for these risks is greater than that of the other members of society, they have a tendency to desire insurance coverage to a greater extent than the remainder of the group. This tendency results in what is known as "adverse selection." Adverse selection is the tendency of the poorer than average risks to purchase or continue insurance. Unless some provision is made to prevent it, predictions based on past experience would be useless in predicting future experience. Adverse selection works in the direction of accumulating bad risks. Since the predictions of future losses are based on the average loss of the past (in which both good and poor risks were involved), if the experience of the future is based on the experience of a larger proportion of bad risks, it will be worse than that of the past, and the predictions will be invalid.

Adverse selection has long caused a lack of interest on the part of insurers with respect to flood insurance. The adverse selection involved in insuring fixed properties against the peril of flood is obvious. Only those individuals who feel that they are exposed to loss by flood are interested in flood insurance, and yet in the event of a flood, there is a likelihood that all these individuals would suffer loss. The element of the sharing of the losses of a few by the many who did not suffer losses would not exist. Although some insurers have written coverage against flood on fixed properties in the past, the coverage was not available for those who needed it most.[7]

The "war risk exclusion" which life insurance companies insert in their contracts during wartime is another example of the adverse selection principle. On the basis of past experience, it has been shown that deaths which result from combat have not been catastrophic, yet it is precisely because the insurance companies prevented adverse selection that they have not been. The war risk exclusion is put into policies during wartime to prevent soldiers who would not otherwise have purchased insurance from doing so when

---

[7]After decades of agitation for the government to "do something" about the flood exposure, a federal flood insurance program was enacted in 1968, under which the federal government cooperates with the insurance industry in making flood insurance available. The flood insurance program is a partnership between the federal government and the Association of Flood Insurers. It is as yet too early to determine how the partnership will work out. In the beginning, flood insurance is to be written only in limited geographical areas scattered around the United States. As of February 19, 1971, flood insurance was available in 417 areas in 36 states.

they are exposed to a greater chance of loss. Policies that are sold before the war begins and do not have the war risk exclusion, cover deaths that result from war. If the policies purchased during the war were based on the same randomness as those sold in peacetime, the war risk exclusion would not be necessary, but in the absence of such a provision, the randomness would not exist and the company would be selected against.

### The "Large Loss Principle"

Sometimes, an additional requirement is listed as one of the elements of an insurable risk—that the cost of the insurance must not be high in relation to the possible loss, or that the insurance must be economically feasible. We can hardly call this a prerequisite for an insurable risk in view of the fact that the principle is so widely violated in the insurance industry today. The four elements of an insurable risk are characteristics of certain risks that permit the successful operation of the insurance principle. If a given risk lacks one of these elements, the operation of the insurance mechanism is impeded. The principle of "economically feasible insurability" is not really an impediment to the operation of the insurance principle, but rather a violation of the principles of risk management and common sense.

## THE FIELDS OF INSURANCE

Insurance is a broad generic term, including the entire array of institutions that deal with risk through the device of sharing and transfer of risk. Insurance may be divided and subdivided into certain classifications on the basis of perils insured against or the fundamental nature of the program. Basically, we make a first distinction between social insurance and private (or voluntary) insurance.

### Social Insurance

Social insurance differs from private insurance in a number of important respects. In the case of social insurance, we use the insurance mechanism for transferring, sharing, and reducing risk, but we do so on a somewhat qualified basis. In the area of social insurance, we qualify the basic insurance principles with the concept of need.

Social insurance is based on the notion that there are some people in the economy who face fundamental risks that they cannot afford to deal with themselves. The occurrence of the losses which these risks entail would place an unbearable burden on a portion of the population, depriving them of what we consider to be an adequate standard of living. One basic purpose of the social insurance programs is a redistribution of income in favor of those who cannot individually cope with these fundamental risks. When contributions are made, they are often supplemented by public funds. This means that we do not enforce the principle of equity in social insurance. As a result of the lack of equity, another departure from the basic principles of insurance is necessary if the plan is to be successful. Social insurance programs must be compulsory for a large portion of the population if they are to work.

Any definition of social insurance must, by its very nature, be rather complex. The following definition of social insurance has been proposed:[8]

> Social insurance is a device for the pooling of risks by their transfer to an organization, usually governmental, that is required by law to provide pecuniary or service benefits to or on behalf of covered persons upon the occurrence of certain predesignated losses under all of the following conditions:
>
> 1. Coverage is compulsory by law in virtually all instances.
> 2. Eligibility for benefits is derived, in fact or in effect, from contributions having been made to the program by or in respect of the claimant or the person as to whom the claimant is dependent; there is no requirement that the individual demonstrate inadequate financial resources, although a dependency status may need to be established.
> 3. The method of determining benefits is prescribed by law.
> 4. The benefits for any individual are not directly related to contributions made by or in respect to him, but instead usually redistribute income so as to favor certain groups such as those with low former wages or large numbers of dependents.
> 5. There is a definite plan for financing the benefits that is designed to be adequate in terms of long-range considerations.
> 6. The cost is borne primarily by contributions which are usually made by covered persons, their employers, or both.
> 7. The plan is administered or at least supervised by the government.
> 8. The plan is not established by the government solely for its present or former employees.

Certain elements in the above definition require clarification. The mere fact that a specific type of insurance is required by law does not make it a social insurance program. Compulsory automobile insurance, for example, does not meet all the above requirements and therefore would not be social insurance. Furthermore, although the government is usually the transferee, this is not a prerequisite. Workmen's compensation insurance constitutes an excellent example of a social insurance coverage that is provided by com-

---

[8] The Commission on Insurance Terminology of the American Risk and Insurance Association.

mercial insurance companies. In the last analysis, it makes little difference whether or not the insurance program is conducted by the government. A number of social insurance programs are provided through private insurance companies; on the other hand, the government provides some insurance coverages that are voluntary in nature.

The fifth condition listed above, that there be a definite plan for financing the benefits that is designed to be adequate in terms of long-range considerations, merely requires that there be some sort of long-run planning. There should be at least some element of actuarial soundness. This does not rule out some contributions to the financing of the plan out of general government revenues, but basically, the contributions by, or on behalf of, the covered individuals constitute the primary sources of financial support.

Within the framework of the above definitions, the following would be considered to be social insurance programs:

1. Old-Age, Survivors, and Disability Insurance (OASDI) and Medicare
2. Unemployment Compensation Insurance
3. Workmen's Compensation Insurance
4. Compulsory Temporary Disability Insurance
5. The Railroad Retirement System
6. Railroad Unemployment and Railroad Temporary Disability Insurance

### Private (Voluntary) Insurance

Private insurance consists for the most part of voluntary insurance programs available to the individual as a means of protecting himself against the possibility of financial loss due to a contingency. The distinguishing characteristics of private insurance are that it is voluntary, and that the transfer of risk is normally accomplished by means of a contract. This voluntary insurance is provided by private firms, but in some instances it is also offered by the government. Perhaps the best example of a private insurance coverage offered by the government is the National Service Life Insurance Program.

Private insurance may be further categorized and subdivided into personal insurance, which provides protection against financial loss in the areas of life and health, and property and liability insurance, which provide protection against perils affecting assets. In general, we may speak of four distinct types of private insurance:

1. Life insurance
2. Accident and health insurance
3. Fire and marine insurance
4. Casualty insurance

**Life insurance.** Life insurance is designed to provide protection against two distinct risks: premature death and superannuation. As a matter of personal preference, death at any age is probably premature, and superannuation (living too long) does not normally strike the individual as an undesirable contingency. From a practical point of view, however, the individual can, and sometimes does, die before he has prepared for the financial requirements of his dependents. By the same token, a person can, and often does, outlive his income earning ability. Life insurance, endowments, and annuities are used to protect against the undesirable consequences for the individual and his dependents that result from premature death and superannuation.

**Accident and health insurance.** Accident and health insurance (or more simply, health insurance), is defined as "insurance against loss by sickness or accidental bodily injury."[9] The "loss" may be the loss of wages caused by the sickness or accident, or it may be the expense involved in doctor bills, hospital bills, medicine, etc. Included within this definition of health insurance are forms of insurance which provide lump-sum or periodic payments in the event of loss occasioned by sickness or accident, such as disability income insurance and accidental death and dismemberment insurance.

**Fire and marine insurance.** Fire insurance is designed to indemnify the insured from loss of, or damage to, buildings, furniture, fixtures, or other personal property against loss as a result of fire, lightning, windstorm, hail, explosion, and a vast array of other perils. Coverage may be provided for both direct loss (i.e., the actual loss represented by the destruction of the asset), and indirect loss (defined as the loss of income and/or the extra expense which is the result of the loss of the use of the asset protected). Originally, only fire was an insured peril, but the number of perils insured against has gradually been expanded until it has reached the present status where "all risk coverage" can be provided.

Marine insurance, like fire insurance, is designed to protect against financial loss resulting from damage to or destruction of owned property, except that here the perils protected against are primarily those connected with transportation. Marine insurance is divided into two classifications: ocean marine and inland marine. Ocean marine policies provide coverage on all types of ocean-going vessels and their cargos. Policies are also written to cover the shipowner's liability. The coverage of the basic policy covers cargo only after it has been loaded onto the ship, but policies are frequently endorsed to provide coverage from "warehouse to warehouse," thus pro-

---

[9] The Commission on Insurance Terminology of the American Risk and Insurance Association.

viding coverage for overland transportation hazards as well as ocean hazards.

Inland marine is something of a contradiction of terms. The field developed as an outgrowth of ocean marine insurance and the "warehouse to warehouse" coverage mentioned above. With the spread of the population across the United States, transportation came to play a crucial role in the development of business. With the spread of transportation facilities, a demand arose for insurance coverage to protect against financial losses involved in damage to products being shipped. As time went by, marine insurers expanded their operations and eventually wrote marine forms on all types of property, moveable or not. Finally, it was agreed that guidelines were needed to outline the types of property which should be insured under the marine forms. In 1933, the National Association of Insurance Commissioners proposed a "Nationwide Definition" with respect to marine coverages, which recognized the following classes of property as being eligible for marine coverage: (a) imports, (b) exports, (c) domestic shipments, (d) instrumentalities of transportation and communication, and (e) personal property floater risks. The first two classes, imports and exports, are strictly limited to the ocean marine category. Inland marine coverages are provided for the three remaining classifications. Domestic shipments include goods being transported by carriers such as railroads, motor vehicles, or ships and barges on the inland waterways and in coastal trade. In addition, provision is made for insuring goods transported by air, mail, parcel post, express, armored car, or messenger. Instrumentalities of transportation and communication include such items as bridges, tunnels, pipelines, power transmission lines, radio and television communication equipment, etc. The final class, personal property floater risks, provides for coverage on a wide range of property, which, by its very nature, is mobile and subject to the perils of transportation; for example, construction equipment, personal clothing, jewelry and furs, agricultural equipment, animals, etc.

**Casualty insurance.** As it exists today, casualty insurance is virtually impossible to define. In a sense, it is the residual class: one commonly proposed definition states that "if it isn't fire, marine, or life, it's casualty." Certainly, what this definition lacks in precision it makes up in scope. Casualty insurance originally included health and accident and liability insurance. As new fields of insurance developed, someone had to accept the underwriting responsibility, and more often than not, the new coverages were adopted and marketed by the casualty companies. As a result, the following coverages, unrelated though they may be, are considered to be casualty insurance: health and accident insurance; automobile insurance; liability insurance; workmen's compensation insurance; boiler explosion insurance; plate glass insurance; burglary, robbery, and theft insurance; credit insurance; title insurance; and fidelity and surety bonds. Although these represent only a partial listing of the coverages that are considered to be casualty insurance, they indicate the wide variety in the field.

Actually, the term "casualty insurance" is gradually being displaced. The older dichotomy between "property" and "casualty" insurance is slowly giving way to the more descriptive division between "property" and "liability" insurance. The term "property" insurance is now used to refer to fire insurance, ocean and inland marine insurance, and those coverages formerly classified as "casualty" insurance which are concerned with losses to real and personal property. "Liability" insurance, of course, refers to those coverages which are concerned with the legal liability exposure.

The coverages discussed below are casualty coverages under the traditional classification system. Using modern terminology (i.e., "property" and "liability"), some are property coverages and some are liability coverages.

*Health and accident insurance* is a traditional casualty coverage, but because of its distribution it is also considered to be a separate field of insurance, as previously discussed.

*Automobile insurance* is the largest field of insurance in the casualty classification, accounting for over half of all property and liability premiums. As it is currently written, automobile insurance provides protection against several types of losses. First, it provides protection against loss resulting from legal liability in connection with the ownership or use of an automobile. The careless operation of an automobile may result in a lawsuit where the defendant is held legally liable, and automobile liability insurance is designed to pay such judgments. In addition, the medical payments section of the automobile policy consists of a special form of health and accident insurance which provides for the payment of medical expenses incurred as a result of automobile accidents. In addition, coverage is provided against loss resulting from theft of the automobile or damage to it by a wide range of causes.

*Liability insurance* includes a wide range of coverages. The form of liability insurance with which most students are familiar is automobile liability insurance, but there are other liability hazards as well. Liability coverage is also available to protect against nonautomobile liability exposures such as the ownership of property, manufacturing, and construction operations, the sale or distribution of products, the operation of elevators, and a vast array of other exposures.

*Workmen's compensation insurance* had its beginning in the United States shortly after the turn of the century, when the various states began to pass workmen's compensation laws. Under the provision of these laws, the employer was made absolutely liable for injuries to workers which arose out of and in the course of their employment. Workmen's compensation insurance provides for the payment of the obligations these laws impose on the employer. In a sense, the workmen's compensation coverage exists not only for the protection of the employer, but also as a guarantee to the employee that his loss will be compensated. Because the benefits are determined by law and the coverage is compulsory, workmen's compensation insurance is considered to be a social insurance coverage, even though it is sold by both private insurers and by state funds.

*Boiler explosion insurance* was one of the earliest casualty coverages. The operation of boilers involves an exposure to life and property because of the hazard of explosion from internal pressure. Furthermore, various forms of machinery are subject to accidental breakdown which may necessitate lengthy and expensive delays in production. Boiler and machinery insurers maintain an extensive inspection service for the purpose of preventing losses, and this inspection service is a primary reason for the purchase of boiler and machinery coverage. Although the contract does not require them to do so, the insurers make periodic inspections of the objects insured. As a result, losses are reduced and the insured benefits.

*Plate glass insurance* is a special casualty coverage that provides for the broadest possible coverage on glass. Glass is also insured under the fire and marine policies, but only against certain specified perils and frequently with numerous exclusions. Plate glass insurance, as developed by the casualty insurers, provides the broadest form of all risk coverage, with only fire and war excluded.

*Burglary, robbery, and theft insurance* are casualty coverages designed to protect the property of the insured against loss resulting from the criminal acts of others. Because a standard exclusion in these crime policies excludes loss caused by an employee of the insured, they are referred to as the "non-employee crime coverages." Protection against criminal acts by employees is provided under fidelity bonds, which are discussed below.

*Credit insurance* is a highly specialized form of coverage (available to manufacturers and wholesalers), which protects against losses resulting from the inability of the insured to collect amounts owed by customers. The coverage is written subject to a deductible equal to the normal bad debt loss, and with a provision which requires the insured to share a part of each loss with the insurer.

*Title insurance* is still another highly specialized form of coverage.[10] Basically, it provides protection against financial loss resulting from a defect in an insured title. The legal aspects of land transfer are rather technical, and the possibility always exists that the title may not be clear. Under a title

---

[10] Title insurance is clearly a form of property insurance, and it may be debated as to whether it should be classified as "casualty" insurance. Historically, it has been written by specialty insurers, but it is generally classified as a casualty coverage by the state insurance codes.

insurance policy, the insurer agrees to indemnify the insured to the extent of his financial loss in connection with transfer to him of a defective title. In a sense, title insurance is unique in that it insures against the effects of some event that has happened in the past, rather than against financial loss which may result from a future occurrence.

*Fidelity and surety bonds* represent a special class of risk transfer device, and there is a difference of opinion as to whether bonds should be classified as insurance. As a matter of fact, there are certain fundamental differences between a bond and an insurance policy, and strictly speaking it can be argued that bonds are not contracts of insurance. In general terms, a bond is an agreement by one party, the "surety," to answer to a third person, called the "obligee," for the debt or default of another party, called the "principal." In other words, the surety guarantees a certain type of conduct on the part of the principal, and if the principal fails to behave in the manner guaranteed, the surety will be responsible to the obligee. Bonding is divided into two classes: fidelity bonds and surety bonds. Fidelity bonds are commonly called "dishonesty insurance" or "employee dishonesty insurance." These are designed to protect the obligee against dishonesty on the part of his employees. In many respects they are closer to insurance than are surety bonds, but like surety bonds, they differ from insurance. There are three parties in the bond, as opposed to two parties in the insurance contract. In addition, if the principal is dishonest and steals, the surety is obligated to pay the obligee, but has the right to attempt to recover its loss from the principal.

Surety bonds guarantee that the principal will carry out, according to plan, the work the obligee has hired him to do. Most surety bonds are issued for persons doing contract construction, those connected with court actions, and those seeking licenses or permits. Basically, the surety bond guarantees that the principal is honest and that he has the necessary ability and financial capacity to carry out the obligation for which he is bonded. If the principal is unable to meet the commitment, after exhausting all his resources, the surety must provide funds to pay for the loss. In this event the surety may take possession of the assets of the principal and convert them into cash to reimburse itself for the loss paid.

As previously noted, there is a difference of opinion as to whether bonds are actually insurance. In Chapter 24 we will discuss more thoroughly the distinctions between bonds and insurance, but at this point we will ignore the differences. Insurance regulatory authorities normally include bonds within the framework of the contracts which they regulate. Furthermore, casualty insurers sell these bonds, and since suretyship is normally considered to be a part of the casualty insurance business, we will consider it so.

## Questions for Discussion and Review

**1.** There are many strikes in the United States, and both employers and workers suffer financially as a result. Would you expect a commercial insurer to provide insurance protection to either the workers or the employers to cover losses resulting from these strikes?

**2.** Many young men belong to army reserve and national guard units. If these units were activated, most of the members would suffer financially. Could the insurance device be used to protect these young men from the financial consequences of this contingency?

**3.** A friend explains to you that he has developed a plan for the formation of an insurance company which will issue insurance policies that will protect a person who buys stock against a decline in the value of that stock. Explain to him that he is out of his tree.

**4.** "Other things being equal, one should prefer to purchase insurance from the largest insurance company possible." On what basis does the author of this statement probably base his conclusion?

**5.** "In view of the operation of the law of large numbers, the most beneficial and logical development in the insurance industry would be the emergence of a monopolistic insurer." Do you agree? Why or why not?

## Suggestions for Additional Reading

Athearn, J. L. *Risk and Insurance*, 2nd ed. New York: Appleton-Century-Crofts, 1969, Chap. 2.

Bickelhaupt, D. L. and Magee, J. H. *General Insurance*, 8th ed. Homewood, Ill.: Richard D. Irwin, 1970, Chap. 3.

Denenberg, H. S., Eilers, R. D., Hoffman, G. W., Kline, C. A., Melone, J. J., and Snider, H. W. *Risk and Insurance*. Englewood Cliffs, N.J.: Prentice-Hall, 1964, Chap. 12.

Denenberg, H. S. "The Legal Definition of Insurance." *The Journal of Insurance* **XXX** (3) (Sept. 1963).

Faulkner, E. J. (ed.) *Man's Quest for Security*. Lincoln, Neb.: University of Nebraska Press, 1966.

Greene, M. R. *Risk and Insurance*, 2nd ed. Cincinnati, Ohio: Southwestern, 1968, Chaps. 2, 3.

Kulp, C. A. and Hall, J. *Casualty Insurance*, 4th ed. New York: Ronald Press, 1968, Chap. 1.

Mowbray, A. H., Blanchard, R. H., and Williams, C. A., Jr. *Insurance,* 6th ed. New York: McGraw-Hill, 1969, Chaps. 2, 5, 6.

Riegel, R. and Miller, J. *Insurance Principles and Practices,* 5th ed. Englewood Cliffs, N.J.: Prentice-Hall, 1966, Chap. 1.

Snider, H. W. (ed.) *Readings in Property and Casualty Insurance.* Homewood, Ill.: Richard D. Irwin, 1959, Chaps. 1–6.

# 3 Risk Management

*It is, generally speaking, all measures con-
ferring security upon the undertaking and
requisite peace of mind upon the personnel.*
—Henri Fayol

## THE NATURE OF RISK MANAGEMENT

Risk management is a scientific approach to the problem of dealing with
the pure risks faced by individuals and businesses. Many business firms
have highly trained individuals who specialize in dealing with pure risk.
In some cases this is a full-time job for one person, or even for an entire
department within the company. Those who are responsible for the entire
program of pure risk management (of which insurance buying is only a
part) are risk managers. Risk management as a profession is older than the
title "Risk Manager," for the risk management technique was utilized by
businesses and individuals long before the term became fashionable.[1]

The risk manager evolved from the insurance manager, and because the
title "Risk Manager" is growing in popularity, many insurance managers
are called risk managers. The terms "insurance manager" and "risk
manager" are often used interchangeably without a great deal of attention
to the actions or the actual functions of the individual. In order to distinguish
between the risk manager and the insurance manager, a functional approach
should be used.

Risk management is something more than insurance management, in

[1]Although the term "risk management" may have been used in the special sense in which it is
used here earlier, the general trend in its current usage began in the early 1950s.

**49**

that it deals with both insurable and uninsurable risks, and the choice of the appropriate techniques for dealing with these risks. Insurance management involves the use of techniques other than insurance (e.g., noninsurance or assumption as an alternative to insurance), but for the most part it is restricted to the area of those risks that are considered to be insurable.

Managers of a business are responsible for the conservation of the assets and income of that business. The risk management responsibility is for the conservation of assets and income from those losses involved in pure risk situations. Thus, while the objective of management in general is the conservation of the assets of the firm and maximizing of profit, the objective of risk management is the protection of the organization's assets and income from serious financial impairment as a result of static losses. The role of the risk manager is to minimize the adverse effects of losses and the uncertainty in connection with pure risk. Implicit in this responsibility is the preservation of the firm as an operational unit in the economy.

Risk management, then, is something more than insurance management, in that it deals with both insurable and uninsurable pure risks, but it is something less than all management, since it does not deal (except incidentally) with business risk.

## DEVELOPMENT OF RISK MANAGEMENT

During periods of high business activity and corporate profits, expenses do not appear as heinous as they do during periods when business losses are prevalent. The 1930s marked an all-time low for many American businesses. In the midst of the greatest depression business has ever experienced, increased pressure for expense reduction and cost control brought management to the recognition of the need for a more objective approach to insurance buying.

Although some companies had already made progress in the development of a professional approach to insurance buying, it was not until 1929 that much consideration was given to the importance of the management of pure risk in business. In that year, insurance buyers met informally in Boston to discuss problems of mutual interest. In 1931 the American Management Association established its Insurance Division for the purpose of exchange of information among members and the publication of news and information of interest to corporate insurance buyers. In 1932 the Insurance Buyers of New York (which later became the Risk Research Institute) was organized. In 1950 the National Insurance Buyers Association was organized; this later became the American Society of Insurance Management.

When these insurance buyer organizations were formed, the insurance companies and agents were not enthusiastic. The organizations were immediately suspect. Agents feared the organizations, because they suspected that they represented the beginning of an attempt to bypass the traditional distribution system, of which the agent had always been the central figure. Insurance companies were concerned that they might come to face a collective force that would insist on practices detrimental to the companies. With time, the true nature and intent of the organizations became evident, and the professional buyers associations earned the appreciation and respect of other segments of the insurance industry.

The professional buyers associations have done a tremendous amount of work in the area of buyer education—holding seminars on risk management and publishing information of interest to insurance buyers. The American Society of Insurance Management publishes a magazine called *Risk Management*, and the Insurance Division of the American Management Association publishes a wide array of reports and studies to assist risk managers. In addition, the Insurance Institute of America has developed an educational program in risk management with a series of six examinations leading to a diploma in risk management.

As the professional risk managers' associations have grown, a large portion of the insurance buying public has become better educated and informed concerning insurance as a product. This has been especially true in the business world, but to a lesser extent it is true even in the area of personal insurance. As the outlay for insurance premiums has come to be a more and more significant item in individual and business budgets, an increasing amount of attention has been devoted to this expenditure. Price consciousness on the part of the insurance buyer has led to a greater interest in matters of proper coverage and total cost. An examination of the principles and techniques that have been developed should prove beneficial at this point.

## THE RISK MANAGEMENT PROCESS

The process by which the risk manager achieves the risk management goal includes five steps:

1. Identification of the risks
2. Evaluation of the risks
3. Consideration of alternatives and selection of the risk treatment device
4. Implementing the decision
5. Evaluation and review of the results

### Identifying the Risk Exposures

Obviously, before anything can be done about the risks the organization faces, someone must be aware of them. In one way or another the risk manager must dig into the operations of the company and discover the risks to which the firm is exposed. It is difficult to generalize about the risks a given organization is likely to face, because the differences in operations and conditions give rise to differing risks. Some risks are relatively obvious, while there are many which can be, and often are, overlooked. In order to reduce the possibility of failure to discover all risks facing the firm, most risk managers use some systematic approach to the problem of risk identification. One approach is the "insurance policy checklist." Lists of available insurance policies are prepared by insurance companies. The risk manager simply consults such a list, picking out the policies applicable to the firm. The major defect of this approach is that it concentrates on insurable risks only, ignoring the uninsurable pure risks.

The preferred method is the risk audit or enumeration approach, where the risk manager also uses a checklist, but the list is designed to include all pure risks, insurable and uninsurable, which may face any firm. Then, through an examination of the firm itself, it is determined which of the risks exist. The examination of the firm would include a systematic analysis of financial statements and a flowchart of the firm's operations, plus a thorough perusal of all aspects of the firm's operations.

### Evaluation of the Risks

Once the risks have been identified, the risk manager must evaluate them. This involves measuring the potential size of the loss and the probability that the loss is likely to occur. The evaluation of risk involves some ranking in order of priorities. Certain risks, because of the severity of the possible loss, will demand attention prior to others, and in most instances there will be a number of risks that are equally demanding. Any risk that involves a loss which would represent a financial catastrophe ranks in the first category. There is no distinction between risks in this class, for it makes little difference if a bankruptcy results from a liability loss or an uninsured fire loss. Therefore, rather than ranking risks in some order of importance such as 1, 2, 3, etc., it is more appropriate to rank them in general classifications such as critical, important, and unimportant.

### Consideration of Alternatives and Selection of the Risk Treatment Device

Once the risks have been identified and measured, the next step is the consideration of the devices and tools that should be used to deal with each risk. The risk management problem is primarily a problem in decision making; more precisely, it is deciding what should be done about each static risk the organization faces. The extent to which the risk manager must make these decisions alone varies from organization to organization.

Frequently, the risk manager is guided in his actions by a "Corporate Risk Policy," which establishes the criteria to be applied in the risk management process. In some instances there is a formal document that outlines the rules within which the risk manager may operate. If the document is rigid and detailed, there is less latitude in the decision making to be done by the risk manager. He becomes an administrator of the program rather than a policy maker, and his responsibility is limited to the execution of the policy. In other instances, where this is no formal policy or where the policy has been drawn loosely to permit the risk manager a wide range of discretion, his responsibility is much greater. Ideally, the risk management policy should be a product of the Board of Directors and the officers of the company, since they are ultimately responsible for the preservation of the firm's assets. The policy should be formulated with the advice of the risk manager, acting as a staff adviser to the Board of Directors.

The techniques available for the treatment of risk were discussed in Chapter 1. These included risk avoidance, assumption, sharing, transfer, and reduction. In practical application, the risk manager focuses on three of these: Assumption, Reduction, and Transfer, the ART of risk management.[2]

In attempting to determine which of these tools of risk management should be used to meet the potential loss, the risk manager considers the size of the potential loss, its probability, and the resources that would be available to meet the loss if it should occur. The benefits and costs involved in each of the alternative tools is evaluated, and then, on the basis of the best information available and under the guidance of the corporate risk management policy, the decision is made.

### Implementing the Decision

The decision is made to assume a risk. This may be accomplished with or without a fund and with or without a reserve. If the decision is to include the accumulation of a fund, the administrative procedures must be inaugurated to implement this decision. If the decision is made to employ loss prevention to deal with a particular risk, the proper loss-prevention

---

[2] Risk avoidance may be viewed as a form of loss prevention. Both risk avoidance and loss prevention are considered here to be a part of risk reduction. Risk sharing is included in the tool of risk transfer, for when risks are shared, there is a transfer of risk from the individual to the group.

program must be designed and implemented. The decision to transfer a risk through the insurance mechanism must be followed by selection of an insurer, negotiations for and placement of the insurance.

### Evaluation and Review

Evaluation and review of the risk management program must be included in the risk management process for two reasons. First, the risk management process does not take place in a vacuum. Things change; new risks arise and old risks disappear. The techniques which were appropriate last year may not be the most advisable techniques this year, and constant attention is required. Second, mistakes are sometimes made. Evaluation and review of the risk management program permits the risk manager to review his decisions and discover his mistakes, hopefully before they become costly.

## THE RULES OF RISK MANAGEMENT

With the development of risk management as a special functional area of business, increased attention has been devoted to formalizing its principles and techniques, so as to provide guidance in the risk management decision-making process. One of the greatest contributions was the development of the "rules of risk management." These guidelines for risk management decision making are quite simply common-sense precepts applied to the pure risk situation. Mehr and Hedges propose the following three basic rules of risk management:[3]

1. Don't risk more than you can afford to lose.
2. Don't risk a lot for a little.
3. Consider the odds.

These rules, simple as they are, provide a basic framework within which risk management decisions can be made.

### Don't Risk More Than You Can Afford to Lose

The first and perhaps the most important of the rules of risk management is "don't risk more than you can afford to lose." If we begin with the recognition that the firm cannot possibly eliminate or transfer all the risks it faces, and that it will be necessary to assume some risks, the fundamental question becomes "Which risks should be assumed?" The obvious answer is explicitly stated in this first rule.

The most important determining factor in deciding what ought to be

---

[3] Robert I. Mehr and Bob A. Hedges, *Risk Management in the Business Enterprise* (Homewood, Ill.: Richard D. Irwin, 1963), pp. 16–26.

done about a given risk is the maximum potential loss which might result from the risk. If this loss is of a magnitude that would result in bankruptcy or serious financial impairment, assumption is not feasible. This amount will obviously vary from firm to firm, just as it varies from one individual to another. Additionally, the level of loss that can be afforded may vary over time, depending on the resources available at the time of the loss.

### Don't Risk a Lot for a Little

The rule "don't risk a lot for a little" provides guidance in two directions. First, it follows the principle of purchasing insurance only when necessary, and of using insurance as a last resort. There should be a reasonable relationship between the cost of transferring the risk and the value that accrues to the transferer. In many cases the cost of transfer is disproportionate to the value. For example, a young man who pays $35 for $50 worth of collision coverage on his automobile is risking a lot for a little. Second, the rule "don't risk a lot for a little" reinforces the first rule. The individual who neglects to purchase a needed insurance coverage is also risking a lot (the possible loss) for a little (the premium saved).

### Consider the Odds

If the risk manager can determine the probability that a loss may occur, he is in a better position to deal with a risk than he would be without such information, but it is possible to attach undue significance to such probabilities. While it is useful to know whether the probability that a loss may occur is almost nil, slight, moderate, or almost definite, such knowledge is of secondary importance when compared with an estimate of the possible size of the potential loss. Once again, the probability that a loss may or may not occur is less important than the financial consequences of the loss if it does occur. If the risk manager discovers through statistical analysis that the probability of a given occurrence is remote, he must still consider the possible severity of that remote loss in deciding what is to be done about the risk. If the risk involves a possible loss that would be a financial catastrophe, the fact that the probability is small is of little significance.

## THE NONPROFESSIONAL RISK MANAGER

In giant corporations, the risk manager can devote his full attention to the problems of pure risk. In smaller firms, he probably has other functions as well. In the smallest firms, the risk manager may very well be the person who manages everything. His job as risk manager is an extremely heavy burden, for it is a job that requires the utmost precision if loss is to be avoided. He must make the decisions as to what kind of insurance is to be purchased, how much, and from whom. If the insurance coverage is inadequate and a loss occurs, the firm will suffer a financial loss. If, on the other hand, the business is overinsured, the loss is just as real in terms of the premiums that should not have been spent, for the legal principle of indemnity states that the insured cannot collect more than the amount of his loss, regardless of the amount of insurance he has paid for.

Certainly, the nonprofessional risk manager needs all the help he can get. He may seek and obtain advice from many sources to assist him in making his decisions, but in the last analysis the decision remains his burden. Unfortunately, risk managers who must depend on the services of others cannot always be certain that their advisers are genuinely interested in advising (as distinguished from selling). For this reason the nonprofessional risk manager should understand and appreciate the principles of risk management. He must know enough about risk management to recognize whether his advisers are any good. He must know enough about risk management and insurance to know when he needs help, and then he must be able to determine if he is getting the kind of help he needs.

### Risk Management and the Individual

Risk management evolved formally as a function of business. Insurance managers became risk managers, and with the transition certain principles of scientific insurance buying, which had always been used to some extent, were formalized. For the most part these principles are common-sense applications of the marginal cost–marginal revenue principle, and they are equally applicable to the insurance buying decisions of the individual or the family unit. Like the business firm, the individual or the family unit has a limited number of dollars which can be allocated to the protection of assets and income against loss. Personal risk management is concerned with the allocation of these dollars in some optimal manner, and makes use of the same techniques as does business risk management. In order to achieve maximum protection against static losses, the individual must select from among the risk management tools of assumption, reduction, and transfer. The primary emphasis in the remainder of this book is on personal risk management and insurance buying.

## BUYING INSURANCE

Both the individual and the business firm face an almost unlimited number of risks, and an almost equally unlimited number of insurance contracts which have been designed to meet these risks. The problem faced by each is the same; how to use the insurance available to the best possible advantage. Since the average individual faces such a wide array of risks, he could not possibly pay for an insurance program that would protect him against all of them. Even if he could, it would probably not be wise to do so, for as we have seen, insurance is only one method for the treatment of risk, and in many cases it is not the best one. Insurance should be used to protect against some risks, but not others. In the last analysis, insurance is purchased when it is the most appropriate and least expensive means of achieving the financial security which the individual desires in the face of uncertain losses. Under what circumstances, then, is it the most appropriate and least expensive means available?

### The Large Loss Principle

The first rule of insurance buying is that the probability that the loss may or may not occur is less important than the possible size of the loss. Since the individual must of necessity assume some risks and transfer others, it seems only rational that he transfer those that he cannot afford to bear himself. One frequently hears the complaint "The trouble with insurance is that those who need it most are the ones who can least afford it." There is a great deal of truth to this statement. The need for insurance is dictated by the inability to withstand the loss in question if the insurance is not purchased, so while it is true that those who most need insurance are those who can least afford it, it is also true that they are the ones who can least afford to be without it. In determining whether or not to purchase insurance in a particular situation, the important question is not "Can I afford it?" but rather "Can I afford to be without it?" The question of whether the individual can afford to be without the coverage in question will depend on the other financial resources available to meet the loss. The large loss principle, that the individual should insure first against those losses which are beyond his margin for contingencies, is simply an application of the first rule of risk management formulated by Mehr and Hedges: "Don't risk more than you can afford to lose." An insurance contract is most meaningful when it is used to insure against losses the individual could not bear himself. Since there are a limited number of dollars available to protect against risk, they should be spent where their impact is most beneficial, in the protection against large losses.

### Insurance As a Last Resort

Insurance should be considered a last resort as a risk management device— it should be used only when absolutely necessary. Insurance coverage always costs more than the expected value of the loss covered. This is because in addition to the expected value of the loss (the pure premium), the cost of operating the insurance mechanism must be paid by the policyholders. If we keep in mind that insurance operates on the principle of averages, we can deduce a great deal about losses that should be insured. On the basis of past experience, the insurance company estimates the amount it will have to pay in order to cover the losses that will occur. In addition to covering the losses, it must recover the costs involved in the operation of the company. Therefore, paradoxical as it may sound, the best buys in insurance involve those losses that are least likely to happen. The higher the probability of the loss, the less appropriate is insurance as a device for dealing with the risk. To illustrate this point, let us take the case of a man who is condemned to die in the electric chair. If an insurance company were to agree to sell him a $100,000 life insurance policy, it would have to charge something more than $100,000. In addition to the amount of the claim (which is relatively certain), they must add the cost of administration, making the cost of the policy more than the amount to be paid out in claims. The purchase of an insurance contract under these terms would be absurd. For the insurance buying public as a whole, the cost of the insurance is also greater than the amount that will be paid out in claims. The higher the probability of the loss, the closer the insurance comes to the situation where the loss is a certainty, and the more expensive the insurance becomes relative to the expected value of the loss. In those instances where the probability of loss is very high, the buyers of insurance simply engage in dollar trading with the insurance companies, paying premiums to collect on losses that are certain to happen. The best buys in insurance are those where the probability of loss is low and the loss severity is high. The worst buys are those in which the size of the loss is low and the probability of the loss is quite high, yet it seems that this is precisely the type of insurance coverage that most people wish to buy.

It is in connection with this latter characteristic that many persons fail to appreciate the true function of insurance. The insurance principle should not be utilized for the purpose of indemnification for small relatively certain losses. These can more desirably be carried as a cost of production in business or as one small cost to an individual of maintaining himself and his family. Why should one want to collect from an insurance company for the two or three shingles that were blown off the roof during a windstorm? Why should a trucking firm want to be indemnified for a $100 collision loss to one of its trucks? Why should the normal family want maternity benefits in a hospitalization policy?[4] Why should an individual with any degree of affluency want $50 deductible collision coverage on his automobile? In

[4]This provides an ideal illustration of the usual misunderstanding of the function of insurance. If a man and a woman get married, what could be more certain than an addition to the family? It is not a highly unpredictable event, and the expenses involved in a normal birth do not usually constitute a financial catastrophe. There should be sufficient time in which money can be saved for the coming expense.

many instances these small relatively certain losses can be eliminated in the insurance operation by excluding them or by using a deductible. Insurance companies, by providing indemnity for such small losses in their contracts are as guilty of a misuse of the insurance principle as are the individual insureds.

It makes good sense to use the deductible in insurance contracts that the individual or the business purchases. The premium reduction normally more than compensates for the risk that is retained. For example, let us take the case of automobile collision insurance. The difference between $50 and $100 deductible coverage may be substantial. The difference will depend on the rates applicable in the area, but as an example, in Davenport, Iowa, for a 25-year-old unmarried male operator, the cost of $50 deductible collision on a new Ford Falcon is $66 per year. The cost of $100 deductible is $41 per year, a difference of $25. Since the difference in cost is $25, the insured is paying $25 for $50 coverage. When examined as a separate transaction, the purchase of $50 deductible hardly seems rational. If the individual who purchased the $50 deductible coverage owned a car worth $50, and he was offered insurance on it for $25, he would reason that the premium was too high relative to the risk. Why is it not also too high when the car is worth more than $50?

There are violations of the large loss principle in virtually every area of insurance, but especially in the field of individual or personal coverages. In the field of hospitalization many individuals purchase "first dollar coverage" plans. In the homeowners insurance area very few people purchase insurance with the optional deductibles. Many car owners would not think of purchasing $100 or $250 deductible collision coverage rather than the more expensive $50 deductible coverage.

There is nothing intrinsically wrong with such coverages; they are just not a very good way to spend the limited number of premium dollars that are available. If the individual's psychological makeup is such that he desires protection against even the smallest type of loss, it is probably alright. The real problem with respect to such coverages is that the individual who insures against such small losses often does so at the expense of exposures that involve losses which would be financially catastrophic. Such individuals spend enough money to obtain an adequate program of insurance, but because the dollars are poorly allocated, they end up with uninsured or inadequately insured exposures.

### Selecting the Agent and the Company

While the selection of an insurance company is an important aspect of the insurance buying process, in most cases the individual is probably well advised to focus his primary attention on the selection of the agent rather than the company. When an insurance policy is purchased, a part of the premium goes to the insurance company to pay for the protection. A second part is compensation to the agent for the service he provides to the insured. The most important part of this service consists of the advice the agent provides. Careful selection of the adviser is a fundamental part of insurance buying. From the point of view of the insured, the primary qualification for a good agent is knowledge and an interest in the needs of the client. One indicator of a knowledgeable and professional agent is a professional designation; the Chartered Property and Casualty Underwriter (CPCU) designation and the Chartered Life Underwriter (CLU) designation both indicate that the agent is sufficiently motivated to work in a formal educational program for professional development. However, there are many competent and knowledgeable agents who do not have these designations.

The insured may receive assistance from his agent in selecting an insurer if the agent represents several companies. In the case of most life insurance agents and certain property and liability agents who represent only one company, the selection of the agent will automatically include the selection of the company. In choosing a company, the major consideration should be the financial stability of the company. In addition, certain aspects of the company's operation, such as its attitude toward claims and cancellation of policyholders, are important. Finally, cost is a consideration.

In view of the importance of the financial stability of the insurer in the selection process, a few comments relative to the determination of financial stability are in order. Actually, analysis of the financial strength of an insurance company follows the same principles used in the financial analysis of any corporation. However, industry accounting practices require certain modifications, making the evaluation of the financial stability of an insurer a somewhat more complicated procedure (see p. 100). For this reason, it is probably advisable for the layman to consult an evaluation service rather than to attempt the analysis himself. Information on the financial stability of insurance companies is available from several sources which specialize in providing information on the financial strength of insurers, the efficiency of their operation, and the caliber of management.

In the property and liability field, the Alfred M. Best Company publishes two reference guides that are useful in determining an insurer's financial position. *Best's Insurance Reports: Property-Liability*[5] is a comprehensive analysis of virtually all property and liability insurers. *Best's Key Rating Guide: Property-Liability*,[6] is a smaller and less comprehensive book, but

[5] *Best's Insurance Reports: Property-Liability* (Morristown, N.J.: Alfred M. Best Company, annual).

[6] *Best's Key Rating Guide: Property-Liability* (Morristown, N.J.: Alfred M. Best Company, annual).

it includes sufficient information to assist in the selection of a company in most cases. Both books include Best's ratings for all companies listed. Two ratings are assigned to each company: a "General Policyholders' Rating" and a "Financial Rating," of which the General Policyholders' Rating is the more important. The General Policyholders' Rating is based on an analysis of five factors: (a) underwriting results, (b) economy of management, (c) adequacy of reserves for undischarged liabilities, (d) adequacy of policyholders' surplus to absorb shocks, and (e) soundness of investments. On the basis of analysis of these factors, the company is assigned one of six policyholders' ratings:

| | |
|---|---|
| A+ | Excellent |
| A | Excellent |
| B+ | Very good |
| B | Good |
| C+ | Fairly good |
| C | Fair |

The majority of property and liability companies are in the top four classifications. The remainder are either not rated or receive C+ or C ratings. In utilizing the Policyholders' Rating, the rating should be checked for a period of years. If there has been a downward trend, further investigation into the cause of the change is warranted.[7]

In the field of life insurance, there are two sources, *The Spectator Life Insurance Yearbook*[8] and *Best's Life Reports*[9] both of which provide detailed financial and historical data on most life insurers. *Best's Life Reports* does not include a Policyholders' Rating such as that assigned to the property and liability companies. However, the results achieved by the companies are classified as "favorable," "very favorable," and "most favorable," and the funds available to offset adverse experience are classed as "considerable," "substantial," "very substantial," or "most substantial." Obviously, the higher the comparative classification assigned to a company with respect to the results achieved or the margin for contingencies, the better.

---

[7] The "Financial Ratings" assigned to property and liability companies indicates Best's estimate of the safety factor of each company, and are based solely on the financial resources of the insurer as indicated by the sum of net worth, conditional reserves, and the redundancy in liabilities. In order to prevent confusion of the Financial Rating with the General Policyholders' Rating, the Financial Ratings in all cases consist of at least two letters, ranging from a rating of "AAAAA" for companies with $25,000,000 or more for a safety factor, down to "CC" for companies with less than $250,000 available as a safety factor.

[8] *The Spectator Life Insurance Yearbook* (Philadelphia: Chilton Company, annual).

[9] *Best's Life Reports* (Morristown, N.J.: Alfred M. Best Company, annual).

### A Note on Insurance Prices

Over 100 years ago, John Ruskin observed, "There is hardly anything in this world, that some man cannot make a little poorer and sell a little cheaper, and people who consider price only are this man's lawful prey." This might easily be reworded concerning insurance, for there is hardly an insurance policy in the world that some company cannot make a little broader for a higher premium, nor is there an insurance policy that cannot be sold more cheaply by reducing the coverage. This is not to imply that all insurance that is less expensive is poor, or that the most expensive policies are the best. It is simply a reminder that insurance prices are based on the law of large numbers and that the broadness or narrowness of the coverage will affect the amount of losses and so the premium. Any increase in the amount the insurance company must pay for losses will be reflected in higher premiums.

Also, insurance companies differ in their degree of efficiency, and there are considerable differences in prices which are based on differing expense factors. In some instances the lower expense factor is a result of a lower commission paid to the agent or the lack of certain services. The cost reduction in such cases must be measured against the lack of the service provided. The most important part of this service consists of the advice the agent provides. In considering the price differences in the insurance market, proper consideration should be given to the need for advice and to whether this service is provided.

### Questions for Discussion and Review

**1.** The principles and rules of risk management appear to be just plain common sense. In view of this fact, how do you account for the widespread violation of these rules in insurance buying today?

**2.** Explain the relationship, if any, among the statements "Don't risk more than you can afford to lose," "Those people who need insurance most are those who can least afford it," and "Insurance should be considered as a last resort."

**3.** It is common practice on the part of many businessmen to divide their insurance among several agents, spreading their business around. The alleged advantage is the good will that it creates. What drawbacks can you think of?

**4.** Discovery of the risks an individual or organization faces is one of the most difficult tasks in the risk management process. How would you go about determining the risks you face?

**5.** What risks do you face as an individual? Which of these risks have you elected to assume and which have you transferred?

## Suggestions for Additional Reading

American Management Association. *The Growing Job of Risk Management,* AMA Management Rept. 70. New York: American Management Association, 1962.

*Best's Aggregates and Averages.* Morristown, N.J.: Alfred M. Best, annual.

*Best's Insurance Reports, Fire and Casualty.* Morristown, N.J.: Alfred M. Best, annual.

*Best's Life Reports.* Morristown, N.J.: Alfred M. Best, annual.

Bickelhaupt, D. L. and Magee, J. H. *General Insurance,* 8th ed. Homewood, Ill.: Richard D. Irwin, 1970, Chap. 29.

Denenberg, H. S. "Is 'A-Plus' Really a Passing Grade?" *The Journal of Risk and Insurance XXXIV* (3) (Sept. 1967).

Insurance Institute of America. *Practices in Risk Management—Selected Readings.* Bryn Mawr, Pa.: Insurance Insitute of America.

Insurance Institute of America. *Principles of Risk Management—Supplementary Readings.* Bryn Mawr, Pa.: Insurance Institute of America.

Long, J. D. and Gregg, D. W. *Property and Liability Insurance Handbook.* Homewood, Ill.: Richard D. Irwin, 1965, Chaps. 72–75.

MacDonald, D. L. *Corporate Risk Control.* New York: Ronald Press, 1966, Chaps. 3, 4.

Mehr, R. and Hedges, B. A. *Risk Management in the Business Enterprise.* Homewood, Ill.: Richard D. Irwin, 1963, Chap. 6.

Snider, H. W. (ed.) *Readings in Property and Casualty Insurance.* Homewood, Ill.: Richard D. Irwin, 1959, Chaps. 28, 29.

Williams, C. A. and Heins, R. M. *Risk Management and Insurance,* 2nd ed. New York: McGraw-Hill, 1971, Chaps. 2–4, 9–13, 23, 24.

# 4 The Insurance Industry

*Tell me thy company, and I'll tell thee what thou art.*

—Cervantes, *Don Quixote*

In spite of the great benefits that accrue to society as a result of the insurance mechanism, it is self-evident that such a complicated and intricate mechanism does not come into existence by itself. Someone makes the estimates of the probability of loss, collects the funds that are necessary to compensate those who suffer loss, makes payments for the losses that occur, and provides for the general administration of the program. These are the functions performed by insurance companies. In addition, insurance is a product; it must be sold. Individuals in the economy must be made aware of their need for the product, and this is the function performed by the agent.

The insurance business in the United States is a tremendous industry, measured by any one of a number of standards. There are approximately 4700 companies conducting operations in the country. These employ over 1,260,000 persons, and have responsibility for assets of more than $200 billion.

We begin our examination of the insurance industry with a quick look at the development of insurance as a business. Although we are primarily concerned with insurance in this country, since insurance has its roots in the Old World, we will consider its development prior to the formation of the United States as well.

## THE HISTORY OF INSURANCE

### Insurance in Antiquity

There is evidence of many practices resembling insurance in the ancient world. As early as 3000 B.C. Chinese merchants utilized the technique of sharing risk. These merchants shipped their goods by boat down river, and because of the treacherous rapids on the river, not all the boats made it safely. To reduce the impact of losses to any one individual, the merchants devised the plan of distributing their goods on each other's boats. When a boat was dashed to pieces on the rocks, the loss was shared by all rather than falling upon a single individual.

About 500 years later the famous Great Code of Hammurabi provided for the transfer of the risk of loss from merchants to moneylenders. Under the provisions of Hammurabi's code, a trader whose goods were lost to bandits was relieved of his debt to the moneylender from whom he had borrowed the money to buy the goods. Babylonian moneylenders undoubtedly loaded their interest charges to compensate for this transfer of risk. This innovation was adapted to the risks of sea trade by Phoenicians and then by Greeks. Loans were made to shipowners and merchants engaged in trade, with the ship or cargo pledged as collateral. The borrower was offered an option whereby, for a somewhat higher interest charge, the lender agreed to cancel the loan if the ship or cargo were lost at sea.[1] Under this technique, the risk of loss was transferred from the owner of the boat or cargo to the lender. These contracts were referred to as *bottomry* contracts in those cases where the ship was pledged, and *respondentia* contracts when the loan involved cargo.

In addition to the risk-sharing techniques of the Chinese and the bottomry and respondentia contracts, there were other risk-sharing practices in the ancient world resembling life insurance, fire insurance and health insurance, but although these resembled insurance, the modern insurance business did not begin until the commercial revolution in Europe following the Crusades.

### Marine and Fire Insurance

Marine insurance, the oldest of the modern branches of insurance, appears to have been started in Italy sometime during the thirteenth century. From Italy it spread to the other countries on the continent and then to England through the Lombard merchants, who came to dominate British commerce

---

[1] The additional interest on such loans was called a "premium," and the term has become a part of insurance terminology, indicating the payment made by the insured.

and finance during the fifteenth century. This early marine insurance was issued by individuals rather than by insurance companies as we know them. A shipowner or merchant who desired protection on his ship or cargo prepared a sheet with information describing the ship, its cargo, its destination, and other pertinent information. Those who agreed to accept a portion of the risk wrote their names under the description of the risk and the terms of the agreement. This practice of "writing under" the agreement gave rise to the term "underwriter." Individual underwriters gradually gave way to corporate insurers and the term "underwriter" retained its meaning as one who selects and rejects risks. Shipowners seeking insurance and the individuals who organized themselves into groups of underwriters found the coffee houses of London a convenient meeting place. One of the coffee houses, owned by Edward Lloyd, soon became the leading meeting place because its proprietor made available paper and pens and information regarding shipping. No one is certain exactly when Lloyd's started, but it is known to have been in existence early in 1688. As Lloyd's became more and more a meeting place for insurers it was moved from its original location on Tower Street to the financial district. In 1771 the underwriters who were using Lloyd's facilities entered into a formal agreement, and the Lloyd's Exchange was formally created.

Fire insurance in the modern era can be traced to Germany, where a fire association known as the *Feuer Casse* was organized in 1591. Several additional proposals for fire insurance companies were made shortly thereafter, but none made any great impression until the middle of the seventeenth century. In 1666 the Great Fire of London broke out. The fire raged for five days, virtually destroying London, and created a good deal of enthusiasm for fire insurance. An English physician named Nicholas Barbon (who had been relatively unsuccessful as a physician) entered into the construction business during the rebuilding of the city and at the same time entered into the business of insuring the newly built houses against loss by fire. At first he operated as a proprietorship, but later, in 1680, he formed a stock company with several associates called "The Fire Office." Other entrepreneurs soon followed his lead.

The first insurance contracts in the United States were marine policies placed with British companies. Shortly after 1750, American underwriters began to issue marine policies. The first successful fire insurance company in the United States was a mutual insurance company founded in 1752 by Benjamin Franklin and a group of his associates, called the Philadelphia Contributionship for the Insurance of Houses from Loss by Fire.[2] The

---

[2]A company founded in Charleston, South Carolina, in 1735, the Friendly Society for Mutual Insuring of Houses, preceded the Philadelphia Contributionship. However, it lasted only a few years and very little is known about it.

first capital stock company in the United States, The Insurance Company of North America, was founded as an association in 1792 and was incorporated in 1794. Its charter gave it broad underwriting powers which permitted it to engage in all lines of insurance.

### Casualty Insurance

The first form of casualty insurance was written in England by a company founded in 1849, to provide accident insurance against injuries resulting from railroad accidents. The Travelers Insurance Company of Hartford was established in 1863 and became the first company in the United States to sell accident insurance.

The Hartford Steam Boiler Inspection and Insurance Company was founded in 1866 and commenced writing insurance on boilers. Corporate sureties began to sell fidelity bonds in 1876. Next came liability insurance in 1886. The first liability policies covered the liability of an employer to his employees and were prompted by the employer liability statutes passed by the various states. By 1889 insurers had begun writing liability insurance on elevators and other public liability hazards. The first automobile liability policy in the United States was written in 1898, and the first physical damage coverage was written in 1899. Workmen's compensation insurance followed the passage of the first New York workmen's compensation law in 1910.

### Life Insurance

On June 18, 1536, a group of marine underwriters in London issued what appears to have been the first modern life insurance policy to a William Gybbons. The policy was a 1-year term policy in the amount of £400. As an interesting footnote to history, Gybbons died within the year and the underwriters paid the £400. Other attempts similar to this were tried from time to time (although probably not by the underwriters who had insured Gybbons).

Although Edmund Halley had prepared a mortality table in 1693, it was not until nearly 100 years later that any degree of accuracy was achieved in the prediction of mortality. The first modern life insurance company, the Society for the Assurance of Widows and Orphans, a London company founded in 1699, charged all insureds the same premium. It and several companies that followed it were unsuccessful. Then, in 1762, the Equitable Society for the Assurance of Life and Survivorship was chartered and began successful operation. It introduced the innovation of premiums which varied with the age of the insured. Following the beginning of the Old Equitable, the number of companies increased slowly, and 40 years later there were only eight in England.

The first life insurance company in America was founded just seven years after Benjamin Franklin's mutual fire insurance company. It was a stock company called "The Corporation for Relief of Poor and Distressed Presbyterian Ministers and the Poor and Distressed Widows and Children of Presbyterian Ministers" (for the sake of preservation of sanity and space we will refer to it as the Presbyterian Ministers Fund). This company is still in operation and is the oldest life insurance company in the world. It presently insures only Presbyterian clergy and laymen.

Between 1759 and 1835, several other stock companies were founded, but they did not survive. The first mutual life insurance company was New England Life, founded in 1835. It was followed by a dozen more companies which have survived to the present day.

### Industry Growing Pains in America

During the early stages of its development, the insurance industry in the United States met many crises and came in for a good deal of criticism, most of which was deserved. In the field of life insurance, abuses crept in and companies got into financial difficulty. Many life insurance companies were operated in a precarious manner. Unsound business practices were prevalent, and many policyholders lost the funds they had paid to the companies. In the property and liability field the catastrophe hazard wiped out many companies. The most famous of these catastrophies were the great New York City fire of 1835 which wiped out 23 of the 26 New York companies and almost wiped out New York, the 1871 Chicago fire which made Mrs. O'Leary's cow famous, and the fire which accompanied the 1906 San Francisco earthquake. Each of these disasters resulted in the disappearance of many companies, and while others were organized to take the place of the bankrupt companies, policyholders suffered. Reforms were pressed for by regulatory authorities, and some improvements were made. The Armstrong Investigation of 1905 and the Merritt Investigation of 1910 were commissioned by the State of New York to consider unsound practices in the life insurance and property insurance fields, respectively. Many abuses were discovered and corrective measures were implemented.[3]

The great depression of the 1930s was extremely hard on the life insurance companies, and to a lesser extent on property and liability companies. In spite of the difficulties, the industry weathered the depression, and the post World War II period has witnessed the greatest expansion of the industry in the history of the country.

[3]The history of insurance regulation is treated in greater detail in Chapter 6.

### Monoline Organization

During the period from the beginning of insurance in the United States until about the time of the Civil War, there was little regulation of insurance companies and few restrictions with respect to the types of coverage they might write. Nevertheless, most companies chose to specialize in one field or another. Even the Insurance Company of North America, which had been granted power to write all types of insurance, dabbled only briefly in the field of life insurance and then abandoned it.

As more and more states began to regulate insurance, state limitations on the underwriting powers of insurance companies became common. The industry became organized on a monoline basis, where companies were restricted by law to the writing of a single line of insurance. A company that wrote fire insurance was not permitted to write casualty insurance; a casualty company could not write fire insurance. Neither fire insurance companies nor casualty insurance companies could write life insurance and life insurance companies were permitted to write only life insurance (including annuities) and health insurance. This monoline form of organization was unique to the United States. British and European companies more often than not received charters which conferred upon them the authority to conduct the business of insurance of all kinds anywhere in the world.

There were three basic reasons for the compartmentalization that was built into the American system. First, it was supposed that the monoline system would permit the insurer to specialize in a particular field of insurance and develop a proficiency that would permit it to cope better with the technical problems to be solved. Second, it was felt that the segregation of classes of insurance would permit a more accurate appraisal of the financial qualification required for each line of insurance, and regulatory requirements could be laid down that would fit the particular requirements of the different phases of the industry. Finally, insurance regulators felt that there was a danger in combining fire insurance, which seemed more subject to catastrophes, with life insurance. The various conflagrations, such as the New York fire of 1835, helped to reinforce this opinion.

Although not all states had prohibitions against multiple-line operations (the writing of more than one line by a single company), the state of New York did have, and through a rather curious administrative ruling made its prohibition effective in other states; a deputy superintendent of the New York Department of Insurance formulated this ruling in 1900, which came to be known as the Appleton Rule. In its simplest form, the Appleton Rule provided that out-of-state companies that desired to do business in New York were required to agree to follow New York's laws not only while operating in New York, but also while operating in any other state. This rule, which was originally an administrative ruling, was made a part of the New York Insurance Code in 1939. More than any other single factor, the Appleton Rule acted to foster and perpetuate the monoline development.

### The Multiple-Line Transition

As early as the beginning of the 1900s there was agitation for a departure from the monoline concept, but it was not until 1944 that any real progress was made. In that year the Diemand Committee of the National Association of Insurance Commissioners[4] submitted a report to the insurance commissioners of the country strongly advocating multiple-line powers for insurance companies. During the latter part of the 1940s the various states began to enact legislation permitting multiple-line operations, and by 1949 the movement to abandon the system of compartmentalization had spread to two-thirds of the states. When New York decided to permit multiple-line operation in 1949, the die was cast. Since the advent of legislation permitting multiple-line underwriting, there has been a rapid expansion of the concept. The greatest benefit from the point of view of the consumer has been the development of the package policy, in which the traditional property coverages are combined with the casualty coverages into a single policy.

The basic idea of multiple-line operation is sound. It extends the concept of product diversification into the insurance field. Just as manufacturers have discovered that it is often better to produce several related products instead of relying only on one, so insurance companies have diversified. The averaging of fire losses with liability losses over a period of time should result in a greater stability of operating results and therefore in greater financial stability for the companies. The spread of loss principle which is basic to all insurance operations is inherent in the notion of the multiple-line concept.

Multiple-line legislation did not completely destroy the underwriting compartmentalization. It merely permitted the companies in the fields of property and casualty insurance to cross the traditional barriers when an insurer met the capital and surplus requirements of each line. It did not, in most cases, destroy the barrier between life insurance and the field of property and casualty insurance. The next step in the development of the insurance industry would appear to be the removal of this barrier and the transition to "all-lines operation," which refers to the combination of property and liability operations with life insurance operations in a single company. There is little doubt that this transition will eventually be made, and with it will come an expansion of the package policy concept.

---

[4] The Diemand Committee was named after its chairman, John Diemand, of the Insurance Company of North America. An explanation of the nature and functions of the National Association of Insurance Commissioners will be made in Chapter 6.

## CLASSIFICATION OF INSURERS

Insurers may be classified according to the type of insurance they sell, their legal form of ownership, or the marketing system they employ.

### Classification by Type of Product

It is possible to distinguish between three types of insurers on the basis of their product. Life insurance companies deal in the area of life contracts and annuities, and, in addition, write health and accident insurance. Property and liability insurance companies write all forms of property and liability (including health and accident), but do not write life insurance. Health and accident insurers represent a special classification of specialty insurers. They write only health and accident coverage. While there are other specialty insurers that write only a single line of property or liability insurance, these may still be classified as property and liability companies.

### Types of Insurer by Form of Ownership

In addition to being classified on the basis of the type of insurance they provide, insurance companies may be classified according to the legal form of their ownership into the following six broad groups:

1. Capital stock insurance companies
2. Mutual insurance companies
3. Reciprocals or interinsurance exchanges
4. Lloyd's associations
5. Government insurers
6. Self-insurers

### Capital Stock Insurance Companies

Stock companies are organized as profit-making ventures, with the stockholders assuming the risk that is transferred by the individual insureds. If the actuarial predictions prove accurate, the premiums collected are sufficient to pay losses and operating expenses and return a profit to the stockholders. The capital provided by the stockholders provides a fund for the operation of the company until premium income is sufficient to pay losses and operating expenses. In addition, it provides a surplus fund which serves as a guarantee to the policyholders that the contracts will be fulfilled. The distinguishing characteristics of a capital stock insurance company are (a) the premium charged by the company is final—there is no form of contingent liability for the policyholder; (b) the Board of Directors is elected by the stockholders; and (c) earnings are distributed to shareholders as dividends on their stock. Capital stock companies more or less dominate the field of property and liability insurance, accounting for approximately two-thirds of the premium volume.

### Mutual Insurance Companies

In contrast to a stock company, a mutual insurance company is owned by the policyholders. Mutual companies are organized for the purpose of providing insurance for its members. Normally, a mutual company is incorporated, and in many states this is a legal requirement. The essential characteristic of the mutual company is its lack of capital stock, and the distribution of earnings. Any money left after paying all costs of operation is returned to the policyholders in the form of a dividend. Included in the concept of "costs" which must be paid is the addition to the surplus of the company. Unlike the capital stock company, the mutual company has no paid-in capital as a guarantee of solvency in the event of adverse experience. For this reason it is essential that a surplus be accumulated to protect against such adverse contingencies as excessive losses or a decline in investment return.

**Pure assessment mutuals.**    Pure assessment mutuals operate on the basis of sharing the losses by members of the group. Under the pure assessment plan, no premium would be payable in advance, but assessments would be made of each member for his portion of losses which occur. The difficulty in making these assessments makes the operation of such a plan impractical. Perhaps the best example of the pure assessment idea of mutual insurance is the burial benefit plan in which each member of the group (which typically consists of 1000 members) sends $1 or $2 to the widow of a deceased member. Obviously, an important aspect of this program is acquiring new members.

**Advance premium mutuals—assessable policies.**    The advance premium mutual, as the name indicates, charges a premium in advance, at the beginning of the policy period. If the original premiums are sufficient to pay all operating expenses and losses, any surplus is returned to the policyholders in the form of a dividend. If, on the other hand, the original assessment is insufficient to meet all contingencies, additional assessments may be levied against the members. Normally, the amount of the assessment is limited, either by state law, or simply as a provision in the bylaws and policies of the mutual. Under this limited assessment arrangement, the amount of an additional assessment normally may not be more than the advance premium, although at times it is specified as double, triple, or some other multiple of the advance premium.

Under an assessment mutual plan, each member of the organization becomes both an insured and an insurer. In becoming a member of the organization, the individual makes himself liable for his share of all losses that occur to members of the group.

**Advance premium nonassessable mutuals.** Until a mutual company has established its financial stability through the accumulation of surplus, it must provide for assessment of its members. However, all states permit mutual insurers to issue nonassessable policies after they have established their financial responsibility. Normally, when a mutual company has the same financial strength required of a capital stock company writing the same type of business, it may be permitted to issue nonassessable policies. An advance premium mutual company issuing nonassessable policies is usually operated in about the same manner as a capital stock company. The advance premium which is collected is intended to be sufficient to cover all losses and expenses. If it is not, the additional costs are paid out of the accumulated surplus. All the larger mutual carriers in the United States operate on this basis. However, unlike the capital stock companies, the premium is not fixed and definite, and any excess of premium income over costs may be returned to the policyholders in the form of dividends. In the field of property and liability insurance, this excess is predicted in advance, and the "return" is made in the form of a lower initial premium.

In the last analysis, there are few practical differences between a mutual company operating on an advance premium basis and issuing nonassessable policies and a capital stock company. Although the policyholders own the mutual company in theory, there are no vested rights of ownership for these policyholders except in the case of liquidation. Furthermore, while the policyholders theoretically control the company, this control is equivalent to the theoretical control of the stockholders over the management in a large corporation with a large number of individual stockholders.

**Fraternals.** Fraternal societies are specialized forms of mutual insurers. Basically, fraternal societies are nonprofit organizations which operate on the basis of a "lodge," with a representative form of government. Fraternals have primarily concentrated their activity in the field of life insurance, although they sometimes sell sickness and accident insurance. Since fraternals are considered to be charitable institutions, they do not pay federal income tax or state premium tax.

### Reciprocals

The reciprocal or interinsurance exchange is a relative newcomer to the insurance industry. It is a particularly American innovation, and while reciprocals are only a small segment of the insurance industry, they are significant. Reciprocal insurance exchanges are often confused with mutual insurers, and while there is a similarity, there is also a fundamental difference. A reciprocal is an unincorporated aggregation of individuals, called subscribers, who exchange insurance risks. Like mutuals, reciprocals are fundamentally cooperative organizations. Each member (or subscriber) is both an insured and an insurer; as a member of the group the individual is insured by each of the other members, and he in turn insures each of them.

In a mutual organization, members of the group assume their liability collectively; in a reciprocal exchange, each subscriber assumes his liability severally as an individual, and not as a member of the group. The advantage inherent in this arrangement is that the liability of each subscriber is limited. Although some reciprocals provide for a limited assessment of the members, one member cannot be called upon to assume the liability of a defaulting member. The premium paid by each subscriber is maintained in a separate account, and the subscriber's share of each loss is paid from his account.

One main characteristic that distinguishes the reciprocal is the chief administrator of the program, who is called the "attorney-in-fact." He derives his authority through a power of attorney granted to him by each of the subscribers; he uses this to commit the members as insurers of each other's property. The power of attorney granted by the members is unusually broad—as a matter of fact, it can be a detrimental aspect of the reciprocal, since an unscrupulous attorney-in-fact could conceivably exploit the subscribers for his own personal gain. The attorney-in-fact receives some percentage of the gross premiums paid by the subscribers (usually about 25%) to cover the expenses involved in operating the program.

With the exception of the compensation of the attorney-in-fact and the expense of operating the plan, the only expense involved for a subscriber is the amount of losses that occur. If there are no losses, there is no cost. Profit is eliminated through a return of the unused premiums to the subscribers. In addition, since the insurers are also the insureds, the expense of commissions or other acquisition costs are also eliminated.

Reciprocals confine their operations to the property and casualty fields. The portion of the total premiums written through interinsurance exchanges is relatively small. In 1970, only about 4.5% of all property and casualty premiums were written through reciprocals.

### Lloyd's Associations

**Lloyd's of London.**    Lloyd's of London is the oldest and perhaps the most famous of all insurance organizations in the world. Generally speaking, Lloyd's is a corporation for marketing the services of a group of individuals. Lloyd's itself does not issue insurance policies or provide insurance protection. The actual insurance is underwritten by the 6000 underwriting members of the association. Technically, each member is a separate "insurance company," issuing policies and underwriting risks separately or collectively with other members. In a sense, Lloyd's is similar to the New York Stock Exchange, in which the actual physical facilities are owned by the stock exchange and made available to members for the transaction of business. It is governed by a group known as "The Committee of Lloyd's" which establishes standards with which members must comply.

Each underwriter at Lloyd's must conduct business as an individual proprietor or as a member of one of 300 syndicates. No corporations or other limitations on liability are permitted, and every member of Lloyd's exposes his entire personal fortune in addition to his business assets.

The fact that Lloyd's is a combination of a great many individual underwriters who assume their liability individually means that each member is liable only for his own commitments. The Lloyd's policy contains the statement, "Each for his own part and not for one another." Normally, policies issued through Lloyd's are issued by a number of the individual underwriters. A single underwriter will not assume the total risk connected with a given policy, but will assume only a fraction. He will be liable only for his portion of the total policy if a loss should occur, and he is under no obligation to assume the portion underwritten by another member. In the past, for public relations, solvent members have assumed the liabilities of defaulting members.

In addition to the individual liability that results from the severability of the underwriters, another problem arises. In the event of a dispute concerning coverage under the policy, it is technically necessary to sue each of the individual underwriters. As a matter of practice, however, if suit is brought against one underwriter under a contract and it is successful, the remaining members pay their portion of the loss without the necessity of further litigation.

Although Lloyd's of London is famous throughout the United States, it is licensed in only two states, Illinois and Kentucky. In each Lloyd's policy issued in the United States, there is a clause in which the underwriters agree to submit to the jurisdiction of either of these two states or any other court of competent jurisdiction in the United States. As a special guarantee to American policyholders, Lloyd's maintains a fund of approximately $450,000,000 in the United States.

In spite of the fact that Lloyd's is licensed in only two states, it provides insurance protection in many other areas. In order to service the needs of individuals who desire protection that is not available from companies licensed in a state, it is permissible in many states for an agent to place coverage with nonadmitted or nonlicensed companies. The insurance obtained in this manner is known as "Surplus Lines Insurance." Basically, an agent may secure coverage for a client with Lloyd's (or any other nonadmitted insurer) provided he has made a diligent effort to place the coverage concerned with licensed insurers.

**American Lloyd's.**   The American Lloyd's are an attempt to emulate the success of (and capitalize on the fame of), Lloyd's of London. An American Lloyd's is simply a group of individuals who operate an insurance mechanism using the same principles of individual liability of insurers that

Lloyd's of London uses. In an American Lloyd's, each underwriter assumes a part of every risk. Each insurer promises to pay a specified amount in the event that the contingency insured against occurs. Each member is liable only for his portion of the risk, and is not bound to assume any portion of a defaulting member. In other words, American Lloyd's operate in essentially the same manner as Lloyd's of London, but without the strict regulation which the original Lloyd's imposes upon its members. Most states have laws which prohibit the organization or licensing of American Lloyd's. Those American Lloyd's which do exist operate almost exclusively in the property insurance field.

### Government Insurers

In addition to a vast array of social insurance programs, both the federal and state governments have become increasingly important in the area of private insurance. In many cases they operate monopolistic insurance programs; in some cases they compete with private insurers. In most instances, the government has entered the insurance area when private insurers were unable or unwilling to provide desired coverages.

**State insurance programs**

1. All the states operate unemployment insurance programs which provide for payment to certain unemployed workers who have qualified on the basis of previous employment.
2. Eighteen states offer workmen's compensation insurance. In six of these, the government fund operates as a monopoly and employers may purchase this coverage only from the state. In the remaining twelve states, the government fund operates side by side with private insurers.
3. Five states (California, Hawaii, New Jersey, New York, and Rhode Island) and Puerto Rico have established compulsory temporary disability programs which provide income to workers who are disabled by a nonoccupational cause. In Rhode Island the state operates a monopolistic insurance program. In the other jurisdictions, competitive state funds or private insurers provide the coverage.
4. Hail insurance funds have been established in the states of North Dakota, Colorado, and Montana, which offer coverage against loss to growing crops from hail damage.

**Federal insurance programs.** The federal government is the largest insurer in the United States, operating a number of social and private insurance programs. Among the most important are the following:

1. The Social Security Program provides life insurance, disability income insurance, retirement pensions, and health insurance to those covered.

Over 90% of the employed persons and their dependents in the country are covered for at least some benefits under this program.

2. The Federal Deposit Insurance Corporation (FDIC), which is technically owned by the member banks it insures, is maintained and operated by the federal government, providing a specialized form of insurance protection on bank deposits.

3. The Veterans' Bureau sells National Service Life insurance to veterans of previous wars.

4. The Federal Housing Authority (FHA) provides mortgage insurance to lenders to protect against default by home purchasers.

5. The Federal Crop Insurance Corporation sells crop insurance to farmers.

Once again, it is important to note that the government provides both social insurance and private insurance. The fact that the coverage is furnished by the government does not necessarily make it a social insurance coverage. The distinguishing characteristic of the private insurance programs offered by the government is that they are voluntary, while the social insurance programs are not. Normally, the private insurance coverages provided by the government involve a contractual relationship, whereas the social insurance programs may or may not involve a contract.

### Self-Insurance

Under some circumstances, it is possible for a business firm to engage in the same activities as a commercial insurance company in dealing with its own risks. However, what many people refer to as self-insurance is not really insurance at all, but rather assumption of risk. In order to be classified as a bonafide self-insurance plan, the elements that we found in our two definitions of insurance must be present:

1. The firm should be large enough to permit the combination of a sufficiently large number of exposure units so as to make losses predictable. The program must involve the operation of the law of large numbers.

2. The plan must be financially dependable. In most cases, this will involve the accumulation of a fund to meet losses that occur, with a sufficient accumulation to safeguard against the possible fluctuation upward of losses from the prediction.

3. The individual units of loss potential must be distributed in such a manner geographically so as to prevent a catastrophe. A loss involving all units should be impossible.

Self-insurance is a somewhat overworked term. Few companies or organizations are large enough to engage in a sound self-insurance program.

In the majority of cases, risks are simply retained without attempting to make estimates of the future losses. In many cases, no fund is maintained to pay for losses. Furthermore, until the fund reaches the size where it is adequate to pay for the largest possible loss, the possibility of loss is not eliminated for the individual exposure units.

## THE AGENT

From many points of view, the most important person in the entire insurance transaction is the agent. The marketing of insurance is a complicated operation, and yet it is an essential part of the insurance business, for without an effective marketing organization, insurers could not obtain a sufficient number of exposure units to permit the spreading of the risk and the calculation of the probability of loss on an accurate basis. With few exceptions, the marketing mechanism in the insurance industry revolves around the agent, however, his role varies in different lines of insurance. In the field of property and liability insurance, on one hand, the agent is "an individual authorized to create, terminate, and modify contracts of insurance." In the area of life insurance, on the other hand, the agent's power is somewhat more limited. Life insurance agents are appointed with the authorization to solicit and deliver contracts of insurance, however, they cannot, as can the property and liability agent, bind the insurance company to a risk.

The agent derives his powers from two sources. He is given express powers by his company in the agency agreement or contract. This gives him express authority to represent the company, and generally contains clauses dealing with such things as the specific and general powers of the agent, the scale of commissions, the ownership of the contracts sold, and a provision for cancellation of the contract. In addition to those expressly granted powers, the agent has certain implied powers. Under the doctrine of "ostensible authority," the courts have ruled that an agent has those powers that the public has come to expect him to have. Because it is accepted by the public that property and liability agents have the power to bind their company to a risk, they have this power, in spite of the fact that the company may not have granted it expressly. Let us say, for example, that the insurance company has told a particular agent not to sell any insurance on match factories, but the agent binds coverage on such an establishment. In spite of the fact that the company has forbidden the agent to bind such coverage, it would be liable for any loss that occurred. As far as the public is concerned, an act by the agent is an act by the insurance company. He acts on behalf of the company in the insurance transaction, and under the laws of agency, his acts are deemed to be those of the company. If he binds the company to a risk, it is bound to that risk until such time as it effects cancellation of the contract.

The insurance agent is first and foremost the representative of the insurance company. An insurance broker, on the other hand, is a representative of the insured. Although he is the agent of the insured, the broker normally receives his compensation in the form of a commission from the company. The fact that the broker is not an agent of the insurance company means that he does not have the power to bind the company to a risk. He merely solicits business from his clients and then places the business with an insurer. Brokers represent an important segment of the insurance marketing mechanism, particularly in large cities, where they control large segments of the market. In some instances, agents also act as brokers, placing coverage through the agents of companies they do not represent.

## MARKETING SYSTEMS

As noted previously, the agent is the central figure in the insurance marketing process. While this is true, the relationship between the agent and the company he represents can be, and is often, quite varied. Through a process of evolution, several marketing forms have developed, each of which has as its goal the attainment of efficiency in distribution and service.

### The Life Insurance Distribution System

With the exception of a small amount of life insurance that is sold through the mail, life insurance companies are represented by agents. Most life insurance companies either insist that the agent represent them exclusively or attempt to encourage him to do so. While there are life agents who represent more than one life insurance company, these are the exception.

The chief differences among life insurance companies in their distribution techniques are centered around the supervision of the agent. Two systems are used: (a) the general agent and (b) the branch office. A general agent is an independent businessman, empowered by the company he represents to sell life insurance in a specified territory and to appoint subagents. At one time, the general agent received no financial assistance from the company he represented, but received a commission on all the business his subagents produced. He in turn paid a part of this commission to the agents and paid his expenses, with the balance representing his personal income. This has gradually changed, and now most general agents receive some sort of financial assistance from their companies in the form of a contribution toward the general agency expense. The fact that the general agent hires, trains, and compensates his subagents makes the general agency a relatively inexpensive and riskless manner of starting in a new area. Unfortunately, however, there are certain disadvantages inherent in the general agency system. One major shortcoming is the lack of supervision and control that the company has over the subagents. For this reason, the general agency operations have gradually been modified with more control from the home office.

The branch manager, in contrast to the general agent, is a salaried employee of the insurance company. Expenses of the branch office are paid by the home office, for in reality the branch office is simply an extension of the home office. At one time, the branch manager received only a salary, but in recent years this has been modified, and in many cases the branch manager now receives additional compensation on the basis of the production of the agents he supervises.

The trend in the supervision of life insurance agents (the sales organization of the life insurance industry) is toward an elimination of the differences between the general agent and the branch manager. Today, the general agent has many characteristics of the branch manager and vice versa.

### Property and Liability Distribution Systems

In the field of property and liability insurance, companies may be classified into two groups based on their distribution system: (a) those who operate through the American Agency System and (b) the "direct writers." The agents who operate through the American Agency System are known as "independent agents," while those who represent direct writers are called "captive agents."

**The American agency system.**   The independent agent normally represents several companies, dividing the policies he sells among those companies according to his choice. He owns his expirations, which means that he may place the renewals of policies he has sold with some other insurer if he chooses to do so. This alternative often gives the independent agent strategic power he can use to the benefit of his clients. However, since even the independent agent is first and foremost a representative of the insurance company, he also has an obligation to the company. One implication of the ownership of renewals by the independent agent is the fact that it prevents the insurance company from attempting to pay a lower commission on renewal business. If a company represented by an independent agent were to attempt to pay a lower commission on renewal business than on new business, the agent could simply place the policy with a different company, making it new business for that company.

**Direct writers.**   Direct writing companies operate through salaried representatives (as in the case of The Liberty Mutual Insurance Company), or through exclusive or "captive agents" (as is the case with Nationwide, State Farm, and Allstate).[5] The compensation of the salesman may be in the form of a salary, or it may be a commission, based on the premium volume. In the case of the exclusive agent, it is normally in the form of commission. The important point is that the agent or the salaried employee does not own the expirations. He has no choice as to where the policy is to be renewed. Since the agent cannot transfer the business he writes to another insurer, the direct writing company can pay an infinitesimally small renewal commission or none at all.

The ownership of renewals is the most important difference between the two types of agents, and from this difference arises still other differences in the method of operation. Since the direct writing agent receives little or no commission on renewals, the production of new business is of crucial importance. In a sense, the life insurance agent is in the same position; he is a captive agent, representing only one company. Since for the life insurance agent, like the direct writing agent in property and liability, the renewal commission is quite low, his income depends on the generation of new business. The independent agent, on the other hand, places greater emphasis on the retention of accounts he presently services. As a matter of fact, the independent agent's interest in his obligation to his clients is one of the essential themes of the advertising program of the independent agents.

## COOPERATION AND COMPETITION IN THE INDUSTRY

### Cooperation in the Insurance Industry

Insurance by its very nature is cooperative. Despite the fact that insurance companies and agents compete vigorously with each other, there are many areas in which both companies and agents cooperate. This cooperation arises out of economic necessity in some cases. Many cooperative organizations are formed and supported by groups of insurance companies to perform functions that would involve a duplication of effort if each company attempted to perform them individually. In other areas, the objective of the organizations is public relations or education. The complicated nature of the insurance business requires cooperation in technical areas such as ratemaking and management, and cooperative organizations have been formed and are supported by insurance companies to serve this end. The extent and nature of the cooperation within the industry can best be shown by examining a number of the most important organizations.

[5]Technically, companies that operate through exclusive agents are not "direct writers," but rather "exclusive-agent companies." However, the term "direct writer" is commonly used in reference to both companies operating through salaried representatives and those operating through exclusive agents.

**Rating organizations.**    One major area of cooperation among insurance companies is in rate-making. As we have seen, the accuracy of the predictions made by actuaries is increased as the number of exposures upon which these predictions are based increases. Numerous organizations called rating bureaus are supported by insurance companies who furnish their loss statistics to these organizations as the raw material for producing rates. Members of the bureau then use the rates that are published by the bureau. A full member of a bureau generally agrees to use all its facilities and to adhere to its rates and forms. In addition to the full bureau members, there are numerous companies that subscribe to the services of the bureau. While they are not members, they use the facilities of the bureau and purchase the right to use the rates published by the bureau as a basis for their own rates. Subscribers to a bureau may use full bureau rates, or, with the permission of the insurance regulatory authorities, they may "deviate" or depart from the bureau rates.

There are, of course, companies that do not belong to the major cooperative rating bodies. These companies pursue an independent course of action, using independently filed rates and forms. A small insurer does not normally have a sufficiently large number of exposures to devise accurate rates, and as a result, only larger companies make independent filings. Many people in the insurance business feel that the cooperative rating bureaus set the standard for the industry on the premises that companies that deviate must have something to deviate from.

Some of the more important rating bureaus and organizations are the following:

1. The Insurance Service Office (ISO) which came into being January 1, 1971, is the largest cooperative rating organization in the property and liability field. It was formed through the consolidation of six previous organizations that had computed rates for individual lines of insurance. The ISO computes and publishes rates in the area of automobile liability, medical payments and physical damage, general liability insurance, boiler and machinery, theft, plate glass, inland marine and package policies such as the homeowners forms.

2. The Mutual Insurance Rating Bureau (MIRB) computes rates to be used by mutual companies in the nonautomobile liability field and other casualty fields.

3. The Transportation Insurance Rating Bureau (TIRB) publishes inland marine rates for mutual companies.

In the area of fire insurance, rates are not made at a national level. The actual rate-making is carried out by fire insurance rating bureaus at the state (and sometimes regional) level. These fire insurance rating bureaus are supported by the companies using the rates in the area. Although the actual rate-making is carried out at the state level, there are two important organizations at the national level that facilitate it.

1. The Inter-Regional Insurance Conference acts in an advisory capacity for fire rate-making organizations, developing suggested rates and policies on their behalf. The programs recommended by the Inter-Regional Insurance Conference must then be adopted by the fire-rating organization.
2. An equally important organization, the American Insurance Association (AIA), studies the construction codes of various cities throughout the United States, the adequacy of their water supply, the competence of their fire departments, and other factors that are of importance in the establishment of proper fire insurance rates. The AIA is a combination of three previous organizations, The National Board of Fire Underwriters, the old American Insurance Association, and the Association of Casualty and Surety Companies.

There are no rating bureaus in the life insurance field; however, the Society of Actuaries, a voluntary association of insurance actuaries, holds periodic meetings for the exchange of information with the goal of improvement of premium determination.

**Public relations organizations.** Each of the three major fields of insurance has its "information institute," which functions as a public relations arm of the industry. The Institute of Life Insurance is primarily a public relations organization financed by member life insurance companies. It prepares and distributes educational materials to teachers and schools, prepares news releases concerning developments in the field of life insurance that are of general interest to the public, and gathers and publishes statistics concerning life insurance. The Health Insurance Institute performs the same functions in the area of health insurance. The property and liability insurance equivalent of the above two organizations is the Insurance Information Institute, which is supported by approximately 300 capital stock insurance companies.

**Educational organizations.** The field of insurance requires continuing education on a scale that is matched by few occupations. A large number of educational organizations exist for the agent or company employee who wishes to improve his knowledge and increase his professionalism.

The American College of Life Underwriters is the leading educational organization in the field of life insurance. It sponsors the course of instruction leading to the professional designation "Chartered Life Underwriter" (CLU). This designation is a symbol of professional attainment that relatively few individuals achieve. The American College of Life Underwriters is supported by contributing life insurance companies.

The American Institute for Property and Liability Underwriters is the equivalent of the American College of Life Underwriters in the area of property and liability insurance. The designation granted by the Institute is Chartered Property and Casualty Underwriter (CPCU). The CPCU, like the CLU, is the highest symbol of attainment granted to a member of the property and liability insurance profession for educational development and professionalism.

In addition to the American Life College and the Institute for Property and Liability Underwriters, two other organizations exist with the purpose of sponsoring education. The Insurance Institute of America offers basic courses in preparation for the rigorous requirements of the CPCU study program. The Life Underwriters' Training Council offers similar instruction in the field of life insurance.

**Agents' cooperative organizations.**    Cooperation in the insurance business is not limited to insurance companies. There is also a substantial degree of cooperation among agents. In the area of property and liability insurance, many agents belong to cooperative organizations at the local level known as local boards of insurance agents. These in turn cooperate by affiliating with a state association of insurance agents (e.g., The Iowa Association of Independent Insurance Agents or The Iowa Association of Mutual Insurance Agents). The state associations further cooperate by affiliating with one of two national associations, The National Association of Insurance Agents or the National Association of Mutual Insurance Agents.

In the area of life insurance, the basic cooperative organization is the local association of life underwriters; each local association affiliates with a state association (e.g., The Iowa Association of Life Underwriters). The national organization with which each of the state associations is affiliated is known as the National Association of Life Underwriters.

In both the property and liability and the life insurance field, agents' associations perform many valuable functions for member agents, particularly in the areas of supporting legislation which is of interest to the public and the insurance industry and guarding against unwise legislation. An equally important function provided by the agents' associations is the promotion of agent education, helping agents to improve themselves and their operations.

### Competition in the Insurance Industry

The competition within the insurance industry today is fierce; perhaps more so than at any time in history. Briefly, this competition takes place in three areas:

1. Price competition

2. Quality competition
3. Service

**Price competition.**    Insurers compete on the basis of price by offering a lower-priced product than other companies dealing in the same line of insurance. It is often puzzling that insurance companies can charge significantly different premiums for identical coverage. The price of insurance coverage, like most prices, is a function of the cost of production. The most obvious answer to the question of how various insurance companies can charge significantly different premiums for the same insurance coverage is that their costs must also vary significantly. The following costs are common to all insurance companies:

1. Payment of losses
2. Loss of adjustment expense
3. Cost of production (sales expense)
4. Administrative expenses
5. Taxes

If a company is successful in reducing any of these costs below those of its competitors, it stands to reason that it will be able to offer its coverages at a lower premium.

The first of the listed costs, the *payment of losses*, can be an area of significant difference between companies. Since the hazards and perils involved in each exposure are different, the exposure units have varying degrees of risk. Some exposures are better than average and some are worse. If a company can succeed in obtaining its customers from a better class of risks, not only will its loss experience be lower, but since the better risks are thus removed from the total of exposure units, the average risk in the remaining group will be worse than previously. So when one company or a group of companies succeeds in lowering its loss payments through the selection of better risks, the loss payments of the remaining companies rise.

If losses decline, then the second cost, the *expense of adjustment*, also declines. In this way, careful selection of the more desirable exposures results in an additional saving.

The third cost, the *cost of production*, can also be altered to reflect substantial premium savings. The bulk of production costs have traditionally been agents' commissions. In addition to the original commission when the policy is first sold, some lines of insurance require commission payments at each renewal, equal to the original commission. Some companies, such as the direct writers, have been able to reduce premium costs by reducing the agent's renewal commission. Even in life insurance, where the agent's commission is a significant cost only in the first years, lower commission scales may permit lower premiums.

Closely connected with the costs of production are the fourth cost, *administrative expenses*. Efficiency in administration, through the use of mechanized billing and automatic renewal procedures, not only saves administrative costs, but also gives the company greater control over policy renewals and permits a reduction of renewal premiums.

Although *taxes* represent only a small percentage of the total premium, some differences in cost are traceable to the tax element. Since the premium tax is levied as a percentage of the total premiums written by an insurer and added to the individual premiums, it tends to magnify the difference among companies in the other costs. Also, the fact that some insurers (e.g., fraternals or Blue Cross and Blue Shield organizations) are exempt from certain taxes gives them a competitive advantage. Finally, some states give preferential treatment to domestic insurance companies by exempting them from the state premium tax or taxing them at a lower rate than the rate at which out-of-state insurers are taxed.

While all savings in the costs of various companies have some effect on the price of their product, the most substantial variations in premium rates are due to the savings made in loss payments. We might add that selection of a better class of insureds is not the only way to save in the area of loss payments.

Price competition in the life insurance field is a complicated operation. Although most companies use the same mortality tables and make the same assumption regarding the return they will make on their investment, the price for a given type of policy varies from one company to another. It does not appear that competition has been an effective device for the protection of the consumer in the field of life insurance. At least one authority maintains that there are excessive prices in the field of life insurance resulting from a lack of competition, which is possible because of the complexities of the contracts and the general lack of sophistication on the part of the buyers.[6] Competition is an effective force only when the consumer is aware of his alternatives, and in most cases it is difficult if not impossible for the layman to compare life insurance contracts and evaluate the differences.

In the area of property and liability insurance, the price competition takes place between various types of companies. Thus, mutual companies compete with stock companies, bureau companies compete with nonbureau companies, and companies operating through the American Agency System compete with the direct writers.

**Quality competition.**    In addition to price competition, insurance companies also compete by offering different forms of policies, with broader insuring agreements or additional provisions which are beneficial to the insured.

---

[6] Joseph M. Belth, *The Retail Price Structure in American Life Insurance* (Bloomington, Ind.: Bureau of Business Research, Graduate School of Business, Indiana University, 1966).

One aspect of the competition which has been beneficial to insureds (and we might add detrimental to the companies in some cases), has been the continuous broadening of coverage under various policy forms.

**Service.**   Essentially, the insurance product is a promise of future performance. The individual seldom knows if the product he has purchased is adequate until he has a loss, and this is a rather inconvenient time to find that it is inadequate. One major area certain types of insurers have stressed is the service and advice the agent gives the individual. Basically, the service consists of advising the client regarding the proper types of insurance he needs, making certain that there are no unprotected exposures, maintaining a constant check on the coverages in effect, and providing prompt and fair settlement of losses.

## Questions for Discussion and Review

**1.**   The economic significance of the insurance industry is indicated by a number of statistical measures, including (a) the total number employed in the industry; (b) the assets held or controlled by insurers; (c) the total premium volume written; (d) taxes paid; (e) the amount of insurance in force; (f) the amount of claims paid annually; (g) the number of people who benefit or hold policies. Which of these, in your opinion, provides the best single measure of the importance of the insurance industry in the American economy? Why?

**2.**   List the types of insurers as classified by legal form of ownership, and briefly describe the distinguishing characteristics of each type.

**3.**   Why do you think that the property and liability distribution system developed along the lines of the American agency system, whereas the life insurance distribution system developed through exclusive agents?

**4.**   Direct writing agents have made tremendous gains in the field of property and liability insurance for the individual, but insurance for business firms is still handled primarily through the American agency system. Why do you think this has been so?

**5.**   Agents frequently emphasize "service" in their advertising. What services should a client legitimately expect from his insurance agent?

## Suggestions for Additional Reading

Athearn, J. L. *Risk and Insurance*, 2nd ed. New York: Appleton-Century-Crofts, 1969, Chaps. 6, 22, 24.

Bickelhaupt, D. L. *Transition of Multiple-Line Insurance Companies.* Homewood, Ill.: Richard D. Irwin, 1961.

Denenberg, H. A., Eilers, R. D., Hoffman, G. W., Kline, C. A., Melone, J. J., and Snider, H. W. *Risk and Insurance.* Englewood Cliffs, N.J.: Prentice-Hall, 1964, Chap. 14.

Greene, M. R. *Risk and Insurance*, 2nd ed. Cincinnati, Ohio: Southwestern, 1968, Chap. 5.

Gibbs, D. E. W. *Lloyd's of London: A Study in Individualism.* New York: St. Martin's Press, 1957.

Magee, J. H. and Serbein, O. N. *Property and Liability Insurance,* 4th ed. Homewood, Ill.: Richard D. Irwin, 1967, Chap. 28.

Mehr, R. I. *Life Insurance Theory and Practice.* Austin, Texas: Business Publications, 1970, Chap. 28.

Michelbacher, G. F. and Roos, N. R. *Multiple-Line Insurers,* 2nd ed. New York: McGraw-Hill, 1970, Chap. 1.

Mowbray, A. H., Blanchard, R. H., and Williams, C. A., Jr. *Insurance,* 6th ed. New York: McGraw-Hill, 1969, Chaps. 24, 26, 33.

National Association of Insurance Agents. *Stanford Report.* New York: National Association of Insurance Agents, 1967.

Nelli, H. O. and Marshall, R. A. *The Private Insurance Business in the United States,* Research Paper 48. Atlanta, Ga.: Bureau of Business and Economic Research, Georgia State College, June 1969.

Pfeffer, I. "The Early History of Insurance." *Annals of the Society of Chartered Property and Casualty Underwriters* **XIX**, 11, 19, 23 (Summer 1966).

*Prices and Profits in the Property and Liability Insurance Industry—Report to the American Insurance Association.* Cambridge, Mass.: Arthur D. Little, November 1967.

Snider, H. W. (ed.) *Readings in Property and Casualty Insurance.* Homewood, Ill.: Richard D. Irwin, 1959, Chaps. 7–10, 53–54.

The Health Insurance Institute. *Source Book of Health Insurance Data* (New York: The Health Insurance Institute, annually).

The Insurance Information Institute. *Insurance Facts, Property-Liability-Inland Marine-Surety.* New York: The Insurance Information Institute, annually.

The Insurance Information Institute. *Life Insurance Fact Book.* New York: The Institute of Life Insurance, annually.

# 5 Functions of Insurers

*What I advise is that each contentedly practice the trade he understands.*
—Horace, *Epistles*

As a part of our study of the insurance mechanism and the manner in which it operates, it may be helpful to examine some of the unique facets of insurance company operations. In general, insurers operate in much the same manner as other firms; however, the nature of the insurance transaction requires certain specialized functions. In addition, financial record keeping of insurers deviates from normal practices. In this chapter, we will examine some specialized activities of insurance companies and the financial aspects of their operations.

## FUNCTIONS OF INSURERS

Although there are definite operational differences between life insurance companies and property and liability insurers, the major activities of all insurers may be classified as follows:

1. Production
2. Underwriting
3. Rate-making
4. Loss settlement
5. Finance

In addition to these, there are, of course, various other activities that are common to most firms, such as accounting, personnel management, market research, and so on.

### Production

The production department of an insurance company, sometimes called the agency department, is its sales or marketing department. This department supervises the external portion of the sales effort, which is conducted by the agents or salaried representatives of the company. The various marketing systems under which the outside salesmen operate were discussed in Chapter 4.

The internal portion of the production function is carried on by the production department or the agency department. It is the responsibility of this department to select and appoint agents and to assist in sales. In general, it renders assistance in technical matters to the agents. Special agents or fieldmen are employed to assist the agent in his marketing problems. The special agent is a technician who calls on agents, acting as an intermediary between the production department and the agent.

### Underwriting

Underwriting is the process of selecting and classifying exposures. It is an essential element in the operation of any insurance program, for unless the company selects from among its applicants, the inevitable result will be adverse selection against the company. As we noted in Chapter 1, the future experience of the group to which the rates are applied will approximate the experience of the group upon which those rates are based only if both groups have approximately the same loss-producing characteristics. There must be the same proportion of good and bad risks in the group insured as there were in the group from which the statistics were taken as the basis for the rate. The tendency of the poorer than average risks to seek insurance to a greater extent than do the average or the better than average risks must be prevented. The underwriter's main responsibility is to guard against adverse selection. It is important to understand that underwriting does not have as its goal the selection of risks that will not have losses, but merely to avoid a disproportionate number of bad risks, and thereby make the actual losses equal the expected losses. In addition to this goal there are certain other objectives. While attempting to avoid adverse selection through rejection of those risks which are undesirable, the underwriter must secure an adequate volume of exposures in each class. In addition, he must guard against congestion or concentration of exposures which might result in a catastrophe. Few factors are as important to the success of the insurance operation as the underwriting function, for it is directly connected with the adequacy of rates. The actuaries of the company or the rating bureau compute the rate for the various classes.

The underwriter must determine into which, if any, of the classes each risk should go. Poor underwriting may wipe out the efforts of the actuary and make a good rate inadequate. For this reason, those who perform the underwriting function must develop a keen sense of judgment and a thorough knowledge of the hazards associated with various types of coverage.

**The agent's role in underwriting.** Since the application for the insurance originates with the agent, he is often called a field underwriter. The use of the term "underwriter" in reference to an agent is more common in the field of life insurance than in the field of property and liability, which is surprising in view of the fact that the agent plays a far more important role in the underwriting process in the field of property and liability. As a matter of fact, a part of the compensation of property and liability insurance agents is based on the profitability of the business they write. This is accomplished through a device known as a "contingency contract" or "profit-sharing contract," under the terms of which the agent receives an additional commission at the end of the year if the business he has submitted has produced a profit for the company. The intent of these profit-sharing agreements is to provide incentive to the agent to underwrite in his office.

**The underwriting policy.** Underwriting begins with the formulation of the company's underwriting policy, which is generally established by the officers in charge of underwriting. The underwriting policy establishes the framework within which the desk underwriter makes his decisions. This policy specifies the lines of insurance that will be written and those exposures that are prohibited, the amount of coverage that will be permitted on various types of exposures, the areas of the country in which each line will be written, and similar restrictions. The desk underwriter, as the individual who applies these regulations to the applications is called, is usually not involved in the formation of the company underwriting policy.

**The process of underwriting.** In order to perform effectively his function, the underwriter must obtain as much information about the subject of the insurance as possible within the limitations imposed by time and the cost of obtaining additional information. The desk underwriter must rule on the exposures submitted by the agents, accepting some and rejecting others that do not meet the underwriting requirements of the company. When the risk is rejected, it is because the underwriter feels that the hazards connected with the risk are excessive in relation to the rate. There are five basic sources from which the underwriter obtains his information regarding the hazards connected with the exposure:

1. The application containing the insured's statements
2. Information from the agent or broker

3. Investigations
4. Information bureaus
5. Physical examinations or inspections

**The application.**   The basic source of underwriting information is the application, which varies for each line of insurance and for each type of coverage. The broader and more liberal the contract, usually the more detailed the information required in the application. The questions on the application are designed to give the underwriter the information he needs in order to decide if he will accept the exposure, reject it, or attempt to acquire additional information.

**Information from the agent or broker.**   In many cases the underwriter places much weight on the recommendations of the agent or broker. This varies, of course, with the experience the underwriter has had with the particular agent in question. In certain cases the underwriter will agree to accept an exposure that does not meet the underwriting requirements of the company. Such exposures are referred to as "accommodation risks," because they are accepted as an accommodation for a valued client or agent.

**Investigations.**   In some cases the underwriter will request an inspection report from an inspection company that specializes in the investigation of personal matters. The inspection report may deal with a wide range of personal characteristics of the applicant, including his financial status, occupation, character, and the extent to which he uses alcoholic beverages (or to which his neighbor says he uses them). All the information is pertinent in the decision to accept or reject the application. For example, the financial status of the applicant is important in both the property and liability field and in the life insurance field, although for different reasons. In the property and liability field, evidence of financial difficulty may be an indication of a potential moral hazard. In life insurance, there is concern because an individual who purchases more life insurance than he can afford is likely to lapse the policy, a practice which is costly to the company.

**Information bureaus.**   In addition to the inspection report the underwriter may seek information from one of the cooperative information bureaus the industry supports. The best example of this is the Medical Information Bureau, which maintains centralized files containing information concerning the physical condition of applicants who have applied for life insurance in a member company. In automobile insurance, the company may obtain a copy of the applicant's motor vehicle record with a list of violations from the state department of motor vehicles.

**Physical examinations or inspections.**   In life insurance, the primary focus is on the health of the applicant. The medical director of the company lays down principles to guide the agents and desk writers in the selection of risks, and one of the most critical pieces of intelligence is the report of the physician. Physicians selected by the insurance company supply the insurer with medical reports after a physical examination, and this report serves as a very important source of underwriting information. In the field of property and liability insurance the equivalent of the physical examination in life insurance is the inspection of the premises. Although such inspections are not always conducted, the practice is increasing. In some instances this inspection is performed by the agent, who sends his report to the company with photographs of the property. In other cases, a company representative conducts the inspection.

### Rate-Making

An insurance rate is the price per unit of insurance coverage. Like any other price, it is a function of the cost of production. In insurance, unlike other industries, the cost of production is not known when the contract is sold, and it will not be known until some time in the future when the policy has expired. The fundamental difference between insurance pricing and the pricing function in other industries is the fact that the price for insurance must be based on a prediction.

Regardless of the type of insurance involved, the premium income of the insurer must be sufficient to cover losses and expenses. To obtain this premium income the insurer must predict the claims and expenses anticipated, and then allocate these costs to the various classes of policyholders. The final premium the insured pays is called the "gross premium." It is composed of the "net" or "pure" premium plus a "loading." The loading is designed to cover expenses, margins for contingencies, and, in the case of proprietary companies, a profit. In spite of the public opinion to the contrary, it does not always work out exactly this way for the companies.

Insurance rate-making is not an exact science. The law of large numbers and the experience of the past permit actuaries to make estimates about the future experience, but these must be qualified. When the actuary makes his estimate of future experience, he implicitly says "If things continue to happen in the future as they have happened in the past, this is what will happen." But things do not happen in the future as they have happened in the past; some adjustments must be made in order to account for any changes that are likely to modify future losses as compared with those in the past. Of course, if the future deviates from the past favorably, there is no great problem. However, if the deviation is unfavorable, the rate predicated on past experience may prove to be inadequate.

A major difference between the fields of property and liability insurance and life insurance has been the differences between past experience and the present. In the case of life insurance, we have seen a continued improvement in the life expectancy; this has benefited insurance companies in two ways. First, since people have lived longer than was originally anticipated, the insurers have been permitted to delay payment of funds which can continue to be invested. In addition, the people who have lived longer than anticipated have paid premiums on their policies longer than anticipated.

In the property and liability field, the estimates of the future have also been somewhat wrong, but in this case the results have not been so favorable to the insurers. Inflationary pressures, which push up the costs of repair and construction, rising medical costs, an increasing rate of automobile accidents, soaring liability judgments, and other factors of the same nature have all acted to the detriment of the insurance companies. Inflationary pressures do not affect the amount of loss under a life insurance policy, because the agreement is to pay a fixed sum of dollars. In the field of property and liability insurance, however, the departures from past experience have caused severe difficulties.[1]

The rate-making function in a life insurance company is performed by the actuarial department, or, in smaller companies, by an actuarial consulting firm. The accuracy in life insurance rate-making is far better than that in any other field. Life insurance rate-making and the actuarial basis for life insurance are treated in greater detail in Chapter 9.

In the property and liability field, rates are made cooperatively through rating bureaus, although in some instances large insurance companies have their own actuarial staffs and compute their rates independently of the rating bureaus. In the field of marine insurance, the rates are frequently made by the underwriter. In the inland marine field, rates for some coverages are computed by the bureaus, and they are computed by the underwriter for other coverages.

### Loss Settlement

One basic purpose of insurance is to provide for the indemnification of those members of the group who suffer losses. This is accomplished in the loss settlement process, but it is a good bit more complicated than just passing out money. The payment of losses that have occurred is the function of the claims department, and the nature of the difficulties that are frequently encountered is evidenced by the fact that the employees in this department are called claims "adjusters."

It is obviously important that the insurance company pay its claims fairly and promptly, but it is equally important that the company resist unjust

---

[1]An additional cause of these difficulties has been a degree of price inflexibility owing to the regulatory system. The regulation of insurance rates is discussed in Chapter 6.

claims and avoid overpayment of claims. The view is rapidly increasing among insurerers that prompt, courteous, and fair claim service is one of the most effective competitive tools available to the company. Most companies in the property and liability field stress this concept in their advertising, and it is not unusual to hear claims adjusters discussing a loss and attempting to find some way a claim can be paid rather than a way not to pay it.

**The adjuster.**    Broadly speaking, an adjuster is an individual who investigates losses. He determines the liability and decides on the amount of payment to be made. Adjusters include agents, staff adjusters, bureau adjusters, independent adjusters, and public adjusters. It is quite common for the agent to function as an adjuster in the case of small property losses. Many agents have been granted "draft authority" by their companies, which means that they are authorized to issue company checks in payment of losses up to some stipulated amount. Even in cases where the amount of the loss exceeds the draft authority, the agent may handle the settlement of the loss.

Most insurance companies employ adjusters who are salaried representatives of the company. The use of a company staff adjuster in a given area is dictated by the amount of work available. In areas where the company has a large volume of claims, it will use a salaried staff adjuster in preference to using an adjustment bureau or an independent adjuster. If the volume of claims is too small to support a full-time adjuster, the company will contract for adjusting service. It is not economically feasible to maintain an adjuster in every area in which the company writes insurance. Likewise, it would be excessively expensive to send an adjuster into a distant area simply for the purpose of adjusting a loss. Under these circumstances, the company may use an adjustment bureau. The adjustment bureaus were originally organized to adjust fire losses, but they now handle other types of insurance claims. The largest of the adjustment bureaus is the General Adjustment Bureau, organized in 1896 and owned by a group of insurance companies.[2]

As an alternative, the company may hire an independent adjuster who does not work for a bureau, but instead contracts his services directly to the insurance company. These adjusters normally do not handle claims for a single company, but work for any company which is involved in the community and does not have a staff adjuster or adjusting bureau available. The independent adjuster bills each company directly for the expense of adjustment.

The public adjuster is quite different from the other types discussed. Unlike the adjusters discussed above, all of whom represent the insurance company

---

[2] Following an investigation by the United States Department of Justice in 1970, the insurance companies that owned the General Adjustment Bureau agreed to divest themselves of their stock in the company.

in the loss settlement process, the public adjuster represents the policyholder. A public adjuster is employed by an insured who has suffered a loss and does not believe that he will be able to handle his own claim. A public adjuster is a specialist available to the insured. The most common method of compensation for public adjusters is a contingency fee basis, under which the public adjuster collects a percentage of the settlement; the usual fee is 10% of the amount recovered from the insurance company. In return for this fee the public adjuster performs the actions normally required of the insured, such as preparing estimates of the loss, presenting the amount of the claim to the insurance company, and negotiating the final settlement. There is a danger in the use of a public adjuster that should be recognized. The public adjuster is considered to be an agent of the insured, which makes the insured responsible for any actions of the adjuster. For example, if the adjusters were to make fraudulent statements in an attempt to increase the amount of recovery, the policy would be voided just as if the insured had made the statements.

**Courses of action in claim settlement.**     There are two basic courses open to the company when confronted with a claim: pay or contest. In most cases there is little question concerning coverage, and payment of the loss is the most common procedure, but in those instances where the company feels that a claim should not be paid, it will deny liability and thereby contest the claim. There are two basic grounds on which the company might deny payment: either because the loss did not occur, or because the policy does not cover the loss. A loss might not be covered under the policy because it does not fall within the scope of the insuring agreement, the loss is excluded, the policy was not in force at the time of the loss, or the insured had violated a policy condition.

**The adjustment process.**     In determining whether to pay or contest the claim, the adjuster follows a relatively set procedure. There are four main steps in the settlement process: notice of loss, investigation, proof of loss, and payment or denial of the claim. The details of these steps vary with the type of insurance involved.

*Notice.*     The first step in the claim process is the furnishing of notice by the insured to the company that a loss has occurred. The requirements differ from one policy to another, but in most cases the contract requires that notice be given "immediately" or "as soon as practicable." Some contracts require that notice be given in writing, but even in these contracts the requirement is not strictly enforced. Normally, the insured gives notice that a loss has occurred by informing the agent, and this satisfies the requirement of the contract.

*Investigation.*     The investigation is designed to determine if there was actually a loss covered by the policy, and if so, the amount of the loss. In determining whether there was a covered loss, the adjuster must determine first that there was in fact a loss, and then whether the loss is covered by the policy. Determination as to whether there was a loss is the simpler of the two. There are, of course, instances in which the claimant attempts to defraud the insurer, and in some instances payment is doubtlessly made where there has not in fact been a loss. Once it has been determined that there was a loss, the question as to whether that loss is covered under the policy must be answered. The first question of importance is whether the policy was in effect at the time of the loss. If the policy is a newly issued policy, there is the possibility that the loss took place before the policy became effective. At the other end of the time spectrum, there is the possibility that the policy may have expired before the loss took place. Once it has been established that the loss took place during the policy period, there is still the possibility that the insured might have violated a condition which caused the suspension or voidance of the contract. If it appears that the policy was in effect at the time of the loss and that there was a loss, the next question is whether the peril causing the loss is a peril insured against in the policy. In the case of property insurance, it must be determined if the property damaged or lost meets the definition of the property insured. The location of the property is still another question, for some contracts cover property only at a specific location, or are applicable only in certain jurisdictions. Finally, the adjuster must determine if the person making the claim is entitled to payment under the terms of the policy.

If all the above questions are answered in the affirmative, the loss is covered. Yet to be determined is the amount of the loss, which in most cases can be far more complicated than the determination of whether or not coverage applied.

*Proof of loss.*    Within a specified time after giving notice, the insured is required to file a proof of loss. The proof of loss is a sworn statement to the effect that the loss has taken place, the amount of the claim, and the circumstances surrounding the loss. The adjuster normally assists the insured in the preparation of this document.

*Payment or denial.*    If all goes well, the insurance company draws a draft reimbursing the insured for his loss. If not, it denies the claim. The claim may be denied because there was no loss or because the policy did not cover the loss, or it may be denied because the adjuster feels that the amount of the claim is unreasonable.

**Difficulties in loss settlement.**    It is inevitable that there will be disagreements regarding loss settlements. In some instances the insured will mistakenly feel that a loss should have been covered under his policy when in fact it is not. Adjusters, being human, also err, and there are occasions when a legitimate claim is denied. In addition to the question of whether the loss is covered, the amount of the loss is a continuing source of trouble. Value in most instances is a matter of opinion, and we should therefore, not be surprised that the insured and the adjuster may have differing opinions regarding the amount of the loss. For these reasons the role of the adjuster is a delicate one. He must be fair, and yet he must try not to leave the insured unhappy. This is difficult when a loss is not covered.[3]

On the surface, it would appear that the insured is relatively powerless against the insurance company in the event of a dispute. This, however, is not the case. In those instances where the disagreement involves the amount of the loss, most policies provide for compulsory arbitration on the request of either party. In the case of a denial based on an alleged lack of coverage, the insured who feels that he is being unfairly treated may appeal to the state regulatory authority, who is charged with the protection of the consumer's interest. Finally, the insured has recourse through the courts. In some instances, the only alternative remaining to the insured is to bring suit against his own company. In general, the provisions of insurance policies require the insured to file suit within a specified period of time, usually 12 months.

### The Investment Function

As a result of their operations, insurance companies accumulate large amounts of money which are to be used for the payment of claims in the future. When these are added to the funds of the companies themselves, the assets total over $200 billion. It would be a costly waste to permit these funds to remain idle, and it is the responsibility of the finance department or a finance committee of the company, to see that they are invested.

Because a portion of their invested funds must go to meet future claims, the primary requisite of insurance company investments is safety of principal. In addition, the rate of interest that is earned is an important variable in the rating process. Life insurance companies assume some minimum rate of interest earning in their computation of premiums. Property and liability rates do not explicitly include interest income in their calculation, but it may be argued that the investment income that is earned subsidizes the underwriting experience and is therefore a factor in rate-making.

**Life insurance company investments.**   In the field of life insurance, the contracts are typically long-term in nature. For this reason, life insurance

---

[3] This admittedly requires a highly developed degree of human relations skill. Not all adjusters are masters in this field. One of the authors knows of a case in which the adjuster, upon being asked for a reason, when he told the insured that his claim was being denied, replied "Because we've got you in the fine print."

companies invest primarily in long-term investments. At the present time, almost one-half of the assets of life insurance companies are invested in bonds. Of this amount, approximately 75% are invested in public utility and industrial bonds, while government bonds represent less than 5% of total assets. Ranking next to bonds in the portfolio of life insurance companies are mortgages, representing approximately one-third of total investments. Common stocks account for less than 5% of total investment holdings.

**Property and liability investments.** Unlike life insurance contracts, the obligations of property and liability companies are generally short-term obligations. Investments of property and liability companies differ from the investment portfolio of life insurers for this reason. Property and liability insurance companies also invest approximately one-half of their assets in bonds, but investments in common stocks are far more common to the property and liability companies. Approximately one-third of the total assets of the property and liability companies are invested in common stocks. Investments in mortgages by property and liability companies are insignificant.

### Miscellaneous Functions

In addition to those already discussed, there are various other functions that are necessary for the successful operation of an insurance company. Among these are the legal function, accounting, and engineering.

**Legal.** The legal department furnishes legal advice of a general corporate nature to the company. In addition, it furnishes legal advice on such matters as policy forms, relations with agents, compliance of the company with state statutes, and the legality of agreements. It may or may not render assistance to the claims department in connection with claim settlement. Many companies have a separate legal staff as a part of the claims department, which is distinct and independent from the staff of the legal department.

**Accounting.** Historically, the primary function of the accounting department has been the recording of company operating results and the maintenance of all accounting records necessary for the company's periodic financial statements, especially the report to the commissioner of insurance. Insurance company accounting is a highly specialized field. In the past, the principal focus has been on external reporting, primarily because of the requirements of the report to the commissioner. In the recent past, several companies have moved in the direction of the development of an internal information system, with greater emphasis on internal or managerial accounting.

**Engineering.** The engineering department, which is unique to the property and liability insurers, is charged with the responsibility of inspecting premises to be insured for the purpose of determining their acceptability. In addition, the engineering department serves a beneficial purpose for the insureds of the company in making loss-prevention recommendations.

## FINANCIAL ASPECTS OF INSURER OPERATIONS

In a general sense, the financial statements of insurance companies are quite similar to those of other business firms. However, because of the requirements imposed by the regulatory authorities, certain modifications of the traditional accounting practices are made in the field of insurance accounting. These changes result in distortions of the financial statements of insurance companies, and the purpose of this section is to point out a few major differences between insurance accounting and the accounting practices of other businesses.

### The Equity Section of the Balance Sheet

The equity section of the balance sheet for any business consists of the excess of assets over the liabilities of the firm. For an insurance company, it consists of either one or two items. In the case of capital stock companies, it consists of the capital stock, which represents the value of the original contributions of the stockholders, plus surplus, which represents amounts paid in by the organizers in excess of the par value of the stock and any retained earnings of the company. Since there is no capital stock in mutual insurance companies, the total of the equity section is called surplus. In both stock companies and mutual companies, the total of the equity accounts is referred to as "policyholder's surplus," indicating that this is the amount available, over and above the amount of the liabilities, to meet the obligations to the public.[4]

### Reserves

The major liabilities of insurance companies are debts to the policyholders; these are called "reserves." In insurance accounting and insurance terminology, the term "reserve" is almost synonymous with liability. Under-

---

[4]The modern trend in accounting terminology is away from the term "surplus." The term "earned surplus" is gradually changing to "retained earnings," and "paid-in surplus" is being replaced by the term "capital paid-in in excess of par." Nevertheless, because of the statutory reporting requirements and the connotation that the policyholder's surplus is the total excess of assets over liabilities, the term "surplus" is, and will probably remain, acceptable in insurance terminology.

standing insurance company financial operations will be greatly simplified if this point is clear.[5]

### Reserves in Property and Liability Companies

Property and liability insurance companies have two major types of reserves, both of which are liabilities to policyholders or to claimants—the loss reserve and the unearned premium reserve.

**The loss reserve.**   Loss reserves are required because of the time lag between the occurrence of a loss and the time the loss is finally paid. In some instances, the time between the loss and the settlement of that loss may be five years or more. Until the loss is paid, the insurance company holds the money, but it holds it as a trust, and this fact must be recognized in the financial statements of the company. The loss reserve, which is a liability to claimants for the funds not yet paid, gives recognition to the claim.

**The unearned premium reserve.**   Insurance is somewhat unique in that it collects in advance for a product that will not be delivered until some time in the future. The regulatory authorities require that the insurance companies recognize this in their accounting systems. Although the premiums are paid in advance, the insurer's obligations under the contracts it issues are all in the future. If the insurance company were permitted to use premiums which are currently being collected for future protection to meet the obligations which had been paid for in the past, it would be perpetrating a fraud on the current purchasers. The only way in which this advance-payment form of operation can be operated safely is to require the insurance companies to make some provision in their financial statements recognizing the fact that although premiums have been collected, they are still the property of the insured and do not belong to the company. This is done by setting up the value of these obligations as a liability called the unearned premium reserve.

The unearned premium reserve is computed by tabulating the premiums on the policies in force according to the year (or month) of issue and the term. It is customary to assume that the policies issued during any period were uniformly distributed over that period. If the income over the period is uniformly distributed, the result is the same as if the business had been

[5]The use of the term "reserve" to indicate a liability will undoubtedly make your accounting professor turn purple. This usage is probably misleading to the layman and is contradictory to modern accounting terminology. In general connotation, the term "reserve" is a fund or asset accumulation. In addition, the term may refer to an asset valuation reserve, such as the "reserve for depreciation," although this term is declining in favor of "accumulated depreciation." Finally, reserve may refer to earmarked retained earnings. Unless otherwise specified, when used in insurance accounting, the term "reserve" always refers to a liability.

written at the midpoint of the period. The policies written during the first month of the year will almost have expired by the end of the year, while those written at the end of the year will still have 11 months to run. Thus, at the end of a given year, the annual policies written during that calendar year are assumed to have been in force, on the average, for one-half of their term, and they have one-half to run. For example, if the insurance company writes $100,000 in premiums each month for a year, the total premium volume written during the year will be $1,200,000. Assuming that all the insurance written consists of annual policies, the company will have earned $600,000 by the end of the year and will have an unearned premium reserve of $600,000.

The unearned premium reserve should be sufficient to meet all the obligations of the company to insureds under the policies which have not expired. This reserve is sometimes called the "reinsurance reserve," for it is the amount required to transfer the insurance to another company if the primary insurer desires to retire from the insurance business.

**Redundancy in the unearned premium reserve.**    When a policy is issued, the entire amount of the premium must be set up as a liability as a part of the unearned premium reserve. In most cases, the company incurs certain expenses which must be paid at the inception of the policy, the most important being the agent's commission. Since these expenses must be paid when the policy is written and before the premium becomes totally earned, and the premium is included in the income computation only as it becomes earned, the net effect is a drain on the company's surplus whenever the unearned premium reserve is increased. To illustrate, let us assume that the company in question increases its premium written during a given year by $100,000. The company will receive $100,000 minus commissions to agents, which we will say amount to $20,000. At the end of the year, 50% of the premiums written will have been earned, and the unearned premium reserve of the company will have increased by $50,000 over the previous year. If we assume that losses equal 50% of premiums earned, the recapitulation would appear:

| | |
|---|---|
| Premiums earned | $50,000 |
| Less commissions | – 20,000 |
| Less other expenses | – 20,000 |
| Less losses | – 25,000 |
| Statutory underwriting loss | $(15,000) |

Looking at the balance sheet, cash will have increased by $35,000 ($100,000 in premiums minus $40,000 in expenses, minus $25,000 in losses), while liabilities will have increased by $50,000. The amount by which the increase in liabilities exceeds the increase in assets represents a reduction in surplus.

Now it is obvious that the company did not really lose money during the year. The $15,000 loss reported at the end of the year is merely an illusion created by the fact that premiums are included in the computation only as they are earned, but expenses are included when they are paid. As the second half of the premiums written become earned, the prepaid expenses locked in the unearned premium reserve are released:

| | |
|---|---|
| Premiums earned | $50,000 |
| Minus losses | − 25,000 |
| Statutory profit | $25,000 |

The loss that appeared at the end of the first year is a result of the legal requirements imposed by the regulatory authorities, and because it is a result of the statutory accounting requirements, it is called a statutory loss, to distinguish it from a real or "trade" loss. Persons familiar with the property insurance industry are aware of the inaccuracy in the figures on operating results shown in a company's official reports, and they make allowance for it. There is no universally accepted formula for doing this, but one method, applied to companies whose business is primarily fire insurance, is based on the assumption that the unearned premium reserve is 40% excess. This method rests on the following reasoning: Under statutory requirements, the entire premium, initially, is credited to the reserve to assure the payment of future losses. However, the premium is large enough to cover not only the losses, but the expenses as well. Since the expenses have already been paid, the unearned premium reserve is higher than need be.

The important point here is that whenever a property and liability company is increasing the volume of premiums it writes, the effect will be a reduction in surplus, for the expenses on the increased premium volume must be paid when the policy is written, but the income is included only as the premiums become earned. During a year when premium volume is increasing, the necessary increase in the unearned premium reserve may result in an understatement of the underwriting gain, and may even cause the company to report a statutory loss. In a year of declining business, underwriting gains will be distorted in the opposite direction. The excess reserve that had been set up will be released, and a part of it, representing prepaid expenses, will not be needed to pay losses and will indicate a statutory underwriting gain. The redundancy in the unearned premium reserve causes the company's operations to appear more profitable than they are during periods of declining business in force and to appear less profitable in periods of rising business in force.

### Reserves in Life Insurance Companies

**Reserve for unpaid claims.**   Not all death claims are payable in a lump sum. Under certain circumstances the beneficiary to the policy may elect to leave the proceeds of the policy with the insurance company and draw only interest or the interest and a part of the principal. Such arrangements are usually evidenced by supplementary contracts for which the company must establish reserves. In addition, the company may have a liability for death claims which have occurred but which have not yet been paid or which are in the process of being paid.

**Policy reserves.**    Unearned premium reserves also arise in life insurance, but here they are called "policy reserves." Under many forms of life insurance, the insured pays more during the early years of the contract than the amount that is required to provide protection against death. The insurer is required by law to set up liabilities (called reserves) representing the amount of the additional or excess payment.

Like the reserves in the field of property and liability insurance, those in life insurance contain a redundant element and are higher than the actual amount of the liability. In life insurance the redundancy arises from the fact that rates and reserves are computed using interest assumptions that are lower than the actual interest earnings and mortality assumptions that are higher than the actual experience.

## REINSURANCE

### The Nature of Reinsurance

Reinsurance constitutes a device whereby an insurance company may avoid the catastrophe hazard in the operation of the insurance mechanism. As the term indicates, reinsurance is insurance for insurers. It is based on the same principles of sharing and transfer as insurance itself. In order to protect themselves against the catastrophe of a comparatively large single loss or a large number of small losses as a result of a single occurrence, insurance companies devised the concept of reinsurance. In a reinsurance transaction the insurer seeking reinsurance is known as the "direct writer" or the "ceding company," while the reinsurer is known simply as the "reinsurer." That portion of a risk which the direct writer retains is called the "net line" or the "net retention." The act of transferring a part of the risk to the reinsurance company is called "ceding," and that portion of the risk that is passed on to the reinsurer is called the "cession."

Reinsurance had a very simple beginning. When a risk was presented to an insurer that was too large for the company to handle within the bounds of safety, it began to shop around for another insurance company that was willing to take a portion of the risk in return for a portion of the premium. A small part of current reinsurance operations are still conducted in this manner, which is called "facultative" or "street" reinsurance. In the case of street reinsurance, each risk represents a separate case for the insurer, and the terms of reinsurance must be negotiated when the direct writer finds another insurer that will accept a portion of the risk. The ever-present danger is that a devastating loss might occur before the reinsurance becomes effective. The cumbersome nature of the facultative system has led to the development of modern reinsurance treaties.

### Types of Reinsurance Treaties

There are two types of reinsurance treaties, facultative and automatic. Under a facultative treaty, the risks are considered individually by both parties. Each risk is submitted by the direct writer to the reinsurer for acceptance or rejection, and the direct writer is not even bound to submit the risks in the first place. However, the terms under which the reinsurance will take place is spelled out, and once the risk has been submitted and accepted, the advance arrangements apply; until then, the direct writer carries the entire risk.

Under the terms of an automatic treaty, the reinsurer agrees—in advance— to accept a portion of the gross line of the direct writing company or a portion of certain risks which meet the reinsurance underwriting rules of the reinsurer. The direct writer is obligated to cede a portion of the risk to which the automatic treaty applies.

### Reinsurance in Property and Liability Insurance

There are two essential ways in which risk is shared under reinsurance agreements in the field of property and liability insurance. The reinsurance agreement may require the reinsurer to share in every loss which occurs to a reinsured risk, or it may require the reinsurer to pay only after a loss reaches a certain size. Quota share treaties and surplus treaties are in the first category, while excess-loss treaties are in the second.

**Quota share treaty.**    Under a quota share treaty, the direct writing company and the reinsurance company agree to share the amount of each risk on some percentage basis. Thus, the ABC Mutual Insurance Company (the direct writer) may have a 50% quota share treaty with the DEF Reinsurance Company (the reinsurer). Under such an agreement, the DEF Reinsurance Company will pay 50% of any losses involving those risks subject to the reinsurance treaty. In return, the ABC Mutual Insurance Company will pay the DEF Reinsurance Company 50% of the premiums it receives from the insureds (with a reasonable allowance made to ABC for the agent's commission and other expenses connected with putting the business on the books).

**Surplus treaty.**    Under a surplus treaty, the reinsurer agrees to accept some amount of insurance on each risk in excess of a specified net retention. Normally, the amount the reinsurer is obligated to accept is referred to as a number of "lines" and is expressed as some multiple of the retention. A given treaty might specify a net retention of $10,000, with five "lines." Under such a treaty, if the direct writer writes a $10,000 policy, no reinsurance is involved, but the reinsurer will accept the excess of policies over $10,000 up to $50,000. These treaties may be "first surplus treaties," "second surplus," etc. A second surplus treaty fits over a first surplus treaty, assuming any excess of the first treaty, and so on for a third or fourth treaty. To illustrate, let us assume that the ABC Mutual Insurance Company (the direct writer), has a first surplus treaty with a $10,000 net retention and five lines with the DEF Reinsurance Company, and a second surplus treaty with the GHI Reinsurance Company, also with five lines. If ABC sells a $100,000 policy, it must, under the terms of both agreements, retain $10,000. The DEF Reinsurance Company will then assume $50,000 and GHI will assume $40,000:

| | |
|---|---|
| ABC Mutual Insurance Company | $10,000 |
| DEF Reinsurance Company | 50,000 |
| GHI Reinsurance Company | 40,000 |

Any loss under this policy would be shared on the basis of the amount of total insurance each company carries. Thus, ABC would pay 10% of any loss, DEF would pay 50%, and GHI would pay 40%. The premium would be divided in the same proportion, again with a reasonable allowance from the reinsurers to the direct writer for the expense of putting the policy on the books.

**Excess-loss treaty.**    Under an excess-loss treaty, the reinsurer is bound to pay only when a loss exceeds a certain amount. In essence, an excess-loss treaty is simply an insurance policy taken out by the direct writer which has a large deductible. The excess-loss treaty may be written to cover a specific risk, or to cover many risks suffering loss from a single occurrence. Such a treaty might, for example, require the reinsurer to pay after the direct writing company had sustained a loss of $10,000 on a specific piece of property, or it might require payment by the reinsurer if the direct writer suffered loss in excess of $50,000 from any one occurrence. There is, of course, a designated maximum limit of liability for the insurer.

**Pooling.**    Still another method of reinsurance is pooling. The pooling arrangement may be similar to that used in aviation insurance, under the terms of which each member assumes a percentage of every risk written by a member of the pool. This pooling arrangement is similar to a quota share treaty. On the other hand, the pool may provide a maximum loss limit to any one insurance company from a single loss, as is the case with the Workmen's Compensation Reinsurance Bureau. After a member of the pool has suffered a loss in excess of a specified amount (e.g., $100,000 as a result of one disaster), the other members of the pool share the remainder of the loss.

### Reinsurance in Life Insurance

In the field of life insurance, reinsurance may take one of two forms: the term insurance approach and the coinsurance approach. Under the term insurance approach the direct writer purchases yearly renewable term insurance equal to the difference between the face of the policy and the reserve, which is the amount at risk for the company. The "coinsurance" approach to reinsurance in life insurance is quite similar to the quota share approach in property and liability. Under this approach, the ceding company transfers some portion of the face amount of the policy to the reinsurer, and the reinsurer becomes liable for its proportional share of the death claim. In addition, the reinsurer becomes responsible for the maintenance of the policy reserve on its share of the policy.

### Functions of Reinsurance

Reinsurance actually serves two important purposes. The first, which is fairly obvious, is the spreading of risk. Insurance companies are able to avoid catastrophe losses by passing on a portion of any risk too large to handle. In addition, through excess-loss reinsurance arrangements a company may protect itself against a catastrophe involved in a single occurrence. Smaller companies are permitted to insure exposures they could not otherwise handle within the bounds of safety.

The second function reinsurance performs is not as immediately obvious— it is a financial function. As we have seen, when the premium volume of an insurance company is expanding, the net result will be a drain on the surplus of the company. With a continually expanding premium volume, a company faces a dilemma. The business it is writing may be profitable, but because of the requirements of the unearned premium reserve, its surplus may be declining and may reach a dangerously low level. We say "dangerously low," because although there is no absolute standard, the amount of new business a company may write is obviously a function of its policyholders surplus. In the absence of some other alternative, a company could expand only to a certain point and would then be required to stop and wait for the premiums to become earned, freeing surplus.

Reinsurance provides a solution to this dilemma. When the direct writing company reinsures a portion of the business it has written under a quota share or surplus line treaty, it pays a proportional share of the premium collected to the reinsurer. The reinsurer then establishes the unearned premium reserves or policy reserves required, and the direct writer is relieved of the obligation to maintain such reserves. Since the direct writer has incurred expenses in acquiring the business, the reinsurer pays the direct writing company a commission for having put the business on the books. The payment of the ceding commission by the reinsurer to the direct writer means that the unearned premium reserve is reduced by more than cash is reduced, resulting in an increase in surplus. Thus, if the direct writer transfers $100,000 in premiums to the reinsurer, the unearned premium reserve of the direct writer is reduced by $100,000. The payment to the reinsurer is $100,000 minus a ceding commission of 40%, or $60,000. Since assets have been reduced by $60,000 and liabilities have been reduced by $100,000, surplus is increased by $40,000. When reinsurance is used on a continuing basis, the net drain on the surplus of the direct writing company is reduced. The market is greatly increased, since excess capacity of one insurer may be transferred to another through reinsurance.

## Questions for Discussion and Review

**1.** "Pricing is much more difficult in insurance than in other business fields, because the costs of production are not known until after the product has been delivered." To what extent is this statement true and to what extent is it false?

**2.** To what do you attribute the different nature of the investments of property and liability insurers as compared with life insurance companies?

**3.** "In view of the relationship of surplus to premiums that may be written, the underwriting losses of the past decade have severely restricted the capacity of the property and liability insurance industry." Explain what is meant by this statement.

**4.** Do you think that loss adjustment would be most difficult in the field of (a) life insurance, (b) property insurance, or (c) liability insurance? What training would you recommend for adjusters in each of these three fields?

**5.** "Increasing premium volume reduces the net profit of an insurer and creates a surplus drain, but this is illusionary rather than real." Suppose a company increases its premium volume by 10% each year; its loss ratio is 50% and its expense ratio is 40%. Will it ever show a profit?

## Suggestions for Additional Reading

Athearn, J. L. *Risk and Insurance*, 2nd ed. New York: Appleton-Century-Crofts, 1969, Chaps. 23, 25.

Bickelhaupt, D. L. and Magee, J. H. *General Insurance*, 8th ed. Homewood Ill.: Richard D. Irwin, 1970, Chaps. 6, 7.

Denenberg, H. S., Eilers, R. D., Hoffman, G. W., Kline, C. A., Melone, J. J., and Snider, H. W. *Risk and Insurance*. Englewood Cliffs, N.J.: Prentice-Hall, 1964, Chaps. 28–30.

Donaldson, J. H. *Casualty Claims Practice*, rev. ed. Homewood, Ill.: Richard D. Irwin, 1959.

Greene, M. R. *Risk and Insurance*, 2nd ed. Cincinnati, Ohio: Southwestern, 1968, Chap. 7.

Kenney, R. *Fundamentals of Fire and Casualty Insurance Strength*, 4th ed. Dedham, Mass. The Kenney Insurance Studies, 1967.

Magee, J. H. and Serbein, O. N. *Property and Liability Insurance*, 4th ed. Homewood, Ill.: Richard D. Irwin, 1967, Chaps. 30–33.

Michelbacher, G. F. and Roos, N. R. *Multiple-Line Insurers*, 2nd ed. New York: McGraw-Hill, 1970, Chaps. 2–12.

Mowbray, A. H., Blanchard, R. H., and Williams, C. A., Jr., *Insurance*, 6th ed. New York: McGraw-Hill, 1969, Chaps. 27–32.

Munich Reinsurance Company. *Reinsurance and Reassurance*. New York: Munich Reinsurance Company, 1963.

Thompson, K. *Reinsurance*, 4th ed. Philadelphia: The Spectator Company, 1966.

# 6 Regulation of the Insurance Industry

*The safety of the people shall be the highest law.*

—Cicero

## THE WHY OF GOVERNMENT REGULATION

The courts have long held that insurance is an industry which, like banking, is "vested in the public interest." This simply means that insurance is a business which affects many people, and the public welfare demands that the insurance industry be regulated in its activities. In the case of public utilities, government regulation is necessary because firms tend toward monopolistic power, and in the absence of government regulation, the consumer would in some instances be forced to pay artificially high prices. In the case of insurance regulation, the problem of monopoly is not acute, but there are still significant reasons for government regulation.

Classical economic theorists held that competition serves the consumer best by forcing the firms in an industry to reach the point of maximum efficiency on the production function. In an economy characterized by perfect competition, the inefficient firms would be forced out of the market. As a matter of fact, according to the *laissez faire* tradition, the benefits gained through competition are the result of the inefficient producers being forced out of the market. The public welfare requires the continued existence of insurance companies in which members of the economy have invested

**110**

their funds. Individuals purchase insurance to protect against financial loss at a later time. It is essential that the insurance firm making the promise to indemnify the insureds for future losses remain in business so that it will be able to fulfill its promise.

While a good deal of government regulation is aimed at enforcing competition and preventing artificially high prices, government regulation of insurance has been aimed in the opposite direction: a basic goal has been prevention of cut-throat competition. It has long been held that in the absence of government regulation, the natural tendency in the insurance industry would be toward the keenest sort of competition. There are two basic reasons for this:

1. The cost of production is not known until the contract of insurance has run its full term.

2. There are classes of desirable and undesirable risks. There is a danger that, in attempting to compete, insurance companies might assume that their risks are from the better class and make unwarranted assumptions about their future costs.

The basic danger of competition in the insurance industry is the possibility that, in attempting to compete, companies may underestimate their costs and fail as a result. The primary purpose of government regulation of insurance companies is to assure the solvency of the insurers.

The insurance product is a promise. In return for the premium the insured pays, the company promises to pay a specified sum upon the occurrence of the event insured against. Insofar as the ability of the company to fulfill its promise is based on the financial solvency of the company, the public welfare requires regulation of that solvency.

In addition to the competitive nature of the industry, there are certain other reasons the industry must be regulated. The complicated nature of most insurance contracts makes them difficult for the insured to understand even if he attempts to do so. The regulatory authority is charged with the responsibility of assuring that the contracts offered by insurance companies are fair.

The function of insurance regulation is quite simple. Insurance is regulated with the goal of promoting the welfare of the public by maintaining sound insurance companies who offer fair contracts at fair prices.

## A BRIEF HISTORY OF INSURANCE REGULATION

Although statutes dealing with insurance activities had been enacted by the states as early as the beginning of the nineteenth century, the history of modern regulation of the insurance industry begins shortly before the Civil War, when several states established bodies to supervise the operation of the insurance industry within their borders. The New Hampshire Board of Insurance Commissioners, which was established in 1851, was the first of these bodies. Massachusetts followed shortly thereafter,[1] and New York established its board in 1859. The panic of 1857, which had been precipitated by the failure of a New York branch of the Ohio Life Insurance and Trust Company of Cincinnati, was probably a leading factor in the establishment of the New York Commission, as well as those of other states that followed.

### Paul vs. Virginia

The case of *Paul vs. Virginia* was an important precedent concerning the regulation of insurance. Samuel Paul was a native of Virginia who represented New York insurance companies in his state. Paul challenged the right of the state to regulate insurance by selling insurance without obtaining a license from the state. The state denied Paul a license, because his insurer would not comply with the demand of the State of Virginia for a security deposit. Likewise, a license for the insurer was denied on the same grounds. When Paul continued to sell insurance without a license, he was arrested and fined $50. The case was carried to the United States Supreme Court, where it was finally decided in 1869. In rendering its decision, the Supreme Court ruled that insurance was not interstate commerce:

> Issuing a policy of insurance is not a transaction of commerce. The policies are simply contracts of indemnity against loss by fire entered into between the corporations and the insured for a consideration paid by the latter. These contracts are not articles of commerce in any proper meaning of the word. They are not subjects of trade and barter, offered in the market as something having an existence and value independently of the parties to them. They are not commodities to be shipped or forwarded from one state to another and then put up for sale. They are like other personal contracts between parties which are completed by their signature and the transfer of considerations. Such contracts are not interstate transactions, though the parties may be domiciled in different states. The policies do not take effect—are not executed contracts—until delivered by the agent in Virginia. They are then local transactions, and are governed by the local law. They do not

---

[1] One member of the Massachusetts board was Elizur Wright, who is often called "the father of insurance regulation." Wright was an abolitionist who turned his energies toward the elimination of unsavory practices in the insurance industry. He was an ardent proponent of federal regulation of insurance and visualized the state department of insurance as a step toward a national insurance bureau.

constitute a part of the commerce between the states any more than a contract for the purchase and sale of goods in Virginia by a citizen of New York, whilst in Virginia, would constitute a portion of such commerce.[2]

The decision of the United States Supreme Court that insurance was not interstate commerce, and, therefore, was not subject to regulation by the federal government stood for 75 years.

### Regulation from 1869 to 1944

During the 75 year period following the *Paul vs. Virginia* decision, the insurance industry was regulated by the individual states. This was a period of rapid development and expansion for the entire economy, and the insurance industry grew with the economy. The quality of regulation varied from state to state, and it was inevitable that abuses would creep into the operation of the insurance business.

During the period following the Civil War, many life insurance companies were operated in a precarious manner. Unsound business practices were common, and advertising claims were greatly inflated. During the depression period of the 1870s, many of these poorly managed companies went out of business. In addition, many innovations were developed in the field of life insurance, some of which were detrimental to the insurance-buying public. One such innovation was the "tontine policy," a life insurance contract with a higher than necessary premium which provided for the payment of dividends at some future time. Dividends on these policies were paid at the end of the tontine period (which was usually 10, 15, or 20 years). The dividends were paid only to those policyholders who survived to the end of the period, at the expense of those who had died or permitted their policies to lapse.

Shortly after the turn of the century, big business was being condemned and investigated, and the rapid growth of the life insurance industry plus these abuses attracted attention. The New York State Legislature appointed a committee to investigate the abuses in the life insurance industry in 1905. The committee was named after its chairman, Senator William W. Armstrong. The Armstrong Investigation turned out to be a sober, responsible examination of the life insurance industry. Many defects were pointed out, and although the investigation caused a temporary loss of confidence among the insurance-buying public, legislation was enacted in New York following the investigation correcting these abuses, which proved to be a benefit to both the public and the life insurance industry.

[2] *Paul vs. Virginia*, 231 U.S. 495 (1869).

In 1910, a second committee was appointed in New York, this time to investigate the property insurance industry. The Honorable Edwin A. Merritt, Jr., was chairman of this committee, which came to be known as the Merritt Committee. This committee did essentially the same thing for the property insurance industry that the Armstrong Committee had done for the life insurance industry. The Merritt Committee concerned itself with the question of fire insurance rates and the basic philosophy of these rates. During the period from 1885 to 1910, over half the states passed laws prohibiting cooperative rate-making. These "anticompact laws," as they were called, prohibited insurance companies from joining together to make rates, a practice which the companies held to be necessary in order to achieve the accuracy inherent in the operation of the law of large numbers. Following the San Francisco fire of 1906, many fire insurance companies went bankrupt, in part because they had charged inadequate rates. Fire insurance rates then increased throughout the country in what appeared to be the result of concerted action. After an extensive study, the Merritt Committee made its recommendations, which became the basis for New York legislation. The committee opposed the anticompact laws and urged that rating bureaus be recognized, and further that a company be permitted to belong to a rating bureau, or to file its rates independently if it chose.

The Armstrong Committee Investigation and the Merritt Committee Investigation proved to be significant events in the development of the industry. Although they were state investigations, the fact that many states patterned their laws after those of New York State (and the impact of the Appleton Rule) made their effect pervasive.

### The South-Eastern Underwriters Association Case

After a period of 75 years, another test of the authority of the federal government to regulate insurance was made. In 1942, the Attorney General of the United States filed a brief under the Sherman Act against the South-Eastern Underwriters Association (SEUA), a cooperative rating bureau, alleging that the bureau constituted a combination in restraint of trade. In its decision of the SEUA case in 1944, the Supreme Court reversed its decision of *Paul vs. Virginia*, stating that insurance is interstate commerce and as such is subject to regulation by the federal government.[3] This decision stands today.

### Public Law 15

During the period of time that the SEUA case was being decided and appealed, the insurance industry arranged to have bills introduced into

---

[3] *U.S. vs. South-Eastern Underwriters Association*, 322 U.S. 533 (1944).

Congress that would have exempted the insurance industry from the provisions of the antitrust laws. These bills were all defeated, but finally a bill was drafted by the National Association of Insurance Commissioners that could be passed. This bill was Public Law 15, or the McCarran–Ferguson Act, which became law on March 9, 1945. Congress insisted that it was the right of the federal government to regulate the insurance industry, but stated in the McCarran–Ferguson Act that the federal government would not regulate insurance as long as the states did an adequate job of regulating the industry. In addition, the law declared a two year moratorium on the regulation of insurance by the federal government, and stated that the federal government would not regulate the industry until after January 1, 1948, at which time it would do so to the extent that the industry was not being regulated adequately by the several states. Following the enactment of Public Law 15, the states attempted to put their houses in order, enacting rating laws, fair trade practices, and extending the licensing and solvency requirements.

## REGULATION TODAY

Insurance is presently regulated by the several states, through the three basic branches of our state governments; legislative, judicial, and executive.

### Regulation by the Legislative Branch

Each state enacts laws that govern the conduct of the insurance industry within its boundaries. These laws spell out the requirements that must be met by persons wishing to organize an insurance company in the state. A company domiciled within the state (i.e., which has its home office in the state) is called a domestic company. The laws also specify certain requirements that a company domiciled in another state (called a foreign company) must meet in order to obtain a license to do business in the state.[4] In addition, the insurance code sets forth the standards of solvency that are to be enforced and provides for the regulation of rates and investments. It also provides for the licensing of agents.

### Regulation by the Judicial Branch

The judicial branch exercises control over the insurance industry through the courts by rendering decisions on the meaning of policy terms and ruling on the constitutionality of the laws of the state and the actions of those administering the law.

[4] A company which is domiciled in a foreign country is called an "alien company."

### Regulation by the Executive Branch— the Commissioner of Insurance

The central figure in the regulation of the insurance industry in each state is the Commissioner of Insurance.[5] In most states the Commissioner of Insurance is appointed by the governor of the state and is charged with the administration of the insurance laws and the general supervision of the business. Few people understand the complicated nature of the position or the tremendous power the commissioner of insurance wields. Although he is a part of the executive branch of the state government, the commissioner frequently makes rulings which have the binding force of law and exercises judicial power in his interpretation and enforcement of the Insurance Code.

### The National Association of Insurance Commissioners

The National Association of Insurance Commissioners (NAIC) has been an active force in the regulation of insurance since it was founded in 1871. Although it has absolutely no legal power over insurance regulation, it is an important force. Through it, the fifty state commissioners exchange information and ideas and coordinate regulatory activities. On the basis of the information exchanged at its two annual meetings, the NAIC makes recommendations for legislation and policy. The individual commissioners are free to accept or reject these recommendations, but in the past the majority of the commissioners have seen fit to accept the recommendations appropriate for their particular states.

### AREAS REGULATED

### Licensing of Companies

The power to license insurance companies (or revoke those licenses) is perhaps the greatest power the Commissioner of Insurance possesses. In effect, when a company is licensed, he certifies the company with regard to its financial stability and soundness of methods of operation. Before licensing a company to conduct business in the state, the commissioner must satisfy himself that the company to be licensed meets the financial requirements specified in the insurance code of the state. In order to qualify for a license, the insurance company making application must have a certain amount of capital and/or surplus. The exact amount required varies from state to state, being relatively small in some states and substantial in others. The amount of capital and/or surplus required also depends on the type of

---

[5]Although the title "Commissioner of Insurance" is the most common, in some states the chief insurance regulator is referred to as the "Director of Insurance" or the "Superintendent of Insurance."

business the firm will conduct and whether the company is a stock or mutual carrier.

In most cases, foreign companies may not be licensed to transact business in the state unless they have the amount of capital and surplus required of a domestic company.

In addition to the capital and surplus requirement, the commissioner normally reviews the personal characteristics of the organizers, promoters, and incorporators of the company in order to determine their competence and experience. The commissioner may deny the application for a license if the organizers or incorporators prove to be unworthy of public trust.

### Examination of Companies

The insurance code requires every licensed company, foreign and domestic, to submit an annual report to the Commissioner of Insurance. This report includes information regarding the assets and liabilities of the company, its investments, its income, loss payments, and expenses, and any other information desired by the commissioner. In addition to the annual report, a periodic inspection of each company conducting business in the state is made by the commissioner's office. The insurance commissioner may examine or inquire into the affairs of any company transacting business in the state at any time, but the insurance code normally requires him to examine domestic companies at least once every three years. The expense of the examination is paid by the insurance company being examined. The examination is a detailed operation, quite often lasting a considerable period of time, during which the examiners scrutinize every aspect of the firm's operation.

In order to eliminate duplication of effort, it is becoming a practice for the commissioner to examine only those companies that are domiciled in his state. To provide for the examination of foreign companies, "zone" examinations are conducted, wherein each state in a zone (there are six zones) accepts the examination of the zone for its foreign companies.

### Rates

To the extent that the insurer's promises depend on the price it charges for these promises, rates must be subject to regulation. All state insurance codes provide for the regulation of insurance rates, requiring that the rates must be:

1. Adequate
2. Not excessive
3. Not unfairly discriminatory

*Adequacy* is the primary requirement. The rates, together with the interest income from investments, must be sufficient to pay all losses as they occur and all expenses in connection with the production and servicing of the business. Competition among insurers on a price basis is often limited through regulation in an attempt to ensure that solvency of the insurance companies is maintained. As we saw in Chapter 4, much of the rating in certain lines of insurance is done on a cooperative basis. The regulatory authorities permit, but do not require, concerted rate-making. Companies may pool their loss statistics in an attempt to achieve greater accuracy in prediction and use the bureau rates which result from this pooling. Yet this practice does not constitute collusion. In most jurisdictions, a company may also file its rates independently or may deviate from the published rates by satisfying the insurance commissioner that there is a basis for such action through presentation of loss experience or expense data.

In addition to the requirement of adequacy, the insurance rates must *not be excessive*. Insurance has come to be regarded as a product that is essential to the well being of the members of the society. Insurers may not take advantage of the need of the members of society in order to realize unreasonable returns.

Finally, insurance rates must *not discriminate unfairly*. The emphasis in this requirement is on *unfairly*, for the very nature of insurance rates requires some degree of discrimination. By unfairly discriminatory we mean that the insurance company may not charge a significantly different rate for two clients with approximately the same degree of risk. Any difference in rates charged must have an actuarial basis.

While all states have legislation requiring that rates must be reasonable, adequate, and not unfairly discriminatory, the manner in which these requirements are enforced varies.

Life insurance rates constitute a special case in the area of rate regulation. Apart from making certain that the companies do not engage in price discrimination, the state regulatory authorities do not directly control life insurance rates. Life insurance companies do not engage in cooperative rate-making, as do the property and liability companies. However, the companies generally begin with the same mortality table and the dictates of competition generally force them to use realistic interest assumptions. A substantial portion of the life insurance in effect in the United States is written on a "participating basis," under which the cost of the insurance depends on the actual experience of the company. Under a participating policy, the company often charges more than the expected cost of the policy, returning the excess to the policyholder in the form of a dividend. In order to ensure that the individual policyholder receives an equitable share of the surplus, most states have legal requirements specifying the basis for the distribution of dividends. In addition, legal restrictions on the expense portion of the premium helps to control the cost of life insurance. The state of New York, for example, limits the amount of commission payable in the first year of a life insurance contract to 55% of the premium. Other companies that are not licensed to sell in New York pay commissions as high as 100% of the first-year premium.

The chief justification for the absence of strict regulation of life insurance rates has been the proposition that competition is an effective regulator. There now appears to be sufficient justification to question this assumption. A study by Joseph Belth[6] has shown that there are wide variations in costs for identical products in the life insurance field, and that the consumer is not generally aware of the price he pays when he buys life insurance. Furthermore, he is seldom if ever aware of the price of available alternatives. This is because the combination of protection and savings in the life contract tends to obscure the true cost of the protection and the rate of return on the savings. Belth maintains that the pricing complexities in life insurance place analysis of the price beyond the reach of even the sophisticated buyer, and he advocates more extensive disclosure by life insurance companies.

In the area of property and liability insurance, most states follow the pattern of the "All-Industry Model Law," which was proposed in 1946 following the SEUA case. Under the provisions of this law, the insurance company must file the rates they intend to charge with the Commissioner of Insurance for his approval. These rates cannot be used until the commissioner has approved them, or until a certain period has expired without his approval. The commissioner retains the right to disapprove the rates after they have become effective.

The effect of these so-called "prior approval" laws is often to make the commissioner the justifier of rates to the public, for once the commissioner has approved a rate increase, he must frequently justify that increase. In many cases, the commissioner has a limited staff to review any rate filing, and as a result, the approval process may take a considerable amount of time. This often leads to a lag in the time between the need for a rate adjustment and its actual approval. During the past few years, there has been a growing interest among industry leaders and insurance regulators in replacing the "prior approval" rate regulatory statutes with state laws under which property and liability rates would be set by the insurance companies themselves, subject to insurer competition. This "competitive rating" concept which is currently receiving such widespread interest follows the pattern of a law that has been in use in California for over two decades. Under the California law, which has been in effect since 1947, companies

[6]Joseph M. Belth, *The Retail Price Structure in American Life Insurance* (Bloomington, Ind.: Bureau of Business Research, Graduate School of Business, Indiana University, 1966).

are not required to file their rates for approval of the Commissioner of Insurance. Insurance companies and rating bureaus may adopt rates and make them effective immediately without prior approval from the commissioner. The fundamental difference is one of a philosophy concerning insurance rates. The "prior approval" laws and other systems of direct government regulation of insurance rates assume that the normal forces of competition in the marketplace cannot be effective in governing insurance rates and that administrative price control must be employed. The California law expressly makes it clear that competition and not government authority is the preferred governor of rates, and that barring the existence of an anticompetitive situation or practice, the insurance commissioner is not to regulate rates as such. The law is intended to encourage and permit competition among insurers on a sound financial basis. The absence of filing and prior approval requirements is intended to remove the procedural deterrents and delays in the rate-making process so as to promote competition and discourage tendencies toward uniform rating. In effect, the position of property and liability insurers under such a law is much the same as that of life insurers, which, as we have noted, do not operate under state rating laws and are subject only to indirect rate controls by the states.

"File and use" laws represent something of a compromise between the prior approval laws patterned after the All Industry Model Law and the no-file system of California. Under the file and use system the insurer must file proposed rate changes, but may use the new rates immediately. The rates may subsequently be disapproved by the commissioner. The chief advantage of the file and use system is that there is no delay between the time a rate adjustment is needed and the time it becomes effective.

Although the prior approval system still predominates, there has been increased interest in the no-file and the file and use approach.[7] Since 1966, prior approval rating laws have been changed to file and use laws or no-file laws of the California type in the states of Connecticut, Florida, Georgia, Idaho, Illinois, Indiana, Minnesota, Missouri, Montana, New York, Oregon, and Wisconsin.[8] We will probably see further changes in this direction.

---

[7] In addition to the prior approval, no-file, and file and use systems, there are two other systems— state-made rates and mandatory bureau rates. In the state of Texas, rates are set by the state rather than filed by insurers. The Texas Insurance Commission sets rates annually, based on statistics furnished by all companies doing business in the state. Massachusetts has state-made rates for compulsory automobile insurance. Mandatory bureau rates are used in the District of Columbia, Louisiana, and Mississippi for fire insurance, in North Carolina for fire and automobile insurance, and in Virginia for fire insurance and automobile physical damage insurance.

[8] The Missouri law applies only to private passenger automobile insurance. The Florida law, which was one of the first competitive laws enacted since 1966, was repealed in 1971.

### Reserves

As we saw in Chapter 4, because the insurance industry operates on the somewhat unique plan of collecting in advance for a product that is to be delivered at some time in the future, it is imperative that some recognition of the obligation to policyholders for unearned premiums be made. The only way the insurance business can be conducted soundly on an advance premium basis is by making some provision for the obligations contracted to be met in the future. As we have seen, this is done by setting up the present value of these obligations as liabilities. In addition to the unearned premium reserves of property and liability insurance companies and the policy reserves of life insurance companies, there are various other reserves (such as the loss reserve) that must be maintained.

The regulation of the reserves is one of the most critical areas in the field of insurance regulation. The insurance code of most states specifies the manner in which the reserves must be computed. In addition, the insurance company is required to deposit cash or securities with the Commissioner of Insurance, based on the amount of the reserves.

The critical importance of the reserves in the financial stability and solvency of a company is apparent when we recognize that the reserves are true liabilities. Although it is common to think of a reserve as a fund set aside to meet expected or unexpected contingencies, as we have already seen, the reserves we speak of in insurance are true liabilities. They are an actuarial measurement of the company's liabilities to its policyholders and claimants which must be offset by assets. If the reserves are understated, the net worth of the company is overstated.

### Investments

To the extent that the insurer's promises to pay depend on the value of its investments, these investments must be sound. It is a basic principle of investment that the return on a given security is a function of the risk inherent in that security. If it were not for outside regulation, insurance companies might turn to investments which entail a greater degree of risk than is desirable in an attempt to increase their investment return. In general, property and liability insurance companies are granted greater latitude in their investments than are life insurance companies. The insurance code of each state spells out the particular type of investments permitted to each type of insurance company in the state. The investments permitted are usually United States government obligations; state, municipal, and territorial bonds; Canadian bonds; mortgage loans; certain high-grade corporate bonds; and, subject to limitations, preferred and common stocks. Life insurance companies are generally permitted to invest only a small percentage of their assets in common stocks. As the reader may recall, common stocks account for less than 5% of the total investment holdings of life insurance companies, while approximately one-third of the assets of property and liability companies are invested in common stocks.

### Policy Forms

Since the insurance product is a contract, by its very nature it is technical. In most cases, the customer is asked to purchase a product in which he becomes a party to a contract which he has not read, and which he would not understand if he did read it. The complicated nature of most insurance contracts makes them appear to be formidable objects to the public, but this is so because as contracts, they must be precisely drawn. If the insurance company wishes to insure against loss by a specified peril, it must make certain that the contract limits coverage to that peril. In order to do this, it is often necessary to devise a complex document. Since the insurance contracts are complicated, they must be approved by the regulatory authorities to ensure that the insurance-buying public will not be mistreated as a result of unfair provisions in the contracts. In addition, the solvency of the insurers must be protected against unreasonable commitments which they might make in the interest of competition. In some states, new policy forms and endorsements need only be filed with the commissioner's office before they are put into use; if the commissioner does not approve of the form, it is then withdrawn from use. In most states, however, the law requires the approval of a form before it is used.

### Competence of Agents

Because of the technical complications in the insurance product, it is particularly important that those selling insurance understand the contracts they propose to sell. Many states require all applicants for a license to take an examination in which the insurance regulatory authority must be satisfied that the applicant understands the contracts he proposes to offer to the public and the laws under which he will operate. Furthermore, the agent must be a respected and responsible resident of his community.

### Practices

An insurer might be sound financially and yet indulge in practices that are detrimental to the public, such as unfairly discriminating against an insured or engaging in "sharp" claim practices. The commissioner attempts to control such activities. Among the many unfair practices that are specifically forbidden by many insurance codes are rebating and twisting. Rebating consists of directly or indirectly giving or offering to give any portion of the premium or any other consideration to an insurance buyer as an inducement to the purchase of insurance. An example of unlawful rebating would be an offer by an insurance agent to give a part of his commission to a prospective insured.

Twisting is the practice of inducing a policyholder to lapse or cancel a policy of one insurer in order to replace it with the policy of another insurer in a way which would operate to the prejudice of the interest of the policyholder. Obviously, there is no crime in a complete comparison without misrepresentation which an agent may make between a policy sold by his company and a policy sold by another company. Unfortunately, many agents are reluctant to even talk about replacement of an existing contract with a new contract. It is unfortunate, because there are a surprising number of cases where replacement of a contract would clearly be beneficial to the policyholder.

## STATE VERSUS FEDERAL REGULATION

The prospect of federal regulation of the insurance industry has existed since the SEUA case in 1944. While the McCarran–Ferguson Act left regulation in the hands of the states, it did so with the implicit condition that the federal government would not regulate insurance as long as the states did a good job. In effect, the federal government permitted the states to continue to regulate insurance, but it stands ready to take over the regulation if state regulation proves inadequate.

### Arguments Favoring Federal Regulation

Those who advocate federal regulation of insurance do so on two basic grounds: that the past regulation by the states has been inadequate, and that federal regulation would bring a desired uniformity. The chief criticism of state regulation has been the lack of uniformity. While it is true that some states have done an outstanding job in their regulatory activities, the quality of the regulation has varied markedly. Some states have imposed rigid financial standards on the insurance companies licensed in the state, but others have been relatively lax. The result in some cases has been the failure of companies and public suffering.

In addition to the inadequacy in some jurisdictions, the lack of uniformity has caused some inconvenience, waste, and duplication of effort. There are 50 different insurance codes, each of which imposes restrictions and limitations on the insurers. An insurance company seeking a rate adjustment or a change in policy form must obtain approval from each of the jurisdictions. This lack of uniformity has been a leading consideration in the pressure for federal standards. A past president of the National Association of Insurance Commissioners stated:

> Positive study and action is needed in many fields, uniformity of laws in the various states is necessary. For instance, the investment laws of the 50 states are so different, complex, and contradictory that (life) insurance companies are confronted with a variety of practices, laws and regulations which often favor domestic over foreign companies. In my opinion, this has been the motivating factor behind the report of the Commission on Money and Credit which recommended overriding Federal charters for insurance companies.[9]

In essence, those who advocate federal regulation maintain that since insurance is interstate commerce, there should be one body to provide for uniform nationwide regulation.

### Arguments Favoring State Regulation

The opponents of federal regulation argue that the individual states have the experience and expertise necessary to meet and solve the critical issues, and that state regulatory authorities, being more familiar with local conditions and problems, are more responsive to local needs. Advocates of state regulation maintain that the NAIC already provides a vehicle for uniformity of regulation to the extent that such uniformity is desirable. Finally, they point out that a system of federal regulation would of necessity be superimposed on the system of state regulation, for many regional insurers not subject to federal regulation (since they do not engage in interstate commerce) would continue to exist.

### The Insolvency Issue and Federal Legislation

Obviously, if state regulation did not evidence certain defects, it would be difficult for proponents of federal regulation to obtain a hearing. From time to time these defects come into focus, and are usually met with threats of federal legislation. During the latter half of the 1960s, congressional attention was again focused on the adequacy of state regulation, asking the question, "How good a job have the states been doing in the field of regulation?" The answer, according to some members of Congress, was "Not very well."

Testimony before the United States Senate Antitrust Subcommittee in 1967 indicated that about 80 insurance companies had been placed in liquidation since 1961. Most of these companies were "high-risk" automobile

[9] Rufus D. Hayes, President of the National Association of Insurance Commissioners, *American Life Convention Newsletter* (Oct. 18, 1962).

insurers, specializing in writing insurance for those persons who could not obtain coverage through the regular market. This testimony sparked renewed interest in federal legislation to deal with the problem of insurance company insolvency, for although insolvency is a small problem statistically, involving only a few companies each year, for the policyholders and claimants involved, it can be catastrophic.

Senator Warren G. Magnuson introduced legislation providing for a Federal Motor Vehicle Insurance Guarantee Corporation, which would guarantee payment of claims against an insolvent insurer, in much the same way that the FDIC guarantees bank deposits.[10] The corporation was to be financed by a tax on the insurance companies, collected in advance, and passed on to the individual insurance policyholders in the form of higher premiums. Virtually all insurers would be required to belong, and would pay an annual fee of one-eighth of 1% of their annual net premiums. The initial financing was to be provided by $50 million in treasury shares. The proposed legislation gave the corporation broad examination powers and also empowered it to remove officers and directors of any member insurer and to settle or adjust any claim against an insolvent member.

Although the proponents of the bill argued that the corporation was intended only to supplement state regulation, the insurance industry and state regulators viewed the legislation as a wedge to further federal regulation. Several arguments were advanced against the legislation. The two major arguments against the Magnuson Bill were (a) that it would force strong efficient companies to subsidize their marginal competitors, and (b) that the existence of such a fund might lead to laxity in prevention of insolvencies.

It soon became apparent that the arguments against the bill were not going to be sufficient to prevent its passage, and that a different strategy was necessary. In an attempt to prevent passage of the bill, the NAIC developed its own model legislation dealing with payment of claimants of insolvent insurers, which it then recommended to the states for passage. New York, New Jersey, and Maryland had had automobile insurance guarantee funds prior to the introduction of the Magnuson Bill. By the end of 1970, the number of states with protection for policyholders in the event of insolvency of an insurer had risen to 29, most of the states following the model legislation of the NAIC. Unlike the federal bill, the NAIC model law operates on a postinsolvency basis. Under the postinsolvency assessment plans, when an insurer operating in the state becomes insolvent, other property and liability insurers operating in the state are assessed according to a formula based on their share of the statewide insurance market. The funds thus

[10]A similar bill had been introduced by Senator Thomas J. Dodd in 1966.

assessed are used to pay off the covered claims and to pay the unearned premiums to policyholders.

The enactment of the state insolvency laws may have forestalled enactment of federal legislation for the Federal Motor Vehicle Insurance Guarantee Corporation. On the other hand, unless and until all states have enacted such legislation, the arguments favoring such a corporation remain. Regardless of the outcome, the Magnuson bill was a valuable landmark in that it underscored the need for state legislation and forced the states to enact such legislation. The entire issue indicates the leadership that the threat of federal regulation can play in improving state regulation. No doubt new issues will arise; the controversy between the proponents of state regulation and those who advocate federal regulation will no doubt continue. The eventual result may well be federal regulation of insurance, but even when and if this takes place, the debate regarding the superiority of one system over the other will not end.

## TAXATION OF INSURANCE COMPANIES

Insurance companies, like all business corporations, are subject to federal, state, and local taxes. At the federal level, insurers are subject to the federal income tax. At the state level, they are subject to income and property taxes like other businesses, and in addition they are subject to a number of special taxes levied on insurers, the most important of which is the premium tax.

### The State Premium Tax

Taxation of insurance companies by the states grew out of the states' need for revenue and a desire to protect domestic insurers by means of a tariff on out-of-state companies. The premium tax spread from state to state as a retaliatory measure against taxes imposed by each state on the insurers of the other states. As time went by, most states came to levy the premium tax on the premium income of both domestic and foreign insurers.[11]

All the states currently impose a premium tax on insurers operating within their state. In essence, this tax is a sales tax on the premiums for all policies sold by an insurer within the state. The amount of the tax varies among the states; the maximum in any state is 4%, with the most typical amount being 2%. The tax paid by the insurer is, of course, added to the cost of the insurance contract and passed on to the policyholder. Most states tax all companies

---

[11] Since the levying of taxes on the premium income of insurers required a system of registration and reporting, the administrative requirements of taxation had a great deal to do with the development of regulation by the states.

alike, but some states still apply the tax only to out-of-state companies, or they tax domestic companies at a preferential rate.[12]

In addition to the premium tax, the states also charge companies and agents license fees before they can solicit business in the state. The total revenue received by the insurance department of the states greatly exceeds the expenditures required to operate these departments; this makes the insurance department an income-producing agency in every state. As a matter of fact, a critical concern of the states in the "state versus federal regulation" issue is one of revenue. It has been said that "the power to regulate is the power to tax," and many state officials fear that should the federal government assume responsibility for the regulation of insurance, Congress would begin to look with growing interest at the state insurance tax revenues, which now amount to approximately $1 billion annually.

### Federal Income Taxes

For the purpose of taxation under the Internal Revenue Code, insurance companies are classified into three categories: life insurance companies, nonlife mutual insurance companies, and insurance companies other than life or mutual. In general, all three classes are subject to the same tax rates as are other corporations. They differ from other corporations, and from each other, in the manner in which taxable income is determined.[13]

**Life insurance companies.**  Until 1959, life insurance companies were exempt from taxes on underwriting profit and were given favorable treatment in the taxation of investment income. The Life Insurance Company Tax Act of 1959 provided a new method of taxation for life insurance companies for 1958 and subsequent years. Under this act, life insurance companies are now taxed on both investment earnings and underwriting profits. However, only 50% of underwriting profit is taxed in the year in which earned, with the taxation of the other 50% deferred until it is paid

---

[12] Most states have reciprocal or retaliatory premium tax laws. Under a retaliatory law, the purpose is to impose equally high taxes on the admitted companies of another state as that state imposes on the companies of the initial state doing business in the foreign state. For example, if Iowa taxes all companies doing business within its borders at the rate of 2% and Illinois taxes the companies organized in Iowa at the rate of 3%, companies from Illinois that are admitted to Iowa would be taxed 3%.

[13] Life insurers are taxed under Code Sections 801–820; mutual insurers other than life or marine are taxed under Code Sections 821–826; and insurance companies (other than life and mutual) and mutual marine insurance companies are taxed under Code Sections 831 and 832. Section 501(a) of the Code provides that fraternal beneficiary societies, voluntary employees' beneficiary associations, federal employees' voluntary beneficiary associations, local benevolent life and mutual associations, and certain small property and liability mutuals are exempt from income taxation.

out to stockholders.[14] The deferral of the tax on one-half of the underwriting profit is accomplished by permitting stock life insurers to divide newly earned surplus into two accounts: policyholders' surplus and shareholders' surplus. The shareholders' account receives all income that has been taxed, and disbursements to shareholders can be made only from this account. Income that has not been taxed goes to the policyholders' surplus account, where it accumulates until it is no longer needed for the protection of policy-holders or until it reaches a specified ceiling. Income accumulated in the policyholders' account must be taxed before it may be transferred to the shareholders' account, and it must be transferred to the shareholders' account before it may be paid to the stockholders.

**Property and liability companies.**     Property and liability capital stock companies pay the usual corporate income tax on net underwriting profit and investment income. The taxation of nonlife mutual insurers is subject to certain modifications. Most mutual property and liability insurers were totally exempt from income taxes until 1942. From that time until 1962, they were taxed under special formulas which did not take into account their underwriting gains or losses. The Revenue Acts of 1962 and 1964 completely revised the taxation of property and liability mutuals, and most mutuals are now taxed in essentially the same manner as capital stock companies, with one important exception. Since a mutual company does not have accumulated profits out of which to pay extraordinary losses, the law permits mutual insurers to set aside a portion of each year's underwriting gain in a special "protection against loss" account. Through this account, the mutual insurer is permitted to defer a portion of its taxable income over a 5-year period, to be used in the event underwriting losses exceed premiums plus investment income. If the income deferred is not needed to absorb losses, the amounts deferred are returned to taxable income in the fifth year after deferral.

Property and liability mutuals with gross income from operations and investment of not more than $150,000 are wholly exempt from the tax. Property and liability mutuals with gross receipts between $150,000 and $500,000 are taxed on investment income only, unless they elect to be taxed on the regular basis so as to take advantage of an underwriting loss.

## Questions for Discussion and Review

**1.**   Explain why the field of insurance has been regarded as a type of business that requires government regulation.

---

[14]The tax on underwriting profits does not generally apply to mutual life insurers, since policy-holders' dividends are used to return any underwriting income earned to policyholders.

**2.** "Competition can be depended upon to keep rates from being excessive, and good management will keep them from being inadequate; regulation of rates is an infringement on the right of management to make business decisions." Do you agree or disagree with this statement? Why?

**3.** In most states the office of Commissioner of Insurance is an appointive office. Do you feel that it would be better if it were an elective office? Why or why not?

**4.** The commissioner of insurance is normally charged with the responsibility of determining the qualification of applicants for agents' licenses. How rigorous should the preparation for this field be? How rigorous do you think the entrance requirements are in your state?

**5.** What, in your opinion, are the major factors that should be considered in evaluating state regulation of insurance as opposed to federal regulation? What advantages do you see to each system?

## Suggestions for Additional Reading

Bickelhaupt, D. L. and Magee, J. H. *General Insurance*, 8th ed. Homewood, Ill.: Richard D. Irwin, 1970, Chap. 8.

Denney, R. L., Rua, A. P., and Soen, R. J. *Federal Income Taxation of Insurance Companies*. New York: Ronald Press, 1966.

Kimball, S. L. *Insurance and Public Policy*. Madison, Wis.: University of Wisconsin Press, 1960.

Kimball, S. L. and Denenberg, H. S. *Insurance, Government, and Social Policy*. Homewood, Ill.: Richard D. Irwin, 1969.

Magee, J. H. and Serbein, O. N. *Property and Liability Insurance*, 4th ed. Homewood, Ill.: Richard D. Irwin, 1967, Chap. 34.

Mayerson, A. L. "An Inside Look at Insurance Regulation." *Journal of Risk and Insurance* **XXXII**, 51–75 (March 1965).

Mehr, R. I. *Life Insurance Theory and Practice*. Austin, Texas: Business Publications, 1970, Chap. 29.

Mowbray, A. H., Blanchard, R. H., and Williams, C. A., Jr. *Insurance*, 6th ed. New York: McGraw-Hill, 1969, Chaps. 34, 35.

Patterson, E. W. *The Insurance Commissioner in the United States*. Cambridge, Mass.: Harvard University Press, 1927.

Strain, R. W. "An Analysis of the Proposed Federal Motor Vehicle Insurance Guarantee Corporation." *CPCU Annals* **XXII** (2) (June 1969).

Williams, C. A., Jr. and Heins, R. M. *Risk Management and Insurance*, 2nd ed. New York: McGraw-Hill, 1971, Chap. 30.

Williams, C. A., Jr. "Insurance Rate Regulation—A New Era." *CPCU Annals* **XXII** (3) (Sept. 1969).

# 7 The Legal Framework

*Even lawyers were children once.*
—Charles Lamb

The transfer of risk from the individual to the insurance company is accomplished through a contractual arrangement under which the insurance company, in consideration of the premium paid by the insured and his promise to abide by the provisions of the contract, promises to indemnify the insured or pay an agreed amount in the event of the specified loss. The instrument through which this transfer of risk is accomplished is the insurance contract, which, as a contract is enforceable by law.

A great deal of the law that has shaped the formal structure of insurance and that has influenced its content has been derived from the general law of contracts. But because of the many unique aspects of the insurance transaction, the general law has had to be modified to fit the needs of insurance. Our discussion will involve a combination of both the general contract law and its modifications relative to insurance, but with particular emphasis on those principles that are peculiar to insurance. And by way of admonition, remember that these legal aspects are important. If you fail to understand them, your knowledge of the operation of the insurance principle will have a substantial void.

## INSURANCE AND THE LAW OF CONTRACTS

### General Requirements of an Enforceable Contract

Insurance law is predominantly derived from the general law of contracts. Insurance policies, as is the case with all contracts, must contain certain

**130**

elements in order to be binding legally. These elements of a contract are the following:

1. Offer and acceptance
2. Consideration
3. Legal object
4. Competent parties
5. Legal form

**Offer and acceptance.** In order to have a legally enforceable contract, there must be a definite, unqualified offer by one party, and this offer must be accepted in its exact terms by the other party. In the case of insurance, the offer is normally made by the applicant when he applies for insurance. The acceptance takes place when the agent binds coverage or when the policy is issued. There is no requirement that the contract be in writing.

Under the Statute of Frauds, some types of contracts must be in writing in order to be enforceable. The only section of this statute that might be construed to apply to insurance contracts is that which requires written-and-signed proof of an agreement which by its terms is not to be performed within one year from its effect date. This provision has been interpreted to apply only to agreements which cannot possibly be performed within one year. Since the insurer's promise may be required to be fulfilled within one year, or even within one day, from the issue date of the policy, an insurance contract falls outside the statute. Hence, it may be said that in the absence of specific legislation to the contrary, an insurance contract can be oral in nature. However, most insurance contracts are written, and only rarely is an oral contract used.

An oral contract is just as binding on both parties as is a written contract. However, the difficulty of proving the terms of an oral contract, or even the existence of such a contract makes it advisable to confine contractual agreements to those that are written whenever possible. In certain instances, however, the situation may arise in which it may be necessary to create an oral contract of insurance. When a prospective insured requests coverage from a property and liability agent, the agent may effect a contract orally, accepting the offer of the prospective insured. In such instances, coverage begins immediately. If a loss occurs before a written "binder" is issued,[1] or before the policy is issued, the company that the agent bound to the risk will be liable for the loss. However, the courts have ruled that if the agent represents more than one company, he must specify the company with

---

[1] A "binder" is a temporary contract, normally issued for 30 days, which an agent uses to give evidence that he has accepted the offer of the prospect. The binder issued by the company is accepted by the insured with the understanding that it provides the same coverage as the policy form in use by the company.

which coverage is bound. The life insurance agent cannot bind the insurance company to a risk.

**Consideration.**   The binding force in any contract is the consideration, which is the thing of value that each party gives to the other. Like all contractual arrangements, the insurance transaction requires that both parties exchange consideration if the contract is to have a proper legal status. The consideration of the insurance company lies in the promises that make up the contract, e.g., the promise to pay if a loss should occur. The consideration on the part of the insured is the payment of the premium or the promise to pay it, plus an agreement to abide by the conditions of the contract. The promise to pay the premium is normally sufficient consideration for a legally binding contract in property and liability insurance. However, in life insurance, the first premium must be paid before the contract will take effect. And in a life insurance contract, only the first premium constitutes the consideration. This means that premiums subsequent to the first are not part of the legal consideration, since otherwise the contract could not come into existence until all the premiums were paid. The subsequent premiums, however, are conditions precedent to the continuance of the contract.

**Legal object.**   A contract must be legal in its purpose. A contract in which one party agreed to commit murder for a specified amount would be unenforceable in court because the object of the contract is not legal. Likewise, an insurance policy that is actually a gambling contract would be unenforceable as contrary to public policy, and a policy that promised to assume the consequences of the insured's criminal acts would also be contrary to public policy. Perhaps the most common example of such an unenforceable insurance contract is one in which insurable interest does not exist. Lack of insurable interest makes the policy a gambling contract, and gambling contracts are not (except in Nevada) enforceable in the courts. However, lack of insurable interest is not the only possibility. For example, a business interruption policy written on the operations of an illegal whiskey still would not be enforceable. It is even possible that an insurance contract providing physical damage coverage on the contents of an illegal gambling establishment would not be enforceable, but here there is a divided legal opinion. Some courts would hold the entire contract unenforceable. Some would hold it unenforceable only with respect to the equipment that can be used only for gambling purposes; other equipment, such as tables, chairs, beds, and the like, if destroyed, would be an enforceable obligation of the insurance company.

**Competent parties.**   The parties to the contract must be capable of entering into a contract in the eyes of the law. In most cases, the rules of competency are concerned with minors and the mentally incompetent. The basic principle involved is that some parties are not capable of understanding the contract they would enter into; therefore, the courts have ruled that they are not bound by such contracts.

A minor generally is considered to be a person under the age of 21, although in some states a female reaches majority at 18, and in others the marriage of a male or a female will give them full contractual capacity. The legal rule respecting a contract with a minor is that, except for contracts involving a reasonable value of necessities of life, the contract is voidable at the option of the minor. Since insurance has never been held to be a necessity of life by the courts, a minor could purchase insurance, repudiate the contract later, and receive a refund of all his premiums. Several states, however, have enacted statutes conferring on minors of a specified age or over the legal capacity to enter into valid and enforceable life insurance contracts. The age limit varies from $14\frac{1}{2}$ to 18. But in the absence of such a statute a minor could, for example, purchase a life insurance policy at age 15 and pay the premiums until age 20, then repudiate the contract, and receive a return of all the premiums he has paid. Most courts would probably not permit the insurance company even to make a deduction for the cost of the pure life insurance protection received while the contract was in force. Or a minor could purchase automobile insurance for a period of a year, and just before the expiration of the policy he could repudiate the contract and receive a return of his premium even though he did have the protection during the time the contract was in existence.

**Legal form.** We have already noted that there is no requirement that the contract be in writing, but in many instances the form and content of a contract are rather carefully governed by state law. Many states, by law, use a standard fire insurance policy. In life insurance, a standard policy is not required in any state, but most require the inclusion of certain standard provisions in all life insurance policies. For example, the policy must provide that it will be incontestable after it has been in force during the lifetime of the insured for two years from the date of issue. Another standard provision also denies the life insurance company the right to void the policy because of a misstatement in age of the insured. In health insurance, the Uniform Law, adopted by practically all the states, requires all individual and family health insurance contracts to include twelve provisions specified and spelled out in the law.

In addition to the use of standard contracts and provisions, states require that all types of policies be filed with, and approved by, the state regulatory authorities before the policy may be sold in the state. This, of course, is to determine if the policy meets the requirements of the law, and to protect the policyholders from an unscrupulous insurance company which otherwise would take advantage of the public.

To be legal in form, then, the insurance contract must have the same wording as the legal standard policy, or must contain, in substance, the intent of the standard provisions. It must also follow the proper legal procedure of being filed and accepted by the state regulatory authority.

### Void–Voidable

The terms "void" and "voidable" are sometimes incorrectly used interchangeably. Actually, to speak of a "void contract" is a contradiction in itself. A contract which is void is not a contract at all, but rather an agreement without legal effect. In essence, it is not a contract at all, for it lacks one of the requirements specified by law for a valid contract. A void contract cannot be enforced by either party. For example, a contract having an illegal object is void, and neither of the parties to the contract can enforce it. A "voidable contract," on the other hand, is an agreement which, for a reason satisfactory to the court, may be set aside by one of the parties to the contract. It is binding unless the party with the right to void it wishes to do so. For example, let us say that a situation develops under which the insured has failed to comply with a condition of the contract. The company may elect, if it chooses to do so, to fulfill its part of the contract, or it may elect to avoid the contract and revoke coverage. Or, let us say that a 13 year old purchases a life insurance contract. While this contract would be binding on the company, in most cases it would be voidable at the option of the insured. A contract may be held to be voidable for any one of a number of legal reasons. If one party was forced into the contract under duress, or if there was an element of fraud involved, the contract may be voided.

## SPECIAL LEGAL CHARACTERISTICS
## OF INSURANCE CONTRACTS

In addition to those principles which apply to all contracts, there are certain legal characteristics that are unique to insurance contracts.

### Insurance Is a Contract of Indemnity

In many forms of insurance, particularly in property and liability, the contract is one of "indemnity." This means that the insured is entitled to payment from the insurance company only if he has suffered a loss and only to the extent of the financial loss sustained. Put in its simplest terms, the principle of indemnity maintains that an individual should not be permitted to profit from the existence of an insurance contract, but should be placed in the same financial condition that existed prior to the occurrence of the loss. Human nature being what it is, the ability to make a profit from the existence of an insurance policy would lead to the destruction of property and other more serious crimes. The principle of indemnity is enforced through legal doctrines and policy provisions which are designed to limit the amount the insured can collect to the amount of his loss. The four most important of these are the doctrine of insurable interest, the concept of actual cash value, and the "other insurance" and "subrogation" provisions of insurance contracts.

**Insurable interest.** We have already discussed the principle that the insured is not supposed to profit from his insurance contract. Insurance contracts are primarily designed to indemnify insureds for financial losses they have suffered. Perhaps the most important legal doctrine giving substance and support to the principle of indemnity is the doctrine of insurable interest.

An insurance contract is legally binding only if the insured has an interest in the subject matter of the insurance and this interest is in fact *insurable*. In most instances, an insurable interest exists only if the insured would suffer a financial loss in the event of damage to, or destruction of, the subject matter of the insurance. To be more specific, an insurable interest involves a relationship between the person applying for the insurance and the subject matter of the insurance, such as a dwelling or a person's life, so that there is a reasonable expectation of benefit or advantage to the applicant from the continuation of the subject matter, or an expectation of loss or detriment from the cessation of that subject matter. In property and liability insurance, this relationship requires a pecuniary interest, and insurable interest is limited to the extent of that pecuniary interest. In life insurance, it is broad enough to recognize a sentimental interest or one based on love and affection.

The doctrine of insurable interest was developed as a means of assuring that the insurance contract would not be used for wagering purposes and also to mitigate the moral hazard. It should be obvious that if Smith can purchase insurance on Brown's house and collect if the house is damaged or destroyed, he would be profiting from the insurance. He might even be inclined to cause the damage. In the absence of the doctrine of insurable interest, an insurance policy might be used as a gambling contract and could be an inducement to commit arson.

The doctrine is used in life insurance as a means of controlling wagering with human lives, and is also intended to reduce the threat of murder, just as it is used in property insurance to reduce the threat of willful destruction of property. If the class of persons who can legally insure the life of another is restricted to those who are closely related to the insured by blood or marriage, or who possess such a financial relationship to him that they stand to gain more by his continued life than by his death, the temptation to murder the insured will be greatly curtailed.[2] There is even a requirement in a few states that the person whose life is to be insured by another must give consent to the transaction.

*Insurable interest in property and liability insurance* is established by means of a pecuniary relationship between the insured and the subject matter of the insurance. Perhaps the most obvious of these relationships is *ownership*. For example, if the insured owns an item of property such as a building or an automobile and if the property is destroyed, the insured will suffer a financial loss. Ownership, however, is not the only relationship that gives rise to insurable interest. If one has an interest in property for which title is held by another, then this interest may establish an insurable interest. An example would be property used as collateral for a debt. Thus, a mortgagee has an insurable interest in the property mortgaged, and a lienholder has an insurable interest in the property upon which he holds the lien. In both cases, damage to, or destruction of, the collateral could cause the creditor financial loss.[3] Legal liability for loss of, or damage to, property of others in the care of someone may also establish an insurable interest. For example, the operator of an automobile-storage garage could become legally liable for damage to, or destruction of, customers' cars in his care if the proximate cause of the loss is his negligence. The fact that a bailee may become liable for the property of the bailor establishes an insurable interest that is of great importance. There are other relationships which will not be mentioned. As long as one can establish a relationship in which a financial loss would arise, the relationship is a proper subject for a legally binding insurance contract.

An important aspect of the application of the doctrine to property and liability insurance involves the time at which the insurable interest must exist. The insurance contract will be valid only if the insurable interest exists at the time of the loss, regardless of whether it did or did not exist at the inception date of the contract.

*Insurable interest in life insurance* requires a somewhat different relation-

---

[2]Murder, of course, may still exist. There are instances in which a greedy and unsatisfied wife will murder her husband for his insurance. If she is caught and makes a well-deserved exit by way of the electric chair, murder of the insured by the beneficiary will not relieve the insurance company of its obligation to pay the proceeds of the policy. The proceeds will not be paid to the murderer–beneficiary, obviously, but will be paid to a contingent beneficiary or to the estate of the insured.

[3]However, the insurable interest of the mortgagee or the lienholder does not extend to the full value of the property used as collateral, but only to the extent of the indebtedness. Obviously, the financial loss of the creditor would be limited to the balance of the debt, including unpaid interest.

ship for its establishment, and it must exist at a different time. Here, a sentimental interest or one based on love and affection is sufficient to satisfy the requirement, even though a financial loss would not necessarily be involved. The family relationship of husband and wife is universally conceded, in and of itself, to satisfy the requirement.[4] A number of courts, although perhaps a minority, have recognized the relationship of parent and child, of brother and sister, of grandparent and grandchild, and the like, as sufficient. But more remote blood relationships, such as cousins, have generally been rejected as insufficient unless a monetary loss would be involved. Other relationships growing out of affinity alone, such as the interest in the life of one's mother-in-law, are also insufficient. In other relationships, particularly those of a business nature, the death of the insured must give rise to a definite and measurable financial loss if insurable interest is to exist. Examples of the latter include the interest of a theatrical producer in the life of an actor, a professional baseball club in the lives of outstanding players, a corporation in the lives of key employees, a partner in the lives of the other partners, and creditors in the lives of debtors. There are many others, but these examples should be sufficient for our purpose at this time.

In contrast to the requirement in property and liability insurance, an insurable interest must exist at the inception of the life insurance contract for the contract to be legal, but it need not be present at the time of the insured's death. For example, if Jones and Smith are partners in a business operation, it is obvious that if Jones should die, the partnership must be dissolved. The heirs of the deceased partner are entitled to his share of the business, even though the sale of the assets will terminate the business and may involve all concerned in substantial losses. Because of this possibility of financial loss, each partner has an insurable interest in the lives of the other partners. But what happens to the life-insurance policy Jones has purchased on Smith's life if a voluntary dissolution terminates the business? Since the rule in life insurance is that insurable interest is not required at the time of the occurrence of the event insured against, Jones could continue to maintain the policy and collect the proceeds at Smith's death. In the same manner, it is also possible for a creditor to maintain insurance on a debtor's life even though the debt has been paid off.

The extent of the insurable interest depends on a number of factors. First, and perhaps most important, it is assumed that an individual has an unlimited insurable interest in his *own* life. This is based on the principle

---

[4] However, one might argue that the relationship is virtually always accompanied by an economic interest arising out of the wife's legal right to support from her husband and the husband's expectation, however ephemeral, of domestic services from the wife.

that one should be able to dispose of his human life value with the same freedom that he can exercise in disposing of his other property after death. So if a person can find a company that will sell him $1 million worth of life insurance, and if he can pay the premiums on this amount, the contract would be legitimate, even though his death would not cause a financial loss to anyone. His insurable interest in his own life is without limit. The insured has the right to designate anyone he so desires as the beneficiary of his life insurance, and it is not required that the beneficiary have an insurable interest in the life of the insured. The beneficiary has a legal claim to a fixed sum of money upon the occurrence of the insured's death, and as a consequence, he need not prove that he sustained a financial loss because of the death. A third-party applicant for the insurance, who is to be the beneficiary, however, must possess an insurable interest, and the amount of the insurance must bear a relationship to the extent of the interest. For example, in most jurisdictions, the insurance procured by a creditor on the life of a debtor must not be disproportionate to the amount of the debt as it existed at the time the policy was issued or as it was reasonably expected to be thereafter. The purpose of this requirement is to prevent the use of a debt as a cloak for a wagering transaction.

**Actual cash value.**    The second doctrine that is used to enforce the principle of indemnity is the concept of "actual cash value." No matter how much insurance an individual purchases, the amount he may recover is limited to the amount of his actual loss. If Mr. Smith owns a dwelling worth $10,000 and he insures it for $20,000, in the event of a loss, he will be permitted to collect only the actual value of the house. Generally speaking, if persons were permitted to collect the face amount of their insurance contracts, regardless of the extent of the financial loss involved, this again would make the operation of the insurance principle impossible. Overinsurance would be common, and this would lead to willful destruction of property. As a result, it would upset any possibility of predicting losses with any reasonable degree of accuracy. Both results would be socially and economically undesirable.

The basis of measuring the financial loss of the insured varies with the type of contract and the circumstances surrounding the loss. In most types of property and liability insurance contracts, the measure is called actual cash value. This term, however, does not have a hard-and-fast meaning, and what constitutes actual cash value in one situation could not be used in another. Perhaps the most frequently used definition is "that amount of money necessary to replace the damaged or destroyed property with new materials at present-day prices, less depreciation." For example, let us assume that a dwelling was constructed in 1950 at a cost of $10,000. Today, the actual cash value of this structure would be the amount required to replace it with new materials at present prices, minus depreciation. If we assume that construction costs are two and one-half times as much as in 1950, then the replacement cost of the dwelling new today would be $25,000. If we assume that the structure has depreciated approximately 15%, then the actual cash value would be $21,250. This is the value the insurance company would consider in determining the financial loss of the insured. If he had purchased physical damage insurance with a face value of $21,250, and a total loss occurred, this is the amount that would be paid. If the insured had purchased insurance with a face amount of $25,000, only $21,250 would be paid for a total loss, because this amount constitutes the actual cash value of the property.[5]

Although actual cash value is the basic measure of the financial loss of the insured in most types of property and liability insurance contracts, it is not the only measure used. In business interruption and in rent insurance, for example, the measure of financial loss is the *loss of income* of the insured which arises because of his inability to use and occupy the premises because of physical damage to the property. In extra-expense insurance, the measure is the amount of *abnormal expense* incurred to make possible the continued operation of a business in the event the business premises have been damaged or destroyed by certain specified perils. In liability insurance, it would be the amount of damages the insured is obligated to pay a third party in cases in which the proximate cause of the injuries of the third party has been the negligence of the insured. But regardless of the method used in measuring the loss, the principle of indemnity is applicable. The insurance company will pay only if a loss has occurred and only to the extent of the financial loss of the insured, not exceeding the limits of coverage purchased, of course.

*Valued policies and cash payment policies* are other possible types of insurance contracts. They are not contracts of indemnity in the strict sense. Under the valued policy principle, the insurer agrees on the value of the property at the time the contract begins, and in the event of a total loss must pay the face amount of the policy. This type of contract is characteristic of ocean marine insurance and insurance on fine arts. Life insurance contracts, on the other hand, are "cash payment policies." There is not neces-

---

[5] Since the insured is presumed to know more about the value of his own property than anyone else, the burden of purchasing the proper amount of insurance is that of the insured. If he overinsures, he has no one to blame but himself, and the insurer is not obligated to return the premium on the excess insurance.

sarily an agreement on the value of the life insured, but the company agrees to pay the face of the policy upon the death of the insured.

In ocean marine insurance, the reason for the use of the valued policy is more a historical consequence that a modern necessity. Many years ago, if a ship were lost at sea, it could be many months before the loss became known, and in many cases it would be virtually impossible to determine exactly where the loss occurred. As a consequence, the disagreements arising from the attempts to determine the value of the destroyed property at the time and place of the loss were insurmountable. In addition, it is obvious that when a ship is lost at sea, there is no physical evidence that could be used to help establish the value at the time of the loss. The practical alternative to actual cash value was the use of an agreed value for insurance purposes. The principle of insuring on the basis of an agreed value was developed in ocean marine insurance in early times and it is still used today.

In those cases where it would be difficult or impossible to determine the amount of the loss after it has taken place (such as might exist in the case of a rare or valuable work of art), the valued policy is used. Under these contracts, the face amount of the policy is paid in the event of a total loss, regardless of the actual amount of financial loss.

*Valued policy laws*—in addition to its use in marine insurance, the valued policy principle has been enacted into law in some form or other in about half of the states. The Nebraska law is an example:

> Whenever any policy of insurance shall be written to insure any real property in this state against loss by fire, tornado, or lightning, and the property insured shall be wholly destroyed, without criminal fault on the part of the insured or his assignee, the amount of the insurance written in such policy shall be taken conclusively to be the true value of the property insured and the true amount of loss and measure of damages.

This is an ill-conceived law and has little, if any, justification. Fortunately, however, it is limited in its application. The student should note carefully that it is applicable only to *real property*, and only to the perils of *fire, lightning, or tornado*, only if the loss to the real property is *total*.

A valued policy law is perhaps based on the mistaken assumption that if an insured pays for a certain amount of insurance, this is the amount he should collect should a total loss occur. If an insured has a dwelling with an actual cash value of $20,000 and if he purchases $30,000 coverage and the dwelling is totally destroyed by fire, the insurer will be obligated to pay the $30,000, even though this will involve the insured in a profit of $10,000, and even though the contract promises to pay only the actual cash value of the destroyed property.[6] To permit the insured to profit through the existence of his insurance contract is in direct contradiction to the principle of indemnity and it is contrary to public policy. Nevertheless, most valued policy laws have been in existence for many decades.

*Cash payment policies*—the principle of indemnity is necessary in most forms of property insurance in order to prevent the insured from profiting on his insurance contract, but in life insurance the principle has little application. Here, the insurance company contracts to pay a stated sum of money in the event of the insured's death, and this sum is payable without reference to any financial loss resulting from the death. The life insurance contract, therefore, is a cash payment policy. In life insurance, not only is it difficult to place a monetary value on a human life, but to the extent that it can be approximated, most individuals would be substantially underinsured. Overinsurance, with the possibility of profiting through the existence of the insurance contract, is not generally an important problem in life insurance.

The principle of indemnity is applicable only partially in the field of health insurance. Policies providing benefits for loss of income due to disability are cash payment contracts and not contracts of indemnity. The coverage is for a fixed amount, as in life insurance, and this amount will be paid if the insured becomes disabled, even though he suffers no financial loss or if the amount of the financial loss is less than the insurance. For example, if X has a disability policy that will pay him $600 per month in the event of total disability arising from sickness or bodily injury by accident, the insurance company must pay the $600 per month, even though the insured has not had employment for some time and suffers no loss of earnings because of the disability. The basic reasons for the use of the cash payment contracts rather than the indemnity principle are much the same in health as in life insurance. It is so difficult to place an exact monetary value on disability or freedom from disability, that any attempts to do so after a disability has occurred would be highly impractical.

**Other insurance.**   A normal insured is customarily obsessed with the discovery of ways of "beating the insurance company." A common attempt involves the purchase of several policies from different companies. When a loss occurs, these "brilliant" individuals discover to their dismay that this possible source of profit is prevented in the form of some type of "other insurance clause" in the contracts. Most insurance contracts, other than life and in most instances health, contain some clause relating to the existence

---

[6]The student is perhaps aware of the fact that if there is a conflict between the provisions of a contract and a statute, the provisions of the statute will prevail.

of other insurance, and the primary purpose of the restriction is that of preventing the insured from profiting from the existence of the other insurance.

One of the most common of the other insurance clauses is one that is known as a "pro rata clause." The provision in the basic fire insurance contract may be used as an illustration:

> This Company shall not be liable for a greater proportion of any loss that the amount hereby insured shall bear to the whole insurance covering the property against the peril involved, whether collectible or not.

An example will clarify the meaning. Let us assume that X has a dwelling with an actual cash value of $20,000. He purchases $10,000 fire insurance coverage from Company A and $10,000 from Company B, and he suffers a fire loss of $5000. If X could collect $5000 from each insurance company, which he has every intention of doing, he would obviously profit from the existence of the insurance. But under the provisions of the pro rata clause in each policy, each insurer will be obligated to pay only that proportion of the loss which its insurance bears to the total fire insurance on the property. Each company will pay $2500. This will rather effectively prevent the insured from profiting.

Another common type of other insurance clause is one that makes the insurance excess over other valid and collectible insurance. A partial statement of the other insurance clause in an inland marine personal property floater is as follows:

> If at the time of the loss or damage, there is other valid and collectible insurance which would attach . . . had this policy not been effected, then this insurance shall apply as excess over all such other insurance and in no event as contributing insurance.

This clause is typical of inland marine insurance contracts and is also found to some extent in other property and liability insurance contracts. The excess other insurance clause is a method of distributing the insurance in those instances where more than one policy covers a specific loss, and, similar in purpose with that of the pro rata clause, it prevents the insured from profiting through the existence of his insurance contract.

It is permissible to include a pro rata clause in a health insurance contract, although the practice of doing so is not general. The clause operates in a slightly different manner in the health contract than in property and liability contracts. The first distinction involves the use of the clause only if the insured did not disclose the existence of the other insurance to the insurance company in question. The second involves a return of the premium on the excess insurance in those cases in which, because of prorating, the full face amount of the insurance is not paid. For example, let us assume that X purchases a disability income policy in Company A which will provide an income of $200 per month in the event of total disability; X did not, however, disclose to Company A that he also had a disability income contract in Company B and that it would pay $300 per month. Now if X becomes disabled and the true facts come to light, Company A will not be obligated to pay $200 per month, but only its pro rata share. Company A, then, will pay only $80 per month, i.e., two-fifths of the income amount purchased. It will be obligated, however, to return 60% of the premium X had paid on the contract.

The ocean marine contract provides still another contrast with the pro rata clauses used in property and liability insurance. Under the United States rule, if there is double insurance, the ocean marine policy with the earliest effective date is the primary insurance.[7] A policy with a subsequent effective date will be applicable only if the primary insurance is insufficient to provide full coverage for the loss.

**Subrogation.** Another contractual provision designed to prevent the insured from making a profit is the subrogation clause. Here, if the insured collects indemnity under his policy and the loss has been caused by the negligence of some third party, the right to collect damages from the negligent party must be relinquished to the insurance carrier. However, relinquishment is required only to the extent of the amount paid by the insurance company. The right of subrogation is based on the principle that if it did not exist, the insured would be permitted to collect twice for his loss, once from the insurance company and once from the negligent party. This, of course, would be profiting from the existence of the insurance contract.

The doctrine of subrogation is applicable only in property and liability insurance. It is never applied in life and health insurance. For example, if X has a $100,000 life insurance contract and is killed while crossing the street as the result of the negligence of the operator of a 10 ton truck, the widow–beneficiary can collect the $100,000 from the insurance company, and in addition could sue the driver and the trucking firm. The insurance company has no right to reimbursement from the negligent party. The inapplicability of the doctrine is based on the principle that in life insurance the policy is not a contract of indemnity. Support is also provided in the

---

[7] The English rule involves prorating regardless of the order of the dates on the contracts. Any company providing the insurance may become liable for the full amount of its coverage. However, if the insured collects from one specific insurer, the other companies would then be liable to this insurer for their pro rata share of the loss.

fact that in terms of one's economic value, most individuals will be substantially underinsured. Therefore, the possibility of profiting from the existence of a life insurance contract is relatively slight. The same principles are true in health insurance. For example, if X had a disability income contract that would provide a payment of $100 per week in the event of his total disability, and if X is injured seriously as a result of the negligent operation of the 10 ton truck, he can collect the $100 per week from the insurance company and he can also collect damages from the trucking firm without reference to the insurance coverage. The disability insurance company would have no rights against the negligent third party.

### Insurance Is a Personal Contract

Although insurance coverage may apply to property, the risk is transferred to the company from an individual. While we speak of "insuring a house" or some other piece of property, the contract is between the company and a specifically named insured. If the insured should sell the property which is "insured," the insurance is not binding in favor of the new owner of the property. Since the company has a right to decide with whom it will and will not do business, the insured cannot transfer his contract to someone else without the written consent of the insurer. The personal characteristics of the insured and the circumstances surrounding the subject matter of the insurance are important to the insurance company in determining whether it will issue the policy. For example, an automobile insurer would much prefer to have an insured who never drives his car in a reckless manner, and whose major operation is confined to driving back and forth to church on Sunday. It would also be desirable if this person did not drink, gamble, or chase women. The insurer would not be too happy, on the other hand, to insure a 17-year-old boy whose major enjoyment in life is competing in such automobile driving games as "chicken" and "crinkle fender."

One important aspect of the application of the personal contract rule to insurance contracts involves the right of the insured to assign his insurance policy to another person. Since the general rule states that one cannot be forced to contract against his will, the right of the insured to assign his policy must require the consent of the insurance company. Otherwise, the insurance company could be legally bound on a contract with an individual to whom they would never have issued a policy originally, and on one in which the nature of the risk is altered substantially. For example, if the automobile owner described above decided to sell his car, he might sell it to the 17-year-old boy. And if it were possible for him to assign the insurance policy to the boy without the consent of the insurance company, the company would then be in a position of contracting with a person with whom originally it would not have dealt. The insured has the right to assign his policy, but in most contracts the assigned policy will be legally binding only with the written consent of the insurance company.

There are instances in which an insured will assign the proceeds of his policy if a loss occurs; for example, to a mortgagee, a lienholder, or another creditor. This type of assignment is valid without the consent of the insurance company; it does not change the contracting parties or the nature of the risk, it merely makes the recipient entitled to a certain amount of money without making him a party to the contract.

The requirement of written consent of the insurance company in the event of an assignment of the policy is not applicable to all insurance contracts. Life insurance policies are freely assignable without permission. The applicable rule is that anyone having an interest in a life insurance contract can transfer this interest, and can transfer it even to a person who does not have an insurable interest in his life and under circumstances in which no financial consideration is involved.[8] Although no restrictions are placed on the right of the insured to assign a life insurance policy, the policy provides that the insurance company will not be bound by any assignment until it has received written notice of the assignment. This is simply for the protection of the company. An owner might, for example, assign the policy, and the company, not being aware of the fact, might make payment to someone other than the person to whom the policy was assigned. In order to avoid litigation and eliminate the possibility of being required to make a double payment, the company requires written notice of any assignment and is not bound by the assignment until the notice is received.

The difference in the application of the rule of assignment in life insurance as contrasted with its application in the property and liability field may be explained largely by the fact that an assignment of a life insurance policy does not alter the nature of the risk to the insurance carrier, but merely changes the ownership of the contract. The person whose life is insured is still the person insured, and the assignment should have no appreciable effect upon the possibility of the insured's death. In property insurance, however, the assignment could have a substantial effect on the possibility of the occurrence of a loss.

### Insurance Is a Unilateral Contract

Only one party to the contract is legally bound to do anything. The insured makes no promises which he can be legally required to keep. It is true that an insurance policy is a conditional contract, and if the insured violates certain conditions of the contract he may be prevented from collecting in the event of a loss.

---

[8] If the assignment is made for a consideration, such as collateral security for a debt, the person to whom the contract is assigned must have an insurable interest in the life of the insured.

### Insurance Is a Contract of Adhesion

This means that it is prepared by one of the parties (the company) and accepted or rejected by the other (the insured). It is not drawn up through negotiation, and if the insured does not particularly like the terms of the contract, he may choose not to purchase it, but if he does purchase it, he must accept it as it is.

Because the insurance company has the right to draw up the contract, the courts have held that any ambiguity in the contract should be interpreted in favor of the insured. It is somewhat like the case of two small children and the device commonly adopted to settle the dispute as to which of the two gets the biggest piece of pie. "One boy cuts and the other gets first pick." The company draws up the contract and the insured gets the benefit of any doubt.

The fact that the insurance policy is a contract of adhesion and the insured must accept or reject the terms as they are written, makes the doctrine of "presumption of intent" rather important in the area of insurance. Under the doctrine of "presumption of intent," the courts have ruled that a person is bound by the terms of a written contract which he signs or accepts, whether he reads the contract or not. In other words, the court assumes that the insured reads his contract and agrees with the terms thereof.

### Insurance Is an Aleatory Contract

Briefly, the term aleatory means that the outcome is affected by chance and that the number of dollars given up by the parties involved will be unequal. The insured pays the required premium, and if no loss occurs, the insurance company pays nothing. If a loss does occur, the insured's premium is small in relation to the amount the insurer will be required to pay. In the sense that it is aleatory, an insurance contract is like a gambling contract.

### Insurance Is a Contract of Utmost Good Faith

Partly due to the fact that the contract is aleatory, the insurer and the insured enter into a contract where mutual faith is of paramount importance. The legal principle of *uberrimae fidei* (utmost good faith) has deep historical roots in its application to insurance. In the early days of marine insurance, an underwriter was often called upon to insure a ship that was halfway around the world, and he had to accept the word of the applicant that the ship was still afloat. The practical effect of the principle of utmost good faith today lies in the requirement that the applicant for insurance must make full and fair disclosure of the risk to the agent and the company. The risk which the company thinks it is assuming must be the same risk that the insured transfers. Any information about the risk which is known to one party should be known to the other. If the insured intentionally fails to inform the insurer of any facts which would influence the issue of the policy or the rate at which it would be issued, the insurer may have grounds for avoiding coverage. The courts have given meaning to the principle of "utmost good faith" through the evolution of the doctrines of misrepresentation, warranty, and concealment.

**Misrepresentation.** A representation is an oral or written statement made by the applicant prior to, or contemporaneously with, the formation of the contract. It constitutes an inducement for the insurer to enter into the contract. Normally, the representations are the answers to certain questions that are given by the applicant concerning the subject matter of the insurance. For example, in the negotiation of a life insurance contract, if the applicant states in answer to a question that he has never had tuberculosis, this statement is a representation. If the statement is false, a misrepresentation exists that may provide grounds for the insurer's avoidance of the contract later on. However, a misrepresentation may give grounds for voidance of a contract only if it involves what is known as a "material fact." A material fact is information that would have caused the insurance company to reject the application had the truth been known, or to have caused the company to issue the policy on substantially different terms. Facts of minor importance, such as the age at which one's grandparents died, if misrepresented, would have had no influence on the terms of the contract had the truth been known, and therefore would not provide a basis for voidance of the contract.

The doctrine of misrepresentation is applied with varying degrees of strictness. In ocean marine insurance, since frequently there is little chance for the insurer to inspect the subject matter of the insurance, the company must place greater reliance on the information supplied by the applicant than would be the case in domestic insurance. Therefore, it has always been a rule in ocean marine insurance that a misrepresentation of a material fact, even though there was no bad faith on the part of the insured, will give grounds for voiding the contract. In other words, even though fraud is not involved, the mere fact that certain conditions are misrepresented and exercise an improper influence is sufficient to exonerate the carrier from its contractual obligation.

In most other forms of insurance the misrepresentation must be made with fraudulent intent before it can be used by the insurer as grounds for voiding the contract. This application of the principle is, of course, based somewhat on the assumption that the subject matter of the insurance can be inspected by the insurance company. The company, then, is not obligated to depend so strictly for its knowledge upon the information provided by the insured, and therefore cannot have grounds for voidance of a contract, unless it can prove a willful intent on the part of the insured to defraud the company. For example, a provision in the basic fire insurance policy states:

> This entire policy shall be void if, whether before or after a loss, the insured has willfully concealed or misrepresented any material fact or circumstance concerning this insurance or the subject matter thereof. . . .

Thus, the fire policy, by its provisions, requires a willful intent on the part of the insured to defraud the company.

Many applicants for insurance are inclined to misrepresent important facts. Naturally, the reason for this is to obtain insurance where otherwise no insurance company would issue a policy at all, or to obtain the insurance at a lower cost.

In some states there is a statutory requirement that the misrepresented or concealed material fact contribute to the loss before it can give grounds for voiding a policy. These are ill-conceived laws and have about as much justification as valued-policy legislation. The illogical result of such legislation may be demonstrated rather easily. For example, in a nonmedical life insurance contract, the insured could misrepresent the fact that he has a serious heart impairment. If the insurer had known this fact, it would not have issued the policy. If the insured dies as a result of an automobile accident, and not because of the heart impairment, the company will be obligated to pay the proceeds of the policy because the misrepresented fact did not contribute to the loss. Such legislation seems to put a premium on fraud or at least make the existence of contracts involving fraudulent intent much more possible. The rule followed in most states, i.e., the possibility of voidance whether the misrepresented or concealed fact contributes to the loss or not, places the insurance contract on a much more logical and justifiable basis.

In life insurance, a misrepresentation may be used as grounds for voiding a policy only if the representation is a part of the written application and only if the application, or a photostatic copy thereof, is attached to the policy. In most other forms of insurance, the application is rarely a physical part of the contractual arrangement; however, even though the application is not attached to the policy, the doctrine of misrepresentation is still applicable.

Some of the best examples of the operation of the doctrine of misrepresentation are to be found in automobile insurance. At present, many automobile insurance companies are using a rather highly refined premium rating plan, in which the premium will depend upon a number of factors. The insured is required to fill out a rather long application form, and he is required to sign it. His signature attests to the fact that he requests the company to issue the policy and any renewals of the contract in reliance upon the information he has provided. The company, then, obtains representations from the insured concerning such facts as the number of moving traffic violations of the insured and members of his household in the three years previous to the issuance of the policy, the ages of the operators in the household of the insured, previous cancellations of automobile insurance, and the like. Since the answers to these questions are representations of the insured and since automobile insurance is so important today, it would be desirable to see how far the courts have gone in permitting automobile insurers to void policies because of misrepresentations in the application.

In *Safeco Insurance Company vs. Gonacha,* the Colorado Supreme Court held a policy to be void because of a misrepresentation by the insured that he had not had a previous cancellation or had not previously been refused insurance.[9] The court considered the false information to be material and considered it as grounds for voiding the policy, even though the application was not attached to and made a part of the policy. In other recent cases, it was held that a misstatement of age is material to the risk and is grounds for voiding the policy,[10] and that a representation that the automobile would be principally garaged in a community which took a lower premium than the large city where it actually was located, would also give grounds for voiding the contract.[11] In *Pittman vs. West American Insurance Company,*[12] the court held that a misrepresentation in the application concerning previous accidents and major traffic convictions constituted material misrepresentations and could thus give grounds for voiding the policy. Here, the applicant stated that he had not had any accidents in the three years preceding the date of the application. Shortly before applying for the insurance he had an accident as a result of which he was fined for careless driving.

These cases emphasize the importance of the doctrine and the necessity of providing complete and accurate information to the insurance company. Students should learn an excellent lesson from these cases, particularly the one involving the representation of the place of principal use of the automobile. Remember that if you intend to leave the rural area or small town in which you reside and go to a relatively large city to attend college, it would be best to reveal this information to the insurance company. Otherwise, you may be operating an automobile in and about the college campus without any insurance coverage at all.

**Warranties.**   When a representation is made a part of the insurance contract,

[9] *350 Pac. (2nd) 189.* Incorrect statements concerning previous cancellations have been held in other cases to be grounds for voiding coverage. *Dragosvich vs. Allstate Insurance Company, 118 N. E. (2nd) 57,* is typical.

[10] *State Farm Mutual Automobile Insurance Company vs. Mossey, 195 Fed. (2nd) 56.*

[11] *Purcell vs. Pacific Automobile Insurance Company, 64 Pac. (2nd) 1114.*

[12] *25 C. C. H. (Auto 2nd) 349.*

usually by physical attachment of the application to the policy, the statements of the insured then become warranties. Warranties, by definition, also include promises of the insured that are set forth in the policy. The promise to maintain certain protective devices, such as burglar alarms, in proper working order at all times would be an example. A breach of warranty may give grounds for voiding a policy and, most important, it may do so without reference to the materiality of the statement or promise. Therefore, whether the insurer was prejudiced by the untruth or nonfulfillment of the promise, is not a consideration. The mere breach of warranty will provide grounds for voiding the contract. The warranty, therefore, is quite different from a representation in that (a) the warranty need not be material, and (b) the warranty must be a part of the contractual agreement.

A breach of warranty as a means of avoiding a contract is in general much too harsh a doctrine to be applied to insurance contracts. As a consequence, its unqualified use is found only in ocean marine insurance. Here, for example, if the insured warrants that his ship will be used only in coastwise trade, any use otherwise, even though the use would not materially increase the risk, would be a breach of warranty and could void the contract. However, in other forms of insurance, the use of the doctrine has been modified substantially. Courts have tended to look with disfavor on the strict application of the doctrine, and in most instances have modified the doctrine by requiring that the breach of warranty materially increase the risk before it may be used to avoid an insurance contract. There have also been some statutory modifications of the use of the doctrine. For example, in life insurance, the statements of the insured, regardless of the fact that they are part of the contract, can have the legal effect only of representations. This means that the breach of warranty must involve a material fact. Other statutory modifications provide that the breach of warranty will prevent recovery by the insured only if it increased the risk of loss, or only if it contributed to the loss. The disfavor into which warranties have fallen and the difficulties of enforcement of their use is gradually leading to an abandonment of their use except in ocean marine contracts. Instead of a promise in the form of a warranty, such as one requiring the insured to maintain certain protective equipment (burglar alarms, for example) in proper working order at all times, the policy may provide an exclusion to the effect that the insurance coverage is not applicable while the equipment is not in proper working order.

**Concealment.** The requirement that the insured answer in good faith all questions put to him by the insurance company is perhaps the most important legal requirement for the maintenance of the doctrine of *uberrimae fidei* in the insurance contractual arrangement. The doctrine of warranty has been so modified that its legal status is much the same as that of a representation. However, the disclosure of proper and accurate information is not all that is required if the knowledge of both parties of the material facts is to be equal. The applicant also has the obligation of voluntarily disclosing material facts concerning the subject matter of the insurance that the company could not be expected to know about. The failure of the insured to disclose such facts constitutes a concealment, and a willful concealment of a material fact will give grounds for voiding the policy.[13]

Since the insurance carrier cannot be expected to inquire about everything that may be material to the subject matter of the insurance, the insured has an obligation to disclose extraordinary facts within the scope of his knowledge. For example, a company normally would not ask the insured in the application whether he has a whiskey still in the basement of his home. However, if the insured has such an apparatus, he must reveal this fact to the company. If he does not do so, he may discover to his dismay that his insurance is without effect. Legislatures have also tampered with this doctrine, and as is the case with representations, some states require that the fact concealed contribute to the loss before it will give grounds for voiding the policy. So if faulty wiring in the attic, rather than the still, were the cause of the loss, the policy would be valid. There are many other possibilities of concealments, yet this example should be sufficient for the student to recognize that any extraordinary fact related to the subject matter of the insurance, of which the insurance company could not be expected to know, requires a disclosure of such fact to the insurance company.

**Waiver and estoppel.**    Directly related to the doctrines of concealment and misrepresentation are the doctrines of waiver and estoppel. These also relate directly to the law of agency and to the power of the agent.

*Waiver* is the intentional relinquishment of a known right. If the agent issues a contract, knowing that the conditions are being violated, he is deemed to have waived the violation. For example, let us assume that the insured takes out an automobile liability policy, and in the application he states that no male drivers under 25 years of age will be operating the car, when the truth of the matter is that his 17-year-old son operates the car almost exclusively (probably in stock car races). Let us assume further that the agent knows full well that this is the case. Since the knowledge of the agent is presumed to be knowledge of the company, the agent is deemed to have waived this violation when he issues the policy.

*Estoppel* prevents a person from alleging or denying a fact the contrary

---

[13] In ocean marine insurance the concealment does not have to be willful. In other forms of insurance, however, the material fact concealed must be with the intent to defraud.

of which, by his own previous action, he has admitted. The waiving of a violation of the contract by the agent *estopps* the company from denying liability on the basis of this violation at some time in the future.

The powers of the life insurance agent, as we have said before, are somewhat more limited than those of the property and liability agent. In reference to the property and liability agent, however, make no mistake, the powers are extremely broad, and the power of waiver on the part of the agent has been extended by court decision. For example, in an attempt to protect themselves from actions on the part of their agents, insurance companies have inserted the following clause in the standard fire policy:

> No permission affecting this insurance shall exist or waiver of any provision be valid, unless granted herein or expressed in writing added hereto.

Does this clause really protect the companies from the waiver powers of agents? Let us suppose that the insured phones his insurance agent and says, "I just put a still in my basement and I wondered if this would affect my insurance." (Naturally it would, for there is a provision in the policy suspending coverage at any time the hazard is increased by any means within the control of the insured.) His agent, however, says, "Don't worry about it—it's OK." If a fire occurs, will the insured be able to collect? The company will probably point to the clause stating that no waiver is valid unless expressed in writing, but this may not do much good. Some courts have ruled that the agent can waive the above quoted clause along with any other clauses in the contract. In other words, the power of the agent is so strong that he can waive the very clause that says that he cannot waive any of the clauses in the contract!

### The Insurance Contract As a Contract

The complicated nature of the insurance contract has made it the butt of many jokes. Why, people often ask, doesn't the insurance company make the policy simple enough for the layman to understand? Why not cut out some of the excess wordage? The answer to both questions is that the insurance policy is in fact a contract. As a contract it is enforceable by law and must set forth as clearly and as unambiguously as possible every condition and obligation of both parties. Many provisions found in insurance policies are for the protection of the insured. In addition, the insurance company must attempt to protect itself against both the insureds and ministerpretations by the courts.

In the chapters that follow, we will examine a number of insurance contracts, and while all these are different, they are similar in that they are all composed of four basic sections:

1. Declarations
2. Insuring agreements
3. Exclusions
4. Conditions

**Declarations.**   The declarations section contains the statements made by the insured. As we have seen, these are usually considered to be representations by the courts. Also included in the declarations section is information about the location of the property insured, the name of the insured, and other matters relating to the identification of the person or property insured.

**Insuring agreements.**   In this section, the company promises to pay for loss if it should result from the perils covered. Coverage may be provided in one of two principal ways. It is either on a *named peril* basis, in which case the policy lists the perils insured against, or it is on an *all-risk* basis. *All-risk* policies cover loss by any perils except those that are specifically excluded.

**Exclusions.**   In this section, the company states what it will not do. The number of exclusions has a direct relationship to the broadness or narrowness of the insuring agreement. If the policy is written on a named peril basis, the exclusions may be few. On the other hand, all-risk policies require more exclusions in order to eliminate coverage for those perils which are uninsurable. The exclusions are a basic part of the contract and a thorough understanding of the contract requires a complete knowledge of the exclusions. Certain perils must be excluded in insurance contracts either because they are not insurable, or because the basic premium does not contemplate the exposure and the coverage must be obtained through the payment of an additional premium or under another more specialized contract.

**Conditions.**   This section spells out in detail the duties and rights of both parties. Most of the clauses contained in it are fairly standard, and they relate to the duties of the insured in the event of loss and protect the insurance company from adverse loss experience through increases in the hazard within the control of the insured.

### The Insurance Contract and the Courts

When members of society who have entered into a contractual arrangement disagree about the terms of the contract, or one of the parties questions the very existence of the contract, either party has recourse to the courts. It is important to recognize that the courts play an important role in the operation of private insurance. Since private insurance is offered through contracts, it is sometimes necessary to turn to the courts.

Court decisions are important in the individual case, because they decide the issue in question, but more important from our point of view, they set precedents which are applied in future instances. Court interpretation of insurance policies make policy interpretation difficult in one sense, in that there is always the distinct possibility that the court will interpret a contract in a way that the insurer had not considered. On the other hand, past decisions are useful in interpreting contracts, for they indicate the intent of the court with respect to certain terms.

Since the insurance contract is a contract of adhesion, the courts normally favor the insured in the event of ambiguity in the contract. Since the insurer has the option of changing future contracts, court decisions often influence the drawing of insurance contracts.

## Questions for Discussion and Review

**1.** The principles of insurable interest, subrogation, actual cash value, and pro rata apportionment all stem from the broader principle of indemnity. Explain what is meant by the principle of indemnity, and indicate specifically in what way each of the four principles mentioned above helps to enforce the principle of indemnity.

**2.** We have noted several instances in which the principle of indemnity is not enforced in the various fields of insurance. List the exceptions to the principle of indemnity with which you are now familiar and explain why each is permitted.

**3.** Rosie LaRue calls her insurance agent at 3:00 AM and asks that the agent increase the coverage on her house from $8000 to $15,000. He agrees to do so. During the night her house burns to the ground. The company will probably deny liability for the additional $7000 in coverage. On what grounds? Should the company be obligated to pay the original $8000?

**4.** The subrogation provision enforces the principle of indemnity by preventing the insured from profiting from the existence of the insurance contract. What other beneficial effect might it have?

**5.** Your roommate and you have automobile insurance policies written by the same insurance company and the coverage is identical. As a matter of fact, you both drive the same year and model car, but his premium is $85 less than yours. He tells you that he was able to obtain the insurance cheaper by having the automobile registered in his father's name and having his father purchase the insurance. Advise him.

## Suggestions for Additional Reading

Beadles, W. T. and Greider, J. E. *Law and the Life Insurance Contract.* Homewood, Ill.: Richard D. Irwin, 1960.

Denenberg, H. S., Eilers, R. D., Hoffman, G. W., Kline, C. A., Melone, J. J., and Snider, H. W. *Risk and Insurance.* Englewood Cliffs, N.J.: Prentice-Hall, 1964, Chaps. 16, 17.

Gordis, P. *Property and Casualty Insurance*, 17th ed. Indianapolis, Ind. The Rough Notes Co., 1970, Chap. 1.

Horn, R. C. *Subrogation in Insurance Theory and Practice.* Homewood, Ill.: Richard D. Irwin, 1964.

Kulp, C. A. and Hall, J. *Casualty Insurance*, 4th ed. New York: Ronald Press, 1968, Chap. 23.

McGill, D. M. *Legal Aspects of Life Insurance.* Homewood, Ill.: Richard D. Irwin, 1959.

Patterson, E. W. and Young, W. F., Jr. *Cases and Materials on the Law of Insurance*, 4th ed. Brooklyn, N.Y.: Foundation Press, 1961.

Patterson, E. W. and Young, W. F., Jr. *Essentials of Insurance Law*, 2nd ed. New York: McGraw-Hill, 1957.

Vance, W. R. and Anderson, B. M. *Handbook on the Law of Insurance*, 5th ed. St. Paul, Minn.: West Publishing, 1951.

# Section II

# LIFE
# AND
# HEALTH
# INSURANCE

# 8 Introduction to Life Insurance

*A man's dying is more the survivors' affair than his own.*

—Thomas Mann

We begin our study of specific types of insurance and insurance coverages with life insurance. We do this for two reasons. First, the life insurance contract is one of the simplest of all the insurance contracts in existence. The insuring agreement is straightforward and to the point, there are relatively few exclusions, and the conditions and stipulations are easily understood. Second, we treat life insurance first in order to follow the philosophy of risk management. This entire course is designed to develop concepts that should be used in dealing with risks the individual faces. We have already noted the first principle of risk management—that the probability a loss may or may not occur is less important than the financial burden which would be imposed if the loss did occur. Following from this principle, the individual should protect against the most important risk first, and for the family unit the risk of the loss of income is of paramount importance. Any well-ordered insurance program should begin with protection of income. It is foolish to insure the property a person owns and neglect to insure the asset that produces the property. The most important asset an individual has is his ability to earn income.

Death is not the only way in which income-earning ability can be destroyed. Disability is equally effective as a means of cutting off income, for it results in unemployment and may entail additional expenses as well. Unemployment resulting from causes other than disability has the same impact, but other forms of unemployment are fundamental risks. Finally, income may be

**159**

stopped as a result of retirement; however, retirement does not have the horrendous implications premature death has. We will deal with the risks of disability and unemployment in later chapters. Here and in Chapters 9–11, we will concern ourselves with the risk of premature death and super-annuation.

It is difficult to know exactly where to begin in the study of life insurance. To understand the various types of insurance policies, it is necessary to know how rates are computed, but to understand the difference in the rate computations between various types of policies, it is necessary to know something about the policies. In this chapter, we will examine the life insurance product in a summary fashion, leaving a detailed analysis for Chapter 10.

## UNIQUE FUNCTION OF LIFE INSURANCE

Life insurance is unique as a means of creating an estate for one's dependents. There is no legal method, other than life insurance, whereby one can create an immediate estate. This conclusion may appear at first to be unwarranted, yet its truth can be demonstrated easily. To illustrate, let us assume that X is 30 years of age, that he is progressing successfully in his professional career, and that his chances for continued success are bright indeed; X has a wife, age 30, and two children. Suddenly it occurs to X that if he should die he would leave his dependents with only the meager standard of living that could be provided with social security benefits. As a result, he decides that he should start accumulating an estate for this possible contingency. His course of action is to be that of saving a definite portion of his paycheck each month with a careful and intelligent investment of his savings. Over a period of time he will accumulate a sizable estate which will provide his dependents with a proper standard of living should he die. Mr. X is to be congratulated for his thoughtfulness, because his desire to make provision for his dependents is noble indeed. However, his perspicacity in utilizing a savings program as the only means of accumulating an estate is sadly lacking in many respects. He is, of course, assuming that he will live for many years and that he will save conscientiously and invest these funds wisely. But X cannot predict the date of his death. He may live for many years or he may be "splattered all over the street" by a 10-ton truck the day after his noble decision is reached. He may save his money consistently, or he may be inclined from time to time to use the money for the normal fringe benefits of a convention or an out-of-town business trip. He may make wise investments, or he may play the stock market with the objectives of achieving quick and substantial increases in his estate and end up with nothing at all.

All these difficulties could have been avoided had X chosen to create his estate by means of life insurance. Had he purchased a $100,000 life insurance policy, he would have created a $100,000 estate the moment he paid the first premium. If he should die a week later, the insurance company would be obligated to pay his beneficiary the $100,000, even though the policy has not as yet been issued. Is there any other legal method whereby an immediate estate can be created at such a small cost?

## SOME UNIQUE CHARACTERISTICS OF LIFE INSURANCE

Life insurance is a risk-pooling plan—an economic device through which the risk of premature death is transferred from the individual to the group. However, the contingency insured against has certain characteristics that make it unique; as a result, the contract insuring against the contingency is different in many respects from other types of insurance. The event insured against is an eventual certainty. No man lives forever. Yet we do not violate the requirements of an insurable risk in the case of life insurance, for it is not the possibility of death itself that we insure against, but rather "untimely" death. The uncertainty surrounding the risk in life insurance is not whether the individual is going to die, but rather when he will die. The risk increases from year to year. The chance of loss under a life insurance contract is greater the second year of the contract, as far as the company is concerned, than it was the first year, and so on, until the insured eventually dies. Yet, through the mechanism of the law of large numbers, as we shall see, the insurance company can promise to pay a specified sum to the insured no matter when he dies.

There is no possibility of partial loss in life insurance as there is in the case of property and liability insurance. Therefore, all policies are cash payment policies. In the event that a loss occurs, the company will pay the face amount of the policy.

### Life Insurance Is Not a Contract of Indemnity

The principle of indemnity does not apply in the case of life insurance. In most lines of insurance, an attempt is made to put the individual back in exactly the same financial position after a loss as he was in before the loss. For obvious reasons, this is not possible in life insurance. The simple fact of the matter is that it is not possible to place a value on a human life.

As a legal principle, every contract of insurance must be supported by an insurable interest, but in life insurance the requirement of insurable interest is applied somewhat differently than in property and liability insurance. When the individual taking out the policy is also the insured, there is no legal problem concerning insurable interest. The courts have held that every individual has an unlimited insurable interest in his own life, and that he may assign that insurable interest to anyone. In other words, there is no legal limit to the amount of insurance an individual may take out on his own life and no legal limitations as to whom he may name as beneficiary.[1]

The important question of insurable interest arises when the person taking out the insurance is someone other than the person whose life is concerned. In such cases, the law requires that an insurable interest exist at the time the contract is taken out. There are many relationships which provide the basis for an insurable interest. Husbands and wives have an insurable interest in each other, likewise partners, and a corporation may have an insurable interest in the life of one of its executives. In most cases, a parent has an insurable interest in the life of a child, although the extent of this interest may be limited by statute. A creditor has an insurable interest in the life of a debtor, although this too is usually limited by statute to the amount of the debt or slightly more.

The question of insurable interest seldom arises in life insurance, because the bulk of life insurance policies sold are purchased by the person whose life is insured. In addition, the consent of the individual insured is required in most cases even when there is an insurable interest. The exception to this requirement exists in certain jurisdictions where a husband or wife is permitted to insure a spouse without the consent of the spouse.

### Effective Date of Coverage

Coverage under the life insurance policy is effective as soon as the contract comes into existence. The fundamental question, then, is when does the policy come into existence. The answer to this question hinges on a relatively small detail in the eyes of many insureds—whether the first premium accompanies the application for insurance. If the application is sent to the insurance company without the premium, the insurance company draws the contract and offers it to the insured. It is not a contract until it has been accepted by the insured, which the insured does by taking the policy and paying the first premium. If the insured should die during the period between making the application and receiving the policy and paying the first premium, no benefits will be paid, for the policy has not yet come into existence. For the most part, this is not the usual procedure.

Normally, the premium accompanies the application for insurance. The

---

[1] While there is no *legal limit*, insurance companies often impose limits for underwriting reasons. Not only is the amount of insurance a company is willing to write on a life limited, but companies are also reluctant to issue a policy with a beneficiary where there is no apparent insurable interest. A company would probably look with disfavor, for example, on an application for insurance made by a middle-aged married executive naming his curvaceous 23-year-old secretary as beneficiary. It may also be noted that it is possible to make an irrevocable designation of a beneficiary, but this type of designation is not often used.

company acknowledges receipt of the premium with a conditional binding receipt. The typical binding receipt makes the policy effective as of the date of application, provided the applicant is found to be insurable according to the underwriting rules of the company. A situation might arise in which the underwriter is forced to determine whether a deceased person would have qualified for insurance if he had not died. If the applicant would have qualified, then the company is bound to pay the death benefit, since the policy went into effect conditionally at the time of the application.

### Rights of Creditors to Life Insurance Proceeds

The proceeds of life insurance policies have long been exempted from the claims of the deceased insured's creditors. While it has sometimes been maintained that this represents discrimination against creditors, it seems justifiable, since the insured also has certain obligations to his dependents which are even more fundamental than his obligations to his creditors. In some states, the exemption applies only if the benefits are payable to certain beneficiaries, such as a wife or children. In some states, the exemption laws are extremely broad, exempting the proceeds of a life insurance policy not only from the claims of the insured's creditors, but also from the claims of the beneficiary's creditors. For example, Section 511.37 of the Insurance Laws of Iowa states:

A policy of insurance on the life of an individual in the absence of an agreement or assignment to the contrary shall inure to the separate use of the husband or wife and children of said individual, independently of his creditors.

The proceeds of an endowment policy payable to the assured on attaining a certain age shall be exempt from liability for any of his debts.

Any benefit or indemnity paid under an accident, health or disability policy shall be exempt to the assured or in case of his death to the husband or wife and children of the assured, from his debts.

The avails of all policies of life, accident, health or disability insurance payable to the surviving widow shall be exempt from liability for all debts of such beneficiary contracted prior to the death of the assured, but the amount thus exempted shall not exceed $15,000.

Laws such as the Iowa law, which exempts the proceeds of an endowment policy from the debts of the insured, and the proceeds from a life or accident policy from the debts of the beneficiary, are extremely rare. In most jurisdictions the proceeds are subject to the claims of creditors of the beneficiary, but not of the insured.

## TYPES OF LIFE INSURANCE POLICIES

Strictly speaking, there are only three types of life insurance policies:

1. Term insurance
2. Whole life insurance
3. Endowment life insurance

Often, a fourth type is included as a separate form, the limited-pay whole life policy, but as we shall see, the limited-pay policy is simply a form of whole life. Contracts involving combinations of these forms are also offered.

### The Term Insurance Policy

Term life insurance is protection against financial loss resulting from death during a specified period of time. It pays only if the insured dies within the given period, which may be 1 year, 5 years, 10 years, 20 years, until the insured is 65 years of age, or any one of a number of other periods. At the end of the policy period, the protection ceases. In many cases, the policy is written with a clause that gives the insured the option of renewing the contract (at a higher premium) for some predetermined period of time. In addition, term policies may be convertible or nonconvertible. A convertible policy may be exchanged at a later date for some form of permanent insurance without taking a medical examination or furnishing other evidence of insurability.

Term insurance is pure protection; it does not develop cash values and there is no saving element. (On some long-term policies a slight cash value does develop, but it disappears before the end of the policy.)

### The Whole Life Policy

The whole life policy (also known as the "straight life" policy, and, even more confusing, "ordinary life") is the basic type of lifetime policy. It provides insurance protection at a level premium for the entire lifetime of the insured. Under the whole life policy, the insured pays premiums for his entire lifetime, and as long as he continues to pay premiums he enjoys protection equal to the face amount of the policy. If he lives to age 100, the age at which the insurance company's mortality tables say he should be dead, they will declare him dead and pay him the face amount of the policy.

### Limited-Pay Whole Life

The limited-payment whole life policy is similar to the whole life policy, in that it provides protection for the entire lifetime of the insured. The difference between the two policies is the manner in which the premiums are paid. Under the limited-pay contract the protection extends to age 100, but the premium payments are made for some shorter period of time. During the period of time that premiums are paid, they are sufficiently high to prepay the policy in advance. Thus, under a 20-payment life policy, the insured pays premiums during the payment period that are high enough to permit him to stop payment at the end of 20 years, and still enjoy protection equal to the face amount of the policy for the remainder of his life.

### Endowment Life Insurance

A pure endowment is a contract that promises to pay the face amount of the policy only if the insured survives the endowment period. The benefits that each survivor receives are contributed to in part by the members of the group who die and do not survive to collect, for if the purchaser of a pure endowment does not survive to the end of the period, there is no return. In most states a pure endowment contract is not permitted under the insurance laws.

Endowment life insurance, in contrast to a pure endowment is a combination of a pure endowment and term insurance for the endowment period. Under the terms of the contract, the company promises to pay the face amount of the policy if the insured dies within the policy period, or to pay the face amount if the insured lives to the end of the specified period, which is known as the endowment period. This is the famous "you win if you live and you win if you die" contract. The endowment portion of the policy pays the face amount if the insured survives, while the term insurance portion pays if he dies during the period.

For example, a 20-year endowment policy provides for the payment of the face amount of the policy to the beneficiary of the insured if he should die during the 20-year period, or for the payment of the face amount to the insured if he should survive to the end of the 20-year period.

### Why Different Forms?

The simplest form of life insurance, but one rarely offered by life insurers today except in connection with group life insurance, is yearly–renewable–term. This type provides protection for a period of one year only, but permits the insured to renew the policy for successive periods of one year, at a higher premium rate each year, without the necessity of furnishing evidence of insurability at the time of each renewal. This is life insurance protection in its purest form.

The easiest way to understand the operation of any mechanism is to try it. In life insurance, as in other forms of insurance, the fortunate many who do not suffer loss share the financial burden of those who do suffer loss. In life insurance, each member of the group pays a premium which represents his portion of the benefit to be paid to the beneficiaries of those who die. At age 21, mortality data tell us that 1.83 persons will die out of every 1000. In order to simplify the operation of the principle, let us assume that there are 100,000 persons in the group. On the basis of past experience, we may expect 183 of them to die, and if we wish to pay a death benefit of $1000 to the beneficiary of each person who dies, we will need $183,000. Ignoring, for the present, the cost of operating the program and any interest we might earn on the premiums we collect, and assuming the mortality table is an accurate statement of the number that will die, it will be necessary to collect $1.83 from each individual in the group, which will provide the necessary fund of $183,000. During the year, 183 members of the group will die and $183,000 will be paid to their beneficiaries.

The next year we would find that the chance of loss has increased, for all the members of the group are now older, and past experience indicates that a greater number will die per 1000. At age 22, it will be necessary to collect $1.86 from each member. At age 30, the cost will be $2.13. At age 40, the cost per member will have almost doubled from the cost at age 21, and it will be necessary to collect $3.53. By the time the members of the group reach age 50, we will have to collect $8.32 from each. At age 60, we will need $20.34, and at age 70, we will need $49.79 from each member. It does not take a great deal of insight to recognize that before long the plan is going to bog down, if it has not done so before the members reach age 70. At age 70, when the probability of death is greater than ever before, the members of the group may find that they cannot afford the premium that has become necessary. At age 80, we will need $109.98 from each member, and at age 90, we will need $228.14. The increasing mortality as the group grows older makes yearly–renewable–term impractical as a means of providing insurance protection at advanced ages. Yet many insurance buyers desire coverage which continues throughout their lifetime. It has been found that the more practical method of providing life insurance for the entire lifetime of the insured is to use a level premium, set at a level that charges more than the cost of protection during the early years, to offset an undercharge during the later years. Under the level premium plan, the premiums do not increase from year to year, but remain constant during the premium-paying period. The level premium for an ordinary life policy of $1000 purchased at age 21, and the premium for yearly–renewable–term insurance beginning at age 21 are illustrated in Figure 8-1. The line that constitutes the level premium is the exact mathematical equivalent of the yearly–renewable–term premium curve. This means that the insurance company will obtain the same amount of premium income and interest from a large group of insureds under either plan, assuming that neither group discontinued premium payments.

The level premium plan introduces features that have no counterpart in term insurance. Death is bound to occur at some time, and in a whole life policy the insurance company knows that a death claim must be paid at some future time. From a glance at Figure 8-1 it should be obvious to the student that under the level premium plan the insured pays more than the cost of pure life insurance protection during the early years the policy is in force. This is evidenced by the difference between the term and the level

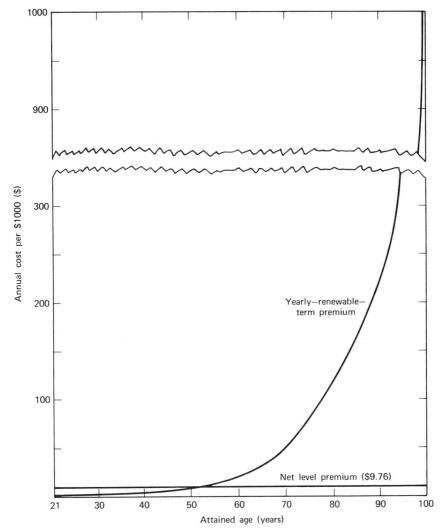

**FIGURE 8-1**
Comparison of net premiums per $1000 in insurance of yearly–renewable–term and whole life. Source: 1958 Commissioners Standard Ordinary Mortality Table, 3% interest assumption.

premium lines. The additional premium is necessary so that the excess portion, when accumulated at compound interest, will be sufficient to provide for the deficiency in the later years of the contract. These redundant premiums create a fund which is held by the insurance company for the benefit and the credit of the policyholders. The fund is the reserve, and it must be accumulated and maintained by the insurance carrier if it is to be able to meet its future obligations on the policies in force.

Referring again to Figure 8-1, it would appear to the student that the reserve would increase for a time and then diminish. It would also appear that the area of the redundant premiums in the early years of the contract will never be sufficient to equal the inadequacy in the later years. Both appearances are false. Not only will the redundant premiums in the early years completely offset the deficiency in the later years, but with the aid of compound interest, the reserve will continue to accumulate throughout the term of the policy and be equal to the face of the contract at the terminal age in the mortality table. Figure 8-2 shows the increase in the reserve on an ordinary life policy purchased at age 20.

The level premium plan introduces the features of the redundant premium during the early years of the contract and the creation of the reserve fund. The insured has the right to withdraw these excess payments at any time through the use of the cash-surrender or loan privilege in his contract. As a consequence, under the level premium plan the insured accumulates an investment element. The result is that the face amount of the policy is composed of a decreasing amount of insurance (the net amount at risk) and the increasing investment element (the growing reserve). The decreasing insur-

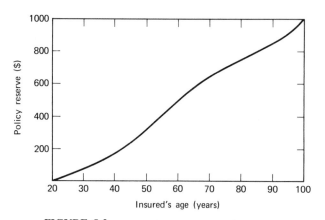

**FIGURE 8-2**

**Increase in reserve on a whole life policy purchased at age 20. Source: 1958 Commissioners Standard Ordinary Mortality Table, 3% interest assumption.**

ance and the increasing investment element always equal the face of the policy. When a policyholder dies, the death claim is composed in part of the reserve on the policy and in part from the current premiums paid by other policyholders in the insured's age and policy classification.

It should be stressed that the policy reserve is not solely the property of the insured. It is his only if and when he surrenders the policy. If he does so, the contract no longer exists, and the insurance company is relieved of all obligations on the policy. As long as the contract is in full force, the reserve belongs to the insurance company and must be used to help pay the death claim if the insured should die. As mentioned above, the reserve must be accumulated by the company to take care of the deficiency in the level premium during the later years of the contract.

From the above analysis, it is obvious that there are two distinct advantages in the use of level premium insurance. First, by paying an amount in excess of the cost of pure life insurance during the early years of the contract, the insured avoids a rising premium in the later years. This will make it financially possible to maintain the insurance until his death, even though it occurs at an advanced age. Second, if the insured survives, he is in the process of accumulating a savings fund which can be utilized for his income needs in his old age.

## ANNUITIES

### The Nature of Annuities

Annuities have been called "upside-down life insurance," and in a sense they are a reverse application of the law of large numbers as it is used in life insurance. While life insurance is a method of scientifically accumulating an estate, an annuity is a device designed for the scientific liquidation of an estate.

The annuity may be defined as a periodic payment to commence at a stated or contingent date and to continue for a fixed period or for the duration of a life or lives. The person whose life governs the duration of the periodic payments is called the "annuitant" and the payment is called the "annuity." If the payments are to be continued for the duration of a designated life or lives, the contract is called a life annuity. But if the payments are to be made only for a specified period, but only as long as the designated person lives, the contract is known as a temporary life annuity.[2]

The basic function of a life annuity is that of liquidating a principal sum,

---

[2] The temporary life annuity is used only infrequently. Therefore, our discussion of annuities will be limited to the whole life annuity.

regardless of how it was accumulated,[3] and it is intended to provide protection against the risk of outliving one's income. Each payment is composed partly of principal and partly of interest earned on the unliquidated principal, and the payments will continue as long as the annuitant lives, even though his life span is much greater than his life expectancy at the time of the purchase of the annuity. In order to illustrate the principle of the life annuity, let us assume that our ubiquitous X attains age 65, retires, and has exactly $25,000 to provide for his needs during the balance of his lifetime. In addition to the physical and mental problems of old age, and particularly an extremely guilty conscience concerning the type of life he has lived, X has a rather difficult financial problem. How much of his $25,000 should he spend each year so that the principal will be used up when he dies? He cannot answer this question, because he does not know how long he will survive. If he decided to spend $1000 plus the interest on the balance each year, he would have sufficient money to last until age 90. But what will he do if he is still alive at this time? If he decides on a little higher standard of living and spends $2000 plus the interest each year, he will have enough to last a little over 12 years. But if X uses his $25,000 principal as a single premium for the purchase of a life annuity, his income from this contract could be as high as $2200 per year, and it will be guaranteed for the balance of his lifetime, regardless of how long he lives.

For the insurance company, it makes absolutely no difference how long the individual lives. Some men who reach age 65 will die before they reach 66. Others will live to be 100. Those who live longer than the average will offset those who live for a shorter period than the average. Every payment the annuitant receives is part interest and part principal. In addition, each payment is part "survivorship benefit," in that it is composed in part of the funds of members of the group who have already died.

Insurance companies have found that annuitants live longer than most people. This is simply a result of selection against the company. People who feel that they have a short life expectancy do not normally purchase annuities, while the individual whose father and grandfather both lived to be 115 will probably look upon an annuity as a good investment. In other words, the principle of the annuity favors people who live a long time, and on the whole, these are the people who purchase annuities. For this reason, insurance companies use different mortality tables for computing the cost of annuities than they do for the cost of life insurance. Since the company promises to

---

[3] It could involve the liquidation of a sum of money derived from a person's savings. This sum could be used as a single premium to purchase an immediate-life annuity. It could also involve the liquidation of the cash values of life insurance contracts, or the liquidation of the proceeds of a life insurance contract after the death of the insured in the form of a life income for the beneficiary of the policy.

pay an income for the life of the annuitant, the longer the annuitant is expected to live, the higher will be the cost for a given amount of annual or monthly income. The higher the age of the annuitant, the lower the cost for a given amount of monthly income. Obviously, there is no requirement that the annuitant be in good health.

### Classification of Annuities

Annuities may be classified in various ways. First, the annuity may be paid only for the duration of a single life or for the duration of two or more lives. This classification involves the single-life and the joint-and-survivor annuities. Second, annuities may be classified according to the time payments are to commence. An annuity may either be immediate, i.e., one in which the first payment is due one payment interval from the date of purchase, or deferred, i.e., one in which normally there is a spread of several years between the date of purchase and the beginning of the annuity payments. The immediate annuity is always purchased with a single premium. The deferred annuity normally is purchased with periodic premium payments made over a period of years, with annuity payments to commence at some specified future date. Third, annuities may be classified according to the method of premium payment. They may be purchased with a single premium, with the annuity to begin immediately or at some future date, or they may be purchased on an installment basis over a period of years. Fourth, annuities may also be classified according to the nature of the insurer's obligation. Under a pure, single-life annuity, payments are made only for the balance of the annuitant's lifetime, regardless of how long or how short this period might be. The annuity is considered fully liquidated at the annuitant's death, with nothing payable to the annuitant's estate. The annuity may contain some sort of refund feature, with a specified amount to be paid to the annuitant's estate if he should die shortly after the commencement of annuity payments. The difference between the total annuity payments and the purchase price of the annuity, for example, could be paid to the annuitant's estate.

The life annuity that provides the maximum income per dollar of premium expenditure is the pure life annuity. This is true particularly if the annuity is purchased above age 60 or if the annuity payments are to commence at an age above 60.[4] This annuity may be immediate, or it may be deferred. It may be purchased on a single life, or jointly on two or more lives. Its outstanding characteristic is that the annuity is payable only for the balance of the lifetime of the annuitant or annuitants. The pure life annuity is perhaps most

---

[4] Below age 60 the annuitant's chances of surviving the typical periods of guaranteed payments are so great that he will gain little in monthly income by eliminating the guarantee-of-refund feature.

attractive for the unmarried individual who has no dependents and who desires the maximum income that is possible on a life annuity basis. If the principal sum used to purchase this annuity was $25,000, it would yield a lifetime monthly income for a male age 65 of approximately $175. If the annuitant is a female, however, the monthly income with the same principal sum and at the same age would be only $150 per month.[5]

Even though the pure life annuity provides the maximum income per dollar of principal sum, many people have strong objections to placing a substantial sum into a contract that promises no return if death should occur shortly after the annuity payments begin. As a consequence, insurers have found it necessary to add some sort of refund feature to annuities in order to make them more salable.[6]

One of the most common refund features involves an annuity with a certain number of payments guaranteed, whether the annuitant lives or dies. For example, if X is age 65 and has a principal sum of $25,000, he could purchase a life annuity with payments guaranteed for a period of 10 years. This would provide him with a life annuity of approximately $150 per month. This is to be compared to the pure life annuity, in which the payments would be $175 per month. But under the annuity with payments guaranteed for 10 years, if X should die at age 70, the insurance company would be obligated to continue the payments to a designated beneficiary or to the annuitant's estate for a period of 5 more years. The beneficiary may or may not have the right to commute the balance of the payments into a lump sum. If the annuitant survives the guaranteed period, the payments will continue for the balance of his lifetime.

Today, guaranteed periods are available for 5, 10, 15, or 20 years. Naturally, the longer the period of guaranteed payments, the greater will be the cost of the annuity. For example, if X had purchased his annuity with 20 rather than 10 years certain, the annuity income would be reduced to an approximate figure of $125 per month.

Another popular type of refund feature is one that provides for annuity

---

[5] Since on the average, women live longer than men, life annuities are more expensive for women. In calculating the cost of life annuities, insurance companies do in fact what women so frequently do in imagination: they rate the age of the woman back by at least 5 years. Therefore, the amount of monthly income to be produced by a given principal sum for a female of age 65 will be approximately the amount produced for a male who is 60.

[6] It appears that most persons are willing to reduce their incomes while alive in order to leave some estate for distant relatives to fight over. It should be obvious that these refund features will increase the cost of the annuity, or, what amounts to the same thing, will reduce the amount of the periodic income purchasable with a given principal sum. If the refund feature is used because of the fear that dependents will be left without income in the event of the early death of the annuitant, then an annuity should not be purchased at all, or an approach such as the joint-and-survivor annuity should be used.

payment at least equal to the purchase price of the annuity; the balance will be paid to a beneficiary or to the annuitant's estate either on a lump-sum basis or in continued installments. If the balance is paid in continued installments, the contract is referred to as an "installment refund annuity." If it is paid in a lump sum, the contract is a "cash refund annuity."

## GENERAL CLASSIFICATIONS OF LIFE INSURANCE

There are four basic classes of life insurance, distinguished on the basis of how they are marketed:

1. Ordinary
2. Industrial
3. Group
4. Franchise

Our treatment thus far has been concerned with ordinary life insurance. The discussion would not be complete without at least a brief description of the other three types. Group life is perhaps the fastest-growing branch of the life insurance industry today, and its specific function and characteristics are so different from those of ordinary life that it has become a separate branch of the industry. Industrial life insurance has also had a tremendous popularity and growth, although it has declined in relative importance in recent years.

### Ordinary Life Insurance

Ordinary life insurance constitutes the oldest and largest of the classes. In ordinary life, individual policies are marketed with a face amount of over $1000. The premiums on these policies are paid annually, semiannually, quarterly, or monthly. The main characteristics of ordinary life are the purchase on an individual basis and the policy amounts in excess of $1000.

### Industrial Life Insurance

By definition, industrial life insurance is a form in which the face value of the policy is less than $1000 and the premiums are payable as frequently as weekly.[7] The most distinctive feature is that the premiums are collected by a representative of the insurance company at the home of the insured. The weekly premium and its collection at the home of the insured are important factors in keeping the policies in force. Most people in the class who purchase industrial insurance will not save the money necessary to pay a monthly or quarterly premium. Also, these persons are not likely to send the premium to the insurance company, as in ordinary insurance. But if a company

---

[7] The average industrial policy today has a face amount of about $300.

representative calls each week at the home of the insured and collects, for example, the 25¢ premium, there is a high degree of assurance that the insurance will be maintained.

In most instances, industrial insurance is sold in premium units and not in units of face amount. Generally, it is decided how much weekly premium the insured can pay. The amount of the insurance will then depend upon the amount this premium will purchase under the plan selected at the attained age of the insured. Generally, the weekly premium will vary from 5¢ to as much as $1.00 per week. The types of policies available include whole life with premiums payable to a specified age such as 65 or 70, 20-payment life, and 20-year endowment. Term insurance is not available. The insurance may be provided for all family members from birth to a specified age such as 70. As a general rule, the insurance is provided without medical examination.

Industrial policies have a number of provisions that are unique. First, when the insured purchases the policy, he has the right to surrender the contract within a specified period, usually two weeks, and receive a return of the full amount of the premium. This provides the insured with a sort of trial period which is designed to protect him against high-pressure salesmanship and to provide him with a reasonable time in which to make a firm decision.[8] Second, the policies contain incontestable clauses which in most instances provide for incontestabllity after the policy has been in effect during the lifetime of the insured for one year from date of issue. However, the application normally is not made a part of the contract, as in ordinary life insurance, and as a consequence, the statements in the application cannot be used as evidence for voiding the contract. However, a safeguard does exist. It is usually provided in the policy that if the insured had medical treatment for a serious mental or physical condition within two years prior to the issuance of the policy and did not disclose this fact to the insurer, the policy would be voidable if the misrepresentation was discovered within the one-year contestable period. The third unique feature of industrial life insurance is a provision known as the *facility-of-payment clause*. The insured may designate a beneficiary in the contract. However, under the facility-of-payment clause, if the beneficiary predeceases the insured, or if the beneficiary fails to make a claim under the policy within 60 days after the death of the insured, or if the beneficiary is a minor, an incompetent, or the estate of the insured, the company shall have the right to pay the proceeds to the insured's executor or administrator or to any relative by blood or marriage appearing

---

[8] Remember, in industrial life insurance one is dealing with rather unusual individuals, and anything within reason that will help these people to maintain some life insurance in force will have a justification.

equitably to be entitled to the proceeds. This provision is necessary in order to avoid holding the small amount of the proceeds until the appointment of an administrator and until the completion of the settlement of the estate.

The assignment of an industrial policy generally is prohibited. The same types of surrender values as in ordinary contracts are provided in industrial policies. However, in many instances, the surrender values are not available until the contract has been in force for 5 years. Because of the low values, loan values are generally not available. Dividends are paid on participating policies, but the insured normally has no choice as to the form of dividend payment. Some companies provide for their use in making future premium payments; others utilize the dividends to purchase paid-up additions to the policy. Settlement options are not available in these contracts primarily because of the small amounts involved. For the same reason, industrial policies do not contain a suicide restriction.

One unfortunate aspect of industrial life insurance is that it is quite expensive. The cost per unit of coverage is substantially higher than that of ordinary life insurance or group life insurance. It is indeed unfortunate that those who are least able to afford life insurance must pay the highest cost per unit. There are, of course, justifiable reasons for the higher cost of industrial life insurance. The death rates at all ages are higher for this class of persons than for those who purchase ordinary life insurance. The absence of the medical examination will produce a rather substantial element of adverse selection, and the greater expense factor arising from the frequent premium payments with collections at the home of the insured will have a substantial influence on the cost of the insurance.

### Group Life Insurance

Group life insurance is a plan whereby coverage can be provided for a number of persons under one contract; the insurance on each life, however, is independent of that on the other lives. Normally, it is provided for the employees of a specified employer without evidence of insurability. In most states, group life insurance is subject to certain requirements established by law. It is customary to require that it be written on not fewer than 25 employees, under a master contract issued to the employer, the premium to be paid by the employer or by the employer and employees jointly, and with the insurance to be provided for all or any class of employees in an amount to be determined by conditions pertaining to the employment. The amount of the insurance must be based upon some plan which will preclude individual selection, and the insurance must be for the benefit of some person other than the employer. If the premium is to be paid in its entirety by the employer, 100% of the eligible employees must be included. However, if the premium is to be paid jointly by the employer and the employees, then not less than 75% of the eligible employees must be insured.[9]

The cost of group life insurance is comparatively low. The reasons are quite simple. First, the basic plan under which most group life insurance is provided is yearly–renewable–term insurance. The student has already learned that term insurance provides the lowest cost per dollar of premium outlay of all the types of life insurance. Second, the expenses of medical examinations and of other methods of determing insurability have been largely dispensed with. Third, group life insurance involves mass selling and mass administration. As a result, the expenses per life insured will be less under group policies than under the marketing of individual policies.

The major problem of the insurance company in the underwriting of group life insurance is that of holding the factor of adverse selection to a minimum. It should be obvious to the student that if group life insurance were provided without any required minimum number or percentage of employees, and if the employees could choose to enter the plan or stay out, only the impaired lives would take the insurance. If the employee could choose the amount of insurance, the impaired lives would tend to take large amounts, while those in good health would take only small amounts. The problem would, of course, be compounded by the elimination of the medical examination and other evidence of insurability. If group life insurance is to be a practical possibility, safeguards must be provided for the prevention or minimizing of the element of adverse selection.

In the underwriting of group life insurance, the contracting parties are the employer and the insurer. The policy issued to the employer is called the *master contract*. Each participating employee will receive a certificate which stipulates the amount of insurance coverage he has under the plan, the designation of his beneficiary, and any rights and privileges he may have under the plan. The coverage is applicable to the employees as long as they remain in the service of the employer, and also applies for 31 days after termination of employment. The employee may, during the 31 days after termination of employment, convert all or a portion of the insurance to any form of individual policy currently offered by the insurance company, with the exception of term insurance. Conversion would be at the attained age of the employee and could not be refused by the insurance company because of uninsurability of the employee.

---

[9]Some states permit group life insurance to be written on groups of as few as ten employees. In addition, many state laws do not limit the use of the group principle merely to groups involving employer–employee relationships. Provision is made for the use of the principle to insure members of other closely knit groups such as labor unions and even professional and trade associations. It may be used by creditors to insure the lives of installment debtors.

There are no exclusions in group life insurance. The proceeds of the insurance will be paid for death arising from any cause, including suicide, without any restriction as to time.

Group life insurance programs may be contributory or noncontributory. The most common arrangement, however, is contributory. Here the employee pays, normally through payroll deduction, a flat rate, regardless of his age, and the employer pays the balance. The customary flat charge paid by the employee is 60¢ a month per $1000 of insurance, although this charge may be higher or lower in some states. The contribution of the employer will be quite substantial for older employees, yet the employer's contribution for all employees may remain relatively constant. As older employees die, retire, or leave the employment, their places are taken by younger employees, and as a consequence, the age composition of the group remains quite stable.

Group life insurance has become an important branch of life insurance today, and its importance undoubtedly will continue to increase. For persons in the lower-income groups, it may be the only insurance. For many persons who would not be insurable for ordinary life insurance, it provides the only means whereby life insurance can be obtained. For others, the low-cost group life insurance is an excellent supplement to the individual life insurance program, and should always be taken into consideration in the formulation of one's individual life insurance program, in the same manner as consideration of coverage under the social security program.

### Group Annuities

The group principle is also applicable in the operation of industrial pension programs in industry today. However, the subject of group annuities and industrial pension plans is too extensive and complicated to warrant more than mere mention in a textbook of this kind. It is important, though, for the student to recognize that group annuities can be an important and highly attractive means of operating an industrial pension program. Since most pension programs provide a lifetime income for the retired employee, the group annuity principle can be a highly attractive means of funding and administering a pension program. A master contract is issued to the employer, as in group life insurance, and each participating employee receives a certificate outlining his rights and benefits. The vast majority of the group annuities are contributory, with the employee's contribution being subject to payroll deduction.

There are two main types of group annuity. Under the first, known as the Unit Benefit Plan, a paid-up unit of benefit is purchased at retirement age for each year of completed service of the employee. For example, if an employee has worked for 30 years for the employer under a $1\frac{1}{2}\%$ benefit plan; he will receive an annual retirement income of 45% of his average annual wages. The unit purchased each year amounts to from 1% in some plans to as much as 2% in others.

In the second type of group annuity, known as the Money Purchase Plan, paid-up units of income at retirement age are purchased each year through fixed annual contributions of the employer and employee. The annual contribution of the employee is normally a fixed percentage of his salary, such as 6%. The employer contributes the same amount as the employee, or some amount proportionate to the employee's contribution. The total contributions are designed to produce a reasonable retirement income.

A death benefit is provided under a group annuity program if the employee should die before attaining retirement age. The amount of the death benefit is at least equal to the total of the employee's contribution, and usually includes interest on these contributions.

Withdrawal benefits are similarly provided for an employee who terminates his employment. In this case, the employee need not withdraw his contributions in cash, but may leave them with the insurer to provide a life annuity when he attains the specified retirement age. The amount of the life annuity will be the amount his contributions will purchase. In many plans today, after the employee has attained a specified age or after he has had a specified number of years of employment, his interest in the employer's contributions may become "vested." This means that if employment is terminated before retirement age, the employee may withdraw the total of his own contributions in cash, or wait until the attainment of the specified retirement age, and his annuity will then be that amount that can be purchased with the total of his own plus the employer's contributions.

### Franchise Life Insurance

Groups that are not large enough to meet the requirements for a group policy may purchase a different form of wholesale insurance called franchise insurance. Basically, franchise life insurance is a mass marketing plan similar to group life insurance. However, franchise plans may be written on a group composed of five lives or more. Individual policies are issued in franchise insurance programs instead of a master policy and certificates as in the case of group insurance. Each policy may vary as to the kind of insurance, the amount of coverage, and the premium.

The most important distinctions between franchise life insurance and group life insurance are that the minimum size of the group is smaller in franchise insurance and that the contract is between the individual insured and the insurance company in franchise insurance, while it is between the employer and the insurance company in group life insurance.

## USES OF LIFE INSURANCE

### Individual Uses of Life Insurance

Life insurance is used for a variety of purposes, but the main one is that of providing financial protection for the family in the event that the wage earner dies. The policy proceeds serve to replace the lost income, and permit the family to continue as nearly as possible the same standard of living they enjoyed before the death. In addition to this primary function, life insurance serves as a vehicle for savings and the accumulation of funds for specific purposes such as retirement or the education of children. The cash value, which accumulates under permanent forms of insurance, represents a form of "near money," highly liquid in form and available for retirement needs or emergencies. The father who would like to guarantee the future financial needs that will arise in connection with the education of his children can do so through the mechanism of life insurance. If the father lives until the children are ready to enter college, the cash values may be used for the expenses.[10] If he dies before that time, the policy proceeds will provide the means for financing the college costs.

In addition to protecting the family against the financial loss which would result from the death of the father, life insurance may be used to protect against the consequences of the death of the mother. While the need for insurance on the father has generally been recognized, the additional costs that may be involved in the death of the mother were often overlooked until recently.

Another important use of life insurance is in the area of charitable bequests. One of the more attractive approaches in this area is the use of life insurance to provide for a gift to a charitable institution. The individual purchases insurance in the amount he desires to give, naming the institution as the beneficiary. While it might be impossible for the individual in question to make an outright gift of, say $5000, to his church, he could probably afford the annual premium of about $65, which the purchase of a whole life contract would entail.

The well-to-do frequently purchase large amounts of life insurance, even though their surviving dependents would not become charity cases if they did not. They do so in order that their estate will be able to meet the heavy estate taxes that will be payable to the federal government at the time of their death. These taxes must be paid in cash, and life insurance provides a ready source, eliminating the need to dispose of assets which might involve unexpected losses.

---

[10] Of course, the amount of protection will be reduced by the amount of the loan if the cash value is borrowed, and the protection will be terminated if the policy is surrendered for the cash value.

Life insurance also provides a basis for support of credit. The lender is primarily concerned about the ability of the borrower to repay a loan, and since the death of the borrower may diminish the chances of repayment, banks and other financial institutions look favorably upon an applicant whose life is insured.

In addition to these uses of life insurance by individuals, there are numerous business uses.

### Business Uses of Life Insurance

The need for life and health insurance in the business enterprise is becoming more and more widely recognized. As managers have become aware of the problems they must face in the event of the death or extended disability of owners or key employees, they have attempted to meet these problems in advance through the purchase of life insurance. Life insurance may be used to fund buy and sell agreements, as a vehicle for funding retirement programs, and as a device to protect against the financial consequences of the loss of a key employee. These business uses of life insurance will be discussed in greater detail in Chapter 11.

### Questions for Discussion and Review

**1.** "Insurance people are always calling things by names which don't apply. What they call health insurance should be called "sickness insurance" and what they call "life insurance" should be called "death insurance." Do you agree or disagree with the author of this statement?

**2.** Explain in detail why insurance purchased on a group basis is less expensive than comparable insurance purchased on an individual basis.

**3.** Under a whole life policy, the overpayment by the insured during the early years of the contract offsets underpayments in later years. This being the case, the reserve should reach a peak and then gradually decline. How do you explain the fact that it does not?

**4.** It is generally agreed that industrial life insurance is a very expensive form of protection, made so by the high costs involved in the system of distribution and collection. Do you think that this form of life insurance should be outlawed? If so, what would you propose as a replacement? If not, on what grounds do you justify your support of industrial insurance?

**5.** "The *whole life policy* is essentially a *term* to age 100 policy," says Tom. "No," says Tim, "it is an *endowment* at age 100." Who is right? In your answer, explain the nature of each of the terms in italics, and indicate the essential characteristics that distinguish one from the others.

## Suggestions for Additional Reading

Eilers, R. D. and Crowe, R. M. *Group Insurance Handbook.* Homewood, Ill.: Richard D. Irwin, 1965.

Gregg, D. W. *Group Life Insurance,* 3rd ed. Homewood, Ill.: Richard D. Irwin, 1962.

Gregg, D. W. (ed.) *Life and Health Insurance Handbook,* 2nd ed. Homewood, Ill.: Richard D. Irwin, 1964, Chaps. 4–7.

Huebner, S. S. and Black, K., Jr. *Life Insurance,* 7th ed. New York: Appleton-Century-Crofts, 1969, Chaps. 2–8.

McGill, D. M. *Fundamentals of Private Pensions,* 2nd ed. Homewood, Ill.: Richard D. Irwin, 1964.

McGill, D. M. *Life Insurance,* rev. ed. Homewood, Ill.: Richard D. Irwin, 1967, Chaps. 3–6.

Mehr, R. I. *Life Insurance Theory and Practice.* Austin, Texas: Business Publications, 1970, Chaps. 4–6.

Pickrell, J. F. *Group Health Insurance,* rev. ed. Homewood, Ill.: Richard D. Irwin, 1961.

# 9 The Actuarial Basis of Life Insurance

*An actuary is a mathematician with a kind of insanity so rare as to be valuable.*

—Anonymous

## INTRODUCTION

In this chapter we will briefly examine the manner in which the insurance company determines the premiums for the various types of contracts it offers. The purpose here is not to attempt to make the readers into competent actuaries. As a matter of fact, the computation of premiums by the insurance actuaries involves substantially more mathematics than many of the readers or the authors are able to command. The reason for this treatment is to assist the reader in gaining an appreciation of the basic differences among the various contracts. As we will see, differences in premiums among the various forms reflect the differing probabilities of payment under the policies, the length of time for which protection is afforded, and the manner in which the premiums are to be paid.

## LIFE INSURANCE PREMIUM COMPUTATION

There are three primary elements in life insurance rate-making:

1. Mortality
2. Interest
3. Loading

The first two (i.e., mortality and interest) are used to compute the net pre-

**182**

mium. The net premium measures only the cost of claims and omits provision for operating expenses. The net premium plus an expense loading is the gross premium, which is the selling price of the contract and the amount the insured pays. For the most part, we will confine our discussion here to the net premium, realizing that the premiums which we develop are in fact "net," and that an additional charge, the loading, must be added to arrive at the final premium.

### Mortality

The mortality table (Table 9-1) is simply a convenient method of expressing the probabilities of living or dying at any given age. It is a tabular expression of the chance of loss of the economic value of the human life. Since the insurance company assumes the risk of the individual, and since this risk is based on life contingencies, it is important that the company know within reasonable limits how many people will die at each age. On the basis of past experience, applying the theory of probability, actuaries are able to predict the number of deaths out of a given number of people at some given age. Table 9-1 was constructed on the basis of data gathered by fifteen large insurance companies. The mortality table is not, as its form might suggest, a history of a group of people from the year they were born until they all die. The information does not come to the actuary in the form shown. The actuary determines the rate of death at each given age (e.g., the number dying per thousand at ages 1, 2, 3, 4, etc.), and on the basis of this information he builds up a table with an arbitrary number of lives at the beginning age. The table starts with 10,000,000 lives; this figure, known as the "radix," is completely arbitrary. Any number could have been used, for it it the ratio of the number dying to the number living that is important. Table 9-1 contains five columns: age; the number living at each age out of the original 10,000,000; the number of those living at the start of a given year who will die in that year; the ratio of persons dying to persons living expressed in terms of deaths per thousand; and the number of years that those living at any given age can expect, on the average, to live.

Given the mortality table (the chance of loss), the problem of computing the insurance premium at any given age becomes a matter of simple arithmetic. According to the table, there are 9,647,694 persons alive at age 21. Of that number, 17,655 will die. Out of every thousand persons at age 21, 1.83 will die before they reach age 22. To insure the 9,647,694 members of the group for $1000 each for 1 year will require $17,655,000 (17,655 × $1000). If we collect $1.83 from each insured (9,647,694 × 1.83), we will have a sufficient fund to pay all claims. The $1.83 represents the net premium (the cost of the losses only) which each insured contributes:

$$\$17,655,000 \div 9,647,694 = \$1.83$$

**TABLE 9-1**

**Mortality Table**

| Age | Number living | Number dying | Deaths per 1000 | Expectation | Age | Number living | Number dying | Deaths per 1000 | Expectation |
|---|---|---|---|---|---|---|---|---|---|
| 0 | 10,000,000 | 70,800 | 7.08 | 68.30 | 50 | 8,762,306 | 72,902 | 8.32 | 23.63 |
| 1 | 9,929,200 | 17,475 | 1.76 | 67.78 | 51 | 8,689,404 | 79,160 | 9.11 | 22.82 |
| 2 | 9,911,725 | 15,066 | 1.52 | 66.90 | 52 | 8,610,244 | 85,758 | 9.96 | 22.03 |
| 3 | 9,896,659 | 14,449 | 1.46 | 66.00 | 53 | 8,524,486 | 92,832 | 10.89 | 21.25 |
| 4 | 9,882,210 | 13,835 | 1.40 | 65.10 | 54 | 8,431,654 | 100,337 | 11.90 | 20.47 |
| 5 | 9,868,375 | 13,322 | 1.35 | 64.19 | 55 | 8,331,317 | 108,307 | 13.00 | 19.71 |
| 6 | 9,855,053 | 12,812 | 1.30 | 63.27 | 56 | 8,223,010 | 116,849 | 14.21 | 18.97 |
| 7 | 9,842,241 | 12,401 | 1.26 | 62.35 | 57 | 8,106,161 | 125,970 | 15.54 | 18.23 |
| 8 | 9,829,840 | 12,091 | 1.23 | 61.43 | 58 | 7,980,191 | 135,663 | 17.00 | 17.51 |
| 9 | 9,817,749 | 11,879 | 1.21 | 60.51 | 59 | 7,844,528 | 145,830 | 18.59 | 16.81 |
| 10 | 9,805,870 | 11,865 | 1.21 | 59.58 | 60 | 7,698,698 | 156,592 | 20.34 | 16.12 |
| 11 | 9,794,005 | 12,047 | 1.23 | 58.65 | 61 | 7,542,106 | 167,736 | 22.24 | 15.44 |
| 12 | 9,781,958 | 12,325 | 1.26 | 57.72 | 62 | 7,374,370 | 179,271 | 24.31 | 14.78 |
| 13 | 9,769,633 | 12,896 | 1.32 | 56.80 | 63 | 7,195,099 | 191,174 | 26.57 | 14.14 |
| 14 | 9,756,737 | 13,562 | 1.39 | 55.87 | 64 | 7,003,925 | 203,394 | 29.04 | 13.51 |
| 15 | 9,743,175 | 14,225 | 1.46 | 54.95 | 65 | 6,800,531 | 215,917 | 31.75 | 12.90 |
| 16 | 9,728,950 | 14,983 | 1.54 | 54.03 | 66 | 6,584,614 | 228,749 | 34.74 | 12.31 |
| 17 | 9,713,967 | 15,737 | 1.62 | 53.11 | 67 | 6,355,865 | 241,777 | 38.04 | 11.73 |
| 18 | 9,698,230 | 16,390 | 1.69 | 52.19 | 68 | 6,114,088 | 254,835 | 41.68 | 11.17 |
| 19 | 9,681,840 | 16,846 | 1.74 | 51.28 | 69 | 5,859,253 | 267,241 | 45.61 | 10.64 |
| 20 | 9,664,994 | 17,300 | 1.79 | 50.37 | 70 | 5,592,012 | 278,426 | 49.79 | 10.12 |
| 21 | 9,647,694 | 17,655 | 1.83 | 49.46 | 71 | 5,313,586 | 287,731 | 54.15 | 9.63 |
| 22 | 9,630,039 | 17,912 | 1.86 | 48.55 | 72 | 5,025,855 | 294,766 | 58.65 | 9.15 |
| 23 | 9,612,127 | 18,167 | 1.89 | 47.64 | 73 | 4,731,089 | 299,289 | 63.26 | 8.69 |
| 24 | 9,593,960 | 18,324 | 1.91 | 46.73 | 74 | 4,431,800 | 301,894 | 68.12 | 8.24 |
| 25 | 9,575,636 | 18,481 | 1.93 | 45.82 | 75 | 4,129,906 | 303,011 | 73.37 | 7.81 |
| 26 | 9,557,155 | 18,732 | 1.96 | 44.90 | 76 | 3,826,895 | 303,014 | 79.18 | 7.39 |
| 27 | 9,538,423 | 18,981 | 1.99 | 43.99 | 77 | 3,523,881 | 301,997 | 85.70 | 6.98 |
| 28 | 9,519,442 | 19,324 | 2.03 | 43.08 | 78 | 3,221,884 | 299,829 | 93.06 | 6.59 |
| 29 | 9,500,118 | 19,760 | 2.08 | 42.16 | 79 | 2,922,055 | 295,683 | 101.19 | 6.21 |
| 30 | 9,480,358 | 20,193 | 2.13 | 41.25 | 80 | 2,626,372 | 288,848 | 109.98 | 5.85 |
| 31 | 9,460,165 | 20,718 | 2.19 | 40.34 | 81 | 2,337,524 | 278,983 | 119.35 | 5.51 |
| 32 | 9,439,447 | 21,239 | 2.25 | 39.43 | 82 | 2,058,541 | 265,902 | 129.17 | 5.19 |
| 33 | 9,418,208 | 21,850 | 2.32 | 38.51 | 83 | 1,792,639 | 249,858 | 139.38 | 4.89 |
| 34 | 9,396,358 | 22,551 | 2.40 | 37.60 | 84 | 1,542,781 | 231,433 | 150.01 | 4.60 |
| 35 | 9,373,807 | 23,528 | 2.51 | 36.69 | 85 | 1,311,348 | 211,311 | 161.14 | 4.32 |
| 36 | 9,350,279 | 24,685 | 2.64 | 35.78 | 86 | 1,100,037 | 190,108 | 172.82 | 4.06 |
| 37 | 9,325,594 | 26,112 | 2.80 | 34.88 | 87 | 909,929 | 168,455 | 185.13 | 3.80 |
| 38 | 9,299,482 | 27,991 | 3.01 | 33.97 | 88 | 741,474 | 146,997 | 198.25 | 3.55 |
| 39 | 9,271,491 | 30,132 | 3.25 | 33.07 | 89 | 594,477 | 126,303 | 212.46 | 3.31 |
| 40 | 9,241,359 | 32,622 | 3.53 | 32.18 | 90 | 468,174 | 106,809 | 228.14 | 3.06 |
| 41 | 9,208,737 | 35,362 | 3.84 | 31.29 | 91 | 361,365 | 88,813 | 245.77 | 2.82 |
| 42 | 9,173,375 | 38,253 | 4.17 | 30.41 | 92 | 272,552 | 72,480 | 265.93 | 2.58 |
| 43 | 9,135,122 | 41,382 | 4.53 | 29.54 | 93 | 200,072 | 57,881 | 289.30 | 2.33 |
| 44 | 9,093,740 | 44,741 | 4.92 | 28.67 | 94 | 142,191 | 45,026 | 316.66 | 2.07 |
| 45 | 9,048,999 | 48,412 | 5.35 | 27.81 | 95 | 97,165 | 34,128 | 351.24 | 1.80 |
| 46 | 9,000,587 | 52,473 | 5.83 | 26.95 | 96 | 63,037 | 25,250 | 400.56 | 1.51 |
| 47 | 8,948,114 | 56,910 | 6.36 | 26.11 | 97 | 37,787 | 18,456 | 488.42 | 1.18 |
| 48 | 8,891,204 | 61,794 | 6.95 | 25.27 | 98 | 19,331 | 12,916 | 668.15 | .83 |
| 49 | 8,829,410 | 67,104 | 7.60 | 24.45 | 99 | 6,415 | 6,415 | 1000.00 | .50 |

SOURCE: 1958 Commissioners Standard Ordinary Mortality Table.

### Interest

Thus far in our computation, we have not introduced the factor of interest into the discussion. All life insurance policies provide for the payment of the premium before the contract goes into effect, but the benefits will not be paid until some time in the future. Since the insurance company collects the premium in advance and does not pay claims until some time in the future, it has the use of the insured's money for some time, and it must be prepared to pay him interest on it. As we all know, the companies collect vast sums of money, and since their obligations will not mature until some time in the future, they invest this money and earn interest on it. Since they do earn interest on the funds they collect, they do not need to collect the full amount of future losses from the members of the group. They can collect something less than the full amount of the losses, invest it, and then pay the losses out of the total fund of principal and interest. Thus, the present value of a future dollar is an important concept in the computation of premiums. In order to simplify computation, the assumption is made that all premiums are collected at the beginning of the year and all claims mature at the end of the year. Obviously, this assumption does not square with the evidence of reality, but in actual practice the fact that this assumption is not valid does not make any significant difference to the insured or the company.

Table 9-2 represents the value of $1 to be received at the end of some specified number of years at various rates of compound interest (i.e., interest upon interest). It tells how much an individual (or an insurance company, for that matter) would have to invest at a given rate of interest in order to receive $1 at some time in the future. The present value of a future dollar is computed by dividing a dollar by the future value of a dollar at the specified rate of interest.

For example, $1 invested at 3% for a year will be worth $1.03 at the end of the year. How much must we have now, so that if we invest it at 3% it will equal $1 at the end of the year?

$$\frac{\$1}{\$1.03} = 0.970874$$

So if we invest 0.970874 at 3%, it will equal $1 at the end of the year. Reading down the table, we can see that we would have to invest only about 55¢ at 3% in order to have $1 at the end of 20 years.

If we bring the interest into the computation of premiums, the net premium will be something less than it would be necessary to charge each insured for his cost of the death claims of the group. Returning to our example of $1000 worth of insurance for 1 year for each of the 9,647,694 persons alive at age 21, the cost of the claims for the group as a whole (with a 3% interest assumption)

TABLE 9-2
Present Value of $1 at Compound Interest

| End of year | 2% | 2½% | 3% |
|---|---|---|---|
| 1 | 0.980392 | 0.975610 | 0.970874 |
| 2 | 0.961169 | 0.951814 | 0.942596 |
| 3 | 0.942322 | 0.928599 | 0.915142 |
| 4 | 0.923845 | 0.905951 | 0.888487 |
| 5 | 0.905731 | 0.883854 | 0.862609 |
| 6 | 0.887971 | 0.862297 | 0.837484 |
| 7 | 0.870560 | 0.841265 | 0.813092 |
| 8 | 0.853490 | 0.820747 | 0.789409 |
| 9 | 0.836755 | 0.800728 | 0.766417 |
| 10 | 0.820348 | 0.781198 | 0.744094 |
| 11 | 0.804263 | 0.762145 | 0.722421 |
| 12 | 0.788493 | 0.743556 | 0.701380 |
| 13 | 0.773033 | 0.725420 | 0.680951 |
| 14 | 0.757875 | 0.707727 | 0.661118 |
| 15 | 0.743015 | 0.690466 | 0.641862 |
| 16 | 0.728446 | 0.673625 | 0.623167 |
| 17 | 0.714163 | 0.657195 | 0.605016 |
| 18 | 0.700159 | 0.641166 | 0.587395 |
| 19 | 0.686431 | 0.625528 | 0.570286 |
| 20 | 0.672971 | 0.610271 | 0.553676 |
| ⋮ | ⋮ | ⋮ | ⋮ |
| 70 | 0.250277 | 0.177534 | 0.126297 |
| 71 | 0.245125 | 0.173223 | 0.122619 |
| 73 | 0.235607 | 0.164876 | 0.115580 |
| 74 | 0.230987 | 0.160855 | 0.112214 |
| 75 | 0.226458 | 0.156931 | 0.108945 |
| 76 | 0.222017 | 0.153104 | 0.105772 |
| 77 | 0.217664 | 0.149370 | 0.102691 |
| 78 | 0.213396 | 0.145726 | 0.099700 |
| 79 | 0.209212 | 0.142172 | 0.096796 |
| 80 | 0.205110 | 0.138705 | 0.093977 |

is $17,140,780, rather than $17,655,000. If we invest $17,140,780 at 3%, it will equal $17,655,000 at the end of 1 year. The cost per individual becomes 1.776 or 1.78 ($17,140,780 ÷ 9,647,694). To recapitulate:

1-year term policy at age 21          1-year term policy at age 21
  *without interest*                     *with interest*

$$\frac{\$17,655,000}{9,647,694} = \$1.83$$

$$\$17,655,000 \times 0.970874 = \$17,140,780$$

$$\frac{\$17,140,780}{9,647,694} = \$1.78$$

Now, if we want to insure the survivors for another year, we will find that the premium is higher, for there are fewer members left to pay the costs, and at the same time the number of deaths will have increased.

Age 22:   $17,912,000 × 0.970874

$$\frac{\$17,390,295}{9,630,039} = 1.806 = 1.81$$

Age 23:   $18,167,000 × 0.970874

$$\frac{\$17,637,868}{9,612,127} = 1.8349 = 1.84$$

Age 24:   $18,324,000 × 0.970874

$$\frac{\$17,790,295}{9,593,960} = 1.8543 = 1.85$$

Age 25:   $18,481,000 × 0.970874

$$\frac{\$17,942,722}{9,575,636} = 1.8737 = 1.87$$

By the time the insured reached age 65, the mortality table indicates that only 6,800,531 of the original 10,000,000 would still be alive, and that 215,917 of those still alive would die before reaching age 66. Thus, the net premium for the 1-year term at age 65 would be

$$\$215,917,000 \times 0.970874 \qquad \frac{\$209,628,201}{6,800,531} = \$30.83$$

Premiums, being based on mortality, increase as the group of insureds grows older, and as the insured reaches advanced ages, the cost becomes prohibitive. On the whole, then, it becomes advisable to level out the cost of protection by charging slightly more during the early years to offset a deficiency during the later years. Contracts that attempt to level out the premium over the policy period must of necessity be longer-term contracts.

### The Net Single Premium

It is possible to compute a lump sum payment, which, if made by the members of the group, will pay all mortality costs over a term longer than 1 year. The computation of all long-term policies involves this concept. The net single premium is a sum, which, if paid when the policy is issued and augmented by compound interest, will pay the benefits as they come due. Let us assume, for example, that instead of purchasing insurance on an annual basis, our 21 year old and the other members of his group wish to purchase a 5-year term contract. How much must we charge each individual at the beginning of the 5-year policy in order to permit us to pay the death claims as they mature?

The process of computing the net single premium for a 5-year term policy is much the same as the process used in computing the premium on an annual basis. However, since the charge will be made at the inception of the policy and all claims will not have been paid until the end of the 5-year period, the company will have the use of the money for varying lengths of time. To compensate for this, we simply compute the present value of all future claims by discounting the claims due at the end of the first year for 1 year, those due at the end of the second year for 2 years, those due at the end of the third year for 3 years, and so on throughout the policy term. For example, we know from our previous computation that we need $17,140,780 now to meet the $17,655,000 in claims that will mature at the end of the first year. At the end of the second year we can expect, according to the mortality table, claims in the amount of $17,912,000, but applying the discount factor for 2 years we find that we will need only $16,883,780 ($17,912,000 × 0.942596) at the beginning of the contract to meet the obligations that will mature in 2 years. Continuing the process for the full 5 years, we obtain the present value of all future claims:

| Year | Claims | Amount of claims | Discount | Present value of claims |
|------|--------|-----------------|----------|------------------------|
| 1 | 17,655 | $17,655,000 | 0.970874 | $17,140,780 |
| 2 | 17,912 | 17,912,000 | 0.942596 | 16,883,780 |
| 3 | 18,167 | 18,167,000 | 0.915142 | 16,625,385 |
| 4 | 18,324 | 18,324,000 | 0.888487 | 16,280,636 |
| 5 | 18,481 | 18,481,000 | 0.862609 | 15,941,877 |
|   |        | $90,539,000 |          | $82,872,458 |

During the 5-year period, the company will be called on to pay $90,539,000 in death benefits. The present value of these claims is $82,872,458. In other words, $82,872,458 is the amount which, when invested will, with the interest earned on it, permit the company to meet the total obligations during the policy period. This is the cost of claims for the group as a whole. To find the cost of claims for each individual in the group, we simply divide the present value of future claims by the number of entrants in the group:

$$\frac{\$82,872,458}{9,647,694} = \$8.59 \qquad \text{(the net single premium for 5 years)}$$

You may notice that the net single premium for a 5-year term policy is somewhat less than the summation of annual premiums for the same 5 years. This reduction in the cost of the coverage is made possible by the fact that the insurance company has a part of the insured's premium for a longer period of time when the policy is purchased for a longer term with a net single premium.

The procedure for computing the net single premium on any of the various policies we have discussed follows the same procedure. In the case of the whole life policy, for example, all the future claims under the policy are discounted (clear to the end of the mortality table), ending at age 99, when we would expect $6,415,000 in claims. A summation of all the present value of future claims divided by the number of entrants at age 21 would give the net single premium for the whole life policy. In a sense, a whole life policy is a term policy to age 100, for the premium computation on the whole life policy follows the manner described above. The only difference is in the number of years involved.

If we carry the computation out to the end of the mortality table, using the same technique as in the 5-year term policy, we obtain the present value of all future claims under a whole life contract:

| Year | Age | Deaths | Total claims | Discount | Present value of claims |
|------|-----|--------|--------------|----------|-------------------------|
| 1 | 21 | 17,655 | $17,655,000 | 0.970874 | $   17,140,780 |
| 2 | 22 | 17,912 | 17,912,000 | 0.942596 | 16,883,780 |
| 3 | 23 | 18,167 | 18,167,000 | 0.915142 | 16,625,385 |
| 4 | 24 | 18,324 | 18,324,000 | 0.888487 | 16,280,636 |
| 5 | 25 | 18,481 | 18,481,000 | 0.862609 | 15,941,877 |
| . | . | . | . | . | . |
| . | . | . | . | . | . |
| . | . | . | . | . | . |
| 75 | 95 | 34,128 | 34,128,000 | 0.108945 | 3,718,075 |
| 76 | 96 | 25,250 | 25,250,000 | 0.105772 | 2,670,743 |
| 77 | 97 | 18,456 | 18,456,000 | 0.102691 | 1,895,265 |
| 78 | 98 | 12,916 | 12,916,000 | 0.099700 | 1,287,725 |
| 79 | 99 | 6,415 | 6,415,000 | 0.096796 | 620,946 |
| | | | | | $2,441,778,045 |

The present value of future claims, $2,441,778,045, represents the amount the insurance company must have now in order to pay all death claims under the whole life contract as they occur. Divided by the 9,647,694 entrants at age 21, the net single premium for the whole life contract is $253.09.

There is no drastic change involved in the computation of the net single premium for an endowment policy. To compute the net single premium for a 5-year endowment, we would use the same figures that we used in the 5-year term policy, except that for the fifth year the number of claims due would be 9,575,636 instead of 18,481. Since the policy agrees to pay the face amount to the insureds who survive as well as to those who die, we will have to pay each of the 9,575,636 persons who are alive at age 25. Death claims will be paid in the fifth year to 18,481 persons and endowment payments will be made to the 9,557,155 persons who survive to age 26:

| Year | Claims | Amount of claims | Discount | Present value of claims |
|------|--------|------------------|----------|-------------------------|
| 1 | 17,655 | $ 17,655,000 | 0.970874 | $ 17,140,780 |
| 2 | 17,912 | 17,912,000 | 0.942596 | 16,883,780 |
| 3 | 18,167 | 18,167,000 | 0.915142 | 16,625,385 |
| 4 | 18,324 | 18,324,000 | 0.888487 | 16,280,636 |
| 5 | 9,575,636 | 9,575,636,000 | 0.862609 | 8,260,029,794 |
|  |  | $9,647,694,000 |  | $8,326,960,375 |

The present value of future claims under a 5-year endowment with a 3% interest assumption is $8,326,960,375. To find the cost of a policy for a single individual, we divide the present value of future claims by the number of entrants:

$$\frac{\$8,326,960,375}{9,647,694} = \$863.10 \text{ per } \$1000$$

### The Level Premium

The net single premium is the basis for computing the level premium on long-term policies. Although some policies are sold on a single premium basis, the single premium is not popular, as it represents a full cash in advance payment for the insurance, and most insureds realize that in the case of an early death the cost of the insurance would be high in comparison with the cost on an annual basis. In addition, most persons cannot afford the single premium.

To determine the net level premium, we first compute the net single premium, and then convert it to a series of annual payments, taking into consideration the number of premiums that can be expected and the year in which the expected premium will be paid. To do this we make use of the concept of the "annuity due." Annuities, as we have seen, are concerned with the number of survivors. The practical question we ask in computing an annuity due is "How much must the insurance company charge now, in order to be able to pay each member of the group $1 for a given number of years?" The same principles of mortality and compound interest apply, but in a somewhat reverse order. Obviously, the promise by the insurance company to pay $1 for the next 5 years to each of the 9,647,694 21 year olds will involve the payment of something less than 9,647,694 × $5. Some entrants will die; in addition, the company will have the money to invest and will make some return on it. If we refer to the mortality table, we find that there will only be 9,630,039 members of the original group alive at age 22 to collect their $1. In addition, if we assume a 3% rate of return, the insurance company needs only about $0.97 now in order to pay each of those at age 22 $1. Every year there are fewer members of the group; in addition, the company needs less per dollar of benefit the longer the time before the dollar must be paid. We compute the value of an annuity due of $1 for 5 years in the following manner:

| Age | Number living | Present value of $1 | Present value of annual payments |
|-----|--------------|---------------------|----------------------------------|
| 21 | 9,647,694 × $1 due now | $1.00 | $ 9,647,694 |
| 22 | 9,630,039 × $1 due 1 year from now | 0.970874 | 9,349,554 |
| 23 | 9,612,127 × $1 due 2 years from now | 0.942596 | 9,060,352 |
| 24 | 9,593,960 × $1 due 3 years from now | 0.915142 | 8,779,835 |
| 25 | 9,575,636 × $1 due 4 years from now | 0.888487 | 8,507,828 |
|    |              |                     | $45,345,264 |

To be able to pay each of the entrants $1 each year for the next 5 years (paying only those entrants who are alive, of course) the insurance company will need $45,345,264 now. Dividing the amount needed by the number of entrants, we get the cost of an annuity due of $1 for 5 years for each entrant:

$$\frac{\$45,345,264}{9,647,694} = \$4.70$$

Once we obtain the cost of an annuity due of $1 for 5 years, the problem of converting the net single premium on a 5-year policy of any type into a level annual premium becomes one of simple proportion. Taking the premium we computed as the net single premium for a 5-year term policy first, we get

$$\$4.70:\$8.59 = \$1:\$X \qquad X = \$1.8276 = 1.83$$

Giving the insurance company $4.70 in return for $1 annually for 5 years is mathematically the same as giving the insurance company $1.83 each year instead of giving it $8.59 at the beginning of the 5 years.

The net single premium for a 5-year endowment, you will recall, was $863.10. This net single premium can be converted into an annual premium through the use of the present value of an annuity due for 5 years also:

$$\$4.70:\$863.10 = \$1:\$X \qquad X = \$183.64$$

The annual net premium for a 5-year endowment is $183.64. This is the amount that the company must collect from each of the surviving members each year to pay all death claims as they occur and to be able to pay each member who survives to the end of the 5 years $1000. It is the actuarial equivalent of a net single premium of $863.10. The net single premium for a whole life contract was $253.09. To convert the net single premium for a whole life contract to an annual level premium, we compute the value of an annuity due of $1 for an entire lifetime, rather than for 5 years, and use the value of the annuity due to convert the whole life net single premium to a level premium on an annual basis.

The value of an annuity due for life is computed exactly in the same manner as the 5-year annuity due, except that the computation is carried out to the end of the mortality table:

| Age | Number living | Present value of $1 | Present value of benefits |
|---|---|---|---|
| 21 | 9,647,694 × $1 due now | $1.00 | $  9,647,694 |
| 22 | 9,630,039 × $1 due in 1 year | 0.970874 | 9,349,554 |
| 23 | 9,612,127 × $1 due in 2 years | 0.942596 | 9,060,352 |
| 24 | 9,593,960 × $1 due in 3 years | 0.915142 | 8,779,836 |
| 25 | 9,575,636 × $1 due in 4 years | 0.888487 | 8,507,828 |
| ⋮ | ⋮ | ⋮ | ⋮ |
| 95 | 97,165 × $1 due in 74 years | 0.112214 | 10,903 |
| 96 | 63,037 × $1 due in 75 years | 0.108945 | 6,868 |
| 97 | 37,787 × $1 due in 76 years | 0.105772 | 3,996 |
| 98 | 19,331 × $1 due in 77 years | 0.102691 | 1,985 |
| 99 | 6,415 × $1 due in 78 years | 0.099700 | 640 |
|  |  |  | $250,132,551 |

$$\frac{\$250,132,532}{9,647,694} = \$25.93$$

The net single premium for a $1 life annuity due at age 21 is $25.93. Using the cost of an annuity due for life of $1, we determine the annual premium for the whole life contract:

$$\$25.93 : \$253.09 = \$1 : \$X \qquad X = \$9.76$$

The net level annual premium for whole life at age 21 is $9.76.

The computation of the limited-pay whole life policies also uses this basic procedure. A limited-pay whole life policy is the actuarial equivalent of a straight life policy, except for the manner in which the premiums are paid. To compute the premium for a 20-payment whole life contract, we begin with the net single premium for a whole life policy. Under a 20-payment policy, we will spread the premiums over a 20-year period rather than over the total lifetime of the insured. To make the conversion from a net single premium to 20 payments, we use an annuity due for 20 years. The net single premium for an annuity due for 20 years at age 21 is $15.06.

$$\$15.06 : \$253.09 = \$1 : \$X \qquad X = \$16.81$$

The net single premium of $253.09 is mathematically the same as a payment of $16.81 from each of the surviving members of the group for a 20-year period. As a matter of fact, each of the three premiums for the whole life policy that we have computed is the equivalent of the other two. It makes no difference to the insurance company whether the insured makes a net single premium purchase by paying $253.09, or if he agrees to pay $16.81 for 20 years, or if he agrees to pay $9.76 for as long as he lives.

## RESERVES ON LIFE INSURANCE POLICIES

If you will recall, when we computed the annual premium on a series of five 1-year term policies, the premiums were

| | | |
|---|---|---|
| Age 21 | $1.78 | |
| Age 22 | 1.81 | |
| Age 23 | 1.84 | $1.83 × 5 = $9.15 |
| Age 24 | 1.85 | |
| Age 25 | 1.87 | |
| | $9.15 | |

Mathematically, there is no real difference in total cost to the insured if he purchases on the level premium plan or an annual basis over the 5-year period. The level premiums ($1.83 × 5) amount to the same total cost as the summation of the individual annual premiums. Under the level premium plan, however, the insured pays more than the cost of the actual protection that he receives during the first 2 years. *The difference between what the insured pays and the cost of the protection represents the unearned premium reserve for his policy*. This represents the prepayment of future premiums and is the basis for the cash value.

On the 5-year term policy which we computed with an annual level premium, the policy reserve for the first year would be $0.05, since the insured pays $1.83; yet the mortality costs amount to only $1.78. In the second year, when the mortality costs are $1.81, an extra $0.02 is added to the reserve, making a total reserve of $0.07. In the third year, mortality costs exceed the level premium by $0.01, making the reserve decrease to $0.06. In the fourth year, mortality costs are in excess of the level premium by $0.02, decreasing the reserve to $0.04, and in the last year, the reserve completely disappears:

| Year | Step-rate premium | Level premium | Policy reserve |
|------|-------------------|---------------|----------------|
| First | $1.78 | $1.83 | $0.05 |
| Second | 1.81 | 1.83 | 0.07 |
| Third | 1.84 | 1.83 | 0.06 |
| Fourth | 1.85 | 1.83 | 0.04 |
| Fifth | 1.87 | 1.83 | 0.00 |

The reserve on a policy at the end of the policy year is known as the *terminal reserve*, and the terminal reserve at the end of a year plus the net premiums for the next year, is known as the *initial reserve* of that next year. The average of the initial and terminal reserves for any year is called the mean reserve for that year. It is the mean reserve for all policies in force that the insurance company is required by law to have on hand at all times.

The policy reserve and its significance can be more easily understood if we look at the reserve on the 5-year endowment policy which we calculated. If the 5-year endowment is written on an annual pay basis, the annual premium is $183.64, yet only a small portion of this premium goes to pay death claims. The remainder represents a provision for future claims under the policies. The complete computation involved in the reserve on the 5-year endowment policy is illustrated in Table 9-3.

If we trace the operation of the 5-year endowment through the 5 years, we find that during the first year, the company receives $1,771,702,526 in premiums ($183.64 × 9,647,694). This amount is invested at 3% interest, so that by the end of the year it has increased to $1,824,853,575. The total death claims the first year are $17,655,000. When these death claims have been paid a reserve of $1,807,198,575 remains. This is the terminal reserve for the first year; it amounts to $187.66 per policy. The second year the company receives $1,768,460,362 in premiums ($183.64 × 9,630,039). Added to the terminal reserve for the first year, the initial reserve at the beginning of the

**TABLE 9-3**
**Reserve Accumulation on a 5-Year $1000 Endowment**

| | |
|---|---|
| 9,647,694 insureds pay $183.64 each | $1,771,702,526 |
| Invested at 3% for 1 year it equals | 1,824,853,575 |
| Minus first year death claims | 17,655,000 |
| Terminal reserve for first year | $1,807,198,575 |

Terminal reserve per policy $\dfrac{\$1,807,198,575}{9,630,039} = \$187.66$

| | |
|---|---|
| Terminal reserve from first year | $1,807,198,575 |
| 9,630,039 insureds pay $183.64 each | 1,768,460,362 |
| Initial reserve for second year | 3,575,658,937 |
| Invested at 3% for 1 year it equals | 3,682,928,667 |
| Minus second year death claims | 17,912,000 |
| Terminal reserve for second year | $3,665,016,667 |

Terminal reserve per policy $\dfrac{\$3,665,016,667}{9,612,127} = \$381.29$

| | |
|---|---|
| Terminal reserve from second year | $3,665,016,667 |
| 9,612,127 insureds pay $183.64 each | 1,765,171,002 |
| Initial reserve for third year | 5,430,187,669 |
| Invested at 3% for 1 year it equals | 5,593,093,331 |
| Minus third year death claims | 18,167,000 |
| Terminal reserve for third year | $5,574,926,331 |

Terminal reserve per policy $\dfrac{\$5,574,926,331}{9,593,960} = \$581.09$

| | |
|---|---|
| Terminal reserve from third year | $5,574,926,331 |
| 9,593,960 insureds pay $183.64 each | 1,761,834,814 |
| Initial reserve for fourth year | 7,336,761,145 |
| Invested at 3% for 1 year it equals | 7,556,863,933 |
| Minus fourth year death claims | 18,324,000 |
| Terminal reserve for fourth year | $7,538,539,933 |

Terminal reserve per policy $\dfrac{\$7,538,539,933}{9,575,636} = \$787.26$

| | |
|---|---|
| Terminal reserve from fourth year | $7,538,539,993 |
| 9,575,636 insureds pay $183.64 each | 1,758,469,795 |
| Initial reserve for fifth year | 9,297,009,728 |
| Invested at 3% for 1 year it equals | 9,575,010,116 |
| Minus fifth year death claims | 18,481,000 |
| Fifth year terminal reserve | $9,557,438,991 |

Terminal reserve per policy $\dfrac{\$9,557,438,991}{9,557,155} = \$1000.02$

SOURCE: 1958 Commissioners Standard Ordinary Mortality Table, 3% interest assumption.

second year is $3,575,658,937. This amount is invested at 3% for the follow-ing year, producing a fund of $3,682,928,667 out of which death claims may be paid. Note that the terminal policy reserve the first year is actually higher than the annual premium ($187.66 compared with $183.64). This is possible because the interest earning on the overpayment is sufficient to meet the death costs. As the example indicates, the policy reserve gradually increases throughout the lifetime of the policy.

| Year | Policy reserve |
| --- | --- |
| First | $ 187.66 |
| Second | 381.29 |
| Third | 581.09 |
| Fourth | 787.26 |
| Fifth | 1000.02 |

After all death claims have been paid in the fifth year, there is still a fund sufficiently large to pay each of the surviving 9,557,155 members of the group $1000. (The terminal reserve for the last year is not exactly $9,557,155,000, but the small difference of $0.02 per policy results from rounding.)

Our illustrations have indicated that under a level premium plan, the reserves on whole life policies, endowments, and limited-pay whole life policies amount to substantial sums over a period of time. Since these reserves represent a payment by members of the group which is in excess of the current cost of the insurance protection, members of the group have a vested interest in these reserves. In effect, the reserves represent a prepay-ment for future protection. If an individual decides that he wants to with-draw from the group, and that he does not wish the future protection for which he has paid, he is entitled to a return of a portion of his premiums. In a sense, the reserve "belongs" to members of the group, and when a member wishes to withdraw from the group, he is entitled to withdraw a portion of the reserve. Permanent insurance contracts such as whole life, limited-pay, and endowment policies all develop a cash saving fund which is the property of the insured. If he wishes to withdraw from the group, he is entitled to a sur-render value which is based on the policy reserve. Normally, policies do not develop a cash value until after the second year, and the surrender value of the policy rarely equals the full amount of the policy reserve until the policy has been in force for 10 or 15 years. Obviously, the reserve required for any given policy depends on the age of the insured at the date of issue, the assumed rate of interest, and the type of policy. Since, as we have seen, the reserve equals an amount which, together with all future premiums and interest that will be earned on these premiums and the reserve, will equal future benefits, the lower the amount of future premiums and the higher the amount of

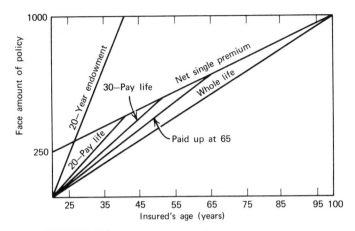

**FIGURE 9-1**
**Reserve accumulation of cash value policies.**

future claims, the higher the reserve must be. A rather simple identity should prove helpful in understanding this relationship:

$$\text{Reserve} = \frac{\text{Present value}}{\text{of future benefits}} - \frac{\text{Present value}}{\text{of future premiums}}$$

In addition to illustrating the nature of the reserve accumulation, the computation of the reserve on the 5-year endowment helps to illustrate once again that the essence of all forms of nonterm life insurance is a combination of decreasing protection and an accumulating fund. When a man purchases $10,000 of whole life coverage, he obtains $10,000 in immediate protection. As he pays on the policy, the cash value accumulates. After 10 years, the policy has a cash value of, say, $3000. The point that is often overlooked is that the actual amount of protection has declined and the "insurance" amounts to only $7000. If the insured dies, his beneficiary will collect $10,000, but $3000 of this amount consists of his "investment."[1] The important point is that under the permanent forms of life insurance, the policyholder does not have $1000 in life insurance protection for each $1000 of face amount, but rather $1000 minus the insured's own accumulated cash value. The actual insurance, or "risk," of the insurance company is constantly being reduced. The major differences among the various forms of cash value life insurance are simply the rates at which the reserve accumulates. Perhaps these differences and the relationship of the policy reserves under the various contracts can be illustrated better graphically. Figure 9-1 illustrates the reserve ac-

[1] An alternative approach would be to say that the beneficiary collects $10,000 and that the "investment" is forfeited to the company. The net effect is the same.

cumulation of various policies purchased at age 21. The lines in the chart indicate the accumulation of the policy reserve for a whole life contract, a 20-pay life contract, a 30-pay life, contract, a paid-up at age 65 policy, and a 20-year endowment policy. The most important line for our purposes is the one designated "net single premium." If the insured purchases a whole life contract with a net single premium of approximately $250, this amount will be sufficient to equal the face of the policy at age 100. The interest on the net single premium will be credited to the reserve, and together with this interest, the net single premium will be sufficient to pay death claims for members of the group and accumulate to the face of the policy at age 100. All the other reserve lines begin at zero, but as the insured overpays his premium, the excess is accumulated as the policy reserve. At any point in time at which the policy reserve equals the net single premium line, premium payments may be discontinued. Remember, there are no additional premium payments due under the net single premium contract, so if the reserve under any other form equals the net single premium line, interest on that reserve will then be sufficient, as in the case of the net single premium, to pay all death claims and still reach $1000 by age 100. Thus, under the 20-pay life policy, the reserve equals the net single premium line at age 41; under a 30-pay life policy, they are equal at age 51. Thus, other things being equal, the reserve on a 20-pay life and a 30-pay life will be the same at the end of 30 years, since the reserve on each policy must by that time be sufficient to pay all future benefits under the policy when credited with interest.[2]

## BENEFIT-CERTAIN AND BENEFIT-UNCERTAIN CONTRACTS

Thus far, we have seen that the procedure for the computation of the premium for all forms of life insurance is essentially the same. The present value of the future claims under the contract is summed, obtaining the net single premium. The net single premium is then distributed over the selected premium payment period, using the concept of an annuity due, which takes into consideration the interest and survival probability.

The present value of the future benefits under a life insurance contract varies with the probability that the insurer will be required to make payment, which varies with the length of time for which the insurance is to be provided and also with the nature of the promise made by the insurer. If the insurer agrees to pay the face of the policy if the insured dies within a specified period

[2] A policy is paid up when there are no further premiums due on it, and the reserve is sufficient, together with the interest on it, to pay all future claims under the policy. Since Reserve = Present value of future benefits − Present value of future premiums, a policy is paid up when Reserve = Present value of future benefits. A policy is mature when the face of the policy is payable. Thus, a 20-year endowment is mature at the end of 20 years, the endowment at age 65 is mature at that age, and the whole life policy matures at age 100.

of time, as in the case of term insurance, the present value of future benefits will be the individual's share of the discounted death claims which are expected to occur during that period. The longer the period of time for which the insurance is to be provided, the greater will be the present value of future benefits. If the insurer agrees to pay the face amount if the insured dies within a specified period and also to make payment if he survives that period, as in the case of an endowment or whole life policy, the present value of future benefits will be the individual's share of the discounted death claims during the period and the discounted value of the endowment benefit. Assuming that the insured persists, the payment of the face of the policy is a certainty.

All forms of permanent life insurance are "benefit-certain contracts." If the insured persists, the face of the policy will inevitably be payable—the probability that the insurer will be required to make payment is 100%. Term contracts, on the other hand, are "benefit-uncertain contracts," in that payment will be made only if the insured dies during the policy period. Since the probability of loss under these contracts is something less than 100%, the present value of future claims is less than that of the present value of future claims under the benefit certain contracts.

In Chapter 8, we noted that the increasing probability of death at advanced ages makes the cost of insurance at those ages prohibitive. The net premium for a 1-year term contract of face amount $1000 at age 70 is $49.79, at age 80 it is $109.98, and at age 90 it is $228.14. Few people would be willing to purchase life insurance coverage at these rates, so the level premium plan was developed to avoid the impact of the increasing mortality.

The perceptive student will note, however, that the level premium contract does not avoid the costs inherent in the higher mortality at advanced ages. The actuarial equivalent of the increasing 1-year term rate must be charged even under the level premium plan, but the higher costs are hidden by premium redistribution and the compound interest on the overpayments made during the early years of the contract. It makes no difference whether the premiums are paid on an annually increasing basis or if they are leveled out via the level premium; the costs are there. The real secret to the operation of the level premium plan and permanent forms of insurance is simply the magic of compound interest rather than the law of large numbers. The level premium plan does not avoid the higher mortality costs at advanced ages; it merely spreads them over a longer period.

Consider the probabilities involved in the various forms of life insurance. A young man, age 21, may purchase a term to age 65 policy. The probability that he will die and that the insurance company will be required to pay the face of the policy is about 30%. If he could purchase a term to age 75 contract, the probability that the company would be required to pay the face of the policy is increased to 57%. Protection to age 85 involves a probability of 86%. What is the probability if a whole life or endowment contract is purchased?

Since the company will inevitably pay the face amount of these policies, the probability is 100%.[3]

The death "risk" at ages past 65 ceases to be a risk. The probability increases each year until the loss becomes a certainty. The exposure under term insurance contracts, on the other hand, is a true contingency—an event that may or may not occur. Mortality costs for the entire life span, i.e., to the end of the mortality table, do not constitute an insurable risk. Mortality costs up to age 65, on the other hand, represent a reasonable approximation of the insurable risk.

There is some question as to whether insurance covering to the end of the mortality table is a proper application of the insurance mechanism. Insuring under a benefit-certain policy such as an endowment or a whole life policy involves the accumulation of an investment rather than a distribution of losses through the law of large numbers. As the insured under permanent forms of life insurance continue their premium payments, the overpayment piles up and the compound interest on the overpayment accumulates, so that the insured builds up a fund which acts to reduce the risk facing the insurance company. While a rational man would probably refuse to purchase insurance at age 75, or 80, or 85, or 90, on an individual year-to-year basis, this is precisely what is done under the whole life contract. However, since the costs involved with the high probability can be hidden by the redistribution of premiums and compound interest, the whole life contract is a saleable product, but the high cost is not avoided. The only way in which the cost of death at advancing ages can be avoided is by refusing to purchase coverage against death at advancing ages.

The most intriguing aspect of the distinction between the benefit-certain and the benefit-uncertain contracts is that it illustrates once again that there is nothing magic or mystical about the insurance equation. The insurance company must collect sufficient premiums to pay the claims it will incur. The benefit-certain contracts are possible only because of the compounding interest on the insured's overpayment of premium during the early years of the contract.

### Questions for Discussion and Review

**1.** "Other things being equal, the lower the interest assumption used in the computation of the premium, the lower will be the reserve on a policy at any point in time." Do you agree or disagree? Why?

**2.** The insurer must estimate in advance both the mortality and the interest

---

[3] The probability of death after age 65 is much greater than the probability of death up to age 65. As a matter of fact, the probability of death during the 10-year period from age 65 to age 75 exceeds the probability for the entire period from age 21 to age 65.

that will be earned on policyholders' premiums. How do insurers attempt to guard against adverse deviations from these estimates?

**3.** The net single premium for a 5-year term policy at age 21 is $8.59 (1958 Commissioners Standard Ordinary Mortality Table, 3% interest assumption). Why can we not compute the annual premium for a 5-year term policy by dividing $8.59 by 5?

**4.** Assume two groups of policies, each consisting of 1000 policies, issued at the same time to groups of the same age. One group of policies consists of single-premium whole life policies and the other consists of 20-payment whole life policies. If mortality is less than anticipated, which group will show the largest mortality savings?

**5.** You have been called upon as a consulting actuary by a tribe of natives in Borneo. Due to warfare with neighboring tribes, the mortality rate is quite high. At the same time, the interest rate is also high. On the basis of the mortality table and the simplified discount table given here, compute (a) the 1-year term rate for ages 21–25; (b) the net single premium for a 5-year term policy at age 21; (c) the net single premium for a 5-year endowment at age 21; (d) the annual premium for the 5-year endowment at age 21.

| Mortality Table | | | Compound Discount Table |
|---|---|---|---|
| Age | Number alive | Number dying | Present value of $1 1 year from now  = $0.90 |
| | | | Present value of $1 2 years from now = $0.80 |
| | | | Present value of $1 3 years from now = $0.70 |
| 21 | 1000 | 10 | Present value of $1 4 years from now = $0.60 |
| 22 | 990 | 20 | Present value of $1 5 years from now = $0.50 |
| 23 | 970 | 30 | |
| 24 | 940 | 40 | |
| 25 | 900 | 50 | |

## Suggestions for Additional Reading

Bickelhaupt, D. L. and Magee, J. H. *General Insurance*, 8th ed. Homewood, Ill.: Richard D. Irwin, 1970, App. J.

Gregg, D. W. (ed.) *Life and Health Insurance Handbook*, 2nd ed. Homewood, Ill.: Richard D. Irwin, 1964, Chaps. 10, 11.

Huebner, S. S. and Black, K., Jr. *Life Insurance*, 7th ed. New York: Appleton-Century-Crofts, 1969, Chaps. 20–25.

McGill, D. M. *Life Insurance*, rev. ed. Homewood, Ill.: Richard D. Irwin, 1967, Chaps. 8–12.

Mehr, R. I. *Life Insurance Theory and Practice*. Austin, Texas: Business Publications, 1970, Chaps. 24, 25.

# 10 The Life Insurance Contract

*Youngsters read it, grown men understand it, and old people applaud it.*

—Cervantes, *Don Quixote*

Unlike many insurance contracts, there is no standard policy form that must be used in life insurance. However, while there is no standard contract, the states have enacted legislation that requires that all life insurance contracts include certain mandatory provisions. The most commonly required provisions include the following:

1. The policy shall constitute the entire contract.
2. There must be a grace period of 30 days or 1 month.
3. The policy shall be contestable only during the first 2 years.
4. Misstatement of age shall adjust the amount of insurance.
5. Reinstatement must be permitted.
6. Participating policies shall pay dividends on an annual basis.
7. Nonforfeiture values must be listed for at least 20 years.
8. The nonforfeiture values to which the insured is entitled must be listed after the payment of three premiums.
9. Loan values must be listed.
10. Installment or annuity tables shall show the amount of benefits to which the beneficiary is entitled if the policy is payable in installments or as an annuity.

**202**

In many cases the exact wording of the provisions is not spelled out, but the final wording adopted must be approved by the commissioner. In addition to those provisions prescribed by law, there are other general provisions which are necessary to complete the structure of the contract. Competition generally requires substantial similarity in these provisions. So, while there is no "standard" life insurance contract, the provisions discussed in this chapter are more or less common to all life contracts.

### GENERAL PROVISIONS

#### Entire Contract Clause

When the application is incorporated as a part of the policy contract, the representations of the insured become contractual provisions and can be used as evidence in a contest of the validity of the contract. To prevent the use of other evidence, most states require the inclusion of a clause in life insurance policies stating that the policy and the application attached to the policy constitute the entire contract between the insurer and the insured. The typical policy provision reads as follows:

> This policy and the application, a copy of which is attached when issued, constitute the entire contract. All statements in the application, in the absence of fraud, shall be deemed representations and not warranties. No statement shall avoid this policy or be used in defense of a claim under it unless contained in the application.

The clause also states that the statements of the insured are to be considered representations and not warranties, thus requiring the insurer to prove the materiality of any misrepresentations by the insured. This provision is clearly beneficial to the insured.

#### Ownership Clause

A life insurance policy is a piece of property. The owner of the policy may be the individual on whose life the policy is written, it may be the beneficiary, or it may be someone else. In most cases, the insured is also the owner of the policy. The person designated as the owner has vested privileges of ownership, including the right to assign or transfer the policy, receive the cash values and dividends, or borrow against the policy. At the death of the insured, the beneficiary becomes the owner of the policy.

#### Beneficiary Clause

The beneficiary is the person named in the life insurance contract to receive all or a portion of the proceeds at maturity of the policy. The designation of the beneficiary is an important aspect of the policy and is designed specifically to reflect the insured's decisions concerning the disposition of his insurance. The beneficiary may be the insured with respect to an endowment or retirement-income policy, or it may be the insured's estate or a third-party beneficiary with respect to the proceeds in the event of his death. In most instances, it is best not to name the estate as beneficiary, particularly when it is intended that the proceeds will go to certain individuals. If a specific beneficiary is named, the proceeds will be paid to the designated person or persons directly after the death of the insured, and they will not be subject to estate administration, with its accompanying costs of probate and the claims of creditors of the insured. But most important, if a specific beneficiary is named, the payment of the proceeds will not be delayed until the settlement of the entire estate has been completed.

The customary type of beneficiary designation is the donee or third-party beneficiary. Here the beneficiary may be a specific individual or a class designation. To make certain that his intentions will be accomplished, the insured should designate the beneficiary or beneficiaries with care. For example, his desire may be that his present wife be the primary beneficiary and that his children by this wife are to be the class-contingent beneficiaries. Proper identification could be accomplished in this case by the designation of "My wife, Elizabeth Hallquist Jones, and our children." The wife would perhaps be named the primary beneficiary and the children contingent. The children then would receive, and share equally, the proceeds if the wife should predecease the insured.[1]

There are many classifications of beneficiaries, but for our purpose the most important involves that in which the insured may or may not reserve the right to change the designation. In this classification, beneficiaries may be *revocable* or *irrevocable*. In the former, the insured reserves the right to change the designation at any time; in the latter, he imposes a restriction upon the use of this right.

The revocable designation is used in the vast majority of life insurance contracts today. Since the insured is the owner of the contract, he has the right to designate anyone as the beneficiary, even if the person named has no insurable interest in his life. If at the inception of the contract, the insured designates a beneficiary and reserves the right to change this designation,

---

[1] There are many reasons for the use of care in the designation of the beneficiary. For example, if the insured designates as beneficiary "My wife, Mrs. John Jones," to whom does he have reference? Is this his present or a former wife? Or if he designates "My children" as a class beneficiary, which children does he desire to include? Would adopted or illegitimate children be included? And what about children of a former wife? These difficulties may be avoided with a little intelligent care. Otherwise, a disgruntled former wife or an illegitimate child may cause considerable difficulty.

then the change may take place any time and any number of times during the term of the policy. This means that the interest of a revocable beneficiary is nothing more than a mere expectancy subject to all the rights and privileges which the insured may exercise in the contract. The insured is the complete owner of the contract and the revocable beneficiary cannot interfere in any manner with the exercise of these rights by the insured. The insured may borrow on the policy; he may surrender the contract for its cash value; he may assign the policy; or do anything else that he wishes without any possible legal interference on the part of the beneficiary. The only time the beneficiary acquires a legal interest in the contract is at the death of the insured. But even here the right of the beneficiary to the proceeds is still subject to the conditions of any settlement options selected by the insured.

If the insured designates an irrevocable beneficiary, he then loses his right to exercise the privileges granted by the contract, except with the consent of the beneficiary; the insured loses his complete ownership of the policy and he and the beneficiary become joint owners of the contract. This means that the insured cannot change the designation of the beneficiary without his consent, and that the acquisition of a policy loan or an assignment of the contract will require the permission of the beneficiary. However, if the irrevocable beneficiary should predecease the insured, most policies today provide that the interest of the beneficiary shall terminate and that all rights in the contract will revert to the insured. As a consequence, the irrevocable beneficiary does not become the complete owner of the policy; his interest is conditionally vested along with that of the insured.

The widespread use of the automobile and the airplane have given rise to a circumstance that could vitally affect the rights of parties in the life insurance contract. What would happen if the insured and the beneficiary were both killed in the same accident? To whom would the proceeds of the insurance be paid if contingent beneficiaries had not been named? The answer depends upon the circumstances. First, if it can be proved that the beneficiary survived the insured, even for a moment, the proceeds will be paid to the estate of the beneficiary, and if the insured survived the beneficiary, the proceeds will be paid to the estate of insured.[2] Second, there are many instances in which it is impossible to obtain evidence that the one outlived the other, so the only conclusion to draw is that they died simultaneously. In order to develop a rule for the disposition of the proceeds in such cases, the majority of states have adopted the provisions of the Uniform Simultaneous Death Act. With specific reference to life insurance, the act stipulates that where the insured and the beneficiary have died and there is not sufficient evidence that they

---

[2] This could in some instances defeat the purpose of the insurance. As a consequence, some companies stipulate that the proceeds will be payable to the beneficiary only if he survives the insured for a specified period, such as 30 days.

died otherwise than simultaneously, the proceeds shall be distributed as if the insured *survived* the beneficiary. It should be obvious, however, that this problem can be dealt with more satisfactorily through the use of contingent beneficiaries. The proceeds will then go wholly to the persons the insured desires to be paid and not partially to some distant relatives who are a part of his estate. Even if the beneficiary survives the insured for a short period of time, the contingent beneficiaries will succeed to his interest.

### Incontestable Clause

One unusual provision that is required in life policies is the "incontestable clause." The usual policy provision reads as follows: "This policy shall be incontestable after it has been in force during the lifetime of the insured for 2 years from the date of issue."[3] This means that the validity of the contract cannot be questioned for any reason whatsoever after it has been in force during the lifetime of the insured for 2 years. The fundamental reason for this restriction is based on the long-term nature of the life insurance contract. It is to assure the person insured and his beneficiary that they will not be harassed by lawsuits long after the original transaction and at a time in which all evidence of the original transaction has disappeared and original witnesses have died. The effect of the clause is not that of justifying a contract involving fraud. The courts justify the clause on the grounds that they are not condoning fraud, but that after an insurance company has been given a reasonable opportunity to investigate the validity of the contract, it should then relinquish its right on the grounds that the social advantages will outweigh the undesirable consequences.[4]

The clause is applicable for only 2 years *during the lifetime of the insured.* This means that the death of the insured during the contestable period will suspend the operation of the clause. If this were not the case, should the claimant know that the insured had purchased the contract and had made many material misrepresentations in the application, he could wait until the

[3] By statute in most states, the incontestable clause must be a provision in all life insurance contracts, and no state permits the period to exceed 2 years from the date of issue of the contract. Some carriers, perhaps for competitive reasons, have shortened the contestable period to 1 year, which is permissible under the law. However, courts have generally refused to uphold a provision that makes the contract incontestable from date of issue, particularly in those cases where fraud is involved.

[4] However, there are a few instances in which fraud would be so abhorrent that impossibility of nullification because of the incontestable clause would be a distinct violation of public policy. For example, courts will permit insurers to deny liability after the contestable period has terminated in those cases in which insurable interest did not exist at the inception of the contract. Liability could also be denied if it is discovered that a healthier person impersonated the applicant in the medical examination, particularly should this person have been the beneficiary under the policy.

termination of the 2-year period before submitting his claim, and thus would be protected against voidance of the contract because of the insured's fraudulent acts.[5]

### Misstatement of Age Clause

The incontestability clause does not apply to the misstatement of his age by the insured. Since the amount of insurance a given premium will purchase varies with the age of the insured, there is a marked tendency on the part of applicants for insurance to understate their age. The misstatement of age clause provides that in the event that the insured has misstated his age, the face of the policy will be adjusted to the amount of insurance that the premium he paid would have purchased at his correct age. In other words, the amount of the policy is adjusted; the contract is not voided. The typical policy provision reads as follows: "If the age of the insured has been misstated, the amount payable shall be such as the premium paid would have purchased at the correct age."

The premium on a certain policy is $20 per $1000 at age 40. The premium on the same policy is only $15 per $1000 at age 31. The insured in question was a particularly youthful looking individual and convinced the agent and the insurance company that he was indeed 31 years old, when in reality he was 40. He purchased a $10,000 policy, paying the annual premium of $150. Upon his death, the insurance company discovered that he was in fact 40 years old when the policy was issued. In this event, the company would pay 15/20 of the face amount, or $7500. This is the amount of insurance the individual could have purchased for the premium that he paid if he had given his correct age.

### The Grace Period

We have already learned that the consideration for the insurance company's promise is the payment of the first premium by the insured. While subsequent premiums are not a part of the legal consideration, they must be paid when due or the contract will not continue to exist. A premium due date is designated in the policy and the premium should be paid on or before that date. The insured may pay his premium on an annual basis, or in semiannual, quarterly, or monthly installments.

If the insured does not pay the premium on the due date, technically the

[5] In years past, the incontestable clause did not contain the language "for 2 years during the lifetime of the insured." In a rather celebrated case, *Monahan vs. Metropolitan Life Insurance Company (283 Ill. 136, 119 N. E. 68)*, an insured had died during the contestable period and the company denied liability, alleging breach of warranty. The beneficiary, however, waited until the 2-year period had expired and then sued the company. The Supreme Court of Illinois held that the policy was incontestable and ordered the insurance company to make payment.

contract will lapse. The time of lapsation, however, is subject to a modification which is in the nature of a "grace period," and which is almost universally required by statute. A typical statement of the grace period clause in a life insurance contract is as follows:

> A grace period of 31 days shall be allowed for payment of a premium in default. The policy shall continue in full force during the grace period. If the insured dies during such period, the premium in default shall be paid from the proceeds of this policy.

Thus, for example, if the premium due date is May 1, and the insured does not pay the premium on this date, the policy allows him a grace period of 31 days before the policy lapses. If he should die on May 15, the proceeds of the policy will be paid, but the amount of the premium in default will be deducted from the proceeds of the policy. If the insured pays the premium before the end of the grace period, the policy continues in effect as if the premium had been paid on time. The purpose of this clause is not to encourage procrastination in the payment of premiums (although it does), but rather to keep the policy from lapsing when the owner of the policy inadvertently neglects to pay the premium.

### Reinstatement

Practially all permanent life insurance contracts permit reinstatement of a lapsed policy. However, the reinstatement is subject to certain specific conditions. The provisions of a typical contract read as follows:

> This policy may be reinstated within 5 years after the date of premium default if it has not been surrendered for its cash value. Reinstatement is subject to (a) receipt of evidence of insurability of the insured satisfactory to the Company; (b) payment of all overdue premiums with interest from the due date of each at the rate of 5% per annum; and (c) payments or reinstatement of any indebtedness existing on the date of premium default with interest from that date.

It is apparent that reinstatement is not an unconditional right of the insured. It can be accomplished only if the risk has not changed for the insurance company and only if, by payment of the back premiums with interest, the reinstated policy would have the same reserve as it would have had if the policy had not been lapsed. The conditions necessary are quite specific. First, reinstatement is possible only if at the time of lapsation the insured did not withdraw the cash value of the policy. Withdrawal of the surrender value in cash terminates the contract forever. Second, reinstatement must be effected within a specific time period, normally 5 years after lapsation. Third, the insured must provide proper evidence of his insurability. Not only must his health be satisfactory, but other factors such as financial income and morals must not have deteriorated substantially. Fourth, it is obvious also that reinstatement can be effected properly only if the insured pays the overdue premium plus interest and pays or reinstates any indebtedness that may have existed. These conditions may appear to be rather burdensome and some may appear unnecessary. However, they are necessary if the contract is to be maintained in its original form, and particularly important if the insurance company is to avoid what would otherwise be a substantial element of adverse selection.[6]

### The Suicide Clause

Almost universally, suicide during a stipulated period after inception of the contract is excluded. A typical exclusion reads as follows: "If within 2 years from the date of issue the insured shall die by suicide, whether sane or insane, the amount payable by the Company shall be the premiums paid." Some companies, however, limit the suicide exclusion period to 1 year. The reason for the exclusion is, of course, that of protecting the insurer against a person who might purchase the insurance with the deliberate purpose of committing suicide.[7] The assumption of the 2 years is that during this length of time, if the insured has not committed suicide, the reason for doing so will probably have disappeared.[8] After the exclusion period is over, death by suicide becomes just another cause of death, and coverage is justified on the assumption that it should be provided for as a hazard of life to which practically all people are subject.[9]

---

[6]The question may arise concerning the application of the incontestability clause to the reinstated policy. Is the entire contract subject to contest for 2 years after the reinstatement, or is the information concerning the reinstatement only subject to contest, or is neither applicable? There is some difference of opinion in the courts. However, the majority opinion is that a reinstated contract is contestable for the same period as prescribed in the original contract, but only with respect to the information supplied for the reinstatement. Representations in the original application for the policy may not be contested.

[7]*Presumption against suicide*—the courts have evolved this doctrine, which states that the love of life in and of itself is sufficient grounds for a presumption against suicide. The burden of proof of suicide is on the company, and the insurance company must prove conclusively that the death was a suicide or pay the face of the policy.

[8]For example, a nagging wife can have a deleterious influence on a husband only for a limited period of time.

[9]Some states have statutes which impose restrictions on the right of the insurer to avoid liability if the insured commits suicide. In Missouri, for example, the law does not permit any exclusion at all. The insurer can deny liability only if it can prove that the insured contemplated suicide at the time he purchased the policy. Needless to say, this intent is difficult, if not impossible, to prove, so insurers in Missouri do not even attempt to do so. This may be an advantage of residing in Missouri.

### Aviation Exclusions

There are as many types of aviation exclusions and restrictions as there are companies. At one time, virtually all life insurance policies excluded death resulting from aviation. Most aviation clauses today are restrictions rather than exclusions, for they do not exclude death by aviation, but only death as a result of certain types of flying. Many policies have no restriction whatsoever; the restrictions found in policies today are usually one of the following types:

1. Exclusion of all aviation deaths except as a fare-paying passenger— this is the broadest exclusion. In most cases, travel in a nonscheduled airline as a fare-paying passenger is covered.
2. Exclusion of pilots, crew members, or student pilots.
3. Exclusion of death in an aircraft operated by or for the military forces.
4. Exclusion of death while on military maneuvers.

The actual exclusion in the policy may consist of one of the above, or it may be a combination of two or more. Most companies will eliminate the aviation exclusion or restriction in their policy if the insured is willing to pay an additional premium.

### War Clause

During time of war, or when war appears imminent, insurance companies usually insert a clause in their policies which provides for a return of premium plus interest rather than payment of the face amount of the policy if the insured is killed as a result of the war. Policies issued during peacetime do not have the war exclusion and therefore, if the insured should be killed as a result of war, they would pay the face amount.

The purpose of the war clause is not so much to avoid payment to beneficiaries of insureds who are killed in the war, but rather to prevent adverse selection. If the clause were not put into policies sold during wartime, those who faced a higher chance of loss (e.g., Second Lieutenants in the Infantry) would obtain larger amounts of insurance than they might otherwise purchase. The result would be selection against the company. As a matter of fact, the war deaths in past wars have not proved to be catastrophic losses as far as insurance companies have been concerned. After both World War I and World War II, many insurance companies found that they could cover the deaths that were excluded under the war clause of policies issued and paid the face amount of these policies retroactively. There is little question that this would not have been true if it had not been for the war clause which prevented adverse selection.

## NONFORFEITURE VALUES

If the insured does not pay the premium within the grace period, the policy will lapse. Years ago, life insurance contracts did not contain nonforfeiture values, and in the event of a missed premium the policy was terminated with no return to the insured. Because of the overpayments which the insured had made under the level premium system, this was extremely unfair to the policyholder and resulted in unjust enrichment of the insurance company. Under the Standard Nonforfeiture Law, today, at any time after the policy has begun to develop a cash value, the insured may discontinue premium payments and obtain the return of a part of the overpayment he has made. Normally, policies do not begin to accumulate a cash value until after the end of the second policy year, and although there is a relationship between the policy reserve and the cash value, the cash value of the policy rarely equals the full amount of the policy reserve until the policy has been in force for 10–15 years.

When the insured decides to stop payment of premiums, he is entitled to the cash value of the policy, which he may take in one of three ways:

1. He may take the cash listed in the table of nonforfeiture values.
2. He may take a paid-up policy in some reduced amount. The amount of the reduced policy will be the amount the cash value would purchase as a net single premium.
3. He may continue the policy in force as term insurance for as long as the cash value will permit. The cash value is used to make a net single premium purchase of a term policy in the face amount of the policy with the nonforfeiture value. If the insured does not request another option, the company will normally provide extended-term insurance.

Table 10-1 is a typical table of nonforfeiture options. It lists the guaranteed values at the end of each policy year. The law requires that these values be listed for at least the first 20 years of the policy, but they are also commonly given for advanced ages of the insured.

### The Cash Option

To illustrate the operation of the surrender provision, let us assume that X purchases an ordinary life policy with a face value of $10,000 at age 21. Let us assume further that he lapses the policy after 10 years and that he chooses to withdraw the surrender value in cash. The insurance company would send him a check for $1148.10[10] If he should decide to lapse the policy and take

---

[10] Remember that the values in the table are for each $1000 of insurance, so if the insured has a $10,000 policy, the cash value and paid-up policy amount will be multiplied by 10.

TABLE 10-1

Illustration of Nonforfeiture Table (Dollar Values Are per $1000 of Face Amount)

| End of policy year | Cash or loan value[a] | Paid-up insurance | Extended-term insurance | |
|---|---|---|---|---|
| | | | Years | Days |
| 01 | $ 0.00 | $ 0 | 0 | 0 |
| 02 | 7.01 | 19 | 2 | 265 |
| 03 | 19.86 | 53 | 8 | 328 |
| 04 | 32.95 | 86 | 15 | 36 |
| 05 | 46.30 | 119 | 19 | 108 |
| 06 | 59.89 | 151 | 22 | 72 |
| 07 | 73.74 | 183 | 24 | 102 |
| 08 | 87.84 | 214 | 25 | 302 |
| 09 | 102.20 | 244 | 27 | 3 |
| 10 | 114.81 | 269 | 27 | 237 |
| 11 | 127.68 | 293 | 28 | 48 |
| 12 | 140.82 | 317 | 28 | 173 |
| 13 | 154.22 | 341 | 28 | 259 |
| 14 | 167.89 | 364 | 28 | 310 |
| 15 | 181.81 | 387 | 28 | 332 |
| 16 | 195.97 | 409 | 28 | 329 |
| 17 | 210.36 | 430 | 28 | 304 |
| 18 | 224.94 | 452 | 28 | 261 |
| 19 | 239.71 | 472 | 28 | 200 |
| 20 | 254.65 | 492 | 28 | 126 |
| @55 | 475.97 | 721 | 23 | 101 |
| @60 | 555.90 | 781 | 20 | 338 |
| @62 | 587.11 | 802 | 19 | 344 |
| @65 | 632.61 | 831 | 18 | 164 |

[a]Paid-up additions and dividend accumulations increase the cash values; indebtedness decreases them.

the surrender value in cash at age 65, the guaranteed amount would be $6326.10[11]

The Standard Nonforfeiture Law requires that a surrender value be made available in cash, but it also premits a company to delay or postpone payment of the cash value for a period of 6 months after surrender of the policy.

[11]The student should note that the figures used are the guaranteed surrender values. If the policy is participating, i.e., dividends are paid on the contract, and if the dividends are left with the insurance company, the actual surrender values could be substantially greater than those shown in the table.

This is known as a *delay clause* and it is now mandatory in all policies. Its purpose is to prevent substantial investment losses in the event that large numbers of insureds cash in their contracts in a relatively short period of time, as might occur during a major economic recession. Insurers pay little attention to the clause and perhaps would use it only under the most unusual circumstances.

A typical policy provision involving the cash-surrender value in cash is as follows:

> The cash value at any time when all premiums due have been paid shall be the reserve on this policy less the prescribed deduction, plus the reserve on any paid-up additions and the amount of any dividend accumulations. The owner may surrender this policy for its cash value less any indebtedness. The insurance shall terminate upon receipt at the Home Office of the policy and a written surrender of all claims. The Company may defer paying the cash value for a period not exceeding 6 months from the date of surrender. If payment is deferred 30 days or more, interest at the rate of $2\frac{1}{4}\%$ per annum from the date of surrender to the date of payment shall be allowed on the cash value less any indebtedness.

If the insured surrenders the policy for its cash value, the entire contract is terminated and the company will have no further obligations.[12]

### Paid-Up Reduced Amount

The second surrender option is paid-up whole life or endowment insurance. Here, in lieu of obtaining the cash-surrender value in cash, with complete termination of any insurance, the insured will receive a reduced amount of paid-up insurance which will be payable under the same conditions as the original policy. For example, referring back to Table 10-1, if the insured lapses the $10,000 ordinary life policy at the end of 10 years, he could use the cash value as a net single premium at his attained age to purchase a paid-up whole life contract with a face value of $2690. At age 65, the reduced paid-up insurance would be $8310. The paid-up contract will have a cash-and-loan value on the same general terms as those of the original policy. If the original policy is a limited-payment contract, the paid-up insurance of reduced amount will be whole life. But if the original contract is endowment insurance, protection in a reduced amount will be granted only for the remainder

---

[12]Annual increments in the cash value of a policy are not subject to federal income tax; there is no tax on cash values until the policy is actually surrendered and the cash value taken out. At the time that the policy is surrendered, the excess of cash surrender value over net premiums paid is taxable as ordinary income, and the gain is eligible for income averaging.

of the endowment period. If the insured survives the endowment period, the payment at that time will also be in a reduced amount.

The "paid-up policy of reduced amount" provision in a typical policy reads as follows:

> In lieu of extended-term insurance this policy may be continued in force as participating paid-up life insurance. The insurance will be for such amount as the cash value will purchase as a net single premium at the attained age of the insured. Any indebtedness shall remain as a lien against the policy. Such paid-up insurance may be requested before or within 3 months after the date of premium default. A request shall be made by written notice filed at the Home Office.

The "paid-up insurance of reduced amount" option perhaps has its greatest attraction for older insureds who no longer have a substantial need for life insurance protection. To be relieved of the burden of continued premium payments and still have a substantial amount of life insurance in force, the policy could be lapsed and the "paid-up policy of reduced amount" option selected. In our illustrative table of surrender values (Table 10-1), at age 65 the insured would have a completely paid-up contract involving $8310 of life insurance. This amount will be paid when he dies.

### Extended-Term Insurance

The third surrender option is paid-up term insurance, and the benefit is commonly referred to as "extended-term insurance." Here, the amount of the term insurance will be the same as the face value of the original contract. The variable will be the length of the term period, rather than the amount of the insurance, and the length of the period will be that which the cash value used as a net single premium will purchase at the insured's attained age. For example, Table 10-1 shows that if the insured lapses the policy at the end of the tenth year and chooses the extended-term option, he would have a paid-up term policy with a face value of $10,000 with a term period of 27 years and 237 days. The contract could continue, then, into the insured's fifty-ninth year of age. If he should die during this term, the insurer will pay the $10,000 to his beneficiary. But if he outlives the term, the commitment of the insurance company will be terminated. If this option is selected where the original contract was endowment insurance, the paid-up term insurance will not extend beyond the maturity date of the original contract. Usually, after the endowment contract has been in effect for a few years, the surrender value will exceed that amount necessary to purchase term insurance for the balance of the endowment period. So rather than extend the term period beyond the original endowment maturity date, the insurance company will use the excess to provide for the payment of a pure endowment should the insured survive the endowment period. This amount, however, will be substantially less than the face amount of the extended-term contract.

A unique feature of the extended-term option is that it normally involves the insurance company in a substantial element of adverse selection. The reason is obvious. What would a relatively intelligent insured do if he was told that he had no more than 3 years to live? Naturally he would lapse the policy and select the extended-term option. Many insureds in poor health will be inclined to do the same thing. As a consequence, the death rates under extended-term insurance will be much greater than normal. For this reason, insurance companies are permitted to calculate net premiums for extended-term policies on mortality factors that are greater than those shown in the mortality table. However, because of competition, most insurance companies have not taken advantage of this provision in the Standard Nonforfeiture Law.

### Policy Loan Provisions

One of the most important secondary benefits of a life insurance contract involves the policy loan provisions. The insured may, at any time, obtain a loan from the insurance company, usually equal to the full amount of the cash surrender value, using the policy as collateral for the loan.[13] The loan will bear interest at some percentage stipulated, and if not paid, will be added to, and become a part of, the loan. If the insured dies while the indebtedness exists, the loan plus interest will be deducted from the proceeds of the policy.

An insured who becomes financially embarrassed and is in need of temporary funds may then borrow on his life insurance policy. For example, in reference to Table 10-1, on the $10,000 ordinary life policy purchased at age 21, the insured could borrow as much as $1148.10 if the policy had been in effect for 10 years, and he could do so merely by assigning the contract to the insurance company as the security for the loan. The advantages of this right should be obvious. First, it would be practically impossible for the insured to borrow elsewhere and pay only a true annual rate of 5% interest. Compare this with the rate he would pay the XYZ Finance Company! Second, the insurance company cannot refuse the loan, regardless of its purpose. For example, the insured could borrow the money for the purpose of gambling and chasing women, and he could inform the insurance company of this intention, and the company could not refuse the loan. Third, there is no legal obligation to repay the loan, and the insured will not be "hounded" for repayment as he would with respect to an overdue loan from a finance company.

[13] The loan provision is also subject to the "delay clause," and, as in the case of the cash-surrender value, the company may delay making the loan for up to 6 months. As in the case of the surrender, the option to delay is rarely exercised.

The policy loan right also involves some substantial disadvantages. The most important is, of course, the ease with which the loan can be acquired and the lack of legal pressure for repayment. If the insured does not repay the loan, the indebtedness will constitute a lien against the contract and will be subtracted from the proceeds when the insured dies. This, of course, could defeat the purpose of the life insurance.

**Automatic premium loan.**    Most policies today contain an automatic premium loan provision. A typical provision reads as follows:

> A premium loan shall be automatically granted to pay a premium in default. A premium for any other frequency permitted by this policy shall be loaned whenever the loan value, less any indebtedness, is sufficient for such premium but is insufficient for a loan of the premium in default. A revocation or reinstatement of this provision shall be made by written notice filed at the Home Office.

If this provision is included in the contract and the insured does not pay the premium on the due date, the company automatically will pay the premium and charge it against the cash value of the policy. The loan will bear interest at the rate applicable to policy loans as stipulated in the contract. The effect of the provision is to extend the original face amount of the insurance, decreased by the amount of the loan plus interest, for as long as the remaining cash value is sufficient to permit the advance of an additional premium. This provision may be very beneficial for the policyholder, particularly for one who inadvertently forgets to pay the premium within the grace period and for one who cannot pay the current premium because of financial difficulties. The most important aspect is that the policy does not lapse. When the insured is again financially able he can start paying the premiums and will not be subject to the conditions imposed in the event of a reinstatement. Another advantage is that any special coverages such as double indemnity and disability coverages will remain in force.[14] And if the policy is participating, dividends will continue to be paid. This would not be true under the extended-term option. After the policy has been in effect for a period of time, it is possible for the increase in cash value each year to exceed the premium payment. In these cases, the policy is capable of sustaining itself, for a loan against the cash value to pay the premium permits an increase in the cash value which is sufficient to pay the next year's premium. Of course, the amount of protection provided by the policy is decreased by the amount of any loans outstanding, so the automatic premium loan provision must be considered as a device which can consume protection under the policy.

---

[14] These coverages of the original contract will not remain in force in the surrender options of paid-up policies of reduced amount and extended term.

There are also disadvantages in the automatic premium loan provision. Most important, if the premium payments are not resumed by the insured and the cash value of the policy is low, the contract may terminate eventually. It is even possible that the period in which the policy will remain in force under automatic premium loan will be less than under the extended-term option, and the amount of insurance coverage will be considerably less. The automatic premium loan feature is also subject to the disadvantage of being used on the slightest provocation. An insured who has the choice of paying the current premium or using the money to finance a Friday night party may be inclined to use the money for the latter. Of course, he will promise himself faithfully that he will pay off the loan in the near future.

Most companies now offer this provision, but the provision is optional and an election must be made at the time the policy is taken out or at least before the premium is in default. Various companies handle the option differently; some specify that the insured must notify the company if he wants the provision to apply, while others make the provision automatic and the insured must notify the company if he does not want it to apply.

## DIVIDEND PROVISIONS

Because of the long-term nature of life insurance contracts, companies must calculate premium charges on a conservative basis. The gross premium for a life insurance contract is composed of three factors: mortality costs, plus the anticipated expenses of operating the company, minus an assumed rate of interest earned on invested funds.[15] Once the premium rate is established, it must be guaranteed for the entire term of the policy. It is not subject to change, even though the basic factors used in determining premiums change substantially. Over a long period of time, substantial changes in the premium factors could occur: mortality rates may change; the expenses of operating the business may increase substantially, particularly if the long-run trend of prices is upward; interest rates may change, and the change could be down as well as up. If current premium rates are to be sufficient to enable insurers to fulfill their obligations on contracts that may exist for many decades in the future, a safety margin must be used in the calculation of the premiums.

Life insurance contracts may be participating or nonparticipating. A participating policy is one on which annual dividends are paid to the policyholder. In this type, a substantial margin of safety is built into the gross premium, sufficient to constitute a willful overcharge but justified on the assumption that if the extra premium is not needed, it will be returned to the

[15] See Chapter 9 for a discussion of the cost factors involved in life insurance rate-making.

policyholder in the form of a policy dividend.[16] This means that policy dividends are not profits, as the term is normally used, but merely the return of an overcharge in the premium. The overcharge, however, does have a logical justification. It will provide the company with a margin of safety which will ensure that its obligations will be fulfilled even in the distant future when underlying conditions affecting premium rates may have changed substantially and adversely. The policyholder is assured of a return of the overcharge as well as the ability of his insurance company to meet its obligations.

Favorable deviations from the assumptions entering into the calculation of the gross premium are the source of surplus from which policy dividends are paid. The savings in mortality, the excess interest, and the savings in expenses will yield a surplus each year. A portion of this gain will be transferred to company surplus or to a special contingency reserve to be used, if necessary, for future losses arising from adverse mortality experience, extremely low interest earnings, and unusually high operational expenses. The balance will be distributed as policy dividends.

In a participating life insurance contract the policyholder is provided with several dividend options. He may take the dividend in cash, he may apply it toward the payment of the current premium on his policy, he may apply it to the purchase of paid-up additions to the policy, or he may leave the dividends on deposit with the insurance company to accumulate interest. The policyholder normally makes an election as to the disposition of the dividends at the time he purchases the policy. However, a new election may be made at any time with just one possible qualification: if the insured does not elect to use the dividends to purchase paid-up additions to the face of the policy at the inception of his contract, he must then file evidence of insurability if this option is selected at some later date.

Several of the options are so simple as to require little explanation. If the insured chooses to receive the dividends in cash, the insurer will send him a dividend check on each anniversary of his contract, and he may use the money as he pleases. If the dividend is to be applied toward payment of the next premium, the insurer will indicate the amount of the dividend on the premium-due notice and the insured will remit only the difference between the gross premium due and the amount of the dividend. If the insured chooses to use the dividend to purchase paid-up additions to his policy, the

---

[16]The safety margin on nonparticipating contracts is much narrower than on participating contracts. This is necessary because the cost of the insurance to the policyholder will not be adjusted by the payment of dividends; hence, the gross premium charged must reflect closely, at least for competitive reasons, the actual cost of providing the insurance. Any profit realized in the operation will be used to provide dividends to stockholders and to provide surplus funds that may be used as a buffer for adverse experience.

dividend will be used as a net single premium at his attained age to purchase whatever amount it could purchase at that age. The additions will be payable under the same conditions as the basic policy, i.e., as whole life or endowment insurance. The paid-up additions, like the basic policy, are participating, and they may be surrendered for their cash value at any time.

The insured may also choose to leave the dividends on deposit with the insurance company. Interest at some guaranteed rate will be paid on the deposit and the insured will also share in the excess interest earnings of the company.[17] If the insured should die, the accumulated deposits will be paid in addition to the face of the basic contract. If he should surrender the policy, the deposits will be added to the surrender value and may be added to the face amount of the paid-up policy of reduced amount or to extended-term.

If the dividends are left with the company either as deposits or to be used to purchase paid-up additions, it is possible for the insured to convert the basic contract into a fully paid-up policy at an earlier date than that called for by the terms of the basic contract. For example, an ordinary life policy might be fully paid up at age 55, a 20-payment life in 15 years, and an endowment at age 65, purchased at age 25, might be paid up by age 50.

A policy is considered to be fully paid up when the reserve of the basic contract plus the value of the dividend additions or deposits equals the net single premium for the policy in question at the insured's attained age. The insurance company will inform the policyholder when this point is reached. The insured will then surrender the paid-up additions or the deposits, and from this time on he will have no premium payment obligation on the policy.

After the basic policy has become fully paid up, it will continue to be participating. It is possible, that in time, the reserve value of the basic policy plus the reserve value of the dividend additions or deposits will equal the face of the policy. In this case, the policy matures as an endowment and the insured may obtain a check for the face of the policy if he so desires.

## SETTLEMENT OPTIONS

The average person, in thinking about the settlement of life insurance policies, normally thinks of a lump sum being paid to the beneficiary of the insured. As a matter of fact, while a great many life insurance policies are paid in this manner, most are not. In addition to the lump-sum settlement, there are certain optional modes of settlement which may be used to pay out the proceeds of the policy. Normally, the owner (who in most cases is also the insured) selects the option under which he wants the proceeds of the policy

---

[17] This interest will be taxable as income to the insured. The dividends themselves are obviously not taxable, for they are not income, but merely the return of an overcharge.

paid. If no election is in force when the policy becomes payable, the beneficiary is entitled to select the option desired. Unless the insured (owner) has made provision which denies the right, the beneficiary may also change to some other mode of settlement.

### The Interest Option

The proceeds of the policy may be left with the insurance company under the interest option, in which case only the interest on the principal amount is paid to the beneficiary. At some later date, the principal may be paid out in a lump sum or under one of the other options. The major shortcoming of the interest option is that the insured must leave a substantial amount of insurance proceeds in order to provide even a minimum amount of monthly income. At a 3% interest assumption, a $100,000 policy would provide only $3000 annually. Normally, the interest option is selected when there are proceeds from other policies available for income, and the principal of the policy is being held for some future need.

### Installments for a Fixed Period

The insured may specify (or the beneficiary may elect) to have the proceeds of the policy paid out over some specified period of time. The insurance company simply computes how much it can pay out of the policy proceeds and the interest on the proceeds during each of the required periods, so that the entire principal and interest will be gone by the end of the period. The rate of interest credited to the unpaid balance is specified in the policy. A typical schedule of installments for a fixed period is reproduced in Table 10-2. The longer the period of time for which the company promises to pay the installments, the smaller each installment must be. According to Table 10-2, a $10,000 policy would provide $177 per month if paid over a 5-year period, and only $93.90 if paid out over a 10-year period. The fixed period selected may be any number of years, usually up to 30. This option is most valuable where the most important consideration is to provide income during some definite period of time, such as the child-raising years.

### Installments of Fixed Amount

The owner of the policy (or the beneficiary) may elect to have the proceeds of the policy paid out in payments of some fixed amount ($50, $100, $200, etc.) per month for as long as the principal plus interest on the portion of the principal which has not been paid will last. Since the amount of each installment is the controlling factor under this option, the length of time for which the payments will last will vary with the amount of the policy. In a sense, the "installment of fixed amount" option is similar to the installment for a fixed period. Under one option, the amount to be paid determines the length of

**TABLE 10-2**
**Monthly Installments for Each $1000 of Net Proceeds**

| Number of years specified | Each monthly payment | Number of years specified | Each monthly payment | Number of years specified | Each monthly payment |
|---|---|---|---|---|---|
| 1 | $84.28 | 11 | $8.64 | 21 | $5.08 |
| 2 | 42.66 | 12 | 8.02 | 22 | 4.90 |
| 3 | 28.79 | 13 | 7.49 | 23 | 4.74 |
| 4 | 21.86 | 14 | 7.03 | 24 | 4.60 |
| 5 | 17.70 | 15 | 6.64 | 25 | 4.46 |
| 6 | 14.93 | 16 | 6.30 | 26 | 4.34 |
| 7 | 12.95 | 17 | 6.00 | 27 | 4.22 |
| 8 | 11.47 | 18 | 5.73 | 28 | 4.12 |
| 9 | 10.32 | 19 | 5.49 | 29 | 4.02 |
| 10 | 9.39 | 20 | 5.27 | 30 | 3.93 |

time the benefits will last, and under the other, the length of time for which the benefits are to be paid determines the amount of the benefits.

### Life Income Options

In addition to the options listed above, the policy gives the insured's beneficiary the right to have the proceeds paid out in the form of an annuity. In such cases, the proceeds of the policy are used to make a single premium purchase of an annuity. Although the various life insurance companies list many life income options, they may be classified into four basic categories.

**Straight life income.**   Under a straight life income option, the proceeds of the policy are paid to the beneficiary on the basis of his life expectancy. The beneficiary is entitled to receive a specified amount for as long as he lives, but nothing more. If the beneficiary dies during the first year of the pay period, the company has fulfilled its obligations and no further payments are made. Beneficiaries who live longer than the average are offset by those who live only a short time.

**Life income with period certain.**   Under this option, the beneficiary is paid a life income for as long as he lives, but a minimum number of payments are guaranteed. If the beneficiary dies before the number of payments guaranteed have been made, the payments are continued to a contingent beneficiary. Normally, the "period certain," as the time for which payments are guaranteed is known, is 5, 10, 15, or 20 years.

**Life income with refund.**   Under the life income with refund option, the beneficiary is paid a life income for as long as he lives, and if the proceeds of the policy have not been paid out by the time the beneficiary dies, the remainder of the proceeds will be paid to a contingent beneficiary. The life income with refund may be either a life income with installment refund, in which case installments are continued until the contingent beneficiary has received the difference between the original policy proceeds and the amount received by the direct beneficiary, or it may be a cash refund. Under the cash refund, installments do not continue to the contingent beneficiary, but instead a lump sum is paid to the contingent beneficiary.

**Joint life income.**   The joint life income option is a somewhat specialized option, designed to provide income to two payees. The joint life income option may provide for payment of a given amount of income during the time that either of the two payees is alive. Under this type of provision the payments continue after the first of the two payees has died and does not stop until the second has died. A modification of this plan provides that the amount of the benefit will be decreased when the first of the two payees dies. The benefit to the remaining payee will then be either two-thirds or one-half (or possibly some other fraction) of the original income amount. The benefit is computed on the basis of two lives and the amount of the benefit depends on the age of both beneficiaries.

**Payments.**   The amount payable under any one of the life income options depends on the age and sex of the beneficiary, plus the plan selected. For obvious reasons, the company cannot afford to pay as high a monthly income if it also guarantees to pay it for some guaranteed period of time. When a period certain is selected, the mortality gains under the annuity are eliminated for whatever length the period certain is. Table 10-3 illustrates a typical life income option table for single lives. Table 10-4 illustrates a joint and survivor life income option.

To illustrate the use of Table 10-3, let us assume that the policy proceeds amount to $10,000, and that the beneficiary is a 65-year-old female. Since the life expectancy of women is greater than that of men, a given number of proceed dollars will provide a higher monthly income to a male beneficiary than to a female. If no period certain is elected, the option will provide a monthly income of $57.20 for as long as the payee lives. With a 5-year period certain, the policy will pay a monthly income of $56.70 for as long as the payee lives, but at least for 5 years. The monthly amount payable under the 5-year certain plan is lower because mortality gains have been eliminated. The fact that some payees will die during the first 5 years does not result in a gain of funds that can be paid to the remaining payees. If a 20-year certain period is elected, the amount of the monthly benefit is reduced even more.

## TABLE 10-3
## Life Income Options

| Age of payee | | Minimum period | | | | | |
|---|---|---|---|---|---|---|---|
| Male | Female | None | 5 Years | 10 Years | 15 Years | 20 Years | Installment refund |
| | 15[a] | $ 2.93 | $ 2.92 | $2.91 | $2.90 | $2.89 | $2.88 |
| | 16 | 2.94 | 2.93 | 2.92 | 2.91 | 2.90 | 2.89 |
| | 17 | 2.96 | 2.95 | 2.94 | 2.93 | 2.92 | 2.91 |
| | 18 | 2.97 | 2.96 | 2.95 | 2.94 | 2.93 | 2.92 |
| | 19 | 2.99 | 2.98 | 2.97 | 2.96 | 2.95 | 2.94 |
| 15[a] | 20 | 3.01 | 3.00 | 2.99 | 2.98 | 2.97 | 2.96 |
| 16 | 21 | 3.03 | 3.02 | 3.01 | 3.00 | 2.99 | 2.98 |
| 17 | 22 | 3.04 | 3.03 | 3.02 | 3.01 | 3.00 | 2.99 |
| 18 | 23 | 3.06 | 3.05 | 3.04 | 3.03 | 3.02 | 3.01 |
| 19 | 24 | 3.08 | 3.07 | 3.06 | 3.05 | 3.04 | 3.03 |
| 20 | 25 | 3.11 | 3.10 | 3.09 | 3.08 | 3.07 | 3.06 |
| 21 | 26 | 3.13 | 3.12 | 3.11 | 3.10 | 3.09 | 3.08 |
| 22 | 27 | 3.15 | 3.14 | 3.13 | 3.12 | 3.11 | 3.10 |
| 23 | 28 | 3.18 | 3.17 | 3.16 | 3.15 | 3.14 | 3.13 |
| 24 | 29 | 3.20 | 3.19 | 3.18 | 3.17 | 3.16 | 3.15 |
| 25 | 30 | 3.23 | 3.22 | 3.21 | 3.20 | 3.19 | 3.18 |
| 26 | 31 | 3.25 | 3.24 | 3.23 | 3.22 | 3.21 | 3.20 |
| 27 | 32 | 3.28 | 3.27 | 3.26 | 3.25 | 3.24 | 3.23 |
| 28 | 33 | 3.31 | 3.30 | 3.29 | 3.28 | 3.27 | 3.26 |
| 29 | 34 | 3.35 | 3.34 | 3.33 | 3.32 | 3.31 | 3.29 |
| 30 | 35 | 3.38 | 3.37 | 3.36 | 3.35 | 3.34 | 3.32 |
| 31 | 36 | 3.41 | 3.40 | 3.39 | 3.38 | 3.37 | 3.35 |
| 32 | 37 | 3.45 | 3.44 | 3.43 | 3.42 | 3.41 | 3.39 |
| 33 | 38 | 3.49 | 3.48 | 3.47 | 3.46 | 3.44 | 3.42 |
| 34 | 39 | 3.53 | 3.52 | 3.51 | 3.50 | 3.48 | 3.46 |
| 35 | 40 | 3.57 | 3.56 | 3.55 | 3.54 | 3.51 | 3.49 |
| 36 | 41 | 3.61 | 3.60 | 3.59 | 3.58 | 3.55 | 3.53 |
| 37 | 42 | 3.66 | 3.65 | 3.64 | 3.62 | 3.59 | 3.57 |
| 38 | 43 | 3.70 | 3.69 | 3.68 | 3.67 | 3.64 | 3.61 |
| 39 | 44 | 3.75 | 3.74 | 3.73 | 3.71 | 3.68 | 3.65 |
| 40 | 45 | 3.81 | 3.81 | 3.79 | 3.76 | 3.72 | 3.70 |
| 41 | 46 | 3.86 | 3.85 | 3.84 | 3.81 | 3.77 | 3.75 |
| 42 | 47 | 3.92 | 3.91 | 3.90 | 3.87 | 3.82 | 3.79 |
| 43 | 48 | 3.99 | 3.98 | 3.96 | 3.92 | 3.87 | 3.84 |
| 44 | 49 | 4.05 | 4.04 | 4.02 | 3.98 | 3.92 | 3.90 |
| 45 | 50 | 4.12 | 4.11 | 4.08 | 4.04 | 3.97 | 3.95 |
| 46 | 51 | 4.19 | 4.18 | 4.15 | 4.10 | 4.03 | 4.01 |
| 47 | 52 | 4.27 | 4.26 | 4.22 | 4.17 | 4.08 | 4.07 |
| 48 | 53 | 4.35 | 4.33 | 4.30 | 4.23 | 4.14 | 4.13 |
| 49 | 54 | 4.43 | 4.42 | 4.37 | 4.30 | 4.19 | 4.20 |
| 50 | 55 | 4.52 | 4.50 | 4.46 | 4.37 | 4.26 | 4.27 |
| 51 | 56 | 4.61 | 4.59 | 4.54 | 4.45 | 4.32 | 4.34 |
| 52 | 57 | 4.71 | 4.69 | 4.63 | 4.52 | 4.38 | 4.42 |
| 53 | 58 | 4.81 | 4.79 | 4.72 | 4.60 | 4.44 | 4.50 |
| 54 | 59 | 4.92 | 4.89 | 4.82 | 4.69 | 4.51 | 4.58 |
| 55 | 60 | 5.03 | 5.01 | 4.92 | 4.77 | 4.58 | 4.67 |
| 56 | 61 | 5.15 | 5.12 | 5.02 | 4.86 | 4.64 | 4.76 |
| 57 | 62 | 5.28 | 5.25 | 5.13 | 4.95 | 4.71 | 4.85 |
| 58 | 63 | 5.42 | 5.38 | 5.25 | 5.05 | 4.77 | 4.96 |
| 59 | 64 | 5.56 | 5.52 | 5.37 | 5.14 | 4.84 | 5.06 |
| 60 | 65 | 5.72 | 5.67 | 5.50 | 5.24 | 4.90 | 5.18 |
| 61 | 66 | 5.89 | 5.82 | 5.64 | 5.35 | 4.96 | 5.29 |
| 62 | 67 | 6.06 | 5.99 | 5.78 | 5.45 | 5.02 | 5.42 |
| 63 | 68 | 6.25 | 6.17 | 5.93 | 5.55 | 5.08 | 5.54 |
| 64 | 69 | 6.46 | 6.36 | 6.09 | 5.66 | 5.14 | 5.69 |
| 65 | 70 | 6.68 | 6.37 | 6.25 | 5.76 | 5.19 | 5.84 |
| 66 | 71 | 6.91 | 6.79 | 6.42 | 5.86 | 5.23 | 6.00 |
| 67 | 72 | 7.17 | 7.02 | 6.59 | 5.96 | 5.28 | 6.16 |
| 68 | 73 | 7.44 | 7.27 | 6.77 | 6.06 | 5.31 | 6.34 |
| 69 | 74 | 7.74 | 7.54 | 6.96 | 6.15 | 5.35 | 6.52 |
| 70 | 75 | 8.07 | 7.82 | 7.14 | 6.24 | 5.38 | 6.72 |
| 71 | 76 | 8.42 | 8.13 | 7.33 | 6.32 | 5.40 | 6.93 |
| 72 | 77 | 8.80 | 8.45 | 7.52 | 6.40 | 5.43 | 7.14 |
| 73 | 78 | 9.21 | 8.78 | 7.70 | 6.47 | 5.45 | 7.37 |
| 74 | 79 | 9.65 | 9.14 | 7.88 | 6.53 | 5.46 | 7.62 |
| 75 | 80 | 10.13 | 9.51 | 8.06 | 6.59 | 5.47 | 7.87 |
| 76 | | 10.64 | 9.89 | 8.22 | 6.64 | 5.48 | 8.14 |
| 77 | | 11.19 | 10.28 | 8.38 | 6.68 | 5.49 | 8.42 |
| 78 | | 11.77 | 10.68 | 8.53 | 6.72 | 5.50 | 8.71 |
| 79 | | 12.39 | 11.08 | 8.67 | 6.75 | 5.50 | 9.02 |
| 80[b] | | 13.04 | 11.48 | 8.80 | 6.78 | 5.51 | 9.35 |

[a]And under.     [b]And over.

**TABLE 10-4**

**Joint and Survivor Life Income Option—Monthly Joint and Survivor Life Income with Payments Certain for 10 Years for Beneficiaries of Equal Age**

| Adjusted age of beneficiary | One male and one female | Two male lives | Two female lives |
|---|---|---|---|
| 25 | $2.65 | $2.70 | $2.61 |
| 30 | 2.75 | 2.81 | 2.70 |
| 35 | 2.87 | 2.95 | 2.81 |
| 40 | 3.02 | 3.12 | 2.95 |
| 45 | 3.22 | 3.35 | 3.12 |
| 50 | 3.46 | 3.63 | 3.35 |
| 51 | 3.52 | 3.69 | 3.39 |
| 52 | 3.57 | 3.76 | 3.44 |
| 53 | 3.64 | 3.83 | 3.50 |
| 54 | 3.71 | 3.92 | 3.56 |
| 55 | 3.79 | 4.00 | 3.63 |
| 56 | 3.86 | 4.08 | 3.69 |
| 57 | 3.93 | 4.16 | 3.76 |
| 58 | 4.01 | 4.25 | 3.83 |
| 59 | 4.09 | 4.34 | 3.92 |
| 60 | 4.18 | 4.46 | 4.00 |
| 61 | 4.27 | 4.57 | 4.08 |
| 62 | 4.38 | 4.69 | 4.16 |
| 63 | 4.48 | 4.82 | 4.25 |
| 64 | 4.60 | 4.96 | 4.34 |
| 65 | 4.73 | 5.11 | 4.46 |
| 66 | 4.85 | 5.23 | 4.57 |
| 67 | 4.97 | 5.35 | 4.69 |
| 68 | 5.11 | 5.49 | 4.82 |
| 69 | 5.25 | 5.64 | 4.96 |
| 70 | 5.40 | 5.80 | 5.11 |
| 71 | 5.53 | 5.95 | 5.23 |
| 72 | 5.69 | 6.13 | 5.35 |
| 73 | 5.85 | 6.31 | 5.49 |
| 74 | 6.01 | 6.49 | 5.64 |
| 75 | 6.19 | 6.69 | 5.80 |

Under the 20-year certain option, the monthly benefit amount will be only $49. At the lower ages in Table 10-3 there is very little difference between a straight life income option and an income option with a period certain. This is because at the lower ages the chance of the payee dying is relatively low and there will be little, if any, gain from mortality.

Table 10-4 indicates the payment that will be made under a joint and survivor life income option. Under this particular agreement, the company will make payments for at least 10 years, and also for the lifetime of each of the beneficiaries. Installments are paid jointly and to the survivor. Under other contracts, provision might be made for a reduction in the benefit at the death of the first beneficiary.

### Taxation of Policy Proceeds under Various Settlement Options

As a general rule, benefits payable to a beneficiary under a life insurance policy are not subject to taxation under the federal income tax, except insofar as the benefits are composed in part of interest on the policy proceeds. The proceeds payable as a lump sum by reason of the death of the insured are not taxable as income except in the case of policies transferred for value. An example of a policy transferred for value would be if A purchases from B an existing policy for $10,000 on B's life, paying B $3000 for the policy. If B then dies, A will be taxed on the $7000 gain. The taxation of policies transferred for value does not apply if the transferee is the person insured, a partner of the insured, or a corporation for which the insured is a director or stockholder.

Proceeds payable under a fixed-installment option involve taxable income. That portion of the installments which represents interest on the principal is taxable. The law seeks to tax only the interest, and a surviving spouse is allowed a $1000 annual exclusion of otherwise reportable interest income. For example, let us say that the proceeds of the insured's life insurance policy amounted to $100,000. His spouse elected to take the proceeds under an installment option, receiving $11,380 for 10 years. Each year she received $1380 in interest on the death benefit. She was taxed on $380 as ordinary income. If the beneficiary were someone other than a surviving spouse, $1380 would be taxable.

## IMPORTANT OPTIONAL PROVISIONS

### The Disability Waiver of Premium Provision

The disability waiver of premium provision is one of the most important options available to a person purchasing life insurance. Under the provisions of this coverage, the company agrees to waive all premiums coming due after the insured has become totally and permanently disabled. The benefits of this provision should be obvious. Once an individual has become disabled, it will undoubtedly be difficult, if not impossible, for him to obtain insurance coverage, and it is therefore essential that he be able to continue the coverage he has. In essence, this benefit provides for the waiving of all premiums on the contract during the period of disability and the continuation of the contract as if the premiums were paid. This means that the cash value will increase and the dividends will be paid to the insured just as if the insured were paying the premiums. The provision is so important and so desirable, while at the same time being so inexpensive, that many companies include it automatically in their policies. If it is not an automatic provision, the insured should certainly elect to have it included.

The most difficult problem in connection with the disability waiver of premium provision is that of determining what constitutes total disability. A typical insurance clause reads as follows:

> Total disability means disability which (a) resulted from bodily injury or disease; (b) began after the issue date of this policy and before the policy anniversary nearest the insured's sixtieth birthday; (c) has existed continuously for at least 6 months; and (d) prevents the insured from engaging for remuneration or profit in any occupation. During the first 24 months of disability, occupation means the occupation of the insured at the time such disability began; thereafter, it means any occupation for which he is or becomes reasonably fitted by education, training, or experience. The total and irrecoverable loss of the sight of both eyes, or the use of both hands, or of both feet, or of one hand and one foot, shall be considered total disability even if the insured shall engage in an occupation.

This definition is carefully worded, but in spite of this care there are difficulties in interpretation.

The disability may arise from sickness or from bodily injury from accident. For example, if the insured contracts a severe case of tuberculosis or has a complete mental breakdown, the disability benefits would be forthcoming. The same is true if the disability is the result of an automobile accident. The disability must occur before a specified age (our definition specifying age 60), although the customary limiting age in most contracts is now 55. [18]

Historically, the intent of the coverage was to provide benefits only if the disability was total and permanent. The term "permanent" strongly implied

---

[18] The student should not confuse the time the disability must begin with the duration of the benefits. If the disability commences before the limiting age, then it could continue for the lifetime of the insured. However, if it should commence after the limiting age, the company would have no liability under the contract.

that the disability would last for the balance of the insured's lifetime. However, because of the difficulties of determining whether a certain disability would or would not be permanent, insurance companies had to compromise and use a definition in which if disability lasted continuously for a specified period, the disability would be presumed to be permanent. Most policies today require that the disability last for more than 6 months if it is to be presumed permanent with benefits forthcoming. For example, if the insured has a serious nervous breakdown which prevents him from engaging in any occupation, it is possible that he may recover in a few years and again become a productive member of society. It is also possible that he may spend the remainder of his life in a mental institution. If the disability arising from the nervous breakdown lasts more than 6 months, the company must presume that it is a permanent condition and provide the benefits promised in the contract,[19] but if the insured should recover, the disability benefits must then cease.

Since the problem of permanency is solved in the 6-month waiting period, the most important problem now becomes that of determining when the disability is total. In most instances, the insured will be considered totally disabled so long as he cannot engage in the major duties of an occupation for which he is or becomes reasonably fitted by education, training, or experience.

The definition given above is more liberal than many, because for the first 2 years total disability is to be determined only with respect to the regular occupation of the insured. For example, if a dentist should lose his right arm in an accident, he will be totally disabled in his occupation of dentistry, and the disability benefits in his life insurance contract will be forthcoming. However, if a college professor in the area of the classics should lose his right arm, the loss presumably would have little effect upon his ability to engage in his occupation. But after a period of 2 years, if the dentist is able to engage in some occupation for which he is reasonably fitted by education, training, or experience, or in which he becomes reasonably fitted, the benefits would then cease. Therefore, if the dentist becomes a faculty member in a dental college or becomes a salesman for a dental supply firm, he would be engaging in an occupation for which he is reasonably fitted by education, training, or experience.

By definition, however, there are certain circumstances in which the benefits will be paid regardless of the insured's ability to engage in an occupation. If the disability arises from the total and irrecoverable loss of the sight of both eyes, or the use of both hands, or of both feet, or of one

---

[19]At this point, the student will probably ask whether the benefits are provided during the 6-month waiting period. In most instances the "waiver of premium" benefit is provided from the commencement of the disability. This means that premiums will be waived even for the first 6 months.

hand and one foot, the disability shall be considered total even if the insured can engage in an occupation. Therefore, if the dentist should lose not only his right arm in the accident, but his left leg as well, the disability benefits in his life insurance policy will be paid even though he teaches in a dental college or works for a dental-supply firm.

The disability waiver of premium benefit is not an indemnity benefit. That is, the benefit is payable even though the insured suffers no monetary loss because of the disability. In addition, the disability provision never becomes incontestable. This means that the insurance company has the right at any time to contest the validity of a claim under the provision. Finally, the normal exclusions are disability resulting from self-inflicted injuries, disability caused by military service in time of war, and in some cases, disability arising out of a violation of the law.

### Accidental Death Benefit

Another coverage, commonly known as double indemnity, can be added to a life insurance contract. Here, if the death of the insured is caused by accident, an additional sum equal to the face of the policy will be paid.[20] A typical insuring clause would read as follows:

> The Company agrees to pay an Accidental Death Benefit upon receipt at its Home Office of due proof that the death of the Insured resulted, directly and independently of all other causes, from accidental bodily injury, provided that death occurred within 90 days after such injury and while this benefit is in effect. This benefit shall be in effect while this policy is in force other than under Extended-Term Insurance, Paid-up Insurance, or Optional Maturity Date provisions, but shall terminate on the policy anniversary nearest the Insured's seventieth birthday.[21]

Payments will be made under the accidental death benefit provision according to the terms of the definition only if three conditions are satisfied. First, death must have resulted, directly and independently of all other causes, from accidental bodily injury. This means that the accidental bodily injury must be the proximate cause of the death and that no other factor, such as sickness, was involved as a cause. For example, if the insured is driving his automobile at a speed of 110 miles an hour and the car gets out of control and collides with a tree, the insured's death would be caused by accidental bodily injury. However, if the insured has a heart attack and as a result loses control of the car and collides with a tree, the proximate cause of

---

[20] Some companies provide triple and quadruple indemnity.

[21] Disability and accidental death benefits are not provided under the surrender options of extended-term and paid-up policy of reduced amount, even though they were applicable in the basic contract prior to its surrender.

his death would be the heart attack, a sickness, and not the bodily injury arising from hitting the tree. In other words, if the heart attack is the proximate cause of the death, the death was not caused directly and independently of all other causes by accidental bodily injury. Second, the death must occur within 90 days after the injury. This limitation is included for the purpose of minimizing the influence of other facts that could contribute to the death. Third, the accidental bodily injury and the death must occur before age 70. This restriction is necessary, because the probability of death from accident increases quite substantially in the older ages, and if an age limitation were not imposed, the coverage would become too expensive relative to its value.

The double-indemnity provision contains several exclusions. The most typical are as follows: (a) death resulting from suicide, whether sane or insane; and (b) death resulting from or contributed to by bodily or mental infirmity or disease. In addition, even though death results directly and independently of all other causes from accidental bodily injury, coverage is excluded if the death results from any act of war. An act of war is defined rather broadly to include that declared or undeclared, as well as armed aggression resisted by the armed forces of any country or combination of countries. Death arising while riding in or descent from any kind of aircraft is also excluded if the insured is participating in training or in any duties aboard the aircraft, or if such aircraft is being operated by or for the armed forces.

There is little to commend and much to criticize in the accidental death benefit. There is no basic economic justification for its existence, since the termination of the insured's income through his death is the same whether death results from an automobile accident or from lung cancer. In addition, its existence will tend to create an illusion of having more insurance coverage than will be the case for most causes of death. In this manner, it is a contributing factor in many of the inadequate insurance programs which exist today. If it is considered only as an adjunct to the life insurance contract and not as a part of the basic insurance program, perhaps the provision should be included in the policy.

### Guaranteed Insurability Option

Many companies now permit an insured to purchase additional amounts of insurance at stated intervals without providing evidence of insurability. The option under which this is possible is known as "guaranteed insurability," "additional purchase option," or some similar designation, and is applicable only to the permanent types of contracts such as whole life and endowment. The insured has the option of purchasing additional insurance, regardless of his insurability, at 3-year intervals and up to a specified age, the most common maximum being age 40. In most cases, the amount of the additional insurance is limited to the face of the basic policy, or $10,000, whichever is the smaller. An extra premium is required for the option that is based on the company's estimate of the extra mortality that will be experienced on policies issued without evidence of insurability. The premium is payable to the last option date and, for the insured, is the cost of insuring his insurability.

For purposes of illustration, let us assume that the insured purchases a $10,000 ordinary life policy at age 21 and that the guaranteed insurability option is a part of the policy. The company automatically agrees to issue an additional policy on the life of this insured, without evidence of insurability, at each option date. The customary option dates are 25, 28, 31, 34, 37, and 40. So if our insured desires, he can add $10,000 insurance at each of these six dates, even though he has become uninsurable. This could result in the addition of $60,000 coverage to the original policy for $10,000.

The option is not standardized, which means that some variation exists in the provisions in use by different insurance companies. One of the most important variations involves the "waiver of premium" and "accidental death benefit" provisions. Naturally, the question must arise as to whether the additional insurance will contain these benefits if they are included in the original contract. If the answer is "yes," will the "waiver of premium" benefit be applicable to the additional insurance should the insured become totally disabled at the time the additional insurance becomes effective? The most liberal options do provide automatically for the inclusion of the "waiver of premium" benefit if it exists in the original contract. For example, the insuring clause may read as follows:

If the Waiver of Premium Benefit is a part of this policy at the time an additional policy is issued: (1) An additional policy of Whole Life or 65 Life plan may contain the Waiver of Premium Benefit even though premiums are being waived under this policy. If premiums are being waived under this policy when such additional policy is purchased, premiums will also be waived under the additional policy. (2) An additional policy on other than the Whole Life or 65 Life plan may contain the waiver of premium benefit only if the premiums are not being waived under this policy. The Waiver of Premium Benefit of such additional policy will apply only if total disability resulted from bodily injury or disease originating after the effective date of such policy.

The insuring clause will provide for "waiver of premium" benefits automatically on the additional insurance, and premiums will be waived on the additional insurance if they are being waived on the basic contract at the purchase option date. This is a liberal benefit which few insurers provide in the purchase option. The reason is quite obvious. For example, if our insured with the $10,000 ordinary life policy purchased at age 21 became so disabled at age 23 that he would never be able to work again, the premiums on the policy would be waived. At each option date he would, of course, add the $10,000 additional insurance, and premiums would be waived on each addition.

Most insurers do not provide a "waiver of premium" benefit as liberal as the above. Some may waive premiums on one or two of the additional amounts. Others will include the "waiver of premium" in the additional insurance only if premiums are not being waived in the basic insurance at the option date. There is a trend, however, toward a more liberal application of the "waiver of premium" benefit to the additional amounts available under the purchase option.

In many of the purchase options in use today it is customary to provide for a change in the option date because of marriage of the insured or birth of a child. For example, one policy provides the right of change as follows:

> If the insured is a male, upon his marriage or upon the birth of his child, the right to purchase an additional policy as of the next available Purchase Date may be exercised immediately. The additional policy shall be in lieu of the policy which otherwise might be purchased as of such date. Each such privilege shall expire on the ninetieth day after it becomes exercisable.

Some companies will also provide automatic term insurance, in an amount equal to what could be purchased as additional insurance, beginning on the date of marriage or of the birth of the child. The term insurance would then terminate on the day preceding the expiration of the privilege to purchase the additional insurance. So if the insured gets married and does not exercise his option immediately and should die before the expiration of the 90-day period, the company would pay the proceeds of the basic contract, plus the proceeds of the term insurance.

The incontestable clause, in general, is not applicable to the additional purchase options, but only to the original contract. However, the suicide exclusion will be applicable to each additional policy and will be effective from the date of issue of each addition.

### Questions for Discussion and Review

**1.** Some life insurance contract provisions are designed for the protection of the insured and some are for the protection of the insurance company. Indicate whether each of the following provisions is designed for the benefit of the insured, the company, or both: (a) the entire contract provision; (b) the incontestability provision; (c) the suicide provision; (d) the mis-statement of age provision.

**2.** Describe the nonforfeiture options. Under what circumstances would you advise the choice of each in preference to the other two?

**3.** Joe Smith purchased a $10,000 whole life policy with an accidental death double-indemnity provision on December 1, 1971. He committed suicide on December 15, 1973. Discuss the liability of the insurance company.

**4.** The settlement option providing a life income with cash or installment refund seems too good to be true. How can the insurance company agree to pay for as long as the beneficiary–annuitant lives and also agree to pay out at least the face amount of the policy?

**5.** Although there is no such thing as a "standard" life insurance policy, certain provisions are generally required; discuss the various optional provisions or modifications which may be added to a life insurance policy. Which of these do you feel should be considered essential by the insurance buyer?

### Suggestions for Additional Reading

Bickelhaupt, D. L. and Magee, J. H. *General Insurance*, 8th ed. Homewood, Ill.: Richard D. Irwin, 1970, Chap. 25.

Gregg, D. W. (ed.) *Life and Health Insurance Handbook*, 2nd ed. Homewood, Ill.: Richard D. Irwin, 1964, Chaps. 13–15.

Huebner, S. S. and Black, K., Jr. *Life Insurance*, 7th ed. New York: Appleton-Century-Crofts, 1969, Chaps. 12–15.

McGill, D. M. *Life Insurance*, rev. ed. Homewood, Ill.: Richard D. Irwin, 1967, Chaps. 27, 32, 33.

Mehr, R. I. *Life Insurance Theory and Practice.* Austin, Texas: Business Publications, 1970, Chaps. 10, 11.

Redeker, H. S. and Reid, C. K., II. *Life Insurance Settlement Options*, Homewood, Ill.: Richard D. Irwin, 1964.

# 11 Special Life Insurance Policy Forms

*Variety's the very spice of life.*
— William Cowper, *The Task*

As we saw in Chapter 8, there are three basic types of life insurance contracts:

1. Term insurance
2. Whole life insurance
3. Endowment life insurance

In addition to these life insurance companies offer a wide variety of policies that combine two or more of the basic types into one contract, or which provide for an unusual pattern of premium payments. In this chapter we will examine a few more specialized contracts that have been developed to fill the particular needs of individuals. These are designed to fit special situations, and while they may or may not offer the same degree of flexibility as do the basic contracts, they may possess advantages that make their use attractive in many situations. The discussion below is not intended to be exhaustive, but is designed only as a description of the more important of these special contracts. The important point to remember is that the forms that will be discussed are nothing more than combinations or modifications of the three basic forms, and the manner in which they may be combined is limited only by the imagination of the policy writers.

## SPECIAL LIFE INSURANCE FORMS

### Renewable and Convertible Term

In its purest form, a term policy is purchased for a specified period and the face of the policy is payable only if the insured dies during this period. Nothing is paid if the insured survives the term period. It is customary, however, for term policies to contain the features of renewability and convertibility. In the *renewable* feature, the insured is provided with the option to renew the policy for a limited number of additional periods, usually of the same length as the original term period. For example, if an insured purchases a $10,000 10-year term policy at age 25 and he survives this period, he has the option of renewing the policy for an additional 10 years without the necessity of proving insurability. The level premium rate for this 10-year period will be higher than the premium rate for the first 10 years. The insured may renew the contract at age 45 and perhaps also at age 55. However, all insurance companies because of the element of adverse selection, impose an age limit beyond which renewal is not permitted.

The most important advantage to the insured is the right to renew even if he becomes uninsurable. In order to illustrate this advantage, let us assume that our insured with the $10,000 term policy becomes ill at age 34, and hospital tests show that he has heart trouble, lung cancer, diabetes, and tuberculosis. If he were told that he could live no more than 3 years, he naturally would renew the policy at age 35. The company would be obligated to accept the renewal, even though the insured informed it of his physical condition and even smiled while providing the information.

The *convertible* feature is also an important aspect of term insurance. In addition to the right of renewal, the policy provides the insured with an option to exchange the term contract for some type of permanent life insurance contract without the necessity of providing insurability.[1] Our insured with the $10,000 term policy could, if he so desired, convert this contract prior to age 35 into a $10,000 ordinary life policy, or into some other form of permanent insurance such as limited-payment or endowment, and the conversion would be accomplished even though the insured was uninsurable at the time.[2]

---

[1] The option to renew regardless of insurability and the option to convert without evidence of insurability provide the insured with complete protection against loss of his insurability.

[2] To minimize the element of adverse selection, most companies impose a time limit within which the conversion must take place. In the 10-year policy, the insured could be required to convert within 7 or 8 years after the date of issue of the original contract. If the policy is renewable, however, the only limitation is that conversion must take place before the limiting age for renewal, or that it be converted within a certain period before the expiration of the last term for which it can be renewed.

The conversion could be effected at the insured's attained age or could be made retroactive to his original age. For example, if the insured decides to convert the term to an ordinary life policy at age 32 and to convert at his attained age, he will pay the premium on the ordinary life contract just as if he had purchased the permanent policy at age 32. The policy could also be converted at the original age of 25, and the premium rates on the converted policy will be those he would have paid had he purchased the permanent contract at age 25. However, the insured will be required to pay a lump sum of money to the insurer equal to the larger of (a) the difference in the reserves under the policies being exchanged, or (b) the difference between the premiums paid on the term and the premiums that would have been paid had the permanent policy been purchased at age 25, plus interest at a rate of 5 or 6%. This means that the insured must pay a rather substantial sum to the insurance company, from which he will receive little real value. Perhaps it would be good advice, if the insured has the funds to pay this difference—which he normally will not have—to use the money to purchase additional insurance or to prepay the premiums on the converted policy.

**Mortgage Redemption Policy**

Actually, we could call any policy purchased for the purpose of retiring a mortgage in the event that the head of the household dies before he has retired it, mortgage insurance. As the term "mortgage insurance" is used in the insurance industry, it refers to a policy designed to provide protection in some amount that will be sufficient to pay off the mortgage at any given time. The long-term mortgage plans that characterize home ownership in our society make life insurance to protect against loss of the home through premature death of the breadwinner increasingly important. The principal of the mortgage normally reduces gradually, leaving the unpaid balance relatively high for many years. Yet the balance is constantly decreasing. Since the amount of the mortgage is constantly decreasing throughout its term, a policy designed to pay off the mortgage in the event of the death of the head of the family may also decrease in face amount over its life. The mortgage protection policy is written on a decreasing basis for the term of the mortgage. If the policyholder lives to pay off the mortgage himself, the policy expires without value at the same time the need for protection has disappeared.

While it is not exactly true to say that mortgage protection insurance reduces at a constant rate, for the purpose of an illustration we can assume it does. Suppose the insured has a $20,000 mortgage on his home, which he has amortized over a 20-year period. If he lives to the end of the 20-year period, he will have paid off the mortgage. However, if he should die before the end of the 20-year period, he would like to leave his beneficiary a sum sufficient to pay off the balance of the mortgage. If he purchases a mortgage redemption policy in the amount of $20,000 for a 20-year period, this goal can be accomplished. Figure 11-1 shows the amount of insurance at any given time during the length of the policy, and the amount of policy proceeds available to pay off the mortgage at any given time. From the example, it should be obvious that the cost of such a policy will be less than the cost of level term insurance for the same period of time. On the average, the amount of risk facing the company is approximately one-half the face amount of the policy. The premium should therefore approximate the premium for a 20-year term policy of one-half the face amount of the mortgage protection policy. Normally, the premiums on the mortgage protection policy are payable for only a portion of the length of the policy (e.g., 16 years on a 20-year policy).

### Family Income Policy

The family income policy also utilizes the concept of decreasing term insurance to fit a need for a decreasing amount of insurance. The family income policy is a combination of some form of permanent insurance (e.g., whole life), with decreasing term insurance. The term insurance makes provision for the payment of some stipulated amount per month from the date of the insured's death until some specific date in the future. The amount payable per month is typically 1% of the amount of permanent insurance, although many companies offer other options. To illustrate the operation of the family income policy, let us assume that the insured in question purchases a $10,000 whole life policy with a 1% family income benefit. The insuring agreement of the family income policy promises to pay $100 per month to the beneficiary of the policy from the date of death of the insured until a date 20 years from the inception of the policy. In essence, the insured has purchased a tremendous amount of protection for a small premium outlay. To be sure, the amount of protection will decline as time passes, but so too will the need for

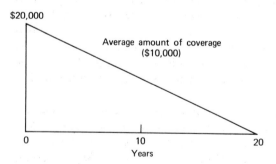

**FIGURE 11-1**
**Mortgage redemption policy.**

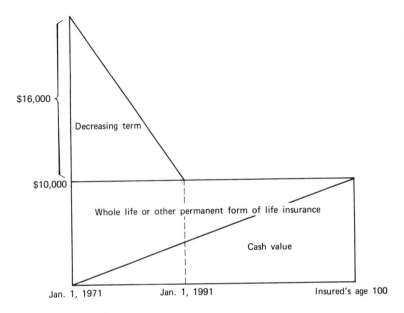

**FIGURE 11-2**
Family income policy.

insurance. Ten years from the inception date of the policy the child-raising period will presumably be half over, and it will take only one-half as much in benefits to pay the required $100 per month for the remainder of the period. The normal family income period is 20 years, although other options such as 10 or 15 years are also available. If the insured outlives the period specified as the family income period, the decreasing term portion of the policy ceases. The insured then has the basic amount of permanent insurance on which he continues to pay premiums.

Figure 11-2 illustrates the family income policy graphically. In our illustration we have assumed that the policy was purchased on January 1, 1971. The amount of whole life insurance in this illustration is $10,000, and a $100 per month benefit will be paid from the date of the insured's death until January 1, 1991. The $16,000 in decreasing term represents the amount the insurance company must have in policy proceeds at the beginning of the family income period in order to pay $100 per month for a period of 20 years. As time goes by, the amount of insurance needed to make the $100 monthly monthly payments for the remainder of the 20-year period declines. The $100 family income benefit comes from two sources: a part of the monthly payment comes from the decreasing term, while another portion comes from interest on the benefits left with the company. It is common under the family income policy to provide for the payment of the basic policy at the end of the income period. Thus, the interest from the basic policy helps provide the monthly income payments.[3] In some instances, the insurance company will permit the beneficiary to take the commutation value of the monthly benefits at the time of the death of the insured. Obviously, the commutation value of $100 per month for any number of months is something less than $100 times the number of months, because the interest that would have been earned is foregone. In addition, many companies will permit the beneficiary to take the basic policy in a lump sum at the death of the insured. If this is done, however, the monthly benefit will be reduced. For example, a $100 benefit might be reduced to approximately $80.

While this is a simplified explanation of the family income policy, it includes most of the essential points about the contract. The policy is most useful when it is used for the purpose for which it was intended, but it can be used for other purposes as well.

### Family Income Rider

The family income rider is merely a variation of the family income policy, but with somewhat more flexibility. The family income rider is a decreasing term rider that is attached to some permanent form of insurance such as whole life or endowment. Some companies will even permit the use of the family income rider with a form of long-duration term, such as term to age 65 or term to expectancy.

One major difference between the family income rider and the family income policy is the amount of term insurance involved. While both the family income policy and the family income rider may provide for the payment of a specified amount (e.g., $100 per month), the actual amount of term insurance required to provide this amount may differ. The determining factor is the time at which the basic policy is payable. As we have seen, it is common under the family income policy to provide for the payment of the basic policy at the end of the income period. In the case of the family income rider, the term insurance is usually sufficient to provide the full amount of the monthly benefit, without the interest from the basic policy. This means that the amount of the basic policy may be paid immediately at the death of the insured, it may be left at interest to increase the amount of the monthly benefit above the designated amount, or it may be left to accumulate at interest until the end of the income period.

---

[3] To provide funds for funeral expenses and the costs of the last illness, some family income policies provide for the payment of a certain amount at the death of the insured if it should occur during the income period. In some contracts, this amount would be $200 per $1000 of the face amount.

### Family Maintenance Policy

The family maintenance policy is a variation of the family income policy. Instead of paying a monthly income from the date of the insured's death until some dates 10, 15, or 20 years from the inception of the policy as does the family income policy, the family maintenance policy pays the monthly income for a period of 10, 15, or 20 years from the date of the insured's death, provided the insured dies during a specified period. The major difference between the family income policy and the family maintenance policy involves the length of the income period. In the family maintenance contract, should the insured die during the income period, the monthly payment will start at the time of death and continue for a period equal in length to the income period, rather than only for the balance of the income period. For example, if X had purchased a $25,000 family maintenance policy at age 30, with an income period of 20 years, and had died at age 40, the income payments of $250 per month would be paid to the widow for 20 years, i.e., until the time the sured would have been 60. Then the face amount would be paid to the beneficiary. In all other respects the two contracts are the same.

The family maintenance policy consists of a basic policy, which is some form of permanent insurance, plus level rather than decreasing term. The term portion of the policy will provide income for the number of years specified. The family maintenance policy is illustrated in Figure 11-3. Note that the amount of term insurance provided does not decrease. The term insurance remains level and provides a sum of $16,000 at the death of the insured, provided the insured dies within the 20-year period. The $16,000 will be sufficient, together with the interest earned on that portion of the benefits held by the company, to pay $100 per month for 240 months. Note also, however, that if the insured does not die before January 1, 1991 (i.e., within the 20-year period) the term expires, and premiums on this portion of the protection cease.

Because of the larger term insurance aspect, the family maintenance policy will cost substantially more than the family income type.[4] However, the family maintenance contract is more flexible than the family income policy. If additional children should be born, the longer income period of the family maintenance contract would provide more adequate protection than would be provided in the family income contract. It is also possible that the longer income period of the family maintenance policy will lessen substantially the gap between the time the income payments cease and the time the widow becomes eligible again for benefits under the Old-Age, Survivors, and Disability Insurance (OASDI) program.

---

[4]At age 30, for example, the premium per $1000 for the family maintenance term portion would be almost double the premium for the decreasing term portion of the family income policy.

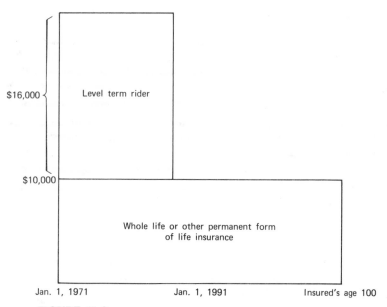

**FIGURE 11-3**
**Family maintenance policy.**

### Family Protection Policy

This special form is known by many names; almost every insurance company offers it in one form or another, and many refer to it by their own trade name. The family protection policy is an attempt to provide insurance on all members of the family. The distinguishing characteristic is that insurance in predetermined proportions is provided for each member of the family. For example, the unit on the husband may be $5000 on an ordinary life basis, with $1000 term insurance on the wife (the term extending to the time the husband is 65), and $1000 term coverage on each child, with coverage to a specified age such as 21. Children born after the inception of the contract are covered automatically without notice to the insurance company upon the attainment of a specified age, e.g., 14 days. The contract may include a "waiver of premium" benefit that provides for the waiver of further premium payments if the husband dies or becomes totally disabled. In addition, an accidental death benefit providing for double indemnity on the life of the husband only may also be included. Surrender and loan values are provided, but paid-up insurance normally is provided only on the coverage applicable to the husband. It is also customary to permit conversion of the term insurance on the lives of the dependents upon the expiration of the specified term. For example, many contracts provide for conversion of the coverage on the children up to as much as $5000 of permanent life insurance for each $1000 of term coverage and without evidence of insurability.

The husband is considered to be the owner of the policy. However, his freedom in disposing of the insurance is normally limited by specific provisions in the contract. The typical arrangement is for the insurance on the husband's life to be payable to the wife, if living. Otherwise, it is payable to his estate. The insurance on the wife is payable to the husband, if living, or to her estate. The insurance on the child is payable either to the father or the mother. If neither is alive, it is payable to the child's estate.

The premium on this form of insurance is based on the age of the husband, with an adjustment made for the additional risk the company accepts. The wife's age also enters into the computation, but on a somewhat different basis. The basic premium computation assumes that the wife is the same age as the husband. If she is not, the face amount of the term insurance covering her is adjusted. The younger the wife relative to her husband, the greater will be the amount of insurance coverage on her life. The older the wife, the less will be the amount of coverage on her life.[5] Table 11-1 indicates the amount of coverage provided for the wife by one company.

All members of the family must be insurable if the contract is to be issued. If the husband or wife should be uninsurable, the contract cannot be issued at all.[6] The only exception involves the children. If one child is uninsurable, the family protection policy may be issued, but with the uninsurable child excluded from coverage.

The family protection policy is extremely popular with young married couples, since it provides some insurance on every member of the family. It can be, and often is, written with a family income rider which provides 1% of the amount of coverage on the father as monthly income during the family income period. One of the more attractive features of the policy is that it guarantees the insurability of the children in the family. In the event that a child should become uninsurable before reaching the conversion age, or if a child were born to the marriage who was uninsurable, this contract would guarantee that the child would be able to purchase at least some minimum amount of permanent insurance upon reaching the conversion age. The conversion does not require evidence of insurability.

### Return of Premium or Cash Value Policy

Some individuals who lack an understanding of the level premium concept feel that the insurance company should pay the face of the policy when the

---

[5]Although this is the standard approach, some insurers leave the amount of insurance on the wife at the standard $1000 and adjust the premium based on her age.

[6]With some insurers, a "parent's policy," covering one parent and the insurable children may be employed.

TABLE 11-1
Wife's Coverage per Unit of Coverage on the Husband under Family Protection Policy

| If the wife is younger than the husband by (years) | Her coverage will be ($) | If the wife is older than the husband by (years) | Her coverage will be ($) |
|---|---|---|---|
| 1 | 1080 | 1 | 930 |
| 2 | 1170 | 2 | 860 |
| 3 | 1265 | 3 | 795 |
| 4 | 1365 | 4 | 735 |
| 5 | 1475 | 5 | 675 |
| 6 | 1600 | | |
| 7 | 1735 | | |
| 8 | 1880 | | |
| 9 | 2030 | | |
| 10 | 2190 | | |
| 11 | 2355 | | |
| 12 | .2525 | | |
| 13 | 2705 | | |
| 14 | 2895 | | |
| 15 | 3095 | | |

SOURCE: *Diamond Life Bulletins* (The National Underwriter Company, Cincinnati, Ohio).

insured dies, plus the cash value. They reason that since the cash value is the insured's saving fund, it is inequitable to pay this to the beneficiary and call it a part of the death benefit. These individuals feel that if the insured dies before the policy matures, the company should be obligated to pay the face amount of the policy plus the cash value. Insurance companies attempt to create a product that is salable, and if people want a policy that will pay the face amount plus the cash value, they are certainly going to get it.

Policies have been issued which purport to pay, in addition to the face of the policy, the cash surrender value at the time of death. It should be obvious from what we have learned about the cash value and its relationship to the level premium that this is impossible unless an additional premium is charged. The policies that agree to pay the cash value plus the face of the policy are nothing more than a combination of two whole life contracts. As Figure 11-4 indicates, there are two amounts of insurance in force at all times. The basic amount is level, being equal to the face of the policy the insured has purchased. The second portion, for which the insured, of course, pays an additional premium, is always sufficient to pay an amount equal to the cash value of the basic policy.

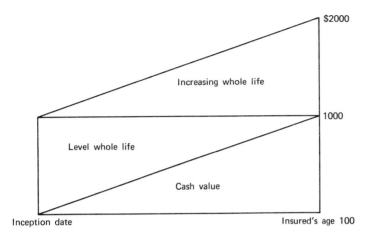

**FIGURE 11-4**
Return of cash value policy.

A variation of this idea is found in the "return of premium" policy (Figure 11-5). There is a strong psychological appeal to most individuals when they are offered something for nothing. The return of premium policy purports to pay the face amount of the policy at the death of the insured, plus all the premiums that have been paid, provided the insured dies within a certain period of time. The return of premium policy is also composed of two amounts of insurance. The basic policy is whole life or some other form of permanent insurance. The second portion is actually increasing term insurance, with a face amount that is always sufficient to pay the total amount of premiums that have been paid for both portions. The insured must die within a certain period (normally 20 years) if the beneficiary is to receive both the face amount and the premiums paid. If the insured does not die until after the 20-year period has passed, the beneficiary will receive only the face amount of the basic policy, and the term portion of the policy expires without value.

### Modified Whole Life

Modified whole life is another combination plan. This form is actually "automatically convertible term." The main characteristic of the policy is the premium level, which changes as the policy becomes 3 or 5 years old. The premium for the first 3 or 5 years is slightly more than the premium on the same amount of term insurance. After the end of the 3- or 5-year period, the premium increases to a level that is slightly more than the whole life premium at the age at which the policy was taken out, but also slightly less than the premium on permanent insurance at the attained age of the insured. This

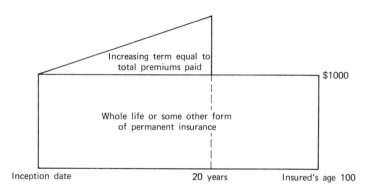

**FIGURE 11-5**
**Return of premium policy.**

policy is particularly attractive to college students and other individuals who feel that their income will increase within a short time. They would like to purchase permanent insurance at their present age, but cannot afford to do so. If they wait until they can afford it, or if they purchase convertible term, the premium on the permanent insurance will be based on the age at conversion. The modified whole life policy helps to solve this problem. To illustrate, we will use the rates of a typical company showing the premiums on whole life, renewable convertible term, and modified whole life. The premium rates used in this illustration are nonparticipating rates.

The company charges the following rates for a 25-year-old male:

| | |
|---|---|
| Renewable convertible term (5-year) | $4.23 |
| Ordinary whole life | $12.68 |
| Modified whole life | $4.58 for first 5 years |
| | $13.54 thereafter |

If a young man purchases a modified whole life contract, he pays $4.58 for the first 5 years. Thereafter, the premium is $13.54. He could have purchased 5-year convertible term for $4.23, but the premium on the whole life when he made the conversion would be the whole life rate for a 30 year old ($14.99). If the insured knows he will be converting to permanent insurance within a short period of time, he can save on the total premium outlay by purchasing a modified whole life contract rather than convertible term. As pointed out previously, this contract is simply a combination of convertible term (with the decision as to whether or not to convert eliminated). During the first 3 or 5 years, the protection is based on term insurance; as a result, the policy does not begin to accumulate cash value until the premium has increased to its higher level.

### Juvenile Insurance

The idea of purchasing insurance on children is especially attractive to many individuals. Often, grandparents or friends make a gift of a life insurance policy to a child. The primary intent of most juvenile policies is thrift. Juvenile insurance policies are widely used by parents to provide a college fund for the child. The forms of insurance most often written to cover children are:

1. 20-year endowment
2. Educational endowment at age 18
3. The jumping juvenile

The *educational endowment at age 18* is quite similar to the *20-year endowment*. The only difference is that the maturity period is shorter, making the face of the policy payable at age 18 so that the benefits can be used for the college education of the child. The *jumping juvenile* is a specially designed policy written for a basic amount of insurance (say $1000) that automatically increases to some multiple of the basic amount when the child reaches age 21. The premium on the contract remains level throughout the life of the policy. It is normal to limit the face of the basic policy to $5000. Many parents purchase this type of contract rather than an endowment policy to provide educational benefits, assuming that the cash value of any permanent form of insurance will be available to finance the college education. A further advantage of the jumping juvenile is the fact that it insures the insurability of the child. Even if the child should become medically uninsurable, the jumping juvenile would assure some minimum amount of insurance equal to five times the base amount of coverage.

Juvenile insurance is an extremely specialized form of insurance. In many cases it is misused. Far too many individuals purchase life insurance on their children when they themselves are inadequately protected. In most cases the premium dollars spent to purchase insurance on children would be better spent in providing protection on the head of the family. As we will see, adequate life insurance programming requires a substantial amount of protection on the breadwinner. While the death of a child is certainly a tragedy, it does not bring with it the horrendous consequences for the family that the death of the breadwinner brings. Dollars spent to provide educational funds for the child can accomplish this purpose almost as well when they are spent to insure the father's life. For the sake of example, let us assume that John Doe, age 21, and his wife have an addition to the family. John immediately wants to set up some type of saving plan that will assure the availability of funds when John Jr. is ready for college in another 18 years. He considers life insurance as a vehicle for this saving fund. When he investigates the rate for an endowment at age 18 on John Jr., he will find that the premium on such a policy is approximately $46 per thousand per year; the annual premium on a $10,000 endowment at age 18 for John Jr. will be $460 per year. On the other hand, John Sr. can purchase a 20-year endowment policy on his own life for only $48 per thousand per year. (Since the probability of death for both John Sr. and John Jr. is quite low, the bulk of the premium under both policies goes to accumulate the fund to be paid at maturity.) It would probably be better for John Sr. to acquire a policy on his own life. This would assure the availability of funds even if John Sr. should die. An even more attractive alternative might be for John Sr. to purchase a whole life policy with himself as the insured. The rate on a participating whole policy at age 21 would be about $15.50 per thousand. Thus John Sr. can purchase $30,000 in whole life coverage for about $465.00, or only slightly more than the $10,000 endowment at age 18 on John Jr. At the end of the 18 years, the whole life policy on John Sr. would have a cash value of approximately $6800. In addition, if the dividends are left to accumulate, the total cash value plus dividends will be in excess of $8000. The exact amount of the cash value plus dividends at the end of the 18-year period will depend on the actual dividends paid by the company. At any rate, through the cash value of the whole life policy, John will have accomplished his goal of providing funds for the education of John Jr., and in addition, his family will have enjoyed the extra protection the whole life policy afforded.

## SPECIAL ANNUITY FORMS

### Retirement Annuity

In our earlier discussion of annuities (Chapter 8) we noted briefly that annuities may be purchased on a deferred basis; under this plan, the insured pays for the annuity prior to the time benefits are to begin. A deferred life annuity is normally purchased in premium installments over a period of years. Premium payments are to terminate and annuity payments are to commence at a stipulated age. The most popular of the deferred life annuities sold by life insurance carriers is one that goes under the name of a retirement annuity. In most instances, the premium for this contract is quoted as the amount necessary to provide a monthly lifetime income of $10 at a designated age such as 65, and it is customary to base the premiums on the assumption that the annuitant will receive the income with payments guaranteed for 10 years. So, if X, age 25, should decide to purchase a retirement income annuity, he could pay $250 per year, and at $2\frac{1}{2}\%$ guaranteed compound interest, he could accumulate a fund over a period of 40 years which would provide approximately $100 per month beginning at age 65 and payable for the balance of his lifetime, but with payments for a period of 10 years. If X should die prior to the selected retirement date, i.e., within the deferred period, the company will pay the accumulated gross premiums, without interest, or the cash value, whichever is larger, as a death benefit.[7] The purchaser may also surrender the policy and withdraw the cash value at any time. The retirement income policy, then, is hardly more than a method of accumulating a principal sum through the use of the investment facilities of an insurance company.

At the maturity date of the contract, X is not obligated to accept a life annuity, but may withdraw the accumulated cash value instead. This is known as the *cash option*, and its existence exposes the insurer to a substantial element of adverse selection. Logically, those in good health will choose the annuity and those whose health is impaired will choose the cash sum. This is an obvious advantage to the insured.

### Retirement Income Policy

Most insurance companies also sell another type of deferred annuity known as a retirement income contract, an endowment annuity, or a retirement endowment. It is similar to the retirement annuity discussed above, except that it provides a rather substantial death benefit during the deferred period. The death benefit in the retirement annuity, as will be recalled, is a return of premiums or the cash value, whichever is larger. Under the retirement income policy, there is $1000 in life insurance for each $10 of monthly income. Then if X, at age 25, purchases this contract with the objective of $100 per month life annuity at age 65, the amount of the life insurance would be $10,000. In the event of his death during the deferred period, the insurance company would pay either the $10,000 or the cash value, whichever is greater. The cash value of the contract probably would exceed $10,000 at approximately age 55. If X should die after age 55, the insurer will then pay the cash value as a death benefit (Figure 11-6).

The retirement income contract is a combination of a retirement annuity and decreasing term insurance. The term insurance, at any age, is the difference between the face amount of the contract, the $10,000 in the above example, and the accumulated cash value. And the term element reaches zero at the point at which the cash value equals the face amount of the insurance. In all other respects the contract is identical with the retirement annuity.

### Joint-and-Last-Survivor Annuity

Annuities may be designed for special purposes, just as life insurance contracts have been. One specialized annuity form is the joint-and-last-survivor an-

---

[7]After the contract has been in effect for several years, the cash value will exceed the gross premiums without interest. This normally takes 10 years or so.

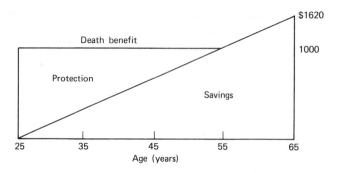

**FIGURE 11-6**
Retirement income policy.

nuity. This is computed on the basis of two lives. Annuities normally cover only one life, but situations arise in which it is desirable to make the payments on the basis of two lives. Under the joint-and-last-survivor annuity, the insurance company promises to make payments until both annuitants have died. This is an especially attractive form of annuity for a retired couple. If, as is likely, one predeceases the other, annuity payments will be continued until the other has died. A variation of this form provides for a reduction in the income payments at the death of the first annuitant, with annuity payments being continued in the reduced amount (usually two-thirds of the original income payments) until the death of the second annuitant.

### Joint-Life Annuity

The joint-life annuity is similar to, but should not be confused with the joint-and-last-survivor annuity. Under the joint-life annuity, payments cease upon the death of the first annuitant to die; the other annuitant then receives no further benefits under the program. This form is useful when there is a secondary source of income which is sufficient to support one, but not both of the annuitants.

### The Reversionary or Survivorship Policy (the Survivorship Annuity)

The reversionary life insurance policy (which is often called either a survivorship policy or a survivorship annuity) is a seldom used form, but in certain circumstances it meets a special need far better than any other form of life insurance. The reversionary or survivorship policy is a program computed on the basis of two lives. Basically, it provides insurance on one person with the benefits payable to the other person under a life income option. The distinguishing characteristic of this form is the fact that if the beneficiary dies before the insured, the policy expires without value. The two individuals upon whose lives the premium is based are referred to as the "annuitant" and the "nominator." The annuitant is the beneficiary of the policy. The nominator is the individual insured. The premium is computed on the basis of both lives. When this policy is written with a young person as the nominator and the annuitant or beneficiary is an older person, the premium is extremely low, for the beneficiary is likely to die before the nominator. In addition, since the amount of insurance required to provide a life income to the annuitant decreases as the annuitant becomes older, the protection is written on a decreasing term basis. In computing the premium for this policy, the company estimates the life expectancy of the annuitant, and then computes the premium on a decreasing term policy at the age of the nominator. The amount of the decreasing term policy will be the amount necessary to provide a life income to the annuitant at any given time, should the nominator die. As mentioned previously, if the annuitant dies before the nominator, the policy expires without value.

## THE VARIABLE ANNUITY

Our discussion of the various forms that have been designed to fill special needs would be incomplete without a discussion of the variable annuity. A comparatively new innovation, the variable annuity represents a classic example of an imaginative approach to a critical problem.

### The Need for the Variable Annuity

The conventional fixed-dollar annuity was developed and is based on the assumption that the value of the dollar is relatively stable. Under this assumption, the fixed-dollar annuity is a good investment for retirement purposes and is the only investment that will guarantee the investor that his income will continue for his entire life. However, since early in the 1940s this country has witnessed a steady increase in the cost of living and a decline in the purchasing power of the dollar. The impact of the upward changes in the price level on the purchasing power of the dollar is illustrated by the consumer price index (Table 11-2).

To appreciate more fully the impact of these price changes, we might review the distinction between real income and money income. Money income is measured in dollars, while real income is measured by the goods and services these dollars can command. Real income is computed by dividing dollar income by a consumers' price index. As prices increase, a given dollar of income represents a shrinking real income, in that it will purchase fewer goods and services.

Because their money income is fixed, persons living on retirement incomes suffer more than most other groups from inflation. Probably no segment of

TABLE 11-2
Consumer Prices—All Items, 1950–1970
$(1957–1959 = 100)$

| | | | | |
|---|---|---|---|---|
| 1949 | = | 83.0 | 1960 = 103.1 |
| 1950 | = | 83.8 | 1961 = 104.2 |
| 1951 | = | 90.5 | 1962 = 105.4 |
| 1952 | = | 92.5 | 1963 = 106.7 |
| 1953 | = | 93.2 | 1964 = 108.1 |
| 1954 | = | 93.6 | 1965 = 109.9 |
| 1955 | = | 93.3 | 1966 = 113.1 |
| 1956 | = | 94.7 | 1967 = 116.3 |
| 1957 | = | 98.0 | 1968 = 121.2 |
| 1958 | = | 100.7 | 1969 = 127.7 |
| 1959 | = | 101.5 | 1970 = 135.3 |

SOURCE: U.S. Department of Labor, Bureau of Labor Statistics, *Monthly Labor Review.*

our population has suffered so much from the inflation and loss of purchasing power, and has been so defenseless against it, as the retired. While the salaries of those who are employed may lag behind price changes, their incomes do rise. The money incomes of the retired remain constant during inflation, for there is little they can do to adjust the money income. Those who have depended on a fixed-dollar retirement plan during the past three decades have learned to their misfortune that they had no protection against changes in the value of the dollar.[8]

Persistent inflation also undermines attempts to save for retirement. Even the prudent individual who makes a serious attempt to provide a fund for his retirement may see his efforts partially wiped out by inflation. If prices are increasing by 5% a year, anyone who invests in a program with a 4% return is crazy. He will eventually accumulate a fund in dollars which are worth less than half the value of the dollars which were saved. Instead of obtaining a positive rate of interest on his money, such an individual is receiving a negative rate.

Many economists feel that there are sufficient inflationary pressures in the economy to cause continued inflation, with little or no possibility of reversal in the long run. The strength of labor unions, the acceptance by both major parties that it is the responsibility of the federal government to maintain full employment, defense costs—all indicate that the greater likelihood is for more inflation rather than deflation.

[8] Those receiving retirement benefits under the Old-Age and Survivors' benefit program of the Social Security system have some protection against inflation, since Congress increases these benefits from time to time.

### The Nature of the Variable Annuity

The variable annuity is an attempt to cope with the problem resulting from changes in the price level over time to the detriment of persons who are retired or who are attempting to accumulate funds for retirement. Under a fixed-dollar annuity, the annuitant is guaranteed a fixed number of dollars at each pay-out date. Under the variable annuity, there is no such guarantee, and the number of dollars that will be paid to the annuitant may vary. The basic intent is to provide a varying number of dollars with constant purchasing power rather than a constant number of dollars with varying purchasing power. This is done by linking the retirement income to the level of stock prices. The basic rationale of the variable annuity is based on the assumption that the value of the dollar will vary from time to time and that the value of a diversified portfolio of common stocks will change in the same direction as the cost of living. While the cost of living has neither remained stable nor increased at a predictable rate, we have seen that the value of common stocks has generally moved in the same direction as the cost of living. There have been times, during periods of accelerated inflation, when the price of common stocks has moved in the opposite direction from that of the cost of living, but there has been no extended period in which the price of common stocks has not moved in the same general direction as the cost of goods and services.

Although individual variable annuity contracts may differ somewhat, the general nature of the variable annuity is the same. Under a variable annuity the annuitant's payments purchase units in a fund of securities, very much like an open-end investment company. These units are accumulated until retirement, and the insurance company promises to pay a variable income based on the value of these units as they fluctuate over time. The number of annuity units to which the annuitant is entitled remains constant, but as the value of these units fluctuates, the number of dollars he receives also fluctuates.

Variable annuities may work in several different ways. Most frequently, the variable annuities include both a variable pay-in and a variable pay-out, as described above. As an alternative, the annuity may provide for a variable accumulation, with a fixed pay-out. Under this plan, the accumulation fund increases or decreases in value prior to retirement, but at retirement, the fund is converted to a conventional annuity and provides a guaranteed income to the annuitant for life. The plan may also provide for a fixed-value pay-in with a variable pay-out, under which the fund is accumulated on a fixed-dollar basis and does not fluctuate prior to retirement, but is converted at retirement to a variable pay-out.

### Development of the Variable Annuity

The variable annuity as we know it today was developed by the Teachers Insurance and Annuity Association of America (TIAA), a nonprofit organization which was founded in 1918 by the Carnegie Foundation for the Advancement of Teaching. The TIAA was originally founded to provide college professors with some means of attaining the retirement security they lacked because of their inability to participate in industry's profit-sharing, stock-option, and bonus plans. The TIAA originally wrote the conventional fixed-dollar annuity until several faculty members at Harvard University pointed out that TIAA offered no protection against inflation. Realizing how vulnerable their retirement program was to inflation, they decided to invest a portion of their retirement dollars in the Harvard Endowment Fund, which invested mainly in common stocks. With a portion of their retirement dollars invested in TIAA and another portion in the Harvard Endowment Fund, these faculty members hedged against deflation and inflation.

Shortly thereafter TIAA began a study of the possibility of equity funded retirement programs as a hedge against inflation. The result of this study was published as *A New Approach to Retirement Income* in 1951.[9] The study reached three major conclusions:

1. It is unwise to commit all one's retirement savings to dollar obligations, since decreases in the purchasing power of the dollar can seriously reduce the value of a fixed-income annuity. Increases in the purchasing power of the dollar, on the other hand, improve the status of the owner of a fixed-income annuity.
2. It is equally unwise to commit all one's retirement savings to equity investments, since variations in prices of common stocks are much too pronounced to permit full reliance on them for the stable income needed during retirement. Changes in the value of common stocks and other equities are by no means perfectly correlated with cost of living changes, but they have provided a considerably better protection against inflation than have debt instruments.
3. Contributions to a retirement plan that are invested partly in debt obligations and partly in common stocks through an equity fund providing lifetime unit annuities offer promise of supplying retirement income that is at once reasonably free from violent fluctuations in amount and from serious depreciation through price level changes.

Another study which appeared shortly thereafter in the Transactions of the Society of Actuaries under the title "A Retirement System Granting Unit Annuities and Investing in Equities" convinced TIAA that it was feasible to develop a system whereby the benefits could be based upon investments in equities. The result was the creation of a companion organization to TIAA, which was called the College Retirement Equities Fund (CREF). The first

[9] William C. Greenough, *A New Approach to Retirement Income* (New York: Teachers Insurance and Annuity Association of America, 1951).

CREF variable annuity was issued in July 1952. Following CREF's innovative lead, private insurance companies became active in the variable annuity field. The first variable annuity written by a life insurance company was issued in 1954 by the Participating Annuity Life Insurance Company of Little Rock, Arkansas. This company sold the variable annuity strictly on an intrastate basis in Arkansas and did not use an agency organization. In the latter part of 1955, the Variable Annuity Life Insurance Company (VALIC) was founded in Washington, D.C. This company was the second to enter the variable annuity field (excluding CREF) and the first to enter the business on an interstate basis. It was also the first to use a life insurance agency organization as a means of marketing variable annuities.

The two most active companies in the early stages of variable annuity development were the Variable Annuity Life Insurance Company and the Prudential Insurance Company of America. The entry of these two organizations into the field of variable annuities prompted the Securities and Exchange Commission (SEC) to intervene, leading to considerable litigation. The first and probably the most important litigation concerning variable annuities involved a dispute between the SEC and the VALIC. The VALIC contended that the variable annuity was an insurance contract, and, under the provisions of Public Law 15, was exempt from federal regulation. The SEC maintained that the variable annuity should be classified as a security. The litigation lasted 3 years and was eventually settled in the Supreme Court of the United States. The Court ruled that the variable annuity was indeed a security and as such was subject to the Securities Act of 1933. This decision was vital to the SEC and opened the way for additional regulation of variable annuities. Variable annuities are currently subject to dual regulation under both the federal government and the individual states. The regulatory authorities of the states and the federal government appear to protect zealously what they conceive to be their own particular sphere of authority, and because of this, there will always be some duplication and overlapping of authority in regulation. However, there have been indications of increasing cooperation.

In addition to the long and involved litigation, the development of private variable annuities has been retarded by another force: opposition within the insurance industry. Life insurance companies have been strongly divided on the question of the variable annuity, with some segments of the industry voicing strong opposition. This opposition is based in part on the "anti-equity bias" of many people in the industry, who consider the variable annuity to be a competing product with the main product of the industry, investment life insurance. In addition, many people in the life insurance industry oppose the variable annuity because they are convinced that there is a danger that the public will not understand the fundamental nature of the variable annuity.

### How Well Has It Worked?

Only one company (CREF) has compiled sufficient experience to permit an appraisal. Although a sample of one is not ideal, the success of this operation may be an indication of the potential for the variable annuity. College professors began purchasing variable annuities from CREF in 1952. There are now over 200,000 participants, and the variable annuity appears to have worked smoothly for those who have participated. Originally, the participants were limited in the amount of their retirement contribution that could be invested in CREF to 50%, with the other 50% invested in TIAA. The present rules permit the participants to invest up to 75% of their retirement contribution in CREF. The professor and his university send a monthly payment to CREF, and in return for this payment the professor is credited with a certain number of accumulation units, depending on the current value of the accumulation unit. This current value is determined in almost exactly the same manner as the value of a share in closed-end mutual fund: the current value of all securities in CREF's accumulation fund is divided by the total number of accumulation units outstanding. Over time, the value of the accumulation unit rises and falls with the market price of the securities held by CREF. By contributing a fixed amount each month regardless of the fluctuations in the value of the securities, the participants make use of the principle of dollar averaging.

When the professor reaches retirement, the accumulation units he has purchased are converted into a lifetime income of annuity units, using a special mortality table for annuitants. The computation is the same as that explained in Chapter 9, except that instead of dollars, the computation yields the number of annuity units payable each month. This number of annuity units does not change over the lifetime of the annuitant, but the income produced by each annuity unit will vary with changes in the value of the annuity unit. The current value of the annuity unit will determine the income the retired professor will receive.[10]

The period since the inception of the CREF program has been marked by continued inflation. As an indication of the performance of the CREF program since it was founded, and as an illustration of the variable annuity in practice, the value of the CREF accumulation unit since 1952 is presented in Table 11-3.

## ADVANTAGES AND DISADVANTAGES OF SPECIAL FORMS

The special policy forms examined in this chapter have certain advantages and disadvantages. Both the advantages and the disadvantages arise from the

[10] The monthly amount remains the same throughout the year because the value of the annuity unit is established on an annual basis by CREF.

TABLE 11-3
Value of the CREF Accumulation Unit,
1952–1970

| 1952 | $10.52 | 1962 | $26.65 |
|------|--------|------|--------|
| 1953 | 10.37 | 1963 | 30.83 |
| 1954 | 14.85 | 1964 | 33.96 |
| 1955 | 18.06 | 1965 | 39.08 |
| 1956 | 19.19 | 1966 | 36.33 |
| 1957 | 17.75 | 1967 | 43.78 |
| 1958 | 24.36 | 1968 | 45.35 |
| 1959 | 27.11 | 1969 | 41.78 |
| 1960 | 27.38 | 1970 | 39.19 |
| 1961 | 31.86 | | |

SOURCE: *TIAA-CREF 1970 Annual Report.*

fact that these policies are designed to meet special needs. Because they are designed to meet special needs, these policy forms meet those needs better than any other policy, but since they are designed for special needs, they are often inflexible and meet other needs poorly. Each individual faces different circumstances, and the danger exists that one of the special policy forms may be used in an attempt to fill a need for which it was not designed. Of course, there are some needs that are almost universal. There is little chance of the family income policy being misused, because of the rather general need for protection during the child-raising years. On the other hand, the juvenile insurance policies are often misused, eating up premium dollars that would be better spent on the father.

In addition to the special policy forms discussed in this chapter, there are a number of other more specialized contracts. A number of the more specialized contracts may be unique with a certain company. In addition, many companies modify the basic provisions of the policy forms discussed here. The point is that the variety and type of special policies is limited only by the imagination of the marketing directors of the insurance companies. When properly used, the special policy forms are extremely useful tools for protecting the members of the insured's family against the financial consequences of premature death, or for accumulating a fund for some specific future need such as retirement or education.

## SOME SPECIALIZED USES OF LIFE INSURANCE IN BUSINESS

Although this chapter is concerned primarily with special policy forms and combinations, the following brief discussion of some of the specialized uses to which life insurance may be put by business firms is also included. These programs are discussed here because of their special nature, and it should be noted that they are designed to make use of the various policy forms that have already been discussed.

### Business-Continuation Insurance

The death or disability of the owner of a business, the member of a partnership, or a stockholder of a close corporation may create serious problems for that business. If the business is a sole proprietorship, it may be necessary to liquidate and sell the specific assets, rather than the going business. Any value based on goodwill or earnings may be wiped out. In the case of a partnership, the executor of the estate of a deceased partner may find it necessary to sell the estate's interest at the best offer he can obtain from the surviving partners. Finally, in the case of the corporation, the corporation will continue, but either the heirs of the deceased stockholder may not desire to continue their ownership, or the remaining stockholders may not wish to share the ownership and control of the corporation with the heirs.

The ideal solution to these problems is to make prior arrangements for the sale of the individual's interest in the business prior to his death through a buy and sell agreement, under the terms of which each owner agrees that his share of the business is to be sold to the remaining owners at his death, and each owner agrees to buy the share of a deceased owner. In the case of a proprietorship, the parties to the purchase agreement may be the owner and an employee or the owner and a competitor. The agreement may contain a formula to be used in setting the value of the business at the time of sale, thus eliminating difficulty at that time.

It is possible to have a business purchase agreement without a funding arrangement. The partners may have sufficient cash or liquid assets to enable a survivor to purchase the interest of the decedent for cash. But this would be a very unusual situation, particularly in a growing business, where the partners have been plowing back the profits into the business. The most satisfactory method of funding is to purchase business life insurance on the lives of the owners; the partners, partnership, stockholders, or the corporation, whoever is to be the purchaser, would pay the premiums and own the policies on the life of the party whose interest in the business is to be purchased upon his death. By this method, it is possible to have the business purchase agreement fully funded at all times.

The operational aspects of the funding may vary, depending on the circumstances. Under the arrangement known as a "cross-purchase plan," each partner or stockholder carries enough life insurance on the lives of the others to permit the purchase of a proportionate share of a deceased member's interest. For example, if Abner, Baker, and Cole each own one-third of a business valued at $300,000, Abner would buy $50,000 in life insurance on Baker and Cole, Baker would buy a $50,000 policy on both Abner and Cole, and Cole would buy $50,000 on each of Abner and Baker. If one partner dies, the remaining two will receive sufficient proceeds from their policies on his life to permit them to purchase his interest.

As an alternative, the policy on each owner could be purchased by the firm itself. Under this arrangement, known as the "entity plan," the firm owns the policies and is the beneficiary. The premiums paid on such insurance is not deductible as an expense for tax purposes, however, the income tax exemption of life insurance proceeds payable by reason of death applies whether the beneficiary is an individual, a partnership, a trustee, or a corporation. Under the entity plan, the partnership or corporation purchases the interest of the deceased owner, and the interest of the survivors is increased proportionately.[11]

### Key Man Insurance

One of the most valuable assets of any business is the skill of its employees. Since every employee contributes to the success of a business, the death of any employee is a source of loss to the firm. The extent of this loss varies with the contribution of the individual to the success of the firm. Those employees who make a critical contribution to this success are key employees, and in the case of these employees the risk of loss to the firm may be sufficiently great to warrant insurance protection. The key man may be a crucial factor in sales, production, finance, management, or some combination of these functions. The determining characteristic is that the success or failure of the firm depends to a great degree on his continued efforts. In many cases, this key man will be the owner; in some he will be a partner or employee; he may even be a stockholder. In any case, when the loss of an individual connected with the business would cause a financial loss through imperiled credit, loss of leadership, reduced profits, or reduced ability to secure new business, the firm has an insurable interest in that individual.

One of the most difficult aspects of insuring a key man is the determination of his value. The valuation may be based on an estimate of the probable loss of income that might result from his loss, based on estimates of the decline in sales or general slowdown of operations. Additionally, it may be based on an

---

[11]There is a distinction between a stock retirement agreement and a stockholders buy and sell agreement. A stock retirement agreement is an agreement between stockholders and a corporation whereby the corporation agrees to purchase the stock of the corporation owned by the stockholder upon his death. There is usually no agreement that the stock will be retired. Such stock may be held in the treasury or canceled. The term "stockholders buy and sell agreement" is generally used to describe an agreement for purchase and sale between stockholders, the survivors to buy the stock of the deceased stockholder.

estimate of the additional expense involved in obtaining a replacement, including the costs of finding, hiring, and training a comparable individual. In the last analysis, the determination of the value of the key man will be an educated guess, based on a combination of the above factors.

The type of insurance used to insure the life of the key man will vary. If the financial indemnification the policy represents is the only objective, then term insurance will probably fill the need as well as any. However, in many situations, other goals are included in the plan. When permanent insurance is selected as the means through which the key man is to be insured, the plan may take the form of a split-dollar plan which is discussed below.

### The Split-Dollar Plan

Split-dollar insurance is the name given to an arrangement whereby an employer and an employee share the premium cost of an insurance policy on the life of the employee. The employer and employee usually enter into an agreement which provides that the employer will contribute a portion of each annual premium equal to the increase in the tabular cash value resulting from such premium payment. The employer will collect the balance of such premium from the employee.

The employer is usually the owner of the policy. The employer is also the beneficiary of the policy to the extent of an amount equal to the cash value as of the date to which premiums have been paid at the time of the employee's death less any indebtedness. The employee's wife or other personal beneficiary is designated as beneficiary to the extent of any balance of the death proceeds. Under the basic split-dollar plan, it is provided that the employer may not change the portion of the beneficiary designation dealing with the insured's personal beneficiary without the consent of the insured. Where the parties wish to have the proceeds of the policy excluded from the insured's gross estate for federal estate tax purposes, it is usually provided that the designation of the insured's personal beneficiary may not be changed without the consent of such beneficiary.

Many concrete benefits accrue to an employee under a split-dollar plan. First, the employee is afforded the opportunity of obtaining additional life insurance with a minimum outlay of his own funds. In addition, split-dollar insurance has the advantage of being permanent insurance—not term insurance—and can be continued beyond retirement age. Finally, split-dollar insurance provides an incentive and an inducement for the employee to remain with the firm.

One drawback to the basic split-dollar plan is that the amount payable to the insured's personal beneficiary decreases year by year as the cash value of the policy increases.

### Deferred Compensation

Deferred compensation is an arrangement in which the employer agrees to make future payments to the employee after retirement or future payments to the employee's widow if he should die before retiring. Such an arrangement usually involves a desire on the part of the employer to retain the services and loyalty of his key personnel. The employee also derives a benefit from such an arrangement, because it defers the receipt of income until a time when the tax burden is usually not as great; ordinarily, a person's income after retirement is lower in amount and he is in a lower income tax bracket. The employee incurs no current federal income tax liability prior to retirement under an orthodox deferred compensation agreement, because the employer's mere promise to pay, not represented by notes or secured in any way, is not regarded as the receipt of income by a cash basis taxpayer.

Employers often find it advisable to obtain a life insurance policy on the life of the employee to fund the deferred compensation agreement. If the employee lives to retirement age, the employer will use the cash surrender value of the policy to make monthly payments to the employee. When the employer surrenders the policy, the amount received by the employer is subject to Federal Income Tax to the extent that it represents a return over the employer's contribution. Amounts payable to the employee are fully taxable when received.

If the employee dies before he retires, the proceeds of the policy on his life provide the amount which will be paid by the employer to the employee's widow. The death proceeds received by the employer are free from income tax, but the amounts paid by the employer to the widow are generally taxable, subject to a $5000 employee death benefit exclusion. The employer may not deduct the premiums paid for the policy as a business expense, but the amount paid out to either the employee or his widow are deductible if reasonable in amount.

### Questions for Discussion and Review

**1.** Recalling the principles of premium computation discussed in Chapter 9, outline the procedure you would use in computing the premium for a 20-year decreasing term policy issued at age 21.

**2.** The variable annuity represents an apparently successful approach to the problem of providing for retirement in the face of a changing price level. What do you think of the concept of variable life insurance, in which the death benefit would fluctuate with changes in the value of common stocks as does the value of an accumulation unit under the variable annuity?

**3.** Many products are brought to the market because, in the words of the seller, "the consumer demanded it." Do you feel that the return of premium policy or the return of cash value policy were the response of the insurance industry to consumer demands, or do you feel that they were developed for competitive reasons? What is your opinion of these two policies?

**4.** Taking any combination of the basic forms of insurance out of which special policy combinations studied in this chapter are constructed, develop a new policy combination you have never heard of and explain the circumstances under which it would be useful.

**5.** "I have just the policy for you," says your friendly life insurance agent, "it was developed specifically for people in your situation."

(a) It provides $10,000 coverage on you for your entire lifetime.
(b) It will pay an additional $100 per month to your family if you die before your youngest child has reached age 21.
(c) It covers your wife until age 65 for $4000.
(d) It covers each of your children for $1000, which may be converted to $5000 anytime before they reach age 21.
(e) It will pay you $5600 in cash at age 65.
(f) If you die before your youngest child is 21, the company will return all the premiums you have paid in addition to the face.
(g) It pays triple the face amount in the event of accidental death.
(h) It guarantees you the right to purchase additional insurance up to $60,000, even if you become uninsurable.
(i) If you become disabled, the company will even pay your premiums for you.

Identify the policy and the additional provisions included in this policy that was "developed specifically for people in your situation."

### Suggestions for Additional Reading

Greenough, W. C. *A New Approach to Retirement Income.* New York: Teacher's Insurance and Annuity Association of America, 1951.

Gregg, D. W. (ed.) *Life and Health Insurance Handbook,* 2nd ed. Homewood, Ill.: Richard D. Irwin, 1964, Chaps. 8, 9, 42.

Huebner, S. S. and Black, K., Jr. *Life Insurance,* 7th ed. New York: Appleton-Century-Crofts, 1969, Chap. 9.

McGill, D. M. *Life Insurance,* rev. ed. Homewood, Ill.: Richard D. Irwin, 1967, Chap. 7.

Mehr, R. I. *Life Insurance Theory and Practice*. Austin, Texas: Business Publications, 1970, Chap. 7.

Riegel, R. and Miller, J. *Insurance Principles and Practices*, 5th ed. Englewood Cliffs, N.J.: Prentice-Hall, 1966, Chap. 8.

Teacher's Insurance and Annuity Association of America. *TIAA-CREF 1970 Annual Report*. New York: Teacher's Insurance and Annuity Association of America, 1970.

# 12 Health Insurance

*He jests at scars that never felt a wound.*
—William Shakespeare, *Romeo and Juliet*

## INTRODUCTION

There are few areas of insurance that are as confusing to the average individual as the field of health insurance. One reason for this confusion is the bewildering number of health insurance contracts available. Health insurance is a generic term, encompassing several types of insurance contracts, which, though related, are intended to protect against different risks. Until recently, there was little general agreement in the terminology used in referring to health insurance. It was called "accident and health," "accident and sickness," "disability," and a number of other terms, all of which are gradually giving way in favor of the general term "health insurance."

### Classification of Health Insurance

There are two separate types of insurance included in the generic term "health insurance":

1. *Disability income (loss of income) insurance* provides periodic payments when the insured is unable to work as a result of sickness or injury. It may provide benefits only in the event of accidental bodily injury, only in the event of sickness (although sickness coverage is rarely written without accident coverage), or it may cover both contingencies in one contract. Benefit eligiblity is based on a presumed loss of income, but in practice this usually is defined in terms of inability to pursue an occupation.
2. *Medical expense insurance* provides for the payment of the expenses for

**262**

medical care which result from sickness or injury. It provides benefits for expenses of physicians, hospital, nursing and related health services, and medications and supplies. Benefits may be in the form of reimbursement of actual expenses up to a limit, cash payment with specified sums, or the direct provision of services. The medical expenses may be paid directly to the provider of the services or to the insured.

While there are two major classifications of health insurance coverage, medical expense insurance may be further subdivided into hospital expense coverage, surgical expense, regular medical expense, and major medical coverage, making a total of five types of coverage.

### Methods of Marketing

All five types of health insurance are marketed in two principal ways: on a group basis and on an individual basis. Approximately two-thirds of the health insurance in the United States is sold on a group basis. Group health insurance involves much the same principle as does group life insurance. A minimum-sized group is required, and the nature of the group must be such that insurance is incidental to its existence. In other words, the group cannot be organized primarily for the purpose of purchasing group insurance.

The coverages offered under group health insurance plans are much the same as those offered in individual policies. However, the cost is substantially less, because the cost to the insurance company is also less. Group health contracts enjoy relative freedom from adverse selection. The administrative costs of group health, like those of group life, are considerably lower than when the contracts are sold on an individual basis. The employer frequently performs the premium collection by deducting the individual's contribution from his paycheck and then making one premium payment to the insurance company. In addition, employers generally screen claims, help employees fill out claim forms, and perform many of the functions which would be performed by the agent or the company under an individual policy. There is also a lower acquisition cost, since the commission rate paid to the agent on a group policy is far lower than the commission rate on individual policies.

### Types of Insurers

Disability income insurance is marketed by property and liability insurance companies, life insurance companies, and specialty companies that specialize in the field of health insurance. These insurers also market medical expense insurance, but in the field of medical expense coverage they are joined by the Blue Cross and Blue Shield plans.

Blue Cross and Blue Shield plans are nonprofit associations organized under special state-enabling legislation to provide for prepayment of hospital and surgical expenses. The legislation exempts these organizations from many of the insurance laws, sets up certain standards, and recognizes them as charitable and benevolent institutions exempt from most state and local taxes. Even though they are exempt from many insurance regulations, the associations are usually under the supervision of the state insurance department. The Blue Cross plans were originally organized by individual hospitals to permit and encourage group prepayment of hospital expenses. Although there is room for controversy concerning the origin of the movement, the Baylor University Hospital Plan which began in Dallas, Texas, in 1929 is generally credited with providing the working model upon which the principles of hospital expense group prepayment plans could exist. There are 78 Blue Cross plans in operation in the United States, of which 76 are members of the Blue Cross Association, and coverage is available in all but two states. Each plan is generally organized with a board of directors or trustees with members representing the hospitals, the physicians of the area, and the general public. Blue Shield plans occupy approximately the same position in the surgical and medical expense field as Blue Cross plans occupy in the hospitalization field. The Blue Shield plans, which came after the Blue Cross plans, were organized by the local medical societies and are approved by the Blue Cross Commission of the American Medical Association. They provide surgical benefits, and in most cases also include provision for payment for other physician's charges. Usually the Blue Cross and Blue Shield organizations in an area work very closely together. Frequently, the Blue Cross organization handles the administration, enrollment, record keeping, and claim administration for Blue Shield on some type of reimbursement basis.

Claim procedures under the Blue Cross and Blue Shield plans generally differ somewhat from insurance company practices. The claim is usually presented to the physician or hospital, who maintain a supply of the claim forms. The insured may fill out the form, but more commonly this is handled by the physician or hospital. The insured merely submits evidence of coverage, and the purveyors of the service do the rest. Payment of insured amounts is made directly by the association to the physician or hospital, and the insured is billed by them for any excess. Other aspects of Blue Cross–Blue Shield operations are discussed later in this chapter.

## DISABILITY INCOME INSURANCE

Disability or "loss of income" insurance is the oldest of the health insurance coverages, and has been marketed for over 60 years. In addition to being the oldest, it is by far the most important of the health insurance coverages as far as the individual is concerned, for disability income insurance undertakes to replace the income which is cut off when the individual is disabled.

Some authorities would argue that loss of income protection should come even before life insurance. When a man is disabled, his income stops just as surely as if he had died. This "living death" of disability can be economically more severe than actual death. If the breadwinner of the family dies, the family's income stops; if he is disabled, not only does the income stop, but expenses remain the same and in most cases increase. In addition, the chance of loss from disability is greater at most ages than is the chance of death. A recently prepared paper of the American College of Life Underwriters entitled "The Economics of Disability" pointed out:

At age 35, the chance of experiencing total disability of three months or more before age 65 is about 33%. The average length of the disability will exceed five years. Moreover, nearly 30% of all disability cases will be permanent.

This is a distressing prediction to say the least. One man out of three who reaches age 35 will be disabled for at least 3 months before he reaches age 65, and one out of every ten will be permanently disabled.

There is little question of the overwhelming need for some sort of disability income protection. The risk of loss of income resulting from disability is one of the most serious risks the individual faces. Logically, the individual's insurance program should include some type of disability protection. It is rather disconcerting to note that by and large, people neglect this relatively more important coverage in favor of hospitalization and medical expense insurance. Approximately 88% of the population enjoys some form of hospitalization protection, while only about 33% is covered for loss of income protection. A part of this difference can be explained by the fact that hospitalization contracts also cover dependents, but only 58% of those covered under the hospitalization contracts are dependents, which means that 88% of the individuals in the labor force are insured for hospitalization benefits, compared with about 68% who are covered for some form of disability income benefits. The hard, cold fact of the matter is that far too many workers have little or no disability income protection. Health insurance plans should have as their primary objective the restoration of income. This restoration of income should certainly come before health insurance plans which take the form of medical expense benefits.

Ideally, the disability income policy should restore the income of the disabled worker as closely as possible to his income before the disability. Normally, the insurance company will not permit an individual to purchase disability coverage in excess of 75 or 80% of his normal earnings. This limit is necessary to prevent moral hazard. If the worker could purchase a policy that would pay him as much or more than his regular income, there would be an incentive to feign illness and contrive accidents. In addition, there would be little incentive for the worker who was collecting benefits to return to work as quickly as possible.

### Length of Time for Which Benefits Are Payable

Disability income policies offer benefits for varying lengths of time. The length of time for which benefits are payable is one primary factor affecting the premium of a disability income policy. Typically, disability income policies may be written on a short-term basis, providing benefits for 13, 26, 52, or 104 weeks, or they may be written on a long-term basis, providing benefits for 5 years, 10 years, until age 65, or even for the lifetime of the insured. Since most disabilities are of a short-term nature, the company's risk decreases as the length of the contract increases. A 26-week plan does not cost twice as much as a 13-week plan. Since most disabilities will not exceed 13 weeks, the company does not have to pay out twice as much in benefits under a 26-week plan as it does under a 13-week plan. The longer the contract, other things being equal, the lower the cost of the additional protection. In spite of the fact that most disabilities are short-term, there are those cases in which the worker is disabled for a long period of time. He may even be disabled for life. For this reason, the long-term contracts are the most desirable.

### Perils Covered

The disability income policy may provide coverage for loss of income caused by accident, or it may be written to provide coverage for loss of income which results from either accident or sickness. Few companies are willing to sell disability income protection covering the peril of sickness only. The reason, of course, is the moral hazard that would be involved. It is relatively easy to feign sickness, but it is more difficult to feign accidental injury. For the same reason, insurance companies will not sell disability income protection to housewives; it is difficult to determine when a housewife is disabled.

When a disability income policy is written to cover both sickness and accidents, the length of time for which benefits are payable may be different, depending on the cause of the disability. Thus, one policy will pay benefits for 2 years if the disability results from illness, and for 5 years if it results from accident. Long-term contracts often pay to age 65 for sickness and for life if the disability results from accident.

### Occupational–Nonoccupational Disability

Some disability income policies exclude payment of the benefits if the illness or accident arose out of the occupation of the insured and if the insured is entitled to receive benefits under a workmen's compensation law. Such contracts are termed "nonoccupational." Other contracts provide for a reduction in benefits equal to the amount received under workmen's compensation, while still others provide payment of the total benefit of the policy regardless of the occupational or nonoccupational character of the injury.

### Definitions of Disability Income Policies

The definitions are of utmost importance in disability income policies, for the broadness or narrowness of the coverage is based on the definitions of "disability" and "injury."

**Definition of disability.** Different companies define disability in various ways, but most definitions fall into one of three categories:

1. The inability of the insured to engage in his own occupation.
2. The inability of the insured to engage in any reasonable occupation for which he is or might easily become qualified.
3. The inability of the insured to engage in any occupation.

In many cases, the definition of disability is a combination of two of these, defining disability as the inability of the insured to engage in his own occupation for the first 2 years, and the inability to engage in any occupation, or any occupation for which he is suited or might become qualified after the first 2 years. Of course, if the insured is hospitalized, or if a sickness or accident keeps him confined to his bed, he would qualify as being disabled under any of the above definitions.

When the disability results from sickness, some policies also make it a requirement that the insured be confined indoors to collect full benefits for the sickness. Other policies do not require that the insured be confined to the house or a hospital. Under those policies that do not require confinement, if the insured is not able to engage in the occupation specified, but is not confined to the house, some policies allow reduced benefits for a short period of time. This is also referred to as a "convalescent benefit."

**Definition of injury.** There is often a considerable difference in the manner in which the policy defines injury. Different companies define the term in various ways. Virtually all definitions take one of the following forms:

1. Accidental bodily injury
2. Bodily injury by accidental means
3. Bodily injury by violent, external, and accidental means

The distinction between accidental bodily injury and bodily injury by accidental means was explained previously in relation to the double-indemnity provision of the life insurance contract, but perhaps it would be well to review the distinction. Accidental bodily injury is the broader term, requiring only that the result (the injury) must have been accidental. The accidental means clause, on the other hand, requires that not only the result must have been accidental, but in addition, the cause of the accident must have been accidental. The "bodily injury by violent, external, and accidental means" is the narrowest of the three definitions, requiring that both the cause and the effect be accidental, and in addition requiring that the cause be violent and external.

### Waiting Period

The waiting period in disability income insurance acts like a deductible, forcing the insured to bear a portion of the loss himself. Almost all disability income policies have a waiting period of some type. When the policy covers both accident and sickness, the waiting period may apply only to the claims arising as a result of sickness. A policy which covers against loss of income as a result of accident may be written without a waiting period.

The purpose of the waiting period on sickness claims is to avoid the small "sniffle" claims which result in a day or two lost from the job, and to discourage workers from simply taking the day off when they are tired. The waiting period eliminates those claims which would be more expensive to adjust than the benefits would be worth. In addition, the waiting period helps to control the moral hazard involved in disability income insurance. If the insured knows he will not collect under his disability income policy until the eighth day of his sickness, he may be more enthusiastic about getting back to his job than if the insurance benefits were payable from the first day of sickness. Waiting periods of 3, 7, 15, 30, 60, 90, 180, and 365 days are available. A 4-day waiting period is about as short as it is possible to purchase under sickness coverage. The insurance companies would prefer at least a week waiting period. It is possible to purchase disability income policies in which the waiting period of sickness is different from that applying to accident disabilities. One widely used plan is the "1-8-26" plan. This coverage provides benefits from the first day if the disability results from an accident, and from the eighth day if the disability results from illness. The "26" indicates the number of weeks for which benefits are payable.

### Accidental Death and Dismemberment Provision

The coverage provided by this provision is in certain respects similar to life insurance. Disability income policies frequently provide that a certain amount, usually expressed as some multiple of the weekly benefit, will be paid to a beneficiary of the insured if the insured dies by accidental means. This coverage is life insurance of a specific type.

The face amount of the benefit is usually 200 weeks, at the rate specified in the policy, to be paid as a lump sum in the event that the insured is killed. In addition, the face amount of the benefit is payable if the insured loses his sight or any two limbs as a result of an accident. There is a scaled-down range of payable benefits in the event that the worker loses only one arm, leg, hand, or foot.

In addition to being written as a supplementary coverage under disability income policies, the accidental death and dismemberment coverage is sometimes written separately as an independent contract. In such cases, the face amount is specified in terms of a given number of dollars rather than in terms of a number of weeks.

### The Cost of Disability Income

The cost of disability income protection varies, depending on the occupation, age, and sex of the insured, and the length of time for which the benefits are payable, as well as the size of the benefits and the length of the waiting period. The longer the waiting period, the lower the premium. As a matter of fact, the judicious use of a waiting period can permit the individual to obtain far better coverage.

For example, a short-term disability contract written by one company on the 1-8-26 plan has an annual premium of $36.40 per $10 of weekly benefit. The cost of a $50 per week benefit under this contract would be $182 per year. On the other hand, a long-term contract providing $200 per month for life for accident and until age 65 for sickness can be obtained with a 30-day waiting period for about $118. With a 180-day waiting period, the cost of the contract would be $96 per year.

For the family in the lower-income group, a short waiting period may be a necessity. However, the individual should take into consideration other disability income protection which he may have from sick leave. If the length of the waiting period can be increased, the premium reduction may well permit a substantial increase in the amount of benefits or the length of time for which the benefits are payable.

Families in the middle-income group, and by this we mean those families with an annual income of between $6000 and $12,000, should consider a waiting period of at least two weeks. Families in the higher-income group, that is, those earning over $12,000, should be able to carry themselves for 3 months, 6 months, or even a year.

## MEDICAL EXPENSE INSURANCE

### Hospitalization Insurance

Hospitalization insurance is sold under two types of contract: the indemnity contract, which is sold by insurance companies, and the service contract, which is marketed by such organizations as Blue Cross. Either plan may be written to cover the individual or the entire family.

**Indemnity contracts.**    Hospital expense policies are designed to pay the cost of room and board, or some portion of the cost, when the insured is confined to the hospital. Hospital room and board is usually written on a flat daily amount basis, for a specified number of days such as 31, 70, 120, or 365. The contract provides that costs up to the maximum benefit per day (e.g., $30, $40, $50, $60, etc.) will be paid for the number of days specified, while the insured or an eligible dependent is in the hospital. Room and board expense in excess of the amount provided in the policy must be paid by the insured himself. As we saw with regard to the disability income policy, the cost does not increase proportionately with the increase in the number of days. A policy with a 120-day limit will be only slightly more expensive than one with a 70-day limit.

In addition to the room benefit, there is usually a lump-sum payment to cover certain incidental hospital expenses such as the use of the operating room, x rays, drugs, anesthesia, laboratory charges, etc. These miscellaneous hospital expenses may be written on an unscheduled basis, in which case the limit for such expenses is usually some multiple of the daily room limit. Alternately, they may be written on a scheduled basis with a certain maximum for each item, such as $25 for x rays, $30 for ambulance, and so on.

Maternity benefits may or may not be included in the contract. If maternity benefits are included, there is usually a specified maximum payment for this benefit. It is also customary to include maternity benefits only after the dependent has been covered under the policy for 9 or 10 months. In group contracts this condition can be and often is waived.

**Service contracts.**    A service plan provides actual services of the hospital to the insured person for a stated number of days rather than a cash benefit. Service benefits are generally purchased on a group basis through service plans such as Blue Cross. There are presently 78 Blue Cross plans providing hospitalization service benefits.

Blue Cross organizations maintain contracts or agreements with the hospitals in the state or region where each operates, which require the hospitals to guarantee to provide service to the subscribers. Such hospitals are called member hospitals. The member hospitals normally agree to accept certain scheduled fees from the Blue Cross organization as full payment for services rendered to the patient. Most Blue Cross plans provide the patient with a semiprivate room for a given number of days. The number of days varies widely in the different Blue Cross organizations, but on the whole, the plans conform to those sold by commercial insurance companies with 70-, 120-, and 365-day plans. Not all hospitals are members of Blue Cross, and service benefits are usually available only in those that are. When a subscriber is admitted to a nonmember hospital, the type of benefits which will be paid are of the indemnity type. The insured will be reimbursed on a dollar basis equal to the Blue Cross organization's cost of a semiprivate room in a member hospital.

Blue Cross plans generally provide all necessary hospital services and facilities required by the patient without any charge being made to the patient. These services and facilities are generally referred to as "hospital miscellaneous expenses" and correspond to the incidental hospital expenses covered under indemnity contracts.

Maternity benefits also are usually covered under Blue Cross programs. There is a specified maximum payable for this benefit. Like indemnity contracts, most Blue Cross plans require coverage for 9 or 10 months before maternity benefits are payable.

Although Blue Cross is written on a group basis, it is possible for a subscriber leaving the group to continue his membership in Blue Cross on an individual basis. In most cases, the coverage for individual subscribers who are no longer members of the group is somewhat more limited after leaving.

### Surgical Expense Insurance

Like hospitalization, surgical expense insurance is written on an indemnity basis by insurance companies and on a service basis by Blue Shield organizations.

**Indemnity contracts.** Surgical benefit plans marketed by insurance companies are written on the basis of a schedule which lists the amount the policy will pay for a variety of operations. The more difficult the operation, the higher the benefit. Less serious operations are scaled down from the maximum. The schedules are referred to by the maximum amount the policy will pay for the most difficult operation. Thus, there are $200, $300, and $400 schedules. Obviously, a $300 schedule is superior to a $200 one, but, of course, it costs more. A typical schedule might provide the following benefits:

| | |
|---|---|
| Appendectomy | $200 |
| Removal of gall bladder | $250 |
| Complete gastrectomy | $400 |
| Pancreatectomy | $275 |
| Tonsilectomy | $125 |

The actual schedule in the policy would be far more complete. In addition, benefits are payable for cutting operations that are not listed in the policy on the basis of the difficulty involved. The surgical schedule also provides, in most cases, a benefit for the obstetrician's charges for prenatal care and delivery of a baby.

**Surgical service plans.** The Blue Shield organizations provide surgical and physicians' services to subscribers in the same way that Blue Cross plans provide hospitalization benefits. Under the original Blue Shield plans, the participating doctors agree to accept the benefit payable by Blue Shield as their total compensation without additional charge to the subscriber, provided the subscriber's income does not exceed a certain level. More recent contracts agree to pay the full physicians' charges, provided they are "usual, customary, and reasonable."

### Regular Medical Expense Insurance

Regular medical expense insurance is not normally written alone, but must be included with one of the other medical expense coverages (hospital or surgical expense). Regular medical expense coverage pays for visits to a doctor's office or for visits by a doctor to the insured at home or in the hospital. Normally, the amount per visit is $3 or $5, with a maximum number of calls per sickness or injury. In essence, regular medical expense insurance is designed to pay a portion of the physicians' fees for nonsurgical care.

### First-Dollar Coverages

The hospitalization and surgical benefit policies and the regular medical expense policies we have been discussing are commonly written on what is called a "first-dollar basis." They are called "first-dollar coverages" because they require the insurance company to pay for the first costs incurred as a result of accidental injury or sickness. During recent years, the first-dollar health insurance plans have become the object of increasing condemnation as an improper application of the insurance principle.

There has been a persistent increase in the cost of medical care for the average American over the past 20 years, and the increasing cost of medical care has been reflected in the cost of health insurance. As the benefits the insurance companies are required to pay increase, the premiums for health insurance also increase. The proportion of disposable personal income which Americans spend on health insurance has shown a steady increase over the past quarter of a century. In 1940, health insurance premiums, including payments to Blue Cross and Blue Shield, amounted to about 0.4% of disposable personal income. By 1945, it had increased only slightly to 0.5%, but during the next 5 years it doubled, reaching 1% by 1950. By 1955, it was 1.6% and by 1960, it was 2.1%. At the present time, over 2.7% of disposable personal income is spent on health insurance premiums.

Medical care data indicate that hospital and other medical care expenses have reached a point where they are a certainty for the majority of the families in the United States, and it is the certainty of medical expenses that makes first-dollar coverage an improper application of the insurance mechanism. Many insurance authorities maintain that the first-dollar coverages are not insurance at all, but rather "medical prepayment plans," and that they result in the insured paying dollars to the insurance company to perform a budgetary function which he could take care of more economically himself.

There is nothing mystical or magic about the insurance equation. The insurance company must take in a sufficient number of premium dollars to pay all claims, plus an additional amount for expenses and profit. Obviously, if the event insured against is certain to happen to each member of the group, then each member must pay a premium equal to the losses he is certain to incur, plus an additional amount to cover the costs of operating the program. In effect, under first-dollar coverage plans the members simply engage in dollar trading with the insurance company. The insured pays a premium to the insurance company which is his share of the losses of the group. But since each family incurs a certain amount of medical expense which is payable under the first-dollar plans, the effect is that each also pays his own claim.

Most people prefer the first-dollar coverages to a contract with a deductible because there is a better chance of "getting the premium back." Yet the simple fact of the matter is that the members of the group as a whole cannot "get their premium back."

Not all the blame for the first-dollar coverage dilemma can be placed with the consumer. One of the biggest causes of the problem rests with the insurance companies, who attempt to create a product that is salable and then train their salesmen to sell that product. The president of a New York life insurance company recently made the following indictment of the insurance industry on this score:

> If the insurance industry properly trained its sales representatives and we could persuade these men to go out and sell on a needs basis, about one-half of the hospital expense policies presently carried by the insurance buying public with commercial companies would be dropped. Instead they would be purchasing major medical contracts.[1]

Yet it is a simple fact of life that first-dollar coverages are far easier to sell to the average consumer than a contract under which the chance of collecting is lower.

There is nothing wrong with purchasing a medical prepayment plan with the realization that it is simply a budgeting of medical expenses. It is not inconceivable that an individual might choose to have an insurance company budget his medical expenses for him. Some individuals have difficulty providing for any future contingency, no matter how slight it might be. However, this coverage should be obtained only after the individual has arranged protection against the more serious medical expenses that would put his back to the wall financially. The real shortcoming of the medical prepayment plans

[1] Michael H. Levy, "Life Insurance: The Need and the Market," *Life Association News* (October 1963). Levy is President of the Standard Security Life Insurance Company of New York.

is not that they are uneconomical; it is that they do not provide protection against the large losses.

There are illnesses and accidental injuries that involve medical bills that would amount to a financial catastrophe for any family. What happens to family finances when a serious sickness or a lingering disease strikes, requiring an extended stay in the hospital? While such catastrophe losses are far less common than pregnancies, they are far more difficult to bear. It is generally preferable to insure that portion of hospital and medical expenses that would constitute a catastrophic burden for the family, and pay directly out of current income those expenses that can be borne by the family budget without serious hardship. In any case, protection against the large serious loss should come first, with protection against the relatively small certain losses only after the major exposure has been dealt with.

### The Major Medical Policy

The major medical policy is the medical contract that is most appropriate for the large expenses that would be financially disastrous for the individual. The major medical policy fits the insurance principle of protection against large losses. It is designed to eliminate the dollar trading inherent in the insurance contracts that are written on a first-dollar basis, and at the same time provide protection against large losses.

One of the chief distinguishing characteristics of the major medical policy is the high limit per loss and the relative absence of exclusions. The maximum limit is usually $10,000 or more for any one illness or accident, and there is no limitation as to how much of this amount may be spent for doctor bills, hospital bills, private nursing, medicines, or other expenses, so long as the expenses are reasonable and necessary. In general, major medical policies go far beyond the usual health insurance contracts, providing payment for blood transfusions, prescriptions and drugs, casts, splints, braces and crutches, artificial limbs or eyes, and even the rental of wheel chairs.

A second characteristic of the major medical policy is its deductible. Since the major medical policy is designed to cover only the serious illnesses or accidents, a deductible is used to eliminate the small claims. The amount of the deductible may be $100, $200, $250, $300, $500, or even $1000. By eliminating the small claims, the insurance company can offer a high limit at a premium that is moderate in comparision with such a plan on a first-dollar basis.

In addition to the deductible, the major medical policy also provides that the insured and the company shall share the loss in excess of the deductible on some stated basis. Normally, the insurance company pays 80% of the loss in excess of the deductible and the insured pays the other 20%. This share loss or "coinsurance" requirement is necessary because of the broadness of the contract. Once the deductible has been met by the insured, virtually all other medical expenses are covered. In the absence of the coinsurance clause, there would be no inducement to the insured or the doctor to keep the expenses within reasonable limits. Every insured would demand three shifts of nurses, a private room, and just about everything else that he could induce his physician to prescribe for him. The provision requiring him to stand 20% of the cost provides him with a realistic incentive to get well as soon as possible and to keep the charges below the maximum limit of the policy.

As an illustration of how the major medical policy operates, let us assume that the insured in our example has a major medical policy with a $250 deductible and an 80% coinsurance requirement. If the insured should suffer a $1250 loss in connection with hospital and doctor bills, the payment would be made on the following basis:

| | |
|---|---|
| Amount of loss | $1250 |
| Less deductible | 250 |
| | $1000 |
| Insurance company pays 80% of the amount in excess of the deductible | $ 800 |
| Insured pays 20% | $ 200 |

The insured pays a total of $450, the company $800.

There are an almost unlimited number of variations to the major medical plan concept. Some companies make the deductible applicable to a certain period of time, such as a calendar year. Under this form the deductible applies only once per member of the family during the time period. Other policies make the deductible apply on a disability basis, providing that the deductible need be paid only once for any single disability. In some instances the deductible applies on a family basis if two or more members of the family are injured in the same accident.

The major medical policy is often used in conjunction with a first-dollar coverage plan, which is called the "base plan" in such cases. Normally, when the major medical policy is written in conjunction with a base plan, a "corridor" deductible is used. The "corridor" represents a specified amount of expense which the insured himself must incur before the major medical plan becomes applicable. The deductible amounts to whatever is paid by the base plan, plus the corridor of $50, $100, or $200. Whenever medical bills not covered by the base plan exceed the corridor deductible, the major medical policy becomes operative. Benefits may be payable before the limits of the base plan have been exhausted, since many items are payable under the major medical policy that are not covered under the base plan. Many individuals purchase a major medical policy in addition to a first-dollar coverage policy. On the other hand, many individuals use the major medical policy as their only form of medical expense insurance, preferring to budget the relatively small certain medical expenses to which they are subjected.

**The cost of major medical.**   The factors determing the premium for a major medical policy are the size of the maximum limit, the size of the deductible, and the coinsurance percentage. In addition, the manner in which the deductible applies also affects the premium. The age of the insured is a factor, as, of course, is the size of the family covered. In addition, the area where the insured resides may enter into the premium determination. One company quotes annual rates on the following basis: $10,000 maximum limit, 80% coinsurance with various deductible options available:

Male, age 25–29 with $100 deductible    $49.20
Add for wife in same age group          $51.60
    For 1 child add                 $24.00
    For 2 children add              $46.80
    For 3 or more children add    $68.40

Male, age 25–29 with $500 deductible    $43.80
Add for wife in same age group          $42.00
    For 1 child add                 $12.00
    For 2 children add              $21.60
    For 3 or more children add    $28.80

Thus for a man with a wife and three or more children, the plan with a $100 deductible would cost approximately $170, while the $500 deductible would cost approximately $115.

### Comprehensive Major Medical

An even more recent development than the major medical plan, the "comprehensive major medical," combines the best features of a base plan and the major medical contract into a single policy. The distinction between the comprehensive major medical and the old major medical policy is the size of the deductible. Under a comprehensive plan, the deductible may be as low as $25. Virtually all comprehensive plans are currently available only on a group basis.

## LIMITED HEALTH INSURANCE POLICIES

There are a substantial number of health contracts on the market that by their very nature are limited. They are normally referred to as "limited policies" and often bear the admonition on the face of the policy, "This is a limited policy. Read the provisions carefully." The nature of the limitation varies. The policy may provide protection against only certain types of accidents, or it may provide coverage against only certain types of disease.

*Travel accident policies* are a good example of the limited health contract. It is important to read such policies carefully to determine the exact extent of the coverage. Some travel accident policies provide coverage only if the insured is killed while a passenger on a public transportation facility. Other travel accident policies provide payment in the event of death as a result of an automobile accident. There is even a limited policy marketed in Chicago that limits payment to the event that the insured is killed in an automobile accident which takes place on one of the city's expressways.

*The dread disease policy* is an example of a limited sickness policy. This contract provides protection against the expense connected with certain diseases such as polio, cancer, meningitis, and certain others.

## INDIVIDUAL HEALTH INSURANCE POLICY PROVISIONS

There has never been a "standard" health insurance policy, and as a result the prospective insured must face a bewildering array of contracts. While it is difficult to state that this type of policy or that type of policy is best, there are certain elements that should be considered.

### Continuance Provisions

The right to continue a health insurance contract may be crucial for the insured, particularly if he has become otherwise uninsurable. Since health insurance contracts provide coverage for a specified term, the absence of a cancellation provision does not guarantee continuing protection, for even when it cannot cancel, the insurer may retain the right to refuse to renew the contract. Individual health insurance policies have a variety of provisions stating the respective rights of the company and the insured to continue or discontinue the policy. There are three types of contracts that cannot be cancelled during the term and in which a guarantee to renew is provided. In addition, there are three forms in which the contract may either be cancelled or in which there is no guarantee of renewability. The six main types of policies, classified according to their continuance provisions are:

1. *Noncancellable.* Noncancellable policies provide the most liberal continuation provision. The noncancellable policy is a continuous term policy which guarantees the insured the right to renew for a stated number of years or to a stated age (normally 60 or 65), with the premium at renewal guaranteed. The guaranteed renewal rate is of critical importance. A provision which permitted adjustment of premiums at renewal time could be the same as a denial of the right

to renew, for a substantial increase in premium might make it impossible for the insured to renew. In trade jargon, these policies are called "noncan."

2. *Guaranteed renewable.* In addition, the policy may be written on a noncancellable basis with the right to renew guaranteed, but with a provision permitting the company to adjust the premium for an entire class of insureds. While the premium rate for renewal is not guaranteed under the guaranteed renewable contract as it is under the noncancellable policy, the company may not increase the rate for a single individual, but only for an entire class.

3. *Conditionally renewable.* Conditionally renewable policies are continuous term policies under which the insurer may terminate the contract by nonrenewal under certain conditions stated in the contract. This form provides some guarantee of continuance, but far less than either of the above.

4. *Renewable at the company's option.* Some continuous term policies are renewable only at the option of the company. This in effect means that the insured has no guarantee whatsoever with regard to continuation.

5. *No provision.* Policies which have no provision with respect to continuation are simply single term policies. They provide coverage for the stated period, with no provision for renewal.

6. *Cancellable.* A contract that may be terminated by the insurer during its term is called a cancellable policy. The provision relating to cancellation normally requires the company to give the insured a specified number of days of notice. Under a cancellable policy, not only does the insured lack a guarantee with respect to continuation at the expiration of the policy, but his coverage may be terminated during the policy period as well.

For rather obvious reasons, the noncancellable policy is more expensive than the guaranteed renewable policy, and the guaranteed renewable policy is more expensive than a conditionally renewable policy. While it has been pointed out that only a very small percentage of the policies not written on a noncancellable basis are refused renewal, the loss of health insurance at the time when it is most needed might be a serious financial blow.

## Uniform Provisions

In an attempt to induce some uniformity in conditions and operating procedures in health insurance contracts, the various states have enacted laws requiring that certain provisions recommended by the National Association of Insurance Commissioners (NAIC) be included in all individual health insurance policies. These laws provide that policies submitted to the state insurance departments must be drafted according to the standards imposed by the uniform provisions proposed by the NAIC and meet certain other requirements. Some requirements of the laws have to do with style, arrangement, and size of type.

There are 23 uniform provisions; 12 of these are required, and must be included in every contract. The other 11 are optional, and in some cases may be omitted. An insurance company may reword any of the provisions, provided it is not less favorable in any respect to the policyholder or the beneficiary.

**Provision 1—entire contract; changes.** This first provision is important to the policyholder because it guarantees that his contract cannot be changed or modified unless the change is authorized by an officer of the company and notice is attached to the contract. As in the case of life insurance, a copy of the application is generally attached to and made a part of the policy. Other papers which may be attached include riders providing additional benefits and waivers excluding specific impairments. The wording of this provision is quite similar to that of the life insurance contract:

Provision 1—Entire Contract—Changes—This policy, including the endorsements and the attached papers, if any, constitutes the entire contract of insurance. No change in this policy shall be valid until approved by an executive officer of the insurer and unless such approval be endorsed hereon or attached hereto. No agent has authority to change this policy or to waive any of its provisions.

**Provision 2—time limit on certain defenses.** This provision is the approximate equivalent of the incontestability provision of the life insurance contract. It provides that except for fraud, misstatements are not grounds for voiding the policy after 3 years. The purpose of this provision is the same as that of the incontestability clause in life contracts. The policyholder has the right to know that when he is disabled, the company will not refuse to pay the benefits. The wording of this standard provision is as follows:

Provision 2—Time Limit on Certain Defenses: (a) After three years from the date of issue of this policy no misstatements, except fraudulent misstatements, made by the applicant in the application for such policy shall be used to void the policy or to deny a claim for loss incurred or disability (as defined in the policy) commencing after the expiration of such three-year period. (b) No claim for loss incurred or disability (as defined in the policy) commencing after three years from the date of issue of this policy shall be reduced or denied on the grounds that a disease or physical condition, not excluded from coverage by name or specific description effective on the date of loss, had existed prior to the effective date of coverage of this policy.

**Provision 3—grace period.** Years ago, insurance policies expired at noon on the day the premium was due if not paid. If the policyholder became disabled that afternoon, he received nothing. Now, policies must allow extra time beyond the due date in which the policyholder may pay his premiums. The number of days specified in the Uniform Policy Provisions Law is not less than 7 for weekly premium policies, 10 for monthly policies, and 31 for all other policies. The provision states:

> Provision 3—Grace Period: A grace period will be granted for the payment of each premium falling due after the first premium, during which grace period the policy shall continue in force. (The length of the grace period may vary depending upon mode of premium payment and company practice.)

A policy which contains a cancellation provision may add, at the end of the above provision: "subject to the right of the insurer to cancel in accordance with the cancellation provision hereof."

**Provision 4—reinstatement.** Although a policy has lapsed for nonpayment of premium, it can be reinstated by the acceptance of an overdue premium by the company or one of its agents unless a reinstatement application is required and a conditional receipt for the premium is given. Then it will be reinstated on approval, or within 45 days without approval except when the applicant has been notified that reinstatement has been refused. The reinstated policy covers accidents occurring only after the reinstatement date and sickness originating 10 days or more after that date. Otherwise, the policy is exactly the same as it was before, unless the company has required any modification in order to justify reinstatement.

**Provision 5—notice of claim.** Under this provision, the policyholder is required to furnish the company with a notice of claim within 20 days, or as soon as reasonably possible. Notice to an agent is considered sufficient. An additional requirement may be inserted in policies paying benefits for more than 2 years, which states that the insured should give the company notice of claim every 6 months, unless he is legally incapacitated.

**Provision 6—claim forms.** This provision places the burden on the company, once it has been notified of the claim, to furnish claim forms within 15 days. If claim forms are not furnished, then the insured shall be deemed to have complied with all requirements of provision 7.

> Provision 6—Claim Forms: The insurer, upon receipt of a notice of claim, will furnish to the claimant such forms as are usually furnished by it for filing proofs of loss. If such forms are not furnished within fifteen days after the giving of such notice, the claimant shall be

deemed to have complied with the requirements of this policy as to proof of loss upon submitting, within the time fixed in the policy for filing of proofs of loss, written proof covering the occurrence, the character and extent of the loss for which claim is made.

**Provision 7—proofs of loss.**    This provision sets the time limit within which a proof of loss must be filed. The policyholder must furnish a written proof of loss within 90 days after the termination of the period for which the company is liable. However, the provision states further that failure to furnish the proof of loss within the 90-day period shall not invalidate the claim if it was not possible for the insured to file the proof of loss. Except in cases of legal incapacity, the proof of loss must be filed within 1 year from the date otherwise required.

**Provision 8—time of payment of claims.**    This provision states that as soon as the proof of loss is received by the company, the benefits are payable. Income benefits are payable at specified intervals not less frequently than monthly.

**Provision 9—payment of claims.**    This provision designates to whom benefits will be paid so that settlement of claims can be made promptly by the company without costly legal investigation. The basic provision provides that payment for loss of life will be made to the insured's estate if no beneficiary has been named.

> Provision 9—Payment of Claims: Indemnity for loss of life will be payable in accordance with the beneficiary designation and the provisions respecting such payment which may be prescribed herein and effective at the time of payment. If no such designation or provision is then effective, such indemnity shall be payable to the estate of the insured. Any other accrued indemnities unpaid at the insured's death may, at the option of the insurer, be paid either to such beneficiary or to such estate. All other indemnities will be payable to the insured.

In addition, a "facility of payment clause," similar to the one used in the field of industrial insurance may be used, which provides that the company may pay up to $1000 to any relative by blood or marriage of the insured or beneficiary who the company believes is entitled to receive it. A second optional addition to the payment of claims clause permits the company to make payment promptly and without red tape directly to a person or hospital rendering service.

**Provision 10—physical examinations and autopsy.**    This provision entitles the company at its own expense to make physical examinations of the policyholder at reasonable intervals during the period of the claim and to make an autopsy when death benefits are payable, provided it is not prohibited by law.

**Provision 11—legal action.** Under certain circumstances, the insured may desire to bring legal action against his own insurance company. Provision 11 imposes two restrictions regarding legal action by the insured. First, the company has 60 days in which to investigate a claim, during which the insured cannot take legal action. Second, no legal action may be brought under the policy unless it is brought within 3 years from the date that the proof of loss is required to be filed.

**Provision 12—change of beneficiary.** Unless the policyholder has specifically denied himself the right to change the beneficiary, he may change the beneficiary or assign the policy as he wishes. The change of beneficiary provision reserves this right to the insured and provides that consent of the beneficiary is not required for surrender or assignment of the policy.

All of the 12 preceding provisions are required by the Uniform Policy Provisions Law.

### Optional Provisions

Any or all of the 11 optional provisions listed below may be included in individual health insurance policies.

**Optional provision 1—change of occupation.** In many types of health insurance the occupation of the insured is an important factor in the rating structure. The change of occupation provision permits an adjustment of the benefit payable if the insured has changed to a more hazardous occupation. In a sense, this provision works much the same as the misstatement of age provision of the life insurance contract. If the insured purchases a policy paying the premium for a relatively unhazardous occupation, and then changes his field of employment, the benefits payable will be reduced to the amount which the premium paid would have purchased at the more hazardous classification. In the event that the insured changes to a less hazardous occupation, the premium rate is reduced accordingly and any overpayment will be refunded to the insured upon request.

**Optional provision 2—misstatement of age.** Under this provision, the policyholder is protected when an error is made regarding age. The policy is not voidable, but like the life insurance contract, the amount of the benefit payable is adjusted.

**Optional provision 3—other insurance in this insurer.** This provision protects a company against excess coverage and the moral hazard by limiting the amount of coverage that will be carried by the company. If a policyholder already has coverage with the company which, with the additional policy provides benefits in excess of some maximum allowed by the company, only the maximum is payable and the excess premiums will be returned to the policyholder or his estate.

**Optional provision 4—insurance with other insurer.**   This provides that if a policyholder has duplicate coverage on an "expense incurred basis" with other companies and does not notify the insurer of the other insurance, the liability of the insurance company will be limited to its proportionate share of the expenses incurred. The premiums for the unused portion are refunded to the insured.

**Optional provision 5—insurance with other insurer.**   This option is the same as optional provision 4, except that it relates to all benefits other than expenses incurred.

**Optional provision 6—relation of earnings to insurance.**   This provision is generally known as the "average earnings clause," and it may be used only in noncancellable and guaranteed renewable contracts. It protects the company from the moral and morale hazard which would result if disability benefits payable were greater than the normal income of the insured. The wording provides that if, at the time disability commences, the insured's total disability income exceeds his earned income, or his average earned income for the preceding 2 years (whichever is greater), the income benefits under the policy will be reduced proportionately. In no case, however, will the benefits under all policies be reduced to less than $200. Premiums for the excess coverage are returned to the insured.

**Optional provision 7—unpaid premium.**   This clause states that the company may deduct from a claim any unpaid premium which is due.

**Optional provision 8—cancellation.**   The cancellation clause gives the company the right to cancel at any time with at least 5 days notice. Excess or unearned premiums must be refunded. Of course, cancellation does not affect any claim originating before cancellation.

**Optional provision 9—conformity with state statutes.**   Although this is an optional provision, some states require that it be included. It amends the policy, if necessary, so that it will conform to minimum state requirements.

**Optional provision 10—illegal occupation.**   This provision states that the company is not liable for loss resulting from any felony or illegal occupation.

**Optional provision 11—intoxicants and narcotics.**   This provision is similar to the preceding clause, and relieves the company of liability for losses while the insured is under the influence of liquor or narcotics. For numerous individuals this is obviously a very restrictive provision.

This long list of policy provisions may seem to the reader to be a tedious exercise in learning, but these provisions are of the utmost importance. The standard provisions outline the rights and privileges of the policy-holder, and do not, in general, present much of a problem in buying insurance. The optional provisions are not included in all contracts, and in examining a contract to be purchased, the existence of any of them should be a consideration. The principles involved in the purchase of health insurance will be discussed in Chapter 14.

## THE PROSPECT OF A NATIONAL HEALTH INSURANCE PLAN

Our discussion of health insurance would not be complete without at least a brief mention of the current discussion concerning the inadequacies of our present health delivery and financing systems and the movement toward a national health insurance program.

### Deficiencies of the Present System

Rapidly rising costs of providing health care, dissatisfaction with current health delivery arrangements, deficiencies in private insurance as a technique for financing health care, and inadequate health care services for the poor and residents of rural and inter-city ghetto areas are among the problems that have raised important questions concerning present methods of financing and delivering these services. Although U.S. medical research in most fields is the most advanced in the world, and in spite of the fact that many U.S. hospitals are the best equipped in the world, the U.S. has been slipping behind other nations in the key indices of national health. Other countries spend a smaller percentage of their Gross National Product on health services and get in return better medical care, lower infant mortality rates, longer life expectancy, and fewer people dying in the productive years of their lives. In infant mortality, the U.S. now ranks fourteenth, behind many Western European countries. Men live longer in seventeen other countries, and women live longer in ten other countries.

It has been pointed out that a part of the poor record is a result of the uneven distribution of health care. In spite of the fact that their need is probably the most acute, the poor have had only limited access to health care. Until 1965, when the Medicare program was added to the Social Security Act, the aged also had only limited access to health care. Even before the 1960s, it was apparent that these two groups (the aged and the poor) were suffering because of inadequate protection against the rising costs of medical care. In 1965, after considerable debate, congress enacted legislation providing some relief for each group. In the case of the aged, the Medicare program provided comprehensive medical care for most persons over 65.[2] The program commonly called Medicaid was designed to provide increased assistance for medical costs of the poor; it was another amendment to the Social Security Act, Title XIX. The Medicaid program is intended to replace previous programs that covered the medical expenses for persons receiving welfare benefits under the state programs for Aid to Families with Dependent Children (ADC), Aid to the Blind, Old Age Assistance (OAA), and the totally and permanently disabled. The intent of the Medicaid program is to encourage the states to increase medical assistance to the indigent, regardless of age, whose income and resources are regarded as insufficient to pay for health care. Under the provisions of the program, the Federal government pays one-half of the administration cost of state medical assistance programs, and 50–83% of the cost of payments to the providers of services to the needy. The fraction depends on the relationship between the state and national per capita income, with the poorer states receiving larger grants. In spite of the Medicaid program, there are still large segments of the population who do not have access to adequate medical care. Their plight is compounded by the fact that poverty and poor health tend to reinforce each other. Poverty accentuates poor health, and poor health can breed poverty.

Assuring access to health care for the poor is only part of the problem, and pressures for change are coming from sources other than the poor and their advocates. Millions of Americans who have access to health care through private insurance are raising questions about the rapidly escalating costs and the lack of control over such costs. For those who are covered by insurance and for those who are not, the most distressing problem is that of costs—not only the absolute level of health care costs, but the escalation from year to year.

Funds provided through the insurance mechanism by both private and social insurance programs, while making it possible for the majority of the population to get some type of health care, have also distorted the system. Evidence indicates that the reduction in out-of-pocket costs resulting from insurance coverage stimulates the use of health services. On the other hand, the poor frequently dispense with medical care as long as possible rather than face medical bills they cannot pay. In addition, insurance tends to make hospitals less concerned about increasing rates, and doctors less concerned about prescribing health services that are covered by insurance. Indeed, many of the problems in the health care area today may be attributed

---

[2] Medicare provides protection against the high cost of hospitalization, skilled nursing, home health services, and other kinds of medical costs for those over 65. In addition, it provides an option whereby those eligible for the basic benefits under the medical program may purchase subsidized medical insurance to help pay for doctors' services and expenses not covered by the basic plan. The entire Medicare program is discussed in detail in Chapter 13.

to the fact that insurance plans tend to emphasize hospitalization. The result has been the use of such facilities, even when care could have been provided at some other place. For example, since health insurance contracts typically pay for hospitalization but do not cover nursing homes and out-patient care, doctors and patients have tended to utilize the hospitals unnecessarily.

Private health insurance presently covers almost 90% of the civilian population under 65 years of age, but this insurance pays only about one-third of the health expenditures of those covered. Private health insurance is available which would pay a higher percentage of the cost of health care for those insured, but the purchasers have been unwilling to pay the premium necessary for the broader coverage. As health care costs have continued upward, other groups have started to demand the same kind of broad protection that Medicare gives to the elderly.

The simple fact of the matter is that the present systems do not deliver to all segments of the public the high levels of health care that the medical profession currently knows how to deliver, and the care that is delivered is not delivered as economically as present technology would permit. The shortage of physicians and other medical manpower, poorly distributed facilities, and the overutilization of facilities prompted by present insurance arrangements have made adequate health care inaccessible to many and expensive for all. The result has been the growing assertion that private health insurance is unable to meet the nation's health care financing needs.

### The Proposed Solution

Clearly, something is lacking in the U.S. health care system. One thing that every other industrialized country has that the U.S. lacks is some form of national health program or insurance that can deliver adequate care to the bulk of its population. Many observers now believe that a health care crisis exists in the U.S., and that a national health insurance program, coupled with more emphasis on coordinated planning of health services is not only inevitable, but highly desirable. More important, the notion that some form of national health insurance is inevitable is now held among even some of the more conservative elements in our society. As a matter of fact, there is no longer even serious debate about whether we want national health insurance; the debate has moved to the stage where we are trying to determine the type of plan most desirable for the nation. There is even little opposition to the concept that there needs to be an enlargement of the federal government's role, for it seems clear that the poor will need assistance in providing themselves with adequate medical care. However, there is a difference of opinion concerning the extent of the government's role, and the national health insurance proposals that have been made reflect this difference. Two broad approaches are under consideration.

**A government system program.** The insurance plan could be government run and tax financed, somewhat along the same lines as Medicare. This approach is favored by the AFL-CIO, among others. Under such a program, universal compulsory insurance coverage would be financed through payroll taxes and general revenues of the federal government and would be administered through a federal agency. The National Health Insurance bill, sponsored by Senator Edward Kennedy (D-Mass) and Representative M. W. Griffiths (D-Mich) is typical of the plans in this category. It would eliminate private health insurance and substitute a federal insurance system with benefits for hospital, dental, optometric, home and nursing care, and rehabilitation, plus a limited amount of nursing home care and psychiatric care. The plan would be financed by payroll taxes and general revenues. Fifty percent of the cost would be paid by general revenues, 36% from a tax levied on employers, 12% from a tax on employees, and 2% from a tax on the unemployed. Medicare and Medicaid would be absorbed under the program, and overall responsibility for the administration of the program would be vested in the Department of Health, Education and Welfare. In addition, the Kennedy–Griffiths Plan would seek to enlarge and improve the delivery system. It would do this by funding special training programs for physicians, dentists, and other health care workers, providing incentives to move physicians into medically deprived areas and expansion of the Health Maintenance Organizations.[3]

**Incentive-stimulated or mandatory private insurance.** The national health insurance program could consist of a comprehensive form of voluntary insurance, with the government providing incentives to induce employers and employees and individuals to purchase private insurance which would conform to legislated standards. As an alternative, the program could require mandatory health insurance purchased from private insurers. In

[3] It should be noted that the solution to the health care problem is not merely a matter of providing financial resources. Financing methods which permit the individual to obtain health care without incurring direct charges might eliminate financial barriers, but they will not necessarily guarantee that people will be able to obtain health care unless measures are also initiated to increase and redistribute the supply of health care services. For this reason, many of the health insurance proposals include measures to improve the health delivery mechanism. Health Maintenance Organizations, or prepaid medical group practice plans, are prominent in several of the national health insurance proposals. Under the prepaid medical group practice plans, subscribers pay an annual membership fee, in return from which they receive a wide range of health care services. The physicians involved in these plans work for salaries paid by the group rather than for fees from the individual patients. The New York Health Insurance Plan (HIP) and California's Kaiser Permanente plans are the two best known of the prepaid medical group plans. Other plans include the United Mine Workers plans, the Ross-Loos Medical Group in Los Angeles, and the San Joaquin plan. There are currently about 7 million members participating in such plans. The plans have generally been popular because of the relatively low annual fees and fairly successful control of costs.

either case the private insurance industry would be used as a base, with the federal government paying the premiums for those too poor to do so themselves.

The American Medical Association program, called "Medicredit," follows the incentive approach and would encourage individuals to purchase health insurance by allowing them to take part of the premium cost as a direct credit from their income tax. The credit against the income tax would vary inversely with the individual's tax level. A credit of 10% of the premium would be allowed to families with a federal tax liability of $1300 or more, and those with a tax of $300 or less would receive credit for their entire premium. Those with incomes so low as to owe no tax would receive a government certificate to pay for their insurance, with the amount of the credit diminishing as income increases. The government would pay for catastrophic illness coverage for everyone, but the benefits available would be related to the insured's income. Medicare would be retained and a part of Medicaid would be absorbed into the program. The American Medical Associations plan makes no provision for change in the current arrangements for organization or delivery of services.

The Nixon administration's National Health Insurance Standards Act and Family Health Insurance Plan are representative of the mandatory private insurance approach. The Nixon plan consists of two parts: the Family Health Insurance Plan (FHIP) for the needy, which would replace Medicaid and be financed entirely by the federal government, and the National Health Insurance Standards Act, which provides for mandatory purchase of health insurance from private insurance companies. The heart of the Nixon proposal is a requirement that employers provide basic health insurance for all employees and their families, including hospital and out-patient services, medical services, maternity, and well-baby care. Initially, the employer would pay 65% of the cost of such coverage, with the employee paying the remainder. Later, the employer's share would increase to 75%. For the poor and the unemployed, the government would provide coverage through the separate FHIP. The coverage under this plan would cost nothing for a family of four with an annual income of not more than $3000, and families with income above that level would pay a sliding scale. Like the Kennedy Plan, the Nixon proposal would encourage the use of Health Maintenance Organizations, for it would require the employer-sponsored plans to offer HMO membership where available as an option to covered workers. The Nixon plan also proposes increased financial assistance for training of doctors and other medical personnel.

### The Future of National Health Insurance

It appears that a comprehensive national health and hospital plan for all Americans is an idea whose time has arrived, and the only remaining question is the form that it will take. It is impossible to determine at this point in time which of the directions outlined above our national health insurance program will take. It will no doubt involve some form of subsidy to the poor. Only time will tell if it will also include the private health insurance industry.

## Questions for Discussion and Review

**1.** Joe Smith is considering the purchase of a disability income policy and is trying to decide between two policies sold by two different companies. Although both will pay until age 65 for disability arising out of sickness and for lifetime for disability resulting from accident, the cost of one policy is almost twice that of the other. What provisions in the two contracts would you advise Smith to compare?

**2.** "Much of the increase in the cost of medical care can be attributed to unnecessary and undesirable overutilization of health services, often prompted by the existence of insurance." Do you agree or disagree? What policy provisions have been designed to control overutilization of health services?

**3.** Suppose you decide to buy a basic hospitalization and surgical expense policy. What points of coverage would you check if you were presented with two apparently similar contracts, but with substantially different premiums?

**4.** "The major medical policy represents catastrophe protection, yet the deductible provision and the coinsurance provision could result in uncovered expenses that would be catastrophic for some people." Do you agree or disagree with this statement? Why or why not?

**5.** Compare and contrast the typical provisions and benefits of a commercial hospitalization policy with a Blue Cross contract, and a commercial surgical expense contract with a Blue Shield contract.

## Suggestions for Additional Reading

Bickelhaupt, D. L. and Magee, J. H. *General Insurance*, 8th ed. Homewood, Ill.: Richard D. Irwin, 1970, Chap. 27.
Dickerson, O. D. *Health Insurance*, 3rd ed. Homewood, Ill.: Richard D. Irwin, 1968, Chaps. 5–16.

Eilers, R. D. *Regulation of Blue Cross and Blue Shield Plans.* Homewood, Ill.: Richard D. Irwin, 1963, Chaps. 1–5, 8–11.

Faulkner, E. J. *Health Insurance.* New York: McGraw-Hill, 1960.

Gregg, D. W. (ed.) *Life and Health Insurance Handbook*, 2nd ed. Homewood, Ill.: Richard D. Irwin, 1964, Chaps. 21–23.

Huebner, S. S. and Black, K., Jr. *Life Insurance*, 7th ed. New York: Appleton-Century-Crofts, 1969, Chaps. 17, 18.

Levy, M. H. "Life Insurance: The Need and the Market." *Life Association News* (Oct. 1963).

Mehr, R. I. *Life Insurance Theory and Practice.* Austin, Texas: Business Publications, 1970, Chaps. 13, 14.

Riegel, R. and Miller, J. *Insurance Principles and Practice* , 5th ed. Englewood Cliffs, N.J.: Prentice-Hall, 1966, Chap. 18.

# 13 Social Insurance

*The essence of social insurance is bringing the magic of averages to the rescue of millions.*

— Winston Churchill

## INTRODUCTION TO SOCIAL INSURANCE

Most of our discussion in the preceding chapters has been concerned with the approach and techniques of private insurance in alleviating the adverse effects of risk. These techniques are all concerned with attempts to attain economic security, i.e., attempts to assure a continuance of income or the replacement of lost or reduced income. We have examined the life and health insurance contracts that commercial insurance companies make available to individuals through the marketplace. Such contracts provide a means whereby many individuals can protect themselves and their dependents against the loss of income and the additional expenses which death, illness, or accident cause. These private insurance contracts permit the owners or their dependents to maintain an adequate standard of living in the face of undesirable contingencies.

Society as well as the individual is concerned with the problems of economic insecurity, and for many years these problems have been given increasing attention in the United States by the federal and state governments. We cannot deal with all the social and economic programs that are designed to alleviate economic insecurity, since this would involve an almost endless discussion and description of programs involving such things as public assistance for the indigent aged, minimum wages, child labor, antipoverty programs, and even monetary and fiscal policies used to promote economic growth and the maintenance of full employment.

**291**

However, we can and should deal with those programs in which the insurance principle is utilized for the purpose of alleviating the adverse effects of certain risks. Such programs may be included in that category of social security known as "social insurance."

There has always been an assumption in our society that an individual should provide for his own economic security. This is a basic principle that undoubtedly has considerable merit and one that should be maintained as a basic factor in the quest for security in our society. However, there are many circumstances in which for various reasons the attainment of a reasonable degree of economic security for individuals or families is impossible or only partially attainable through the efforts of individuals themselves. In such instances, government programs involving such diverse approaches as the relocation of persons in economically backward areas, minimum wages, and the vast operations of the social insurance programs, have been set up to provide a basic amount of economic security. These programs involve an assumption, not necessarily modern but more formalized and more extensive than before, that if an individual cannot provide for a reasonable level of living through his own efforts, then society should make the attainment of this objective possible.[1]

Social insurance is based on the notion that there are some people in the economy who cannot provide themselves with an adequate standard of living, and that we have a moral obligation to protect any segment of the economy from undue hardship. There are two basic philosophies that relate to the problem of the security of those who are not able to provide themselves with some minimum, adequate standard of living: the social insurance approach and the welfare approach. For better or for worse, our government is going to help the indigent, and the manner in which this help is provided is going to involve some combination of these two approaches. Under the welfare approach, money is taken from those who are not in need and given to those who are, on the basis of demonstrated need. Under the insurance approach, all the people who are not in need at any given time are required to contribute regularly to the insurance fund, out of which some minimum income is paid, *regardless of need*, to those whose regular income is interrupted. The more the social insurance approach is used, the less will be the burden of welfare.

Social insurance differs from private insurance in many respects, but

---

[1] We must admit that many persons, including many students, would disagree with the magnitude of the social approach to the attainment of the objective. However, the various social security programs and their principles have become rather firmly entrenched in our society today. It seems safe to conclude that society is becoming increasingly aware of the necessity of guaranteeing some minimum degree of security to those individuals and families who otherwise would not have a minimum or subsistence level of living.

the most fundamental differences are based on the above purpose of social insurance, i.e., to assure the members of society a minimum standard of living.

### Social Insurance Definition

The Committee on Social Insurance Terminology of the American Risk and Insurance Association defined social insurance as

> A device for the pooling of risks by their transfer to an organization, usually governmental, that is required by law to provide pecuniary or service benefits to or on behalf of covered persons upon the occurrence of certain pre-designated losses under all of the following conditions:
>
> 1. Coverage is compulsory by law in virtually all instances.
> 2. Except during a transition period following its introduction, eligibility for benefits is derived, in fact or in effect, from contributions having been made to the program by or in respect of the claimant or the person as to whom the claimant is dependent; there is no requirement that the individual demonstrate inadequate financial resources, although a dependency status may need to be established.
> 3. The method of determining the benefits is prescribed by law.
> 4. The benefits for any individual are not usually related directly to the contributions made by or in respect of him but instead usually distribute income so as to favor certain groups such as those with low former wages or a large number of dependents.
> 5. There is a definite plan for financing the benefits that is designed to be adequate in terms of long-range considerations.
> 6. The cost is borne primarily by contributions which are usually made by covered persons, their employers, or both.
> 7. The plan is administered or at least supervised by the government.
> 8. The plan is not established by the government solely for its present or former employees.[2]

While this definition is somewhat detailed and complicated, it is an excellent one. In applying the definition to the many and varied social security programs in the United States today, social insurance would encompass the following:

1. Workmen's Compensation Insurance
2. Unemployment Compensation Insurance
3. Old-Age, Survivors, Disability, and Health Insurance

[2] Commission on Insurance Terminology of the American Risk and Insurance Association.

4. Compulsory Temporary Disability Insurance
5. The Railroad Retirement System, Railroad Unemployment, and Railroad Temporary Disability Insurance

**Principles of Social Insurance**

The definition of social insurance given above not only defines social insurance, but in addition indicates many of the areas in which social insurance differs markedly from private insurance. There are certain fundamental principles inherent in the nature of social insurance. The first, and perhaps the most important, involves the emphasis upon the social adequacy of the benefits rather than individual equity in the relationship of costs and benefits. This principle could not be used in private insurance because of the legal requirement, among other things, that premiums must not be unfairly discriminatory. In private insurance, the actuarial value of the benefits under an insurance policy must be related closely to the actuarial value of the premiums paid. Thus, on a comparable basis, if X pays twice the premium for a life annuity as Y, then the life annuity benefit for X must be twice that of Y. Private insurance companies are also obligated to distribute the loss costs of the group to the various insureds in proportion to the loss-producing characteristics of each insured or each relatively homogeneous class of insureds. For example, it would be inequitable to charge a single male operator of an automobile who is age 20 the same premium for automobile insurance as a single female, age 35, who uses her car only for driving to and from Sunday school.

In social insurance, individual equity is secondary in importance to the social adequacy of the benefits. This means that benefits are weighted in favor of certain groups in order that all persons will be provided a minimum floor of protection. In the Old-Age, Survivors, and Disability Insurance program, for example, the benefits are weighted in favor of the low-income groups, individuals with large families, and persons who have been covered under the program for a relatively short period of time. If this were not the case, i.e., if the benefits were directly and proportionately related to average earnings, then the benefits of the substantial number of persons in the low-income groups would not be sufficient to provide the minimum floor of protection. In the basic approach of social insurance, however, the benefits are not divorced entirely from contributions, but are at least loosely related to the earnings of the individual. Therefore, even though social adequacy rather than individual equity is stressed, a second principle involves at least a loose relationship between earnings and benefits.

Third, with few exceptions, social insurance programs are compulsory. This means that, unlike the voluntary choice in private insurance, a person has no alternative but to be a member of the program whether he likes it or not. Compulsion, however, is necessary to the success of a social insurance program because a substantial number of persons, if given their choice, would not use the program at all. The need for compulsion is based, of course, on the lack of equity.

A fourth important principle of social insurance involves the amount of the benefits. In general, the programs are designed to provide only a minimum floor of protection. In private insurance, it is possible in many instances to purchase full protection for a possible loss. However, in social insurance a person must be content with the basic limited benefits prescribed by law. This means that the principle of individual responsibility for his own economic security is still an important principle in our society. Persons are expected, if possible, to supplement the government programs with their own personal savings, investment, and insurance programs.

The fifth principle of social insurance is concerned with the right to benefits. The right is essentially a statutory right and is not based upon a "needs" or "means" test.[3] This means that for an individual to be entitled to benefits, there is no necessity for him to establish a need for the benefit. Therefore, a retired president of a huge corporation will be entitled to benefits even though he will have little need for the income. The right to the benefit, however, is based upon presumed need. For example, a recipient under most programs will discover that continued earnings will have an adverse effect upon the benefits, in that benefits will be reduced or eliminated altogether after a certain level of earnings is attained.

The sixth principle involves what is known as the "self-supporting contributory principle." This means that the social insurance programs are generally self-supporting, and in most instances the support is derived from contributions from employees, employers, and the self-employed. Administrative and benefit costs, then, are not financed from the general revenues of the treasury, but are financed primarily by those who expect to benefit from the programs.[4] This approach is justified on the grounds that it will encourage a more responsible attitude on the part of the program participants in that they will be more inclined to take a personal interest in the sound operation of the program. It could also induce a more responsible attitude on the part of the elected representatives to government.

The seventh principle concerns the funding of the obligations under the programs, i.e., the extent to which reserves are currently accumulated to

---

[3] In many social security programs, e.g., the Public Assistance programs in all states today, the right of a person to benefits is based strictly upon need.

[4] This method of financing is unique to American social insurance programs, because in most other countries in which an extensive program exists, a part or all of the financing comes from general government revenues.

provide for future obligations. In private life insurance, reserve funds normally must be sufficient to equal the difference between the present value of benefits and the present value of future premium payments on the policies involved. In all types of insurance, the reserves must be sufficient so that if the insurance company decided to discontinue business operations, the present reserves plus interest earned upon these funds would meet all obligations on existing policies as they came due in the future. In social insurance, the future obligations are rarely fully funded. This means that the reserves plus interest are only partially sufficient to pay future benefits plus administrative costs. The funding of future benefits in social insurance programs is not as important an aspect of the soundness of the program as in private insurance, because the permanency of the programs along with the taxing power of government makes funding or precise funding unnecessary. However, partial funding does have a leveling effect upon future payroll tax rates. This is important because without the funding, there could be a necessity in the future for substantial increases in tax rates that could have adverse effects upon the operation of a sound program.

The last principle concerns the benefits themselves. These are strictly prescribed by law, and the recipient has no choice as to the type or the amount of benefits.

With these principles in mind, we can now proceed to a discussion of the social security system.[5] Before doing so, however, we must caution the student that the provisions of many of the programs are subject to quick and drastic change, and any description of specific benefits must be considered as subject to change at any time.

## THE SOCIAL SECURITY ACT

The Social Security Act of 1935 stands as the most comprehensive piece of social legislation of its kind in the history of the country. Although social security programs had been in effect in leading European countries for a long time, little progress was made prior to 1935 in promoting such plans in the United States. After a considerable amount of debate in the Congress, the Social Security Act was passed in August of 1935.

Most people think of the Social Security law in terms of the Old-Age, Survivors, and Disability Insurance program and Medicare. In reality, the Social Security Act provided for a substantial number of other important social security programs. Among the more important programs established under the provisions of the Social Security Act of 1935 were:

[5] In this chapter we will limit our discussion to one of the social insurance programs, the Old-Age, Survivors, Disability, and Health Insurance program. Unemployment Insurance and Workmen's Compensation will be discussed in Chapter 23.

1. The Old-Age Retirement Program, later expanded to include survivors' benefits, disability benefits, and most recently, medicare benefits—it is now referred to as the Old-Age, Survivors, Disability, and Health Insurance (OASDHI) program
2. Unemployment insurance programs
3. Federal grants to the states for old-age assistance, aid to dependent children, and aid to the blind
4. Federal grants to the states for maternal and child welfare, for public health work, and for vocational rehabilitation

While the terms "social security" and "social insurance" are often used interchangeably, this is not technically correct. The term social security is somewhat broader than social insurance, including all government measures that are designed to provide a minimum standard of living for members of society. Social insurance consists of measures designed to accomplish this end through the operation of the insurance mechanism.

Old-age assistance, aid to dependent children, aid to the blind, and the other public assistance programs that constitute a part of the nation's social security program are not social insurance programs; they are social security but not social insurance. The basic difference between the social insurance and public assistance programs is that the public assistance programs are designed to meet the "needs of dependent persons not covered under social insurance and of those whose minimum needs exceed their insurance benefits."[6] To receive benefits under old-age assistance, aid to dependent children, or other public assistance programs, the individual must meet a *means test*, which involves proof of actual need on the part of the recipient. There must be a budgetary deficiency or a difference between what is necessary for a minimum standard of living and the income of the individual. Under the social insurance programs, the individual does not have to demonstrate need; he is entitled to benefits as a matter of right under the law. Normally, this right is based on an employment experience. Workers derive their rights to social insurance benefits from the taxes they pay and the taxes or premiums their employers pay on their behalf.

### Old-Age, Survivors, Disability, and Health Insurance

Under the Old-Age, Survivors, Disability, and Health Insurance section of the Social Security Act (commonly called OASDHI), eligible workers and their dependents are insured against the financial disasters connected with death, disability, superannuation, and sickness in old age. Every covered employee enjoys a substantial amount of insurance protection under the social security system. The benefits payable under this law, to

[6] U.S. Department of Health, Education and Welfare, *Annual Report, 1961* (Washington, D.C.: Government Printing Office, 1962), p. 49.

the survivors of a worker when he dies and to the worker and his dependents when he retires, constitute an important part of the individual's life insurance protection. The disability benefits are likewise a crucial part of the individual's health insurance program. Any attempt to fit insurance to the needs of the family must obviously take cognizance of the benefits available under the social security program. The OASDHI program provides four distinct types of insurance coverage.

**Old-age portion.**   Provides a lifetime pension beginning at age 65 for each eligible worker and certain eligible dependents. The amount of this pension is based on his average earnings at some period of time during his working life. There is a flexibility with regard to the selection of the base earning period which permits the worker to select those years which would be most advantageous to him.

**Survivors' portion.**   Provides each eligible worker with a form of life insurance coverage, with the proceeds payable to his dependent children and/or his spouse in the event of his death.

**Disability portion.**   Any worker meeting the eligibility requirements who is totally and permanently disabled is treated as if he had reached retirement age, with benefits payable to him and to his eligible dependents.

**Medicare portion.**   This was added by the 1965 amendments, and was a long-awaited extension of the social security concept in the United States. This newest social insurance program offers people over 65 protection against the high cost of hospitalization, skilled nursing, home health services, and other kinds of medical care. In addition, it provides an option whereby those eligible for the basic benefits under the medical program may purchase subsidized medical insurance to help pay for doctors' services and other expenses not covered by the basic plan.

### Eligibility and Qualification Requirements

Only about 60% of the civilian work force was covered under the original act. The major classes not included were the self-employed, agricultural workers, government employees, and the employees of nonprofit organizations. The coverage of the law has gradually been expanded until virtually all private employment and self-employment is covered under OASDHI—the self-employed, members of the armed forces, previously excluded agricultural workers, employees of nonprofit organizations, and many government employees are now covered. The most recent additions took place in 1965 and 1967. In 1965, medical doctors and interns and persons who earn their living by tips rather than wages were added. In 1967, the clergy and certain previously noncovered state employees were added.[7] Even railroad workers, who have their own retirement system, are permitted to come under OASDHI.[8] Over 93% of the labor force is covered, and most are covered on a compulsory basis. Those not covered under the act are not covered either because they are state, local, or federal employees who are covered under a separate retirement program, or because they work only irregularly and do not meet the earnings requirement for coverage. To qualify for benefits, those who are eligible must have credit for a certain amount of work under social security.

When a worker is covered under the law, a tax is paid on a portion of his wages. In the case of wage earners, the employer and the employee each pay an equal tax on wages. Self-employed persons pay a tax which is slightly less than one and a half times the employee's contribution. In the original act of 1935, the tax was 1% by the employer plus 1% by the employee, which was levied on the first $3000 of earnings. Both the taxable base and the tax rate have gradually been increased over the years as the coverage of the program has been expanded. The base was increased from $7800 to $9000 in 1972. To support the program over the long-range future, the social security tax is scheduled to increase gradually in the future, going from 4.8% of the $9000 base in 1972 to 6.05% of the same base by 1987. This schedule of tax rates is included in the law and is designed to provide sufficient funds to pay the cost of the benefits now provided by the law, and to pay the administrative cost of the program. The schedule of contribution rates is shown in Table 13-1.

Certain costs are financed from general funds of the U.S. Treasury, including the cost of hospital insurance benefits for people who are not insured for cash social security benefits, the government's share of the cost of supplementary medical insurance, and cash payments to certain uninsured people over age 72.

The law makes a distinction as to what constitutes qualification for the various programs under the law. A worker may be "fully insured," "currently insured," or both. The different degrees of qualification are deemed necessary to provide some protection for the families of younger workers. Basically, the current insured status entitles dependents to survivor benefits in the event that the worker dies. Fully insured status is required for the retirement benefits. To become currently insured, the worker must have

[7] Members of the clergy could elect coverage on an optional basis prior to 1967. The 1967 amendments made coverage for clergy compulsory unless they have taken a vow of poverty or file an application for exemption based on religious principle or conscience.

[8] Railroad workers with over 10 years of service are entitled to benefits under a separate program administered by the Railroad Retirement Board. If a worker has less than 10 years of railroad service, his earnings are treated as covered wages under OASDHI for benefit purposes.

TABLE 13-1
**Social Security Contribution Rates**

| Years | Contribution rate schedule for employees and employers (each), percent of covered earnings[a] | | | Contribution rate schedule for self-employed persons, percent of covered earnings[a] | | |
|---|---|---|---|---|---|---|
| | For retirement, survivors, and disability insurance | For hospital insurance | Total | For retirement, survivors, and disability insurance | For hospital insurance | Total |
| 1969–1970 | 4.2 | 0.6 | 4.8 | 6.3 | 0.6 | 6.9 |
| 1971–1972 | 4.6 | 0.6 | 5.2 | 6.9 | 0.6 | 7.5 |
| 1973–1975 | 5.0 | 0.65 | 5.65 | 7.0 | 0.65 | 7.65 |
| 1976–1979 | 5.15 | 0.7 | 5.85 | 7.0 | 0.7 | 7.7 |
| 1980–1986 | 5.15 | 0.8 | 5.95 | 7.0 | 0.8 | 7.8 |
| 1987 and after | 5.15 | 0.9 | 6.05 | 7.0 | 0.9 | 7.9 |

SOURCE: *Your Social Security* (U.S. Department of Health, Education and Welfare, Social Security Administration, March 1971, p. 35.

[a] Contribution rates apply to earnings up to $9000 a year.

had Federal Insurance Contribution Act (FICA) taxes paid on $50 of income for 6 out of the last 12 calendar quarters. A calendar quarter is defined as the first, second, third, or last 3 months of the year. If the employee's total wages for a calendar year equal or exceed the maximum social security base for that year, he is granted 4 quarters of coverage, even though he received no wages in some of the quarters. A self-employed person receives a quarter of coverage for each quarter in which he has $100 in self-employment income. However, a self-employed person must have $400 in net earnings from covered self-employment in a taxable year before any of such net earnings can be counted as self-employment income. Ordinarily, a self-employed person with $400 in net earnings will receive credit for 4 quarters.

To become fully insured, the worker must have had taxes paid in 40 quarters during his working years. Ten years of work in covered employment qualifies the worker for retirement income. In addition, as a concession to those workers who were older when they came under the program, the number of years required for fully insured status may be reduced, depending upon the year the worker reaches age 65 or dies. Under the provisions of the law, an individual may achieve fully insured status if he has 1 quarter in covered employment for every four quarters that have elapsed since 1950 or since December 31 of the year in which the worker

**TABLE 13-2**
**OASDI Qualification Requirements**

| Year worker reaches age 65 or dies (age 62 for women) | Number of quarters required for fully insured status |
|---|---|
| 1970 | 19 |
| 1971 | 20 |
| 1975 | 24 |
| 1979 | 28 |
| 1983 | 32 |
| 1987 | 36 |
| 1991 or later | 40 |

SOURCE: *Your Social Security* (U.S. Department of Health, Education, and Welfare, Social Security Administration, March 1971), p. 8.

became 21. Under this optional qualification basis, it is possible for some individuals to acquire fully insured status with as few as 6 quarters of covered employment. An individual reaching age 65 must have the number of quarters specified in Table 13-2 to be fully insured.

No worker can acquire fully insured status with fewer than 6 quarters of covered employment, and no worker needs more than 40 quarters of covered employment for fully insured status.

### Categories of Benefits

**Retirement benefits.**   The old-age portion of the OASDHI program provides a retirement income at age 65 to those workers who have met the requirements of the law.[9] A fully insured status is required for retirement benefits. If the worker chooses, he may retire at age 62 rather than at age 65. In the case of retirement at age 62, or at any age between 62 and 65, the amount of the retirement benefit is permanently scaled down. The dependents of retired workers may also be entitled to benefits.

*Wife of a retired worker's benefit.*   The wife of a retired worker is entitled to a benefit at age 62. The amount of her benefit is based on the amount of the benefit her husband is receiving.

*Children's benefit.*   The children's benefit is payable to three classes of dependent children of a retired worker.

[9]The amount of the benefits is discussed in the following section of this chapter.

1. Unmarried children under age 18
2. Unmarried children 18 or over who are disabled, provided they were disabled before reaching age 18
3. Unmarried children between 18 and 22 who are full-time students

*Mother's benefit.* The wife of a retired worker who has not yet reached age 62 may still be entitled to a benefit. A mother's benefit is payable to the wife of a retired worker who has in her care a child under 18, or a disabled child over 18, who is receiving a benefit.

*Husband's benefit.* In those cases in which the husband was dependent upon his wife for support, the husband of a retired worker is entitled to a benefit at age 62, based on the amount of his wife's benefit.

**Survivor's benefits.** Benefits are payable to certain dependents of a deceased worker under the survivor's portion of the program, provided the worker meets the requirements of insured status. The benefits which are payable under the survivor's program are the following.

*A lump-sum benefit.* The lump-sum benefit is payable at the worker's death, provided the worker was either fully or currently insured. The amount of this lump-sum benefit is ordinarily three times the amount of the worker's monthly retirement benefit at age 65, or $255, whichever is less.

*A children's benefit.* The children's benefit is payable to three classes of dependent children of a deceased worker:

1. Unmarried children under age 18
2. Unmarried children 18 or over who were severely disabled before they reached 18 and who continue to be disabled
3. Unmarried children between 18 and 22 who are full-time students

The children's benefit is payable if the deceased worker was either fully or currently insured.

*A mother's benefit.* A Mother's benefit is payable to the wife of a deceased worker who has in her care a child under 18 who is receiving a benefit, or a disabled child over 18 who is receiving a benefit. The mother's benefit is not payable to the mother of a full-time student between 18 and 22 who is receiving a child's benefit. The mother's benefit is payable if the deceased worker was either fully or currently insured.

*The widow's benefit.* The widow of a deceased worker is entitled to a benefit at age 62, or a somewhat reduced benefit at age 60. The widow's benefit is also payable to a widow 50 or older who becomes disabled not later than 7 years after the death of the worker or not later than 7 years after the end of her entitlement to the mother's benefit described above. The worker must have been fully insured.

*The widower's benefit.* A widower is entitled to a benefit at age 62, but this benefit requires that the working wife must have been fully insured, and the widower must have been dependent upon his wife for support.

*The parent's benefit.* The parent's benefit is payable to the parents of a deceased worker who are over 62, provided they were dependent upon the worker for support at the time of the worker's death. The worker must have been fully insured.

**Disability benefits.** Disability benefits are payable to disabled workers and their dependents, provided the worker meets certain qualifications under the law. Prior to the amendments of 1967, disability benefits were payable only if the worker was both fully insured and had also worked 20 out of the last 40 quarters. This meant that most young workers did not enjoy disability coverage. The 1967 amendments to the Social Security Act liberalized the qualification requirements under the disability section. If the worker becomes disabled before reaching age 24, he need only have been currently insured in order to collect disability benefits. He must have had 6 quarters of coverage out of the 12 quarters ending when the disability began. If the worker becomes disabled between ages 24 and 31, he must have 1 quarter of coverage for each 2 quarters beginning at age 21 and ending when he became disabled. Workers over age 31 must have 20 out of the last 40 quarters, and must be fully insured. To be eligible for disability benefits, the individual must meet the definition of disability required by the law. Disability consists of a mental or physical impairment which prevents the worker from engaging in "any substantial gainful activity." Thus, if the individual is disabled to the extent that he cannot perform any of the duties connected with his own job, but can still qualify for employment in some other type of work, he would not be considered eligible for disability benefits. However, a person with a severe medical condition might still be eligible and would not be denied benefits if he managed to do a little work. In addition, the disability must have lasted (or be expected to last) for 12 months or longer or be expected to result in the death of the worker.

Everyone who applies for social security disability benefits is referred to the state vocational rehabilitation agency for possible help. These agencies help many people to return to productive employment. If the state vocational rehabilitation agency is satisfied that the worker is disabled, as defined by the Social Security Act, it will certify him as such and he will receive benefits. Disability benefits do not start until the worker has been disabled for 6 full calendar months. After this waiting period, the disabled worker receives a benefit equal to the benefit he would have received at retirement. In addition, his dependents, as defined above under the retirement benefits section, also receive the benefits to which they would be entitled if the worker had retired.

**Medicare benefits.** Almost all persons 65 and over are eligible for health insurance coverage under the medicare benefits portion of OASDHI. Everyone who is 65 or older and who is entitled to a monthly cash social security or railroad retirement benefit is covered automatically. In addition, many persons who do not have enough credit for work covered by social security to qualify for monthly cash benefits are also eligible for the medicare coverage.

The amendment which added medicare coverage to the social security program blanketed-in and provided coverage for almost everyone who became 65 before 1968, regardless of whether they were entitled to social security retirement benefits. For those persons who became 65 in 1968 or later, and who do not qualify for cash benefits under social security or railroad retirement, a special eligibility requirement was established (Table 13-3). Such persons must have some work credit in order to qualify, with the amount of credit required depending on the age of the individual. Eventually, the requirement for medicare will be the same as for retirement (i.e., 40 quarters).

Although this discussion may have seemed complicated, the nature of

**TABLE 13-3**
**Special Medicare Qualification Requirements for Persons Reaching Age 65 after 1968**

| Year age 65 is reached | Quarters required | |
| --- | --- | --- |
| | Male | Female |
| 1968 | 3 | 3 |
| 1969 | 6 | 6 |
| 1970 | 9 | 9 |
| 1971 | 12 | 12 |
| 1972 | 15 | 15 |
| 1973 | 18 | 18 |
| 1974[a] | 21 | 20 |
| 1975[a] | 24 | 21 |

SOURCE: *A Brief Explanation of Medicare* (U.S. Department of Health, Education and Welfare, Social Security Administration, May 1969), p. 3.

[a]A woman reaching age 65 in 1974 or after, or a man who reaches age 65 in 1975 or after needs the same number of quarters to qualify for medicare as is required for fully insured status. See Table 13-2.

**TABLE 13-4**
**Insured Status Required for OASDHI Benefits**

| Benefit | Insured status required of worker |
| --- | --- |
| Survivor benefits | |
| Children's benefit | Fully or currently insured |
| Mother's benefit | Fully or currently insured |
| Dependent parent's benefit | Fully insured |
| Widow age 60 or over | Fully insured |
| Widower age 62 or over | Fully insured |
| Lump-sum death benefit | Fully or currently insured |
| | |
| Retirement benefits | |
| Retired worker | Fully insured |
| Wife of retired worker | Fully insured |
| Child of retired worker | Fully insured |
| Husband of retired worker | Fully insured |
| | |
| Disability benefits | |
| Disabled worker | 6 of last 12 quarters if under age 24 |
| Dependents of disabled worker | 1 of every 2 quarters since age 21 if between ages of 24 and 31; 20 of last 40 quarters and fully insured if over age 31 |
| | |
| Medicare benefits | Entitled to cash benefits under social security or railroad retirement or have reached age 65 before 1968, or meet special eligibility requirements |

SOURCE: *Your Social Security* (U.S. Department of Health, Education and Welfare, Social Security Administration, March 1971), p. 34.

the qualification requirements can be summarized rather concisely, and while all the qualification requirements are important, some seem to be more so than others. The children's and mother's benefits require only that the worker have been fully or currently insured. To be eligible for any retirement benefits, the worker must have been fully insured. Table 13-4 summarizes the qualification requirements for the various benefits under OASDHI.

### Amount of Retirement, Survivors, and Disability Benefits

All benefits under the old-age, survivors, and disability portion of the program are based on the past earnings of the insured worker. The process used in determining the amount of benefits under any of the programs involves the same technique, for all benefits are based on the amount of the benefit to which the worker is entitled at retirement. The amount of the retirement benefit for each worker is based on his annual average earnings during a portion of his income earning years. Only earnings after December 31, 1950 are counted in estimating the annual average earnings of the individual. To compute the annual average earnings of the insured, simply divide his earnings during the period of time since 1951 by the number of years:

1. Count the number of years beginning with 1951 up to the year the individual dies or retires. (The year he dies or retires is not included.)
2. Take the total taxed earnings in each year. The total income of the insured is not counted, only that portion of total earnings upon which taxes were paid.

| | |
|---|---|
| 1951–1954 | $3600 was the maximum taxable |
| 1955–1958 | 4200 was the maximum taxable |
| 1959–1965 | 4800 was the maximum taxable |
| 1966–1967 | 6600 was the maximum taxable |
| 1968–1971 | 7800 was the maximum taxable |
| 1972– | 9000 was the maximum taxable |

3. The insured is permitted to ignore up to 5 years if he chooses. This permits him to eliminate any years in which he has had low earnings or in which he did not have taxable income.
4. Divide the income taxed for the period since 1951 (excluding 5 years) by the number of years in which this income was earned.

The insured in the example has annual average earnings of $5400. The years 1951, 1953, 1962, 1966, and 1969 are dropped, since they are the five lowest. The remaining years total $91,800. Divided by the number of years (17), the annual average earnings are $5400.

Once the average annual earnings of the worker have been determined, they are converted into a "Primary Insurance Amount," using a table prescribed by law. The table provides for a higher percentage of the annual average earnings at lower income levels than it does for higher incomes.

All other benefits are based on the worker's Primary Insurance Amount. If the worker chooses to retire at age 62, he will receive a scaled-down benefit, based on a percentage of his Primary Insurance Amount. Benefits payable to dependents of a retired worker or to the survivors of a deceased worker, or to a disabled worker and his dependents are also based on the worker's Primary Insurance Amount. Some of the more common benefits are the following:

**Example**

| Year | Earnings | Taxable | Amount taxed |
|------|----------|---------|--------------|
| 1951 | $3000 | $3600 | $3000 |
| 1952 | 4000 | 3600 | 3600 |
| 1953 | 3500 | 3600 | 3500 |
| 1954 | 3600 | 3600 | 3600 |
| 1955 | 4200 | 4200 | 4200 |
| 1956 | 4200 | 4200 | 4200 |
| 1957 | 5000 | 4200 | 4200 |
| 1958 | 5000 | 4200 | 4200 |
| 1959 | 5000 | 4800 | 4800 |
| 1960 | 6000 | 4800 | 4800 |
| 1961 | 6000 | 4800 | 4800 |
| 1962 | 2500 | 4800 | 2500 |
| 1963 | 5000 | 4800 | 4800 |
| 1964 | 6000 | 4800 | 4800 |
| 1965 | 7000 | 4800 | 4800 |
| 1966 | no earnings | 6600 | 0 |
| 1967 | 7000 | 6600 | 6600 |
| 1968 | 8000 | 7800 | 7800 |
| 1969 | 3000 | 7800 | 3000 |
| 1970 | 8000 | 7800 | 7800 |
| 1971 | 8000 | 7800 | 7800 |
| 1972 | 9500 | 9000 | 9000 |

SOURCE: *Your Social Security* (U.S. Department of Health, Education and Welfare, Social Security Administration, May 1970), p. 12.

1. The wife of a retired worker is entitled to 50% of the worker's Primary Insurance Amount when she reaches age 65. If she chooses to collect at age 62, she will receive a scaled-down benefit, also based on the Primary Insurance Amount.
2. The children of a retired worker who are under 18 (or under 22 if attending school) are entitled to a benefit equal to 50% of the worker's Primary Insurance Amount.
3. The wife of a retired worker who has not reached age 62, but who has a child entitled to a benefit in her care, is entitled to a benefit equal to 50% of the worker's Primary Insurance Amount.
4. Surviving children of a deceased worker are entitled to a benefit equal to 75% of the deceased worker's primary insurance amount.
5. The wife of a deceased worker is entitled to a benefit equal to 75%

of the worker's primary insurance amount if she has dependent children in her care.

6. The wife of a deceased worker is entitled to a benefit equal to $82\frac{1}{2}\%$ of the Primary Insurance Amount at age 62.
7. All disability benefits are the same as for a retired worker.

All these benefits are subject to a maximum family benefit. The actual dollar amount of benefits at various annual earnings are listed in Table 13-5.

The benefit levels listed in Table 13–5 are those that were in effect in January of 1972. In view of the rather frequent changes in the level of benefits in the past, it is advisable for the reader to check to see if the level of benefits has been changed. An excellent source providing up-to-date data is *Your Social Security*, a free pamphlet that is available from any Social Security office.

Although the table indicates benefits that would be payable to persons with annual average earnings of $7800 and $9000, annual average earnings will usually not reach these amounts. The exception would be in the case of a deceased worker who had earnings only since 1968.

### Loss of Benefits—Retirement, Survivors, or Disability Programs

A person receiving benefits may lose his or her eligibility for benefits in a number of ways. The conditions which cause a loss of eligibility under the law are the following:

1. *Conviction of treason, sabotage, or subversive activity.*
2. *Deportation.* If the dependents of the deported person choose to remain in the United States, they may retain their right to benefits.
3. *Aliens living outside the United States for 6 months or longer.*
4. *Work in foreign countries unless that work is also covered under OASDHI.* One month's benefit is lost for any part of 7 days during which the individual is employed. Work for an entire month would disqualify the individual for benefits for 4 months.
5. *Refusal of vocational rehabilitation by a disabled recipient.*
6. *Divorce from a person receiving benefits.* For example, the wife of retired worker who is receiving a benefit based on the qualification of her husband would lose the right to her benefit if she divorces him.
7. *Attainment of age 18 by a child receiving benefits.* The child's benefit is payable to the children of a retired or deceased worker who are under the age of 18. When a child who is entitled to benefits reaches age 18, the payments automatically stop. The exception to this rule is that payments may continue if the child is shown to be mentally or physically incapacitated. The wife of a deceased or retired worker

**TABLE 13-5**
**Social Security Benefits—Examples of Monthly Cash Payments**

| | | Average yearly earnings after 1950 | | | | | | |
|---|---|---|---|---|---|---|---|---|
| | $923 or less | $1800 | $3000 | $4200 | $5400 | $6600 | $7800 | $9000 |
| Retired worker—65 or older ⎫<br>Disabled worker—under 65 ⎭ | 70.40 | 111.90 | 145.60 | 177.70 | 208.80 | 240.30 | 275.80 | 295.40 |
| Wife 65 or older | 35.20 | 56.00 | 72.80 | 88.90 | 104.40 | 120.20 | 137.90 | 147.70 |
| Retired worker at 62 | 56.40 | 89.60 | 116.50 | 142.20 | 167.10 | 192.30 | 220.70 | 236.40 |
| Wife at 62, no child | 26.40 | 42.00 | 54.60 | 66.70 | 78.30 | 90.20 | 103.50 | 110.80 |
| Widow at 60 | 61.10 | 80.10 | 104.20 | 127.20 | 149.40 | 171.90 | 197.30 | 211.40 |
| Widow or widower at 62 | 70.40 | 92.40 | 120.20 | 146.70 | 172.30 | 198.30 | 227.60 | 243.80 |
| Disabled widow at 50 | 42.80 | 56.10 | 72.90 | 89.00 | 104.50 | 120.30 | 138.00 | 147.80 |
| Wife under 65 and one child | 35.30 | 56.00 | 77.10 | 131.20 | 181.10 | 194.90 | 206.90 | 221.60 |
| Widowed mother and one child | 105.60 | 167.90 | 218.40 | 266.60 | 313.20 | 360.60 | 413.80 | 443.20 |
| Widowed mother and two children | 105.60 | 167.90 | 222.70 | 308.90 | 389.90 | 435.20 | 482.70 | 517.00 |
| One child of retired or disabled worker | 35.20 | 55.60 | 72.80 | 88.90 | 104.40 | 120.20 | 137.90 | 147.70 |
| One surviving child | 70.40 | 84.00 | 109.20 | 133.30 | 156.60 | 180.30 | 206.90 | 221.60 |
| Maximum family payment | 105.60 | 167.90 | 222.70 | 308.90 | 389.90 | 435.20 | 482.70 | 517.00 |

SOURCE: *Your Social Security* (U.S. Department of Health, Education and Welfare, Social Security Administration, March 1971), p. 12; *Social Security Manual* (The National Underwriter Company, Homewood, Ill., 1971), pp. 111, 124–135.

is entitled to a benefit, even if she is not 62, if she has a child in her care who is receiving a benefit. When the child reaches age 18, the payments to the child stop and, since she no longer has a child in her care, the mother's benefit also stops. If the child is a full-time student, the child's benefit will continue until age 22, but the mother's benefit will stop when the child reaches age 18. The widow of a deceased worker therefore faces a period of time during which no benefits are payable to her. Between the time that the youngest child reaches age 18, and the time that the widow reaches age 60, she is not entitled to any benefits under the act. This period of time is commonly referred to as the "black-out period."

8. *Marriage.* As a general principle, if a person receiving a monthly benefit payment as a dependent or survivor marries a person who is not also a beneficiary, his or her payments stop. Thus, payments to a dependent child would stop if the child married.

9. *Adoption.* If a child is adopted by anyone except a step-parent, grandparent, aunt or uncle, the payment to the child stops.

10. *Disqualifying income.* In some cases, individuals who are drawing social security benefits continue to work. In some instances, this work is on a full-time basis; others work only on a part-time basis. The social security administration provides that in the event a person receiving benefits receives additional income, he or she may lose a part or all of his benefits.

If the earnings of the individual do not exceed $1680 for the entire year, the full benefits to which he is entitled under the law are payable. Even if the earnings are in excess of $1680, the individual may still be eligible for some social security benefits. The law provides that $1 in social security benefits are withheld for each $2 in earnings between $1680 and $2880. An additional $1 in benefits is withheld for each $1 in earnings in excess of $2880. Thus, a surviving spouse entitled to a benefit of $142.50 would lose that entire benefit if she earned $333.00 or more per month. No matter how much the individual may earn in a year, he is still entitled to social security benefits for any month in which he does not earn over $140 as an employee and does not render substantial services as a self-employed person. In addition, after age 72, the individual may earn any amount, and no benefits will be withheld. Since additional earnings can diminish the amount of the social security benefit to which the individual is entitled, it is important to distinguish those types of income which do not disqualify the individual from receiving social security benefits. Among the items that do not count as disqualifying income are (a) pensions and retirement pay; (b) insurance annuities; (c) dividends from stock (unless the individual is a dealer in stocks); (d) interest on savings; (e) gifts or inheritances of money or property; (f) gain (or loss) from the sale of capital assets; (g) rental income (unless the individual is a real estate dealer or a participating farm landlord).

### Amount of Benefits—Medicare Program

There are two separate programs under Medicare: Part A, hospital insurance, which provides coverage for all eligible persons over 65 and pays for the cost of hospital care, nursing home care, and home visits; and Part B, supplemental medical insurance, an optional coverage for which the insured must pay and which covers doctors' fees and certain other costs.

**Part A—hospital insurance.**   The basic benefits under the hospital insurance coverage fall into three broad categories: hospital care, care in a nursing home or extended-care facility, and home health services.[10]

*Hospital care.*   The hospital insurance coverage provides up to 90 days of hospital care in a participating hospital for each spell of illness (also called a benefit period). A spell of illness starts on the first day the insured receives covered services as a bed patient in a hospital or extended-care facility and ends when he or she has been out of the hospital or skilled nursing home for 60 consecutive days. The benefits include room and board in the hospital, x rays, laboratory tests, and ordinary nursing services. The patient pays the first $60 of hospital costs, Medicare pays the full cost in excess of this $60 deductible during the first 60 days in the hospital. From the sixty first to the ninetieth day, the hospital insurance pays all but $15 per day. In addition to the 90 days per spell of illness, the insured has a 60-day "lifetime reserve," which may be used after the 90-day limit has been exhausted in a spell of illness. However, hospital insurance pays all but $30 per day during the reserve days.

*Nursing home benefits.*   The hospital insurance coverage provides up to 100 days of care in a participating extended-care facility during each benefit period, provided the insured has been confined to a hospital for at least 3 days and enters the facility within 17 days after discharge from the hospital. The insurance covers all costs for the first 20 days of care. After the first 20 days, the insured must pay $7.50 of the costs per day for the next 80 days.

*Home health benefits.*   Home health benefits are provided to those

---

[10]To participate in the Medicare program, health facilities must meet certain standards which help to assure that they will be able to provide quality health care. In addition, they must not charge the Medicare beneficiary for services provided by the program and must abide by the provision of the Civil Rights Act, which prohibits discrimination based on race, color, or national origin.

insureds who require home health care such as part-time nursing, physical, occupational, or speech therapy, or part-time services of a home health aide, after having been confined to a hospital for at least 3 days. The home health care must be prescribed by a doctor within 14 days after the discharge from a hospital or extended-care facility and must be for the further treatment of a condition for which the insured received services as a bed patient in the hospital or extended-care facility. Custodial care is not covered, but only that care the primary purpose of which is to meet the medical needs of the patient. The benefit provides up to 100 home health visits by nurses (but not doctors) or other health workers from a home health agency during the 365 days following release from the hospital or extended-care facility.

**Part B—supplementary medical insurance.**    The medical insurance part of medicare is a voluntary program financed jointly through monthly premiums paid by those persons over 65 who have elected the coverage and an equal contribution for each by the federal government. No one is covered automatically under Part B of Medicare, and to obtain coverage the individual must sign up and pay the designated premium. The individual's monthly premium (which is matched by the federal government) was originally set at $3 a month. It was increased to $4 a month in April of 1968, to $5.30 a month in July of 1970, and to $5.60 a month in July of 1971. This medical insurance premium rate is reviewed annually and may be further changed if necessary to guarantee that the total amounts collected will continue to meet the cost of the program.

The coverage under the supplementary medical insurance program is much like a major medical contract. Coverage is subject to a $50 annual deductible, and nothing is paid until this deductible has been met by the insured. Medical insurance covers 80% of the covered expenses in excess of the deductible. Covered expenses include the following:

1. Physicians' and surgeons' services, no matter where rendered, including services in a hospital, clinic, doctor's office, or even in the home.
2. Home health services even if the insured has not been in the hospital, up to 100 visits during the calendar year.
3. Diagnostic tests, surgical dressings, splints, and rental or purchase of medical equipment.
4. All outpatient services of a participating hospital, including diagnostic tests and treatments.

In addition to the above expenses, medical insurance will pay 100% of the cost of radiological and pathological services when the insured is an in-patient in a participating hospital. These expenses are not subject to the deductible or the coinsurance provision.

## IS IT REALLY INSURANCE?

There is an additional aspect of social insurance, often discussed in terms of a criticism, that should at least be mentioned at this juncture—the question of whether social insurance is really insurance, or whether it is merely a unique method of providing benefits without the use of the basic principles of insurance. Any answer to this question could be subject to considerable debate. However, in spite of the rather substantial differences between the operational features of social and private insurance, it is our conclusion that the basic principles of insurance are just as applicable in one as in the other. As you should recall, insurance is essentially a process whereby existing risks of financial loss are transferred by individuals to a group or a pool. In the grouping of relatively homogeneous exposure units, it then becomes possible by means of statistical techniques and judgment to obtain a reasonable approximation of the probability of loss. Loss costs are then distributed in some equitable manner among the members of the group. Since insurance involves risk transfer and pooling, and since social in-surance programs utilize both devices, social insurance is "insurance."

Critics of this conclusion, however, compare the use of the insurance principle in private and in social insurance and assume that the latter is not insurance for two major reasons. First, in the private insurance approach there is a direct and proportionate relationship between the costs and the benefits. This relationship must exist because of competitive reasons and because the law requires that premium rates should not be unfairly dis-criminatory. However, since social insurance programs do not stress this relationship, but place the emphasis upon the adequacy of benefits, it is assumed that social insurance is not true insurance. There is little justifica-tion for this argument. Insurance is essentially a risk transfer and risk pooling device, and what constitutes an equitable distribution of the loss costs must depend upon the circumstances and the objectives. The term "equity" does not have a precise meaning that is applicable in the same manner in all circumstances. In the area of public finance, for example, it is considered equitable to distribute the burden of taxation upon the basis of ability to pay rather than upon benefits received. This same principle is applicable to social insurance. Since in the latter the objective is that of providing a minimum amount of economic security, then ability to pay, rather than contributions made, can constitute an equitable distribution of the loss costs of the group. Therefore, the stress upon the adequacy of the benefit in social insurance as compared with the direct and proportionate relationship between costs and benefits in private insurance means only that the term "equity" has a somewhat different application in the two areas. In both cases, however, transfer of risks and pooling of risks still exist.

Second, many critics maintain that social insurance programs are "actuarially unsound" and therefore cannot be insurance. The effectiveness of such an argument must, of course, depend upon the definition of "actuarial soundness," and to these critics an insurance program is "actuarially sound only if it is possible to measure the probability of loss with a high degree of accuracy and only if proper reserves are maintained to provide for future obligations. If this high degree of precision in measuring probabilities does not exist, according to the argument, then actuarial soundness does not exist, and thus any program falling into such a category should not be called insurance. For example, the OASDHI program involves so many variables—population growth, the aging of the population, inflation, politics, and the like—that a precise prediction of long-range future obligations is not possible. Therefore, the critics would assume that the OASDHI program is actuarially unsound and is not insurance.

It is true, perhaps, that the success of the insurance principle must depend upon the ability to obtain at least a reasonable approximation of the probability of loss. However, a precise prediction is not necessary. For example, there are many forms of private insurance, such as windstorm, hail, earthquake, and even automobile, in which precise statistical calculations of probabilities are impossible. In some cases, probability calculations are nothing more than enlightened guesses. To the extent that a reasonable approximation of loss can be obtained, these types of private insurance are actuarially sound. To the extent that the future obligations under social insurance programs are capable of approximation for a reasonable time in the future, they are also actuarially sound. Actuarial soundness involves specifically a prediction of future obligations and has nothing basically to do with the maintenance of reserves. Therefore, an insurance program can be actuarially sound whether the future obligations are funded or not just as long as there is sufficient income to pay for the obligations. The partial funding of many of our social insurance programs, then, does not remove these from the category of insurance.[11]

[11] Critics frequently ask how long the unemployment insurance reserves would last during a prolonged depression. The implication is that they would not last very long and, therefore, unemployment insurance is actuarially unsound. This criticism is unjustified, since no intelligent person would ever expect any type of insurance to provide coverage for every conceivable catastrophe that could occur. If World War III were imminent, for example, one could be certain that all life insurance companies would insert war clauses in all their new policies. Thus, life insurance companies would not feel that they could provide coverage for the catastrophe of war. And there are no health insurance companies that will provide for medical and hospital expenses on an unlimited basis. Social insurance, like private insurance, cannot be expected to

### The Soundness of the Program

Originally the Social Security Act was designed to provide for a compulsory saving by members of the economy. One central issue of debate concerning the passage of the act was the question of financing. Many authorities proposed that the federal government support the program out of general revenue, while others maintained that the program should be financed completely by the contributions of the workers and their employers. The decision was eventually made that no revenue would be used to pay benefits except that provided by the social security taxes. The intent at that time (and the principle has been carried down to the present) was that the OASDHI program should be self-supporting from the contributions of covered workers and their employers. The reasons for this decision are quite complex, but at least one of the reasons was expressed by Franklin D. Roosevelt:

> Those taxes were never a problem of economics. They are politics all the way through. We put those payroll contributions there so as to give the contributors a legal, moral, and political right to collect their pensions and their unemployment benefits. With those taxes in there no damn politician can ever scrap my social security program.[12]

Once the issue of a self-supporting program had been settled, there was a considerable amount of disagreement as to whether the program was to be funded, with a reserve similar to those used in private insurance, or whether it was to be operated on a "pay-as-you go" basis. The proponents of a fully funded program won a short-run victory, for the original act provided for a fully funded program, with each generation of workers accumulating funds collectively to be used for their retirement benefits. However, in 1939 the system was revised and put on a pay-as-you-go basis.

At the present time, benefits are paid to those who are eligible out of the social security taxes which are being paid by those who are working. In turn, those who are now working will receive benefits upon retirement from funds that are being paid in by the labor force at that time. There is a logical rationale to this approach. Presumably, both productivity and income will continue to increase in the future. The constantly increasing social security benefits which will be required to keep pace with the increasing price level

---

provide benefits under all circumstances. Unemployment insurance, then, is actuarially sound within the limits of its objectives, and to criticize it for not providing benefits under the catastrophic circumstances of a prolonged depression is an unjustified criticism. We might also state that this criticism has less merit today than was true when the program was started because the greater knowledge and use of fiscal and monetary policies in creating full employment will reduce substantially the possibility of a prolonged depression.

[12] Quoted in Arthur M. Schlesinger, Jr., *The Coming of the New Deal* (Boston: Houghton Mifflin, 1959), pp. 308f.

could not be paid out of a funded program, but as long as the benefits payable during each period can be collected from the then working labor force, the solvency of the program is assured.

It is not at all unusual to hear the OASDHI program criticized because it is not a fully funded program. Such criticism indicates a lack of faith in the future performance of the American economy. As long as the income generated by the laboring members of the economy is sufficient to permit taxation to meet the benefits payable to former workers, the program can be operated on a pay-as-you-go basis. There is no need for a fully funded program in social insurance as there is in the private insurance industry, and many make the mistake of assuming that there is. The question of future solvency which is applicable to private insurance firms has little validity for the government with its power to tax and create money.

### The Future of Social Security

The social security system of the United States was originally developed on the principle that the amount of the social insurance benefit should be sufficient to provide a "floor of protection," meaning a benefit amount that is sufficient to maintain a minimum standard of living. This floor of protection was then to be supplemented by the individual through private insurance or other devices. As inflationary pressures in the economy have increased

**TABLE 13-6**
**Social Security Earnings Base and Benefits, 1939–1970**

| Year | Monthly earnings base | Maximum primary insurance amount benefit | Minimum family benefit | Maximum family benefit |
|------|------|------|------|------|
| 1939 | $250.00 | $ 60.00 | $25.00 | $ 85.00 |
| 1950 | 300.00 | 80.00 | 40.00 | 150.00 |
| 1952 | 300.00 | 85.00 | 45.00 | 168.75 |
| 1954 | 350.00 | 108.50 | 50.00 | 200.00 |
| 1958 | 400.00 | 127.00 | 53.00 | 254.00 |
| 1961 | 400.00 | 127.00 | 60.00 | 254.00 |
| 1965 | 550.00 | 168.00 | 66.00 | 368.00 |
| 1967 | 650.00 | 218.00 | 82.50 | 434.40 |
| 1970 | 650.00 | 250.70 | 96.00 | 434.40 |
| 1972 | 750.00 | 295.40 | 105.60 | 517.00 |

SOURCE: *Social Security Bulletin, Annual Statistical Supplement, 1967* and *Your Social Security* (U.S. Department of Health, Education and Welfare, Social Security Administration, March 1971).

the cost of living and wages in general, the social security benefit has also increased. The benefit amount has been increased as a result of changes in the earning base upon which taxes are levied and average monthly wages are computed, and changes in the formula which specifies the percentage of the average monthly wage that becomes the primary insurance amount. Table 13-6 traces the increases in the earnings base and the benefit amounts since the inception of the program. The upward trend in benefits will undoubtedly continue in the future. As a matter of fact, the proposal has been made to provide for an automatic adjustment of the social security benefit, based on changes in the price index. To many this has great appeal, for it would take the magnitude of the changes out of the hands of congress and tie them to changes in the price level.

In addition to increases in the amount of benefits, it appears very likely that other aspects of the program will be liberalized, including further expansion of the Medicare program to provide benefits to additional groups.

## Questions for Discussion and Review

**1.** Social security provides protection to wage earners against financial loss to dependents resulting from premature death of the wage earner, and also provides retirement benefits. Do you think that the enactment or expansion of the Social Security Act has adversely affected life insurance sales? Why or why not?

**2.** "If I could take the money my employer and I pay for my social security tax and put it into a private insurance plan, I could do much better with my money than I will do in OASDHI." Do you agree or disagree with this statement? Indicate the fundamental philosophy involved here.

**3.** The medicare amendment to the social security act represented a significant expansion of the concept of social security. In your estimation, could the provision of medical insurance for the aged have been left in the hands of private industry? Why or why not?

**4.** What is the "real" cost of the OASDHI program from the point of view of the economy as a whole? What are the redistribution effects of the OASDHI program?

**5.** What benefits would be available under the social security program to the dependents of a deceased worker who was only currently insured? In the case of a deceased worker, does it make any difference whether the insured status was currently insured or fully insured?

## Suggestions for Additional Reading

Brinker, P. A. *Economic Insecurity and Social Security*. New York: Appleton-Century-Crofts, 1968.

Burns, E. M. *Social Security and Public Policy*. New York: McGraw-Hill, 1956.

Carlson, V. *Economic Security in the United States*. New York: McGraw-Hill, 1962.

Haber, W. and Cohen, W. *Social Security Programs, Problems, and Policies*. Homewood, Ill.: Richard D. Irwin, 1960.

Myers, R. J. *Social Insurance and Allied Government Programs*. Homewood, Ill.: Richard D. Irwin, 1965.

Rejda, G. E. "Social Security and the Paradox of the Welfare State." *The Journal of Risk and Insurance* **XXXVII** (1) (March 1970).

Schlesinger, A. M., Jr. *The Coming of the New Deal*. Boston: Houghton Mifflin, 1959.

Turnbull, J. G., Williams, C. A., Jr., and Cheit, E. F. *Economic and Social Security*, 3rd ed. New York: Ronald Press, 1967.

U.S. Department of Health, Education, and Welfare. *Annual Report, 1961*. Washington, D.C.: Government Printing Office, 1962.

# 14 Buying Life and Health Insurance

*We first survey the plot, then draw the model*
*Then must we rate the cost of erection*
*Which if we find outweighs ability*
*What do we then but draw anew the model*
—William Shakespeare, *King Henry IV, Part II*

A knowledge of the contents of a life insurance policy or a health contract, or an understanding of the differences between the various types of life and health insurance contracts is meaningful only when it is put to use. We study such things as the settlement options and cash values in life insurance contracts not as an end in itself, but rather to acquire the tools that can be used in constructing an adequate program of protection against the loss of the individual's income producing ability. The process of constructing such a program of protection is called "programming," and consists of fitting the insurance products available to meet the needs of the individual. In the case of life and health insurance programming, we are concerned with the task of providing protection against loss of income from death, disability, and retirement.

## PROGRAMMING LIFE INSURANCE

Life insurance programming consists of a study of the individual's needs for capital resources. It includes an assessment of the person's present financial position and future obligations, and the life insurance that should be used to meet these obligations. It is an approach to life insurance buying

**319**

that places the emphasis on planning, and is to be contrasted with the piecemeal approach of purchasing one policy at one time and another when the urge strikes. The latter approach results in a hodgepodge of policies that all too often do not accomplish the intent of the insured. Perhaps the worst aspect of insurance marketing today is the manner in which prospecting and selling is done. In far too many cases not enough attention is paid to the total overall needs of the prospect. On the other hand, many agents maintain that the public is not yet prepared for the "right way" of insurance buying. Some maintain that the total needs of the family must be ignored if the prospect is to be induced to buy at all, for the amount of insurance he really needs may overwhelm him. As a result, salesmen tend to emphasize the sale of a specific policy. As we shall see, it takes a substantial amount of life insurance to provide adequate protection in most cases. The vast majority of the families in the United States today are inadequately insured. If total life insurance in force in the United States were divided equally among all American families, each family would have only slightly over $21,000 in protection. Simple arithmetic tells us that $21,000 would not provide an adequate income for very many years, yet many individuals feel properly insured with even less insurance.

The first and most obvious step in programming life insurance is to determine the amount to be purchased. The willingness of the individual to spend hard-earned dollars on insurance will depend on his subjective orientation and his desire to provide protection for his family. This is an individual matter, and in the last analysis the decision must rest with the individual. However, there are at least two generally accepted approaches which can be of assistance in determining the amount of life insurance needed: the life value and the needs approaches.

### The Life Value

One of the foundations of life insurance is the concept of the economic value of human life. Every human life in some respect has an economic value, which is measured in terms of the pecuniary advantage which persons or businesses may derive from the continued existence of the person involved. Most authorities credit S. S. Huebner with the creation of the concept. Huebner felt that the human life value could be defined as

> ... the capitalized monetary worth of the earning capacity resulting from the economic forces that are incorporated within our being: namely, our character and health, our education, training and experience, our personality and industry, our creative power, and our driving force to realize the economic images of the mind.[1]

[1] S. S. Huebner, *The Economics of Life Insurance*, 3rd ed. (New York: Appleton-Century-Crofts, 1959), p. 5.

The human life value is the insurable value of the individual's income earning ability. The insurable value of the income producing capacity of an individual may be viewed as the maximum potential earnings of the individual that would be lost if the individual died. It is the present value of the income lost by his dependents as a result of his death. We can estimate this insurable value by discounting the expected stream of income that would accrue to the dependents as a result of continued employment. If we deduct the amount of the income earned which would be consumed by the producer himself, and discount the remainder, we have a notion of the present value of the stream of income that will be lost. The emphasis here is on the income that would be lost by the dependents. Thus, if the individual earns $15,000 and consumes $5000 himself, the insurable value of his income producing ability is $10,000 per year discounted to the date of his retirement.[2]

The practical value of the concept may be illustrated in the following manner: Let us assume that X has graduated from college and is embarked on a career. He has already "accumulated," or is destined shortly to do so, a wife and family, with all the obligations this situation will involve. He should purchase life insurance, and the ideal amount should be the equivalent of his economic value to his dependents; this is what they would lose if X should die prematurely. Let us also assume that X plans to retire at age 65, that his average earnings will be $15,000 per year, and that two-thirds of his gross earnings will be used by his family. If X is now 25, this would amount to a total of $400,000 over a period of 40 years. His economic value at age 25, however, is not measured by this total figure, but by that amount which if invested at some conservative rate of interest would yield an income of $10,000 per year for 40 years. If we assume a rate of 3% compound interest, this sum would be $231,100.[3]

The life value of different individuals will probably not reach its maximum at the same point in time. Changes in income, which might be expected as the individual progresses upward in his field of endeavor, will change the insurable value. Increased earnings will be offset to a certain extent as the

---

[2]Some approaches also discount for life expectancy. The above measure of insurable value differs from the Huebner approach in this respect. It does not (and we believe should not) discount for mortality. See Juan B. Aponte and Herbert S. Dennenberg, "A New Concept of the Economics of Life Value and the Human Life," *The Journal of Risk and Insurance* XXXV (3), Sept. 1968.

[3]Compound interest tables should be readily available to the student. In our calculation, the tables show that the present value of $1 per annum for 40 years, using 3% compound interest, is $23.11. This means that a present investment of $23.11 at 3% compound interest will yield an income of $1 per year for 40 years. By multiplying $10,000 times $23.11, we will obtain the sum which will yield $10,000 per year for 40 years. This sum is $231,100. This calculation should also provide a young lovesick male with some food for thought concerning certain aspects of matrimony.

number of years the individual has left to work decreases. Other things being equal, the insurable value of the 25 year old under consideration would decrease with the number of years until his retirement as indicated in Table 14-1. The life value generally decreases over time and eventually disappears at retirement age. It should be obvious to the student that this method of calculation of the economic value of a life is fraught with so many difficulties that a mere enlightened guess is the only result that can be achieved. The first major difficulty is that of determining the future earnings of an individual. At best it can be nothing more than a projection based upon present earnings in the person's occupation or in comparable occupations.

The main problem is that many factors influence the future earnings of an individual. The second difficulty is that of determining the portion of one's income that is used for his own maintenance. A rule-of-thumb criterion places this figure at 50% of gross personal earnings. However, this figure may vary considerably, and 50% is probably excessive. Perhaps the most important factor is the size of the family and particularly the number of female children. The unfortunate father of a large family of girls could possibly have a self-maintenance figure that is negative, particularly if his wife is a normal woman. Another difficulty involves the amount of personal income taxes that must be paid out of income in the future. Perhaps the only factor of certainty here is the direction of the amount of income taxes; that is, upward! The difficulties involved in the calculation do not, however, invalidate the concept. Even though considerable guesswork is involved,

**TABLE 14-1**
**Present Value of Future Income Illustrated**

| Age | Years until retirement | Present value of $1 per year flow | Present value of $10,000 per year |
|---|---|---|---|
| 20 | 45 | 24.52 | $245,200 |
| 25 | 40 | 23.11 | 231,100 |
| 30 | 35 | 21.49 | 214,900 |
| 35 | 30 | 19.60 | 196,000 |
| 40 | 25 | 17.41 | 174,100 |
| 45 | 20 | 14.88 | 148,800 |
| 50 | 15 | 11.94 | 119,400 |
| 55 | 10 | 8.53 | 85,300 |
| 60 | 5 | 4.58 | 45,800 |

this is still the most acceptable method of calculating the economic value of a human life.

The fact that the insurable value of the individual's income producing ability is a given amount does not necessarily indicate that this is the amount for which it should be insured. There may be instances in which the loss of the income earning ability of the person in question would not cause deprivation for anyone, and under such circumstances there may be no need for insurance. Additionally, it will probably not be necessary to provide protection in the full amount of the insurable value. Remember, in determining what should be done about a given risk the individual should take into consideration other resources available to meet the need if the loss should occur. A part of the income lost through the death of the person may be replaced by social security. If it is, the amount of insurance necessary to replace the income may be reduced. For example, if X desires to provide an estate by means of life insurance that would equal a high percentage of his economic value, it would be necessary to provide only a portion of this amount through his own individual efforts. If he dies or becomes totally disabled, benefits of a substantial amount will be provided under the Old-Age, Survivors, Disability, and Health Insurance program (OASDHI) of the federal government. For example, if X should die and his survivors are a widow, age 30, and one child, age 2, and if his average annual earnings have been at least $6600, it would take about $50,000 of life insurance to provide the same benefits his survivors will receive under the OASDHI program, plus a capital sum of approximately $20,000 to provide the widow with a life annuity beginning at age 60. Thus, the OASDHI program provides a substantial amount of life insurance. It is also possible that life insurance coverage will be provided under the group life insurance program in effect at the place of X's employment; X might have coverage of as much as $10,000–$20,000 under this program. The amount of life insurance that must be purchased voluntarily by an individual in order to have a total that approximates a relatively high percentage of his economic value must be determined with a consideration of other sources of life insurance protection. The OASDHI benefits and coverage under group life insurance programs are the most common sources of additional life insurance protection.

### The Needs Approach to Life Insurance

Another method, and one that may be more practical than the use of the economic value concept, is commonly called the "needs" approach. Here, the amount of life insurance purchased is based on an analysis of the various needs that would be experienced by the family should the income producer die. In reality, the needs approach is directly related to the life value concept. In summarizing the needs that would exist in the event of the wage earner's death, we are merely looking at the other side of the family income–expenditure equation. While the life value concept focuses on the income that would be lost, the needs approach attempts to identify the allocation of that income and summarize the most critical prospective expenditures. In addition, the needs approach attempts to recognize unusual or non-regular expenditures that may result from the death of the wage earner and the additional expenses that may accompany the period of readjustment following the wage earner's death.

There are various ways in which the needs may be classified; the traditional approach includes the following:

1. Fund for last expenses
2. Funds for readjustment
3. Dependency period income
4. Mortgage payment funds
5. Educational funds
6. Life income for the wife

The nature of the *fund for last expenses*, also called "the clean-up fund," is relatively obvious. Death may be accompanied by high medical expenses, funeral costs, and other unplanned expenses, and the fund for last expenses is intended to cover these additional costs. The *readjustment expense fund* is provided on the assumption that the period immediately following the death of the wage earner will be accompanied by certain nonrecurring expenditures incurred as the family adjusts to its new way of life.

Income needs during the *dependency period* bulk largest in most programs. The amount of income needed during this period is often much greater than is supposed, primarily because the incremental cost of the wage earner himself is often overestimated. With the death of the wage earner, certain expenses will undoubtedly cease, but the reduction may be far less than expected. Many individuals underestimate the amount of insurance they must provide during the dependency period. Moreover, it is not at all uncommon to completely ignore the need for insurance during this critical period. What about the possibility of the widow obtaining work to support the family after the father has died? This may be a possibility, but there are a number of factors that deserve consideration. While a widow without children can probably get a job and fend for herself, a widow with small children must sacrifice a great deal if she is forced to work. First, if the mother does work, she will lose a portion of the social security benefit to which she is entitled as a widow with a dependent child in her care. As a matter of fact, assuming a maximum social security benefit, a widow with one child who earned $400 or more a month would lose over $200 in social security benefits a month. In other words, since earnings in excess of $1680 per year reduce the social security benefit, a widow earning $4800 or more a year would lose $2400 in benefits, leaving a net gain of only $2400.[4] There is an even more important factor to be considered. It has been said that the greatest gift a father can leave to his children is "a mother's time." If the mother is forced to work to support the family, time which would otherwise have been spent with the children must be spent working. If sufficient income is provided through life insurance, the mother will be able to spend time with her children just as she would have if the father had not died.

The *mortgage payment fund* may be a particularly effective way to reduce the amount of income needed during the dependency period. If the mortgage permits prepayment without penalty, substantial savings in future interest payments may be gained by paying off the mortgage at the death of the husband.

Although *educational needs* are typically listed as a separate need, this is arbitrary. As an alternative, the planner might continue the income of the dependency period until the youngest child is past college age. Since social security benefits are payable to dependent children until age 22 if they are attending college, this seems to be a more appropriate approach.

The *life income for wife* need is composed of two components. The period from the time the children leave home or complete their education until social security benefits begin again is called the "black-out period," indicating that social security benefits cease and will not resume until age 60 or 62. Following the resumption of social security benefits to the widow, a lesser amount of supplementary income will again be necessary, but during the black-out period the entire income of the wife must come from life insurance, employment, savings, or some other source.

Under the needs approach, these income requirements of the family are usually listed on a month-to-month basis over time, in a graphic presentation indicating the amount of income needed, the amount available from social security and other sources, and the extent of the unfilled need. The chief benefit of this graphic analysis is that it helps the individual to visualize the amounts needed as a flow of income. A typical "needs analysis" chart is shown in Figure 14-1.

[4] The exact amount of the benefit lost would of course depend on the level of the mother's benefit. Social security benefits are reduced $1 for every $2 of income between $1680 and $2880, and $1 for every $1 earned over $2880. For example, using the benefits payable to the widow and child of a deceased worker with annual average earnings of $7800, which were in effect in January 1972, the widow and child would be entitled to receive $413.80 ($206.90 for the child and $206.90 for the mother). The first $2880 in earnings would reduce the mother's benefit by $600, leaving $1882.80 of her $2482.80 annual benefit. The next $1882.80 in earnings would wipe out the mother's benefit. The child's benefit, however, would be unaffected by the mother's earnings.

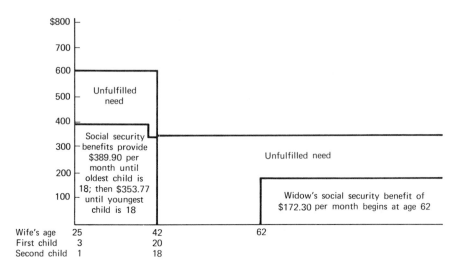

**FIGURE 14-1**
**Needs analysis chart.**

### A Continuing Task

The major defect of both the life value and the needs approaches as they are most frequently used is that they rely on static analysis, determining the amount of insurance at a specific point in time. This results in the purchase of an amount of insurance that may be correct at that point in time, but which will be inaccurate as time goes by. Because the life value of the individual decreases over time as the individual approaches the end of his income earning years, the fixed amount may be excessive. The needs of each individual will vary, depending on age, the number of children, responsibilities, and financial assets. In addition, the needs of the individual may change over time, for during each period of life there are different needs that appear to be more crucial. We can subdivide the average person's life into the following four periods: the premarital period, the pre-child-raising years of marriage, the child-raising years, and the years approaching retirement. For most individuals, needs will vary with each of these periods.

**The premarital period.**   A young man or woman who has not yet married has no great need for death protection. Unless there are parents who are dependent on such a person, there is no need for a flow of income to replace the income which stops. Enough life insurance to cover an indebtedness and a fund for last expenses really constitute the extent of the need. However, it may still be advisable for the young individual to acquire life insurance because of the fact that such a person cannot be certain that he will be able to purchase life insurance at a later time. The real justification for life insurance purchases early in life is to guarantee insurability.

**The pre-child-raising years of marriage.**    Like an unmarried man, the need for death protection is relatively slight for the childless couple. A widow without children can probably make out alright by herself if something should happen to the husband. However, if the need to guarantee future protection was important during the premarital period, it is even more crucial now that the individual has married and the possibility of future responsibilities has increased.

**The child-rearing years.**    The need for death protection is greatest in most cases during the period when there are small children in the family. The amount of the need during the child-raising years increases as the expenses that would continue in the event of the death of the wage earner increase, and the amount of these expenses increase with the number of children and the standard of living that would be maintained. The life insurance needs of the individual therefore increase with the birth of each child and will reach a maximum after the last child is born. Determination of the amount required deserves careful thought, for the amount must take into consideration not only the standard of living to which the survivors have become accustomed, but should also recognize future changes in the purchasing power of the dollar.

**The years approaching retirement.**    After the end of the child-raising years (they do come to an end, we are told; it only seems like they are eternal), the need for death protection declines, while the need for retirement income becomes more apparent. During this period, the need for death protection consists primarily of provision for the widow in the event of the husband's death. The retirement income need (to be discussed shortly) is composed of the funds required to maintain both the husband and the wife.

Not only do the needs for insurance change with the different periods of life that the individual passes through, but in addition, the ability to pay for insurance varies. During the child-raising years, when the need for death protection is greatest, the resources to pay for it are the lowest. For this reason a compromise must be made. The individual must either postpone the goal of accumulating retirement income funds, or he must leave a portion of the death needs unprotected. In keeping with the protection-first approach to life insurance, death protection takes precedence.

Since needs and the ability to meet these needs both change over time, management of a personal insurance program is a continuous task. As needs change, provision for the needs must also change. As income changes, new purchases can be made to provide for needs that were neglected. Proper insurance planning requires a considerable amount of foresight. The provision made during one period of time to provide protection against the greatest risk may not be appropriate at a later time. The insurance program that is ideal is one that meets the current needs, and at the same time permits enough flexibility for future changes as income and needs change. For example, during the premarital period young people often purchase life insurance because of the saving feature. Yet if a young man purchases a life insurance policy with a high saving potential, such as a 20-year endowment, he may find later that his needs have changed and that the premium is too high in proportion to the protection. For this reason, many authorities advocate the whole life policy as the best buy for young people. It is a reasonable compromise between the saving and protection functions of life insurance. Since the future needs for insurance are of concern to the individual at this point in his life, the contract should include the additional purchase option.

The same flexibility can be attained by the individual who faces the dilemma of limited resources and unlimited wants during the child-raising years. A father may feel that he cannot provide an adequate amount of protection if he purchases a contract that has a high saving feature (or any saving feature, for that matter). By purchasing convertible term he can achieve the protection he needs, yet retain the right to change to a permanent form of insurance that has a cash value when the children are older and he can afford to do so.

## PROGRAMMING HEALTH INSURANCE

The art of programming health insurance is far less well developed today than is the art of life insurance programming. As a matter of fact, it has been estimated that programming of health insurance stands at approximately the same stage as life insurance programming stood 35 years ago. Yet, it is important to recognize that the needs in the event of a disability require the same type of planning that death needs require. No matter how complete a life insurance program may be, it does not provide total protection against loss of income. A true income protection program must provide protection against loss of income from both death and disability. In addition, most disabilities are accompanied by some medical expense, regardless of whether they are caused by accident or sickness. To the extent that the amount of these medical expenses is in excess of the amount the family can affordto bear, some provision for protection must be made. Thus, in programming health insurance we are concerned with protection against two types of losses. In addition to the loss of income that may accompany sickness or accident, protection must be provided against the additional expenses that accompany the sickness or accident.

As in the case of life insurance, the disability income insurance should be viewed as a potential flow of income, capable of replacing the income lost as a result of the inability to work. In determining the amount of income necessary, the same needs as those discussed in connection with life insurance programming are appropriate. In selecting the amount of weekly or monthly indemnity, and the length of the waiting period, consideration should be given to other sources of income that may be available under social security or other sources, such as sick leave or disability benefits provided by the employer. Inasmuch as it is impossible to determine in advance the possible length of the period of disability, protection should be provided for the worst possible eventuality, a disability that is permanent in nature. A disability policy should therefore provide benefits for life or until retirement age in an amount that will permit the individual to continue the accumulation of a retirement fund in the same manner as if he had not been disabled.

The major consideration in the area of medical expense coverage should be protection against the catastrophic loss. In this connection, medical expense insurance has a direct relationship to the life insurance program. The amount of the clean-up fund discussed in connection with life insurance is difficult to determine, primarily because the amount of the final medical expenses cannot be determined with any degree of accuracy. For this reason, these final medical expenses are more appropriately insured through health insurance contracts rather than by means of a fixed amount of life insurance. A major medical policy is likely to be the best choice for most individuals. In many instances hospitalization and surgical coverage may be provided in whole or in part by the employer, and the availability of such coverages should be taken into consideration in selecting the medical expense coverage to be purchased. If the individual chooses to insure ordinary medical expenses through first-dollar contracts, he should recognize that he is merely having the insurance company budget these expenses for him, and that the cost of such coverage is not a part of what we may call the insurance budget.

## LIFE AND HEALTH INSURANCE PROGRAMMING ILLUSTRATION

### Life Insurance

For the purpose of illustrating the life insurance programming technique, we will construct a life insurance program for an average American family. Our subject is Tom Jones, average American, age 25. His wife Mary is also 25. They have two children, ages 3 and 1. Tom has an annual income of $12,000 and a mortgage which has 20 years to run with an unpaid balance of $25,000. Although Tom is in the third period of his insurance-buying life, "the child-raising period," we will assume that he does not presently have any life insurance. He is fully and currently insured under OASDHI, and his average earnings amount to $5400.[5]

In determining the need for life insurance, the needs of the family for funds in the event of Tom's death are measured. The first need chronologically would be for a clean-up fund. This fund would provide Mary with money to pay off any last debts and to meet the funeral expenses. The lump-sum payment of $255 under social security represents far too little to meet the need. In addition, most authorities advise providing for a "readjustment income," which will help the family over the financial difficulties that arise in adjusting to the new life that will come after the death of the wage earner. The exact amount needed for these two funds is difficult to determine, but for the sake of illustration we will determine the amount needed for both funds to be $4000.

Next, chronologically, and probably of primary importance, will be the need for an income for the family during the period when the children are growing up. Since the youngest child is now 1 year old, it is not unrealistic to assume that this need will continue for at least the next 17 years, when the youngest child will be 18 years old. The period may well extend beyond that point if the insured wishes to provide additional income past age 18 to permit continued education. The amount of income needed during this period will depend on a number of things. If Tom decides to provide insurance protection to pay off the balance of the mortgage at his death, the amount of income needed each month for living expenses will be somewhat reduced. As a matter of fact, it will probably be a good idea to pay off the mortgage at the death of the insured, provided that the mortgage permits prepayment. The differential between the interest that could be earned on death proceeds and the interest charges on the mortgage make this an economical means of reducing the amount of insurance needed. Assuming that the mortgage will be paid off at the death of the insured, we will set the income needed by the family during the dependency period at $600 per month. At this point we are concerned only with a summation of the needs and will defer until later the provision we will make to meet these needs.

One of the most perplexing problems that we must face is the decision at this point concerning the provision, if any, that should be made for Mary after the children are grown. When the youngest child reaches age 18, Mary will be 42 years old. She may seek and find employment. She may remarry. As a matter of fact, she may have done one or both before the children are grown. In either case, it would not seem necessary to provide life in-

[5] The social security benefits used in this illustration are those that were in effect in January 1972. See Table 13-5.

surance benefits to provide her with a lifetime income. Tom is inclined to believe that it would be difficult for Mary to obtain work or to find a new husband.[6] He therefore decides to provide her with an income of $350 a month for the remainder of her life.

Finally, after these needs have been met, Tom would like to provide an accumulation of funds that would permit him to retire without being dependent upon his children or charity. He would like to have $500 a month for his retirement income, assuming that the price level is approximately the same as it is now. If it has changed, he would like to have a proportionate change in his retirement income.

Once the needs have been determined, the means already available to meet these needs is subtracted. As stated previously, the insured is fully and currently insured under OASDHI, and in the event of his death, the widow and children would be entitled to the survivor benefits discussed in Chapter 12. In addition, the wife would be entitled to retirement benefits at age 62.

The task of the insurance programmer is to fill those needs which OASDHI does not meet. The program must, of course, start at the beginning, but starting at the beginning, it must also look to the end. Proceeds from the insurance that is purchased to provide income after the children are raised will not be needed immediately upon the death of the insured and may be left at interest under the interest option. The interest earned on these funds can be used to meet a part of the need during the dependency period. For this reason, the amount of insurance purchased to provide for the wife's black-out period and retirement period will determine the amount required for the dependency period. Therefore, we will begin with the last chronological need, the retirement income for Tom's widow.

Upon reaching age 62, Mary will be entitled to a widow's benefit under OASDHI in the amount of $172.30 per month. To provide $350 per month, life insurance proceeds must supply an additional amount of $177.70 per month. The question now is "How much life insurance does it take to provide a monthly income of $177.70 to a woman at age 62?" By quick reference to the life income option in the settlement table of a policy, we find that a woman, aged 62, will receive $5.25 per month under the life income with 10 years certain option, for each $1000 of policy proceeds.[7] Simple division indicates that if $1000 will provide $5.25 a month, it will require about $34,000 to provide $177.70 a month:

$$\frac{\$177.70}{\$5.25} = \$33,847$$

If Tom purchases $34,000 worth of insurance, it will provide $179.50 per

[6] He knows her much better than we do.
[7] Refer to Table 10.3.

month for Mary at age 62. Added to the $172.30 social security benefit, this will provide a monthly income of $351.80.

During the black-out period (i.e., the time between the end of the social security benefits for the youngest child and the time Mary reaches age 62) no social security benefits will be payable. During this period, there is a need for $350 a month. In this particular instance, the black-out period will last for 20 years, from Mary's age 42 until age 62. During this period, the interest on the policy proceeds that are to be used for the widow's retirement income will be available. The interest option generally guarantees a minimum rate of interest, with provision for a greater amount if it is earned on the company's investments. Assuming that the rate guaranteed by the contract is 3%, the policy purchased to provide the retirement income to the widow will produce a minimum of $1020 a year under the interest option. This amounts to $85 per month, leaving $265.00 to be met through additional insurance. Once again, we turn to the settlement options of the policy, this time with the question, "How much insurance is needed to provide $265 a month for 20 years?" Under the installments for a specified period option, we find that the policy will pay $5.27 per month for each $1000 of face amount. The amount of insurance needed to provide $265 a month is:

$$\frac{\$265}{\$5.27} = \$50,284$$

If Tom purchases $51,000 worth of insurance, the face amount of the policy will provide $268.77 per month for a 20-year period. This, together with the interest on the proceeds which will provide the retirement coverage, amounts to $353.77 per month during the black-out period.

Turning to the dependency period, there is a need for income in the amount of $600 per month. Social security benefits will provide $389.90 per month until the 3-year-old child reaches age 18, and then $313.20 until the 1 year old is 18. In addition, the interest on the funds intended for the black-out period ($51,000) and the wife's retirement income ($34,000) will also be available. Again assuming the 3% interest that is guaranteed as a minimum, the $85,000 will produce $2550 a year in interest, or $212.50 a month. The OASDHI benefits plus the interest will amount to $602.40 per month until the first child reaches age 18, and then $525.70 per month until the second child reaches age 18.

We have not provided a specific fund for educational expenses; however, if the children desire to continue their education and attend college, funds will be available. We have programmed the wife's lifetime income to begin at age 42, when the youngest child reaches age 18. The children's OASDHI benefits will continue until age 22 if the children attend college, and these funds should be sufficient to meet the educational costs. Presented graphically, the program would appear as shown in Figure 14-2. In total, we have determined that Tom must purchase a $25,000 policy to provide for the payment of the mortgage, plus $4000 for a clean-up and readjustment fund, plus $51,000 for the black-out period, and $34,000 for the wife's retirement period. The total amount of insurance needed under the program is $114,000.

Obviously, the preceding illustration is not the only way that the needs of this individual could have been programmed. As a matter of fact, it may not even be the best way, but it illustrates the use of the settlement options in programming and gives a rough idea of the amount of insurance required to provide a flow of income to surviving dependents.

Up to this point, we have not commented on the type of insurance Tom should purchase to fill the needs we have outlined. As a matter of fact, there is a wide range of possibilities, as the figures in Table 14-2 indicate. If Tom decides to purchase nothing but 10-year renewable convertible term, the annual cost of the program will be $482.22 (114 × $4.23). If he decides to purchase nothing but whole life, the annual cost will be $1419.30 (114 × $12.45). He could spend as much as $3040.38 a year if he chooses

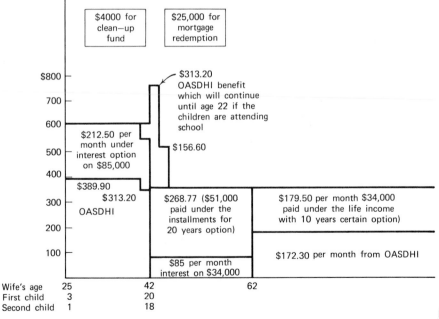

**FIGURE 14-2**
Life insurance programming illustration.

TABLE 14-2
Life Insurance Rates—Nonparticipating[a]

| Age | Whole life | Paid up at 65 | 20-Pay whole life | 10-Year term | Mortgage protection, 20 years | Family income rider[b] | Retirement income policy |
|---|---|---|---|---|---|---|---|
| 20 | $10.65 | $11.63 | $19.02 | $4.00 | $3.16 | $4.35 | $22.08 |
| 21 | 10.98 | 12.04 | 19.45 | 4.03 | 3.18 | 4.37 | 22.91 |
| 22 | 11.32 | 12.46 | 19.89 | 4.06 | 3.20 | 4.38 | 23.78 |
| 23 | 11.67 | 12.90 | 20.33 | 4.10 | 3.22 | 4.40 | 24.68 |
| 24 | 12.05 | 13.38 | 20.80 | 4.16 | 3.24 | 4.45 | 25.64 |
| 25 | 12.45 | 13.89 | 21.29 | 4.23 | 3.26 | 4.53 | 26.67 |
| 26 | 12.88 | 14.44 | 21.81 | 4.32 | 3.30 | 4.64 | 27.74 |
| 27 | 13.32 | 15.01 | 22.35 | 4.42 | 3.34 | 4.76 | 28.86 |
| 28 | 13.79 | 15.62 | 22.91 | 4.54 | 3.40 | 4.92 | 30.04 |
| 29 | 14.29 | 16.27 | 23.50 | 4.69 | 3.48 | 5.11 | 31.31 |
| 30 | 14.83 | 16.99 | 24.12 | 4.86 | 3.59 | 5.36 | 32.69 |
| 31 | 15.40 | 17.76 | 24.77 | 5.06 | 3.74 | 5.66 | 34.17 |
| 32 | 16.00 | 18.59 | 25.44 | 5.29 | 3.91 | 6.00 | 35.74 |
| 33 | 16.63 | 19.46 | 26.14 | 5.54 | 4.11 | 6.33 | 37.41 |
| 34 | 17.29 | 20.40 | 26.87 | 5.83 | 4.34 | 6.81 | 39.20 |
| 35 | 17.99 | 21.40 | 27.61 | 6.15 | 4.59 | 7.29 | 41.14 |

SOURCE: *Diamond Life Bulletins* (The National Underwriter Company: Cincinnati, Ohio).

[a]Nonparticipating rates are used in the illustration for the sake of simplicity. There is no intent to imply that nonparticipating rates provide insurance at the lowest cost, but for the sake of illustration it is simpler to use net rates, and since dividends are not guaranteed, and normally change as the policy ages, nonparticipating rates were selected. As a matter of fact, since the insurance company has the use of the "overcharge" for a year, the interest on this portion of the premium will probably reduce the participating premium below nonpar rates.

[b]Family income rider rates are for $10 per month for a 20-year period which commences at the beginning of the policy. Benefits are paid from the death of the insured until the predetermined date 20 years from the inception of the policy. This is essentially decreasing term insurance.

retirement income policies. We will leave the discussion of the type of policies that should be purchased until later in the chapter.

In addition, we have not discussed the question of the retirement income needs which will exist if Tom survives to age 65. Tom has stated that he would like to have $500 a month at that time. The social security benefit tables indicate that Tom and Mary will be entitled to a combined benefit of $313.20, leaving about $200 to be met out of savings accumulated by age 65. Reference to a settlement option table indicates that an insurance company will pay $4.73 per month for each $1000 in policy proceeds under the joint-and-survivor life annuity option if both persons are age 65. This means that Tom must accumulate an amount in excess of $42,000 to provide the retirement income he has specified in his goal. The life insurance policies he purchases to provide protection against the financial loss to his family which would result from his premature death may be used as a vehicle for this accumulation. We will also defer the question of life insurance as an investment or as a means of accumulation until later in the chapter.

### Health Insurance

**Disability income.**   The needs of the family for income in the event that the wage earner should be disabled are certainly as great as they would be if he died. As a matter of fact, they will probably be greater. As in the case of life insurance, the needs vary with the number of children in the family and with other responsibilities the insured may have. Also as in the case of life insurance, there are benefits available under OASDHI that may be available in the event of disability and which must be considered in determining the need for disability income insurance.

Suppose, for the sake of example, that we determine that the minimum income the family would need in the event of the disability of the wage earner is $700 per month during the child-raising years, and $500 per month thereafter for life. In the event of a total disability of a permanent nature, Tom would be entitled to disability benefits under OASDHI equal to the maximum family benefit for his taxable earnings of $389.90 until the children were grown. At that time, the disability benefit would be reduced to $208.80 per month until his wife reaches age 62, at which time it would increase to $287.10 per month.

There may be a gap in the benefits payable under social security, however. The definition of disability under social security requires that the disability be total, and also that it must be expected to continue for a period of 1 year or result in death. A situation might easily arise under which Tom could be deprived of income for up to a year, without becoming eligible for disability benefits under the act. In addition, there is the problem of the waiting period under social security. Disability benefits are not payable until the insured has been continuously disabled for a period of 6 months. If we assume that Tom's net pay after taxes is about $800, the 6-month waiting period would represent a loss of almost $5000. We ought, therefore, to recommend disability coverage to protect against the loss of income during the waiting period under social security and also against disabilities of less than 1 year, in addition to providing disability coverage to supplement the social security benefits during disabilities of longer duration.

Coverage to supplement the social security benefits may be provided under a long-term disability contract. A disability income policy paying

$300 per month for life in the event of accident and until age 65 in the event of illness, with a 30-day waiting period, will cost about $175 per year.

To protect against disability that is total, but which may not be expected to last for a full year and which consequently does not qualify for OASDHI benefits, and also to insure the exposure in connection with the 6-month waiting period under social security, Tom can purchase a policy paying benefits for 1 year, in an amount equal to his social security disability benefit. The cost of a policy paying $400 per month for 1 year for either sickness or accident, again subject to a 30-day waiting period, would be about $95. This policy, in addition to the lifetime policy proposed above, will provide reasonably adequate protection against the loss connected with a short-term disability not covered under OASDHI. Such a program would provide $700 per month during the first year of disability (plus any social security benefits which might be payable) and $300 per month thereafter. After the first year, the insurance benefit would be supplemented by OASDHI benefits, providing a total income of $689.90 per month until the children were grown, then $508.80 until Mary reaches age 62, and then $587.10 for retirement. Graphically, our program would appear as in Figure 14-3. The total cost of the disability income protection would be about $270.

**Medical expense coverage.**    The violations of good sense in the allocation of premium dollars in the field of health insurance have already been discussed. At this point, we will add little more, except to state that the only medical insurance we are concerned with in our program is major medical insurance. If the insured wishes to budget his medical expenses on a first-dollar basis, he may certainly do so, but these expenditures are fixed medical expenses and not a part of our insurance budget.

Tom should purchase a major medical contract with as high a maximum and as high a deductible as he can afford. The higher the deductible, the lower the premium outlay will be. For the sake of illustration, we will assume that Tom selects a major medical policy with a $10,000 maximum, $100 deductible, and an 80% coinsurance provision, covering all members of the family. The premium on this policy will be approximately $145.

### The Cost of the Program

Now let us summarize the cost of the income protection plan we have designed for Tom. In the area of life insurance we have a wide range of alternatives. The decision as to the types of policies Tom should purchase to meet his needs will depend on how much he can afford to spend and his investment goals. A mortgage protection policy appears to be an obvious choice to provide the $25,000 needed for mortgage retirement. The cost

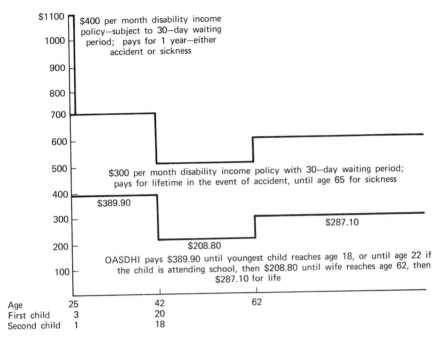

**FIGURE 14-3**
Disability income insurance programming illustration.

of such a policy will be $79.50 per year. If we assume that Tom purchases $89,000 in 10-year renewable convertible nonparticipating term to fill the remainder of the $114,000 need, his income insurance expenditure will be as follows:

| | |
|---|---|
| Mortgage protection policy ($25,000) | $ 79.50 |
| 10-year term ($89,000) | 376.47 |
| Disability income insurance | 270.00 |
| Major medical insurance | 145.00 |
| | $870.97 |

With a total premium outlay of $870, Tom may feel "insurance poor." On a monthly basis, the program would require about $73 a month, which may be more than Tom feels he can afford to spend on income insurance protection. In this case, the question becomes one of where to cut. Perhaps we could select a longer waiting period under the disability income policy, or a higher deductible under the major medical. A third alternative would be to reduce the amount of life insurance protection, leaving a portion of the need unprotected.

As a matter of fact, the $870 we have committed Tom to pay seems to be a reasonable amount. The total cost of the programs might have been much higher if we had selected permanent insurance rather than term, and many would criticize the above program as "term heavy" arguing that some form of permanent insurance should have been used.

## CHOOSING THE TYPE OF POLICY AND THE COMPANY

### Buy Term and Invest the Difference?

"Buy term and invest the difference" are the six most controversial words in the area of life insurance buying. They summarize the philosophy of those who have argued that the individual would be better off if he were to purchase term insurance and invest, separately, the difference in premiums between term insurance and permanent insurance. The long-raging controversy between the proponents of permanent insurance for the sake of investment and those who advocate insurance for the sake of pure protection will probably never be settled.

If it were not for the fact that the risk management process must also deal with the risk of outliving one's income, we could leave the question of term versus cash-value insurance for the finance professors and their growth yield tables. But the individual must concern himself with the possibility that he may live beyond his income earning years, and recognizing this contingency, he must plan to meet it. If the individual foresees that his income will cease at some time in the future and that his need for income will remain, the logical course of action is to provide for the accumulation of a fund which can be used to replace the income. Life insurance is one vehicle that can be used for the accumulation of that fund, and we ought therefore to discuss the merits of this form of accumulation.

There are, as we have seen, two separate risks which can be met through life insurance: premature death and superannuation. Yet these two risks are diametrically opposed. If the individual dies before reaching retirement age, there is no need to have accumulated a fund for retirement income. On the other hand, if he does not die before reaching retirement age, he could have done without the death benefits. Unfortunately, from an insurance-buying point of view, we do not know what the future holds, and so the individual must attempt to make preparations for both contingencies.

Many persons do not have sufficient income to provide adequate death protection and at the same time accumulate funds for retirement, forcing a choice between death protection and the saving element. As Table 14-3 indicates, there is an inverse relationship between the amount of insurance protection and the cash value of the various forms of life insurance. The higher

TABLE 14-3

Protection and Cash Values Available per $100 in Premium—Nonparticipating Rates

| Type of policy | At age 21, a $100 premium will purchase the following amount of death protection | The cash value of the policy at the end of 20 years will be |
|---|---|---|
| 20-Year mortgage redemption | $35,714 | $ 0 |
| 10-Year term | 26,470 | 0 |
| Term to age 65 | 14,128 | 1,215[a] |
| Whole life | 8,310 | 1,860 |
| Paid up at age 65 whole life | 7,481 | 1,893 |
| 20-Pay whole life | 4,658 | 1,942 |
| 20-Year endowment | 2,182 | 2,182 |

SOURCE: *Diamond Life Bulletins* (The National Underwriter Company: Cincinnati, Ohio).

[a]While this is the cash value the insured would receive if he discontinued the policy at this point, it is technically a reserve that gradually lessens and disappears after this point until at age 65 it is completely gone.

the cash value, the lower the amount of death protection that can be purchased for a given number of premium dollars.

The decision involved in the purchase of insurance should be divided into two separate and unrelated decisions. First, and this is the more important risk management decision, what should be done about the risk of premature death? How significant is this risk relative to the other risks the individual faces? Measuring the loss potential here involves determination of the amount of insurance needed. If the amount of the potential loss that is beyond the family's margin for contingencies is $125,000, then $125,000 is the amount of risk that ought to be transferred to the insurance company.

The first question, then, is not what kind of life insurance should be purchased, but rather how much is needed. In many instances the answer to this first question will provide an answer to the second question, the type of insurance that should be purchased. If the amount of insurance needed is substantial, term insurance may be the only alternative. When the amount of money available for life insurance is limited (and it usually is limited), the savings feature of permanent insurance forces the individual into a compromise in protection for his family during the critical years. If the individual follows the proper techniques of risk management, he will seek to transfer that portion of the risk of loss of income earning ability which his family could not afford to bear. If insurance is purchased in the amounts needed to replace the income that would be lost, term insurance may be the only thing that the individual can afford. In other words, as we have seen from our programming example, the arguments about term versus other forms of life insurance are meaningless for a substantial portion of the population, for with limited resources available for expenditure on insurance, there is normally very little "difference" left after providing complete protection.

In the cold realism of mathematics we noted that the insurable value of a young man earning $15,000 a year might be as much as $230,000 or even more. If this individual chooses to purchase cash value coverage for this amount, the premiums would be in excess of $2000 a year. Even on the basis of the needs approach, we saw that $114,000 would be required after deducting that portion of the need met by OASDHI. If the buyer chooses permanent life insurance, he must make a choice between savings and protection. Because the cost of life insurance at ages past age 65 becomes prohibitive, the purchase of benefit-certain contracts such as whole life involves the purchase of less protection than could be obtained through the purchase of term insurance. This is not intended as a criticism of cash value life insurance. It is a criticism of the misuse of cash value life insurance and the violations of good risk-management practice that it entails. As a matter of fact, the major criticism that can be levied against cash value life insurance is that it frequently leads to a violation of all three of the rules of risk management. With a limited number of dollars available for the purchase of life insurance, cash value life insurance involves an opportunity cost in terms of the death protection that must be foregone. As a result, many individuals leave their families in financial straights. They fail to consider the odds by purchasing coverage against an event that is not a contingency at all, and in so doing, they risk more than their family can afford to lose. They risk a lot for a little by underinsuring their income earning ability, leaving a serious exposure unprotected in exchange for interest on the funds that should have been used to protect against that exposure.[8] They commit the great error of permitting the question of the type of policy to purchase to determine the answer to the question of how much to purchase instead of vice versa. The first and most important decision to be made is the amount of protection needed, which is made without reference to the type of coverage that will be obtained to provide the protection.

In deciding on the form of life insurance to be purchased, we leave the area of risk management and enter the field of finance. The question of term insurance versus permanent cash value insurance is a separate question,

[8] Wouldn't it be absurd if an insurance company approached the owner of a $200,000 building with the proposal that he purchase $50,000 in coverage on the building and use the money he saved for a savings program? Yet this is precisely what is done time and time again in the field of life insurance when the individual is induced to purchase high-premium benefit-certain life insurance.

unrelated to the problems of risk management. Once the individual has made the decision to transfer the risk of the possibility of the loss of $114,000 in income earning ability to an insurance company, the rules and principles of risk management are no longer helpful. The choice as to the type of insurance contract that should be used is an investment question and should be evaluated in terms of the same standards that are applied in ranking investments of other types. As a matter of fact, the question is not really one of term versus permanent insurance at all, but rather a choice between permanent insurance and alternative forms of investment. The only logical reason for the purchase of cash value insurance is that it is superior to the other investment alternatives available to the insured for his purpose.

In many instances, the purveyors of life insurance attempt to pose the choice between term and permanent insurance in terms of "protection" rather than an investment decision, by pointing out that term insurance cannot be continued beyond age 65 or 70. "Term insurance is only temporary protection," they criticize, as if there were something inherently good about insurance that is not temporary. When one recalls that the income earning period and the economic life value of an individual are also temporary, it is "permanent" that takes on the undesirable connotation. By age 65, the economic value of the individual has declined to zero in most cases; in addition, by this time the economic responsibility to dependents is also normally fulfilled. A man has little need for protection at this age; yet it is during the 35-year period following this age that the cost of life insurance becomes prohibitive. Nothing could more clearly be a violation of the principles of risk management than insuring an asset that no longer has value.[9]

After the individual has provided a reasonably adequate insurance program from the point of view of the protection it affords, he may wish to implement his savings through life insurance. In this case, life insurance is probably as good a long-term saving program as many others, and even better than some. The outstanding characteristic of cash value life insurance as an investment is the compulsion that it entails. Most individuals do not have the self-discipline and determination required to follow through with their plans for the regular accumulation of a savings fund. Once a policy is

---

[9] Another criticism of term insurance, which hardly deserves comment, is that "you have to die to collect," undoubtedly the most absurd criticism that can be made. The implication is that if you do not collect under an insurance policy, you have somehow lost in the transaction. One might just as well say that your house has to burn down in the case of fire insurance, or that you have to run over someone to collect under your automobile liability insurance. The best approach to use on the person who makes such a comment is to refer him to any insurance textbook that explains the operation of the insurance principle. Perhaps he will learn that the insured receives something under an insurance policy even when he does not collect.

taken out, the individual will pay the premiums rather than deprive his family of the protection involved in the policy, and in paying the premiums he makes regular contributions to the saving element of the contract. History indicates that even in the depths of the Great Depression of the 1930s, men gave up almost every kind of obligation before they stopped paying their life insurance premiums.

In addition, there are certain tax advantages under life insurance which some other forms of investment do not enjoy. Increments to the cash value are not taxable until they are actually received by the insured. At the time the policy is surrendered, the excess of the cash surrender value over net premiums paid is taxable as ordinary income, and the gain may be spread over a 3-year period. To earn a net return on alternative investments equal to that under a life insurance contract, the gross rate of return on the alternative investment must be higher than that available under the life contract.[10]

Finally, there is a safety of principal that does not exist in certain other investments. The major criticism levied at life insurance as an investment is the relatively low rate of return—usually between 4% and 5%, and perhaps the rate of return is low, but low relative to what? Common stocks represent a risk form of investment. The investor hopes to have gains, but on the other hand, he may suffer losses. Life insurance cash values are a guaranteed form of investment, with both safety of principal and a guaranteed rate of return. For this reason, and the other reasons cited above, life insurance may be the most attractive and dependable investment for many individuals. On the other hand, there are individuals who are not content with the fixed-dollar nature of the life insurance investment, preferring equity investments with their potentially greater rate of return. The choice, however, is a matter of finance rather than an insurance decision.

The major legitimate criticism of life insurance as an investment is that inflation may seriously errode the value of the dollars contributed, but this criticism is a legitimate criticism of all fixed-dollar instruments. We should point out that whenever anyone makes a statement about the "goodness" or "badness" of a given type of investment vehicle in the long run, he is making an implicit judgment concerning the future trends in the economy. If the future of the economy is marked by inflation and increases in the

[10] M. Albert Linton, former chairman of the board of the Provident Mutual Life Insurance Company and a past president of the Actuarial Society of America, calculated that a man investing in a life insurance program for 20 years beginning at age 35 would have to receive a net return, after taxes and expenses, of 4.78% on an alternative investment to equal the accumulation under permanent life insurance. To obtain a 4.78% net rate of return on the alternative investment, the gross rate would have to be 6.83% if the man were in a 30% bracket and 7.97% in a 40% tax bracket.

price level, then life insurance (or any other fixed-dollar investment) will be less attractive than those investments which ride the inflationary trend.

### Choosing between Companies

In spite of the fact that most life insurance companies invest in approximately the same securities and use the same mortality tables, there are significant differences in the premiums charged by different companies for the same type of policy. The wide range of premiums charged by different companies makes selection of a company and a policy a complicated and intricate process. The fact that the premium for a whole life policy with Company A is $14 per $1000 and the cost of a whole life policy with Company B is $16 per $1000 does not necessarily mean that Company A is offering the best "deal" and that Company B is overcharging its customers. The cash value of Company B's policy may increase at a more rapid rate than that of Company A, the settlement options may be more liberal, or other internal policy provisions may be more liberal. Unfortunately, however, it is also true that the provisions of Company A's policy may be more liberal or that its cash value may increase more rapidly.

One of the commonest fallacies in connection with the differences in premiums among companies is that these differences can be traced to the actuarial differences in the benefits of the contracts and that in the field of life insurance you get exactly what you pay for. This misconception is based on a misplaced faith in the principle of competition. Some people maintain that the marketplace will effectively keep a company from over-charging the public and that competition will result in an equality of value between companies. But is competition truly an adequate device for the protection of the consumer in the field of life insurance? At least one authority indicates that there are excessive prices in the life insurance field, and to the extent that those excessive prices exist, it seems that competition is not effective.[11] In other words, one cannot always be certain when purchasing life insurance that he is getting what he is paying for or that other more attractive alternatives are not available. It should be pointed out that competition is effective only when the consumer is aware of his alternatives, and the complexity of price analysis in life insurance generally precludes this condition. Competition does not effectively protect the consumer from excessive prices in life insurance because of the lack of buyer sophistication and the distortion inherent in the traditional life insurance sales approach, which tends to conceal the price differentials.

[11] Joseph M. Belth, *The Retail Price Structure in American Life Insurance* (Bloomington, Ind.: Indiana University Press, 1966).

While some differences in premiums between companies may be traced to differing rates at which the saving element of the contracts accumulate, to differences in dividends, and to differences in the liberality of policy provisions,[12] the differences in premiums may also be due to differing levels of expense and efficiency of operation. Since the operating expenses of the company must in the last analysis be borne by the insureds, the levels of these expenses are important determinants of the price. Not only is the internal efficiency an important determinant of price, but commissions and other acquisition costs may also differ significantly between companies, resulting in wide differentials in the actual cost to the insured. New companies, in particular, which are attempting to grow rapidly, pay substantially higher commissions to their agents; and these higher commissions must be passed on to the consumer in the form of higher premiums.

The simple fact of the matter is that there are wide variations not only in the premiums charged by different companies, but in the cost as well. This is particularly true in the cash value policies. Obviously, here the premium paid by the insured does not represent his true cost, since a part of that premium goes toward the accumulation of the cash value or may be returned in the form of a dividend. Calculation of the true cost to the insured must make allowance for the saving element inherent in permanent forms of insurance.

Only in a term policy can we get a look at the difference in the cost of coverages between companies. If we compare a term policy in which there is no accumulation (savings), we can determine the difference in the cost between the companies for this policy only. The difference may not exist on the same basis in other contracts sold by the two companies. Even in making a comparison between two different term policies, we must make certain adjustments. For example, if we are attempting to compare a participating policy with a nonpar policy, we must make allowance for the dividends that will be paid on the participating policy, and since the dividends normally increase as time goes by, we must consider the dividends over the long run. At the same time, we should recognize that future dividends cannot be guaranteed and are mere projections based on past experience.

### Note on Net Cost Comparisons

One frequently used method of selling life insurance is on an illustrative projected net cost basis. Such proposals are not only misleading, but the manner in which they are usually presented is fundamentally invalid. The

---

[12] The first point to recognize in attempting comparisons between companies is that the policy provisions are probably not identical. Disregarding cash values and dividends for the moment, there are other differences of great importance, and a price comparison of two different contracts is valid only if the two contracts are identical in other respects.

basic technique is to make a summation of the total premiums paid, sub-tract any dividends that have been paid, then subtract the cash value (which the insured may at his option withdraw), and call the answer the net cost of the policy. The fallacy in such proposals is that they completely ignore the value of the use of money. Accurate appraisal of a proposed contract must include consideration of the opportunity costs involved.

For example, the existence of participating and nonparticipating policies in life insurance may result in considerable confusion to a prospective life insurance purchaser, particularly if a somewhat unscrupulous agent makes comparisons for the prospect that are fallacious. For the sake of example, let us consider two term contracts, one a nonparticipating contract with a $4 per $1000 premium and the other a participating contract at $6 per $1000. The net cost of the participating contract can be made to appear lower than that of the nonparticipating policy: Company A charges $4 per $1000. The premium for a $50,000 policy will be $200 per year, and at the end of a 20-year period the net cost will be $4000. Company B, on the other hand, charges $300 for the $50,000 policy and returns the "overcharge" at the end of the year in the form of a dividend. It has the use of the $100 overcharge for a full year. Assuming that the company can earn 4% on the $100 overcharge, it can return a dividend of $104, making the "net cost" to the policyholder $196 for the year and the net cost over the 20-year period $3920. Thus, the overcharge on participating policies can permit a "net cost" com-parison, which, ignoring the interest on the insured's overpayment, makes the cost appear lower. When dividends are left to accumulate, the oppor-tunity cost becomes even greater. [13]

The same approach may be used to illustrate the "advantages" of those policies which have a high element of investment as opposed to those which have little or no investment. Under those policies that accumulate cash values, the interest on the saving portion of the policy is used to show how the cash value reduces the "net cost." The same fallacy creates this apparent advantage. If we ignore the insured's opportunity cost in terms of interest foregone, the net cost of the policies with a high saving element will be lower than those with a low saving element.

There are, of course, techniques of comparison that are used by the experts to compare the prices of life insurance contracts, but they are by no means simple. The basic approach is to disaggregate the cost of the saving element from the cost of the protection element. There are two basic ap-proaches that can be used to do this:

---

[13] Carried to its logical conclusion, the company could charge a premium of $5000 per year, invest it at 4%, earning $200, use the $200 to cover the cost of the insurance, and return a $5000 dividend. In this case, the net cost of the policy over the 20-year period would be zero.

1. Treat the policy as a combination of protection and savings, make an assumption concerning the yield on the saving element, and then compute the cost of the protection element.
2. Treat the policy as a combination of protection and savings, make an assumption about the cost of the protection element, and then calculate the yield on the savings element.

These two approaches are really just different ways of looking at the same thing.[14] Unfortunately, the process is rather involved and complicated and is impractical for the individual faced with a choice between two policies.

In the opinion of a leading authority on the subject, the solution to the problem is a system of price disclosure in connection with life insurance pricing which would make it possible for the insurance buyer to make an informed decision.[15] In the absence of such a price disclosure system, the average consumer can only attempt to avoid the pitfalls of the more obvious distortions discussed above and hope that the near future will bring some techniques which will make meaningful price information available to prospective buyers of life insurance. There is reason to hope that such information may soon be available. In order to overcome the inadequacies of the traditional methods of cost comparison, the life insurance industry itself has developed a more accurate cost comparison method, known as the "interest-adjusted method." This new method takes into consideration the time value of money by applying an interest adjustment (at a 4% rate) to the annual premiums, dividends, and cash value increases. The special committee appointed by the life insurance industry that developed the interest-adjusted method recommended its use by all companies for cost comparisons in life insurance. Unfortunately, the recommendation has not yet been followed widely.

## ESTATE PLANNING

Estate planning is the process of arranging a person's affairs so as to produce the most effective accumulation, management, and disposition of capital and income, planning so as to reduce the shrinkage of the estate and provide that the maximum number of dollars will be transferred from the decedent to the survivors. At one time, it was felt that estate planning involved nothing

---

[14] A third approach would be to compute the present value of the benefits under the contract and to compare this figure with the present value of the money to be paid by the policyholder. This is somewhat more complicated, and other things being equal, will yield the same result as the above techniques.

[15] See Joseph M. Belth, *The Retail Price Structure in American Life Insurance* (Bloomington, Ind.: Indiana University Press, 1966).

more than making out a will, but today most people recognize that making a will is just one part of a more elaborate process. While the will is certainly one of the more critical tools in the estate planning process, there are other tools as well, including life insurance, outright gifts during the lifetime of the individual, gifts in trust created during the owner's lifetime, and trusts created at death.

### Causes of Estate Shrinkage

Estates shrink as they pass from one individual to another, and several factors are responsible for this. First, there is the shrinkage that results from the debts of the decedent, for all debts must be paid before the estate may be passed on to the heirs. In addition, the administrative cost involved in probate and administration generally amounts to between 4% and 5% of the estate. Finally, and frequently the most burdensome, there is the cost of the federal estate tax and the state inheritance tax.[16] All these costs must be paid in cash, and they must usually be paid rather promptly. The debts, state taxes, and administrative costs must usually be paid within 1 year after death. The federal estate taxes must be paid within 9 months, or they incur interest costs and sometimes penalties. For this reason, in addition to reducing the shrinkage, the estate planner should make certain that the estate contains sufficient liquidity to meet these costs; otherwise, forced sale of assets might be necessary.

The greatest shrinkage of the estate usually comes as a result of the federal estate tax, which is levied on all taxable estates of over $60,000. Before the reader dismisses the threat of the estate tax, let us briefly list what is included in the $60,000. Estate tax laws refer to the gross estate. This means the fair market value of all real and personal property the individual owns at the time of his death. In addition to his house, its contents, automobiles, jewelry, cash, stocks, bonds, mortgages, and notes he may own, the gross estate also includes the proceeds of life insurance policies on the individual's life, no matter how payable, if the deceased possessed any incidents of ownership in the policies.[17] Many people are under the mistaken impression that since life insurance proceeds are not generally taxable under the personal income tax, they are also exempt from the federal estate tax. This is not the case. The proceeds of a life insurance policy payable to a named beneficiary

---

[16] The estate tax is a tax on the right to transmit property at death, whereas the inheritance taxes levied by the states are a tax on the right of the heir to receive a bequest.

[17] By "incidents of ownership" is meant such rights as the right to change beneficiaries, to borrow against the cash value of the policies, or the right to collect the cash values. If the insured does not possess any incidents of ownership, the proceeds may not be subject to the tax even though the insured may have paid the premiums. The premium would be considered a gift to the beneficiary and taxable under the provisions of the federal gift tax.

passes outside the will, and is therefore not subject to probate costs, but such proceeds are still included in the gross estate and may be subject to the estate tax. Additionally, property that is held in joint ownership with right of survivorship passes outside the will, but such property is still taxable under the estate tax law to the extent of the deceased's original contribution to the purchase price or other interest therein.

The gross estate is subject to certain deductions in determining the portion that is taxable. These include credit for death taxes paid to the states and foreign death taxes, credit for taxes previously paid under the federal gift tax,[18] a basic exemption of $60,000, and a marital deduction. The marital deduction provides that the individual may leave up to one-half of his adjusted gross estate to a surviving spouse if the survivor receives all the income at least annually and has the power to dispose of the property during his or her lifetime or upon death. In computing the amount of the taxable estate, we deduct the basic $60,000 exemption and that part of the adjusted gross estate[19] left to the surviving spouse (up to 50% of the adjusted gross estate). For example, if Jones dies leaving a $120,000 estate to his spouse, the estate would receive credit for the $60,000 exemption plus the marital deduction of $60,000, and no tax liability would exist. On a $200,000 estate, the marital deduction would amount to $100,000, making a total of $160,000 in deductions and leaving a taxable estate of $40,000. The current federal estate tax rates are contained in Table 14-4.

### Intestacy and Estate Shrinkage

An individual who dies without having left a will is said to have died "intestate." In such cases, the individual is frequently deprived of some of the exemptions available to him under the federal estate tax which would have helped to reduce shrinkage of the estate. When an individual dies without having left a will, the property he owned at the time of his death is distributed in accordance with the fixed provisions of the laws in the state in which he lived, and while this distribution may vary from state to state, in general it may be said that such distribution may act to the detriment of

---

[18] In addition to the taxation of transfers taking place at the time of death of the individual, the estate tax is also imposed on transfers made in contemplation of death. Gifts which were made within 3 years of the death of the deceased are included in the taxable estate unless the executor can prove that they were not made in contemplation of death. If it is possible to establish that such gifts were not made in contemplation of death, they are subject to the federal gift tax.

[19] The "adjusted gross estate" is the gross estate minus funeral expenses, estate administration expenses, debts (including accrued taxes and unpaid mortgages on property included in the estate), and casualty losses not compensated by insurance and which have not been deducted under the income tax. See Sections 2031, 2053, 2054, Internal Revenue Code.

**TABLE 14-4**
**Federal Estate Tax**

| Amount of taxable estate[a] | Tax on amount in (A)[b] | Amount of taxable estate in excess of (A) but not in excess of (C) is taxed at rate shown in (D)[c] | |
|---|---|---|---|
| (A) | (B) | (C) | (D) |
| $ 0 | $ 0 | $ 5,000 | 3% |
| 5,000 | 150 | 10,000 | 7 |
| 10,000 | 500 | 20,000 | 11 |
| 20,000 | 1,600 | 30,000 | 14 |
| 30,000 | 3,000 | 40,000 | 18 |
| 40,000 | 4,800 | 50,000 | 22 |
| 50,000 | 7,000 | 60,000 | 25 |
| 60,000 | 9,500 | 100,000 | 28 |
| 100,000 | 20,700 | 250,000 | 30 |
| 250,000 | 65,700 | 500,000 | 32 |
| 500,000 | 145,000 | 750,000 | 35 |
| 750,000 | 233,200 | 1,000,000 | 37 |
| 1,000,000 | 325,700 | 1,250,000 | 39 |
| 1,250,000 | 423,200 | 1,500,000 | 42 |
| 1,500,000 | 528,200 | 2,000,000 | 45 |
| 2,000,000 | 753,200 | 2,500,000 | 49 |
| 2,500,000 | 998,200 | 3,000,000 | 53 |
| 3,000,000 | 1,263,200 | 3,500,000 | 56 |
| 3,500,000 | 1,543,200 | 4,000,000 | 59 |
| 4,000,000 | 1,838,200 | 5,000,000 | 63 |
| 5,000,000 | 2,468,200 | 6,000,000 | 67 |
| 6,000,000 | 3,138,200 | 7,000,000 | 70 |
| 7,000,000 | 3,838,200 | 8,000,000 | 73 |
| 8,000,000 | 4,568,200 | 10,000,000 | 76 |
| 10,000,000 | 6,088,200 | | 77 |

SOURCE: *1954 Internal Revenue Code*, Section 2001.

[a]Column (A) shows the amount of the taxable estate; that is, the total gross estate less all deductions and an exemption of $60,000.

[b]Column (B) shows the estate tax on the corresponding taxable estate in column (A).

[c]Column (D) shows the rate applicable to any amount in excess of the taxable estate shown in column (A) but not in excess of the taxable estate shown in column (C).

the survivors. Under the laws of many states, if the husband dies leaving a spouse and children, the estate is divided one-third to the spouse; and the remaining two-thirds is divided equally among the children. This disposition deprives the estate of the full benefit of the marital deduction.

For example, suppose the individual leaves an estate of $240,000 but does not leave a will. Under the provisions of the law dealing with intestacy in his particular state, one-third of the estate is distributed to the spouse and two-thirds goes to the children. The estate tax will be levied on a taxable estate of $100,000 ($240,000 minus one-third of $240,000 minus the $60,000 basic exemption). The tax on the $100,000 estate will be $20,700. If the deceased had left a will providing that the entire estate go to his spouse, the marital deduction would have been $120,000 rather than $80,000, leaving a taxable estate of only $60,000, with an estate tax of $9,500.

Aside from the fact that intestacy is likely to increase the shrinkage of the estate, there are a number of other reasons that make a will advisable. When an individual dies without having left a will, the family becomes unnecessarily involved in certain court procedures. The widow may be appointed to administer the funds belonging to the children, but she will probably be required to post a bond and make periodic reports to the court. Overall, the inadequacies of intestacy are so apparent and inequitable, that a person planning for the disposal of his estate and the protection and welfare of his family should provide for the execution of this plan through a will.

### Trusts

Another method of reducing administrative costs and death taxes is to reduce the value of the estate by making living transfers to someone of a portion of the individual's assets. Under the present tax laws, a person may give away what he owns while he is alive—to his wife or children, for example—and as a result gain a substantial tax advantage. Although a federal tax is also imposed on gifts, the tax on gifts is lower than the tax on estate property. Further saving results from dividing the taxation of property between the estate tax and the gift tax because each tax has its own exemptions and its own increasing rate schedule.[20]

A common tool for such transfers of assets and for the administration of an estate is a trust. A trust is an arrangement under which the holder, called the trustee, undertakes the job of managing another's property for the benefit of designated persons or organizations. These persons are called the benefi-

---

[20]A person may give up to $3000 a year to as many individuals as he desires without being subject to the gift tax. In addition, a person may give away $30,000 during his lifetime (in addition to the annual $3000 exclusion) without incurring the gift tax.

ciaries of the trust, and the original owner is called the grantor, trustor, or creator of the trust.

The most widely used trusts are the testamentary trust, which is a part of the will and, as the name implies, takes effect after death, and the living trust, or *inter vivos* trust, which is established during the life of the creator and which may be revocable or irrevocable in nature.

A *testamentary trust* will not reduce estate taxes upon the death of the testator, nor will it reduce estate settlement costs. The potential trust property remains in the estate of the testator until the distribution of the trust after the will is probated. It is handled and taxed like all other property. However, it can reduce taxes and administration costs upon the death of the trust beneficiary. If a testator leaves his estate to his widow outright, an estate tax will be payable at his death. When his widow dies, there is a further estate tax on her estate including the property left her by her husband. If the property is left in trust at the death of her husband, with the income payable to the widow for life, and the distribution of the trust made to remaindermen upon the death of the widow, the estate tax is levied only once, at the death of the husband.

A *revocable inter vivos trust* is one in which the creator reserves the right to terminate the trust and reacquire the property. The creator can reduce estate administration cost if the trust remains in force after his death, for the property will pass outside the will. The beneficiaries will not have to wait until the will is probated to receive their allotted income and principal. The revocable trust does not, however, reduce the estate tax liability.

An *irrevocable inter vivos trust* is one in which the creator has not retained the right to terminate the trust and reacquire the property. An absolute and irrevocable trust takes the property out of the grantor's estate, and the administration costs and the estate tax on the property are eliminated.

In addition to the tax advantages which may result, trusts are often used for other reasons. The testamentary trust, which is a trust established under the will of a deceased person, may be set up to relieve the widow of the burden of managing the funds of the estate, just as the settlement opions may be used in regard to insurance policy proceeds.

The purchase of life insurance has become more and more complex as a result of its ever-increasing relationship to wills, trusts, and taxes; and the stern practicalities of law, taxation, and other factors require the individual to make far-reaching decisions in this area which are often irrevocable. It should be apparent that the entire field of estate planning is a complicated and highly specialized area. The complexity dictates that the individual seek not only expert insurance advice when setting up his insurance program, but skilled legal guidance as well, so as to guarantee that his intentions will be realized.

## Questions for Discussion and Review

**1.** Assume that you have finished college and that you are now married with two children, ages 1 and 2. Your income is $12,000 a year and you have been working in employment covered under social security for $2\frac{1}{2}$ years. You live in a $25,000 house with a $22,000 mortgage. Your employer provides group insurance equal to two and one-half times your annual salary. Prepare an income-protection program for yourself.

**2.** It is often stated that one of the most neglected areas in the life insurance field is that of insurance on mothers. Certainly the loss of the mother would be a serious loss in terms of the services she provides. In facing the risk-management decision regarding life insurance for the family, where do you feel insurance on the wife should fit?

**3.** Income may be divided into two components: consumption and savings. Into which of these components do you feel expenditures on insurance should be put?

**4.** What underlying assumptions are embodied in the advice, "Buy term and invest the difference"? What do you think of this advice?

**5.** When deciding on the type of insurance to buy, "the question is not really one of term versus permanent insurance at all, but rather a choice between permanent insurance and alternative forms of investment." In comparing permanent insurance with alternative forms of investment, what do you consider to be the most attractive features of insurance?

### Suggestions for Additional Reading

Aponte, J. B. and Dennenberg, H. S. "A New Concept of the Economics of Life Value and the Human Life." *The Journal of Risk and Insurance* **XXXV** (3) (Sept. 1968).

Belth, J. M. "The Cost of Life Insurance to the Policyowner—A Single Year Attained Age System." *The Journal of Insurance* **XXVIII** (4) (Dec. 1961).

Belth, J. M. "The Rate of Return on the Savings Element in Cash Value Life Insurance." *The Journal of Risk and Insurance* **XXXV**(4) (Dec. 1968).

Belth, J. M. *The Retail Structure in American Life Insurance*. Bloomington, Ind.: Bureau of Business Research, Graduate School of Business, Indiana University, 1966.

*Diamond Life Bulletins*. Cincinnati, Ohio: The National Underwriter Company.

*Fundamentals of Federal Income, Estate and Gift Taxes*, 15th ed. Indianapolis, Ind.: The Research and Review Service of America, 1969).

Greene, M. R. *Risk and Insurance*, 2nd ed. Cincinnati, Ohio: Southwestern, 1968, Chap. 22.

Gregg, D. W. (ed.) *Life and Health Insurance Handbook*, 2nd ed. Homewood, Ill.: Richard D. Irwin, 1964, Chaps. 55–59, 61, 63, 64.

Hofflander, A. E. "The Human Life Value: An Historical Perspective." *The Journal of Risk and Insurance* **XXXIII**(3) (Sept. 1966).

McGill, D. M. *Life Insurance*, rev. ed. Homewood, Ill.: Richard D. Irwin, 1967, Chap. 34.

Mehr, R. I. *Life Insurance Theory and Practice*. Austin, Texas: Business Publications, 1970, Chaps. 7, 20, 21.

Reynolds, G. S. *The Mortality Merchants*. New York: David McKay, 1968.

Shoup, C. S. *Federal Estate and Gift Taxes*. Washington, D.C.: Brookings Institution, 1966.

Williams, C. A., Jr. and Heins, R. M. *Risk Management and Insurance*, 2nd ed. New York: McGraw-Hill, 1971, Chap. 29.

# Section III

# PROPERTY
# AND
# LIABILITY
# INSURANCE

# 15 Property Insurance for the Family Part I

*Behold how great a matter a little fire kindleth.*

— *New Testament,* James 3:5

In this chapter we begin our study of those insurance coverages that are designed to protect the individual in connection with loss of or damage to his property. Property may be damaged or lost as a result of a wide variety of perils, and we will examine the insurance coverages available to protect against most of those perils that are insurable. We will begin our study of these coverages with the area of fire insurance. The fire insurance policy may be endorsed to provide protection against a wide range of perils. It is the basic contract in the property insurance area, and many other forms of property insurance incorporate its provisions. It seems logical, then, to begin our study of property insurance with the standard fire policy.

## THE STANDARD FIRE POLICY

At one time, there was no such thing as a "standard" fire policy; the attorneys of each insurance company drew up the contract their respective companies were to use in insuring property against loss by fire. Frequently, the contracts were intentionally drawn in a complicated manner, with the purpose of the complication being the confusion of the insureds. To further complicate the situation, the early contracts were frequently revised. When a

**357**

court decision was handed down ruling that coverage existed in a given situation in which it had not been intended by the insurance company, an amendatory provision was inserted in new policies to eliminate such coverage. Contracts became increasingly complicated; they almost always consisted of many pages of small print, making it difficult for anyone who might have wanted to read the contract to do so. Eventually, no one, not even the attorneys who had drawn the contracts, could be certain what the policy covered and what it did not. The loss adjustment difficulties became so great that even the insurance companies favored the development of a standard contract. The first standard fire policy law was passed in Massachusetts in 1880. In 1886, the New York Board of Fire Underwriters drew up a standard contract which was adopted first in New York, and later throughout the country. This 1886 form was revised in 1918, and again in 1943.

The 1943 New York Standard Fire Policy is now used in almost all states. Three states, Texas, Massachusetts, and Minnesota, use different forms; and twelve states have minor variations from the New York Standard Form. The differences in the form in use in the twelve states that have modified the New York Standard Form are so insignificant that it can be said that the form is used in all states except Texas, Massachusetts, and Minnesota. The form is "standard" in two respects. First, its wording is prescribed by law. In each jurisdiction any insurer wishing to write fire insurance must use the form that has been approved by the regulatory authorities, and most jurisdictions prescribe the New York Standard Policy. In addition, the widespread use of this form throughout the United States justifies the term "standard."

### Not a Complete Contract

It is important to understand at the beginning that the Standard Fire Policy is not a complete contract in itself. To be made complete, it must have a form attached. The terms "form," "endorsement," and "rider" are used rather loosely in fire insurance terminology. A form and an endorsement are normally considered to be about the same—a printed form which tends to be uniform throughout a given jurisdiction. "Riders," in contrast with forms and endorsements, are usually typewritten and vary with the individual policy. The purpose of all three attachments to the basic policy is to tailor the insurance to the specific risk being insured. There are over 200 forms and endorsements designed for use with the Standard Fire Policy, giving it extreme flexibility. The form used to complete the contract describes the property insured and modifies the basic policy to meet the requirements of insuring that specific type of property. With one form, the Standard Fire Policy may be used to insure a barn in western

Iowa, while with another it may be used to insure a large industrial plant in Detroit. There are forms for insuring dwellings, household goods, apartment houses, mercantile buildings, schools, churches, warehouses, and practically every other type of insurable risk. Forms may also be used to provide additional coverage by adding perils insured against to the insuring agreement.

### Policy Format

The face of the fire policy includes the declarations section and the insuring agreement. The declarations section includes such items as the name of the insured, the description of the property and its location, the amount of coverage, the amount of the premium, the term of the policy, and the inception and termination dates. Immediately following the declarations is the insuring agreement. The conditions and exclusions are on the second page of the contract in 165 numbered lines; these set forth the obligations of the insured and the company, specify the requirements in the case of loss, exclude certain uninsured perils, and provide the general framework of the contract.

### Insuring Agreement

The insuring agreement of the Standard Fire Policy could provide us with enough material for a full-length book. However, time and space permit only a brief examination of its provisions. The insuring agreement reads as follows:

IN CONSIDERATION OF THE PROVISIONS AND STIPULA-TIONS HEREIN OR ADDED HERETO AND OF the premium above specified, this Company, for the term of *years specified above* from *inception date shown above* At Noon (Standard Time) to *expiration date shown above* At Noon (Standard Time) at location of property involved, to an amount not exceeding the amount(s) above specified, does insure *the insured named above* and legal representatives, to the extent of the actual cash value of the property at the time of loss, but not exceeding the amount which it would cost to repair or replace the property with material of like kind and quality within a reasonable time after such loss, without allowance for any increased cost of repair or reconstruction by reason of any ordinance or law regulating construction or repair, and without compensation for loss resulting from interruption of business or manufacture, nor in any event for more than the interest of the insured, against all DIRECT LOSS BY FIRE, LIGHTNING AND BY REMOVAL FROM PREMISES EN-DANGERED BY THE PERILS INSURED AGAINST IN THIS

POLICY, EXCEPT AS HEREINAFTER PROVIDED, to the property described herein while located or contained as described in this policy, or pro rata for five days at each proper place to which any of the property shall necessarily be removed for preservation from the perils insured against in this policy, but not elsewhere.

Assignment of this policy shall not be valid except with the written consent of this Company.

This policy is made and accepted subject to the foregoing provisions and stipulations and those hereinafter stated, which are hereby made a part of this policy, together with such other provisions, stipulations and agreements as may be added hereto, as provided in this policy.

Each of the more important features of the insuring agreement will be discussed.

**Consideration.**   The consideration on the part of the insured consists of both the provisions and stipulations of the policy, and the premium. In addition to paying the premium, the insured agrees to abide by the conditions with respect to such things as furnishing proof of loss and cooperating with the company in certain other areas. Since the promise to abide by the conditions is a part of the insured's consideration, failure to abide by these conditions relieves the insured company of the obligation to pay in the event of a loss.

**Policy term and time effective.**   In most jurisdictions, policies may be written for 1, 2, or 3 years. The term of the policy (i.e., the period of time for which the insurance company agrees to provide protection) begins at "Noon (Standard Time)" at the location of the property. Of course, the agent can bind coverage at any time, but in the absence of some other designated time, the coverage begins at noon. This being the case, if an insured requests coverage effective immediately at 8:00 AM on February 10, the agent will bind coverage pending the issuance of the policy. When the policy is issued, it should be dated with an effective date of February 9.

**Persons insured.**   The insuring clause provides coverage for the insured named in the policy, but it also provides coverage for the legal representatives of the insured. If the insured should die, any loss covered under the policy would be payable to his estate.

**Valuation.**   From the point of view of both the insured and the company, one of the most important portions of the insuring clause is that part which concerns the amount of money to be paid by the insurance company in the event of loss. The insuring agreement of the Standard Fire Policy imposes four limits on the amount payable:

1. Face amount of the policy
2. Actual cash value of the property
3. Amount it would cost to repair or replace the property with material of the same type
4. Interest of the insured

The limitation of the face amount of the policy requires little explanation at this point. It is the amount of insurance that the insured has elected to purchase and for which a premium has been paid. A dollar amount is generally specified for each type of property or structure, although it is also possible to insure several items with one amount of insurance. The actual cash value of the property may be interpreted as "replacement cost minus depreciation" in most cases. The phrase "not exceeding the amount which it would cost to repair or replace" is merely a limitation on the amount that may be collected. It is not a requirement to be met by either party.

The necessity for an insurable interest on the part of the insured is referred to by the provision "nor in any event for more than the interest of the insured." The insured can collect only to the extent of his insurable interest in the property, regardless of the amount of the damage. To illustrate the importance of this provision, let us say that White and Brown have a joint ownership in a building valued at $50,000, each having 50% interest. If White insures the building for $50,000 with himself as the only insured, the maximum he could collect in the event of a loss would be $25,000, for this is the extent of *his* insurable interest. For this reason, it is important that all persons having an interest in the property be designated in the policy. It is a good rule to list the insureds in the policy as they are listed in the title to the property.

**Other restrictions.**    The insuring clause lists two restrictions excluding losses which might otherwise increase the cost of a loss. First, the indemnity does not include "allowance for any increased cost of repair or reconstruction by reason of any ordinance or law regulating construction or repair. . . ." This is to protect the insurance company from an increase in the amount of a loss that might result from a change in the building code of the city in which the building is located. For example, let us say that the insured has a frame warehouse and that the city fathers have enacted a statute that requires all new warehouses to be constructed of brick. In the event of a loss to the frame warehouse, the loss would be settled on the basis of the replacement cost minus depreciation of the frame warehouse, and not of the replacement cost of the brick building. The second limitation, "without compensation for loss resulting from interruption of business or manufacture" is inserted to indicate that the nature of the Standard Fire Policy is to provide for direct loss. Such indirect loss as business interruption may be insured under the policy by the addition of a modifying form.

**Perils insured against.**   The insuring agreement also specifies the perils against which coverage is provided. The policy insures against "direct loss by fire, lightning and by removal from premises endangered by the perils insured against in this policy. . . ."

*Fire.*   The first of these three perils, fire, is the basic peril the policy was originally designed to provide protection against. It is rather surprising that the term "fire" is nowhere defined in the policy. Although the term is not defined, court decisions over many years have established the fact that the "fire" which is contemplated in the fire policy is a fire of a specific type. Fire, according to the courts, is "combustion proceeding at a rate rapid enough to generate flame, glow, or incandescence."[1] In other words, there must be light. Mere smoke, scorching, or charring is not sufficient to establish the presence of a fire.

Not all fires are covered under the fire policy. The courts have made a distinction between a "friendly fire" and a "hostile" or "unfriendly" fire. A friendly fire is one that is within the confines for which it was intended; the friendly fire was intentionally kindled and is where it is supposed to be. A "hostile fire," on the other hand, is a fire that has escaped the confines for which it was intended. Only hostile or unfriendly fires are covered under the Standard Fire Policy.

One of the best illustrations of both the distinction between a friendly fire and a hostile fire, and the existence of a fire that produces "flame, glow, or incandescence," is the cigarette that is inadvertently left on the edge of a table. The glow at the end of the cigarette is a fire—there is no question about that. However, the fire is exactly where it is supposed to be—on the end of the cigarette. If the cigarette chars the table, there has been damage, but it has been the result of a friendly fire. On the other hand, if the table itself begins to glow, a new fire, and this time an unfriendly fire has come into existence, and the damage would be covered.[2]

In addition to the damage by the actual fire itself, the "direct loss by fire" peril provides coverage for any damage that results from the smoke from a hostile fire, or damage caused by water or firemen in attempting to extinguish a hostile fire.

*Lightning.*   Lightning may cause damage to property, and in addition it may cause fire that in turn will cause damage. At one time, the fire policy did

---

[1] *Western Woolen Co. vs. Northern Assurance Co., 139 Fed. 637.*

[2] Damage caused by cigarette burns have been a constant source of difficulty. Since the extent of the damage is normally slight, companies usually pay them even when no coverage exists, in order to prevent ill will. One decision by a court, which appears to be the only decision on the matter, ruled that a lighted cigarette which had fallen on a rug was a hostile fire; the movement of the cigarette from the ashtray to the rug took the fire out of the confines for which it had been intended. *Swering vs. Connecticut Fire Insurance Company, 180 Atl. 343.*

not include the peril of lightning, which caused considerable difficulty in the adjustment of fire losses which were caused by lightning. Since the insuring agreement promises to pay on the basis of the "actual cash value of the property at the time of loss," when a house was struck by lightning and a fire ensued, the loss settlement became virtually impossible. It was necessary to estimate the actual cash value of the house after it had been struck by lightning, but before it burned. The inclusion of the lightning peril has simplified the process by making the damage covered regardless of whether it was the lightning or the fire that caused the damage.

*Removal.*   Often, property that is insured may be damaged while attempting to preserve it from destruction by removing it from a building that is threatened by an insured peril. It would be grossly unjust to penalize the insured for attempting to prevent a loss to the property or to reduce the amount of loss if the property was somehow damaged in the process. For this reason, the Standard Fire Policy provides for coverage of damage to property that is being removed to protect it from one of the perils insured against. The coverage provided under this peril is quite broad, and provides protection for almost anything that results in a loss when the property is being removed under the described conditions.[3] The following example will serve to illustrate the broadness of the coverage: Property removed from a burning building or a building exposed to loss by any insured peril may be left outside temporarily, exposing it to many types of losses. Suppose that Mr. Brown arrives home to discover his house on fire. To reduce the amount of loss, he decides to empty the house of its furnishings. While carrying his color television set down the front steps, he misses his footing, falls, and spreads the television set all over the sidewalk. Next, Brown asks two college students who are passing by to help him. The "boys" carry the stereo set out, and while Brown goes back for another load, they depart with the stereo. Finally, Brown succeeds in emptying the remainder of the house. Shortly before the fire department arrives, a cloud burst occurs which completely ruins most of the furniture. Brown will be able to collect for all the losses described under the removal peril. Even the loss of the stolen stereo is covered, in spite of the fact that the policy specifically excludes theft elsewhere. The courts have held that in spite of the exclusion of theft, such losses are covered under the removal insuring agreement.

Closely related to the removal coverage is an extension of coverage to property at new locations when it has been removed because of a fire or other peril. The Standard Fire Policy covers property while it is located or contained as described in the policy. It is specific location coverage and covers

---

[3] The perceptive student will note that removal is not a peril at all, but rather a hazard. Technically speaking, we should state that the Standard Fire Policy insures against two perils and a hazard.

property elsewhere only as provided by endorsement or in this removal extension. The extension provides that property removed from the premises for preservation from the perils insured against is automatically covered at each location to which it is removed. The extension is effective for 5 days, covering the property at each location on the basis of the percentage of total values that the values at each location represent. Thus, if 20% of the total property is stored at one location, 20% of the insurance in force will apply there. The extension of coverage applies only for 5 days, and within that time the insured is expected to have the coverage transferred.

**The assignment clause.**   Immediately following the removal extension is the assignment clause, which provides that "Assignment of this policy shall not be valid except with the written consent of this company." While we often speak of the property as being insured, an insurance contract is a personal contract, agreeing to indemnify a specific insured in the event of loss. Coverage does not transfer to the new owner of property when it is sold, and moreover, through this clause, the insurance company reserves the right to decide if it wishes to continue the insurance for a new owner.

### Conditions and Exclusions

*Lines 1–6* state that the policy shall be void if the insured has willfully concealed or misrepresented any material fact concerning the insurance. In addition, provision is made for voiding the policy if the insured is fraudulent about the amount of the loss, other insurance, or the extent of his insurable interest, regardless of whether this false swearing takes place before or after the loss.

*Lines 7–10* excepts certain property from coverage. Accounts, bills, currency, deeds, evidences of debt, money, or securities are excluded. In addition, bullion and manuscripts are also excluded unless they have been specifically named as insured property in writing. The reason for this exclusion of course is to prevent fraudulent claims. The drafters of the contract felt that in the absence of this exclusion, every fire loss would involve a considerable amount of money. In addition, it is difficult to determine the actual value of documents and evidences of debt. Other contracts are available to provide coverage on the property excluded in this section.

*Lines 11–24* list certain perils that are not covered. If a fire or other peril insured against in the policy is a result of one of these excluded perils, there will be no coverage: (a) enemy attack by armed forces; (b) invasion; (c) insurrection; (d) rebellion; (e) revolution; (f) civil war; (g) usurped power; (h) order of civil authority; (i) neglect of the insured at or after loss; (j) loss by theft. The first seven exclusions are relatively obvious. By their nature, such losses are catastrophic and uninsurable.

The exclusion of damage by fire as a result of civil authority "except acts of destruction at the time of and for the purpose of preventing the spread of fire, provided that the fire did not originate from any of the perils excluded by this policy," requires some further explanation. Fires may be ordered by civil authorities for a number of reasons. Slum destruction or clearance projects might be accomplished by burning the old buildings. Such fire losses would not be payable under the fire policy. On the other hand, if property is burned by order of civil authority in an attempt to prevent the spread of fire (as might be done to create a firebreak), the loss would be paid, provided that the fire being prevented from spreading did not originate from one of the other excluded causes.

The reason for the exclusion of damage at or after a loss which results from the negligence of the insured should also be obvious. The insured cannot collect for damage which he has a reasonable chance to prevent. He is expected to take any steps which a reasonable man would take if he did not have the insurance and was going to be forced to suffer the loss himself.

*Lines 25–27* deal with the subject of other insurance covering the property insured under the policy. The limitation in these lines do not constitute a prohibition of other insurance, but merely reserve the right to prohibit other insurance to the insurance company.

*Lines 28–37* set forth certain conditions which suspend or restrict the insurance coverage:

1. While the hazard is increased by any means within the knowledge or control of the insured
2. While the described building, whether intended for occupancy by owner or tenant, is vacant or unoccupied for over 60 days
3. As a result of explosion unless fire ensues, and then the company is liable for the damage by the fire only

Note that these restrictions merely provide that the coverage is suspended during the period of time that the hazard is increased or while the building is vacant; once the increase in hazard has been removed and the building is again occupied, the suspension is lifted. As we will see, most modern dwelling forms permit vacancy and unoccupancy without limit of time and also modify the "increased hazard" restriction.

*Lines 38–48* deal with the modification of the policy by endorsements and riders. This section provides that the policy may be expanded to provide coverage against additional perils by endorsement. It also provides that no provision of the policy may be waived, unless it is subject to change by the terms of the policy.

*Lines 49–55* have been the subject of conflicting court opinions. The lines provide that no waiver affecting the policy is valid unless expressed in writing and attached to the policy. Some courts have upheld the provision, while others have maintained that not only are oral waivers by the agent valid, but that the agent can waive the very clause that says he cannot waive any of the provisions of the policy.

*Lines 56–67* provide for the cancellation of the contract by either party. If the company elects to cancel, the insured is entitled to a return premium computed on a "pro rata" basis, which means that he is charged only for the protection he has received. If a 1-year policy is cancelled after 6 months, the insured is entitled to a full 50% of the original premium. If the insured cancels, the return of premium is computed on a "short-rate" basis, and the insured receives a less than proportionate return of premium. For example, the short-rate return premium after 6 months of coverage would be about 40% of the annual premium. When the policy is originally written, both the insured and the company expect it to continue for the term specified, and the premium is computed on this basis. If the company decides to terminate the contract, a proportionate return of premium is made. If the insured decides to terminate the contract, the short-rate return provides some compensation to the company for the administrative work involved in the cancellation.

The policy requires that the company give the insured 5 days written notice of cancellation. The insured may cancel immediately upon notification. Most insurers cancel by registered mail with a return receipt requested. The 5 days required begins at midnight following the receipt of the notice.

*Lines 68–85* contain provisions that govern the rights and obligations of a mortgagee named in the policy. A mortgagee occupies an unusual position in the fire insurance contract. Although the mortgagee does not enter into the formation of the contract, any mortgagee listed in the policy becomes a party to the contract with certain rights distinct from those of the insured. When a mortgagee is named in the policy, a Standard Mortgage Clause is added to the policy granting certain rights to the mortgagee and imposing certain obligations. (This clause is included in the dwelling forms). The rights of the mortgagee are:

1. To receive any loss or damage payments to the extent of its interest in the property, regardless of any default of the property owner under the contract, and regardless of any change in the occupancy or increase in the hazard. (This right is granted in the Standard Mortgage Clause.)
2. To receive 10 days written notice in the event of cancellation instead of the 5 days afforded to the insured. (This right is granted in the basic policy and is repeated in the Standard Mortgage Clause.)
3. To sue under the policy in its own name. (This right is granted in the basic policy.)

The obligations imposed on the mortgagee are:

1. To notify the insurer of any change in occupancy or ownership or any increase in hazard. (This obligation is imposed in the Standard Mortgage Clause.)
2. To render proof of loss to the insurer if the owner fails to do so, and to thereafter abide by the policy provisions with respect to appraisal, time of payment, and bringing suit. (This obligation is imposed in the basic policy.)
3. To pay premiums due if the owner fails to do so. (This obligation is imposed in the Standard Mortgage Clause.)
4. To surrender to the insurer any claim it has against the mortgagor to the extent that it receives payment in those cases where the company has ruled that no coverage exists for the owner. (This obligation is imposed in both the basic policy and in the Standard Mortgage Clause.)

Note that these are conditional obligations. They must be met only if the mortgagee wishes to enjoy the coverage of the policy; they are not conditions which the mortgagee can be required to keep.

*Lines 86–89* deal with pro rata liability of the insurer in the event that there is more than one policy covering the property. If more than one policy covers the same property, the insured is limited in his recovery under each policy to its proportion of the loss, based on the percentage of all insurance that the insurance of each policy represents. For example, property valued at $20,000 is insured in Company A for $15,000 and Company B for $5000. In the event of a $4000 loss,

$$\text{Company A would pay} \quad \frac{\$15,000}{20,000} \times \$4000 = \$3000$$

$$\text{Company B would pay} \quad \frac{\$5000}{20,000} \times \$4000 = \$1000$$

The pro rata liability clause enforces the principle of indemnity by making certain that all insurance covering property shares only a percentage of the loss, and that this sharing is on an equitable basis.

*Lines 90–122* should be read in their entirety. These list the obligations the contract imposes on the insured in the event of loss. As an examination of the requirements will indicate, they appear to be dishearteningly burdensome and exacting. However, all that is required in most cases is reasonable compliance with three fundamental requirements:

1. The insured is required to give immediate notice of loss. Although the policy specifies that this notice is to be in writing, normally the insured gives notice of loss by calling his agent, and the courts have accepted this as meeting the requirement.

2. The insured is required to protect the property from further damage. This is a reasonable obligation. Any further damage would be due to the neglect of the insured and would not be covered.

3. Within 60 days, unless this time is extended by the company, the insured is required to file a "proof of loss." This is a certified statement, signed and sworn to by the insured, which contains information concerning the loss, the interest of the insured in the property, the total amount of insurance, the actual cash value of the property, and the amount claimed by the insured.

*Lines 123–140* provide a framework for the settlement of losses in those cases where the company and the insured cannot agree on the amount of loss. In this event, the policy provides that each party shall select a competent and disinterested appraiser. Together, the two appraisers select an umpire. If the appraisers cannot agree on an umpire, one will be appointed by the court. The appraisers then appraise the loss, each appraiser stating what he estimates the actual cash value to be. Their differences are submitted to the umpire, and an agreement in writing of any two of the three persons is binding on both parties. The cost of the appraisers is paid by the party they represent and the cost of the umpire is paid by both parties. This provision provides a means whereby the amount of a loss can be determined. It is not used when the company and the insured disagree as to whether a loss actually has occurred, or whether or not the loss is actually covered under the policy. Such disagreements can be settled through the courts.

*Lines 141–147* specify the options the company may exercise in settling the loss. The policy provides that the company may pay for the loss in cash, or, at its option, it may repair, rebuild, or replace the property destroyed or damaged with property of like kind and quality. The purpose of this condition is to protect the company against inflated loss claims. Normally, the company exercises its cash option, however, the right to repair or replace the property operates as a safeguard against unreasonable cash claims. In addition, the provisions of these lines give the company the option to take all or any part of the salvage at the agreed or appraised value.

*Lines 148–149* relate to the practice of taking salvage. In loss adjustment, it is the practice to agree on the value of salvage. As we have seen, the company has the option to take the salvage at the agreed value; however, the abandonment clause of the policy states that the company cannot be forced to take salvage, and the insured cannot abandon the property to the insurance company.

*Lines 150–156* require the insurance company to pay for any loss under the policy within 60 days after it has received the insured's proof of loss and the company and the insured have agreed on the amount of the loss.

*Lines 157–161* place a limit upon the time within which the insured must bring suit in a court of law. The policy provides that no suit shall be sustainable in any court of law unless the requirements of the policy have been complied with, and unless the suit is brought within 12 months of the loss.

*Lines 162–165* contain the subrogation provision. The company may require the insured to assign the right to sue a third party to it, to the extent that it has made payment for loss that was caused by the third party and for which the insured has a claim against the third party. If the insured decides to collect under his fire policy, he gives the insurance company the right to sue in his name and collect the sums he would have been able to collect. If he decides not to collect under the fire policy, he may retain the right and sue the third party himself. If the amount of the loss is greater than the amount of the insurance, the insured may assign a part of the right to sue to the insurance company and retain his right to sue for the remainder of his loss.

Previously, it was noted that the Standard Fire Policy is not a complete contract in itself, and must be combined with a form. Different forms are required for different types of property, and there are often several forms available for a given type of property. In addition to forms that are used to describe the type of property insured, there are forms that are used to provide coverage against certain other perils which are not covered by the basic fire policy. Three of the forms used to insure private dwellings and their contents will now be examined briefly.

## THE DWELLING BUILDING(S) AND CONTENTS FORM

The Dwelling Building(s) and Contents Form (usually referred to as the Dwelling and Contents Form) is the basic form used to modify and complete the fire policy when providing coverage on dwelling property. It may be used to provide coverage on one- and two-family dwellings and certain other property.[4] As its title indicates, it can be used to provide coverage on both the dwelling and the personal property of the insured.

### Dwelling Coverage

When the form is used to provide coverage on the dwelling, it provides coverage on the dwelling itself, and in addition provides coverage on building equipment and fixtures and outdoor equipment pertaining to the service of the premises. This form does not provide any coverage on trees, shrubs,

[4]Technically, the eligibility requirements for this form state that it is to be used to insure dwellings designed for occupancy by not more than four families or containing more than four apartments, for boarding and rooming houses with not more than 20 rooms for lodging or not more than 20 boarders, and nurses' and sisters' homes with not more than 10 sleeping rooms.

plants, or the lawn. If the insured wishes coverage on these items, they must be listed on the face of the policy as specifically insured items, and an additional premium must be paid.

### Contents Coverage

Contents is defined as household goods and personal property usual and incidental to the occupancy of a dwelling. This means that anything that one would expect to find in or around a dwelling is covered, so long as it is not specifically excluded. The form excludes aircraft, motor vehicles, boats (except rowboats and canoes), animals, birds, and fish. Thus, in addition to furniture and clothing, coverage would apply to books, food, tools, cameras, sporting equipment, and anything else which might conceivably be in or around a dwelling.

### Extensions

The Dwelling and Contents Form provides certain extensions of coverage which constitute an important part of the insured's protection. Although these extensions are often overlooked, they are one of the most important parts of the form. There are six extensions under the form, extending coverage to certain additional property or types of losses.

**The appurtenant structures extension.** The insured may apply up to 10% of the amount of insurance on the dwelling to cover other structures on the permises. The only restrictions are that the building cannot be used for mercantile, manufacturing, or farming purposes, and that they may not be rented to anyone except a tenant of the main dwelling. A private garage which is used for private garage purposes only does not come under the rental exclusion and may be rented to anyone. The 10% extension applies to such garages. This 10% is not an additional amount of insurance. If the insured has a $10,000 dwelling and the house and garage both burn, coverage will be limited to $10,000.

**Rental value extension.** When a dwelling is damaged by fire or some other peril, the owner faces not only the loss that results directly from the damage, but he also faces an indirect loss. During the period of time required to restore the building to tenantable condition, he loses the use of the dwelling. The rental value extension provides that the insured may apply up to 10% of the amount of insurance on the dwelling to cover the rental value, with a 1/12 per month limit of recovery. Rental value is defined as the amount for which the dwelling could have been rented at the time of loss, completely furnished, whether or not it was rented. In other words, if the insured himself was living in the house at the time of the loss, he would still be entitled to collect the amount he could have rented the building for during the period of time it takes to restore the building to livable condition. The 1/12 per month limitation imposes a maximum on the amount recoverable during any one month. Suppose that the insured has a dwelling valued at a $300 per month rental value. If the insured has a dwelling insured for $24,000, the 10% extension provides $2400 coverage to cover rental value, but the 1/12 limitation permits only a $200 per month recovery. On the other hand, assuming the same insurance coverage, if the dwelling has a rental value of $150 per month, this is the maximum the insured can collect, regardless of the fact that the policy extension provides up to $200 per month. Like the extension on structures, this 10% is not an additional amount of insurance.[5]

**Off-premises extension.** In discussing the fire policy, it was noted that the coverage afforded is at the location listed in the policy except in the case of removal or extensions under the forms attached to the fire policy. The Dwelling and Contents Form provides that up to 10% of the amount of coverage on contents may apply to property belonging to the insured or residents of the insured's household while such property is away from the premises but still in the United States or Canada. Rowboats and canoes, which are covered on premises, are excluded under this extension. Note that the coverage under the off-premises extension, like the appurtenant private structures extension and the rental value extension, is not additional insurance.

This extension is particularly meaningful to college students who are away from home attending school. Such students are considered to be residents of their parents' household, and any personal effects they have with them are covered under their parent's policy (but with the 10% limit). If the student's father has $5000 worth of contents coverage, the student's effects are covered under the extension for up to $500.

This extension also covers personal property off-premises which is in the hands of repair shops, laundries, dry cleaners, or others. However, the insured must file a claim against any bailee or carrier in whose possession the insured's property was at the time of loss. In other words, the off-premises extension cannot be used for the benefit of a bailee or carrier.

**Improvement, alterations, and additions.** If the insured is a tenant and he installs improvements or betterments at his own expense and for his own convenience and use, he has an insurable interest in these expenditures, even though by law any property attached to the dwelling or any improvements made by the tenant become the property of the owner. The improvements, alterations, and additions extension provides that the insured, if a tenant, may apply up to 10% of the amount of coverage on contents to cover such improvements, but not as additional insurance.

[5] Under previous editions of the Dwelling and Contents Form, the 10% extensions on appurtenant private structures and rental value were additional amounts of insurance.

**Property removal extension.** The Dwelling and Contents Form provides that if the insured moves to another location within the state, and it is to be the residence of the insured, the insurance on the contents will cease to cover at the old location and will cover the property at the new location. During the period of removal, the property at each location is covered on a pro rata basis; the coverage applies at each location on the basis of the total amount the values at that location represent to the total values at each location. For example, if the individual has $10,000 worth of contents, which is insured for $10,000, and he has moved $4000 worth of furniture to the new location, he has $4000 in coverage at the new location and $6000 in coverage at the old one. Property in transit is covered only to the extent of the off-premises extension.

**Debris removal extension.** This extension provides that the policy will cover expenses incurred in removing debris of insured property which is damaged by any of the perils insured against under the policy. It does not increase the limits of the policy, and all expenses charged for removing debris will apply against the face amount of insurance in the same manner as direct loss of property.

### Other Important Provisions

In addition to these six extensions, there are certain other important clauses in the form which are of particular importance.

**Consequential loss.** Consequential loss, in contrast to direct loss, results in damage or loss that is a result of damage to other property. The best example of consequential loss as it applies to the dwelling risk is that of frozen food in a deep freeze. Suppose that as a result of a fire, the deep freeze is damaged. In all probability, the damage to the deep freeze will represent only a part of the loss sustained by the insured. He may lose $200 or $300 worth of frozen food. The Dwelling and Contents Form provides some coverage for this loss. The policy provides, in an exception to one of the exclusions, that loss due to a change in temperature will be covered, if the change in temperature is a result of actual physical damage to power, heating, or cooling equipment on the premises. Of course, the damage must be caused by an insured peril. Suppose that lightning strikes the house and destroys all the wiring, with the result that the meat in the freezer is ruined. This loss would be covered. However, if the lightning does not strike the house and damage the wiring, but instead knocks out the power plant 2 miles away, the loss would not be covered because of the requirement of damage to the building or equipment in the building.

**Inherent explosion clause.** The inherent explosion clause adds another peril to the three which are covered by the basic policy. This clause extends the policy to cover direct loss to the property of the insured caused by explosion occurring in the described building or other buildings on the premises, even if fire does not ensue. The inherent explosion clause specifically lists explosion of accumulated gases or unconsumed fuel within the firebox or combustion chamber of a furnace or other fired vessel as covered and excludes specifically explosions of a steam heating system, machinery, bursting of water pipes, electrical arcing, or water hammer. Virtually all other explosions emanating from an insured dwelling are covered.

**The loss clause.** The Dwelling and Contents Form, like most other fire forms, states that any loss under the policy will not reduce the amount of the policy. Following a loss the insured still has the same amount of insurance coverage as he had before the loss, and the policy does not need to be reinstated in any manner.

**Permission granted clause.** The basic policy suspends coverage at any time during an increase in the hazard within the knowledge or control of the insured. The permission granted clause grants permission for certain things that might otherwise suspend coverage as increases in the hazard. In this clause permission is granted:

1. For such use of the premises as is usual or incidental to the described occupancy.
2. For the described premises to be vacant or unoccupied without limit of time.
3. To make alterations, additions, and repairs, and to complete structures in the course of construction.

**Electrical apparatus clause.** The form excludes damage to electrical appliances by artificially generated currents. If an appliance is damaged by an abnormally high or low surge of power, there is no coverage under the contract unless fire ensues, and then only the ensuing damage is covered.

**Liberalization clause.** The liberalization clause provides that if, during the term of the policy, the company adopts any form or endorsement that would broaden the policy without an additional premium, the broader provisions of such form are made a part of the policy.


### THE EXTENDED COVERAGE ENDORSEMENT

Up to this point, we have discussed only the basic fire policy and one of several forms that are used to make it a complete contract. In addition to forms that complete the contract, there are forms available which extend the coverage of the policy to include certain additional perils. One of the more important of these endorsements is the Extended Coverage Endorsement.

In the early 1900s it was the custom for insurance companies to offer windstorm damage to the public as a separate coverage. As people became increasingly aware of the possibility of property damage as a result of windstorm and certain other perils, the Extended Coverage Endorsement was eventually developed.

The Extended Coverage Endorsement adds nine perils to the policy. It does not increase the limit of the policy. It merely expands the number of perils insured against. The insured who purchases $10,000 fire and extended coverage does not have $20,000 in coverage; he has $10,000 coverage against twelve perils. Extended coverage is written for the same amount as the fire insurance in the policy.

Most forms that are used to complete the fire contract (e.g., the Dwelling and Contents Form, the Building and Contents Form, etc.)[6] include the provisions of the Extended Coverage Endorsement. The coverage of the endorsement is effective, however, only if the insured pays the additional premium the coverage requires.

### Perils of Extended Coverage

The extended coverage insuring agreement modifies the insuring agreement of the Standard Fire Policy. It states:

> In consideration of the premium for this coverage, and subject to the provisions herein and in the policy to which this Extended Coverage is attached, including endorsements thereon, this policy is extended to insure against direct loss by WINDSTORM, HAIL, EXPLOSION, RIOT, RIOT ATTENDING A STRIKE, CIVIL COMMOTION, AIRCRAFT, VEHICLES, AND SMOKE.

The cost of the combined perils is far less than the cost of purchasing them individually. By selling all the coverages as a combined unit, the insurance companies are able to avoid the adverse selection that would result if the individual purchased only perils he felt he needed most.

**Windstorm and hail perils.** Coverage is provided by the Extended Coverage Endorsement for damage caused by direct action of the wind or hail. The majority of the courts have held the position that objects propelled by the wind, which cause damage, are a result of "direct action by the wind."

---

[6] The reader should recognize that although the treatment of the Extended Coverage Endorsement appears in this section, which deals with dwelling coverages, the provisions of the Extended Coverage Endorsement used to insure other forms of property are exactly the same as those explained here.

If the wind blows a tree branch through a window, or blows a tree over on the insured's dwelling, the resulting damage would be covered.

The provisions of the endorsement specifically exclude any damage caused by rain, snow, sand, or dust, to the interior of the building unless the exterior walls or the roof are first damaged by direct action of the wind or hail. Thus, if the insured leaves a window open and the wind blows rain into the house damaging the furniture and rugs, such damage would not be covered. However, if the window had been broken by the wind, the damage would be covered.[7]

**Windstorm and hail deductible.** The windstorm and hail perils are subject to a $50 deductible, which applies separately to each building or structure including outdoor radio and television antennas. It does not apply to contents or to rental value. In some jurisdictions, this deductible may be waived by the payment of an additional premium. In other jurisdictions a $50 deductible is applicable to all perils.

**Explosion peril.** The coverage provided for damage caused by explosion under the Extended Coverage Endorsement is considerably broader than the inherent explosion coverage of the Dwelling and Contents Form. Explosions are covered whether they originate within or outside the building. The endorsement states that the following are not considered to be explosions within the definition of the contract:

1. Shock waves caused by aircraft (Sonic Boom)
2. Rupture or bursting of steam boilers, steam turbines, steam engines if owned or operated by the insured
3. Rupture or bursting of rotating parts of machinery or electrical arcing
4. Rupture or bursting of water pipes or pressure relief devices
5. Rupture or bursting due to explosion or swelling of the contents of any building or structure caused by or resulting from water.

**Perils of riot, riot attending a strike, and civil commotion.** Although the term "riot" and the other related terms are not defined in the contract, various courts have provided definitions. One court defined a riot as follows:

A tumultous disturbance of the peace by three persons or more assembling of their own authority with an intent mutually to assist one another against anyone who shall oppose them in the execution of some enterprise of a private nature, and afterwards actually executing the same in a violent and turbulent manner to the terror of the people, whether the act intended were of itself lawful or unlawful.[8]

---

[7] It does not take a member of the bar to figure out how to cope with this exclusion. In many such losses the insurance company ends up paying for the water damage and a broken window.

[8] *Symonds vs. State, 66 Okla. Cr. 49, 54, 88 P 2d 970, 973.*

Damage caused by rioters is covered under the provisions of the Extended Coverage Endorsement with very few exceptions. Even "pillage and looting" is covered, if it occurs during and at the place of the riot. The main question that arises is in connection with the distinction between a riot and an insurrection. The Standard Fire Policy excludes losses caused by insurrection, so the distinction is very important. The feature that distinguishes an insurrection from a riot is the intent in an insurrection to overthrow the government and take possession of the powers of government.

**Aircraft damage peril.**  Damage to property resulting from a crashing plane is likely to be severe. The aircraft damage peril provides coverage for loss to property resulting from physical contact of an aircraft or an object falling from an aircraft. The requirement of physical contact between the aircraft and the insured property eliminates coverage for damage caused by "sonic boom."

**Vehicle damage peril.**  As under the aircraft peril, physical contact is required. "Vehicles" are defined as including those which run on land or tracks, but not aircraft. There are two very important exclusions applicable to the vehicle damage peril.

1. All damage caused by vehicles owned or operated by the insured or a tenant of the property is excluded.
2. Damage to fences, driveways, walks, trees, lawns, and shrubs are excluded from coverage by any vehicle, as are vehicles and the contents of vehicles.

It should be recognized that the coverage afforded is somewhat limited. The greatest exposure consists of damage which might be caused by the insured himself.

**Smoke damage peril.**  As the reader will no doubt recall, the Standard Fire Policy provides coverage for damage caused by smoke from a hostile fire. The Extended Coverage Endorsement broadens this slightly by providing coverage for smoke damage which results from the "sudden, unusual, and faulty operation of a heating or cooking unit." Furthermore, it is required that such heating or cooking unit be connected to the chimney by a smoke pipe or vent pipe, and that it be on the described premises. Smoke from fireplaces and industrial apparatus is excluded.

### Apportionment Clause

In examining the pro rata liability clause of the Standard Fire Policy, it was determined that when more than one policy covers the property insured, each policy participates on the basis of the percentage of all insurance that it represents. The apportionment clause of the Extended Coverage Endorsement provides for settlement when the policies on the loss do not all cover against the same perils. Losses covered by the policy written with extended coverage are apportioned as if all policies were written with extended coverage. If all policies are not written alike, the insured may suffer a penalty in the loss settlement. This is accomplished through the simple device of apportioning losses covered by the perils of extended coverage on the basis of the percentage of all fire insurance which the extended coverage represents. For the sake of illustration, suppose that the insured has purchased two policies, each in the amount of $10,000 to cover his $20,000 building. To save on his premium, he has purchased one policy with both fire and extended coverage and one policy with the peril of fire only. This might be a logical approach, were it not for the apportionment clause. Most losses covered under extended coverage tend to be partial losses, and the $10,000 protection against these perils would probably be adequate to cover most such losses. However, because of the provisions of the apportionment clause, in the event of a loss caused by one of the perils of the Extended Coverage Endorsement, the insured will collect only 50% of the amount of the loss, for this is the proportion of all fire insurance that the policy written with extended coverage represents.

When all policies covering the same property are not written exactly alike, they are said to be "nonconcurrent." Concurrency in property insurance is of utmost importance, for virtually all policies with broad or extended perils coverage provide for the apportionment of losses with other insurance on the basis of the face amount of all policies covering against the peril of fire.

## THE DWELLING AND CONTENTS BROAD FORM

Following the development of the Extended Coverage Endorsement, broader forms of coverage were developed, especially in the dwelling field. In 1951, an endorsement known as Additional Extended Coverage was made available, which, when combined with the Extended Coverage Endorsement, provided protection against an exceedingly wide range of perils. The next step was to combine the Dwelling and Contents Form, the Extended Coverage Endorsement, and the Additional Extended Coverage Endorsement into one form. Certain additions and modifications were made, and the result was the Dwelling and Contents Broad Form.

Due to the fact that the coverage is considerably broader under the Dwelling and Contents Broad Form than under the basic form, the eligibility requirements are more exacting. To qualify for coverage under the Broad Form, the amount of insurance on the dwelling must be at least $8000. When the Broad Form is used to provide coverage for a tenant, the minimum amount of coverage on contents is $4000.

### Perils Added under the Broad Form

In addition to those perils covered under the basic fire policy and those included in the Extended Coverage Endorsement, the Dwelling and Contents Broad Form adds coverage against loss from the following perils:

1. Steam or hot water heating system explosion
2. Vandalism and malicious mischief
3. Damage caused by burglars
4. Falling objects
5. Weight of ice, snow, and sleet
6. Collapse of the dwelling
7. Leakage or overflow of plumbing, heating, or air-conditioning systems
8. Breakage of glass constituting a part of the dwelling
9. Freezing of plumbing
10. Injury to electric appliances and wiring by artificially generated currents

A complete analysis of these additional perils requires a close examination of the form itself, but briefly the perils provide the following.

**Heating system explosion.**  Coverage is provided against "sudden and accidental tearing asunder, cracking, burning, or bulging of a steam or hot water heating system." There are two separate insuring agreements dealing with such explosion damage. One covers explosion of any appliance used for heating water for domestic consumption and is subject to a $50 deductible; the other covers any other type of steam or hot water system and does not have a deductible.

**Vandalism and malicious mischief.**  Vandalism and malicious mischief is covered, but the peril excludes loss by pilferage, theft, larceny, or burglary. Glass breakage is also excluded under this peril, but is covered under a separate peril, subject to a $50 deductible. Finally, there is no coverage for vandalism and malicious mischief damage if the dwelling has been vacant for over 30 days.

**Damage caused by burglars.**  Only the damage caused by burglars is covered. There is no coverage for loss of property that is taken by the burglars. Like the vandalism peril, the burglary damage peril excludes loss if the dwelling has been vacant for over 30 days.

**Damage by falling objects.**  This peril covers damage caused by falling objects such as tree limbs, but of course is not limited to this. There is an exclusion of damage to the interior of the building or the contents of the building unless the exterior first sustains damage. In addition, damage to trees, plants, shrubs, television and radio antennas, cloth awnings, gutters and downspouts is excluded.

**Weight of ice, snow, and sleet.** Damage which results from the weight of ice, snow, and sleet is covered, but the damage must actually be the result of such weight. For example, melting snow which leaks into the dwelling causing damage would not be covered. Damage to trees, shrubs, plants, lawns, outdoor equipment, fences, radio and television antennas, cloth awnings, gutters, and downspouts is excluded.

**Collapse of the dwelling.** Direct loss as a result of the collapse of the building or any part of the building is covered. This insuring agreement is actually a promise to indemnify for a type of loss rather than for loss caused by a specific peril. Collapse from any cause is covered, but mere settling, cracking, shrinking, bulging, or expansion are excluded.

**Water damage.** This peril provides coverage for accidental discharge, overflow or leakage of water from a heating, plumbing, or air-conditioning system or appliance, including the cost of tearing out and replacing part of the building to make repairs. Only the loss of the plumbing itself is ex-excluded. Vacancy is limited to 30 days, as in the case of vandalism and malicious mischief.

**Glass breakage.** Like the collapse of building insuring agreement, the glass breakage insuring agreement covers a type of loss rather than a peril. The breakage need not be a result of a specific cause. Breakage of glass constituting a part of the building, including glass in storm doors and windows is covered. Vacancy is limited to 30 days.

**Freezing of plumbing.** Loss resulting from freezing of plumbing, heating, or air-conditioning systems or domestic appliances is covered, provided that the building has not been left vacant or unoccupied for over 4 days unless the system was drained and the water shut off. If the insured was careful in attempting to maintain heat in the building, or if the system was drained and the freezing still occurred, the loss would be covered even if the building had been vacant or unoccupied for over 4 days.

**Injury to appliances by artificially generated electricity.** Sudden and accidental injury from artificially generated electric currents to wiring and appliances is covered as an insured peril. This is in contrast to the Dwelling and Contents Form which specifically excludes such damage. The major exclusion with respect to artificially generated electricity is damage to tubes, transistors, and similar electronic components.

### Perils Broadened under the Broad Form

Not only does the Broad Form add perils not covered by the Dwelling and Contents Form, but many of the perils of the Dwelling and Contents Form are considerably broadened under the Broad Form.

**The smoke peril.** The smoke peril of the Dwelling and Contents Form is quite restrictive. The Broad Form, on the other hand, covers all sudden and accidental smoke damage from any source except industrial or smudging operations. There is not even an exclusion of smoke from a fireplace as in the Dwelling and Contents Form.

**Explosion.** The explosion peril does not exclude explosion of a steam boiler as does the Dwelling and Contents Form. As a matter of fact, steam boiler explosion is specifically insured under the heating system explosion peril discussed above.

**Aircraft.** The aircraft peril of the Dwelling and Contents Form requires actual physical contact of the airplane or an object falling from an aircraft for loss to be covered. The Broad Form makes no such requirement; therefore, sonic boom would be covered under the aircraft peril of the Broad Form.

**Vehicles.** The Dwelling and Contents Form provides no coverage whatsoever for damage caused by a vehicle owned or operated by the insured or a tenant of the property. The Broad Form provides coverage for such damage, subject to a $50 deductible. Damage to trees, shrubs, plants, lawns, walks, and driveways is excluded if the damage is caused by a vehicle owned or operated by an insured or a tenant of the property, but otherwise all damage is covered.

While the examples given above are not exhaustive, they serve to illustrate the manner in which the perils of the Dwelling and Contents form have been broadened under the Broad Form.

### Deductibles

Like the Dwelling and Contents Form, the Broad Form includes a $50 deductible applicable to the perils of windstorm and hail. In addition to the wind and hail deductible, the Broad Form contains a $50 deductible applicable to most of the perils which are not contained in the Extended Coverage Endorsement. In many jurisdictions, one or both of these deductibles may be waived by the payment of a higher rate or an additional premium. However, there is a deductible applicable to damage caused by a vehicle owned or operated by an insured or a tenant, and a deductible which applies to vandalism and malicious mischief or burglary damage at a seasonal dwelling, which cannot be removed.

**Extensions**

Like the Dwelling and Contents Form, the Broad Form includes certain extensions of coverage. The extensions of the Broad Form are:

1. Appurtenant structures
2. Additional living expense
3. Off premises
4. Improvements, alterations, and additions
5. Property removal
6. Debris removal
7. Trees, shrubs, lawns, and plants
8. Replacement cost

Most of these are essentially the same as the extensions discussed in connection with the Dwelling and Contents Form, so we will confine our discussion to those which differ from the extensions already discussed.

**Appurtenant structures extension.** The appurtenant structures extension is similar to that of the basic form, except that in the Broad Form the 10% extension is an additional amount of insurance.

**Additional living expense extension.** The additional living expense extension is the Broad Form equivalent of the rental value extension of the Dwelling and Contents Form. The insured may apply up to 10% of the amount of insurance on the dwelling to cover both the rental value and additional living expense. Under the Broad Form, rental value applies to that portion of the dwelling which the insured does not occupy, while additional living expense covers that portion occupied by the insured. Under the additional living expense portion, the insured is entitled to collect the amount by which his living expenses increase as a result of untenantability of the premises. The 1/12 limit per month contained in the Dwelling and Contents Form does not appear in the Broad Form, and the 10% extension is an additional amount of insurance. Thus, if the insured has purchased $10,000 in coverage on his dwelling and the dwelling is totally destroyed, he might collect up to a total of $11,000 for the loss of the dwelling and the additional living expense. The only limitations are that the payment for additional living expense is on an indemnity basis; the insured is to maintain as nearly as practicable his same standard of living after the loss as before, and the time is limited to the period that would be required with due diligence and dispatch to restore the property to tenantable condition. The period for which the additional living expense is payable is not limited by the expiration of the policy.

**Trees, shrubs, lawns, and plants extension.** The Broad Form also provides that the insured may apply up to 5% of the amount of insurance on the dwelling to cover trees, shrubs, lawns, and plants against the perils of fire, lightning, riot, riot attending a strike, civil commotion, vandalism and malicious mischief, damage by burglars, aircraft, smoke, collapse of the building, and damage by vehicles not owned or operated by the insured or a tenant. Windstorm and hail are specifically excluded. There is a maximum of $250 payable for any one tree, shrub, or plant. The $250 limit does not apply to lawns, so lawns are covered for up to a full 5% of the amount on the dwelling.

**Replacement cost extension.**    The replacement cost extension is one of the most attractive features of the Broad Form. It provides that if at the time of a loss the amount of insurance covering a building is at least 80% of the replacement cost of the building, the loss will be paid on the basis of replacement cost (without any deduction for depreciation) rather than on an actual cash value basis. The extension applies only to buildings, and contents are covered on an actual cash value basis. In addition, the provision does not apply to outdoor equipment, domestic appliances, cloth awnings, carpeting, and roof surfacing.

In its simplest aspect, the extension eliminates depreciation in settling losses, provided the insured has maintained insurance equal to 80% of replacement cost. In effect, the replacement cost extension furnishes the insured with an option to purchase insurance equal to the amount of depreciation which the building has suffered. If the amount of coverage on the building is less than 80% of the replacement cost, the company will pay the larger of the following two amounts:

1. The actual cash value
2. The proportion of the replacement cost of the loss that the amount of insurance bears to 80% of the replacement cost value of the building

If the loss is more than $1000 or 5% of the amount of insurance, the building must actually be repaired or replaced before the insured can collect on a replacement cost basis.

While on the subject of replacement cost, it might be well to discuss some problems involved in determining the insurable value of property. The fact that most insureds have a somewhat distorted notion of what is meant by insurable value often results in improper insurance coverage. There are two basic measures of insurable value in dwelling property: replacement cost and actual cash value. By this time, we all have a reasonably good estimate of what is meant by actual cash value—it is replacement cost less depreciation; it is based on replacement cost value and is therefore more difficult to compute. Replacement cost, on the other hand, is simply the cost of replacing the building with materials of like kind and quality at current prices. Replacement cost may be computed by application of a construction cost index to original construction cost or by application of average construction costs in the area to the building under consideration.

Quite often, the insured considers insurable value to be some other inappropriate measure of value such as loan value or market value. The mortgagee normally requires insurance equal to its interest in the property, reinforcing the mistaken notion that market value somehow coincides with insurable value. There is no guarantee that market value will be the same as either actual cash value or replacement cost; there is even good reason to assume that it will not. Market value is based on the supply and demand for real estate of the particular type involved. It includes the value of the land on which the building is located, yet the value of the land is not a part of insurable value.

Let's take a simple example and examine some of the aspects of this insurable value problem. The dwelling under consideration was built 30 years ago at a cost of $8000. It has just been purchased for $12,000. On the basis of current construction costs and a construction price index, we estimate the current replacement cost to be $20,000. For the purpose of illustration, we will assume an expected life length of 60 years for the building and linear depreciation amounting to 50%. Thus, we have an original cost of $8000, a replacement cost of $20,000, a market value of $12,000, and an actual cash value of $10,000.

If the building is insured under the Dwelling and Contents Form, the coverage is on an actual cash basis and it should be insured for $10,000. In the event that it burns down, the insured will collect $10,000, which is the depreciated value of the building. In the event of a partial loss, payment will be made with a deduction for depreciation. If a fire damages a part of the house and the cost of repairing the damage amounts to $2000, the $2000 represents the replacement cost of the loss, and the insured will be compensated with a deduction for depreciation. In the case of our example, he might collect as little as $1000. On the other hand, if the insured purchases replacement cost coverage under the Broad Form, insuring for at least 80% of the replacement cost,[9] payment for the same $2000 loss would be made in full without deduction for any depreciation. Finally, if the insured purchased coverage under the Broad Form using the market value as the basis for the amount of insurance, he would collect only a portion of the replacement cost of the loss. He will collect that proportion of the full

[9] It should be noted that while the form requires only 80% of the replacement cost to be insured, this does not and should not preclude the insured from purchasing 100% replacement cost coverage.

replacement cost which the amount of insurance carried bears to the amount required. Since 80% of the replacement cost is $16,000 and he has purchased only $12,000, he will collect 12/16 of the $2000 or $1500, and he will be forced to bear $500 of the loss himself.

## THE DWELLING BUILDING SPECIAL FORM

The Dwelling Building Special Form is designed to provide all risk coverage on the dwelling and other buildings on the premises. It covers damage from any cause except those perils which are specifically excluded. It cannot be used to cover contents, and when this form is written for an owner–occupant, the contents are normally covered under the Broad Form. Like the Broad Form, eligibility is limited to dwellings with a value of at least $8000.

It is important to keep in mind the distinction between "named peril" coverage and the "all-risk" form of coverage. On a named peril basis, a loss is not covered unless the occurrence falls within the definition of one of the perils insured against. Under the Special Form, a loss is covered unless it is specifically excluded. For this reason, the exclusions of the all-risk form deserve special attention.

The number of exclusions required in an all-risk form is quite large, for all uninsurable perils must be excluded. Even the named peril forms exclude war, flood and water damage of the same nature, earthquake and landslide, and loss by nuclear reaction, nuclear radiation, or radioactive contamination. In addition to these exclusions, the Special Form excludes damage or loss which results from the following:

1. Wear and tear, deterioration
2. Rust, mold, wet or dry rot
3. Contamination, smog
4. Smoke from industrial or agricultural operations
5. Mechanical breakdown
6. Damage by birds, insects, vermin, or domestic animals
7. Settling, cracking, shrinkage, bulging or expansion of pavement, patios, foundations, walls, roof, floor, or ceiling

Anything not excluded under the contract is covered. Note, for example, that there is no exclusion of theft. If fixtures constituting a part of the house were stolen, coverage would exist.

Since each of the successive forms incorporates the extensions and liberalizations of each of the lower forms, the Special Form includes all the extensions and provisions of the Broad Form, except those which apply to the contents coverage.

## Questions for Discussion and Review

**1.** Rosie LaRue has just purchased a 20-year-old dwelling for $25,000. The mortgagee insists that she purchase insurance in an amount at least equal to the amount of the $20,000 mortgage. Rosie protests that the lot on which the dwelling is located is worth $10,000, making the value of the house $15,000. Finally, she comes to you for advice. Advise her.

**2.** The Dwelling Building Special Form covers the dwelling on an all-risk basis. What perils that are not covered under the Dwelling and Contents Form or the Dwelling and Contents Broad Form would be covered under the Special Form?

**3.** Due to a power transformer burnout, the entire city in which you live is without power for 4 days. There is some inconvenience, but your greatest loss is the damage to your freezer, which resulted when the meat within the freezer spoiled. The freezer is no longer usable, and the meat is a total loss. Would you expect the loss of either the freezer or the meat to be covered under the Dwelling and Contents Broad Form?

**4.** The Standard Fire Policy excludes loss resulting from insurrection; the extended coverage endorsement specifically covers loss resulting from riot. Are these provisions in conflict? What, if anything, is the difference between a riot and an insurrection?

**5.** What are the rights and obligations of a mortgagee under the standard fire policy endorsed with the standard mortgage clause? Are there any provisions in the mortgage clause that deprive the mortgagee or restrict any of the rights which it would otherwise have?

## Suggestions for Additional Reading

Bickelhaupt, D. L. and Magee, J. H. *General Insurance*, 8th ed. Homewood, Ill.: Richard D. Irwin, 1970, Chap. 10.

*Fire, Casualty, and Surety Bulletins,* Fire and Marine Volume, "Dwellings" Section. Cincinnati, Ohio: The National Underwriter Co.

Gordis, P. *Property and Casualty Insurance*, 17th ed. Indianapolis, Ind.: The Rough Notes Co., 1970, Chaps. 2, 3, 5.

Long, J. D. and Gregg, D. W. *Property and Liability Insurance Handbook.* Homewood, Ill.: Richard D. Irwin, 1965, Chaps. 4–6.

Magee, J. H. and Serbein, O. N. *Property and Liability Insurance*, 4th ed. Homewood, Ill.: Richard D. Irwin, 1967, Chaps. 5–8.

Vaughan, E. J. "What Is Insurable Value?" *The American Agency Bulletin* (Sept. 1965).

# 16 Property Insurance for the Family Part II

*The things are most dear to us which have
cost us most.*

—Montaigne, *Essays*

In Chapter 15, one of the forms used to modify the standard fire policy
was examined in detail, and two additional forms were briefly mentioned.
In spite of the wide range of perils included in these forms, more attractive
alternatives may be available to the individual. This chapter continues our
discussion of property insurance for the family with a brief discussion of the
Homeowners policies and inland marine coverage.

## THE HOMEOWNERS POLICIES

The multiple-line transition was discussed in Chapter 4. As the reader will
recall, this transition resulted from the removal of the legal barriers which
had separated the writing of property insurance from casualty insurance.
One of the most significant results of the multiple-line transition has been
the development of the package policy, in which property and casualty
coverages are combined in a single contract. The Homeowners policies,
which combine those coverages available under the separate dwelling forms
with theft insurance and personal liability insurance, are the most widely
sold and by far the best known of the package policies.

Prior to the introduction of the Homeowners policy, an extremely limited portion of the population carried adequate insurance coverage on their property. Insurance on the dwelling was usually limited to coverage against the perils of fire and extended coverage, and many people carried no insurance whatsoever on their contents. In the case of the few who did insure their contents, the coverage was also usually restricted to fire and extended coverage, and the amount of coverage purchased was far below the actual value of the property. The more prudent individuals purchased personal liability insurance, but a surprising number neglected this coverage. Finally, personal theft insurance was purchased by an infinitesimally small number. The Homeowners policy, with its "packaging" of these coverages, has resulted in the almost universal purchase of the previously neglected coverages. The basic approach of the Homeowners policy is to require certain minimum amounts of coverage on both the dwelling and the contents, including theft coverage as a part of the mandatory coverage. Comprehensive personal liability insurance is also included on a mandatory basis.[1] The net result has been insurance to value and better insurance to exposure, with a reduction in the adverse selection which existed when the insured was permitted to pick and choose.

The aspect of the package policies that is most attractive from the consumer's point of view is the discount that is involved when these coverages are combined into a single package. In the past, the discounts have ranged upward to 40% of the cost of the coverages when purchased separately. The discounts reflect the savings that result from reduced policy writing and handling costs, the higher amounts of insurance per policy, mitigation of adverse selection, and the effect of exacting eligibility and underwriting rules.

The Homeowners program was developed in 1958 by the Multi-Peril Insurance Conference, an advisory and rating organization. The program was revised slightly in 1962 and more extensively in 1968.

### General Nature of the Program

In most jurisdictions there are five Homeowners forms, designated HO 1, HO 2, HO 3, HO 4, and HO 5. Four of these forms are designed for individuals who own their own homes (forms 1, 2, 3, and 5), while the fifth (form 4) is designed for tenants. There are rather strict eligiblity requirements under the program. Forms 1, 2, 3, and 5 may be written only for the owner occupant of a dwelling which is used exclusively for private residential purposes (although the rules permit incidental office or pro-

---

[1]A policy quite similar to our Homeowners policy has been available in England since about 1916. It is called the Householders Comprehensive Policy and includes all the coverages of the Homeowners policy plus accident insurance on the insured and his wife and their servants.

fessional occupancy, as in the case of a physician who may have an office in his home). The dwelling may not contain more than two families, and not more than two boarders or roomers per family. Homeowners form 4 may be written for a tenant who does not own his own home or for a homeowner who owns his own home but does not meet the eligibility requirements for one of the other forms.

Each of the five forms is composed of two sections: Section I, which provides coverage on the insured's own property, and Section II, which provides liability coverage. Under Section I there are four items of coverage, designated A, B, C, and D, and it is with respect to these coverages that the forms differ. The coverage under Section II is identical under all the forms.[2] As noted above, the basic philosophy of the Homeowners program is to require certain minimum amounts of coverage, and under Section I each of the four coverages not only has certain minimums, but there is a relationship between the coverages:

*Coverage A* provides coverage on the dwelling. A minimum of $8000 is required on the dwelling under forms 1, 2, and 3. Form 5 requires a minimum of $15,000 on the dwelling. Form 4, which is designed for tenants, does not cover the dwelling.

*Coverage B* provides a specific amount of insurance equal to 10% of the amount on the dwelling to cover the garage and other appurtenant private structures on the premises. It is quite similar to the extension under the Dwelling and Contents Broad Form.

*Coverage C* provides a specific amount of insurance to cover personal property or contents. Under form 4, the minimum amount of coverage on contents is $4000. Under the other forms it is 50% of the amount of coverage on the dwelling. In addition to the basic amount of coverage on the contents, forms 1, 2, 3, and 4 provide off-premises coverage on contents equal to 10% of the amount of contents coverage, with a minimum of $1000. This 10% or $1000 is additional coverage and applies anywhere in the world. Under form 5, the entire coverage on contents applies on a worldwide basis, so there is no need for an off-premises extension.

*Coverage D* provides a specific amount of insurance to cover additional living expense and loss of rental which results from untenantability of the premises because of damage by an insured peril. This coverage is the equivalent of the additional living expense extension of the Broad Form. The amount of this coverage is 10% of the amount on the dwelling under form 1, and 20% of the amount on the dwelling under forms 2, 3, and 5. The limit under form 4 is 20% of the amount of coverage on contents.

[2] There are two mandatory coverages under Section II, designated E and F. Coverage E provides personal liability coverage and coverage F provides medical payments coverage. Here we are concerned only with the Section I coverages. Section II coverages are discussed in Chapter 18.

It is in the area of perils insured against that the forms differ markedly. In a sense, each Homeowners form is somewhat comparable to one of the dwelling forms which have already been examined:

*Form 1* is the approximate equivalent of the Dwelling and Contents Form. It provides coverage against fire and extended coverage, plus three additional perils of vandalism and malicious mischief, glass breakage, and theft.

*Form 2* is the approximate equivalent of the Dwelling and Contents Broad Form. It covers against all the perils of that form, plus loss by theft.

*Form 3* provides all risk coverage on the dwelling, and is therefore the equivalent of the Dwelling Building Special Form. It also provides coverage on the contents against the perils covered under form 2.

*Form 4* provides coverage against the same perils as does form 2, but it covers contents only. It is written to insure the personal effects of a tenant and does not therefore provide any coverage for the dwelling.

*Form 5* is a luxury contract which provides all risk coverage on both the dwelling and the contents. It is the equivalent of the Dwelling Building Special Form and a Personal Property Floater.[3]

In addition to the perils described above, provision was made in 1968 for endorsement of the Homeowners policies to cover loss resulting from earthquake. The Homeowners forms include an exclusion of loss resulting from any form of earth movement. This exclusion may be eliminated in part through the earthquake endorsement, which provides coverage against loss resulting from earthquake or volcano, subject to a deductible equal to 2% of the amount of insurance.

For the convenience of the reader, the coverages of each of the five Homeowners forms, the minimum amounts of coverage, and the perils covered under each form are summarized in Table 16-1.

### Coverage on the Dwelling and Appurtenant Sturctures

The dwelling coverage of the various Homeowners forms is almost identical with their equivalent dwelling forms. The definition of the dwelling includes building equipment, fixtures, and outdoor equipment which pertain to the service of the premises, if the property of the insured and not otherwise covered. In addition, the definition of structures includes materials and supplies located on the premises or adjacent to the premises which are intended for use in construction, alteration, or repair of the dwelling.

[3]As in the case of most all risk forms, the exclusions are of special importance under form 5. There are three sets of exclusions under this form: one set applies to both building and contents (vermin, insects, wear and tear, etc.), one set applies to the building only (the same exclusions discussed in connection with the Dwelling Building Special Form), and a third set applies to the contents only. The exclusions applicable to the contents only are essentially the same as those discussed later in this chapter in connection with the Personal Property Floater.

TABLE 16-1
## Comparison of Homeowners Forms

| Coverage[a] | Form 1 | Form 2 | Form 3 | Form 4 | Form 5 |
|---|---|---|---|---|---|
| A | $8000 minimum | $8000 minimum | $8000 minimum | Not covered | $15,000 minimum |
| B | 10% of A | 10% of A | 10% of A | Not covered | 10% of A |
| C | 50% of A | 50% of A | 50% of A | $4000 minimum | 50% of A |
| D | 10% of A | 20% of A | 20% of A | 20% of C | 20% of A |
| E | $25,000 minimum | $25,000 minimum | $25,000 minimum | $25,000 minimum | $25,000 minimum |
| F | $500 minimum | $500 minimum | $500 minimum | $500 minimum | $500 minimum |

*(handwritten: Form 6 / Condim)*

*Perils Covered under Section I*

| Form 1 | Form 2 | Form 3 | Form 4 | Form 5 |
|---|---|---|---|---|
| Fire | Fire | All-risk on dwelling | Same named perils | All-risk on both |
| Lightning | Lightning | —same named | as form 2, except | dwelling and |
| Removal | Removal | perils as form 2 | glass breakage, | contents |
| Windstorm | Windstorm | on contents | which is not | |
| Hail | Hail | | covered | |
| Explosion | Explosion | | | |
| Riot | Riot | | | |
| Civil commotion | Civil commotion | | | |
| Aircraft | Aircraft | | | |
| Vehicles | Vehicles | | | |
| Smoke | Smoke | | | |
| Vandalism | Vandalism | | | |
| Glass breakage | Glass breakage | | | |
| Theft | Theft | | | |
| | Bursting of a steam or hot water heating system | | | |
| | Falling objects | | | |
| | Collapse | | | |
| | Weight of ice, snow, and sleet | | | |
| | Freezing pipes | | | |
| | Damage to appliances by artificially generated electricity | | | |
| | Leakage of a plumbing or heating system | | | |

[a]Coverage key: A, dwelling; B, appurtenant structures; C, contents; D, additional living expense and rental value; E, personal liability; F, medical payments.

As in the case of the separate dwelling forms, the appurtenant structures coverage excludes any buildings which are used for business purposes or which are rented to anyone except a tenant. Again, an exception is made in the case of rental of a garage to be used exclusively for garage purposes.

**Replacement cost coverage.**   The coverage on the dwelling and appurtenant private structures may be written on a replacement cost basis under all the Homeowners forms. Each of the forms which includes coverage on buildings contains a condition which is quite similar to the replacement cost extension of the Broad Form, discussed in Chapter 15. There are some points of difference, however. The Homeowners replacement cost condition specifically excludes outdoor radio and television antennas and aerials, carpeting, awnings, domestic appliances, and outdoor equipment. The Homeowners forms *do not*, as do the Broad Form and the Special Form, exclude roof surfacing from replacement cost.

In connection with the replacement cost condition of the Homeowners policy, a new endorsement, called the "inflation guard endorsement," was adopted in many states in 1969. Under the provisions of this endorsement, the amount of insurance under the policy is automatically increased by 1% of the original amount every 3 months, for a total of 4% annually. The intent of the endorsement is to help the insured to meet the provisions of the replacement cost condition and protect against underinsurance which might result from inflation and increasing costs of construction. The increase applies not only to the building but also to the other items of coverage as well.

### The Contents Coverage

The insured is permitted little choice with regard to the minimum amount of coverage he may purchase on contents. The basic amount of contents coverage under the Homeowners forms 1, 2, 3, and 5 is 50% of the amount of coverage on the dwelling. Thus, for a homeowner with the minimum $8000 coverage on the dwelling, the automatic amount of contents coverage is $4000. This amount may be decreased to 40% of the amount on the dwelling if the insured does not own personal property equal to 50% of the value of his dwelling, but it cannot be decreased below 40%. Under form 4, the minimum amount of coverage provided on the contents is $4000. Form 5 provides 50% of the amount of coverage on the dwelling on contents, and since the minimum on the dwelling under this form is $15,000, the minimum on contents is $7500. Of course, the amount of contents coverage may be increased under any of the forms if the need exists.

The contents coverage of the Homeowners forms is considerably more liberal than that of the separate Dwelling and Contents forms. Certain items of property which are excluded under the separate forms are covered under the Homeowners policy. The basic definition of contents provides coverage on "property usual or incidental to the occupancy of the premises as a dwelling and owned or used by an insured. . . ." Coverage is provided on both owned and borrowed property. For example, if the insured or a member of his family should borrow property from a friend, and that property is damaged or lost as a result of an insured peril, the Homeowners policy will cover the loss as if it had been property owned by the insured.

Classes of property specifically excluded include animals, birds, fish, motorized vehicles (except vehicles used in the maintenance of the premises and not licensed for road use), aircraft, property of roomers not related to the insured, property carried or held as samples for sale, and any property which is separately described and specifically insured under the Homeowners or any other insurance. In addition, business personal property is excluded while away from the described premises. Most of these excluded classes are self-explanatory, but three may require clarification. First, the exclusion of motorized vehicles excludes not only automobiles, motorcycles, motor-scooters, and the like, but also go-carts, golf carts, and snowmobiles. The exception to the exclusion of vehicles used in the maintenance of the premises affords coverage for vehicles such as riding lawn mowers or garden tractors, as long as they are not licensed.[4]

The exclusion of property which is specifically described and insured is of special importance. The coverage for personal property is entitled Unscheduled Personal Property and is intended to provide coverage on the insured's personal effects on a blanket basis, insuring all items except those that are specifically excluded. In addition, the insured may desire to insure some items of high value (for example, boats, furs, jewelry) specifically, by listing them individually in a separate contract. The Homeowners form states that if property is insured under another contract, or if it is listed as a specific item in a schedule under the Homeowners, the blanket personal property coverage provided under Unscheduled Personal Property will not apply to that item at all.[5]

The exclusion of business personal property while away from the premises also deserves comment, primarily because of misinterpretation in the past. Although the Homeowners policy was designed primarily to provide coverage on the personal effects of the insured and the family, it does provide some coverage on business property, as long as that property is on the described premises.

Unlike the other forms that have been examined, there is no exclusion of money, bills, manuscripts, or boats under the Homeowners forms. As a matter of fact, they provide coverage on these items, but with a dollar maximum listed for each:

1. There is a $100 limit on money and bullion.
2. There is a $500 limit on bills, deeds, and valuable papers.
3. There is a $1000 limit on manuscripts.

[4] Under the old Homeowners program, the forms contained an exclusion of "vehicles licensed for road use." The exclusion was changed to "motorized vehicles" in the 1968 revision, and this change constitutes one of the major differences between the old and the new Homeowners. Under the old forms, certain motor vehicles were covered because they were not licensed. Most notable among these were golf carts and snowmobiles. Certain nonmotorized vehicles were not covered because they were licensed for road use, as in the case of trailers.

[5] The need for scheduling such items and the coverage afforded when they are scheduled will be discussed later in the chapter.

4. There is a $500 limit on boats and their equipment.
5. There is a $500 limit on trailers.

The coverage on money may be increased to $500 for an additional premium. The coverage on boats is not limited to rowboats and canoes under the Homeowners policy, as it is under the separate dwelling forms, but applies to any boat and its equipment (including a trailer) up to $500. Under a special exclusion, the policies provide that windstorm and hail losses to boats (other than rowboats and canoes on premises) are covered only if the boat is in a fully enclosed building.

The off-premises coverage of the Homeowners forms is also somewhat broader than that of the separate dwelling forms. Under forms 1, 2, 3, and 4, the off-premises coverage is 10% of the amount on the contents or $1000, whichever is greater. This is an additional amount of insurance, and coverage applies anywhere in the world. This limit may be increased by as much as $5000 for an additional premium if the insured has need for more coverage off-premises than the amount automatically provided. Under form 5, the entire contents coverage applies on a worldwide basis, so there is no need for an off-premises extension.

### Theft Coverage under the Homeowners Policy

The fact that most of the perils included in the Homeowners forms are also included in the separate dwelling forms already treated eliminates the need to discuss them in detail. However, the peril of theft is covered under only one of the separate dwelling forms (the Special Form), and since that form applies only to the dwelling item, the coverage is not particularly extensive.

The major difference between the separate dwelling forms and the coverage provided under Section I of the various Homeowners forms is the theft coverage of the latter. All the Homeowners forms include coverage for theft as an insured peril applicable to both the building and contents. Under form 1, theft is defined as any act or attempt of stealing. Under forms 2, 3, and 4, this definition is expanded to include "loss of property from a known place under circumstances where a probability of theft exists," a provision which is intended to reduce the burden on the insured of proving that the loss actually resulted from theft. The wording in forms 2, 3, and 4 provides coverage where there is a strong presumption of theft, but no conclusive proof.[6] Although the theft coverage is quite broad, it is

---

[6] It is important to note that the forms provide that "Upon knowledge of loss under this peril or of an occurrence which may give rise to a claim for such loss, the Insured shall give immediate notice to this Company or its authorized agents *and also to the police* [italics added]."

subject to a number of exclusions that should be noted. There are three sets of exclusions under forms 1, 2, 3, and 4: a set of general theft exclusions, a set of exclusions which apply if the insured rents to someone else that portion of the dwelling which he customarily occupies, and a set of exclusions which apply to property while it is away from the premises.

**General theft exclusions.**    There are four general theft exclusions. Any theft committed by an insured is excluded. If Jones Jr., hard-pressed financially on the night of the Junior–Senior Prom, steals $20 from his father's wallet, there is no coverage. Second, the policy excludes theft of materials from a building under construction. This could be an important exclusion in the situation where a Homeowners policy has been written to cover a dwelling while it is being built. The third of the general theft exclusions is the exclusion of loss "arising out of or resulting from the theft of any credit card, or check, draft, promissory note, bill of exchange or similar written promise, order or direction to pay a sum certain of money." The widespread use of credit cards in the American economy is a fact of life, and at one time the loss potential connected with unauthorized or fraudulent use of such cards was catastrophic. However, federal legislation, effective since October 1970, provides a maximum limit of $50 for a credit-card holder's liability in the event of unauthorized use of the card. This limitation on losses resulting from credit cards has reduced the importance of the credit-card exclusion of the Homeowners policy, but in view of the fact that the limitation applies to each card, substantial losses may still exist. Coverage for loss resulting from forgery in connection with credit cards may be added to the Homeowners policy by endorsement.[7] The last of the general theft exclusions excludes loss of a precious or semiprecious stone from its setting. The purpose of this exclusion is to avoid controversy over whether such a lost stone was or was not stolen.

**Theft exclusions while the dwelling is rented.**    The second set of exclusions applies only in the event that the insured rents to someone else the portion of

---

[7]The Credit Card Forgery and Depositors Forgery Endorsement to the Homeowners policy provides four items of coverage: credit card forgery, depositors forgery, court costs, and counterfeit money coverage. The credit card coverage provides for payment up to the limit of the endorsement ($1000–$10,000 limits are available) for losses resulting from forgery in connection with a credit card. It makes no difference whether the card was stolen, lost, or simply misplaced; as long as the loss involves forgery, there is coverage. On the other hand, there is no coverage for cards where charges are permitted without a signature, for there is no forgery. The depositors forgery coverage protects against loss resulting from forgery or alteration of any check drawn on or by the insured. The court cost coverage pays legal expenses in connection with suits brought against the insured to enforce payment of a forged instrument. The counterfeit coverage covers losses through acceptance of bogus currency up to $50 per occurrence with a $100 aggregate. The cost of the endorsement is nominal, about $3 per year for $1000 in coverage.

the dwelling he customarily occupies. Such a situation might arise if the insured were leaving town for an extended period of time. When the situation does exist, the policy excludes theft of money, bullion, numismatic property, bank notes, securities, and other valuable papers, jewelry, and furs, plus theft of any other property committed by a tenant or members of his household.

**Theft exclusions applicable to property away from the premises.**    There are five exclusions applicable to property away from the described premises. First, property at any location owned, rented, or occupied by an insured is not covered for theft, except while an insured is temporarily residing at that location. For example, if the insured has a summer cottage, the contents of that cottage are covered under the off-premises extension of his homeowners policy, but the theft coverage does not apply except while the insured is actually residing at the cottage. This exclusion may be of particular importance to students. A dormitory, sorority, or fraternity is a location occupied by an insured, which means that the theft coverage of the parents' Homeowners policy does not cover the student's property except while the student is actually residing in that location. Obviously, there would be no coverage on property at the dormitory during the summer while the student is at home. Other situations, such as Christmas, Thanksgiving, and Easter vacations, when students leave the campus, may or may not result in an exclusion of theft losses. Interpretation varies from company to company, but in general we should conclude that there is probably no coverage.

The second and third off-premises theft exclusions are related, so we may discuss them together. There is no coverage for theft of property while unattended in any motor vehicle or trailer, unless there is evidence of forcible entry into the vehicle.[8] In addition, there is no coverage for theft of property while in or on watercraft unless the loss is a result of forcible entry into a securely locked compartment. In either case, the forcible entry must be evidenced by visible marks of forcible entry. Both these exclusions may be deleted under forms 2, 3, and 4 through the use of the Theft Coverage Extension Endorsement which requires an additional premium.[9] This endorse-

[8] The policy provides that the automobile is not "unattended" if the insured is required to surrender his keys to a bailee, as in the case of a parking lot. Under all the Homeowners forms except form 1, the requirement of forcible entry does not apply if the entire car is stolen and not recovered within 30 days.

[9] The older forms also excluded theft from unlocked, unattended vehicles, and under forms 2 and 4, this exclusion could be removed by the payment of an additional premium and the attachment of the old Extended Theft Endorsement, which included an additional peril called "mysterious disappearance." Numerous problems arose in connection with this peril, since the courts were inclined to interpret it more broadly than the companies had intended. The mysterious disappearance peril is not included in the present Theft Coverage Extension, although since it is not excluded, it probably exists under form 5.

ment cannot be used with form 1, and it is not needed with form 5, since form 5 does not exclude theft from unlocked, unattended vehicles or watercraft. The Theft Coverage Extension Endorsement simply deletes the exclusions of theft from unlocked, unattended vehicles and boats.

The fourth off-premises theft exclusion excludes theft of watercraft, and their furnishings, equipment, and outboard motors; and the fifth excludes trailers, whether licensed or not.

The theft coverage of form 5 is subject to only two exclusions: theft of materials and supplies in connection with a building under construction and loss arising out of the theft of a credit card, both of which were discussed above. Since none of the other exclusions discussed above are contained in this form, losses arising from such thefts would be covered.

**Limitation on jewelry and furs under the theft coverage.** One of the most important provisions relating to theft coverage under all the Homeowners forms is a limitation on loss by theft of jewelry and furs. Recovery for loss of jewelry and furs is limited to $500 per loss, regardless of the number of items stolen.[10] This makes it essential that valuable items of jewelry and furs be scheduled. The most important consideration in connection with scheduling under the Homeowners is the amount of coverage that must be obtained when an item is scheduled. It is important to remember that when an item is scheduled, the coverage of the basic Homeowners Form no longer applies to that item. The Homeowners policy excludes property which is "separately described and specifically insured in whole or in part by this or any other insurance." Some agents mistakenly schedule valuable furs or jewelry for less than the full value, expecting the basic coverage to provide a part of the protection. If the insured has a ring worth $2000, it must be scheduled for $2000, for the contents coverage of the Homeowners policy will not apply to the ring at all after it is scheduled.

### The Homeowners Deductible

In most states, there is one deductible under the Homeowners policy which applies to loss by any peril under Section I except "additional living expense."[11] The Homeowners deductible is a disappearing deductible; it becomes increasingly smaller as the amount of the loss becomes larger, and in those cases where the loss is $500 or more, the deductible does not apply. Under forms 1, 2, 3, and 4, the amount of the deductible is $50. The provisions

[10] Under the old Homeowner forms, the limit was $1000 per item, except under form 5, in which the limit was $250 per item.

[11] In some jurisdictions, provision is made for two deductibles: one which applies to wind and hail and the other which applies to other perils. In these states, the insured may select between a deductible on all perils except fire and lightning and a deductible applying to windstorm and hail losses only. The windstorm and hail deductible of these jurisdictions normally applies only to buildings, structures, and personal property in the open.

of the deductible clause provide that the company will pay 111% of the loss in excess of the deductible up to $500. Thus, in the case of a $100 loss, the company would pay 111% of $50, or $55.50, making the deductible $44.50. On a $200 loss, the company would pay $111% of $150. Losses of higher amounts produce progressively lower deductibles:

1. On a $100 loss, the deductible is $44.50.
2. On a $200 loss, the deductible is $33.50.
3. On a $300 loss, the deductible is $22.40.
4. On a $400 loss, the deductible is $11.50.
5. On losses of $500 or more, there is no deductible.

Under form 5, the deductible is $100, and the company will pay 125% of the loss in excess of the deductible, up to $500, with no deductible on losses over $500. For an additional premium, the form 5 deductible may be reduced to $50.

The 1968 Homeowners program makes provision for higher optional deductibles. Under the rules of the program, the Homeowners policy may be endorsed to provide a flat (nondisappearing) deductible, which is applicable to any loss under Section I except losses under the additional living expense coverage. Under Homeowners forms 1, 2, 3, and 4, the insured may elect an optional flat deductible of $100, $250, or $500; under form 5, the optional deductibles are $250 and $500. Substantial premium credits are allowed for these higher deductibles.

### Other Provisions

In addition to those provisions already discussed, the various Homeowners forms include all the extensions that were discussed in connection with the Dwelling and Contents Broad Form, including the automatic removal extension, the replacement cost condition, the trees, shrubs, lawns, and plants extension, the debris removal extension, and the improvements and betterments extension in form 4.

This analysis of the Homeowners forms has been quite brief and somewhat limited, because of the close relationship between the Section I coverages of the Homeowners policy and that of the separate dwelling forms. It is hoped that this brief discussion has served to illustrate the comprehensive nature of the forms and the manner in which they provide protection for eligible homeowners against loss of property.[12]

[12]A similar program, the Farmowners program, has been developed for farm occupancies. The Farmowners policy is an extension of the Homeowners concept into the farm field and in many respects is quite similar to the Homeowners. It provides coverage on the insured's dwelling, garage, unscheduled personal property, additional living expense, and liability coverage in a single package. The essential difference between the Homeowners and Farmowners policies is the provision in the Farmowners for inclusion of coverage on farm barns and buildings and farm personal property such as grain, machinery, and equipment.

## INLAND MARINE COVERAGES FOR THE INDIVIDUAL

Although the Homeowners forms do a reasonably adequate job of insuring the personal property of the average individual, in some cases it may be desirable to insure specifically certain items of personal property under inland marine forms. Obvious examples would include items of property that are specifically excluded under the Homeowners policy, such as automobiles and recreational motor vehicles or items on which the coverage afforded under the Homeowners policy is limited. For example, coverage on boats and trailers is limited to $500, and the theft peril does not apply away from the premises. Theft coverage on jewelry and furs under the Homeowners policy is limited to $500 per loss. Perhaps not so obvious is the need for broader coverage on certain classes of property than that afforded under the named peril coverage of the Homeowners or for valued coverage in the case of fine arts or antiques.

Coverage on such property is provided under inland marine forms purchased either as a separate contract or by endorsement to the Homeowners forms. The Homeowners "Scheduled Personal Property Endorsement," which may be attached to the Homeowners policy, provides all risk coverage on nine classes of property[13] under the same terms as if separate contracts were purchased for each type of property. Regardless of whether the coverage is purchased as a separate floater policy or by endorsement to the Homeowners policy, it is extremely broad and provides an attractive means of insuring valuable types of personal property. We shall not attempt to discuss all the personal floater policies available but shall limit our discussion primarily to those coverages which may be included in the Homeowners Scheduled Personal Property Endorsement.

### Personal Furs Floater

The Fur Floater policy was one of the earliest of the all-risk personal contracts. The extreme broadness of this policy, and its equivalent coverage afforded under the Scheduled Personal Property Endorsement, is attested to by the fact that there are only three exclusions. The first excludes loss caused by wear and tear, gradual deterioration, insects, vermin, or inherent vice; the second excludes loss by nuclear radiation or radioactive contamination; and the last excludes war. The garment must be a fur garment; i.e., it must be the dressed pelt of some animal and not a man-made fabric, or it must be a garment trimmed with fur. Each item must be scheduled and an amount of insurance applicable to each. The insurance company generally will require an appraisal of each item before it can be insured; however,

---

[13] Jewelry, furs, cameras, musical instruments, silverware, golfers' equipment, fine arts (including antiques), stamp collections, and coin collections.

the sales slip on a recently purchased item is sufficient to establish a value. The coverage is on a worldwide basis.

### Personal Jewelry Floater

Personal jewelry also may be scheduled under the Homeowners policy providing the same coverage as is available under a separate Jewelry Floater. The Personal Jewelry policy is also an all-risk contract. Each item must be scheduled with an amount of insurance applicable to each, and the indemnity may be on a valued or an actual cash value basis. Here again, an appraisal is mandatory, or at least some verification of the cost price must be established. In addition to the normal exclusions, this contract has a "pairs and sets" clause which is an important condition. This clause prevents the insured from collecting for a total loss if one item in a pair or set is lost or destroyed. The loss payable then becomes a fair proportion of the total value of the set, giving consideration to the importance of the article or articles. This coverage is also worldwide.

### Silverware Floater

Another class of property which may be insured under the Homeowners Scheduled Personal Property Endorsement or under a separate inland marine floater is silverware. Coverage is provided on valuable silverware, silverplated ware, and the like. The coverage is essentially the same as that provided for jewelry as described above.

### Golfer's Equipment

Golfer's equipment may also be insured under a separate policy, or it may be covered under the Homeowners Scheduled Personal Property Endorsement. Either form provides coverage for golfing equipment, including clubs, golf clothing (but excluding watches and jewelry), and other clothing which is contained in a locker in a clubhouse or other building used in connection with the game of golf. The description of eligible property is quite broad and could even include a motor-driven golf cart. The coverage is on an all-risk basis for most items of property and most generally is written on a blanket basis. However, the coverage for golf balls is definitely not all-risk but is limited to the perils of fire and burglary.

### Camera Floater

Cameras and all the appropriate equipment used therewith such as projection machines, moveable sound equipment, films, binoculars, telescopes, and the like may be insured on an all-risk basis under the Camera Floater or the Homeowners endorsement. As usual, the various items are scheduled, and a blanket item may be included to provide coverage for miscellaneous articles such as sunshades, filters, etc. Additionally acquired property is insured automatically but subject to a limitation of 25% of the amount of insurance or $10,000, whichever is less, and with the requirement that the acquisitions be reported within 30 days and the additional premium paid. The only exclusions are those of the wear and tear variety, war, and radioactive contamination.

### Fine Arts and Antiques

A Fine Arts Floater is written to cover objects of art such as paintings, statuary, rare manuscripts, and antiques.[14] The coverage is all-risk, with the usual exceptions. It is customary to issue the policy on a valued rather than an actual cash value basis. Since this means that the insurance company agrees to the value of each item insured and that this is the value paid in the event of a loss, the greatest of care must be used in determining these values. Appraisals normally are mandatory, and some insurance companies even have art appraisers who advise them on the values. Each insured item is scheduled with an amount of insurance applicable. Newly acquired property is insured automatically but subject to a percentage limitation relative to the aggregate amount of the schedule. However, reports of additional items must be made within 90 days and the proper pro rata additional premium paid.

### Stamp and Coin Collection Floater

A stamp and coin collection may be an extremely valuable piece of property. The appropriate all-risk coverage is provided in the Stamp and Coin Collection Floater or the Homeowners Schedule Endorsement. The property eligible involves postage stamps including due, envelope, official, revenue, match and medicine, covers, locals, reprints, essays, proofs, and other philatelic property owned by or in the custody or control of the insured, including the books, pages, and/or mountings. The eligible coins include rare and current coins, medals, paper money, bank notes, tokens of money, and other numismatic property owned by or in the custody or control of the insured, including coin albums, containers, frames, cards, and display cabinets in use with such collection. The property in both cases may be insured on a schedule or on a blanket basis. There is no automatic coverage of newly acquired property. In addition to the customary exclusions, there are several unique to this contract. For example, damage resulting from fading, creasing, denting, scratching, tearing, thinning, transfer of colors, or damage

---

[14] For an item of property to be eligible as an antique, it must have a real antique value, i.e., the value must be something more than just sentimental. An arbitrary rule followed by most insurance companies requires that the object be at least 100 years old before it can be considered an antique.

arising while the property is being worked upon is excluded. The policy also excludes mysterious disappearance of individual stamps unless the item has been specifically scheduled or mounted in a volume and the page to which the stamp is attached is also lost. Loss by theft from an unattended automobile is also excluded except when a package is being shipped by registered mail. The policy also contains a limit of no more than $250 on any one stamp or any one pair, block, or series, and $1000 on unscheduled numismatic property.

### Musical Instrument Floater

The owner of expensive musical instruments needs the broad type of coverage that can be provided under an inland marine contract. Musical instruments may be scheduled under the Homeowners policy or insured under a separate contract; either approach provides all-risk coverage. One of the major conditions of the contract involves an agreement on the part of the insured that none of the instruments insured will be played for remuneration during the term of the policy unless permitted by endorsement and the payment of an additional premium.

### Wedding Present Floater

In many cases, wedding presents can accumulate to a considerable value, and the Wedding Present Floater is designed to provide coverage for the presents during the temporary period in which they are accumulated before the bride and her new husband are settled in their home.[15] The presents are considered to be the property of the bride, and she purchases the contract. Coverage commences at the time the presents begin to accumulate and continues up to a maximum of 90 days after the wedding. The coverage is the usual all-risk coverage; in addition to the customary exclusions, certain types of property are excluded. The classes of property excluded include realty, animals, automobiles, motorcycles, aircraft, bicycles, boats, money, notes, securities, and stamps.[16] Unlike the other floater classes that have been discussed, there is no provision for insuring this class of property in the Homeowners Schedule Endorsement.

### Personal Property Floater

As we have seen, named perils coverage is available for tenants under the Homeowners form 4. In some instances, however, an individual who does not own his home may desire a broad form of all-risk coverage on all his personal property rather than only on the classes of property discussed above

---

[15] We are including this contract in our discussion not because it has the importance of the other personal coverages discussed, but because it may be of interest to some students.

[16] Some of these might be considered as rather unusual presents, but many strange things happen.

which can be scheduled. The Personal Property Floater (PPF) is designed to provide all-risk coverage on all personal effects owned by the insured. It covers all personal property owned, used, or worn by the insured. Under certain circumstances, it is extended to cover property of guests on the premises of the insured. In addition, it may provide some coverage on real property. It may be written to cover unscheduled property only, or it may be written to cover both scheduled and unscheduled property. Scheduled property consists of those items of property which are specifically described and insured for a specific amount (e.g., a valuable ring or fur coat). Unscheduled property, on the other hand (which is also referred to as "blanket"), refers to all the other property of the insured that is not listed item by item. The policy covers *any* property owned by the insured and not specifically excluded against loss by theft or attempted theft. Thus, loss by theft or damage by attempted theft to trees, shrubbery, or fixtures attached to the building would be covered. By the same token, damage caused by thieves or burglars to the building would also be covered.

The insuring agreement provides coverage against "All risk of loss of or damage to property covered, except as hereinafter provided. . . ." This is a perfect example of an all-risk insuring agreement. The policy provides for a single amount of insurance to cover all the insured's unscheduled personal property, subject to three important limitations:

1. There is a limit of 10% of the amount of insurance applicable to unscheduled personal property on property located at a secondary residence of the insured.
2. The maximum collectible for any loss of jewelry or furs is $250. (Note that this is for any loss and not for any item. The intent is to require the insured to schedule valuable items.)
3. There is a limit of $100 for loss of money including coin collections. There is a $500 limit of liability on accounts, bills, deeds, evidences of debt, and other valuable papers.

Since this is an all-risk form, the most important provisions in the contract are the exclusions. The following are the more noteworthy exclusions in the contract.

*Breakage of fragile articles* is excluded unless such breakage results from fire, windstorm, explosion, falling aircraft, riot, earthquake, collapse of buildings, flood, accident to conveyances, theft, attempted theft, or vandalism and malicious mischief.

*Damage to processing* is excluded—there is no coverage for loss which results from work on property in the course of refinishing, renovating, or repairing the property. (This exclusion does *not* apply to jewelry, watches, or furs.)

*Wear and tear, and mechanical breakdown* are excluded.

*Damage caused by insects and vermin* is excluded.

*Damage of atmosphere or extremes of temperature* are excluded.

*Flood or underground water seepage* are excluded, but damage to fragile articles caused by flood may be covered.

*Damage by pets* excludes damage caused by animals or pets owned by or kept by the insured or a resident employee of the insured.

*Property on exhibition* is excluded unless the premises are described in the policy.

In addition to the exclusions, the policy is always written with a deductible, which may vary in amount from $15 to $50. This is deemed necessary because of the broadness of the coverage.

The PPF is a luxury contract and is used primarily for wealthy individuals who desire the ultimate in protection and who do not own their own homes. If the individual owns his home, the Homeowners form 5 will provide the same coverage on contents as the PPF. For this reason, the PPF has become less and less important as a personal lines coverage.

### Insurance on Boats

In view of the fact that there are 40 million people who engage in the sport of boating, the question of insurance coverage on boats is of some importance. As we have seen, the Homeowners policy provides coverage up to $500 on boats and their equipment but excludes coverage for loss by theft away from the premises. Because of the dollar limitation, and to a lesser degree because of the theft exclusion, it may be necessary to purchase specific insurance on a boat. Although the coverages marketed to insure boats are not standard forms, in general they may be subdivided into two separate classes of coverage: yacht insurance policies, which are designed for in- boards, and outboard motorboat policies. The essential distinction between the two divisions has become somewhat clouded, but basically the yacht policies are considered ocean marine coverages, while the outboard motor- boat coverages are considered inland marine. Our discussion here will focus primarily on the outboard motorboat program.

Under the most popular outboard motorboat program, the physical damage coverage provides all-risk coverage on the hull, the motor or motors, the trailer, and the boat's equipment. The coverage is written on an actual cash value basis, subject to a deductible. Even the deductible amounts are not standardized and range from $10 to $50, and, in some cases, are even higher. Since the coverage is written on the actual cash value basis, it may be neces- sary to adjust the amount of coverage downward as the boat ages. Market value is a reasonable approximation of actual cash value in the case of boats and motors.

When the coverage is not written on an all-risk basis, it is usually written on a broad named perils basis. At one time, a very limited form also was used (which covered against fire and lightning, collision or overturn during transportation, windstorm on land and theft of the entire boat or motor). This limited form has virtually disappeared. The broad named perils form adds "perils of the sea" to the perils listed above for the limited form. The perils of the sea include heavy seas, high wind, flood, stranding, collision with another vessel, striking of submerged objects, and sinking, if the sinking results from one of the perils insured against.

## BUYING PROPERTY INSURANCE FOR THE INDIVIDUAL

### Pricing and Cost Considerations

Before discussing the purchase of property insurance for the individual or family, a brief review of the factors that affect the cost of such insurance seems in order. Aside from the differences in prices among companies which exist in the cases of those companies that deviate from bureau rates or file independent rates, there are differences in cost based on the characteristics of the individual exposure.

As the reader will recall, the "rate" is the cost per unit of insurance. In the property field, rates are generally stated in terms of the cost per $100 or $1000 of coverage. The premium is determined by multiplying the amount of insurance purchased by the rate. The rate varies with the scope of the perils insured against and the loss potential involved in those perils. The loss potential (i.e., the likelihood that a loss will occur and the extent of damage if a loss does occur) is a function of the property itself, and is measured in part by the characteristics of the property. For example, the type of construction is an important consideration in the case of some perils: the rate for fire insurance is lower on a brick or masonry building than on a wood building. Rates also vary with the loss experience of each locality. Again, in the case of fire insurance, rates vary with the fire protection provided by the city. Cities and towns are evaluated with respect to certain factors such as the fire department and water supply, and placed in one of ten classifications, numbered 1 through 10, with class 1 towns being the lowest rated and class 10 towns the highest rated.[17] The rates for other coverages also vary by locality; extended coverage rates are higher in those areas subject to severe loss experience (e.g., from windstorms) just as crime rates are usually higher in large cities, reflecting the greater incidence of crime.

---

[17]These classifications are assigned by the American Insurance Association to cities over 25,000 in population and by the local rating bureaus to towns under that size.

**TABLE 16-2**

**Comparison of Cost of Various Personal Forms—Annual Premiums for $20,000 on Dwelling, $10,000 on Contents for a Frame, One-Family Dwelling, Class 4 Town, $50 Deductible Applicable**

| | |
|---|---|
| Dwelling and Contents Form | $109 |
| Dwelling and Contents Broad | 126 |
| Special Form on Dwelling, Broad Form on Contents | 132 |
| Homeowners form 1 | 62 |
| Homeowners form 2 | 74 |
| Homeowners form 3 | 88 |
| Homeowners form 5 | 157 |

SOURCE: *The Iowa Rapid Rater* (Hollywood, Florida: The Rapid Rater Company).

In the case of dwelling property, rates are based on three major factors: the type of construction, the number of families, and the fire protection of the city.[18] Under the Homeowners program, the same three considerations are involved, however, the package policies use an "indivisible premium" concept, in which the premium is the cost of the entire package, without allocation of parts of the premium to the different sections of coverage.

With these rather basic notions of the cost factors involved in mind, we may now consider the differences in the cost of the various forms which have been examined. Table 16-2 indicates the cost of coverage on a $20,000 dwelling and $10,000 in contents on a frame, one-family dwelling in a class 4 town in one of the midwestern states. Coverage under each form is subject to a $50 deductible.

It is interesting to note the relationship of the cost of the separate dwelling forms to the Homeowners forms, particularly in view of the fact that the premium for the Homeowners policy includes the cost of theft and liability insurance. The higher cost of the separate forms for less coverage is due primarily to the fact that there are strict eligibility rules under the Homeowners program, resulting in a poorer class of exposures under the separate forms. In a sense, most of the good risks are insured under the Homeowners program, leaving the poorer risks, with their higher loss experience, to be insured under the separate forms.

If the dwelling is eligible, coverage should be obtained under one of the Homeowners forms. The choice of the particular form to be purchased is somewhat more complicated, but in most cases the choice should not be

[18] There are actually four factors that are used in the determination of fire rates: construction, occupancy, protection, and exposure. The fourth, "exposure," which reflects the hazard created by neighboring property, is used in the rate structure for nonresidential property.

difficult. Form 5 provides the most extensive coverage, but the cost is quite high, precluding it from consideration for most property owners. Of the remaining three forms, form 3 represents the ideal. It is only slightly more costly than form 2, yet it provides all-risk coverage on the dwelling. In the instances where the incremental cost of form 3 seems to be a problem, the insured should consider a larger deductible. The choice of a form 3 policy with a $100 deductible in preference to a form 2 policy with a $50 deductible is in keeping with the principles of risk management. In general, since each additional peril included reduces the possibility of an uninsured catastrophe, the insured should prefer broader coverage with a deductible to narrower coverage without the deductible. By sacrificing coverage on the potential $50 loss, the purchaser secures coverage against catastrophies involved in losses caused by perils which are not listed in form 2, but which would be covered under form 3.

### Tailoring the Coverage under the Homeowners Policy

The greatest errors in the area of purchasing insurance on the dwelling and its contents are usually in connection with the amount of insurance. As we have noted previously, the dwelling should be valued on the basis of its replacement cost. If the dwelling is relatively new, determination of the replacement cost should not pose a great problem. Original cost may be inflated to present replacement cost using a construction price index. In the case of older dwelling property, replacement cost may be calculated with the aid of a replacement cost estimator, available from many insurance agents and companies. These replacement cost estimators are simple to use and permit the individual to reach a reasonable approximation of the value of his dwelling by the application of stated cost factors to the various items of construction. In most cases, the cost estimators make provision for differing types of construction and regional differences in cost, resulting in a reasonably accurate estimate.

Even though the replacement cost condition of the Homeowners forms requires that the amount of insurance on the dwelling be 80% of the full replacement cost value, it is good practice to insure for 100% of the replacement cost value. This cushion, plus the Inflation Guard Endorsement should prevent underinsurance that might result from inflation and increases in the cost of construction.

The Homeowners forms provide coverage on the contents equal to 50% of the value of the dwelling. Yet there is no reason that the actual value of contents will be this amount, and the insurance buyer should estimate the value of his personal property, so as to avoid underinsurance. The problem of estimating insurable value of contents is an even more difficult problem than estimating building replacement cost. An inventory of personal property, with the replacement cost of each item provides a starting point. Since the coverage on contents is an actual cash value basis, depreciation should be taken into consideration. While any system of depreciation is probably arbitrary, the age of the article and its expected life may be used to roughly determine depreciation.

The inventory of personal property which is compiled in estimating the value of contents should also point out any valuable jewelry and furs or other items on which all-risk scheduled coverage is needed. Specific insurance should be purchased on those items of personal property that are not covered under the Homeowners policy (such as snowmobiles and golf carts) or on property which has a greater value than the amount provided under the Homeowners policy (e.g., boats or trailers valued at more than $500).

Finally, the insured should consider adding other perils or broadening those that are included under the form selected. For example, the earthquake peril may be added to the Homeowners forms through the use of the "Earthquake Damage Assumption Endorsement." The "Extended Theft Endorsement" is probably also a worthwhile addition, and individuals who use credit cards should consider the addition of credit card coverage.

## TITLE INSURANCE

Before leaving the subject of insurance for the home, we should at least briefly mention title insurance, which is a form of property insurance designed to protect against losses resulting from a defective title to land and improvements. The legal principles connected with the transfer of title to real estate are quite complicated, and because of the technical details involved, it is possible for a defective title to be transferred in a real estate transaction. A person may purchase a home and after many years find that the one who conveyed the title to him was not the rightful owner, and did not in fact have the right to transfer the title. If a person with a superior claim to the land comes forward to exert his right, the purchaser to whom the defective title was transferred may suffer.

Defects in a title may result from a number of causes, including forgery of titles, forgery of public records, invalid or undiscovered wills, or liens and encumbrances. All rights in real property such as encumbrances, liens, and easements are generally recorded in the public records of the jurisdiction in which the real estate is located. One approach to dealing with the risk of defective titles is therefore the examination of these public records. A buyer may protect himself by procuring an abstract of title, which is a summarized report of the history of the title as shown by the records, together with a report of judgments, mortgages, and similar claims against the property that have been recorded. An attorney is generally retained to render an opinion on the accuracy and validity of the abstract. The major shortcoming of this procedure is that it only partially reduces the possibility of loss. Even if the abstractor or attorney is careful in his examination, there may be defects that are not discovered, such as a right to the property granted in an undiscovered will or a forged transfer document which appears to be genuine. If the abstractor or lawyer is free from negligence, he cannot be held liable even if it is later determined that the title was defective.[19]

If no other alternative is available, an examination of the abstract and a title search serve as a means of loss prevention. However, in some areas, title insurance may be available as a more attractive alternative. Title insurance companies are generally local in the scope of their operations and insure titles only within a limited territory. This is a natural result of the nature of title insurance. The basic asset of the title insurance company is the "abstract plant," which consists of an index of the various plots of land in the area and the history of each. All transactions and transfers that affect the title to the property are recorded in the records of the company on a day-to-day basis, so that when an application for insurance is received, most of the information regarding the title to the property is already on hand. When an application is received, the title insurance company engages in a title search, attempting to determine if the title is valid. Any defects in the title that are discovered by the title insurance company in its research are listed in a schedule which is included in the policy. A contract is then issued under which the title insurance company agrees to indemnify the insured for any loss arising out of undiscovered defects in the title. Those defects scheduled in the policy are excluded from coverage.

This guarantee by the insurer differs from most other lines of insurance in that it relates to occurrences in the past rather than in the future. If an undiscovered defect later causes financial loss to the insured, the insurer will indemnify him. The remedy to the insured in the event of a defective title is a dollar indemnification and not possession of the property. In addition, the insurer agrees to defend the insured in the event of legal action against him in connection with losses that are not excluded under the policy.

A single premium is payable for the title insurance policy, and it is fully earned once it is paid. The policy term is indefinite, terminating only when the property is again sold. For rather obvious reasons, title insurance may not be transferred to a new purchaser, but a new purchaser may obtain a policy at a reduced "reissue rate" if it is purchased within a short period after the previous policy was issued.

---

[19] If the abstractor or attorney was negligent, the property "owner" who suffered the loss would have a right of action and could sue for damages.

### The Torrens System

We should perhaps mention briefly an alternative to the system of title insurance just described, the Torrens System. This system was originally developed in Australia by Robert Torrens. It provides that title to property is vested in the purchaser. Fees are collected at the time the title is registered, and an insurance fund is created from these fees. If someone can later show a claim to the property, he is reimbursed for his loss out of the fund, and the title remains with the person who has registered it. Many persons feel that this system is superior to the alternatives discussed above, because the purchaser is granted a clear title.

### Questions for Discussion and Review

**1.** Rosie LaRue has a collection of valuable antique furniture. She has never given any thought to the insurance coverage; she has a Homeowners policy with $10,000 on the dwelling and standard percentages on the other Section I coverages. Explain to her what you think she should do and the reasons you feel the course of action you recommend would be advisable.

**2.** Your Homeowners policy is ready to be renewed. It is written to cover your dwelling for its original construction cost. The policy is standard in all respects; the percentages of coverage are the standard percentages, and there are no endorsements or alterations. What modifications to this basic contract should you consider?

**3.** Your parents are planning a 2-month trip to Europe. Your father, assuming that you are now an expert in the field of insurance, asks you if the fact that the house will be empty for 2 months will affect the coverage under his Homeowners policy. You examine the policy and find that it is a form 3. What will you tell him?

**4.** As a single college student living in the dorm, you have some coverage under your parent's Homeowners policy. Discuss the extent and nature of his coverage. Be as specific as possible, assuming that your father's policy is a Homeowners form 2.

**5.** If the purpose of a deductible is to eliminate small claims, is it logical to apply the deductible to a total loss? Why do you suppose that the deductible approach used under the Homeowners policy has not been adopted in the field of automobile insurance?

## Suggestions for Additional Reading

*Fire, Casualty and Surety Bulletins,* Fire and Marine Volume, "Dwellings" Section. Cincinnati, Ohio: The National Underwriter Co.

Gordis, P. *Property and Casualty Insurance,* 17th ed. Indianapolis, Ind.: The Rough Notes Co., 1970, Chaps. 34, 18.

Johnstone, Q. "Title Insurance." *Insurance Counsel Journal* (July 1959).

Long, J. D. and Gregg, D. W. *Property and Liability Insurance Handbook.* Homewood, Ill.: Richard D. Irwin, 1965, Chap. 49.

Magee, J. H. and Serbein, O. N. *Property and Liability Insurance,* 4th ed. Homewood, Ill.: Richard D. Irwin, 1967, Chap. 22.

Riegel, R. and Miller, J. *Insurance Principles and Practices,* 5th ed. Englewood Cliffs, N.J.: Prentice-Hall, 1966, Chap. 40.

# 17 Negligence and Legal Liability

*That man may err was never yet denied.*

—John Dryden, *The Hind and the Panther*

A risk confronting almost every person or business is that of behavior that could result in an injury to another person or damage to property of others. The basis of the risk is the liability imposed by law upon one responsible for injury or damage to the property of others. It is a risk that can, and in many instances has, attained catastrophic proportions, and one that can occur at any time. There is no way of estimating the amount of legal liability in advance. It may be a mere thousand dollars, or it could be a half-million dollars. It is a risk that has no maximum predictable limit.[1] Before we examine the role of insurance in protecting the individual from the legal liability hazard, we will examine the hazard itself, with emphasis on the doctrines of negligence that give rise to the liability exposure.

## CRIMINAL AND TORTIOUS BEHAVIOR

Basically, a person can commit two classes of wrongs: public and private. A public wrong is a violation of one of the laws that govern the relationships

[1]For many risks, the maximum predictable loss is subject to careful calculation. For example, the ownership of an automobile entails the possibility of the loss of the value of the auto itself, a loss with a maximum limit equal to the value of the car. But with respect to the legal liability arising from the operation of the car, the loss will depend upon the severity of the accident and the amount the jury is willing to provide for the injured parties.

of the individual and the rest of society; it is called a crime and is the subject of that field known as criminal law. Crimes include a wide range of acts: treason, murder, rape, arson, larceny, trespass, disorderly conduct, vagrancy, and so on. Criminal acts are prosecuted by the state as the moving party (plaintiff) against any citizen for the violation of a duty prescribed by statute or common law,[2] and they are punishable by fine, imprisonment, or death.

A private wrong, on the other hand, is an infringement of the rights of another individual. A private wrong is called a tort, and the person who commits a tort is called a *tort feasor*. Commission of a tort may give the person whose rights were violated a right of action for damages against the tort feasor. Such an action is called a *civil* action. Torts may be subdivided into those that are intentional and those that are unintentional. Intentional torts include such infringements on the rights of others as assault and battery, libel, slander, false arrest or imprisonment, trespass, or invasion of privacy. Persons who suffer injury as a result of these intentional torts have the right to sue for damages.[3] Unintentional torts are those that result from negligence or carelessness, and in these cases the injured party may also be entitled to damages in a civil action, even though the tort feasor had no malicious intent as in the case of the intentional tort.

Liability insurance is rarely concerned with the legal penalties resulting from criminal behavior or intentional torts, for it would be contrary to public policy to protect an individual from the consequences of the intentional injury or damage he inflicts. Although insurance is available to protect against loss resulting from some of the intentional torts listed above, most liability policies exclude injury or damage caused intentionally or at the direction of the insured. In liability insurance, we are primarily concerned with unintentional torts or losses arising from negligence.

## NEGLIGENCE AND LEGAL LIABILITY

We have already determined that there are many causes of legal liability.[4] The most important, and the most significant for insurance, is that of *negligence*. Most people have a responsibility to behave in the same manner as would a reasonable and prudent individual. Failure to behave in this manner constitutes negligence, and if this negligence leads to an injury to another, or to the damage of property belonging to another, the negligent

[2]Statutory law is written law, enacted by federal and state legislatures. Common law, on the other hand, consists of the body of rules based on customs and decisions of the courts which recognize and enforce such customs. It is unwritten law in the sense that it has not been codified and can be found only by referring to the various decisions of the courts. Under the doctrine of *stare decisis*, the courts, in attempting to decide an issue, look at previous decisions by other courts on the same point. If there is no precedent available, the court must then decide the issue, and in so doing, creates a precedent. At times the courts may deviate from previous

party may be held liable for the damage. Legal liability is imposed by the courts when it has been established that all the following occurred:

1. There was negligence.
2. There was actual damage or loss.
3. The negligence was the proximate cause of the damage.
4. The person injured was free from fault.

### There Must Be Negligence

The basic concept of our law holds that unless a party is at fault—unless he has unreasonably and unlawfully invaded the rights of another—he is not liable. The basic question in all cases concerning liability must be "Has there been negligence?" Negligence is defined as the failure of a person to exercise the proper degree of care required by the circumstances.

**Who may be held liable?**    To be held to have been legally negligent, it must be established that the individual had a duty to act and that he failed to act or that he acted incorrectly. The duty to act is the first of the prerequisites.

At the beginning of this discussion, we stated that "Most people have a responsibility to behave in the same manner as would a reasonable and prudent individual." The question arises, "What persons do not have this obligation?" There are certain classes of individuals and certain institutions which are excepted from the obligation.

*Infants.*    To be bound by the obligation to behave in the reasonable and prudent manner, the individual must be capable of determining what is reasonable. The person must have, in the terms of the law, reached the "age of reason." In some states this has been set by law at 7 years of age; in other jurisdictions the court determines what constitutes the age at which the individual can distinguish between right and wrong.

There is a popular misconception regarding the legal liability of minors arising from confusion between the terms "infant" and "minor." While infants are immune from legal liability, a minor who has attained the age of reason may be held legally liable for his own negligent acts.[5] Although

---

precedents on the grounds that the circumstances are different, or that such deviation is necessary in order that the ends of justice be served.

[3] It is possible for an act to be both a crime and a tort. If Brown assaults White, he commits a crime and he may go to jail; but in addition he has committed a tort and he may be liable for civil damages if White decides to sue.

[4] Liability may also arise from contracts. Civil law is composed of two branches: the law of contracts and the law of torts. Here we are concerned primarily with the area of torts.

[5] In addition to the liability of children itself, the liability of a parent for the acts of his children is often misunderstood. Fundamentally, a parent is not liable for the acts of his children. This point will be discussed in greater detail later in the chapter.

minors can be held legally liable, the degree of care required of a child is often different from that required of an adult.

*Mentally incompetent.* For obvious reasons, certain mentally incompetent persons are not required to exercise the care required of a sane person. In the eyes of the law, a mentally incompetent person is approximately the same as an "infant." However, if it can be shown that the mentally incompetent could have been expected to exercise some degree of care, the courts will hold him to that degree of care.

*Government bodies.* At common law, sovereign powers can be sued only with their permission. Any government unit that shares in the factor of sovereignty is immune from liability unless they are engaging in proprietory functions. When engaging in strictly government functions, they are normally immune from liability. This government immunity is based on the old common law maxim that "the king can do no wrong." There is little doubt that the doctrine, as applied today, is harsh and inequitable and somewhat anachronistic, for it frequently deprives injured persons of any right to damages. The doctrine is being modified significantly today — both by statute and by court decision. One of the most important qualifications is the Federal Tort Claims Act,[6] which provides that the United States shall be liable for money damages to the same extent as a private individual. Government immunity also has been modified at the state level in many jurisdictions by similar state statutes.[7] Finally, the courts, in a growing number of instances, have attempted to find exceptions to the doctrine of government immunity, and a few courts have rejected it entirely.

It should be noted that even in those areas where the doctrine has not been abrogated, the immunity does not extend to the employees of the government unit who are acting in their capacity as employees. If Mr. Brown is struck by a city vehicle and the damage is the result of the negligence of the driver of the city vehicle, the city itself may not be held liable, but the driver of the vehicle does not enjoy the same immunity.

*Charitable institutions.* At one time, there was a distinct difference between the liability exposure of a charitable institution and that of a profit-making one, but this distinction has gradually disappeared. At one time, the courts were reluctant (and some still are) to hold charitable institutions liable, but the recent trend has been to hold them liable in the same manner as profit-making institutions.

---

[6] The Act is set forth in Title 28, United States Code, Sections 1346(b), 2401, and 2671–2680.

[7] For example, the Iowa legislature passed a bill in the 1967 session which removed all vestiges of sovereign immunity in that state. Other states in which government immunity has been substantially affected by statute include Alaska, California, Connecticut, Maryland, Minnesota, New Jersey, New York, North Carolina, Oregon, Washington, and Wisconsin.

**What constitutes negligence?**   As we noted previously, negligence is defined as the failure of a person to exercise the proper degree of care required by the circumstances. The duty to use care is a duty that is owed to all persons. As a general rule, it is owed to anyone who might suffer injuries as a result of a person's breach of duty, even if the negligent party could not have foreseen a risk of harm to someone because of his behavior.

One of the major problems is to determine what constitutes correct action in any given situation. To make this determination, the courts apply what is known as "the prudent man rule," which seeks to determine what would have been a reasonable course of action under the circumstances. The mere fact that some other course of action might have avoided the accident does not make the individual liable. The negligent person is entitled to have his actions judged on the basis of this "prudent man standard" rather than hindsight. The judge and jury are not permitted to look back at the situation in light of what happened and judge liability on the basis of whether some other course of action would have prevented the accident. The action must be judged on the basis of what a reasonable and prudent individual, confronted with the same situation, might normally and properly have done.

Since the standard is rather vague and since no hard-and-fast rules can be used because of the variety of circumstances and conditions, in the final analysis the determination as to whether the duty has been breached will be one for a court of law to decide.[8]

Normally, the burden of proof of negligence is on the injured party. However, there are also certain doctrines which impose liability by statute or which shift the burden of proof from the injured party to the defendant.

**Negligence per se.**   In many circumstances, what constitutes the standard of care of an individual is set arbitrarily by statute. For example, speed limits in most states set the rate of speed at which an automobile may be operated. These speed limits amount to the establishment of a rule that no reasonable man should violate. If the law is violated, it is referred to as "negligence per se" (negligence of itself), and the injured party is relieved of the obligation to prove that the speed was unreasonable.

**Absolute liability.**   Under certain circumstances, liability may be imposed simply because "accidents happen," and it is imposed regardless of whether anyone was at fault. In such cases we have the application of the rule of

---

[8]Obviously, not all situations involving negligence, particularly those in which insurance is involved, become subjects of court litigation. Adjusters can determine the existence or non-existence of legal liability in the vast majority of cases without court action. Only those in which the facts or issues are debatable reach court, and these constitute a relatively small percentage of the total.

strict liability. The injured party will be provided damages even though there was nothing legally wrong in what the other person was doing or the manner in which he did it.

One of the most important cases of absolute liability exists in the area of employment connected injuries. All the states have enacted workmen's compensation laws, which impose absolute liability on employers for injuries to employees who are covered under the laws. In this sense, there is a departure from the basic laws of negligence in the case of an injured worker, for there is no need for the worker to prove negligence on the part of the employer. Workmen's compensation laws then represent an exception to the rule that there can be no liability without fault, and the injured worker is entitled to indemnity regardless of the negligence or lack of negligence on the part of his employer.

The second application of the rule of strict liability is with respect to extra-hazardous activities. The principle is that one who maintains a dangerous condition on his premises, or who engages in an activity which involves a high risk or harm to the person or property of others, in spite of all reasonable care, will be strictly liable for the harm it causes. Customary examples are keeping wild animals,[9] blasting, explosives manufacture, oil-well drilling, crop spraying by airplane, and containment of water.

**Res ipsa loquitur.**    A significant doctrine in the operation of the law of negligence is that of *res ipsa loquitur*. This means that "the thing speaks for itself" and is concerned with circumstances and types of accidents that afford reasonable evidence, in the absence of some specific explanation, that negligence existed. The accident is of a type that normally does not occur in the absence of someone's negligence and is one that recognizes the persuasive force of a particular kind of circumstantial evidence. The characteristics of the event constitute an inference or *prima facie* evidence of negligence. In the operation of the doctrine, the law reverses the burden of proof. When the instrumentality which causes the damage was under the exclusive control of the defendant, and the accident is of the type that would not ordinarily happen if it were not for negligence on the part of the person exercising control

---

[9] In many jurisdictions the principles involved in liability with respect to animals represent a separate case. Obviously, an animal cannot be held legally liable, but if the animal causes damage to a person or property, the law may hold the owner or keeper of the animal liable. For example, in the case of wild animals, as noted above, the law imposes absolute liability on the owner or keeper for injury caused by such an animal. In many jurisdictions the owner of domesticated animals such as cattle is liable for any damage they cause if they escape from their enclosure. Pets represent a separate case. One of the most interesting principles of old English common law was the doctrine which permitted a dog "one free bite." Under the legal doctrine of *scienter* (knowledge), the owner of the animal is held liable for injuries caused by the animal only if the animal is known to be viscious. Hence the one "free bite." How can the owner know that his dog bites people until he has bitten one?

over that instrumentality, the law says that the very fact that the accident happened is proof that there was negligence on the part of the defendant. For example, if Mr. Brown walks down the sidewalk and a 2000-lb. safe which was being lowered by a rope falls on him, he is not required to prove that the person or persons lowering the safe failed to exercise due care. The fact that the safe fell on him (or that he is 18 inches shorter) is evidence of this. The burden of proof is shifted, and the defendants must prove that care *was* exercised.

For the doctrine to be applicable, certain conditions are generally required. First, the event must be of a type that normally does not occur in the absence of negligence. Second, the instrumentality causing the injuries must be shown to have been under the defendant's exclusive control. Finally, the injured party must in no manner have contributed to his own injuries. He must be completely free from fault.

### There Must Be Actual Damage or Loss

The mere fact that carelessness existed is not sufficient cause for legal liability. There must be actual injury or damage suffered by the party seeking recovery. In most cases it is not difficult to establish the fact that injury or damage has occurred, but the establishment of the amount of damages may be difficult indeed.

It is difficult to determine the financial loss of a person who is injured by the negligent act of another. In the final analysis, the financial loss will be determined by a court of law, and what the jury is willing to assess against the guilty party is almost anyone's guess. A seemingly slight injury may result in many thousands of dollars in damages, while an obviously serious injury may bring only a relatively small amount. It should be obvious to the student that there is no set criterion that can be used to measure the various types of losses. The judgment of the court must be relied upon to provide what it considers reasonable.

The tort may result in two forms of injury to another: bodily injury and property damage. In the case of property damage, the extent of the loss is relatively simple to determine. In most cases it is measured by the actual monetary loss the injured party suffers.

If, as an example, a normal driver should negligently collide with your automobile and the loss to your car is total, it is relatively simple to place a value on the automobile. Market or depreciated value would be a possible measure. However, an additional loss could involve the loss of use of your car. If you needed the automobile in your business and had to rent a substitute car, the expenses of the substitute automobile would be included in the damages. The loss of use of property could amount to a large sum in instances in which, for example, you might destroy a large building.

In the case of bodily injury, it is often difficult to place a monetary measure on the loss. Bodily injury may result in claims by the injured party for medical expenses, loss of earnings, disfigurement, pain and suffering, mental anguish, and loss of consortium.

Most of these are self-explanatory, and only the last requires comment. Loss of consortium is a term which refers to the loss of companionship of the wife. Under a common law rule which is retained in most states today, a husband has the right to the services and consortium of his wife. If a third person should tortiously injure his wife, the husband has an ancillary cause of action against the party responsible for the loss of the wife's services and consortium, as well as reasonable expenses incurred for her care.[10] In most cases, the courts have not recognized the right of the wife to file for loss of consortium, although it now appears that there may be a trend in the direction of permitting the wife to file for loss of consortium in connection with the loss of the husband's companionship.

The great difficulty in determining the amount to be awarded for each of these losses should be obvious, and in the usual personal injury case, several types of losses must be considered. First, the medical and hospital expenses incurred by the injured party must be included as part of the compensatory damages. These are subject to fairly accurate measurement, although an injury that will require the incurrence of expenses for many years in the future could pose some difficult problems of valuation at the time the determination is being made. Second, the injured party will demand reimbursement for his loss of earnings. Here again, if the injury is such that the injured party will never be able to work again, the problem of determining the present value of his probable future earnings becomes somewhat complicated.

A third factor in consideration of the amount of damages involves the existence of a permanent partial injury that would lead to a permanent reduction in the earning capacity of the injured person. For example, suppose the injury is to a beautiful girl and that one of the results is a rather odious disfigurement. This naturally will seriously impair her ability to obtain employment in Hollywood or to land a husband, and she should be compensated specifically for this loss. This is also a difficult loss on which to place a value. A fourth factor to be considered is reimbursement for pain and suffering and mental anguish. It is here that we really enter the world of fancy. For example, what is the pain and suffering and mental anguish "price" on loss of a leg? The best answer is the amount that an attorney can convince a jury it is worth.

---

[10]Perhaps the discussion of this rule should be brief. The fertile imagination of the student will provide innumerable examples and appropriate comments. We might suggest that the value of the consortium in dollars may be difficult to determine, and perhaps more will be obtained in damages than the extent of real worth.

As a final factor, particularly in cases in which the injuries were caused by willful, malicious, wanton, and reckless conduct, the court may add exemplary and punitive damages. Exemplary damages represent a sum assessed by the jury in a tort action, over and above the compensatory damages described above, as punishment, to make an example of the wrongdoer and to deter like conduct by others. Punitive damages are those assessed as punishment for a wrongful injury that is willful and malicious.

### The Negligence Must Be the Proximate Cause of the Damage

The negligence must have been the proximate cause of the damage if the injured is to collect for the damage. This means that there must have been an unbroken chain of events beginning with the negligence and leading to the injury or damage. The negligence must have been the cause without which the accident would not have happened.

The negligent person is usually held to be responsible not only for the direct consequences of his action, but for the consequences which follow naturally and directly from the negligent conduct. Even if an intervening force arises, the negligent party may still be held responsible for the damage if the intervening force was foreseeable. For example, let us say that Mr. Brown decides to burn his leaves but takes no precautions to confine the fire. The wind begins to blow (an intervening cause), which causes the burning leaves to set Brown's neighbor's house on fire. The negligence began the direct chain of events, and in spite of the intervening cause Brown could be held liable. The blowing of the wind is an intervening cause, but one that Brown should have foreseen and for which provision should have been made.

### The Injured Party Must Be Free from Fault

**Contributory negligence.**  As an outgrowth of the idea that every person has an obligation to look out for his own safety and cannot blame someone else for damage if he himself is to blame, the common law principle of "contributory negligence" developed. The injured party must come into court with clean hands if he is to collect. Under the contributory negligence doctrine, any negligence on the part of the injured party, even though slight, will normally defeat his claim.

Contributory negligence, then, is the first and most important defense available in most jurisdictions. It may be defined as conduct on the part of the injured party which is a contributing cause of his own injuries and which falls below the standard of care to which he is required to conform for his own protection. Any person has a duty to exercise reasonable and prudent care in all circumstances and to avoid exposing his interest to injury at the hands of another.[11] His negligence in exposing his interests to injury at the hands of another is a contributing cause of his injury, and proof of its existence will, in most jurisdictions, constitute a complete bar to his recovery. And it is important to appreciate the fact that the degree of contributory negligence is of no consequence. Its existence on the part of the injured party, even though slight, will defeat his claim.

Contributory negligence is an important and effective defense, but it is an extremely harsh doctrine to apply in modern society. It seems rather unfortunate that most courts continue to follow the common law maxim of refusal to apportion blame. For example, one could seriously question the virtue of a legal doctrine under which a person 90% to blame for an accident should be free of liability just because the injured party was 10% to blame.[12] But in spite of its harshness, it is the doctrine that applies in most states today, and its use has been subject to little significant modification.

The number of instances in which contributory negligence has qualified as a defense is practically infinite. One of the most common examples in liability concerning automobiles is jaywalking. Failure to signal a turn could be contributory negligence on your part, even though your car was rear-ended by an oncoming automobile. Being drunk, running down poorly lighted stairs, teasing an animal, and horseplay, have all qualified at one time or another, to name just a few examples of contributory negligence.

**Comparative negligence.**    The doctrine of contributory negligence has been modified in a few states by comparative negligence statutes.[13] Here, contributory negligence on the part of the injured party will not necessarily defeat his claim but will be used in some manner to mitigate the damages payable by the other party. The Nebraska statute is an excellent example:

> In all actions to recover damages for injuries to a person or to his property caused by the negligence of another, the fact that the plaintiff may have been guilty of contributory negligence shall not bar a recovery when the contributory negligence of the plaintiff was slight and the negligence of the defendant was gross in comparison, but the contributory negligence of the plaintiff shall be considered by the jury in the mitigation of damages in proportion to the amount of contributory negligence

---

[11] Contributory negligence is a defense only to torts based upon negligence. It is not a defense to intentional torts such as assault and battery or to any tort predicated on strict liability.

[12] Because of the obvious and unjust harshness of the doctrine, some courts by judicial interpretation use the rule of comparative negligence discussed below. In practice, many courts are inclined, perhaps, to ignore slight degrees of contributory negligence.

[13] The states that have adopted comparative negligence laws are Arkansas, Georgia, Nebraska, Mississippi, South Dakota, and Wisconsin.

attributable to the plaintiff; and all questions of negligence and contributory negligence shall be for the jury.[14]

The statute is quite clear. The jury is obligated to determine the degree of the negligence of each party, and if that of the injured party—the plaintiff—is slight and that of the other party—the defendant—is gross in comparison, damages will be awarded the plaintiff; but his recovery will be reduced by the extent of his contributory negligence.

The comparative negligence principle does have a justification. Its use is not extensive, although its adoption is under serious consideration in many states today. It at least has the effect of tempering the harshness of the contributory negligence doctrine, particularly in situations in which a slight degree of contributory negligence will defeat an injured party's claim. It seems unfair to disallow a claim in cases in which the negligence of the injured party is slight, yet it is not logical to allow one to recover complete damages in such instances. If the jury can separate degrees of negligence, the comparative negligence principle will produce logical and fair results.

**Last clear chance.** The doctrine of "last clear chance" is an additional modification of the doctrine of contributory negligence. Under this doctrine, as utilized in practically all legal jurisdiction, it is recognized that the contributory negligence of an injured party will not bar his recovery if the other party immediately prior to the accident had a "last clear chance" to avoid the accident and failed to avail himself of that chance. Its logic is obvious. If one can avoid an accident and does nothing to prevent its occurrence, he should be legally liable for damages, regardless of the contributory negligence of the injured party.

To illustrate the operation of the doctrine, let us assume that X drives onto a highway from where he had been stopped at a stop sign. He gets partially on the highway and his automobile stalls. He tries frantically to get the car started, but to no avail. A car driven by Y is proceeding down the highway at a high rate of speed. Although Y notices X's car well in advance of the accident, he slows down very little and makes no attempt to drive to the other side of the road. From the resulting collision, X may be entitled to collect a considerable amount in damages, even though he had no right to be on the highway and even though he knew that his car was in the habit of stalling. Here, Y was negligent because of his failure to use reasonable care in the operation of his automobile. He had knowledge of X's predicament and could have avoided the accident by slowing down, or, if necessary, by coming to a halt. He could also have driven to the other side of the road if it had been clear of oncoming traffic. One of the most difficult lessons for an automobile

---

[14] Section 25-1151, Revised Statutes of Nebraska, Reissue of 1964.

operator to learn is that just because one has the right-of-way does not mean that he is permitted to use this right without reasonable regard for the safety of other people, even though the other people have placed themselves negligently in situations which may imperil their person or property.

### Obligations of Property Owners to Others

As a general rule, a land occupier has the right to do as he pleases with his land, but it is important to note at the outset that the owner of property or the person occupying the property has an obligation to persons who come onto the land. The duty of care does apply, and the degree of care that must be taken will depend upon the specific circumstances and upon the status of the person who comes onto the land. The law generally recognizes four classes of persons and the degree of care that must be shown to them.

**Trespassers.** A trespasser is a person who comes onto the property without right and without consent of the owner or occupier. As a general rule, the land occupier has no duty to exercise due care to protect trespassers upon his land from injury. His only obligation is to avoid doing the trespasser intentional injury.[15] This is particularly true of an ordinary trespasser whose presence on the land is unknown. There is not even any duty to discover the presence of such individuals.

**Licensees.** A licensee is a person who comes onto the property with the knowledge or the toleration of the owner but for no purpose of or benefit to the owner. This classification would include door-to-door salesmen, business visitors who have strayed from the part of the premises they were invited or authorized to enter, and perhaps visiting friends and relatives.[16] As in the case of a trespasser, the property owner must avoid intentional harm to a licensee, and in addition must warn the licensee of, or make safe, conditions or activities involving risk or harm which would not be obvious to a reasonable man coming onto the land. For example, the land occupier has a duty to protect licensees from wild or domestic animals on his premises which he

---

[15]The fact that the person was a trespasser is not a defense for injuries caused intentionally; intentional injury to another is permitted only in self-defense. The rule is that a person is privileged to use force likely to cause death or serious bodily harm only if he reasonably believes the behavior of the other party would cause his death or serious bodily harm. For example, if someone were coming at you in an insane frenzy with a meat cleaver in one hand and a double-bitted axe in the other, you would be privileged to use force for your defense which could result in serious bodily harm to the other party. In addition, if someone intrudes on your land, you have the privilege to use force not likely to cause death or serious bodily harm if you have demanded that the intruder leave or desist and the demand has been ignored.

[16]The situation with respect to social guests varies in different jurisdictions. The majority of the courts hold that a social guest is a licensee, while some courts have held that a social guest is an invitee.

knows about or should know are dangerous. Therefore, if the family dog has a nasty disposition and has displayed this characteristic previously, the occupier of the premises must take care to protect licensees from this animal, or strict liability may result.

If the land occupier knows that persons continuously or habitually trespass on his land, then he has a higher degree of responsibility to such persons than he would have for ordinary trespassers. This is based on the principle that since the owner knows that persons are in the habit of trespassing and he does nothing to stop it, their presence is tolerated and he has given implied consent to their presence, thus changing their status to that of licensees. Perhaps the best evidence of this implied consent is a beaten path. The land occupier might overcome the implied consent by posting "no trespassing" signs.

**Invitees.**    An invitee is a person who has been invited in or onto the property for some purpose of the owner. If the person coming onto the premises of the land occupier is a business visitor—an invitee—rather than a licensee, the degree of care required of the land occupier is significantly increased. Invitees, as a classification, include customers and any person on the premises held open for admission to the general public, free or paid—such as theaters, churches, railroad stations, and the like. It also includes postmen, deliverymen, workmen, garbage collectors, and similar persons, who come onto the land to further the use to which the land occupier is putting his premises. With respect to invitees, the person occupying the land has a duty to inspect and discover the presence of natural and artificial conditions or activities involving any risk of harm, and he should exercise due care to warn them of such dangers or make them safe. This is more of an onerous burden than the care he is obligated to exercise with respect to licensees in that it applies to more than just the extraordinary or unusual. Any condition that could cause harm to an invitee is a possible cause of legal liability.

**Children.**    The law imposes a greater responsibility with regard to the degree of care that must be exercised with regard to children. It is an accepted fact that children do not always act prudently, and this being the case, the law requires the property owner to protect children from themselves, regardless of their status as trespassers, licensees, or guests. Under the doctrine of an "attractive nuisance," a high degree of care is imposed on the land occupier with respect to certain conditions on his land—attractive nuisances—where children who are unable to recognize the danger involved may be injured thereby. The doctrine is based on the principle that there is a greater social interest in the safety of children than in the land occupier's right to do as he pleases with his land. For the doctrine to be applicable, the child must be so immature as to be unable to recognize the danger involved. Or, with respect to the land occupier, it must be something one would realize could involve an unreasonable risk of harm to such children.[17]

In the application of the doctrine, the land occupier is obligated to use due care to discover children on his property. If he discovers them, or is charged with such knowledge, then he owes a duty to exercise care to warn them or to protect them from artificial conditions involving a risk of death or serious bodily harm. Many types of artificial conditions have been held to be attractive nuisances. However, there does not appear to be any consistent criterion that the courts have utilized. Unattended vehicles have been considered in this category. Explosives, guns, window wells in basements, trees, construction machinery, and fences have been held to qualify. In fact, almost anything in or about premises has at one time or another been considered as qualifying. We might note that it is difficult to eliminate the possibility of legal liability from an attractive nuisance even by dying, because gravestones have even qualified under the doctrine.

### Vicarious Liability

There are circumstances in which one person may become legally liable for the negligent behavior of another person. This type of liability is known as "imputed" or "vicarious" liability and is based on the common law principle of *respondeat superior* (let the master answer). For example, the principal is liable for the negligent acts of his agent. The employer is liable for the negligent actions of his employees when they are acting within their capacity as employees. In some instances, vicarious liability is imposed by statute. For example, in many states the owner of an automobile is held liable for the negligent acts of anyone operating his automobile with his permission. Note that this does not involve liability without negligence; there is negligence; the negligence of one person makes another person liable.

To illustrate the principle involved in vicarious liability, let us assume that an employee owns his own automobile, has no automobile liability insurance, and is using the car in the business of his employer. Through his negligent operation, a pedestrian is injured seriously. The injured party has a right of action against both the employee and the employer, and any judgment would be binding on both.[18] If the employee is financially irresponsible, the vicar-

---

[17]The courts regard the doctrine either as an exception to the general rules of negligence, or as an application of the rules of negligence to a special class of persons, i.e., children. The doctrine, however, is rarely applicable to a child over age 12.

[18]The injured pedestrian will probably sue both, or, in legal parlance, "everybody in sight." The purpose of the doctrine of *respondeat superior* is to permit the inclusion of other parties who probably will have a greater ability to pay for the injury. Note that vicarious liability does not relieve the agent of his liability. It merely makes it possible to impute his negligence to additional persons.

ious liability rule will obligate the employer to pay the damages.[19]

Under English common law, a husband was liable for the torts of his wife. This liability is not recognized today, and the wife is liable for her own torts. As a general rule, parents are not liable for torts committed by their children. Here again, the child is liable for his own torts. While this is true as a basic principle, there are some circumstances in which the parents may be held liable for the acts of their children. First, the parent may be held liable if it can be shown that the parent himself was negligent in the supervision of the child. For example, if the parent was aware of the fact that the child's hobby was breaking picture windows and did not at least tell him to stop, the courts would probably consider this to be negligence on the part of the parent. In the same manner, in allowing a child to possess a dangerous weapon, the parent may be considered to be negligent and be held liable for any injuries committed by the child with the dangerous weapon.[20] As a consequence, it might not be too desirable to give your child a machette or a 16-ft blacksnake whip for a birthday present. In addition, the parents may be held liable under the doctrine of *respondeat superior* if the child were acting as an agent of the father. Several states have enacted statutes which hold that the child is considered to be acting as an agent of the father when operating the family automobile. Finally, many states have enacted special statutes which impose liability upon the parents for willful and malicious destruction of property by their children. For example, the law in Nebraska reads as follows:

> The parents shall be jointly and severally liable for the willful and intentional destruction of real personal property occasioned by their minor or unemancipated children residing with them, or placed by them under the care of other persons.[21]

The statutes may impose liability without limit, as in Nebraska, or the vicarious liability of the parent may be subject to a maximum, as in Kansas. The limit there is $300.

---

[19]The matter does not necessarily end at this point. Perhaps the best procedure is not that of firing the employee. Under agency law, if the agent through his negligence or through his failure to follow reasonable instructions, causes a financial loss to the principal, the principal can hold his own agent liable to him for the amount of the loss. It would be best to keep the person at work and force him, at least to some extent, to reimburse the principal.

[20]Surprisingly enough, the automobile is not considered to be a "dangerous weapon" in this context. The entire question of legal liability arising out of the ownership and use of automobiles will be discussed in Chapter 18.

[21]Section 43-801, Revised Statutes of Nebraska, Reissue of 1960. Unemancipated means that the child is not freed; an emancipated child would be one that has left home and is making his own living.

### Defenses to Negligence

In our previous discussion of the nature of negligence, we have been concerned with the existence of a duty owed to others and a breach of that duty. But the existence of negligent behavior on the part of an individual does not necessarily mean that he has a legal liability. For many torts predicated on negligence alone, the presumed negligent party may have certain defenses that could free him from legal liability in spite of his negligent behavior. As we have already seen, the injured party may have contributed to his own injuries through his own negligent behavior and for this reason he may be denied recovery.

Another excellent defense for negligent behavior is that of assumption of risk by the injured party. If one recognizes and understands the danger involved in an activity and voluntarily chooses to encounter it, his assumption of the risk will bar any recovery for injury caused by negligence. Perhaps the most common example of the use of this doctrine is attendance at certain types of sporting events such as baseball and hockey. Courts have held that, in seeking admission, a spectator must be taken to have chosen to encounter the well-known risk of having his face smashed by a baseball or a hockey puck. Another rather common example concerns the guest rider in an automobile. If the automobile is operated in a grossly negligent manner and the guest fails to protest the grossly negligent operation of the car, he may be considered to have assumed the risk of injury.

### Survival of Tort Actions

Under common law, tort actions do not survive the death of the person committing the injury or the person injured. This obviously prevents any recovery by the deceased individual's estate or personal representative. This rule has been changed to some extent in almost every jurisdiction. Some statutes provide merely that cause of action for damage to property survives the death of either the plaintiff or the defendant. But most go further and allow the survival of causes of action for personal injuries as well.[22] At common law, then, no action could be brought for wrongfully causing the death of a human being. The one responsible could be held criminally, but not civilly, responsible. It is rather obvious therefore, that this rule had the unusual characteristic of making it more profitable to kill a person than to maim him.[23]

---

[22] However, only a few jurisdictions allow survival of actions for the invasion of intangible personal interests as defamation, right of privacy, and the like.

[23] This is also true in states which today impose a monetary limit for actions involving a wrongful death. In Colorado, for instance, the jury may award such damages as it may deem fair and just, but not to exceed $25,000.

Every jurisdiction now has some sort of statute of wrongful death. The most common creates a new cause of action for the benefit of particular surviving relatives—usually the spouse, children, or parents—which permits the recovery of the damage sustained by such persons. The new cause of action, however, does not eliminate any defenses available to the responsible party. Thus, the decedent's contributory negligence, assumption of risk, or a release executed by him before death for the full recovery of a judgment by him, are all held to bar wrongful death actions in most states.

### Legal Liability and Bankruptcy

The risk of legal liability is one in which catastrophic losses are possible. With all the various factors used in determing damages in a tort action added together, the result could be astounding. Naturally, the question must arise as to whether the guilty party, confronted with a large judgment, has any alternative but to pay, even if it takes the balance of his lifetime to make complete settlement.[24] Bankruptcy is, of course, a possible alternative, and perhaps is the only possible course of action. The negligent party will lose most of what he has accumulated up to this point in his lifetime, but he will be released from the balance of the judgment. The discharge of the judgment may appear to be desirable to the guilty party, but the stigma of bankruptcy will follow him the remainder of his life and will constitute a harassment in practically all his future business and personal activities.

A judgment for liability arising from a willful or malicious tort, on the other hand, cannot be discharged by bankruptcy, and here the guilty party will be obligated to pay the judgment if it takes the balance of his lifetime. That bankruptcy will not discharge a judgment arising from a willful or malicious act is a fact that should be appreciated, particularly by young people who are inclined to operate cars in a manner that could amount to willful and malicious behavior. Anyone whose willful and malicious behavior results in a serious injury to someone else may find his future existence rather disconcerting, indeed, with a huge judgment that cannot be discharged by bankruptcy.

Although we have surveyed only the more fundamental aspects of legal liability, the tremendous exposure that the individual faces in this area should be evident. The catastrophic proportions that the liability loss may assume dictate that the risk management device used to deal with it be risk transfer. This is accomplished for the most part by transfer of the risk to an insurance company through the purchase of liability insurance, the subject of Chapter 18.

---

[24]This problem would never arise if the guilty party had used his foresight and had purchased liability insurance with adequate limits of coverage.

## Questions for Discussion and Review

**1.** At one time, it was felt that liability insurance would undermine the tort system, which has as its central theorem the concept that the individual responsible for injury to another should be made to pay for that injury. Do you think that the existence of liability insurance causes one to be less careful than he might otherwise be?

**2.** Distinguish between the concepts of contributory negligence and comparative negligence. Which doctrine is used in your state? Which do you feel is the more reasonable?

**3.** Explain fully what is meant by the term "vicarious liability," giving examples of several situations in which vicarious liability is likely to exist.

**4.** Bodily injury awards have increased at an almost incredible rate during the past three decades. To what do you attribute this increase? Were previous awards inadequate, or are the current awards excessive?

**5.** What major liability exposures do you as an individual in your current status as a student face? How are your exposures likely to change after you have completed your education?

## Suggestions for Additional Reading

Anderson, R. A. *The Insurer's Tort Law.* Ocean City, N.J.: Insurance Press, 1964.

Bickelhaupt, D. L. and Magee, J. H. *General Insurance*, 8th ed. Homewood, Ill.: Richard D. Irwin, 1970, Chap. 14.

Gordis, P. *Property and Casualty Insurance*, 17th ed. Indianapolis, Ind.: The Rough Notes Co., 1970, Chap. 23.

Harper, F. V. and Fleming, J. *The Law of Torts.* Boston: Little, Brown, 1956.

Kulp, C. A., and Hall, J. *Casualty Insurance*, 4th ed. New York: Ronald Press, 1968, Chap. 4.

Long, J. D. and Gregg, D. W. *Property and Liability Insurance Handbook.* Homewood, Ill.:  Richard D. Irwin, 1965, Chap. 31..

Prosser, W. L. *Handbook of the Law of Torts*, 3rd ed. St. Paul, Minn.: West Publishing, 1964.

# 18 General Liability Insurance for the Individual

*He that scatters thorns, let him not go barefoot.*
—Benjamin Franklin, *Poor Richard*, 1736

### LIABILITY INSURANCE IN GENERAL

In Chapter 17, we examined the principles of negligence that give rise to the legal liability exposure. We noted that the risk of legal liability is a pervasive aspect of the life of every individual, and that it is a risk of catastrophic potential. In this chapter, we will examine some fundamentals of liability insurance, that form of protection designed to protect against the financial consequences of negligence and legal liability which it may cause.

In its simplest form, liability insurance undertakes to assume the obligations imposed on the negligent party in the event of legal liability. The liability policy agrees to pay the sums which the insured becomes legally obligated to pay, up to the limit of the policy, when such liability arises out of acts of the insured which are included in the definition of coverage. It is commonly called "third party coverage," since it undertakes to compensate someone who is not a party to the contract, the injured party to whom the insured is liable. It is important to recognize at the outset that this "third party" is not an insured under the policy and that he has no direct claim against the insurance company. Under the contract, the company is bound to pay only when the insured has become *legally obligated* to pay, and the insured becomes so obligated only when a judgment has been granted in court.

**429**

In addition to the promise to pay all sums which the insured becomes legally obligated to pay, most liability policies include a promise to defend the insured in any lawsuit involving the type of liability insured under the contract. Thus, automobile liability insurance will pay for defense in connection with lawsuits involving the ownership, operation, or maintenance of an automobile; a premises liability policy will pay defense costs connected with suits alleging liability in connection with the premises. The insurance company is obligated to pay the defense costs even if the grounds of the suit are false or fraudulent. The basic principle is that the company must pay defense costs if it would be obligated to pay the damages should the insured be found liable.

As a practical matter, very few liability claims ever reach trial. The insurance companies realize that the interest of all concerned will be served best if a settlement can be reached without litigation, and the company normally attempts to reach an out-of-court settlement with the injured party. Most liability policies reserve this right to the insurer. In spite of the fact that the insurance company often deals directly with the injured party, it should be remembered that the injured party's claim is against the negligent insured and not the company. Technically, the company is not bound to make payment until actual liability has been determined in a court of law.

### Types of Liability Insurance

Most people recognize the liability exposure in connection with the operation of an automobile. The size of the judgments we see in newspapers act as a constant reminder of this exposure. Recognizing the exposure, most individuals purchase automobile liability insurance to protect themselves against the tremendous losses that can result from legal liability arising out of the use of an automobile. Yet at the same time, many fail to recognize that the basis of the liability exposure—i.e., the negligent act—is also the basis for liability for acts that have no connection with an automobile. The individual needs protection against the consequences of any negligent act, not just those connected with the automobile. There are various forms of liability insurance available to meet the liability exposure from various sources.

For our purposes, we will divide liability insurance into three classifications:

1. Automobile liability
2. Employer's liability and workmen's compensation
3. General liability

In general, these three classes of liability insurance are provided under separate contracts. Most general liability policies exclude liability to employees, benefits that are required to be paid by a workmen's compensation law, or liability that arises out of the operation of an automobile. By the same token, the employer's liability and workmen's compensation or the automobile liability policy cover only these exposures. In this discussion, we will be concerned primarily with the third of these classifications, general liability. The remaining two will be treated separately.

General liability insurance can be subdivided further into the coverages that are designed for the protection of business firms and similar institutions and the coverage available to protect the individual against loss resulting from legal liability. In this chapter, we will confine our discussion to coverage for the individual. Coverages available to business firms will be discussed in Chapter 22.

### The Comprehensive Personal Liability Policy

The Comprehensive Personal Liability Policy, or, as we will refer to it from this point on, the CPL, is designed to provide protection for the individual against claims arising out of his premises and of his and his family's actions. The coverage of the CPL can be purchased in one of three ways:

1. It may be purchased as a separate CPL.
2. It is a basic part of the Homeowners policy—Section II provides the individual with essentially the same coverage that he could obtain through a separate CPL.
3. It may be added to other casualty contracts by endorsement; for example, the individual's automobile policy may be endorsed to provide the coverage.

In most cases, the coverage is purchased as a part of the Homeowners contract.[1] Since the most widely used means of purchasing the contract is the homeowners policy, we will use the provisions of Section II of the homeowners as the basis for our discussion.[2]

The CPL is designed to provide much of the necessary liability insurance for a homeowner or for a tenant in an apartment or in a rented dwelling. Insurance protection exists for legal liability arising in connection with the dwelling and also from that arising as a result of the personal activities of the insured, both on and away from the insured premises.

There are three separate coverages in Section II of the Homeowners policy, with three separate insuring agreements.

[1] The general aspects of the Homeowners policy were discussed in Chapter 15. The student will recall that the CPL is the mandatory Section II of the policy and that reference was made in Chapter 16 to a discussion of this coverage here.

[2] There are some minor differences in coverage between the separate Comprehensive Personal Liability Policy and the comprehensive personal liability coverage provided in Section II of the Homeowners form.

**Coverage E—liability.**   Under the insuring agreement of this coverage, the company promises to pay all sums which the insured becomes legally obligated to pay either because of bodily injury or property damage. There is a single limit of liability for both property damage and bodily injury.[3] The minimum limit of liability, which may be increased, is $25,000.

**Coverage F—medical payments.**   The medical payments insuring agreement requires the insurer to pay all reasonable medical expenses (defined as including funeral expenses) incurred within 1 year from the date of an accident to or for anyone who is injured while on the premises with the permission of the insured or who is injured away from the premises if the injury results from an activity of the insured or a member of his family. The basic limit under the Homeowners for this coverage is $500 per person, which may be increased.

**Supplementary coverages, coverage 1—damage to property of others.**   The damage to property of others coverage contained in the supplementary coverages section of the policy provides some coverage for damage to the property of others which is caused by an insured but for which the insured may not be legally liable. It is intended to provide some coverage for damage for which the insured feels a moral obligation, even though there is no legal one. The limit of this coverage is $250, and the limit *cannot be increased*.

### The Liability Insuring Agreement

The liability insuring agreement is simple and straightforward:

COVERAGE   E—PERSONAL   LIABILITY
This Company agrees to pay on behalf of the Insured all sums which the Insured shall become legally obligated to pay as damages because of bodily injury or property damage, to which this insurance applies, caused by an occurrence. This Company shall have the right and duty, at its own expense, to defend any suit against the Insured seeking damages on account of such bodily injury or property damage, even if any of the allegations of the suit are groundless, false or fraudulent, but may make such investigation and settlement of any claim or suit as it deems expedient. This Company shall not be obligated to pay any claim or judgment or to defend any suit after the applicable limit of this Company's liability has been exhausted by payment of judgments or settlements.

---

[3] Under a "single limit" of liability, the insurance company will pay up to that limit for either bodily injury or property damage arising out of a single occurrence. This is in contrast with "split limits" such as those in the automobile policy. Automobile limits of $10,000/$20,000/$5000 mean that the company will pay up to $10,000 for each person injured, up to $20,000 for all persons injured, and up to $5000 for property damage arising out of a single occurrence.

The agreement to defend, which is included with the agreement to pay damages, is an important element of the coverage. Most liability policies agree to defend the insured against suits which are brought against him alleging negligence. However, the policy will provide defense coverage only if the damages will be payable under the policy if the insured is held to be liable. For example, since this policy is not designed to cover liability arising out of the use of automobiles, if the insured is involved in a suit which involves the operation of an automobile, the CPL will not provide defense.

**Persons insured.** One of the most important parts of any liability policy is the definition of "persons insured," for the promise of the company is to pay the sums that the "*insured* becomes legally obligated to pay. . . ." As is the case in many liability policies, coverage is provided under this contract for certain individuals other than the person listed in the declarations of the policy. The definition of "Insured" in the liability section of the Homeowners policy is as follows:

"Insured" means
(1) the Named Insured stated in the Declarations of this policy
(2) if residents of the Named Insured's household, his spouse, the relatives of either, and any other person under the age of twenty-one in the care of any Insured; and
(3) under Coverage E—Personal Liability and Coverage F—Medical Payments to Others;
> (a) with respect to animals or watercraft to which this insurance applies, owned by any Insured, any person or organization legally responsible therefor, except a person or organization using or having custody or possession of any such animal or watercraft in the course of his business or without the permission of the owner; and
> (b) with respect to any vehicle to which this insurance applies, any employee of any Insured while engaged in the employment of the Insured.

This definition is quite broad. It includes the named insured listed in the declarations, his or her spouse, any relatives of the husband or wife who are residents of the household, and anyone else under 21 in the care of the insured. There are only a few problems of interpretation that may arise. Obviously, the parents are insureds. The children living at home are also insureds; even a great aunt or grandparents will be insured, if they are residents of the named insured's household. But what about a son or daughter away attending college? Do such persons have to be actually living under the same roof in order to qualify as residents of the named insured's household? In general, the answer is "no." There have been a number of court decisions in which a child who is in residence at a college or university and who expects to return during vacations and weekend visits is to be considered as residing in the same household as the named insured. There have even been cases in which a son was considered to remain a resident of his parents' household while he was temporarily in the Armed Services.[4] This is an important aspect of the coverage, because one would hardly dispute the need for liability insurance on the part of son or daughter while he or she is away attending college.

The definition of the insured also includes any other person under the age of 21 in the care of an insured. On the surface, this may appear to have some intriguing possibilities. It applies to some person other than a resident relative who has become established in the household. It could include, for example, a child whose parents have gone on an extended vacation, a ward, a foreign-exchange student, a foster child, and persons in similar situations. It does not include a mere guest in the household. For example, if the neighbors are to be in court all day and they ask the insured to take care of their children during the day, the children will be in the nature of guests and will not be insureds. This may have importance because, as will be discovered later, the medical payments coverage of the policy is not applicable to insureds. If one of the children fell down the basement steps and injured himself, the insured could use the medical payments coverage to pay for the medical and hospital bills of the injured child. However, if the neighbor's children were to reside with the insured for several months while their parents were on an extended vacation, they would become insureds.

**Severability of insureds.**   One condition in the policy states: "The insurance afforded under Section I applies separately to each insured against whom claim is made or suit is brought, except with respect to this Company's limit of liability." This is known as the severability of insureds clause. Since the insurance is stated to apply separately to each insured, it is possible for one insured to bring suit against another insured, with any resulting judgment payable under the policy. For the sake of example, let us say that the insured has a gardener. As the definition of "Insured" states, such an employee would be covered as an insured while operating a tractor for the insured. Suppose the gardener runs over the insured. In this case, the insured could bring suit

---

[4] Until recently there was little disagreement on this point. However, there have been a few decisions to the contrary. For example, in *State Farm Automobile Insurance Company vs. Hanna 30 C.C.H. (Auto 2nd) 1291*, the court held that a son in residence at the college he was attending was not a member of his father's household, even though he returned to the home of his parents during summer vacation each year, and returned also during Thanksgiving, Christmas, and Spring holidays. The weight of opinion, however, is to the contrary, and, as a consequence, we may conclude that son or daughter will have coverage from the parents' insurance, both physical damage and liability, during a "sojourn" at college.

against the gardener, and if the suit were successful, he could collect under his own policy.[5]

### Liability Exclusions

Obviously, exclusions will be applicable to the liability coverage, and these will include those normally applicable to liability insurance in general. There are four sets of exclusions under Section II of the Homeowners policy: one set of six exclusions which applies to both liability and medical payments; one set of five which applies to liability coverage only; one set of two, which applies to medical payments only; and one set of four, which applies to the damage to property of others coverage.

**Aircraft, motor vehicles, and recreational motor vehicles.** The first major exclusion involves aircraft and motor vehicles. Generally, there is an exclusion (l.a.) for liability arising out of the ownership, maintenance, use, loading, or unloading of any aircraft, motor vehicle, or recreational motor vehicle. Each aspect of the exclusion will require some explanation. First, legal liability arising from the ownership, maintenance, or use of *aircraft* is excluded in all respects. Naturally, the relatively nominal premium charged for the CPL does not contemplate the assumption by the insurer of a risk of this magnitude. If the insured owns or rents a private airplane, he must purchase aircraft insurance specifically designed for this purpose.

Second, liability arising out of motor vehicles is excluded. "Motor vehicle" is specifically defined and means a vehicle designed for travel on public roads. It does not include vehicles which are not subject to motor vehicle registration and which are designed for use principally off public roads.

Third, the exclusion of recreational motor vehicles was added in 1968. A recreational motor vehicle is defined as a golf cart, snowmobile, or, if not subject to motor vehicle registration, any other land motor vehicle designed for use off public roads. Note that while "motor vehicles" are excluded both on and off premises, the exclusion of "recreational motor vehicles" applies only away from the premises. In addition, an exception to the exclusion states that the exclusion does not apply (and hence coverage is afforded) to a golf cart even while away from the premises while it is being used for golfing purposes.

---

[5] Of course, if the right of one insured to sue another does not exist, the provision has no effect. The common law rule is, for example, that one spouse may not sue the other spouse for tort. This has been modified in some states. Those states in which a suit may be brought by one spouse against the other are Alabama, Arkansas, Colorado, Connecticut, Nevada, New Hampshire, New York, North Carolina, North Dakota, Oklahoma, South Carolina, South Dakota, and Wisconsin. In Kentucky, an administrator may sue a surviving spouse on behalf of the children. In Louisiana a spouse cannot sue the other spouse, but may sue the insurer of the spouse.

**Boats.**    Exclusion l.b. excludes liability arising out of certain types of boats. First, inboard or inboard–outboard motorboats of over 50 horsepower or any sailing vessel of over 26 feet in length owned by, or rented to, the insured are excluded. In addition, any boat powered by an outboard motor or motors in excess of 25 horsepower is excluded if such motor or motors were owned by the insured at the inception of the policy and not listed or reported to the insurance company. Note that the exclusion with respect to outboard motors, unlike that with respect to inboards or sailing vessels, does not apply to rented motors. Coverage applies to boats below these limits, and the exclusion with respect to larger units may be removed for an additional premium.

**Business and professional pursuits.**    The CPL is designed to provide coverage for legal liability arising from dwelling premises and personal activities of insureds. As a consequence, it is not designed for business and professional activities. Two specific exclusions (l.c. and l.d.) make this clear. The coverage does not apply:

to bodily injury or property damage arising out of the rendering of or failing to render professional services;

to bodily injury or property damage arising out of business pursuits of any Insured except activities therein which are ordinarily incident to non-business pursuits.

It is perfectly clear that the policy will not provide coverage for legal liability arising in the process of conducting the operations of a grocery store, a drug store, or the professional activities of a lawyer, medical practitioner, or real estate agent. These exposures may be insured under separate business and professional liability policies.

Considerable difficulty may arise in cases involving part-time remunerated activities, particularly of minors who are insureds under the policy. Are newspaper delivery, lawn cutting, baby-sitting, and part-time after-school and vacation jobs to be considered business pursuits? As is usual, the answer must "depend on the circumstances." It is intended that normal part-time activities of minors shall not be considered business pursuits. These may include newspaper delivery, lawn cutting, snow removal, baby-sitting, after-school jobs, and the like. On the other hand, if a minor is employed full-time, the activity must be considered a business pursuit. These principles also apply to part-time employment of the named insured and to adult relatives residing with him. Thus, if the insured's son has a paper route and should heave a newspaper negligently through a customer's glass door, the property damage would be paid because this part-time activity is not considered a business pursuit. Or if the insured's wife bakes rolls for a church dinner and inadvertently but negligently uses powdered rat poison for flour and all the diners become seriously ill, the legal damages would be paid under the CPL. At some point, however, the part-time activities may be sufficiently extensive to become business activities, probably when the income from the part-time activity becomes substantial. It is difficult to determine just when this point is reached, yet an income of $100 a month for baby-sitting could be considered substantial and thus a business activity.

It is possible, under certain circumstances, to endorse liability arising from business pursuits to the CPL. Provision is made specifically for clerical office employees, salesmen, collectors, messengers, and teachers. Thus, if the insured is engaged in any of these pursuits and desires liability insurance, it is available by endorsement to his CPL under the Business Pursuits Endorsement. The liability of a teacher is an excellent example of a business pursuit which can be added to the CPL. Here, the insurance provided under the personal liability and medical payments coverages of the CPL will apply to acts or omissions of the insured in connection with his business pursuits as a member of the faculty or teaching staff of any school or college. Consequently, legal liability for injuries to pupils or members of the general public arising from activities as a teacher would be covered. The endorsement could even include bodily injury to any pupil arising out of corporal punishment. This is, needless to say, delightful. The exasperated teacher who administers corporal punishment, and in the process relocates the teeth of the recalcitrant pupil, can have insurance coverage for a possible legal liability.

The endorsement excludes coverage for acts of the insured in connection with a business owned, or financially controlled by, the insured or by a partnership or joint venture of which the insured is a partner or a member. A regular business liability policy should be purchased for this type of risk.

This coverage obviously is intended to be applicable to an employee in a business firm who desires liability insurance for legal liability that could arise in his business activities for his employer. But why would an employee want this insurance? The answer is quite simple. In many, and perhaps most, instances the employer does not include his employees as additional insureds in his general liability insurance. So, if an employee were taking a deposit to the bank and somewhat inadvertently "ground up" a beautiful girl in the revolving door at the bank, the girl could sue both the employee and the employer. With the Business Pursuits Endorsement, the carrier of the employee's CPL would be obligated to defend the employee and, if he were liable, to pay the judgment. Or if the girl sues only the employer, and the employer's insurance carrier pays the judgment and then subrogates against the employee, the employee's Business Pursuits Endorsement would provide coverage for the legal obligation. The only other exclusion in the endorsement involves bodily injury to a fellow employee of the same employer in the course of the employment. This risk is designed to be covered under workmen's compensation insurance.

**Uninsured premises.**    As long as the insured has disclosed the ownership and location of all premises that he owns and paid the appropriate premium, coverage is afforded for liability arising out of such premises. However, a specific exclusion (l.e.) excludes liability arising out of any premises other than "insured premises" which are owned, rented, or controlled by an insured. The definition of "insured premises" found in the general conditions states that insured premises means:

(1) the residence premises described in the Declarations of this policy and

(2) Under Section II only;

(a) any other residence premises specifically named in this policy;

(b) any residence premises acquired by the Named Insured or his spouse during the term of this policy;

(c) any residence premises which are not owned by any Insured but where an Insured may be temporarily residing;

(d) vacant land, other than farm land, owned by or rented to any Insured; and

(e) individual or family cemetery plots or burial vaults.

The definition in the policy includes, first, the named residence premises and all *other* residence premises listed in the policy. This portion of the definition needs little analysis. The definition next includes any other residential premises the named insured may require during the policy term. The latter could even include the acquisition of a cottage on a lake to be used by the named insured and his family for vacation purposes on weekends and during summer months.[6]

Perhaps the most interesting aspect of the definition of insured premises is the part that includes premises in which an insured is temporarily residing but which are not owned by the insured. This would include a hotel or motel room, as well as a cabin on a lake that has been rented for the two weeks' vacation of the insured and for other purposes. Legal liability obviously could arise with respect to some condition of the premises over which the insured has some control, and in addition, the medical payments coverage could be made applicable to guests injured because of some condition involving the temporary premises.

The definition also includes vacant land, other than farm land, owned by, or rented to, any insured. Thus, legal liability arising in connection with a vacant lot owned by the insured would be covered automatically in the policy. An example could involve injuries to children playing on the vacant lot,

[6] Excluded premises would include premises owned but not declared at the inception of the policy. Coverage on additional premises acquired during the policy period is automatic. However, a small additional premium must be paid by the insured for each premises.

particularly if the situation involved an attractive nuisance. Coverage is also provided under the supplementary coverages in connection with vacant land following the commencement of construction operations thereon of a one- or two-family dwelling if the dwelling is intended as a residence for an insured. We all know that children like to play in, or on, a dwelling under construction. If a child were injured and a suit followed, everybody in sight would be named, including the owner and the contractor. The insurance carrier, under the CPL, would be obligated to defend the owner, and if a judgment were levied against the owner, it would be paid, up to the limits of the policy.

The final portion of the definition includes individual or family cemetery plots or burial vaults. This is interesting and may seem somewhat unusual. However, since the plot is owned by the insured, if somebody should be injured there, the insured could have a legal liability. It would also seem desirable to provide medical payments indemnity for a guest viewing grandfather's grave, who steps in a hole on the cemetery lot and breaks his leg.

**Intentional injury.**    As noted in our discussion of intentional torts, it would be contrary to public policy to protect an individual from the consequences of intentional injury which he causes another. For this reason, the policy also excludes bodily injury which is either expected or intended from the standpoint of the insured. It is interesting to note that the business pursuits endorsement for teachers which includes corporal punishment specifically states that administration of corporal punishment is not considered injury caused intentionally or at the direction of the insured.

**Contractual liability.**    In addition to the imposition of liability because of negligence, liability may be incurred as a result of contractual agreements. For example, a common clause in many leases shifts the liability in connection with the premises from the landlord to the tenant or from the tenant to the landlord. Such agreements are called "hold-harmless agreements" because one party agrees to hold the other harmless from liability arising out of the premises. To illustrate the operation of such agreements, assume that Brown, the tenant, has agreed to hold Smith, the landlord, harmless from liability arising out of the premises. Jones is injured as a result of a defect in the premises and brings suits against Smith as the owner. Smith is held liable and is required to pay a judgment in the amount of $25,000. Under the terms of the hold-harmless agreement, Brown will be required to reimburse Smith. The CPL excludes liability assumed under any contract not in writing or any contract or agreement in connection with the insured's business. Since it excludes only nonwritten contracts, coverage would be afforded for liability assumed under a lease agreement of the type discussed above.

**Workmen's compensation.**    There is no intention of providing coverage under a CPL for legal liability of an employer for injuries of domestic servants arising in the course of the domestic employment in his home if these domestic servants are covered under the state's workmen's compensation law. In a special exclusion (2.b.), liability for bodily injury to any person, including a residence employee, is excluded if the insured has a policy providing workmen's compensation or occupational disease benefits for such bodily injury or if benefits for such bodily injury are in whole or in part either payable or required to be provided under any workmen's compensation or occupational disease law.[7] We must not conclude, however, that the employer would not have any legal liability for injuries of a servant arising during the course of the employment or that such liability is not covered. If domestic employees are not covered under the workmen's compensation law of the state in which the insured resides, the employer may still be held liable in a suit at common law. This type of liability is determined under what is known as Employer's Liability Law. The CPL does not provide coverage for legal liability arising under workmen's compensation, but does provide coverage for legal liability arising under Employer's Liability Law. Thus, protection is provided for the insured in his CPL for possible legal liability arising from his employment of butlers, maids, gardeners, and similar domestic employments.[8] However, in another exclusion the policy excludes liability for bodily injury to a domestic employee unless written claim is made or suit is brought within 36 months after the end of the policy term. It should be obvious that this is merely to provide reasonable protection for the company in investigation and preparation of a defense.

**Property owned by, rented to, or in the care of the insured.**     The CPL, similar to most liability insurance contracts, excludes property damage to property owned by the insured (2.c.) and to property occupied or used by the insured or rented to or in the care, custody, or control of the insured (2.d.) Although the first of the two exclusions is easily understood, the rationale of the second is difficult to grasp.

Remember, this is a liability contract. An individual cannot be liable to himself, so the exclusion of property owned by the insured seems logical. Because it is difficult to separate interest and because the policy is not designed to promote carelessness, the policy also excludes damage to property which the insured may not own but which he has in his care. If the insured should borrow an outboard motor from a friend and allow it to drop into

---

[7] In most states domestic servants in a private home are not subject to the workmen's compensation law. It is possible, however, for the employer voluntarily to bring his servants under the law.

[8] Coverage is provided automatically for two full-time domestic employees in the basic premium. An additional premium is charged for each employee in excess of two.

600 feet of water, legal liability would exist but without the benefit of liability insurance coverage. Or, if the insured should borrow a neighbor's lawn mower and ruin the shaft by hitting a rock, even though the neighbor might sue and obtain a judgment, the policy would not cover the loss because of the care, custody, and control exclusion.

This exclusion does have one important qualification, however, with respect to property damage included within the fire hazard. Under the supplementary coverages section of the policy, the policy affords what is known as "Fire Legal Liability," which covers damage to premises rented to the insured and to house furnishings therein if such damage arises out of fire, or explosion, smoke, or smudge caused by sudden, unusual, and faulty operation of a heating or cooking unit. The care, custody, and control exclusion does not apply to this coverage, and this qualification could be important to an insured who has rented a dwelling or apartment.[9]

### Medical Payments to Others

In addition to the rather broad coverage for liability, the CPL includes medical payments coverage that applies to injuries to others even in those cases in which the insured is not legally liable. The insuring agreement provides that medical payments will be paid under a variety of circumstances:

COVERAGE F—MEDICAL PAYMENTS TO OTHERS
This Company agrees to pay all reasonable medical expenses, incurred within one year from the date of the accident, to or for each person who sustains bodily injury to which this insurance applies caused by an accident, while such person is:
  1. on an insured premises with the permission of any Insured; or
  2. elsewhere, if such bodily injury
     a. arises out of a condition in the insured premises or the ways immediately adjoining,
     b. is caused by the activities of any Insured, or by a residence employee in the course of his employment by any Insured,
     c. is caused by an animal owned by or in the care of any Insured, or
     d. is sustained by any residence employee and arises out of and in the course of his employment by any Insured.

The definition of medical payments is quite liberal, and includes medical, surgical, x-ray, and dental services, including prosthetic devices, ambulance, hospital, and nursing services. The definition even includes payment for funeral expenses, but of course the expenses again must be reasonable.

[9] If the tenant negligently sets fire to the apartment or dwelling, he might be sued by the landlord. On the other hand, the landlord may not sue, but collect instead from his fire insurance carrier. What do you suppose the fire insurer will do?

It is important to stress that medical payments is not a liability coverage. The medical payments portion of the policy provides payment even though the insured is not legally liable. As a matter of fact, the policy specifies that the benefits are payable "to or for each person who sustains bodily injury." This means that anyone injured within the scope of the coverage may claim directly under the policy. They do not have to have the consent of the named insured to enter a claim. In addition, since the medical is a separate coverage, the injured party can technically collect benefits under the medical payments portion of the policy and in addition bring suit against the insured.

### Medical Payments Exclusions

The liability exclusions discussed above relating to aircraft, motor vehicles, recreational motor vehicles, boats, business pursuits, uninsured premises and intentional injury also apply to the medical payments coverage. In addition, there are two more exclusions which apply to the medical payments coverage.

**Workmen's compensation.**   Just as liability imposed under any workmen's compensation law is excluded under the liability section of the policy, medical benefits payable or required to be paid under any workmen's compensation or occupational disease law are excluded. In addition, the policy excludes bodily injury to any person if there is a workmen's compensation policy in effect which would cover the injury. This excludes, for example, injuries to workmen who come on the premises and who are covered under a workmen's compensation policy purchased by their employer.

**Certain persons excluded.**   One of the most important of the exclusions dealing with medical payments (3.b.) provides that medical payments are not applicable to certain classes of individuals. There are three classes of excluded individuals. The coverage is inapplicable to the named insured, and to the residents of the insured's household.[10] In addition, the policy provides that medical payments are not applicable to any other persons, other than a residence employee, who is regularly residing on any part of the insured premises. An example would be a college student to whom a room has been rented.[11] The final class of individuals excluded under medical payments are persons on the premises because a business is conducted or professional services are rendered thereon. For example, some individuals maintain an office in their dwelling from which they conduct business. Business visitors would not be covered for medical payments.

---

[10] This is an important point. If a neighbor child falls and breaks his arm, the medical expenses would be covered, but if one of the insured's own children falls in his own yard and breaks his arm, the expenses would not be covered.

[11] The liability coverage would be applicable, however, if the college student were injured as a result of a condition in the premises.

### Physical Damage to Property Coverage

Physical damage to property, like medical payments, is a nonliability coverage. It pays for damage to the property of others that is caused by an insured, regardless of whether the insured is legally liable. The insuring agreement of this coverage is worth examining in detail:

> Damage to Property of Others: This Company will, at its option, either pay for the actual cash value of property damaged or destroyed during the policy period by any Insured, or repair or replace such property with other property of like quality and kind, but in no event shall this Company's limit of liability exceed $250 in any one occurrence.

Note that the damage must have been caused by an insured, and that the property must have actually been damaged. If the insured borrows his neighbor's golf clubs and loses one, the loss would not be covered.

### Damage to Property of Others Exclusions

There are four exclusions relating to this coverage.

**Intentional damage.**    The coverage does not apply to damage to, or destruction of, property that is caused intentionally by any insured who has attained the age of 13. The intentional damage exclusion under the liability coverage does not specify any age limit, thus excluding all intentionally caused damage. Under the damage to property of others coverage, there is coverage up to the limit ($250) for intentional damage caused by insureds under the age of 13.

**Owned and rented property.**    Damage to property owned by, or rented to, any insured, any tenant of the insured, or any resident of the insured's household is also excluded. This exclusion is less restrictive than the exclusion of damage to property in the care, custody, or control of the insured which applies to the liability coverage. The physical damage to the property of others exclusion, like the liability coverage exclusion, excludes damage to property owned or rented, but it does not mention property in the care, custody, or control of the insured. This means that coverage would exist for damage to borrowed property under the physical damage to property of others coverage up to $250.

**Business pursuits and vehicles.**    The third exclusion relating to this insuring agreement excludes completely any damage arising out of business pursuits or professional services, and also excludes all damage resulting from the ownership, maintenance, or use of any land motor vehicle, trailer or semi-trailer, farm machinery or equipment, aircraft, or watercraft. The exclusion relating to vehicles and watercraft is more extensive than the similar exclusion under the liability coverage. If any of the equipment listed is involved in the damage, there is no coverage.

**Losses covered under Section I.**    Finally, the policy excludes under the damage to property coverage any loss for which insurance is provided under Section I of the policy. As the student will no doubt recall, the definition of insured property under Section I includes not only owned property, but also any property which is used by an insured. If the insured borrows personal property, it may be considered insured property just as if it were owned by the insured. If such property is damaged by one of the perils insured against under Section I, the insured must collect for the damage under that section of the policy, for Section II will not apply. Of course, the insured would be indifferent as to which section of the policy covered the damage unless Section I included a deductible. In this case, he would still be required to collect under Section I, and the recovery would be subject to the deductible.

**Loss illustrations.**    Several illustrations will clarify the intent of this coverage. First, let us assume that the insured borrows his neighbor's power lawn mower. While mowing the lawn, he inadvertently runs over a large rock and damages the machine extensively. Our insured will be legally liable for the damage, but his liability coverage will not be applicable to the loss because of the care, custody, or control exclusion. But since the loss involved physical damage to the property of others and is caused by an insured, the physical damage coverage will be applicable up to $250. The insurance is designed, then, to provide coverage for property damage for which the insured is liable but which is excluded elsewhere in the contract.

The student, however, should recognize that not all losses involving property of others in the care, custody, or control of the insured are covered. To illustrate, if the borrowed lawn mower had been placed in the insured's garage overnight and had been stolen, the loss would not be paid, because it did not involve physical injury or destruction caused by an insured. Or if lightning had struck the garage and burned it to the ground, destroying the lawn mower, this loss would not be paid for the same reason.[12]

As a second example, assume that the insured, his wife, and his 2-year-old son are visiting some friends. While the adults are engaged in conversation, the child explores the house. He finds a bottle of laundry bleach, comes back into the living room with it, and before anyone can react, he slams the bottle down on the top of a glass-topped coffee table. The table is broken, as is the bottle of bleach, and the contents of the bottle damage a part of the rug. The facts as presented would strongly imply that there is no legal liability on the part of the child or his parents, but still his parents might feel a strong moral

---

[12] Both the stolen lawn mower and the one destroyed in the fire would be covered under the physical damage, Section I, of the insured's Homeowners policy.

obligation to pay for the property damage. If no legal liability exists, obviously the liability section of the policy would not apply. However, since the loss was caused by an insured, the son, payment would be made up to $250 under the physical damage to property coverage. The coverage is designed to indemnify for certain moral obligations such as the one described above, even though no legal obligation exists.

As a final illustration, assume that the insured's 10-year-old son has a girlfriend next door and that the insured and the girl have a fight. The son obtains vegeance by heaving a brick through the neighbor's plate glass picture window. This loss would not be paid under the liability coverage because it was an intentional act on the part of the insured.[13] However, the damage to property of others coverage would pay up to $250, since only intentional acts of insureds who have reached the age of 13 are excluded.

The damage to property insuring agreement provides an important extension to the basic liability policy. It provides a limited amount of coverage (up to $250) for damage to the property of others which the insured may have in his care, custody, and control. In addition, it provides a limited amount of coverage for intentional damage which is caused by minor children of the insured, provided that they are under the age of 13. Finally, it provides some coverage in those cases where there is no legal liability, but in which the insured feels a moral obligation.

### The Cost of the Comprehensive Personal Liability Policy (CPL)

The cost of the CPL is far less than one might imagine. In most jurisdictions, the cost per year for the basic $25,000 limit of liability with $500 medical payments is about $10. Increasing the limits of liability only slightly increases the cost of the policy.

| Limit of liability | Annual premium |
|---|---|
| $ 25,000 | $10.00 |
| 50,000 | 11.30 |
| 100,000 | 12.50 |
| 300,000 | 15.80 |

---

[13] In those states having special statutes making the parents liable for willful, malicious, destructive acts to property by their minor and unemancipated children, perhaps this loss would be paid under the liability section because of the parent's vicarious liability. In *Arenson vs. National Automobile and Casualty Insurance Co., 286 Pac. (2nd) 816,* the court held that coverage applied in the case where the parent was held liable for his son's intentional damage, in spite of the exclusion of damage caused intentionally by the insured. The court based its decision on the fact that the insured who was held liable (the parent) had not caused the damage intentionally.

The basic Homeowners premium includes a charge for the $25,000 limit of liability, and increased limits for about the same incremental premiums as above are available.

## OTHER PERSONAL LIABILITY CONTRACTS FOR INDIVIDUALS

Although the liability coverage afforded under the Homeowners contract satisfactorily insures the nonautomobile liability exposures of the average individual, there are certain classes of persons who need additional liability coverage. Although time does not permit an exhaustive analysis of these contracts, they should at least be noted.

### Professional Liability Insurance

Professional liability insurance is insurance against liability resulting from the failure to use due care and the degree of skill expected of a person in a particular profession. In cases where there is exposure to bodily injury (as is the case with physicians, surgeons, and dentists), professional liability insurance is normally called malpractice insurance. In cases where the risk involves property damage (including intangible property), the coverage is referred to as errors and omissions insurance; this is applicable to such professions as insurance agents, attorneys, accountants, architects, and real estate agents.

**Malpractice insurance.**    Malpractice insurance, which is written for physicians, surgeons, dentists, and hospitals, provides the best example of professional liability insurance. The policies have certain special provisions which illustrate the nature and intent of the professional policies in general.

The need for professional liability insurance coverage on the part of medical and dental practitioners is obvious. In addition to liability which may arise as a result of a professional mistake or error, members of the profession are subject to suits alleging assault and battery for actions taken without the consent of the patient, libel and slander in connection with breach of professional confidence, false imprisonment or wrongful detention, and invasion of privacy through undue familiarity. The list of professions for which malpractice insurance is written is almost overwhelming. There are special forms of professional liability coverage for anesthetists, barbers, beauticians, chiropodists, chiropractors, dental hygienists, dentists, manicurists, masseurs, morticians, nurses, opticians, optometrists, osteopaths, pharmacists, physiotherapists, psychiatrists, psychologists, radiologists, surgeons, and veterinarians. Time and space does not permit a detailed analysis of the various coverages that are designed to insure the professional exposure of these many professions, but a brief examination of the Physicians', Surgeons', and Dentists' Professional Liability coverage should suffice to illustrate their nature.

The Physicians', Surgeons', and Dentists' Professional Liability Policy is an extremely broad form of coverage, designed to cover a wide range of professional liability exposures. The insuring agreement is quite broad:

> The company will pay on behalf of the insured all sums which the insured shall become legally obligated to pay as damages because of: injury arising out of the rendering of or failure to render, during the policy period, professional services by the individual insured or by any person for whose acts or omissions such insured is legally responsible, except as a member of a partnership, performed in the practice of the individual insured's profession described in the declarations including service by the individual insured as a member of a formal accreditation or similar professional board or committee of a hospital or professional society.

Several features of this insuring agreement deserve comment. First, the policy is not limited to bodily injury or property damage; it includes liability for personal injury losses such as mental anguish where there is no bodily injury. A second unusual feature is the fact that the policy applies to occurrences during the policy period, with no time limit on discovery of the injury. Since considerable time may pass between the treatment and the appearance of injury, losses may be covered under policies that have long expired. Still another important feature of the insuring agreement is the exclusion of liability of the insured as a member of a partnership.

There is only one exclusion in the form:

> This insurance does not apply to liability of the insured as a proprietor, superintendent or executive officer of any hospital, sanitarium, clinic with bed and board facilities, laboratory or business enterprise.

This exclusion is included in the policy because such liability is more properly covered under an institutional professional liability policy like the Hospital Professional Liability Policy. There is no exclusion of property in care, custody, and control, and damage to such property arising out of rendering or failure to render professional services would be covered.[14] There is not even an exclusion of intentional acts. There is logic in this unusual feature, since the act which gives rise to the liability may be precisely the act which the physician or dentist intended.

---

[14] The damage must arise out of rendering or failure to render professional service. Liability which arises from any other cause is not covered under the policy; therefore the professional liability policy is not a substitute for other forms of liability insurance. It is a coverage which is purchased in addition to other general liability coverage.

A special feature with respect to defense and settlement requires the insurer to obtain the consent of the insured before settling any claim out of court. As the reader will recall, under the comprehensive personal liability coverage (and most other liability contracts), the company has the right to make any settlement which it deems expedient. The requirement that the insurer must have the consent of the insured before making settlement is an important provision and one of great value to the insured, since the voluntary payment of a claim by the insurance company could be interpreted as an admission of fault and be injurious to the reputation of the physician involved.

**Errors and omissions insurance.**   There are a wide range of professions in which there exists a possibility of property damage resulting from the rendering or failure to render professional services. Included within this range are such varied professions as abstracters, accountants, insurance adjusters, architects, collection agents, consultants, county clerks and recorders, directors and officers of corporations, engineers, land surveyors, insurance agents and brokers, lawyers, masseurs, real estate agents, stockbrokers, and travel agents. In the case of all these professions, errors and omissions insurance coverage is available that promises to pay all sums which the insured becomes legally obligated to pay as damages arising out of the performance of professional services, caused by error, omission, or negligent act. In addition to the coverage available to individuals engaged in these professions, there are a wide range of error and omissions policies designed for business firms.

### The Umbrella Liability Policy

Many persons, particularly professional and well-to-do members of our society, are subject to liability claims which reach catastrophic proportions. These claims may arise in connection with personal activities or as a result of professional or business activities and can exceed by hundreds of thousands of dollars the limits of the basic liability forms. The affluent person is subject to jury awards of high amounts, since such persons are always looked upon as those from whom large settlements can be obtained.

To provide catastrophe liability protection for this type of individual, insurance companies have developed a personal catastrophe liability contract, or as it is more commonly called, the umbrella liability policy. This policy was originally developed for large business firms, and at one time was written almost exclusively by Lloyd's. It was introduced into the United States in 1947, and was soon written by American companies who adapted it and developed forms for the use of the individual. While there is no standard form for the umbrella liability policy, in general it may be described as a broad form of liability insurance, covering both general liability and automobile liability, which is purchased in addition to the separate basic liability contracts.

To qualify for an umbrella liability policy, the insured is required to purchase certain underlying liability insurance. For example, the insurance company may require the individual to have a personal insurance program somewhat like the following before assuming the catastrophe liability exposure:

| | |
|---|---|
| Automobile liability | $100,000/$300,000/$10,000 or $300,000 single limit |
| Comprehensive personal liability | $300,000 single limit |

If other special exposures exist, coverage will be required for these also in the basic program. For example, if the applicant owns watercraft of the type excluded under the basic CPL, they must be insured. If the individual has a professional exposure, as in the case of physicians, dentists, accountants, etc., the company also will require underlying professional liability insurance. The umbrella policy is then written as excess coverage over the limits of the basic policies. The limit of liability under the umbrella may range from $1 million to $5 million.

The umbrella liability policy performs two separate functions, the net effect of which is to provide a blanket or umbrella of protection superimposed on the individual's other liability coverages. The first function is that of providing additional or "excess" coverage in those instances where a liability loss covered under the basic policies exceeds the limits of those policies. In this role, the umbrella "sits on top" of the basic coverages, responding for any losses in excess of their limits. For example, if the insured is involved in a liability claim in the amount of $500,000 which is covered by either his Homeowners policy or his automobile insurance, the basic liability policy involved would respond for the first $300,000, and the umbrella would pay the remaining $200,000.

The second function of the umbrella is that of providing broader coverage than that provided under the basic contracts. There are fewer exclusions in the umbrella, and the coverage is on a much broader basis, so that many losses that are normally excluded under the basic contracts are covered under the umbrella. In the event of a liability claim which is not covered under any of the basic contracts but which is covered under the umbrella, the umbrella will respond, subject to a self-insured retention or deductible. This self-insured retention is subject to considerable variation among companies. On most personal umbrellas it was originally $5000 or $10,000, but several companies now market policies with a retention as low as $250. It should be noted that this deductible or self-insured retention applies only in those cases in which the loss is not covered by the basic contracts. If the loss is covered under the basic contracts, the umbrella responds after the basic policies are exhausted from the first dollar.

**Exclusions under the umbrella liability policy.** While the coverage under the umbrella liability policy is far broader than that of the individual contracts, it is not all risk. There are exclusions, and some of the exclusions are rather important. There is an exclusion of owned or leased aircraft, watercraft of the type excluded under the basic Homeowners policy, business pursuits, and professional services—unless coverage for these exposures has been provided in the underlying insurance program. If such coverage is afforded by the underlying program, these exposures are covered by the umbrella. In addition, workmen's compensation obligations are generally excluded; however, as in the case of the underlying CPL or Homeowners policy, employers' liability coverage is provided. Any act committed by, or at, the direction of the insured with the intent to cause personal injury or property damage is excluded also. With the exception of aircraft or watercraft, there is no exclusion of property rented to, or in the care, custody, and control of, the insured; however, damage to rented or borrowed aircraft and watercraft is excluded. Finally, damage to property owned by the insured is excluded.

Several illustrations of the operation of the umbrella liability policy will demonstrate its attractiveness. First, the coverage with respect to automobiles is much broader than that provided in the basic automobile contracts. The coverage is on a worldwide basis, and there is no restriction for the named insured as to the type of automobile or the use of the automobile.[15] If the insured drove his car into Mexico and had a serious accident, his basic policy would not apply, since the automobile policy restricts coverage to the United States, its territories and possessions, and Canada. The umbrella policy, however, would pay, subject to the retention. In addition to the fact that it is broader than the basic automobile coverage, the umbrella provides excess coverage in the case of automobile liability in excess of the limits of the basic policy. If the insured is involved in an accident for which he is liable and the claims total more than $300,000 for bodily injuries, the basic policy will pay the first $300,000, and the umbrella will be applicable for the excess up to the limit of the policy.

The umbrella is also broader than the liability coverage of the Homeowners policy or CPL. For example, the umbrella liability policy does not exclude damage to property of others in the care, custody, or control of the insured. Occasionally coverage for damage to such property may be important. For example, if the insured's wife borrows a $10,000 mink stole from a friend and it is destroyed as a result of her negligence, the CPL would not afford coverage because of the care, custody, and control exclusion. The

---

[15]As the reader will become aware in Chapter 19, there are such restrictions in the automobile policy.

catastrophe insurer would be required to pay the loss, subject to the self-insured retention.

Furthermore, the basic CPL is written strictly on a bodily injury basis. This means that the personal injury hazard including libel, slander, false arrest, invasion of privacy, humiliation, defamation of character, and the like are not covered exposures. However, such coverage is provided for this exposure in the umbrella. If the insured's wife, in her usual inimitable manner, should humiliate and defame the character of the neighbor's wife to the extent that a liability claim would arise, the catastrophe policy would be applicable.

The personal umbrella liability policy even provides blanket contractual liability coverage. As the student will recall, the CPL excludes nonwritten contracts. While the need for blanket contractual liability coverage is less in personal activities than in business operations, the possibility of contractual liability still exists. For example, suppose that the insured takes a cub pack on a camping trip and agrees with all the fond mothers that he will be liable for the safety of the boys as well as for their behavior. The liability for injuries sustained or injuries caused could be tremendous.[16]

Since the personal catastrophe policy is designed primarily for those individuals engaged in professions, perhaps the most attractive aspect of the catastrophe contract is its provision of excess liability insurance over the basic professional liability insurance. Malpractice claims are growing substantially in number, and the amounts of the judgments are becoming greater with the passage of time. Most catastrophe policies, however, will not be applicable to professional liability losses that are not covered under the basic professional liability contract. In other words, here the catastrophe policy provides only excess coverage, and under no circumstances will its coverage be primary. It is important, then, that the insured purchase a basic professional liability policy that provides a broad coverage rather than one that has many kinds of limitations and qualifications.

In spite of the high limits of liability involved and the extreme broadness of the insuring agreement, the cost of the umbrella liability policy is not excessive. Although the premium will vary somewhat with the occupation of the insured and certain other variables such as the number of automobiles in the family, in most cases the annual premium is less than $100.

### Questions for Discussion and Review

**1.** For each of the following losses, indicate whether or not coverage would exist under coverage E, the liability coverage, of Section II of the Home-owners policy: (a) a young lady of the insured's acquaintance brings suit

---

[16]This is a dedicated man, and also one who apparently has lost some of his marbles.

against him because of scurilous remarks that he made about her virtue; (b) a cleaning lady slips on the wet bathroom floor in the insured's home and brings suit to collect for her injuries; (c) the insured borrows a motorboat powered by a 50 horsepower outboard motor and runs over a water skier who brings suit; (d) the insured's wife borrows a friend's mink stole and negligently burns a hole in it with a lighted cigar—the friend demands reimbursement.

**2.** For each of the following losses, indicate whether or not coverage would exist under coverage F, the medical payments coverage, of Section II of the Homeowners policy: (a) the insured's 65-year-old mother-in-law, who is living with him, falls down the basement stairs and is injured; (b) the insured's dog playfully nips the postman in the leg, requiring fourteen stitches; (c) the insured's maid cuts her thumb while opening a can of beans she is preparing for the insured's dinner; (d) the insured's baby-sitter slips on a loose throw rug while carrying the insured's child, and both are injured.

**3.** For each of the following losses, indicate whether or not coverage would exist under the damage to property of others supplementary coverage of the Homeowners policy: (a) the insured borrows a neighbor's lawn mower, and while it is left outside overnight it is stolen; (b) the insured's 9-year-old son pours sugar in his teacher's gas tank, resulting in extensive damage to the engine; (c) the insured accidentally spills a glass of bourbon on his neighbor's dress, which is ruined as a result of the chemical reaction; (d) the insured backs his car over a neighbor child's wagon, and although it is hardly worth a law suit, the insured would like to pay for the damage.

**4.** A friend, in explaining his position on liability insurance states, "I don't feel that I really need high limits of liability, because I don't make that much money. If I were a doctor or a lawyer, I would carry higher limits of liability, but since I am not, the $25,000 minimum is enough." Would you agree with him or not?

**5.** Explain the nature of the personal umbrella liability policy. In your explanation, be sure to point out the relationship of the umbrella to the underlying coverage and the application of the deductible.

### Suggestions for Additional Reading

*Fire, Casualty and Surety Bulletins,* Casualty and Surety Volume, "Public Liability" Section. Cincinnati, Ohio: The National Underwriter Co.

Gordis, P. *Property and Casualty Insurance*, 17th ed. Indianapolis, Ind.: The Rough Notes Co., 1970, Chap. 25.

Long J. D. and Gregg, D. W. *Property and Liability Insurance Handbook*. Homewood, Ill.: Richard D. Irwin, 1965, Chap. 32.

# 19 Automobile Insurance Part I

*It's the Model T Ford, made the trouble.*

—Meredith Wilson, *The Music Man*

## INTRODUCTION

The automobile is probably the most widely owned major asset in the United States. It is also one of the major sources of economic loss. The ownership or operation of an automobile exposes the individual to a wide range of loss; he may be killed or injured while operating or being struck by an automobile, with resulting medical expenses and loss of income; he might be held legally liable; the automobile itself may be damaged, destroyed, or stolen. Automobile insurance does a remarkable job of protecting against the financial consequences of such losses. Although almost everyone who owns or drives an automobile is protected by some form of automobile insurance, few people really understand the contract which provides this protection. In this chapter, we will begin our examination of the field of automobile insurance. It will be concluded in Chapter 20. Before we turn to automobile insurance itself, it might be well to discuss some basic principles of legal liability as they apply to the automobile.

### Legal Liability and the Automobile

The liability of the owner or operator of an automobile is largely dependent on the principles of negligence discussed in Chapter 16. However, special laws affecting automobile liability have been enacted which modify some of the basic liability principles. Several of these laws relate to the responsibility

**453**

of others when the driver is negligent. In additon, some laws deal with the liability of the operator toward passengers.

**Vicarious liability and the automobile.**   As you will recall from Chapter 16, vicarious liability involves a situation in which one party becomes liable for the negligence of another party. When the average individual thinks of his possibility of being held legally liable for the operation of a motor vehicle, he normally has in mind a situation in which he is the driver. However, because of the vicarious liability laws and doctrines, it is entirely possible that an individual may be held legally liable in a case in which he is not the operator. First, if the driver of the automobile is acting as an agent for some other individual, the principal may be held liable for the acts of the agent. In addition to the possibility of this imputed or vicarious liability, the owner of an automobile being operated by someone else might be held liable because of his own negligence, either in furnishing the automobile to someone he knew to be an incompetent driver, or in lending a car which he knew to be unsafe. In addition to these situations based on common law principles, vicarious liability laws have been enacted by various states which greatly enlarge the exposure of imputed liability in connection with the automobile.

Under the "family purpose doctrine," applicable in 18 states and the District of Columbia,[1] the owner of an automobile is held liable for the negligent acts of the members of his immediate family or household in their operation of the car. The family purpose doctrine is basically a part of the principal–agent relationship, in that any member of the family is considered to be an agent of the parent–owner when using the family car, even for his or her own convenience or amusement. Somewhat related to the family purpose doctrine, a large number of states[2] impose liability on the parents of a minor or any person who signs the application for a driver's license for a minor for any liability arising out of the operation of any automobile by that minor. Note that in this situation it is not only the operation of the family automobile, but of any automobile that gives rise to the vicarious liability. Other states[3] have enacted statutes which go somewhat further and provide that any person furnishing an automobile to a minor is responsible for the negligent acts of that minor in the operation of the automobile. The most extensive vicarious liability laws are the "permissive use statutes," applicable in 12 states and the District of Columbia, which impose liability on the owner

[1] Arizona, Colorado, Connecticut, Georgia, Kentucky, Michigan, Minnesota, Nebraska, Nevada, New Jersey, New Mexico, North Carolina, North Dakota, Oregon, South Carolina, Tennessee, Washington, West Virginia, and the District of Columbia.

[2] Alaska, Arizona, Arkansas, California, Colorado, Delaware, Florida, Hawaii, Idaho, Indiana, Kentucky, Maryland, Mississippi, Montana, Nevada, New Mexico, North Dakota, Ohio, Oklahoma, Rhode Island, South Carolina, Tennessee, Texax, Utah, and Wisconsin.

[3] Delaware, Idaho, Kansas, Maine, Pennsylvania, and Utah.

of an automobile for any liability arising out of its use by someone operating it with his permission, regardless of the age of the operator.[4]

One additional point bears mention again. The vicarious liability laws and doctrines do not relieve the driver of his liability; they merely make the other party (owner or parent) jointly liable.

**Guest hazard statutes.**    The second statutory modification of the principles of legal liability with respect to the automobile involves the liability of a driver or owner toward the passengers of his automobile. So-called "guest laws" have been enacted in many states,[5] which restrict the right of the passengers of an automobile to sue the owner or the driver. The obvious reason for this modification is the opportunity which such suits present for defrauding insurance companies. In the absence of such laws, the guest in an automobile who is injured might easily induce the driver to admit liability in return for a portion of the settlement which the driver's insurance company might make with the injured guest. Under a standard guest law, the injured guest can collect from the negligent driver only if the driver was operating the automobile in a grossly negligent manner, or, in some jurisdictions, if the driver was intoxicated. Gross negligence is defined as a "complete and total disregard for the safety of one's self or others." Even in the event of gross negligence, the guest may be denied recovery if he assumed the risk involved in the gross negligence. Some laws require that the guest must protest against the grossly negligent manner in which the automobile was being operated.

The most difficult problem in the operation of guest hazard statutes is that of determining the status of the rider. Several rules have been developed. First, if no compensation of any kind has been paid, and there is no common business venture with the driver, the rider is to be considered strictly as a guest and liability must be predicated on gross or wanton negligence in the operation of the car. An example would be your Friday night date. If the rider has paid for the transportation either in money, services, or property, and this payment is the motivating influence in the driver's furnishing of the transportation, the rider becomes a passenger and may hold the driver liable on straight principles of negligence. For example, if a friend agrees to take you to see a young lady in another city and you pay him for the ride,[6] and if the payment is the only motivating factor in furnishing the transportation, you are then a passenger and not a guest. The situation with respect to car

[4]California, Connecticut, Florida, Idaho, Iowa, Massachusetts, Michigan, Minnesota, New York, North Carolina, Rhode Island, Tennessee, and the District of Columbia.

[5]Alabama, Arkansas, California, Colorado, Delaware, Florida, Idaho, Illinois, Indiana, Iowa, Kansas, Michigan, Montana, Nebraska, Nevada, New Mexico, North Dakota, Ohio, Oregon, South Carolina, South Dakota, Texas, Utah, Vermont, Virginia, Washington, Wyoming.

[6]You are probably not using your own car because the state has suspended your driver's license.

pools and similar share-ride arrangements is unclear. Some courts have held that guest laws do not apply to passengers in such arrangements, while other courts have held the opposite. Finally, in the case of a joint business venture, the guest statute does not apply, since the passenger is, in a sense, a partner in the venture, rather than a guest.

**Automobile liability insurance and the law.**   When they become aware of the fact, many persons are surprised to find that the state has not taken more positive steps toward requiring the operator of a motor vehicle to carry automobile liability insurance. At the present time, only three states, Massachusetts, North Carolina, and New York, have compulsory automobile insurance laws. Most states have attempted to solve the problem of the financial responsibility of automobile drivers through what are known as "financial responsibility laws." Such laws have been enacted in all states. The financial responsibility law in effect in most states today is known as a "security-type" law. Here, the law provides that anyone involved in any manner in an automobile accident which causes bodily injury or property damage (the latter must exceed a specified minimum, usually $50 or $100) to other than the person or property of the owner or driver, will have his driver's license and automobile registration suspended, unless he can prove that he is able to pay any judgment that may result from the accident. It is necessary for the operator and owner to comply with the provisions of the law even though it may appear that he is not at fault. The law provides that proof must be furnished the proper authorities within a limited period of time, for example, 90 days after the accident. Security must be posted to satisfy claims for the present accident, or the driving privilege will be removed; and if this occurs, then security for future accidents must also be posted.

The requirements of the law may be met if the operator, at the time of the accident, had automobile liability insurance in effect in an amount that would meet the state's requirements. The requirements vary from state to state, the most common requirement today being $10,000/$20,000/$5000. If a person is involved in an accident, his insurance carrier will submit a certificate, commonly known as an "SR-21," to the appropriate authority, thus attesting to the existence of proper insurance at the time of the accident. Many states also provide that the requirement may be satisfied with a deposit of security (money, etc.) with the specified authority, in an amount to be determined by him, or by filing with the authority signed releases from liability for all claims resulting from the accident, or by filing with the authority a certified copy of a final judgment of nonliability, or by executing a written agreement with all claimants providing for payment of an agreed amount in installments for claims resulting from the accident. If, however, the person involved does not have liability insurance at the time of the accident and cannot make any other arrangements for settlement, his driving privileges will be removed.[7] These privileges remain suspended until the claims are paid and proof of financial responsibility for future accidents is demonstrated.[8] Proof of financial responsibility for future accidents normally is demonstrated by the purchase of automobile liability insurance in the limits prescribed by the state. The insurance carrier then submits a certificate, an "SR-22," showing that the insurance is in effect. Financial responsibility may also be demonstrated by certification of a surety company that a bond guaranteeing payment to the same limits is in effect. Or, as a final resort, the deposit of a stipulated amount of cash or securities (e.g., $10,000 or $20,000) with the proper authorities may be used to satisfy the requirement. The length of time for which proof is required varies from state to state, but the most usual time is 3 years.

In many states, the driving privilege may also be revoked if a person has been convicted of a certain number of traffic violations. After the period of suspension has elapsed, the return of the license will require proof of financial responsibility. This can be accomplished as above. Offenses leading to suspension vary among the states. However, practically all states suspend licenses for driving while intoxicated, reckless driving, conviction of a felony in which a motor vehicle was used, operating a car without the owner's permission, and the like.

### Automobile Insurance Forms

There are many automobile forms in use in the United States today. Some of these policies were designed to cover specialized types of exposures, and others were differentiated for the purpose of competition. Many companies have developed independent forms which differ in some details from the "bureau forms" (i.e., those forms developed by the national rating bureaus). Since most policies are patterned after the bureau forms, we will confine our discussion to the three more or less standard forms in use today.

**The Family Automobile Policy.** This policy is available only to individuals (or a husband and wife) for insuring private passenger automobiles (in-

---

[7] The financial responsibility law of a particular state applies to nonresidents who have accidents within the state. The suspension of the license and registration of a nonresident normally involves driving privileges only in that state. But some states have reciprocal provisions, and if the nonresident's home state has reciprocity, his license and registration will be suspended in his home state.

[8] In most states, if a judgment is returned against a guilty party, not only must he pay the damages before his license and registration are restored, but he must supply proof of financial responsibility for future accidents. Usually this provision applies to judgments in any state or Canadian province, and not merely to judgments within the state in which he is licensed. Judgments are deemed satisfied, regardless of the amounts involved, when the amount paid is equal to the required liability limits.

cluding station wagons and jeeps), 3/4-ton farm trucks, and 3/4-ton utility trucks. The Family Automobile Policy constitutes the broadest form of protection available to the individual.

**The Special Automobile Policy.** The Special Automobile Policy is designed for the same classes of business as is the Family Automobile Policy. It is distinguished by a single limit of liability (e.g., a $25,000 limit rather than the more familiar "split limits" of $10,000/$20,000/$5000). Many of the provisions of the Special Automobile Policy are more limited than the provisions of the Family Automobile Policy. The Special Automobile Policy is often written on a continuous form, under which the policy remains in force as long as the premiums are paid. In many cases, the premium is paid directly to the insurance company rather than to the agent under a so-called "direct billing" approach. The Special Automobile Policy is also often written with a "safe driver rating plan," under which the insured is rewarded with a discount at renewal if he has not had any accidents.

**The Standard or Basic Automobile Policy.** This contract, which is far more limited than either the Family Automobile Policy or the Special Automobile Policy, is used to insure most commercial vehicles. It is also used to insure any other vehicles owned by an individual which do not qualify for either the Family Automobile Policy or the Special Automobile Policy. In most respects, the coverage is more limited than that of either the Family Automobile Policy or the Special Automobile Policy.

## THE FAMILY AUTOMOBILE POLICY

The automobile policy that will be examined in detail is the Family Automobile Policy. It is by far the most widely sold of the automobile forms, broadest of the three forms, and by far the most important from an educational point of view.

As noted previously, the automobile insurance policy is one of the most complicated of all insurance contracts. The complicated nature of the contract results from the need to provide a contract that will provide coverage against different types of losses, and under many differing circumstances. The ownership or operation of an automobile involves three possibilities of loss:

1. Legal liability
2. Injury to the insured or members of his family
3. Damage to, or loss of, the automobile

The Family Automobile Policy is a package policy, providing protection against all three of these losses. The policy is a combination of three types of insurance: liability insurance, accident insurance, and property insurance on the automobile itself.

In addition to the various types of losses protected against, the policy must provide protection in various situations. In a highly mobile society such as ours, most people operate motor vehicles, and in many cases the automobile being operated may not be owned by the operator. For example, Jones may loan his automobile to Smith, and as we have seen, Jones may be held liable with Smith if Smith is negligent. Therefore, it is necessary to devise a contract that will protect the owner when someone else is operating his automobile. In addition, it is deemed desirable to provide protection for the insured when he is operating someone else's automobile. Both these requirements add to the complicated nature of the contract.

The Family Automobile Policy is composed of four basic types of coverage, and is divided into four sections. Each of the four sections constitutes a different form of insurance, and two of the sections are further subdivided into various coverages. The Family Automobile Policy is a 5-page contract, with 25 definitions, 26 exclusions, and a large number of extensions, conditions, provisions, and stipulations. A specimen of the Family Automobile Policy should be referred to in following the discussion of the contract (Appendix G).

For our purposes, the important portions of the contract will be the following:

| | | |
|---|---|---|
| Section I | Coverage A | Bodily injury |
| | Coverage B | Property damage |
| Section II | Coverage C | Medical payments |
| Section III | Coverage D | Comprehensive |
| | Coverage E | Collision |
| Section IV | Coverage J | Uninsured motorists |

### Section I—Liability

Basic coverage in connection with the automobile begins with adequate limits of liability coverage. Unless the individual has adequate limits of liability, a judgment could very easily wipe out the entire assets of the family. The question of what constitutes "adequate" limits has become more and more pertinent in recent years as the size of damages assessed has increased. In spite of the unreasonableness of such a course of action, many persons operate motor vehicles without any liability coverage at all.

Section I of the Family Automobile Policy is the liability coverage. It is composed of two coverages designated Coverages A and B. Coverage A, which covers bodily injury liability, has two limits of liability, one limit which is the maximum the company will pay for injury to any one person, and a second, which is the maximum the company will pay for all persons injured in one accident. The "per occurrence" limit is two or three times as large as the per person limit. Thus, the insured has an option of the various combinations of limits for bodily injury listed below:

$ 10,000 per person/$ 20,000 per occurrence
25,000 per person/ 50,000 per occurrence
50,000 per person/ 100,000 per occurrence
100,000 per person/ 300,000 per occurrence

The property damage limit of liability is the maximum amount the company will pay for damage to the property of others as the result of one occurrence. The options available under the property damage insuring agreement are $5000, $10,000, $25,000, $50,000, and $100,000.

**Insuring agreement.**    The liability insuring agreement is extremely broad, promising to pay all sums the insured becomes legally obligated to pay as damages because of either bodily injury or property damage, arising out of the ownership, maintenance, or use of either an owned or a nonowned automobile.[9] Since the policy agrees to pay all sums "the insured" becomes obligated to pay, the section of the Family Automobile Policy entitled "Persons Insured" is one of the most crucial portions of the contract. There are four types of individuals covered under the liability section of the policy, and this coverage is provided for both owned and nonowned automobiles. The Family Automobile Policy includes a "severability of insureds" provision similar to that of the CPL, which states that the insurance afforded under the policy applies separately to each insured against whom suit is brought. Thus, one insured under the policy could sue another insured and the insurance company will be required to respond for any damages that are assessed by the court.

**Persons insured—owned automobile.**    The following persons are insured with respect to the owned automobile:

1. The named insured (including a spouse if a resident of the same household)
2. Residents of the same household
3. Any other person using the owned automobile with the permission of the named insured
4. Any other person or organization who might be held vicariously liable because of negligence on the part of one of the three above listed insureds

[9] The terms "owned automobile" and "nonowned automobile" have precise meanings and are defined in the policy. For the present, we may consider an owned automobile to be the automobile described in the policy, and a nonowned automobile to be any other automobile not owned by the insured or a member of his family.

Note that the definition of "named insured" in the policy includes the spouse of the person listed in the declarations. This is an important point, since the coverage afforded under the policy for a "named insured" is considerably broader than the coverage for other insureds.

Residents of the insured's household other than a spouse are also covered as insureds under the policy, and do not need the permission of the named insured to be covered while operating the owned automobile. The term "resident" has a special legal connotation and may extend beyond the named insured's household. If a relative, such as a son, is temporarily away from home, he is still considered to be a resident, if he considers the named insured's home to be his residence and intends to return to it.

In addition to the coverage provided for the named insured and residents of his household, the policy provides coverage for any other person using the owned automobile, provided that they have the permission of the *named insured.* Note that only the named insured (including a spouse if a resident of the same household), can give permission and have coverage apply. Although children residing in the insured's household are "insureds" under the policy, they are not "named insureds" and they cannot therefore permit friends to drive the owned automobile and have coverage apply.[10]

The inclusion of any other person who might be held vicariously liable because of the negligence of an insured is intended to provide liability protection for the employer of anyone who might be operating the automobile as an "insured" (i.e., the named insured, a resident of the same household, or someone else who is operating the automobile with the permission of the named insured). Employers often request that they be named as additional insureds under their employee's automobile policy, but this provision makes such action unnecessary.

**Persons insured—nonowned automobile.**     The named insured or members of his family may occasionally borrow automobiles from others. The Family Automobile Policy makes provision for this possibility by providing coverage on nonowned automobiles which are being operated by the named insured or resident relatives with the permission of the owner of the nonowned auto. If is important to note that there is a difference between the drive other car or use of nonowned automobile coverage of the named insured and that of an insured. An insured (as contrasted with a named insured), is covered only while operating a private passenger automobile with the permission of the owner. The named insured, on the other hand, is covered while operating any automobile (a truck, for instance).

---

[10]The general rule is that the permission must be given expressly by the named insured, but from time to time the courts have recognized "implied permission," as in a case where the father knew that the son permitted his girlfriend to drive the car on many occasions and gave tacit consent.

The coverage granted for nonowned automobiles can be a source of great difficulty as far as the liability coverage of the Family Automobile Policy is concerned. Let's take a simple example and explore the possibilities. Let us assume that Mr. Jones has a Family Automobile Policy with himself as the named insured, with liability limits of $10,000/$20,000/$5000. His neighbor, Mr. Smith, also has a Family Automobile Policy with the same limits. Mr. Jones has a son and Mr. Smith has a daughter. On the evening in question, Jones Jr. is driving his father's car. Of course, he is insured, since he is a resident of his father's household. Smith's daughter asks Jones Jr. to teach her how to drive and Jones Jr. agrees. This proves to be a serious mistake, for shortly after Miss Smith gets behind the wheel, she smashes into a bus, caroms into three other vehicles, and finally hits a pedestrian. The lawsuits may very well be substantial, and Miss Smith is in real trouble. Is there any coverage under either of the two policies to protect her from the liability she incurs? Unfortunately, the answer is "no." Jones' policy will not provide any protection, because she did not have the permission of the named insured. Children may be insured under their parents' policies, but they do not enjoy the right to grant permission to others. Furthermore, Miss Smith will not have coverage under her father's policy, for the drive other car coverage of his policy requires that the nonowned automobile be operated with permission of the owner. Since she does not have the permission of the named insured, Jones' policy will not provide coverage. Since she does not have permission of the owner of the nonowned automobile (who in this case is Jones Sr.), she does not have coverage under Smith's policy. If she had had the permission of Jones Sr., then both policies would have applied.[11] In such situations, that is, in those cases where there are two policies that may cover the loss, the insurance on the car being driven is primary. It will pay first; after the limits of liability under the policy covering the automobile being driven have been exhausted, the excess policy will apply.

**Definition of owned automobile and nonowned automobile.**    After the definition of "persons insured," the most important definitions in the Family Automobile Policy are the definitions of an "owned automobile" and a "nonowned automobile." Under the Family Automobile Policy, an *owned automobile* is defined as:

---

[11] Some students may say "This may all be very true, but the only thing that Miss Smith has to do is to get Mr. Jones to say that she had his permission. If he will just do this, then both policies will cover her." As you will recall from the discussion of vicarious liability as it relates to the automobile, the owner of an automobile may be held liable for the operation of his automobile by someone else who is operating the automobile with his permission. Since by admitting that Miss Smith had his permission, Jones would leave himself open for a substantial amount of legal liability, he may be reluctant to say this.

(a) a private passenger, farm or utility automobile described in this policy for which a specific premium charge indicates that coverage is afforded,

(b) a trailer owned by the named insured,

(c) a private passenger, farm or utility automobile ownership of which is acquired during the policy, provided

    (1) it replaces an owned automobile as defined in (a) above, or

    (2) the company insures all private passenger, farm or utility automobiles owned by the named insured on the date of such acquition and the named insured notifies the company during the policy period or within 30 days of the date of such acquisition of his election to make this and no other policy issued by the company applicable to said automobile, or

(d) a temporary substitute automobile

The portion of this definition that deserves attention is the part dealing with the acquisition of a new automobile during the policy period. As the provisions of the definition indicate, there is automatic coverage on a new car purchased by the insured, if it replaces a car that was insured under the policy. Even in the case of an additional automobile, the policy will provide automatic coverage, provided that all the automobiles owned by the named insured are insured by the company. For instance, if Mr. Jones has a 1969 Ford and he trades it on a 1970 Ford, the 1970 Ford will be covered automatically. If, on the other hand, he *keeps* the 1969 Ford *and* buys a 1970 Ford, the additional car will be covered only if Jones does not have any other cars which are not insured or which are insured in some other company. Of course, the company is entitled to an additional premium for covering the additional automobile, but even if Jones has an accident before he notifies the company about the additional automobile, the policy will cover him. Note that notice to the company is required only during the policy period or within 30 days; notice within either period will generally provide coverage.

A *nonowned* automobile is defined in the policy as an automobile or trailer not owned by, or furnished for, the regular use of the named insured or a relative who is a resident of his household. This means that the liability coverage of one member of the family will not apply to an automobile owned by another member of the family. If the father has an automobile insured in his name, and the son owns an automobile insured in his name, the father's insurance will not cover him while he is driving the son's car. As far as the father's policy is concerned, the son's car is not a "nonowned automobile," for it is owned by a relative who is a resident of the same household. At the same time, it is not an "owned automobile," since it does not meet the definition of "owned automobile" in the father's policy. In the event that the father drives the son's car, only the insurance on the son's car will apply. This can be an important factor. Most insurance companies are unwilling to write high limits of liability on automobiles operated by youthful drivers. If the father has high limits of liability on his own car, he may feel adequately protected while driving the son's car, which might have minimum limits. In the event of an accident, the father will find to his dismay that his policy does not protect him while driving the son's car.[12]

On the other hand, if either the father or the son is operating a private passenger automobile which qualifies as a nonowned automobile, both policies will apply. For example, let us say that both Jones and Jones Jr. have their automobiles insured under the Family Automobile Policy, each with $10,000/$20,000/$5000 limits of liability. If Jones Jr. is involved in an accident while driving a friend's private passenger automobile with permission, both policies will provide coverage on an excess basis (after the insurance on the car being driven). Jones Jr. has drive other car coverage under his own policy, and as a resident of his father's household, he also has drive other car coverage for a private passenger automobile under his father's policy.

**Trailers.**    Under the liability section, the definition of both an "owned automobile" and a "nonowned automobile" include a "trailer." A trailer is defined as:

> a trailer designed for use with a private passenger automobile, if not being used for business or commercial purposes with other than a private passenger, farm, or utility automobile, or a farm wagon or farm implement while being used with a farm automobile

This definition is sufficiently broad to include virtually any type of trailer. The only restrictions imposed are that the trailer must be designed for use with a private passenger car, and if it is being used for business, it must be used with a private passenger, farm, or utility automobile. If it is not being used for business, a trailer is covered when used with any automobile.

The coverage afforded under the Family Automobile Policy for trailers is an important feature of the policy. Under the basic automobile policy, and the Special Automobile Policy, the liability coverage on the automobile is suspended if the car is used with any trailer (except a utility trailer), which is not specifically insured in the same company. Not only are both owned and nonowned trailers covered under the liability section of the Family Automobile Policy, but there is no additional premium required for such coverage.

---

[12] There is one exception to this statement. The son's automobile might qualify as a "temporary substitute automobile," if it is being used by the father while his own car is withdrawn from use because of mechanical breakdown, servicing, or repair. A temporary substitute automobile may be owned by a resident of the insured's household, although it may not be an automobile owned by the named insured himself.

**Motorcycles and motorscooters.**    Because of their increasing popularity, the question often arises as to whether there is any coverage under the Family Automobile Policy with respect to the operation of a motorcycle or motor-scooter. Of course, a motorscooter or motorcycle is not eligible for insurance under the Family Automobile Policy and must be insured under the basic automobile policy, so a vehicle of this type could not be covered as an "owned automobile."

The case of the "nonowned automobile" coverage is somewhat different. The definition of a "nonowned automobile" includes, as we have seen

> an automobile or trailer not owned by or furnished for the regular use of either the named insured or a relative, other than a temporary substitute automobile

This definition is circular, defining a "nonowned automobile" as an automobile that is not owned. While there is a definition of an "owned automobile," a "nonowned automobile," a "temporary substitute automobile," and a "private passenger automobile," the term "automobile" itself is not defined in the policy. The question is, could a motorcycle be considered to be an "automobile?" One authority, *Black's Law Dictionary*, defines an automobile as "a vehicle for the transportation of persons or property on the highway, carrying its own motive power and not operated on tracks." A motorscooter or motorcycle would seem to fit this definition. Furthermore, in its definition of a "private passenger automobile," the Family Automobile Policy specifies that such a vehicle is a "four-wheel private passenger, station wagon, or jeep type automobile." Yet none of the other definitions specify that the vehicle must have four wheels. Although there have been several court cases in which it was held that a motorcycle or motorscooter is not an automobile,[13] many authorities do not consider these cases to be conclusive, for there are also court cases which have ruled the other way. Many authorities in the field of property and liability insurance maintain that the definition of a "nonowned automobile" is suffi-

---

[13] There are five noteworthy cases with respect to the motorcycle as an automobile. A Pennsylvania court held that the term "automobile" did not include a motorcycle in a 1958 case, *Paupst vs. McKendry, 145 Atl 725*. This case concurred with a previous Pennsylvania decision, *Deardorff vs. Continental Life Insurance Co. 151 Atl, 814*. A Texas court took a position that a motorscooter is not an automobile in *Texas Casualty Insurance Co. vs. Wyble, 333 S.W. (2nd) 668*. A Georgia court has also concurred with the opinion that a motorscooter or a motorcycle is not an automobile in the case of *Whiddon vs. Cotton States Mutual Insurance Co., 135 S.W. (2nd) 521*. On the other hand, in a Minnesota case [*Lang vs. General Insurance Company of America, 127 N.W. (2nd) 541*], the court held that a motorscooter was an automobile. Although this case involved the definition of an automobile under the provisions of the homeowners policy, it seems to indicate that according to this decision, a motorscooter or motorcycle would be covered as a nonowned automobile under the Family Automobile Policy.

ciently broad to include a motorcycle or a motorscooter for the named insured. Since residents of the named insured's household have coverage only for a nonowned private passenger automobile, and a private passenger automobile is defined as a four-wheeled vehicle, they would not be covered while operating a motorscooter or motorcycle.

**Supplementary payments.**    As is the case with most liability policies, in addition to paying the sums that the insured is legally obligated to pay, the liability section includes another set of promises that are extremely important. First, the company promises to defend the insured in any suit that is brought alleging negligence in the operation of an owned or nonowned automobile. This promise is in effect a legal retainer that is always available to the insured in the event that he is sued for negligence in connection with the operation of an automobile, provided that the judgment in such suit would be payable under the terms of the policy. The promise to defend is in addition to the promise to pay any judgment, and any expenses incurred in investigation or defense are payable in addition to the maximum limit of liability. To illustrate, let us say that Jones has a Family Automobile Policy with the basic $10,000/$20,000/$5000 limits of liability, and that he is sued for $20,000 by an injured party. The policy will pay $10,000 of the judgment under insuring agreement A, and will pay any court costs and defense costs in addition to this.

Second, the policy promises to pay the cost of any appeal bonds, bonds to release attachments, or bail bonds which are required from the insured because of an accident or traffic law violation connected with an automobile. This last provision, relating to bail bonds, is often overlooked simply because insureds do not know that it exists. If the insured is arrested for speeding, drunken driving, or any other traffic violation, the policy will pay the cost of his bail bond.[14]

Finally, the company agrees to pay any expenses incurred by the insured at the time of an accident in providing immediate surgical or medical care to a person injured in an accident involving an insured automobile, or any other expenses incurred by the insured (except loss of earnings), which are at the company's request.

**Liability exclusions.**    There are ten exclusions under the liability section of the Family Automobile Policy. Exclusion (a) excludes liability while the insured automobile is used as a public or livery conveyance. There is no

[14]However, the company is not required to furnish the bond; it will merely pay the cost of the bond. Suppose Mr. Jones is arrested for speeding, taken to jail, and his bond is set at $500. Shortly after his incarceration, he will probably be visited by a bondsman, who will post his bond for a fee. If the bondsman charges 10% of the bond, the insurance company will pay the $50 fee which the bondsman charges for posting the $500.

intent under this exclusion to exclude coverage when the insured uses his automobile in a car pool or a similar arrangement. The basic characteristic of a public or livery conveyance is the fact that the insured has no control over whom he carries. If the insured carries fellow workers to the job and charges them, this does not make his automobile a public or livery conveyance.[15]

Exclusion (b) deals with damage caused intentionally or at the direction of the insured. As noted previously, such coverage would be contrary to public policy.

Exclusion (c), which deals with nuclear energy liability, and exclusion (d), which excludes liability arising out of the operation of farm machinery, are self-explanatory.

Exclusions (e) and (f) both deal with liability in connection with persons who are entitled to workmen's compensation benefits. Exclusion (e) excludes bodily injury liability to employees of the insured if workmen's compensation benefits are payable or required to be paid under a workmen's compensation law. Exclusion (f) deals with liability to fellow employees of the insured, and excludes liability to fellow employees if they are injured as a result of the operation of an insured automobile in the business of the employer. However, the exclusion states that it does not apply to the named insured. In other words, if the named insured should be sued by a fellow employee who was entitled to workmen's compensation benefits, the policy would protect the named insured. The basic intent of this provision is to exclude the employer from coverage for bodily injury to a fellow employee of the named insured.

Exclusion (g) excludes liability completely when the automobile is used in the automobile business by anyone except the named insured, a resident of the same household, a partner of the named insured, or an agent or employee of the named insured. The basic intent is to deny liability coverage for a garage or other automobile business which might have custody of the automobile. This liability must be covered under a separate business contract. If Mr. Jones takes his automobile into a garage to have it serviced, his Family Automobile Policy will not provide protection to the garage or to an employee of the garage who is driving or testing the automobile.

Exclusion (h) is similar to exclusion (g), in that it deals with business use of automobiles. This exclusion excludes any nonowned automobile from coverage while it is being used in the automobile business, or any other business of the insured. The exclusion states that it does not apply to the named insured with respect to a private passenger automobile operated by the named in-

[15] The case of *Allstate Insurance Co. vs. Roberson, 5, C.C.H. (Auto 2nd) 389* clearly held that ride-sharing arrangements do not violate the policy provisions and do not constitute use of the automobile as a "public or livery conveyance."

sured in a business other than the automobile business. Thus, the exclusion would not provide coverage for the named insured while operating a nonowned automobile in the automobile business, but it would cover him while operating a nonowned private passenger automobile in any other business. The intent of this provision is to exclude coverage for automobiles that should be insured under a business liability policy. If the named insured works for a garage, his Family Automobile Policy will not provide protection while he is driving a nonowned auto in connection with his occupation.

Exclusion (i) is one of the most important of all of the exclusions. It states:

This policy does not apply under Part I to injury to or destruction of (1) property owned or transported by the insured or (2) property rented to or in charge of the insured other than a residence or private garage

This is the "care, custody, and control" exclusion of the Family Automobile Policy. It is important because it modifies the coverage that is provided with respect to "nonowned automobiles." When the insured borrows or rents an automobile, the liability exposure connected with the operation of that nonowned automobile is covered, *except* with respect to damage to the nonowned automobile itself. For example, let us say that Mr. Jones rents a car from Hertz. His Family Automobile Policy will pay for any damage he causes in connection with the use of the rented automobile, but it will not pay for damage to the Hertz car itself, for the car is property which is "rented to or in charge of the insured." It is important to remember that the liability coverage of the Family Automobile Policy will not provide indemnification for damage to an automobile that is borrowed or rented.

Exclusion (j) provides that the automatic coverage applicable to replacement and additionally acquired automobiles does not apply if the insured has purchased other automobile liability insurance applying to the replacement or additional automobile.

### Section II—Medical Payments Coverage

Medical payments coverage has been available in one form or another in the automobile policy since 1939. This section of the policy provides coverage for necessary medical, surgical, dental, and funeral expenses that are incurred within 1 year from the date of an accident. The coverage is divided into two sections, designated Division 1 and Division 2. *Division 1* of the medical payments coverage provides protection for the named insured and each relative who suffers bodily injury caused by accident, while occupying, or through being struck by, an automobile. According to the definition in the policy, the term "occupying" includes the acts of entering the automobile or alighting from it. One of the most important features of the Division 1 coverage is the fact that coverage is provided to the named insured and resident relatives if stuck by an automobile; there is no requirement that they be occupying an automobile when struck for coverage to apply.

*Division 2* provides coverage for persons other than the named insured and members of his household, but the coverage is not as broad as that provided under Division 1. Persons covered under Division 2 are covered only when they are injured while occupying an insured automobile. This means they are covered, first, if occupying an owned automobile while it is being used by the named insured, a resident of the household, or any other person who has the permission of the named insured; and second, if occupying a nonowned automobile, provided the injury results from the operation or occupancy of the nonowned automobile by the named insured or a resident relative. As under the liability section, the relative has coverage only for a nonowned private passenger automobile, while there is no such restriction with respect to the named insured. Both the named insured and resident relatives must have the permission of the owner of the nonowned automobile, and the operation must be within the scope of the permission.

It is important to note that the insuring agreement that provides the medical payments coverage is a separate insuring agreement. Unlike the medical payments of the CPL, the medical payments of the Family Automobile Policy are designed to pay for members of the insured's family and others who are occupying an automobile operated by the named insured or a resident relative, or who are occupying the owned automobile with the permission of the named insured. Medical payments coverage *does not* apply to persons who are injured by the insured unless they are occupants of an insured automobile.

One of the important features of the medical payments coverage is that it applies to the named insured or resident relatives when they are struck by an automobile, even though they may not be in an automobile at the time. A child of the insured might be struck by an automobile while crossing the street. In such a case, the medical payments of the Family Automobile Policy would pay for the medical expenses involved, up to the limit available.

The basic limit of liability under the medical payments portion of the policy is $500 per person, with no maximum limit per accident. For a small additional premium (a few dollars per year), this limit can be increased to any amount up to $5000 per person, with no aggregate limit per accident.

**Exclusions under medical payments.**    There are relatively few exclusions under the medical payments section of the Family Automobile Policy. Exclusion (a) excludes injury sustained while occupying an owned automobile which is being used as a public or livery conveyance, or a trailer that is being used as a residence, such as a house trailer.

Exclusion (b) excludes injury sustained by the named insured or a resident relative as a result of being struck by a farm-type tractor or other equipment designed for use off public roads unless it is on public roads, or as a result of being struck by a vehicle operated on rails or crawler treads.

Exclusion (c) deals with persons covered under Division 2, and excludes payment to such persons while occupying a nonowned automobile which is being used as a public or livery conveyance or in the automobile business. In addition, there is no coverage if the injury results from the use of a nonowned automobile in any business unless the injury results from the operation or occupancy of a private passenger automobile by the named insured, his private chauffeur, or a domestic servant.

Exclusion (d) deals with injuries sustained by a person who is entitled to workmen's compensation benefits. The coverage is extremely broad in this respect. Medical payments are payable in addition to any benefits payable under workmen's compensation unless the individual is employed in the automobile business.

Exclusion (e) excludes loss due to war.

Many people underestimate the importance of adequate limits under the medical payments portion of the automobile policy. Those who have hospitalization policies often feel that they can do without this coverage. Yet this coverage is probably one of the best insurance buys available. It is designed to cover not only the members of the insured's family, but also guests in the car. Every responsible motorist feels a sense of obligation to his passengers, yet if these passengers are injured due to the negligence of the driver, a guest hazard statute might prevent them from collecting. A driver who has high medical limits can meet the obligation he feels without forcing the guest to resort to legal action. This is probably one of the most important points concerning medical payments coverage: it is not a liability coverage. There need have been no negligence or liability in order to collect under the medical payments portion of the policy. The medical payments coverage provided under the Family Automobile Policy is simply a specialized type of health insurance which has been made a part of the automobile policy. The benefits under this coverage are payable in addition to benefits which may be received from other sources. For example, if Mr. Smith is struck by an automobile, his medical payments coverage will pay any medical expenses which result, up to the limit of the coverage. In addition, Mr. Smith may sue the driver of the vehicle which struck him and collect for his medical expenses, for there is no subrogation provision applicable to the medical expense coverage. In addition, medical payments under the Family Automobile Policy are made regardless of coverage under any other health and accident policy the insured may have.

### Section III—Physical Damage Coverage

The physical damage section of the Family Automobile Policy provides coverage against loss of the automobile or damage to the automobile. There are six coverages available:

| | |
|---|---|
| Coverage D | Comprehensive |
| Coverage E | Collision |
| Coverage F | Fire, lightning, transportation |
| Coverage G | Theft |
| Coverage H | Combined additional coverage |
| Coverage I | Towing and labor costs |

We will confine our discussion, for the most part, to the first two of these six coverages, comprehensive and collision; these are the most frequently purchased. As we shall see, Coverage D (comprehensive) includes protection against all the perils insured against under Coverages F, G, and H. These are seldom used, simply because the difference in cost between them and comprehensive (which is an all-risk coverage) is so small.[16]

**Coverage D—comprehensive coverage.** Comprehensive coverage is essentially an all-risk type of property insurance. Under the comprehensive insuring agreement, the insurance company promises to pay for "loss caused other than by collision to the owned automobile or to a non-owned automobile." The purpose of excluding collision under the comprehensive insuring agreement, and then providing this coverage under a separate insuring agreement, is to permit the application of a deductible to collision losses. If it were not desirable to use a deductible on collision losses from an underwriting and price standpoint, it would be possible to combine comprehensive and collision into one insuring agreement. The comprehensive insuring agreement states that

> for the purpose of this coverage, breakage of glass, and loss caused by missiles, falling objects, fire, theft or larceny, explosion, earthquake, windstorm, hail, water, flood, malicious mischief or vandalism, riot or civil commotion, or colliding with a bird or animal, shall not be deemed to be loss caused by collision.

In other words, since these losses are not deemed to be losses caused by collision, they are losses covered under the comprehensive insuring agreement. The insured would prefer to have any losses that occur covered under the comprehensive insuring agreement rather than the collision coverage, since the collision coverage is written with a deductible. To illustrate the intent of the above provision, suppose that Mr. Jones has a Family Auto-

[16]About the only time that Coverages F, G, and H are sold is in the case of an older car, such as an antique. In such a situation, the owner may want physical damage coverage, but the insurance company is unwilling to provide comprehensive coverage because of the broadness of the insuring agreement. As an alternative, the owner can purchase the separate named peril coverages.

mobile Policy with comprehensive and collision, and that the collision coverage is written with a $50 deductible. If Mr. Jones' car is stolen and later found wrecked, the insurance company will be obligated to pay the entire loss, without any deductible, for the policy specifically states that a loss due to theft shall not be deemed to be a loss due to collision.

The comprehensive coverage also provides some limited coverage on personal effects of the insured while they are in or upon the owned automobile. The coverage for personal effects is widely misunderstood, particularly in the case of the Family Automobile Policy, which will pay for loss to personal effects, up to $100, while they are in or upon the owned automobile, provided they are damaged by fire or lightning. It should be noted that this coverage is extremely limited. Fire and lightning are the only insured perils with respect to the contents of the automobile. Many persons who have their automobile insured under a Family Automobile Policy mistakenly think that the policy provides coverage for theft of articles from the automobile. Comprehensive coverage includes theft coverage, but this applies to the automobile itself, and not to articles stolen from the automobile.

**Coverage E—collision coverage.**    The collision coverage of the Family Automobile Policy is simple to understand. The company promises

> To pay for loss caused by collision to the owned automobile or a non-owned automobile but only for the amount of each such loss in excess of the deductible amount stated in the declarations as applicable hereto.

The insuring agreement further provides, and this is an important provision that is often overlooked:

> The deductible amount shall not apply to loss caused by a collision with another automobile insured by the company.

The deductible amount is normally either $50 or $100, although other options are available.

Under the collision portion of the policy, the company promises to pay for damage to the owned automobile (and to nonowned automobiles, a provision which will be discussed later), which is caused by collision with another object or by upset, no matter whose fault the accident is. Collision coverage can therefore be a valuable coverage even if the accident is not the insured's fault. In those cases where the driver of the other automobile is at fault, we would expect his liability coverage to respond for damages to the owned automobile. However, the other party may not have insurance. If the innocent driver has collision coverage, he can collect the amount of the loss (less any deductible) and then leave the task of collecting from the negligent driver to his insurance company. The physical damage section of the Family Automobile Policy includes a subrogation provision, under which the insured is required to assign to the company all right of claim against a negligent third party, to the extent that he collects from his insurance company. Also, in the case where the insured is at fault, his collision coverage will pay for the damage to his automobile, in addition to the payment made under liability for damage to the other party's automobile.

**Coverage on nonowned automobiles under Section III.** "Drive other car" coverage similar to the liability coverage is also provided under the physical damage section of the policy. The insured is protected from the financial consequences he might suffer if he damages an automobile which he has borrowed or rented. As you will recall from our discussion of the liability section of the policy, there is a liability exclusion relating to the property of others in the care, custody, or control of the insured. If Mr. Jones borrows Smith's car, his liability coverage will provide protection for any damage he causes, but it will not provide coverage for damage to Smith's car. However, if Jones also has comprehensive and collision coverage, these coverages will apply to Smith's automobile as a nonowned automobile. Coverage is provided with respect to a nonowned automobile regardless of whether or not the insured is legally liable.

The coverage with respect to a nonowned automobile is excess. In other words, if Smith has a collision coverage, Jones' collision coverage will apply only after Smith's policy has paid. If Smith has no collision coverage, then Jones' policy will pay for the loss, less the deductible. If the deductible on the nonowned automobile is higher than the deductible on the policy which is excess, the excess policy will pay the difference between the deductibles. Perhaps another example will serve to illustrate the point.

Mr. Smith has a 1972 Chrysler, which he has insured under a Family Automobile Policy with a $100 deductible on the collision coverage. Jones, who wishes to impress a young lady he has just met, borrows Smith's car. Jones has a 1937 Nash, also insured under a Family Automobile Policy, but with a $50 deductible under the collision coverage. While showing the young lady what a superior driver he is, Jones piles the Chrysler into a brick wall and totally demolishes it (the car, not the wall). Since the coverage on the automobile being driven is primary, Smith's policy will pay for the damage to the Chrysler, less the $100 deductible. As excess coverage, Jones' policy will pay the amount of the remaining loss ($100), less his deductible ($50). Jones' policy will therefore pay an additional $50. Jones will probably have to pay the remaining $50 himself or lose Smith's friendship (or possibly both).

The drive other car coverage under Section III of the policy is somewhat more limited than the drive other car coverage of the liability section. Under the physical damage coverage, the named insured and resident relatives are covered for physical damage to an automobile which they are driving or which is in their possession, however, a nonowned automobile is defined more narrowly under the physical damage section than it is under the liability section. As you will recall, the named insured has drive other car liability coverage for any type of automobile, while the resident relatives are covered only for a private passenger automobile. Under the physical damage section, both the named insured and resident relatives are covered only for nonowned private passenger automobiles. Again, as under the liability section, a non-owned automobile is defined as an automobile which is not owned by, or furnished for, the regular use of the named insured or a resident relative.

**Trailers under Section III.**    Under the physical damage section of the Family Automobile Policy, an owned trailer is covered against loss under collision or comprehensive coverage only if the trailer is listed and a premium is paid therefore. In addition, the definition of a trailer is somewhat more limited under Section III than under the liability coverage. Under the physical damage coverage, a trailer is defined as

> a trailer designed for use with a private passenger automobile, if not being used for business or commercial purposes with other than a private passenger, farm, or utility automobile, and if not a home, office, store, display or passenger trailer.

Under the definition of a nonowned automobile in the physical damage section, a nonowned utility trailer is covered against loss under comprehensive and collision coverage, but with a maximum limit for any loss of $500.

**Physical damage supplementary payments.**    This section of the coverage provides certain additional benefits to the insured without additional premium. The supplementary payments are in a sense "fringe benefits" which have been added to the contract over a period of time as competitive devices. The most important of the supplementary benefits under the physical damage section is the promise to pay for loss of use following the theft of the owned automobile; the company agrees with the insured

> to reimburse the insured for transportation expenses incurred during the period commencing 48 hours after a theft covered by this policy of the entire automobile has been reported to the company and the police, and terminating when the automobile is returned to use or the company pays for the loss; provided that the company shall not be obligated to pay aggregate expenses in excess of $10 per day or totaling more than $300.

The payment for loss of use as a result of the theft of the automobile is payable in addition to the applicable limit of liability for the automobile.

The physical damage coverage under both comprehensive and collision is on an "actual cash value" basis. The company is not required to replace the used automobile with a new one. As a matter of fact, the company may not replace the automobile at all. The policy provisions give the company three options in loss settlement; it may

1. Pay for the loss in cash
2. Repair the damaged property
3. Replace the damaged property

The choice of which option it elects is up to the company. If the insured and the company cannot agree on the amount of a loss, either party may, within a period of 60 days after the submission of the proof of loss, demand an appraisal of the loss. The procedure used in appraisal is the same as that used under the fire policy. Each party selects a competent and disinterested appraiser; the appraisers then select a competent and disinterested umpire. The appraisers independently determine the amount of the loss, and failing to agree, they submit their differences to the umpire. An agreement on the part of any two of the three parties involved in the appraisal is binding.

**Coverage I—towing and emergency road service.**    The towing and emergency road service coverage is available for a nominal premium. This coverage is designed to pay for any on-the-road service or charge for towing the automobile to a garage which may be necessary due to a mechanical failure. Towing is not a crucial coverage; the insured can probably afford to pay such expenses himself rather than purchase insurance protection. However, as in the case of many insignificant losses, many individuals prefer to purchase this protection rather than budget such expenses. The normal limit for this coverage is $25.00 per disablement.

**Exclusions under Section III.**    Taken together, Coverages D and E (i.e., comprehensive and collision) provide a broad form of all-risk coverage on the automobile. There are eight exclusions applicable to the coverage under Section III of the Family Automobile Policy.

Exclusion (a) excludes loss to any automobile when it is being used as a public or livery conveyance. As we have seen, participation in a car pool, or carrying friends, even though a charge might be made, does not constitute use as a public or livery conveyance.

Exclusion (b) excludes any loss due to war.

Exclusion (c) excludes loss to any nonowned automobile arising out of its use by the insured while he is employed in the automobile business. If the insured works for a garage, his Family Automobile Policy will not provide coverage on customers' automobiles which he may be driving.

Exclusion (d) excludes loss to any automobile owned by the insured, which is not described in the policy, if the insured has other valid and collectible insurance against such a loss. Essentially, this exclusion eliminates coverage for additionally acquired automobiles, if the insured purchases insurance to cover such automobiles.

Exclusion (e) excludes damage which is due to wear and tear, freezing, mechanical or electrical breakdown or failure, unless such loss results from a theft covered by the policy. If the insured's automobile is stolen, and when recovered is found to have suffered substantial wear and tear, the loss would be covered as a loss due to theft.

Exclusion (f) excludes loss to tires, unless they are damaged by fire, malicious mischief, or vandalism, or stolen, or unless the loss be coincident with, and from the same cause as, other loss covered by the policy. For instance, if the insured suffers a blowout while driving down the road, the loss would not be covered. However, if the blowout happened as a result of a collision, the loss to the tire would be covered.

Exclusion (g) excludes loss due to radioactive contamination.

Exclusion (h) states that breakage of glass is excluded under Coverage E (collision) if insurance with respect to such loss is otherwise provided. In other words, if the insured has purchased comprehensive coverage, glass breakage will be covered under that section. If he has not purchased comprehensive coverage, but carries collision coverage, the glass breakage which is a result of a collision will be covered under the collision section, subject to the deductible.

### Section IV—Uninsured Motorists Coverage

Uninsured motorist coverage, designated Coverage J in the Family Automobile Policy, is designed to protect the insured and members of his family from the acts of financially irresponsible motorists. In spite of the financial responsibility laws and the dictates of common sense, some people still drive without automobile liability insurance. Uninsured motorist coverage is designed to meet the need for protection against *bodily injury* which an insured may suffer as a result of being struck by an uninsured driver or a hit-and-run driver.[17]

In its simplest terms, Section IV promises to pay the amount which an

[17] In most states, the uninsured motorist coverage applies only to bodily injury, but in the states of Georgia, New Jersey, New Mexico, North Carolina, Virginia, and West Virginia it includes property damage liability as well. In these states, the property damage portion of the coverage is subject to a deductible ranging from $100 to $300. Property damage caused by uninsured motorists is covered under the individual's collision coverage in other states.

insured person could have collected from the insurance company of an un-insured driver or a hit-and-run driver, if such a driver had carried auto-mobile liability insurance.[18] The coverage is an attempt by the insurance companies to provide a solution to the problem of uninsured drivers and forestall compulsory automobile insurance.

**Persons insured.** Under Section IV, an insured person includes:

1. The named insured and resident relatives
2. Any other person while occupying an insured automobile
3. Any person, with respect to damages he is entitled to collect because of bodily injury to the named insured, a resident relative, or any other person occupying an insured automobile

Note that the named insured and resident relatives are covered even when they are not occupying an automobile. If the insured or a resident relative is struck by an uninsured automobile, there is coverage. Others are covered only while actually in an automobile which is covered under the policy as an "owned automobile" or a "nonowned automobile."

There are five situations in which the coverage does not apply:

1. When the insured is involved in an accident with an automobile that is insured for an amount at least equal to the minimum limits of liability required by the financial responsibility law of the state.
2. When the insured is involved in an accident with an automobile which is owned or operated by a qualified self-insurer.
3. When the insured is involved in an accident with a government-owned vehicle, even though the government vehicle may be uninsured.
4. When the insured is involved in an accident with an automobile owned by the named insured or any resident of the named insured's household, regardless of who is operating the uninsured auto.
5. When the insured or his representative makes any settlement with the guilty party without written consent of the insurance company.

The limit of liability under this coverage is normally $10,000 per person and $20,000 per accident. This limit may not be increased.[19]

[18] In an increasing number of states, the definition of "uninsured automobile" includes one on which a policy was in effect at the time of the accident, but the insurer became insolvent within 1 year from the date of the accident.

[19] Other limits are prescribed in some states. The limits in California are $15,000/$30,000; in Virginia the limits are $20,000/$30,000 and $5000 property damage. In North Carolina limits of $10,000/$20,000/$5000 are mandatory, but the bodily injury limits may be increased to $15,000/-$30,000 if the insured has purchased bodily injury limits in at least this amount. In Connecticut, New Hampshire, Minnesota, and Virginia, as of January 1971, the insured has been permitted to purchase uninsured motorists coverage in limits equal to the bodily injury liability limits of the policy.

There is a possibility that the insured and the company may not be able to agree as to whether the operator of the uninsured automobile is legally liable, or on the amount to which the insured would have been entitled to collect. The policy specifically provides that a judgment against the negligent party is not taken to be conclusive proof of the amount to which the insured is entitled under Section IV. In the event that the insured and the company cannot agree, the policy provides that settlement is to be made through arbitration in accordance with the rules of the American Arbitration Association.

Uninsured motorist coverage is an essential part of the Family Automobile Policy. In some jurisdictions, this coverage has been made mandatory on all policies sold. In view of the relatively low cost of the coverage (about $3 per year), it is exceedingly worthwhile and should be included in every policy.

### Conditions of the Family Automobile Policy

There are 18 conditions to the Family Automobile Policy. In addition to those which have already been noted, the following are a few of the more important.

**Policy period and territory.**   One of the more important conditions limits the territory in which the policy applies to the United States, its territories and possessions, or Canada, or while the automobile is being transported between ports thereof. Note that there is no coverage under the policy in Mexico, a rather important exception in this day of travel. If the insured drives into Mexico, he must obtain coverage from a company writing automobile insurance in Mexico.

**Two or more automobiles.**   The Family Automobile Policy is often used to insure two automobiles which are owned by the same individual. When two or more automobiles are insured under the same policy, the terms of the policy apply separately to each automobile. An automobile and a trailer which are being used together are considered to be one automobile for the liability coverage, and two automobiles with respect to the physical damage coverage. Thus, since they are considered to be one automobile for liability, only the limits of liability listed in the policy are available to the insured. Since they are considered to be two automobiles for physical damage coverage, the deductible would apply to each.

**Cancellation.**   The Family Automobile Policy has a limited cancellation provision. The insured may, of course, cancel the policy at any time he desires. In the event that the insured decides to cancel, the return premium is computed on a short rate basis. If the company cancels, the return premium is computed on a pro rata basis. The company's right to effect cancellation is limited after the policy has been in force for 60 days. After the policy has been in effect for 60 days, or, if the policy is a renewal, effective immediately, the company cannot cancel Section I (the liability coverage) except in certain instances specified in the policy:

1. Failure of the insured to pay the premium
2. If the insurance was obtained through fraudulent misrepresentation
3. Violation of any of the terms or conditions of the policy
4. Suspension or revocation of the driver's license of the named insured or any other resident of the same household
5. Epilepsy or heart attacks on the part of any operator of the automobile
6. Conviction or forfeiture of bail during the 3 years immediately preceding the effective date of the policy or during the policy period for any felony, drunken driving, criminal negligence in the operation of a motor vehicle, leaving the scene of an accident, or making false statements in an application for a driver's license
7. A third violation within eighteen months of any speed law or other traffic law.[20]

No attempt has been made to discuss all the provisions of the Family Automobile Policy. However, sufficient treatment has been provided to permit the reader to appreciate the scope of the coverage under the contract. Further knowledge may be obtained from a more thorough study of the contract itself, or from more advanced texts.

## Questions for Discussion and Review

**1.** Rosie LaRue presently owns a 1937 Nash, which she has insured under a Family Automobile Policy with liability limits of $10,000/$20,000/$5000, medical payments of $1000, and uninsured motorists coverage. She has loaned the Nash to her sister Queenie, who is currently living with Rosie. Queenie has just lost her driver's license, but Rosie agrees to let her drive the car anyway. While driving the car in a negligent manner, Queenie smashes into a station wagon full of little old ladies. The Nash is totally demolished, Queenie is injured, the station wagon is demolished, and each of the little old

---

[20] Many insurers have introduced programs of voluntary restrictions of the right to cancel automobile policies which go beyond the provisions of this condition. In addition, several states have enacted laws which impose greater restrictions on the right to cancel. Under these programs, effective in many, but not all jurisdictions, the policy may be cancelled only for nonpayment of premium or suspension or revocation of the license or registration of the named insured or a resident of the household.

ladies brings suit. Who could be held legally liable in this situation? What coverage, if any, exists to cover the losses involved?

**2.** Queenie finally buys a car of her own, a 1970 Dodge Charger, which she insures under a Family Automobile Policy with liability limits of $100,000/-$300,000/$50,000, medical payments in the amount of $5000, full comprehensive, $100 deductible collision coverage, and uninsured motorists coverage. Shortly after purchasing the Dodge, Queenie enjoys a financial windfall and decides to purchase a Rolls Royce. She drives the car home, parks it in the driveway, and goes into the house to call her insurance agent and report the purchase. Rosie, who is driving Queenie's Dodge Charger, wheels into the driveway and is unable to stop, thereupon colliding with the new Rolls, causing extensive damage to both vehicles. Queenie is heartbroken, because the agent's line was busy and she had not yet completed her call. Attempt to console her by explaining the coverage that exists in this situation. What coverage, if any, exists?

**3.** Assuming the coverage on Rosie's car as described in question 1, and coverage on Queenie's car as described in question 2, what coverage would apply if Rosie borrows her neighbor's car?

**4.** The agent delivering a Family Automobile Policy to a client tells him, "This policy will cover you when you are driving any car and it will cover anyone when they are driving your car." How accurate is this statement?

**5.** Rosie finally obtains insurance coverage on her Rolls. She obtains a Family Automobile Policy with $100,000/$300,000/$50,000 liability limits, $5000 medical payments, comprehensive, and $100 deductible collision, and uninsured motorists coverage. Which of the coverages would apply to each of the following losses (if there is no coverage, indicate why not): (a) Rosie parks the Rolls on a riverbank, but forgets to set the brake or put the car in "park"—it rolls into the river and the damage amounts to $800. (b) Rosie is changing a tire—the car slips off the jack and breaks her leg. (c) Thieves break into the car and steal the car radio, the spare tire, and an overnight bag full of clothing.

### Suggestions for Additional Reading

Bickelhaupt, D. L. and Magee, J. H. *General Insurance*, 8th ed. Homewood, Ill.: Richard D. Irwin, 1970, Chap. 18.

Brainard, C. H. *Automobile Insurance*. Homewood, Ill.: Richard D. Irwin, 1961.

*Fire, Casualty and Surety Bulletins,* Casualty and Surety Volume, "Auto" Section. Cincinnati, Ohio: The National Underwriter Co.

*Fire, Casualty and Surety Bulletins,* Fire and Marine Volume, "Auto" Section. Cincinnati, Ohio: The National Underwriter Co.

Gordis, P. *Property and Casualty Insurance,* 17th ed. Indianapolis, Ind.: The Rough Notes Co., 1970, Chaps. 26, 28, 29.

Kulp, C. A. and Hall, J. *Casualty Insurance,* 4th ed. New York: Ronald Press, 1968, Chap. 10.

Long, J. D. and Gregg, D. W. *Property and Liability Insurance Handbook.* Homewood, Ill.: Richard D. Irwin, 1965, Chap. 37.

Magee, J. H. and Serbein, O. N. *Property and Liability Insurance,* 4th ed. Homewood, Ill.: Richard D. Irwin, 1967, Chap. 19.

# 20 Automobile Insurance Part II

*Can we ever have too much of a good thing?*
—Cervantes, *Don Quixote*

In Chapter 19, we began our discussion of the field of automobile insurance with a brief treatment of the special principles of legal liability related to the automobile and its operation. In addition, the Family Automobile Policy was discussed in some detail. In this chapter, we continue our discussion of automobile insurance by briefly examining some of the other automobile insurance policies available, and discussing the pricing of automobile insurance. Finally, we will discuss some of the problems frequently encountered in the purchase of automobile insurance and some of the proposals that are currently under discussion for alternative systems to our present methods of compensating the victims of automobile accidents.

## OTHER AUTOMOBILE POLICY FORMS

At this point, it is assumed that the reader is reasonably familiar with the provisions of the Family Automobile Policy. As noted previously, it is only one of several bureau forms available. It was studied in detail, because it offers the broadest coverage of the standard forms. Our discussion of the other bureau forms will focus on the differences between the Family Automobile Policy and those forms.

### The Special Automobile Policy

Next to the Family Automobile Policy, the Special Automobile Policy, which has already been described briefly, is the most widely sold form of auto insurance. The Special Automobile Policy was introduced in 1959, and has

**482**

since been revised twice (once in 1963 and again in 1967); it marks a departure from many of the principles of the Family Automobile Policy. Although the eligibility requirements are technically the same as for the Family Automobile Policy, the underwriting requirements are more exacting in most companies.

The policy is usually written for a period of 6 months, and is renewed by a certificate of renewal rather than by being replaced with a new policy. The renewal premiums are paid by the insured directly to the insurance company, giving rise to the descriptive term "direct bill policy."

There are a number of changes in coverage. In some instances, the coverage is broader than that of the Family Automobile Policy, while in other areas it is considerably narrower. In those instances where the coverage is narrower, it is primarily a result of an attempt to avoid duplication of coverage and elimination of those situations under which an injured party might collect more than once for the same injury. The most important differences in coverage between the Family Automobile Policy and the Special Automobile Policy are the following:

1. The Special Automobile Policy is a package in the sense that there are certain mandatory coverages, and the insured has less choice with respect to the limits. Liability, medical payments, uninsured motorists coverage, and an accidental death benefit come as a package, and the insured must purchase all of them. A single limit of liability under the Special Automobile Policy gives the insured a choice of $25,000, $50,000, $100,000, $200,000, or $300,000,[1] with medical payments coverage of $1000, $2000, $3000, $4000, or $5000, respectively. The accidental death benefit is a relatively simple insuring agreement which requires little in the way of explanation. It applies to the named insured and spouse and agrees to pay $1000 in the event of death caused by accident, directly and independently of all other causes, as a result of being struck by an automobile or while occupying an automobile.

2. Residents of the named insured's household must have permission of the named insured to be covered while driving the owned automobile. They do not need such permission under the Family Automobile Policy.

3. A person related to the named insured and residing in his household is not a relative under the terms of the Special Automobile Policy if he owns a private passenger automobile. This means that such a person does not enjoy the coverage afforded a relative. For example, he would not have drive other car coverage under the Special Automobile Policy

[1] This single limit is preferable from the point of view of the insured. Under a Family Automobile Policy written with limits of $10,000/$20,000/$5000, the insured would have only $10,000 in protection for injury to a single person, or only $5000 in coverage for property damage. Under a single limit, he would have the $25,000 for either of these occurrences.

while operating a nonowned automobile. Under the Family Automobile Policy, he would have coverage under both his own policy and that of the relative.

4. Notice must be given to the company within 30 days for coverage to apply to an additional automobile, or for physical damage coverage to apply to a replacement automobile. Under the Family Automobile Policy, notice is required only during the policy period.

5. An automobile is defined as a "four wheel land motor vehicle designed for use principally upon public roads." This could not include a motorcycle or a motorscooter (but might include a truck). Under the Family Automobile Policy, the named insured might be covered while operating a nonowned motorcycle or motorscooter, since automobile is not defined.

6. Medical payments are paid only if the injured party executes a written statement that the medical payments will be applied toward the settlement of any claim against the insured under the liability section of the policy.

7. Medical payments are made only to the extent that expenses are not paid or payable under (a) other automobile or premises medical payments insurance; (b) individual, blanket, or group accident and health; (c) medical or surgical reimbursement plans; (d) workmen's compensation. Under the Family Automobile Policy, medical payments are made regardless of other coverage which the insured may have or workmen's compensation benefits (except workmen's compensation benefits for persons engaged in the automobile business).

8. The insurance company may require a subrogation right against a third party equal to medical payments paid. Under the Family Automobile Policy, there is no provision with regard to subrogation for medical payments.

9. Comprehensive and collision coverages are applicable to a nonowned private passenger automobile only if the insured is legally liable for the loss (and without regard to the insurance on the nonowned automobile). Under the Family Automobile Policy, coverage is afforded on nonowned private passenger automobiles regardless of the insured's liability, to the extent that coverage does not exist on those automobiles.

10. There is no automatic coverage on physical damage to nonowned trailers under the Special Automobile Policy. Under the Family Automobile Policy, there is automatic coverage on nonowned trailers up to $500 (when physical damage on the owned automobile has been purchased).

11. The Special Automobile Policy pays for loss by fire, lightning, flood,

falling objects, explosion, earthquake, theft of the entire automobile and collision (if collision coverage is purchased) for robes, wearing apparel, and luggage (including the contents), belonging to the insured or a relative while in or upon the owned automobile for up to $200 per loss. The Family Automobile Policy covers only against the perils of fire and lightning, and the limit is only $100.

12. The Special Automobile Policy provides coverage for reimbursement for bail bonds up to $250. The Family Automobile Policy provides only $100.

13. The Special Automobile Policy provides for reimbursement for loss of wages up to $25 per day, when incurred at the request of the company because of attendance at trials and hearings.

14. There is an exclusion providing that there is no liability coverage on any automobile (even one that is specifically insured), when that automobile is being used to tow a trailer (other than a utility trailer) that is not specifically insured with the same company. This exclusion, called the "cross trailer exclusion," has existed in commercial automobile policies for many years, but it is only with the introduction of the Special Automobile Policy that the individual became exposed to the dangers it may involve. The Special Automobile Policy provides automatic coverage only on a "utility" trailer, which is defined in the policy as: "A trailer designed for use with a private passenger automobile, if not a home, office, store, display, or passenger trailer." The exclusion is of special importance to those who may own house trailers. In addition, it may be important in certain other instances. For example, the widespread use of camping trailers may present a problem. There are two types of trailers used for camping: the "camping trailer," which is a small unit, frequently of the "fold-down" type, and the "travel trailer," which is much the same as a mobile home of 20 years ago. The distinction between these two types of vehicles may be of critical importance. The camping trailer is a utility trailer, but what about the travel trailer? This may vary with the individual trailer, its equipment, and perhaps company interpretation. Those trailers which are equipped with refrigeration, cooking, and bathing facilities are probably a "home" within the context of the above definition, and are, therefore, not covered automatically under the Special Automobile Policy. Under the Family Automobile Policy, such trailers would be covered automatically for liability without additional premium. Under the Special Automobile Policy, not only would the trailer not be covered, but the automobile pulling the trailer would not be covered. Such a trailer may be covered under the Special Automobile Policy by listing it in the declarations.

### The Basic Automobile Policy

Although the Family Automobile Policy and the Special Automobile Policy have been specifically designed to cover the automobile exposure of the individual and the family, instances may arise in which yet another contract must be used to afford coverage for these classes. Due to the rigid underwriting and eligibility requirements of both the Family Automobile Policy and the Special Automobile Policy, there are some automobiles and some drivers that do not qualify for these contracts. In such instances, coverage must be provided through the use of the basic automobile policy. As you will recall, only private passenger, farm, or utility automobiles owned by an individual or by a husband and wife are eligible for the Family Automobile Policy or Special Automobile Policy. The Basic Automobile policy, although narrower in coverage than either the Family Automobile Policy or Special Automobile Policy, is much broader in terms of eligibility. It may be used to insure any type of automobile, including not only private passenger automobiles, but motorcycles, motorscooters, trucks, buses, and the like. In addition, some drivers are not eligible for the broad coverage of the Family Automobile Policy or the Special Automobile Policy because of bad driving records. In such cases, they can obtain coverage only under the Basic Automobile Policy. For example, insurance obtained through the "assigned-risk pool" is usually written on the basic form. In addition, coverage offered by the substandard carriers (or so-called "distress" carriers) is usually written on this form. Obviously, there is a distinct possibility that some students will be required to obtain automobile insurance under circumstances that will necessitate the use of the basic policy. For this reason, we will look at the principal differences between the basic policy and the Family Automobile Policy. Many of the differences between the basic policy and the Family Automobile Policy are the same as those between the Family Automobile Policy and the Special Automobile Policy; the major differences are:

1. The coverage of the basic policy is written on an "accident" basis rather than an "occurrence" basis as is the Family Automobile Policy.
2. Residents of the named insured's household are not covered automatically when driving the owned automobile. They must have specific permission from the named insured. (This same provision exists in the Special Automobile Policy.)
3. Drive other car coverage is afforded only for the named insured and his spouse (and is afforded only if the insured is an individual or husband and wife). Members of the insured's family are not covered when driving a nonowned automobile. (Coverage for such use of nonowned automobiles can be provided for members of the named insured's family by adding the Drive Other Car Endorsement for an additional premium.)

This is one of the most significant differences between this policy and the others. *There is no automatic drive other car coverage for resident relatives.*

4. Notice must be given to the company within 30 days for coverage to apply to an additional automobile or for physical damage coverage to apply to a replacement automobile. (This same provision exists in the Special Automobile Policy.)

5. Contractual liability is excluded. Therefore, any liability assumed under a contract (as, for example, in the case of a rent-a-car agreement) would not be covered. There is no such exclusion in either the Family Automobile Policy or the Special Automobile Policy.

6. There is no liability coverage on any automobile (even one that is specifically insured) when that automobile is being used to tow a trailer (other than a utility trailer) not specifically insured with the same company. (This provision also exists in the Special Automobile Policy.)

7. Persons having custody of the owned automobile are not additional insureds under the physical damage (collision–comprehensive) section of the policy. This means that when making payment for damage to the owned automobile, the insurance company may require an assignment of the right to sue the borrower of the owned automobile. To illustrate the effect of this provision, let us look at an example. Mr. Brown, who is insured under a Basic Automobile Policy for collision, loans his automobile to Mr. Smith. Smith is involved in an accident and demolishes the car. Brown will collect from the insurance company, but the company will then subrogate against Smith, seeking damages equal to the amount which was paid to Brown. This possibility is eliminated in the Family Automobile Policy, by making the person who has custody of the owned automobile an insured (provided, of course, that the custody is with permission of the named insured, and the use is within the scope of that permission).

There are other miscellaneous differences between the Family Automobile Policy and the Basic Automobile Policy. However, those discussed above are the most significant differences.

### Other Automobile Forms

The policies discussed above are the so-called "bureau forms," which have been developed by the national rating bureaus. It is important, therefore, to recognize that many insurance companies use contracts that differ from the bureau forms, and that the forms discussed in this text are not the only ones available. Although the trend has been for the bureau and the independent forms to become more and more alike, it is nevertheless important to bear in mind that there may be significant differences between the forms discussed above and those marketed by independent companies.

## BUYING AUTOMOBILE INSURANCE

### The Cost of Automobile Insurance

One of the most distressing aspects of automobile insurance, as far as youthful drivers are concerned, is the difficulty in obtaining adequate coverage and the cost of the coverage when it can be obtained. Because younger drivers have been an unprofitable class of business for the insurance companies, most companies are reluctant to write coverage for them. When a company accepts a young driver, in most cases it will provide only the minimum limits of liability. Because youthful drivers have had a higher proportion of accidents, their premium rates are higher by far than the average.

Like all insurance rates, the rates for automobile insurance are based on averages. The premiums collected by the insurance company are designed to be sufficient to cover the cost of all claims, plus the expenses involved in the operation of the program. To provide for an equitable assessment of cost, a large number of classifications have been established, and the drivers in each class are charged a premium that reflects the experience of the drivers in their class.

Although the rating systems used in the field of automobile insurance are both numerous and varied, the pattern and the factors used in determination of the rate for an individual are quite similar in most cases. Virtually every rating system in use is patterned after one of the two systems discussed below, and while the details may vary by area and with individual companies, most rating systems are simply variations of these systems. The first rating system to be discussed is the traditional classification system, which has been in use for many years. In addition, a revised classification system, adopted in 1965 by the bureau companies in most states, will be discussed. The revised system is the result of an attempt to refine the premium classifications so that the rate for each class will be a more accurate measure of the loss costs of the group comprising the class.

**Traditional classification system.**     The traditional classification system, still used in some jurisdictions and by a number of companies in those jurisdictions in which the new system has been adopted, classifies private passenger automobiles according to three factors:

1. Use of the automobile
2. Distance driven to and from work
3. Age and sex of the driver

In addition to these factors, the rates vary with the territory in which the automobile is principally garaged, the limits of coverage desired, and, for physical damage coverage, the value of the automobile, and the deductible selected.

Under the traditional system, drivers are classified 1A, 1B, 1C, 2A, 2C, 3, or 1AF, 2AF, 3AF. The traditional class 1A involves an automobile owned by an individual or hired under a long-term contract by the individual. It is not customarily used in the business or occupation of anyone and is not even used for driving to and from work, but is used for pleasure only. Most important, there is no male operator in the household less than 25 years of age. Class 1B is the same, except that the car is driven to work and back, but less than 10 road miles one way. Class 1C is also the same, except that the road mileage in driving to and from work one way is 10 miles or more. Class 1B premium rates are about 10% higher than class 1A, and class 1C rates are approximately 45% higher than 1A.

Class 2A, with premium rates approximately 90% higher than 1A, is designed for those families in which there are one or more male operators under 25 years of age in the household, but the underage male operator is not the owner or principal operator of the automobile. In addition, the class 2A group of the traditional system includes a male operator under age 25 who is married.

The highest rated class is class 2C. The premium here is approximately $3\frac{1}{2}$ times that for class 1A. This classification is applicable to male owners or principal operators who are unmarried; the classification is applied whether the automobile is used in business, driving to and from work, or for pleasure only.[2]

Class 3 involves business uses of private passenger automobiles, i.e., the automobile is actually used by the insured in his business or occupation. In most territories, the premium rate for this class is approximately $1\frac{1}{2}$ times the class 1A rate. The classification is applicable to private passenger automobiles owned by individuals, used in business, and with no under-age male operator. It is also used for private passenger cars owned by corporations, partnerships, and unincorporated associations regardless of the age of the operator.

If an automobile is principally garaged on a farm or ranch and is not used in any other business and is not customarily used in driving to and from work in any business except farming, special classifications then

---

[2] The question may arise as to what premium rates apply to an insured who owns two or more automobiles with one male member of the household under age 25. The rule is that class 2 rates apply to not more than the same number of automobiles as there are under-age drivers. Therefore, if there are two automobiles in the family and one male operator under age 25, one automobile is rated the applicable under-age class rate and the other the proper class 1 or class 3 rate.

exist, with premium rates approximately 30% lower than comparable city rates. The classes are 1AF, 2AF, and 2CF, corresponding to the 1A, 2A, and 2C classes.

**Revised classification system.**    The revised classification system, which went into effect in most states in January 1965, greatly increases the total number of classifications. The starting point for this system is the "base premium" for each coverage, which varies with the territory. This is the premium that is charged for an automobile with no youthful drivers and which is used for pleasure only. The premiums for all other drivers and uses of the automobile are expressed as a percentage of this base premium. Each driver is assigned a rating factor that expresses the percentage of the base premium he is to be charged. The rating factors are expressed as multiples of the base premium. Thus, a rating factor of 1.55 means that the driver would pay 155% of the base premium, and a 3.30 rating factor would require a premium equal to 330% of the base premium. There are six general driver classifications under the new plan:

1. No youthful operator
2. Only operator female, age 30–64
3. Female operator under age 21, unmarried
4. Male operator under age 25, married
5. Male operator under age 25, not married, owner, or principal operator
6. Male operator under age 30, not married, owner, or principal operator

Several changes from the traditional system are immediately evident. First, special consideration has been given to female operators between the ages of 30 and 64 who are the only operators of their automobiles; they have been separated from other adult drivers and given the lowest rated classification. In addition, under the revised system, unmarried female operators under age 21 have been surcharged. Married males under age 25 and incidental male operators age 25 (the traditional class 2A) have been separated, with the married males receiving a lower rate. The surcharge for unmarried males who are the owners or principal operators of the automobile has been extended to age 29.

One of the most significant changes is the fact that underage drivers are further subdivided by age, with a decreasing surcharge as the individual becomes older. One major criticism that can be aimed at the traditional system is the lumping of all male drivers in a given classification regardless of age. For example, under the traditional system, an unmarried male operator pays the same surcharge whether he is 17 or 24. Under the new rating system, under-age drivers are still surcharged, but the charge is reduced each year. Figure 20-1 illustrates the relationship of the surcharges based on the age of the driver and the manner in which they decline with the age of the individual.

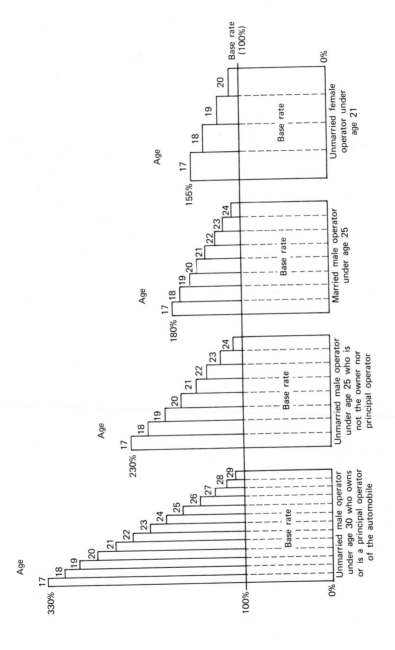

**FIGURE 20-1**

**Rating surcharges on youthful drivers. Source: The Insurance Information Institute, A Family Guide to Property and Liability Insurance (New York).**

Under the traditional system, only the adult classifications were rated with respect to the use of the car. Under the revised system, use classifications apply to all age groups. The basic classification is pleasure use only. If the automobile is driven to work or school more than 3 but less than 10 miles one way, the rate is surcharged 10% of the base rate. For driving to work more than 10 miles one way, the surcharge is 40% of the base rate. If the automobile is used in business, the surcharge is 50%. The final use classification is farm use, which pertains to an automobile principally garaged on a farm or ranch and not used in any other business or in going to or from any other work. For farm use, the basic pleasure classification is discounted 25%. The surcharges for the use of the automobile are added to the rating factor based on the age, sex, and marital status. This means that the additional charge for business use is the same regardless of the age or marital status of the driver. For example, the adult male pleasure factor is 1.00 and the business use factor is 1.50. For a 22 year old who is the owner of the automobile, the pleasure factor is 2.30, and the business factor is 2.80. Each driver would pay the same number of additional dollars for business use.

The rating program contains two features which work to the benefit of some under-age drivers.[3] The first of these is the driver training credit. If the youthful driver has completed an approved driver training course, his rating factor is reduced by 5–20 percentage points, depending upon his basic classification factor. The higher the basic factor, the greater the credit for drivers training. In some states, the discount is applicable when all male drivers have had driver training, while in other states both male and female under-age drivers must have had driver training.

A second feature of considerable interest to some youthful drivers is the good student discount. Introduced by many companies in several states in the fall of 1967, the good student discount applies to full-time students, 16 years of age or older, who are high school juniors or higher, upon certification that the student, for the preceding semester or comparable period:

1. Ranked in the upper 20% of his class, or
2. Had a B average or higher, or
3. Had a 3-point average or higher, or
4. Was on the dean's list, honor roll, or similar list

Like the discount for driver training, the good student discount varies with the individual's basic rating factor. The discount results in a reduction in the rating factor by 10–80 points, depending upon the basic rating factor. This credit is in addition to the driver training credit. Table 20-1 indicates the

[3] These discounts may also be used with the traditional system in some jurisdictions by some companies.

**TABLE 20-1**
**Rating Factors for Underage Drivers**

| Age | Under age 30, unmarried male owner or principal operator | | | | Under age 25, unmarried male not owner or principal operator | | | |
|---|---|---|---|---|---|---|---|---|
| | Without good student rating | | With good student rating | | Without good student rating | | With good student rating | |
| | No driver training | With driver training | No driver training | With driver training | No driver training | With driver training | No driver training | With driver training |
| 17 | 3.30 | 2.70 | 2.50 | 2.05 | 2.30 | 2.05 | 1.75 | 1.55 |
| 18 | 3.10 | 2.65 | 2.35 | 2.00 | 2.10 | 1.90 | 1.60 | 1.40 |
| 19 | 2.90 | 2.60 | 2.20 | 1.95 | 1.90 | 1.75 | 1.45 | 1.30 |
| 20 | 2.70 | 2.55 | 2.05 | 1.90 | 1.70 | 1.60 | 1.30 | 1.20 |
| 21 | 2.50 | 2.50 | 1.85 | 1.85 | 1.55 | 1.55 | 1.15 | 1.15 |
| 22 | 2.30 | 2.30 | 1.80 | 1.80 | 1.40 | 1.40 | 1.10 | 1.10 |
| 23 | 2.10 | 2.10 | 1.75 | 1.75 | 1.25 | 1.25 | 1.05 | 1.05 |
| 24 | 1.90 | 1.90 | 1.70 | 1.70 | 1.10 | 1.10 | 1.00 | 1.00 |
| 25 | 1.70 | 1.70 | 1.70 | 1.70 | 1.00 | 1.00 | | |
| 26 | 1.50 | 1.50 | 1.50 | 1.50 | | | | |
| 27 | 1.35 | 1.35 | 1.35 | 1.35 | | | | |
| 28 | 1.20 | 1.20 | 1.20 | 1.20 | | | | |
| 29 | 1.10 | 1.10 | 1.10 | 1.10 | | | | |
| 30 | 1.00 | 1.00 | 1.00 | 1.00 | | | | |

| Age | Under age 25, married male operator | | | | Under age 21, unmarried female operator | | | |
|---|---|---|---|---|---|---|---|---|
| | Without good student rating | | With good student rating | | Without good student rating | | With good student rating | |
| | No driver training | With driver training | No driver training | With driver training | No driver training | With driver training | No driver training | With driver training |
| 17 | 1.80 | 1.60 | 1.35 | 1.25 | 1.55 | 1.40 | 1.30 | 1.20 |
| 18 | 1.70 | 1.55 | 1.25 | 1.20 | 1.40 | 1.25 | 1.20 | 1.10 |
| 19 | 1.60 | 1.50 | 1.20 | 1.15 | 1.25 | 1.15 | 1.10 | 1.05 |
| 20 | 1.50 | 1.45 | 1.15 | 1.10 | 1.10 | 1.05 | 1.00 | 1.00 |
| 21 | 1.40 | 1.40 | 1.05 | 1.05 | | | | |
| 22 | 1.30 | 1.30 | 1.00 | 1.00 | | | | |
| 23 | 1.20 | 1.20 | | | | | | |
| 24 | 1.10 | 1.10 | | | | | | |
| 25 | 1.00 | 1.00 | | | | | | |

SOURCE: The Insurance Rating Board, *Automobile Insurance Rating Manual* (New York, 1968, 1969).

rating factors for under-age drivers, with and without driver training and the good student discount. These factors are for the pleasure use only classification, and would be surcharged the appropriate percentage of the base for other use. The percentages listed in Table 20-1 apply if the driver has not had any chargeable accidents during the previous 3-year period. If there are chargeable accidents and the company uses the safe-driver rating plan, there will be additional percentage surcharges.

**Safe-driver rating plan.**    The safe-driver rating plan is a program in use by many companies and in many jurisdictions today, whereby the premium will depend on the driving record of the insured involved. It was originally introduced with the Special Automobile Policy and was designed specifically for use with that contract. However, its use is not limited to the Special Automobile Policy; it may be used with the Family Automobile Policy or any other policy form under both the traditional and revised systems. It was originally designed to be applicable to the liability and collision premiums, but in the revised rating system it is applicable to all coverages except uninsured motorist coverage.

The plan is based on the principle that the driving record with respect to motor vehicle violations and accidents during an experience period will be indicative of the characteristics of the insured as an automobile operator in the future.[4] Therefore, premiums in the various classifications are to be based on the operator's record during the experience period. For most plans, the experience period is the 3 years immediately preceding the date of the application for the insurance or the inception of the renewal policy. Points are assigned for traffic violations or accidents involving bodily injury or death or $100 or more of property damage which the applicant or operator resident in the household has had or for which he has been convicted during the experience period. Three points are assigned for a conviction of drunken driving, for driving under the influence of drugs, for failure to stop and report when involved in an accident, for homicide or assault arising out of the operation of a motor vehicle, or for driving during a period while the license is suspended or revoked. Two points are assigned for an accumulation of points under a special state motor-vehicle point system or from a series of convictions requiring evidence of financial responsibility under a state financial responsibility law. One point is assigned for any other conviction or any other motor-vehicle law violation as a result of which the operator's license is suspended or revoked, and the filing of financial responsibility is required as of the effective date of the policy. One point

---

[4] It has been established quite conclusively that the operator who cannot drive a car without accidents or traffic violations, as demonstrated in the past, will be no different in the future. Therefore, if the premium rate depends on the past driving record, the result will produce a higher degree of equity in the premium charges. For example, why should a male operator under age 25, who is a reasonable and careful operator as shown by the fact that he has never had an automobile accident or even a ticket for speeding, pay the same premium as another male operator under age 25, who has had many accidents and who has lost his driver's license twice? It is obvious that the latter should pay a much higher premium.

also is assigned for each accident involving bodily injury or death or $100 or more in property damage. And one point is assigned if there were two or more accidents during the experience period, each of which resulted in damage to property in an amount of $100 or less. No points are assigned, however, under the following circumstances:

1. If at the time of the accident the automobile was lawfully parked
2. If the injured party was reimbursed by the responsible party or a judgment was obtained against him
3. If the car was struck in the rear and the applicant or operator was not convicted of a moving traffic violation in connection with the accident
4. If the operator of the other automobile involved in an accident was convicted of a moving traffic violation and the applicant or operator was not convicted of a moving traffic violation in connection therewith
5. If the damage was caused by a hit-and-run driver, providing the accident is reported to the proper authorities within 24 hours

If the individual has one point under the plan, his rating factor is increased by 30 points. For the second point, there is an additional surcharge of 40 points. The third point involves an additional 50-point surcharge, and the fourth point an additional 60 points. Thus, a driver with four points would incur a total surcharge of 180 percentage points.

The safe-driver plan has many commendable features, particularly because of the greater element of equity in the determination of premium rates which it produces. It is becoming more firmly established in the private passenger automobile rating process as time goes on, and perhaps it may become a compulsory feature of all rating plans in the future.

**Cost of increased limits.** There is little doubt that automobile insurance can be costly, and it promises to become more so in the future. The premiums charged by the companies reflect the accident experience of the drivers they insure. As the number of automobiles increases and the size of liability judgments increases, automobile insurance premiums will also increase.

One of the poorest ways of attempting to save in the purchase of automobile insurance is to purchase only the minimum limits of liability. When a driver is held legally liable for damages, it does not make any difference to the court whether the driver has enough insurance to cover the judgment. If the amount of the judgment is $100,000 and the liable party has only $10,000 in coverage available to meet the judgment, he will have to pay the additional $90,000 himself.

Fortunately, higher limits of liability costs far less proportionately than the basic limits. As an example, the adult rate for basic liability coverage and the cost of increased limits in one major midwestern city are as follows:

| | |
|---|---|
| If $10,000/$20,000 bodily injury limits cost | $39 |
| Then $25,000/$50,000 bodily injury limits cost | $46 |
| $50,000/$100,000 bodily injury limits cost | $51 |
| $100,000/$300,000 bodily injury limits cost | $55 |
| If $5000 property damage limit costs | $34 |
| Then $10,000 property damage limit costs | $36 |
| $25,000 property damage limit costs | $37 |
| $50,000 property damage limit costs | $38 |
| $100,000 property damage limit costs | $40 |

Likewise, increased medical payments cost relatively little. In the same city, for the same driver,

| | |
|---|---|
| $500 medical payments cost | $ 7 |
| $1000 medical payments cost | $ 9 |
| $2000 medical payments cost | $11 |
| $5000 medical payments cost | $14 |

### Automobile Insurance Plans (Assigned-Risk Plans)

A discussion of purchasing automobile insurance would hardly be complete without at least some reference to automobile insurance plans (formerly called assigned-risk plans). There are many people who for one reason or another have difficulty in obtaining automobile liability insurance. A person may attempt to purchase the insurance and discover that no insurer will assume his risk. This is particularly true of youthful male owners or operators and of people who must demonstrate financial responsbility under the laws of the state. It is true also of a person who, because of his driving record, has demonstrated that he is more hazardous as a risk than the average of the classification to which he otherwise would normally belong.

Automobile insurance companies, as in most other businesses, would like to make a profit, or at least to cover all expenses of their business operation. This cannot be accomplished by accepting a relatively large number of insureds in which the possibility of loss is considerably greater than the average. However, many of the undesirable risks may be politically powerful, and if private insurers will not underwrite the insurance, the state may be called upon to do so. If the state should set up a fund to underwrite undesirable risks, it perhaps would not be too long until it would be insuring all automobiles, and private insurers might disappear altogether. Assigned-risk plans have been developed whereby private insurers can provide insurance on some equitable basis for risks they would not otherwise underwrite in the normal course of business operations.

An assigned-risk plan is a voluntary organization of all automobile insurance companies operating in a particular state. Its purpose is twofold:

First, it will provide automobile liability insurance, within limits, to those who cannot obtain it through normal channels. Second, it establishes a procedure for the equitable distribution of these risks among all the automobile liability insurers operating in the state.

With respect to the first function, the applicant must certify on a prescribed form that he has attempted, within 60 days prior to the application, to obtain liability insurance and has been unable to procure it. Not all applicants are eligible for coverage under the plan, and while the eligibility requirements vary from state to state, in general, criminals, persons without driver's licenses, and habitual traffic violators are ineligible. If the applicant is eligible, a company will be assigned to underwrite the insurance. The designated company will be obligated to provide liability coverage with limits equal to the requirements of the financial responsibility law.[5]

A risk cannot be assigned to a company for a period in excess of 3 years, and the insurer may cancel an assigned risk under certain circumstances. The right to cancel is based on facts which demonstrate that the risk ceases to be eligible in good faith for the insurance—nonpayment of the premium, and the like. A number of major offenses and convictions obviously would result in a justifiable cancellation.

The second function of the plan is to provide an equitable procedure for the distribution of risks among all the automobile insurers operating in the state. This is accomplished by assigning to a particular insurer the percentage of assigned-risk premiums that its total liability premiums bear compared to the total liability premiums of all automobile insurers operating in the state. Thus, if a particular company has 1/20 of all liability premiums written in the state, it would be assigned 1/20 of the risks. This perhaps is the only equitable method available, and it appears to be working reasonably well.

For those persons who are unable to obtain liability insurance even through assigned risk, the best procedure would be to give up driving a car. But to some people this is not a practical possibility, or at least they imagine such. To purchase insurance coverage to meet the requirements of a state financial responsibility law, these persons must turn to what is commonly known as a "distress risk" company. In many instances, these insurers will specialize in this type of insurance. They have special rating plans in which the premium can attain almost incredible proportions, and special policy forms that may be highly limited. The distress risk companies perform a service, at least to the extent that they are making automobile liability insurance possible at some price.

---

[5]In many jurisdictions, the coverage available under the automobile insurance plans has been greatly increased in the recent past. Under the plans of many states the applicant may obtain not only liability coverage, but medical payments and physical damage coverage as well.

## THE AUTOMOBILE INSURANCE PROBLEM AND
## THE ATTACK ON THE TORT SYSTEM

It is not at all unusual to hear complaints about automobile insurance today. Almost everyone connected with the automobile insurance business has what they consider to be a legitimate complaint. The insurance companies complain that they are losing money because of inadequate rates. The buyers complain that the rates are too high. Young drivers (and, more recently, older drivers) complain that they frequently have difficulty in obtaining coverage. Finally, many who have suffered losses maintain that settlements do not measure up to the economic loss. With all this dissatisfaction, it is not surprising that every proposal for change meets with widespread acclaim in one corner or another.

All these problems are the backdrop for the recent discussion about automobile insurance and the tort system in general. Many critics of automobile insurance contend that the problem today is not so much with insurance as such, but rather with the system we use to compensate the injured persons. These critics maintain that out tort system is wasteful, expensive, unfair, and excessively time-consuming, and they recommend that we abolish it in connection with automobile accidents. The effectiveness and rationale of the negligence system has been questioned since the *Columbia Report* of 1932,[6] which pointed to many shortcomings of the tort system. One major criticism of that report, and of today's critics, is that many persons who are injured remain uncompensated or are inadequately compensated. The victim in an accident may be unable to obtain compensation because he himself was negligent, because the guilty party is insolvent, or because the guilty party is unknown, as in the case of a hit-and-run accident. Additionally, the amount of compensation that is finally awarded may depend more on the ability of the victim's attorney than on the facts. Other criticisms of our present system include the high cost of providing benefits to those who are injured because of the cost of operating the insurance mechanism, the courts, and the contingency fee system, and the congestion of the courts, which results in long delays in providing the final compensation to those who are injured. Furthermore, the critics maintain that our present system is inequitable. Insurance companies intentionally overpay small claims to avoid litigation, but they resist large claims in which the victim was seriously injured. For these reasons, the tort system has been under attack, and numerous proposals have been made to substitute a no-fault compensation system. Such proposals are not new, but there has been increased

---

[6]Committee to Study Compensation for Automobile Accidents, *Report to the Columbia University Council for Research in the Social Sciences* (Philadelphia: Committee to Study Compensation for Automobile Accidents, 1932).

interest in them since the middle of the 1960's. We will discuss a number of the proposals that are currently prominent, so that the student may be aware of their general nature. It should be pointed out that this discussion includes only the highlights of the programs, and does not include the complete details that may be necessary for a full evaluation of the plans.

### The Keeton–O'Connell Plan

One of the landmark proposals for modification of the tort system, and the one that has received the most attention in the recent past, is the Keeton–O'Connell plan, which the authors call Basic Protection. The details of the Basic Protection plan, together with the documentation of the need for it as seen by the authors, are presented in their book, *Basic Protection for the Traffic Victim*.[7] The Keeton–O'Connell plan seeks to rectify the defects of the present automobile system by providing for compensation of all parties involved in automobile accidents without regard to anyone's fault or lack thereof, up to certain specified limits. In the event of injuries involving losses in excess of the specified limits, tort liability would be retained. Briefly, the features of the plan are given below.

**A new form of automobile insurance coverage.** Under the Keeton–O'Connell plan, a new form of compulsory automobile insurance would compensate all persons injured in automobile accidents without regard to fault or anyone's lack of it. It would pay whenever a motorist carrying this insurance was involved in an accident and he, or a guest, or a pedestrian was injured. The Basic Protection coverage would pay up to $10,000 per person and $100,000 per accident, for any out-of-pocket expenses (primarily lost wages and medical costs). The coverage would be subject to a $100 deductible.

**Partial exemption from tort liability for basic protection insureds.** The second feature of the proposal is a law which would make those insured under Basic Protection exempt to some extent for legal liability for negligence in the use of the automobile. If tort damages for pain and suffering would not exceed $5000 and other tort damages (principally for medical expenses and lost wages) would not exceed $10,000, an action for basic protection under the injured party's own Basic Protection policy would replace any tort action against the negligent driver. In cases of more severe injury, where economic loss is in excess of $10,000 or pain and suffering is in excess of $5000, the tort action is preserved, but the recovery is to be reduced by these amounts. In addition, tort action would be preserved in cases where the loss is less than $100.

---

[7] Robert E. Keeton and Jeffrey O'Connell, *Basic Protection for the Traffic Victim—A Blueprint for Reforming Automobile Insurance* (Boston: Little Brown, 1966).

**Reimbursement limited to "net loss."**    Basic Protection benefits would be designed to reimburse for net economic loss only. Overlapping would be eliminated and any benefits collected from other sources would be subtracted from the gross loss in determining the net loss. Net economic loss would include work loss and expenses. Work loss would consist of loss of income from work (for example, wages) and expenses reasonably incurred for services in lieu of those the injured person would have performed without income. The policy would pay some percentage of the lost wages (say, 85%), the deduction being made to allow for the tax-free nature of the benefits, with a maximum of $750 per month.

**Periodic reimbursement.**    Benefits would be payable month by month as the losses accrued, rather than at some distant time in the future after the injured party had actually paid them all.

**Optional pain and suffering coverage.**    While the basic protection coverage would limit recovery to economic loss only, an optional coverage would be available to compensate for pain and suffering to the insured in amounts of less than $5000. Pain and suffering over $5000 would be recoverable through tort action.

**The assigned-claims plan.**    Through what is referred to as an "assigned-claims plan," Basic Protection benefits would be available even when the vehicles involved in an accident are either uninsured or hit-and-run automobiles. Nonresidents without Basic Protection coverage would also be paid under the assigned-claims plan.

**Liability coverage.**    Optional liability coverage would be available to cover liability incurred by the insured out of the state or in excess of amounts of Basic Protection.

### The American Insurance Association Plan

In June of 1967, the American Insurance Association (AIA) formed a committee to undertake an immediate study of the Keeton–O'Connell plan. In October of 1968, this committee released the result of its study and at the same time announced the AIA's own reform proposal. Under the Complete Personal Protection Automobile Insurance Plan, as the new proposal is known, the AIA goes further than Keeton and O'Connell, proposing abolition of the tort system for automobile accidents without regard to the amount of the damage. The chief points of the AIA proposal are discussed below.

**A new form of compulsory automobile insurance.**    Like the Keeton–O'Connell plan, the AIA plan involves a new form of first party insurance designed to cover the family. The policy would cover the owner and his family for their loss in any accident, and in addition would cover the occupants of the car and any pedestrians not otherwise covered. The policy would provide unlimited medical expense benefits and coverage for lost wages or work loss up to $750 per month, without limit of time. Lost wages would be reduced by 15% to reflect the tax advantage. In the event of a death claim, economic loss benefits would be payable to survivors subject to the same limitations. In addition, funeral and burial expenses would be paid up to $1000.

**Abolition of tort liability for automobiles.**    Tort liability in connection with the automobile would be totally abolished for anyone who purchased a Complete Protection Policy. Uninsured drivers would be subject to tort liability. Jury trial would be preserved for settling disputes between the claimant and the insurance company as to the amount of benefits, and the cost of such suits would be borne by the claimant unless his claim was sustained by the courts.

**Elimination of compensation for pain and suffering.**    The AIA proposal recommends elimination of compensation for pain and suffering, but includes a recommendation of an extra lump sum payment in the event of permanent impairment or disfigurement. The additional compensation for disfigurement or impairment would not exceed 50% of the claimant's hospital or medical expense.

**Coverage in other states.**    Accidents occuring to insureds in states not covered by the AIA proposal would still be subject to the tort liability system. In these cases, the insured would have residual automobile liability insurance for limits most commonly in use under state financial responsibility statutes.

**Property damage.**    Owners of property other than automobiles that is damaged by an insured car would be covered and reimbursed under the policy on the insured car. Each motorist would be responsible for damage to his own vehicle, and physical damage coverage would be available as an option.

**Uninsured persons and vehicles.**    An assigned-claims plan would be supported by all companies and would pay losses of uninsured persons even when an automobile accident involved uninsured or hit-and-run vehicles. Uninsured *drivers* would be subject to tort liability. Loss benefits would be subtracted from any tort recovery against an uninsured driver and repaid to the insurer, who would make payment under the assigned-claims plan.

### The Cotter Plan

The Cotter plan has been hailed in many corners as the least radical and perhaps most workable of the changes that have been proposed. Conceived by Connecticut Insurance Commissioner Willian R. Cotter and announced in January of 1969, the Cotter plan consists of a group of legislative proposals directed at the major problems affecting automobile insurance. The essential features of the plan are described below.

**Medical and disability benefits.** Every private passenger automobile policy would automatically include a minimum of $2000 in medical payments coverage and 1 year of disability benefits, which would be applicable not only to the motorist and his family and guests in the automobile, but to pedestrians struck by the automobile as well. This would provide for immediate payment of most economic losses. At the same time, those who were injured by a negligent driver would retain their right to file suit for additional damages, and the insurance company would have subrogation rights against the negligent driver to recover any money it had paid out. This means that the tort system would remain essentially intact.

**Negligence.** A comparative negligence law would be adopted.

**Small-claims arbitration.** Mandatory small-claims arbitration would be adopted for cases of less than $3000. This would help to relieve the congestion of the courts and would guarantee equitable treatment of those injured on an economical basis. Advance payments would be made for expenses of claimants as they were incurred.

**Pain and suffering coverage.** Standards for assessment of damages for pain and suffering would be adopted. In those cases where hospital and medical bills are less than $500, the plan would pay up to 50% of that amount for additional damages. In cases where medical expenses exceeded $500, the plan would pay up to 100% of that amount for additional damages. In the event that medical testimony demonstrated that such amounts would not justly compensate for the actual pain and suffering experienced, additional amounts could be awarded.[8]

### The Massachusetts Personal Injury Protection Plan

Massachusetts became the first state to enact a compulsory no-fault automobile compensation plan when the Massachusetts legislature, in August

---

[8] The Cotter Plan has received wide support in insurance industry circles, and many of its features have been incorporated into other plans. Although the American Insurance Association favors the no-fault approach (as evidenced by its program discussed above), the other two major insurance company associations, the American Mutual Insurance Alliance (AMIA) and the National Association of Independent Insurers (NAII), have proposed their own plans, both of which retain the tort system and incorporate many features of the Cotter Plan. The AMIA Guaranteed Protection Plan would provide $50,000 in medical expense coverage ($2000 in the first version of the plan) and $6000 in disability income benefits. The NAII Dual Protection Plan proposes medical expense benefits of $2000 and disability income coverage

of 1970, enacted the Personal Injury Protection Plan as an amendment to the compulsory automobile insurance law of that state. As the provisions of the plan presented below indicate, the Massachusetts plan is a modified no-fault plan, and does not go nearly as far as most of the other plans that have been proposed in abrogating the fault system. In essence, the plan provides for direct reimbursement of medical expenses and lost wages by the injured party's own insurance company up to $2000, with limited immunity from tort action.

**Basic benefits.** Personal Injury Protection applies to the named insured, members of his or her household, any authorized operator or passenger of the insured's motor vehicle, and any pedestrian struck by the insured motor vehicle. Members of the insured's household are also covered if struck by an automobile that is not covered by Personal Injury Protection. Insurance protection up to $2000 per person applies to cover medical expenses (including funeral expenses) and loss of wages. Payment is also made for loss of personal services when someone other than a member of the insured party's family is paid to perform such services. This would include, for example, wages paid to someone hired to perform an injured housewife's normal duties.

**Lost wages coverage.** Coverage for lost wages is limited to the actual loss sustained and further to 75% of the injured party's average weekly wage for the year immediately preceding the accident. No benefits are payable if the injured person is entitled to workmen's compensation benefits, and benefits for lost wages are reduced by any amounts received under a wage continuation plan.

**Tort immunity.** Immunity from tort action is provided to the extent of expenses recoverable under the Personal Injury Protection Plan. Tort recovery for pain and suffering is allowed if medical and funeral expenses exceed $500. In addition, in those instances where the accident results in death, loss of a body member, disfigurement, loss of sight or hearing, or fractures, pain and suffering claims are not limited.

**Exclusions.** Certain types of conduct preclude the injured party from

---

of $6000. These benefits would be payable to the named insured, residents of his household, the occupants of his car, and any pedestrian injured by the car. Tort action would be permitted when medical or wage loss exceeded the plan limit and would also be permitted for pain and suffering in cases of disfigurement, dismemberment, or permanent loss of a bodily function. Where no permanent damage resulted from the injury, payment for pain and suffering would be limited to a percentage of the medical expense. Most important, the insurer paying the medical expense and disability benefits would be entitled to subrogation rights against the third party at fault.

collecting under the plan. Specifically, benefits are not payable under the Personal Injury Protection Plan to persons operating a motor vehicle:

1. While under the influence of alcohol or narcotics
2. While committing a felony or seeking to avoid arrest by a police officer
3. With the intent of causing injury or damage to himself or others

**Subrogation.**   Insurance companies are subrogated to the rights of any person to whom benefits are paid, and may seek recovery directly from the insurer of the negligent party. This recovery may include the cost of claim adjustment expense and legal costs.

**Coverage of uninsured persons.**   The plan is applicable only in Massachusetts. Drivers must carry liability insurance to protect against losses in excess of the limited immunity from tort and losses which occur outside of Massachusetts. An assigned-claims plan provides coverage for persons who do not carry Personal Injury Protection (e.g., drivers from other states or persons who do not own automobiles). If such a person is injured, the claim is assigned to one of the insurers operating in the state for payment. The insurer then assumes subrogation rights against the negligent party.

**Deductibles.**   Personal Injury Protection coverage may be purchased subject to a deductible. Deductible options of $250, $500, $1000, or $2000 are available. The deductible applies only to the named insured and members of his household. Deductible amounts are not recoverable in a tort action, and the inclusion of a deductible does not affect the immunity from tort liability.

In addition to the provisions outlined above, the Massachusetts plan includes certain other provisions with respect to the fixing of rates and a system of surcharges for individuals with bad driving records. It also imposes certain limitations on the rights of the insurance companies to cancel or refuse renewal of insurance contracts.

**Property damage.**   Although the original Massachusetts plan did not include property damage, effective January 1, 1972, it was extended to include no-fault property damage coverage. Under this newest aspect of the Massachusetts plan, called Property Protection Insurance (PPI), drivers are responsible for damage to their own automobiles. Every insured must elect one of three first party options with respect to their automobile:

1. Collision or upset coverage
2. Restricted collision coverage
3. No coverage for insured vehicle

Having selected one of these options, the PPI insured is exempt from liability for damage to any vehicle required to come under the plan. The first option, "collision or upset coverage," is ordinary collision coverage as it has traditionally been written. The second option, "restricted collision coverage," applies only when the driver of the other vehicle is at fault. In a sense, it takes the place of the other driver's property damage liability coverage. As the title of the third option indicates, the insured would have no coverage for his own vehicle, and he would have no right of action against another party carrying PPI for any damage suffered. Property damage liability coverage is mandatory, and the exemption from tort liability does not apply to out-of-state vehicles or other property.

### Differences among the Proposals

The programs discussed above by no means exhaust the array of suggested options. They were selected for discussion from among the many programs currently under consideration because they typify the main classifications into which automobile reform proposals fall. There are significant differences among many of the current proposals, and it is important to distinguish among the approaches. Basically, the proposals for reform fall into one of three classifications:

1. *No-fault proposals.* Under a true no-fault plan, the tort system would be abolished generally in handling automobile accident losses. Anyone who suffered loss would seek recovery for medical expenses, loss of income, or other expenses from his own insurer. The AIA Plan is typical of this approach.
2. *Modified no-fault proposals.* Modified no-fault proposals would provide limited immunity from tort action to the extent that the injured party was indemnified under a first party coverage. Tort action would be retained for losses in excess of the recovery under the first party coverage. Under some modified no-fault proposals, payment for pain and suffering would be limited or eliminated. The Keeton–O'Connell Plan and the Massachusetts Plan are examples of this approach.
3. *Expanded first party coverage.* Here there is no exemption from tort liability. Instead, the injured party collects benefits under a first party coverage, retaining the right to sue for losses in excess of the amount recovered under the first party coverage. Most important, the financial responsibility of the negligent driver is retained by permitting subrogation by the insurer paying the first party benefits. The Cotter Plan, the AMIA Plan, and the NAII Plan follow this approach.

Unfortunately, the "no-fault" label is frequently applied to all three approaches. It is clearly a misnomer to refer to the expanded first party coverage approach as a no-fault approach. Plans in this category would not involve any change in the tort system, and are not no-fault plans any more than fire insurance, health insurance, or even life insurance are no-fault plans.

## The Future of the Tort System and the Automobile

As of January 1972, seven states had enacted some type of legislation dealing with the compensation of automobile accident victims, and the majority of the remaining states are considering such legislation.[9] Although many important groups have gone on record as favoring the abolition of the tort system as it relates to the automobile, the trend appears to be in the direction of expanded first party coverages, with only minor modifications, if any, in the tort system. All of the plans enacted to date expand the use of first party medical and wage benefits, but retain to varying degrees the right to bring suit and to collect for pain and suffering.

Some proponents of the no-fault approach maintain that the programs thus far enacted or under consideration will prove to be inadequate to cope with the problem, pointing out that if the states fail to act, or if they act inadequately, federal legislation may take the matter out of the hands of the states. Federal legislation has already been introduced to this end. The Hart–Magnuson bill, first introduced in the U.S. Senate in 1970 and then amended in 1971, would create a national no-fault system. Tort liability would be abolished (except for persons engaging in criminal acts), and every motor vehicle owner would be required to purchase first party coverage as a condition to operating the motor vehicle on the nation's highways.[10] Most informed observers feel that it is unlikely that this legislation will be passed in the immediate future, and so for the present the states will continue in their attempts to find a way to cope with the automobile insurance problem. Whether the plans thus far enacted and currently under consideration will provide a workable solution to the dilemma remains

[9] These states are Delaware, Florida, Illinois, Massachusetts, Minnesota, Oregon, and South Dakota. The Florida and Massachusetts plans are modified no-fault plans. The programs in Delaware, Minnesota, Oregon, and South Dakota add first party coverage to the automobile policy, but do not limit the injured person's right to sue. For a concise comparison of the provisions of these plans and other programs in effect or under consideration, see *The Journal of Insurance*, **XXXII** (6) (November–December 1971).

[10] The Hart–Magnuson bill (S-945) is entitled *The Uniform Motor Vehicle Insurance Act*. The provisions of the plan are quite similar to the AIA plan. It would provide unlimited medical and rehabilitation benefits and payment for loss of income up to $1000 a month. Additionally, it would include no-fault benefits with respect to property damage (other than a motor vehicle being operated). No-fault benefits would be reduced by the amount of benefits collected under any other insurance plan. Optional pain and suffering coverage and collision coverage would be available. As in the case of the AIA plan, victims of uninsured vehicles would collect under an assigned claims plan.

to be seen. It would appear, however, that the automobile and the problem of spreading the financial losses which result from our mechanized society will remain a pressing problem for both the insurance industry and society for some time to come.

## Questions for Discussion and Review

**1.** Most people would probably agree with the statement, "Anyone who operates an automobile should carry automobile liability insurance." In view of the reasonableness of this statement, how do you account for the fact that compulsory automobile insurance laws are not more widespread?

**2.** The Special Automobile Policy is more a contract of indemnity than is the Family Automobile Policy. Briefly describe the areas in which the coverage of the Special Automobile Policy is more limited than the Family Automobile Policy.

**3.** There seems to be general dissatisfaction with the field of automobile insurance in general. Some authorities maintain that the problem is not with automobile insurance at all, but rather with the system we use to compensate those who are injured. Do you agree or disagree with this position?

**4.** The insurance mechanism is based on the principle of loss sharing, with those who do not suffer losses paying to meet the cost of those who do suffer losses. In view of this notion, would it make more sense to group all ages together for rating purposes, with older drivers subsidizing the cost of the losses incurred by younger drivers? Explain why insurance companies divide drivers into different classifications with preferential rates for some groups.

**5.** Which of the plans modifying the tort system do you favor? Why? Do you think that perhaps a combination of the features of several of the plans would be the best solution? What features would you include in a no-fault or modified no-fault plan?

## Suggestions for Additional Reading

Bickelhaupt, D. L. and Magee, J. H. *General Insurance,* 8th ed. Homewood, Ill.: Richard D. Irwin, 1970, Chap. 17.
Brainard, C. *Automobile Insurance.* Homewood, Ill.: Richard D. Irwin, 1961.

Denenberg, H. S., Eilers, R. D., Hoffman, G. W., Kline, C. A., Melone, J. J., and Snider, H. W. *Risk and Insurance*. Englewood Cliffs, N.J.: Prentice-Hall, 1964, pp. 598–610.

*Fire, Casualty and Surety Bulletins,* Casualty and Surety Volume, "Auto" Section. Cincinnati, Ohio: The National Underwriter Co.

Keeton, R. E. and O'Connell, J. *After Cars Crash*. Homewood, Ill.: Dow-Jones-Irwin, 1967.

Keeton, R. E. and O'Connell, J. *Basic Protection for the Traffic Victim*. Boston: Little, Brown, 1965.

Kulp, C. A. and Hall, J. *Casualty Insurance,* 4th ed. New York: Ronald Press, 1968, Chaps. 11–13.

Long, J. D. and Gregg, D. W. *Property and Liability Insurance Handbook*. Homewood, Ill.: Richard D. Irwin, 1965, Chap. 37.

Mowbray, A. H., Blanchard, R. H., and Williams, C. A., Jr. *Insurance*, 6th ed. New York: McGraw-Hill, 1969, Chap. 39.

Rokes, W. *No-fault Insurance*. Santa Monica: Insurors Press, 1971.

United States House of Representatives Antitrust Sub-Committee., *Automobile Insurance Study—A Report by the Staff,* House Rept. 815 90th Congress, 1st Session. Washington, D.C.: Government Printing Office, 1967.

Williams, C. A., Jr. and Heins, R. M. *Risk Management and Insurance,* 2nd ed. New York: McGraw-Hill, 1971, Chap. 33.

# 21 Commercial Property Coverages

*By a small sample, we may judge of the whole piece.*

—Cervantes, *Don Quixote*

## INTRODUCTION

In this chapter we will discuss the major insurance coverages that have been designed to protect the business firm from the financial consequences of damage to, or loss of, its property. As the student will no doubt recall from Chapter 15, the damage or destruction of property may be the source of two types of losses: the direct loss, which involves the loss of the value of the asset itself, and the consequential or indirect loss, which results from the loss of use of the asset. Here we are concerned with both.

## FIRE INSURANCE—DIRECT LOSS

Business firms are not nearly as homogeneous a group as are homeowners. As a result, the forms used to insure dwelling property are multiplied many times over to meet the needs of business firms. A detailed analysis of all these forms is impractical, but the student should at least be aware of some of their main features.

### The Building and Contents Form

The Building and Contents Form is the commercial equivalent of the Dwelling and Contents Form. Like the Dwelling and Contents Form, it contains the definitions of property insured, certain permissive clauses,

**509**

and the provisions of the Extended Coverage Endorsement. However, it does not contain many of the extensions included in the dwelling forms. For example, there are no extensions covering appurtenant structures, improvements and betterments, rental value, or extra expense. When the need exists for such coverage, these items must be specifically insured. The off-premises coverage of this form is also more limited than that of the dwelling forms, applying only when the property has been removed from the premises for repair, renovation, or refinishing. The fact that the off-premises coverage does not apply to stocks of merchandise creates a need for special insurance coverage on property away from the premises. Such coverage will be discussed later in the chapter.

The form does not, as does the Dwelling and Contents Form, grant permission for the building to be vacant or unoccupied beyond the 60 days specified in the fire policy. If a commercial building becomes vacant or unoccupied for a period in excess of 60 days, coverage is suspended unless a special permit is attached to the policy.[1]

### Additional Perils

While the Building and Contents Form includes only the perils of extended coverage, the peril of vandalism and malicious mischief is often added by endorsement. The coverage of the Vandalism and Malicious Mischief Endorsement is essentially the same as the vandalism and malicious mischief coverage of the broader dwelling forms. In addition to the Vandalism and Malicious Mischief Endorsement, other forms are available which include the broader coverage of additional perils, and many properties are eligible for all-risk coverage similar to that provided under the Dwelling Building Special Form.

### Replacement Cost Coverage

Some business property is eligible for replacement cost coverage similar to the replacement cost coverage that was examined in connection with the Broad Form Dwelling Forms and the Homeowners Contracts. In the case of commercial buildings, however, the underwriting requirements are considerably more stringent. Like the dwelling form extensions, the replacement

---

[1] When a mercantile, warehouse, or other nonmanufacturing building is vacant or unoccupied, a Vacancy or Unoccupancy Permit must be attached to the policy. This endorsement provides coverage on the vacant or unoccupied building for a specified period of time, which may not exceed 6 months. If the building is a manufacturing risk, a somewhat different permit must be used which permits unoccupancy only, also for a period not to exceed 6 months. The legal distinction between vacancy and unoccupancy is fairly well defined. A building is vacant when it has neither occupants nor contents. A building is unoccupied when it has contents, but no occupants.

cost endorsement applicable to other forms of fire insurance provides that no deduction will be made for depreciation in the event of a loss, provided that the insured has maintained insurance equal to a specified percentage of the replacement cost value of the building. Under the replacement cost endorsements used for commercial property, it is normally a requirement that the building must be rebuilt on the same premises for the same occupancy before the insured can collect on a replacement cost basis.

### Coinsurance

Coinsurance is one of the most misunderstood topics in the entire area of commercial fire insurance, yet this principle is not really difficult. To understand the basis for the coinsurance concept, it is necessary to understand something about fire insurance rates. It is a well-documented fact that most fire losses are partial.[2] Since the fire rate is based on the ratio of the amount of losses to the amount of coverage provided, the rate will be higher if individuals insure a lower percentage of their property values than if they insure the property to some high percentage of its value. The relationship between insurance to value and fire insurance rates can best be illustrated by the example below.

We will assume that the insurance company in question has insured 10,000 buildings worth $10,000 each for 100% of their value. On the basis of past experience, the company estimates that it will experience the following losses:

| | |
|---|---|
| 30 partial losses at $1000 each | $30,000 |
| 2 total losses at $10,000 each | 20,000 |
| | $50,000 |

Since the company can expect $50,000 in losses out of a total of $100,000,000 worth of buildings, it computes the pure rate to be 0.05 per $100:

$$\frac{\$50,000}{\$100,000,000} = 0.0005 \text{ per } \$1 \text{ or } 0.05 \text{ per } \$100$$

If the company assumes that the loss ratio will be 50% of the gross premiums, it will load the pure rate as follows:

| | |
|---|---|
| Pure rate | 0.05 per $100 |
| Loading | 0.05 per $100 |
| Gross rate | 0.10 per $100 |

[2] Statistical data gathered by the fire insurance rating bureaus indicate that about 85% of all fire losses involve less than 20% of the value of the property, and only about 5% of the losses involve over 50% of the value of the property insured.

If the 10,000 buildings worth $10,000 each are insured 50% to value, the rate per $100 will be considerably higher.

$$10,000 \text{ buildings insured for } \$5000 \text{ each } = \$50,000,000$$

Assuming the same losses:

| | |
|---|---:|
| 30 partial losses at $1000 each | $30,000 |
| 2 total losses at $5000 each | 10,000 |
| | $40,000 |

$$\text{Pure rate} = \frac{\$40,000}{\$50,000,000} = 0.08 \text{ per } \$100$$

Assuming once again that the loss ratio will be 50% of gross premiums, the gross rate is 0.16 per $100.

If the two groups we have just examined were lumped together, the total losses are $90,000, and the amount of insurance is $150,000,000. A rate computed on the basis of all insureds would be 0.12 per $100 [($90,000/-$150,000,000) × 2]. In this event, those insureds who insured their property 100% of value would be discriminated against, in that their rate, which should be 0.10 per $100, is 0.12 per $100. In effect, those who insured 100% of their property values would be subsidizing those who did not insure to value.

Since insurance to value has a definite relationship to the equity of fire insurance rates, some concession must be made in the rating structure for those who insure their property for some high percentage of its value. The coinsurance clause, which provides for a rate reduction if the insured purchases insurance equal to some high percentage of the value of his property, is designed as such a concession.[3]

**Coinsurance clause.**     Under the provisions of the coinsurance clause, the insured agrees to maintain insurance equal to some specified percentage of the value of his property (e.g., 80%, 90%, or 100%) in return for a lower rate. In effect, the coinsurance rate is a quantity discount.

If the insured agrees to purchase insurance equal to the agreed percentage, the rate he must pay per $100 of coverage is reduced. If the insured fails to maintain the amount of insurance he agreed to maintain, he may suffer a penalty at the time of a loss. The provisions of the coinsurance clause are as follows:

> In consideration of the reduced rate and the form under which this policy is written, it is expressly stipulated and made a condition of this

---

[3] The coinsurance clause and coinsurance rates are not generally used in the field of dwelling property; coinsurance is used only for commercial coverages.

contract that in the event of loss, this company will be liable for no greater proportion thereof than the amount hereby insured bears to the specified percentage of actual cash value of the property described herein at the time such loss shall happen.

More simply, at the time of a loss the insurance company will make payment on the following basis:

$$\frac{\text{Amount of insurance carried}}{\text{Amount of insurance required}} \times \text{Loss} = \text{Amount paid}$$

The application of the provision is simple—as long as the insured carries insurance equal to the required percentage, all losses covered by the policy will be paid in full. If he does not maintain the insurance to value required, he will collect only a part of his loss.

To illustrate, let us assume that the insured in question has purchased insurance on a $100,000 building, with an 80% coinsurance clause. In keeping with the requirement of the coinsurance clause, he purchased $80,000 in coverage. In the event of a $5000 loss, the company would pay

$$\frac{\text{Amount of insurance carried (\$80,000)}}{\text{Amount of insurance required (\$80,000)}} \times \$5000 = \$5000$$

Now let us assume that as time goes by, construction costs increase and increases in the price level act to increase the replacement cost of the building. In spite of the fact that the actual cash value of the building has increased, the insured continues to maintain $80,000 in coverage. At the time that his next $5000 loss occurs, it is determined that the actual cash value of the building has increased to $200,000, and to comply with the 80% coinsurance clause, the insured should have been carrying $160,000 in coverage. In this case, he becomes a coinsurer, and suffers a penalty equal to the coinsurance deficiency:

$$\frac{\text{Amount of insurance carried (\$80,000)}}{\text{Amount of insurance required (\$160,000)}} \times \$5000 = \$2500$$

Two important points are illustrated by the above examples. First, the coinsurance requirement is applied at the time of loss, and the amount of insurance required to comply is based on the actual cash value of the property at the time of loss and not the value of the property when the policy is originally taken out. Second, the burden of maintaining the proper amount of insurance is on the insured. The insurance company does not check to see if the insured has kept his promise until a loss takes place.

The coinsurance clause penalty is applicable only in the case of partial losses. In the event of a total loss, the face of the policy is payable, even though the insured has a coinsurance deficiency.

## Blanket Insurance

Thus far, we have discussed only one form of fire insurance, that form known as "specific" insurance. Specific insurance applies a definite amount of insurance to a stated item. In addition to specific insurance, insurance also may be written on a "blanket" basis, under which one amount of insurance covers more than one type of property or property at more than one location. Blanket insurance is designed for firms with insurable property composed of different elements or at different locations. It is used when the individual elements that make up the total fluctuate, but the total values remain stable. Under these circumstances (where the total remains stable but the components fluctuate), specific insurance is inconvenient, for it would be necessary to constantly adjust the amount of insurance as the values changed. If the specific amounts of coverage were not adjusted, the insured might find that he had too much insurance on one item and not enough on some other.

As an illustration of the manner in which blanket insurance operates, let us say that the insured has three warehouses, and while the maximum value of goods at the three locations remains stable at about $150,000, the values at each location fluctuate from $20,000 to $70,000. This insured can purchase $150,000 in blanket coverage at the three locations, and the values at each location will be covered in full, regardless of the proportion of the total $150,000 those values represent.

When coverage is written on a blanket basis, with less than 90% coinsurance, the coverage is subject to the "pro rata distribution clause." This clause provides that the total amount of insurance is to be divided among the locations on the basis of the percentage of total values that the property at each location represents. Suppose the insured purchases $120,000 in blanket coverage, and at the time of a loss he has $150,000 in stock distributed as follows:

Warehouse #1 values $45,000     (30% of the total value)
Warehouse #2 values $45,000     (30% of the total value)
Warehouse #3 values $60,000     (40% of the total value)

The $120,000 in coverage would be divided among the locations on the basis of the above percentages. If the property at location #1 were totally destroyed, the insured would collect only $36,000 (30% of $120,000). The need for the pro rata distribution clause is obvious; without it the insured could purchase a small amount of insurance equal to the maximum value at any one location and use it for insurance at the additional locations as well. The clause forces the insured to maintain insurance to value at all locations.

## Reporting Forms

For a large number of mercantile risks, the value of stock on hand fluctuates substantially during the year. A specific amount policy is unsatisfactory in such instances because it either underinsures or overinsures the property at risk during the year. If insurance is purchased in an amount sufficient to cover the peak value, the stock is overinsured most of the time, and the insured is paying for more insurance than he will be permitted to collect. If some amount of insurance less than the peak value is selected, there will be occasions when the insured will be underinsured and exposed to the possibility of an uninsured loss.

The reporting form is specifically designed to meet the needs of such business firms. The amount of insurance in effect during the year moves up and down with the values on hand. The policy is written with a maximum limit of liability that is sufficiently high to cover the maximum expected values, and the amount of insurance automatically adjusts to the values exposed to loss, subject to this maximum. The insured makes monthly reports of his current values, and is charged on the basis of these reports, paying only for the values exposed to loss, not for the limit of liability. The premium cannot be known until the year is over, so a provisional premium is paid at the inception of the policy and then adjusted at the end of the year to reflect the true cost of the protection that was provided.[4]

The insured is required to report 100% of the values of the property insured. Any violation in late reporting or underreporting of values, whether intentional or otherwise, is a violation of the policy conditions and may result in a penalty in the event of loss. In the case of a late report, the amount of insurance is limited to the values reported in the previous report. In addition, the Full-Value Reporting Clause (also called the Honesty Clause) provides that if the insured underreports the values, the liability of the insurance company is limited to the percentage of the loss that the last values reported bear to the values that should have been reported. Thus, if the insured reports values of $100,000 when in reality the value of the property is $200,000 and then suffers a loss of, say $2000, he would collect only the percentage of the loss that the values reported represent to the actual values (50% or $1000).

### ALLIED LINES

Allied lines is a term used to describe coverages which are closely associated with, and usually sold in conjunction with, fire insurance. In general, the following are forms of insurance that are considered to be allied lines:

1. Sprinkler leakage
2. Water damage

[4] When the fluctuation in value is limited to an identifiable period, an alternate approach, the Peak Season Endorsement, is used. Here the amount of insurance is increased by some specified amount to cover the increased values during the period. A pro rata premium charge is made for the additional amount of insurance.

3. Earthquake
4. Radioactive contamination
5. Standing timber
6. Rain insurance

Any classification system is arbitrary, and other types of insurance might be included in the allied lines classification. For our purposes, we will consider the six classes listed above, and we will discuss only four of these — sprinkler leakage and water damage insurance.

### Sprinkler Leakage

A sprinkler system is one of the most effective means available for keeping a fire under control once it has broken out. A sprinkler system consists of pipes that carry water to sprinkler heads, which are valves designed to open when temperatures reach 135–165°F or higher. Sprinkler systems are installed to protect against the fire hazard and to help reduce fire insurance rates. While they do aid in fire loss prevention, they also create another possible source of loss. The basic fire policy will cover any damage caused by water from a sprinkler system when the discharge is caused by a fire, however it does not cover the damage caused by accidental leakage. Accidental leakage must be covered under the sprinkler leakage coverage.

Like the fire policy, the coverage under the Sprinkler Leakage coverage is on the basis of the actual cash value of the property at the time of the loss. Sprinkler leakage is usually written subject to a coinsurance clause but with a much wider range of coinsurance options. The insured has a choice of coinsurance percentages of 5%, 10%, 25%, 50%, 80%, or even higher. The higher the coinsurance percentage selected, the lower the rate. Different coinsurance percentages may be applied to specific insurance written on different items. For example, the coinsurance on the building might be 10%, while the coinsurance on the contents might be 25%.

### Water Damage

Water damage coverage is designed to cover the accidental discharge or overflow of water or steam from within any of the following sources:

1. Plumbing systems (excluding sprinkler systems, which as noted above are covered under the sprinkler leakage policy)
2. Plumbing tanks for the storage of water for the supply of a plumbing system, a heating system, elevator tanks and cylinders, standpipes for fire hose (except when supplied by a sprinkler system)
3. Industrial or domestic appliances
4. Refrigerating or air-conditioning systems

In addition, the policy covers the accidental admission of rain or snow directly to the interior of the building through defective roofs, leaders, or spouting, or through open or defective doors, windows, skylights, transoms, or ventilators. Subject to certain exclusions, the policy also covers direct loss caused by collapse or fall of a tank or any component part thereof which forms a part of the plumbing system. Finally, the policy covers accidental discharge or leakage of water from underground water supply mains and fire hydrants.

### Earthquake Insurance

As the student will no doubt recall, the Homeowners policy may be extended to cover earthquake damage through the use of the Earthquake Assumption Endorsement. In the eight Pacific Coast states (Arizona, California, Idaho, Montana, Nevada, Oregon, Utah, and Washington), earthquake insurance is written on commercial buildings by endorsement to the standard fire policy. In the rest of the country it is generally written under a special Earthquake and Volcanic Eruption policy. The Pacific Coast form requires a deductible of at least 5% of the value of the property, and higher deductibles are frequently used. In addition, a minimum of 70% coinsurance is generally required under the Pacific Coast form, while 50% coinsurance is required elsewhere. The separate policy used in areas other than the Pacific Coast states provides an independent amount of insurance, whereas the Pacific Coast endorsement extends the fire insurance to cover the additional peril. This is an important point of difference, since the apportionment clause used in the earthquake endorsement to the standard fire policy has the same effect as the apportionment provisions of the Extended Coverage Endorsement: any earthquake loss is pro-rated with all fire insurance on the property, whether or not all of the fire policies provide earthquake insurance. There is no apportionment clause in the separate earthquake policy.

### Rain Insurance

Rain insurance has traditionally been classified as an Allied Line coverage; actually it is a consequential loss coverage, for it does not protect against damage to property, but against loss of income or extra expense due to rain, snow, sleet, or hail. The coverage is generally sold to cover outdoor events of all kinds which are scheduled to take place on a certain day and which are dependent upon favorable weather for success. There are several forms of the coverage available: one form covers the income lost as a result of rain, another covers the expense incurred by the insured that will be lost if the event must be abandoned, and still another form is written on a valued basis. Payment is made for the anticipated income lost or the actual expenses incurred if the peril insured against occurs. In some instances the contract specifies the amount of rain that must fall before payment will be made, while in other contracts any amount of rain will require payment by the insurer. Generally, the policy must be taken out at least 7 days before the event, and the policy is not subject to cancellation by either party.

## FIRE INSURANCE—CONSEQUENTIAL LOSS COVERAGES

Unlike the dwelling forms, commercial fire forms do not provide coverage for the consequential loss resulting from damage to the insured property. Such coverage must be provided by endorsement or in a separate policy, with an additional premium charge. The major consequential loss coverages are business interruption, contingent business interruption, extra expense insurance, leasehold interest insurance, rent or rental value insurance, and profits and commissions insurance.

### Business Interruption Insurance

If a business is forced to suspend operations because of a fire or some other insured peril that damages the building or the contents of the building, there will be no income and the business will be forced to dip into its capital funds to pay continuing expenses. In addition, profit will be discontinued during the period of interruption. It is the purpose of business interruption insurance to pay both the continuing expenses and the profits that would have been earned during this period of interruption.

Business interruption insurance is designed to indemnify the insured for his loss of income during the period of time that it takes to restore the property to a useful condition. It undertakes to replace income, minus expenses that do not continue, which would have been earned if the property had not been damaged. The insurance company agrees to pay for this loss of income for the period of time that would be required "with due diligence and dispatch" to rebuild, repair, or replace that part of the building or other property that was damaged by an insured peril. Business interruption is generally written as a contract of indemnity, limiting the recovery to the actual expenses (including a normal profit) that continue.

**General provisions of business interruption insurance.** Under the provisions of the business interruption forms, the insured is reimbursed for the actual loss sustained from the date of the loss to the date of restoration but in no event for more than the amount stated in the policy. The restoration period for which payment is made ends when the location is again occupied by the insured, and the machinery and equipment in the building are returned to operating condition. In determining the amount of the loss, the insurance company considers the insured's experience before the loss and probable experience after the loss if no loss had occurred. The peril causing the interruption must be an insured peril under the policy, and the damage must have occurred during the policy period. The period of time for which a recovery may be obtained is not limited by the expiration of the policy.

**Expense to reduce loss.** One of the general provisions in the business interruption forms requires the insured to use all reasonable means to get back into operation as soon as possible. If it is possible for the insured to start business at a temporary location, even on a reduced scale, he is required to do so. A policy provision, Expense to Reduce Loss, provides for the payment of costs incurred to reduce the amount of the loss. These are payable so long as the total amount paid does not exceed the amount which would have been paid out under the interruption coverage if the costs had not been paid.

Business interruption insurance may be written to provide coverage against the same perils as the direct damage coverages: fire and lightning; fire, lightning, and extended coverage: fire, lightning, extended coverage, and vandalism and malicious mischief; and even all-risk coverage. The coverage may be written on a coinsurance basis under one of the Gross Earnings Forms, or without coinsurance under the Earnings or "No-coinsurance" Form.

**Gross earnings forms.** The standard form of business interruption coverage is called the Gross Earnings Form. There are two Gross Earnings Forms available, one for mercantile and nonmanufacturing risks and one for manufacturers. Although the wording is slightly different in the two forms, gross earnings are defined as net sales minus the cost of merchandise or raw materials.

Coinsurance options of 50%, 60%, 70%, and 80% are available under both of the Gross Earnings Forms. The coinsurance clause of the business interruption forms (also called a "contribution clause") serves the same function as the coinsurance clause of the fire insurance direct damage coverage—to induce the insured to carry a high percentage of insurance to value. The clause operates in much the same manner as in the direct damage policies. If the amount of insurance carried is less than the required percentage at the time of a loss, the insured will be penalized. The rate for business interruption coverage varies with the coinsurance percentage selected. The higher the percentage of the annual gross earnings insured, the lower is the rate per $100. The percentage of the total annual gross earnings that should be selected will depend on the period of time that will be required for restoration of the premises and the maximum potential earnings that will be lost during the period required for restoration. This means that a business which is seasonal in nature should insure a higher percentage of its annual gross earnings.

**Earnings (no-coinsurance) form.**    A second form of business interruption coverage, called the Earnings Form, is an easy-to-understand coverage, designed to insure loss of earnings of mercantile and nonmanufacturing risks. It is especially designed for the relatively small firm and is characterized by its simplicity. Many insureds do not understand the coinsurance mechanism and find it distasteful. Since there is no coinsurance requirement in the Earnings Form, many insureds are more willing to use it.

To determine the amount of insurance required under the Earnings Form, it is only necessary for the insured to determine the monthly loss of earnings if he were forced to close during his busiest season. Once this figure has been determined, the amount of insurance purchased is some multiple of this amount. Instead of a coinsurance requirement, there is a limit of the face of the policy, expressed as a percentage, which the insured can collect during any one month of shutdown. In the basic loss of earnings endorsement, this limitation is 25%. Thus, if the insured purchases $10,000 in coverage under the loss of earnings endorsement, he can collect up to $2500 per month. Since there is no coinsurance requirement to be met, the insured cannot suffer a coinsurance penalty. If the insured underestimates the amount of his future earnings, the only penalty is that the amount of insurance will be insufficient to cover his total loss.

### Contingent Business Interruption

Contingent business interruption insurance is a means of protecting the firm against loss as a result of interruptions that are caused by a fire or other insured peril at premises that are not owned, controlled, or operated by the firm. There are three situations in which this coverage is used:

1. When the insured depends on one or a few manufacturers or suppliers for most of the materials or services to conduct his business. The firm upon which the insured depends in this situation is called *contributing* property.
2. When the insured depends upon one or a few businesses to purchase the bulk of his products. The business to which the bulk of the insured's production flows is called the *recipient* property.
3. When the insured depends upon a neighboring business to help attract customers to his place of business. A common way of referring to the business is the *leader* property.

Basically, the policy covers the interruption of the insured's business that is caused by fire or other insured peril at the other nonowned property. It is not necessary that the contributing or recipient property be shut down in order to cause a contingent business interruption loss to the insured. A supply of finished goods intended for the insured may be destroyed at the plant of the contributing firm, forcing the insured to shut down. The insured would collect, even though the contributing firm was not shut down for so much as an hour. Conversely, the fire might close the contributing plant; but the insured, having stocked up in advance, might not be affected. In this situation there would be no business interruption loss. The essential point is that the insured's business is interrupted because of damage to someone else's property.

### Extra Expense Insurance

It may be impossible for some types of businesses to shut down their operations in the event of a fire. Under certain circumstances it might be necessary for the business to continue its operations at some other location. Extra Expense insurance is an alternative and sometimes a supplement to business interruption insurance for those businesses that can continue operations through the use of other facilities. The Extra Expense policy provides payment for expenses over and above the normal expenses, when such additional expenses are incurred to continue operations after damage to the insured premises by an insured peril. The insuring agreement provides for reimbursement of those expenses involved in continuing operations, including the expense of temporary premises and equipment, moving, extra labor, advertising, printing, travel for employees, etc.

The Extra Expense Form does not include a coinsurance clause, but instead includes a schedule of cumulative monthly limits of the face amount of the policy. The period of indemnity may not be less than 3 months, and no more than 40% of the amount of insurance purchased may be used during any one month. The most commonly used percentages are:

Up to 40% of the face of the policy payable during the first month
Up to 80% of the policy payable during the first 2 months
Up to 100% of the policy payable during the first 3 months

An insured who anticipates a more extended period during which extra expenses would be required may select a smaller monthly percentage of the face amount. For example, the form might provide that 10% of the face amount of the policy could be collected the first month, 20% during the first 2 months, 30% during the first 3 months, and so on. The rates for this coverage are based on the building rate, with a decreasing rate charged as the percentage of the face amount collectible in the first month decreases.

### Leasehold Interest Insurance

Leasehold interest insurance is designed to provide protection against loss due to the termination of a favorable lease as a result of fire or other insured peril. The lessee or the lessor may suffer financial loss as a result of the termination of a favorable lease, and many lease of premises agreements provide that the lease is to be cancelled in the event of destruction of the property or damage which renders the property untenantable. For example, a property leased for $100 a month, with a provision for automatic cancellation in the event of partial destruction of the property, when prevailing conditions make it impossible to secure similar quarters at less than $250 a month, would create a leasehold interest of $150 per month.

The amount of insurance under a leasehold agreement decreases month by month, with the amount of insurance always approximately equal to the insurable value of the insured's interest in the lease. In the event of a loss which terminates the lease, the insured is paid a lump sum equal to the discounted value of the leasehold interest for the remaining months of the lease.

### Rent or Rental Value Insurance

Rent or Rental Value Insurance is insurance against the loss of rental income or rental value of property made untenantable by fire or some other insured peril. In general, the term Rent Insurance applies to property which is occupied by the renter, and Rental Value applies to property occupied by the owner. Rental Value or Rent Insurance may be written in a separate policy, or it may be endorsed onto a policy covering direct damage to the building. The policy then agrees to cover the loss of rents when a building insured is rendered untenantable by a peril insured against. The company is liable to the insured for an amount not exceeding the actual loss sustained, based upon rents or rental value of the untenantable property, less expenses that do not continue, up to the face amount of the insurance. The period of untenantability is computed from the date of the fire for the period that would be required with due diligence and dispatch to restore the premises to tenantable condition. If a loss occurs during the term of the policy, liability may continue through the period of untenantability which extends beyond the expiration date of the policy.

### Profits and Commissions Insurance

A manufacturer or a selling agent who has on hand a large stock of goods insured against the perils of fire and extended coverage or other perils under a typical fire form is still exposed to loss in a way that may not be recognized— the loss of expected profits or commissions if some peril should destroy the goods. The typical fire policy provides for payment only on the basis of the actual cash value or replacement cost of the goods, not their selling price. If the goods are destroyed, expected profit may never be earned because the customers may turn elsewhere to purchase the goods. Business interruption coverage would not cover this loss because it agrees to pay only for lost profits and expenses as a result of the failure to continue operations. It does not protect against the loss of goods already finished.

The loss of profits can be insured by including a provision in the fire policy to cover the goods for market value; as an alternative, the insured may purchase Profits and Commissions Insurance. The Profits and Commission coverage agrees to pay the difference between the replacement cost of the goods destroyed and their market value. The coverage is not available to wholesalers or retailers, but is designed primarily for manufacturers and warehousers of goods that cannot be replaced within a reasonable time. If the goods can be replaced easily, there would probably be no need for the profits insurance.

## BOILER AND MACHINERY—DIRECT LOSS COVERAGES

Boiler and machinery insurance insures against losses resulting from an "accident" to a specified "object." The terms "accident" and "object" are defined in the schedule attached to the boiler and machinery policy. An object may include such items as a boiler, boiler piping, pressure vessels, or machines. Since different objects insured under the boiler and machinery policy are subject to different types of occurrences which may cause loss, the term accident has a special definition for each type of object insured. With respect to a boiler, the insured may choose between the so-called "broad" form of coverage and a "limited" form. The definition of accident on a broad form is

a sudden and accidental breakdown of the object, or a part thereof, which manifests itself at the time of its occurrence by physical damage to the object that necessitates repair or replacement of the object or part thereof

The limited form coverage is restricted to explosion. Under the limited form, the definition of accident is

a sudden and accidental tearing asunder of the object, or a part thereof, caused by the pressure of the water or steam therein

The definition of the limited form is obviously less liberal, and the premium for this form of coverage is lower than for the broad form.

The most important aspect of boiler and machinery insurance is the inspection service provided by the insurance company. The insurance companies that write boiler and machinery insurance maintain inspection services for underwriting and loss-prevention purposes. The policy provides that the insured shall permit the insurance company to make inspections at all reasonable times during the policy period. Two such inspections are usually made annually: one during the heating season and one when the boiler is not in use. In addition, before issuing the policy, the company inspects the object to determine if it is safe enough to provide insurance. The primary service provided by the company in connection with boiler and machinery coverage is the loss-prevention service. The boiler and machinery policy insures against the four types of losses described below.

*Section I* covers loss to all property of the insured damaged directly by an accident to the insured object. Replacement cost coverage may be purchased which eliminates deduction for depreciation. As the reader will recall, the extended coverage endorsement covers explosion but excludes explosion resulting from a steam boiler. The boiler and machine coverage of Section I of this policy fills this gap by insuring the insured's own property against loss by a boiler listed in the policy.

*Section II* covers expediting expenses. Subject to the limits stated in the policy, this coverage provides reasonable funds to pay for the extra cost of making temporary repairs and for the expediting of permanent repairs. Payment under this section is limited to the amount of any coverage remaining after payment under Section I has been made or $1000, whichever is less.

*Section III* covers property damage liability. This protects the insured against liability for damage to the property of others caused by an accident involving an insured object. If the insured has liability coverage, the boiler and machinery policy will share the loss with the liability policy.

*Section IV* covers bodily injury liability, which protects the insured against liability for bodily injury to any person (except employees of the insured) which is caused by an insured accident. If the insured has other bodily injury liability insurance, it will apply first, the bodily injury liability coverage of the boiler and machinery policy will apply on an excess basis.

The Boiler Machinery Policy is somewhat unique in that it provides one amount of insurance which can be used for all four of the losses listed. The entire amount of the policy is available to pay for loss under item I, damage to the property of the insured. If the limit of the policy is not exhausted by the payment under item I, payment is then made under item II, then under item III, and if payments do not exceed the limit, under item IV.

Like most liability policies, the Boiler and Machinery Policy provides for the payment of defense services, payment of court and other costs of investigating claims under Sections III and IV, including payment of interest on judgment and premiums on appeal bonds and release of attachment bonds. All such expenses are covered, regardless of the limit per accident.

The policy provides for automatic coverage on newly acquired objects; it provides automatic coverage for up to 90 days on any object similar to the object already insured under the policy. Such newly acquired objects may be newly installed at existing locations, or it may be in newly acquired premises.

There are two methods of insuring objects under boiler and machinery policies. Objects may be insured under the blanket group plan, or each object may be specifically insured. The blanket group plan provides automatic coverage at each location for all objects covered by the blanket group description. The blanket group plan provides for annual premium adjustment on a pro rata basis.

## BOILER AND MACHINERY—CONSEQUENTIAL LOSS COVERAGES

Indirect loss coverages may be added by endorsement to the general Boiler and Machinery Policy in the same manner in which they may be insured under the fire policy. The indirect loss coverages provided under the Boiler and Machinery Policy are an essential part of the total coverage against indirect loss. The loss of income sustained by the firm will probably be the same regardless of whether the shutdown is occasioned by a fire or a boiler explosion. Actually, there are three consequential loss coverages available under the Boiler and Machinery Policy, two of which are time-element coverages. The third, called "consequential damage" insurance, covers loss caused by spoilage of specified property resulting from an accident to an object.

*Use and occupancy coverage* provides indemnity for loss due to a total or partial interruption of business or for expense incurred to reduce loss resulting from such interruption. Use and occupancy, or as it is sometimes called "U and O," is the boiler and machinery equivalent of fire business interruption coverage.

*Outrage coverage* is, in a sense, the boiler and machinery equivalent of Extra Expense insurance. It provides a specified indemnity for each working hour during which an insured object is not available for service because of an accident. For example, a firm utilizing a conveyor in an assembly line system of production might suffer a significant loss in the event of breakdown of that conveyor. There is no requirement that the business be interrupted.

*Consequential damage* coverage provides indemnity for actual loss of specified property of the insured and also for such amounts as the insured is obligated to pay by reason of his liability for property of others, when such loss is due to spoilage from lack of power, light, heat, steam, or refrigeration at specifically described premises caused solely by accident to an insured object. A freezing plant or a meat locker may, for example, purchase consequential damage coverage to cover the indirect loss resulting from breakdown of its freezing equipment.

## ACCOUNTS RECEIVABLE AND VALUABLE PAPERS INSURANCE

Accounts receivable insurance was originally written by the Special Risk Department of a small number of fire insurance companies, and then through the Inland Marine Department and the Burglary Department of casualty companies. It is a consequential loss coverage because it protects not against the loss of the accounting records themselves, but against the inability to collect amounts owed to the insured because of destruction of the records by fire or some other insured peril. Today the coverage is usually written as an inland marine coverage on a broad all-risk basis. Both a reporting form and a nonreporting form are available. The coverage is on an indemnity basis and in the event of destruction of the insured records, the insurance company will pay any amounts (with allowance for normal bad debts) that the insured is unable to collect because of damage to or destruction of the records. In addition, payment is made for expenses incurred to reconstruct the records, collection expense in excess of normal collection cost, and the interest charges on any loans taken out by the insured to offset the impaired collections.

Valuable papers and records consist of written, printed, or otherwise inscribed documents and records, including books, maps, film, tape, wire or other recording media, drawings, abstracts, deeds, mortgages, and manuscripts. Such items may be insured on a broad all-risk basis under a Valuable Papers policy. Property may be scheduled or covered under a blanket amount. Items that are specifically scheduled are insured on an agreed amount basis, with the amount listed the agreed amount for loss adjustment. Property covered under the blanket amount are insured for their actual cash value.

## PLATE GLASS INSURANCE

Although fire insurance policies on buildings cover glass which constitutes a part of the building, the coverage is on a named peril basis and is subject to certain exclusions. For example, we have seen that the vandalism and malicious mischief coverage excludes loss to glass. Because of the limited coverage afforded on glass under the fire policy, individual business owners may wish to purchase broader coverage afforded under a Comprehensive Glass Policy, which covers glass on an extremely broad all-risk basis. Under the Plate Glass Policy, the insured is indemnified for damage to the glass, insured lettering, or ornamentation caused by accidental breakage (except by fire) and acids of chemicals accidentally or maliciously applied, provided the glass, lettering, or ornamentation is unfit for further use. This is probably the broadest insuring agreement in existence, covering all breakage and excluding only fire and war. However, only those plate glass panels specifically insured are covered, and lettering is not covered unless it, too, has been specifically insured.

The Plate Glass Policy does not cover marring or scratching of the glass, except as provided under the coverage with respect to acid or chemicals. The insuring agreement covers "breakage," and unless the break extends through the entire thickness of glass, it is not considered to be breakage. The policy provisions give the company the option of replacing the broken glass or paying for the glass in cash. Normally, the company elects to replace the glass.

The policy also covers the cost of repairing or replacing frames or sashes up to $75, the cost of boarding up or installing temporary plates in broken windows up to $75, and the cost, not exceeding $75, of removing and replacing fixtures or other obstructions.

## INSURANCE AGAINST DISHONESTY

The broad field of dishonesty insurance includes all cases in which the cause of the loss is the wrongful taking of property belonging to the insured. Historical development led to two distinct classes of dishonesty coverage:

1. Crime coverages, designed to cover dishonest acts of persons who are not employees of the insured
2. Fidelity bonds, designed to cover theft or dishonesty on the part of employees of the insured

Each of these provides incomplete protection against the peril of dishonesty. To provide complete protection, they must be combined, so it is well to discuss them together. The artificial distinction between "employee dishonesty insurance" and "nonemployee dishonesty insurance" is gradually disappearing, and with the advent of package crime policies, both types of criminal losses are frequently insured in the same contract.

### Nonemployee Crime Coverages

Policies designed to cover against loss of property or money through dishonest acts of persons other than employees may be classified on the basis of the perils they insure against. There are policies designed to protect against loss by robbery, burglary, theft, forgery, or larceny. In addition, there are broad form, all-risk policies designed to insure money and securities. Each of the above classes insures against a specific peril or set of perils. Since the terms "burglary" and "robbery" have technical definitions in these contracts, it is important to determine at the outset what each of these terms means. Burglary is defined as felonious abstraction of property from within a building, safe or vault by someone who has made unlawful entry therein by force and violence, of which there must be visible marks at the place of such entry, or by someone making forcible exit from the premises, of which there must be visible marks of such exit on the interior of the premises

Robbery is defined as

felonious or forcible taking of property by violence inflicted upon the person having care or custody or rightful access to the property; or by putting such person in fear of violence; or by any other overt felonious act committed in the presence of such person and of which such person was actually cognizant

Theft is much broader in meaning than either burglary or robbery. It is intended to be broad in scope and include any illegal taking of the property of another without his consent. Theft includes both burglary and robbery.

There are various types of burglary and robbery forms available, each of which is designed to afford protection against designated perils for designated types of property. Only the specified type of criminal activity insured against is covered, and the coverage exists only when the loss occurs under conditions which meet the definition of the peril insured against.

**Mercantile Open-Stock Burglary Policy.** This form covers loss of merchandise, furniture, fixtures, or equipment as a result of burglary. It does not cover loss of money or securities. Damage caused by burglars to the premises is also covered. In addition, the policy is extended to cover loss caused by robbery or attempted robbery of a watchman employed exclusively by the insured while on duty within the premises. Coverage under the Mercantile Open-Stock Burglary Policy applies only when the premises are not open for business.

The coverage is subject to certain exclusions. First, the loss must be the result of burglary (or robbery of a watchman). Unless there are marks of forcible entry into, or exit from, the premises, coverage for loss does not apply. Losses resulting from employee infidelity are not covered. In addition, losses resulting from war are excluded. Any burglary which occurs during a fire in the premises is also excluded.

Coinsurance applies to the Mercantile Open-Stock Burglary Policy in a special manner. There are two coinsurance requirements: a territorial coinsurance requirement, expressed as a percentage, which reflects the severity of the crime exposure in the territory, and a trade group coinsurance requirement, which is expressed in dollars and varies with the stealability of the merchandise. For example, the territorial coinsurance requirement in the state of Iowa is 50%. In urban areas the territorial coinsurance requirement might be 60% or 70%. The trade group requirement varies with the class of goods: it is $15,000 for jewelry and only $7500 for hardware. The insured may satisfy the coinsurance requirement of the policy by meeting either of these two requirements. If the coinsurance requirement is not met, the insured is penalized in the event of loss just as in the case of fire insurance.

**Mercantile Open-Stock Theft Policy.** In some instances, the Mercantile Open-Stock Burglary Policy may be extended by the use of the Mercantile Open-Stock Theft Endorsement to include the additional perils of robbery, theft, and larceny. When this endorsement is added to the policy, it covers whether or not the store is open for business. The form includes a $50 deductible; however, this deductible is not applicable to the losses covered under the basic Mercantile Open-Stock Burglary Policy. While the endorsement extends the policy to cover theft, mere disappearance is not covered. There must be some evidence of theft. For the same reason, inventory shortages are not covered unless there is some evidence of theft.

**Mercantile Safe Burglary Policy.** The Safe Burglary Policy covers loss of any property, including money and securities, when such property is lost as a result of forcible entry into a safe or vault. Again, the loss must be the result of *forcible* entry; if the burglar opens the safe by manipulation of the dial, there is no coverage. Removal of the entire safe from the premises is construed as safe burglary, and such losses are covered. The policy also covers damage to the safe or vault, furniture or fixtures, equipment, or other property owned by the insured which are damaged by safe burglary or attempted safe burglary. So long as an attempt at safe burglary is made, any other property damaged is also covered. In this connection, it is important to note that forcible entry into the premises does not constitute safe burglary unless there is also forcible entry (or attempt) into the safe. There is no requirement that the premises be entered forcibly.

**Mercantile Robbery Policy.** The coverage of the Mercantile Robbery Policy is restricted to the peril of robbery, as defined at the beginning of this section. Robbery consists of taking property in one of three ways:

1. By violence inflicted upon a custodian or putting him in fear of violence
2. From one who has been killed or rendered unconscious by injuries inflicted maliciously or sustained accidentally
3. By any other overt act committed in the presence of the custodian of the property of which he is actually cognizant

The last of these would include taking of property even where no violence is inflicted or threatened. For example, if an employee sees a thief grab an item and run out of the store, the loss would be considered robbery, since the overt felonious act was committed in the presence of the custodian and the custodian was aware of the act. For this reason also, loss resulting from smashing of a show window while the premises are open for business would be considered robbery.

The coverage is written in two separate sections, each of which is independent of the other; the two sections are robbery within the premises and robbery outside the premises. The insured may select either or both of these, and separate amounts of insurance are purchased for each.

The Mercantile Safe Burglary Policy and the Mercantile Robbery Policy are often combined into a Mercantile Robbery and Safe Burglary Policy.

**Money and Securities Broad Form.** The Money and Securities Broad Form provides all-risk coverage on money and securities and somewhat more limited coverage on other property. Like the other crime coverages discussed, employee infidelity is excluded. In addition, there are the normal exclusions of war and nuclear perils. Money and securities are covered under two separate coverages; Coverage A, which applies to loss within the premises, and Coverage B, which applies to loss outside the premises. As in the case of the Mercantile Robbery Policy, each section is independent of the other, and the insured may elect to insure for either or both.

The on-premises coverage covers any loss or destruction of money or securities. In addition, other property on the premises is covered, but only for the perils of robbery and burglary. Theft of merchandise is covered only if taken by robbery or from a closed and locked safe. Robbery is defined in the same manner as under the Mercantile Robbery Policy, and includes kidnapping losses and stealing from a show window by a person who has broken the glass when the premises are open for business.

The off-premises coverage applies within the United States, the District of Columbia, Virgin Islands, Puerto Rico, Canal Zone, and Canada. There is no coverage for losses occurring outside these limits. Coverage applies to money and securities in the custody of a messenger, while being conveyed by an armored car company, or while within the living quarters of a messenger.

### Employee Crime Coverages—Fidelity Bonds

Each year, thefts by employees amount to several times the amount lost by burglary, robbery, and other forms of larceny. Less than 10% of these losses are insured. Fidelity bonds are designed to protect the insured against loss resulting from dishonesty on the part of his employees. They cover loss or damage to money, securities, or other property resulting from the acts (fraud, forgery, embezzlement, theft) of the person bonded, up to the face amount of the bond, which is called the "penalty." The penalty under a bond is never cumulative from year to year, and always applies to the loss when it is discovered. The dishonesty must result while the bond is in effect,[5] although a provision called the "discovery period" provides that losses discovered within a specified period after the bond is cancelled (usually 1–2 years) will be covered, provided the actual loss took place during the policy period. Fidelity bonds are continuous, running until cancelled by the insured or the company. The various forms which the bond may be written are described below.

**Name Schedule Bonds.** Originally fidelity coverage was written on an individual basis, with the person to be bonded specifically named. This type of bond is seldom written today, having been replaced by other forms. Under a Name Schedule Bond, employees to be bonded are all listed by name. Only those persons listed are covered, and only for the amount of the penalty on each person named. The obvious disadvantages of this form of bond are the lack of coverage on employees not scheduled, and the need for constant revision.

**Position Schedule Bonds.** Under the Position Schedule Bond, all the positions to be covered are listed, rather than the individuals. Thus, if a person leaves the firm or moves to another position, his replacement is covered for the same position. Only those positions listed are covered. A provision in this form of bond states that if there are more individuals occupying a listed position than the number originally specified, all are covered, but on a decreased basis. For example, if the bond provides for two cashiers, with a $10,000 penalty applicable to each, and there are actually four cashiers, loss caused by any one of these cashiers would be covered, but only up to $5000.

**Blanket bonds.** The broadest form of fidelity coverage is provided under blanket bonds, which are designed to cover all employees, regardless of position. Changes in the composition of the force of workers does not affect the coverage, for all employees are covered and new workers are covered automatically. The two major forms of blanket bond are the Primary Commercial Blanket Bond and the Blanket Position Bond. Although they are very similar, there are two major points of difference: application of the penalty and the discovery period.

The *Primary Commercial Blanket Bond* is designed to cover all employees on a blanket basis. Its chief characteristic is the manner in which the penalty or face amount of the bond is applied. The bond provides coverage up to the

---

[5] The Discovery Bond, a special type of blanket bond, covers losses which took place before the bond was issued, provided the loss is discovered while the bond is in force. In other words, a Discovery Bond (which should not be confused with the discovery period) will cover a loss which occurred prior to the inception of the bond, if the loss is discovered during the period of the bond.

face amount for any loss caused by one or more employees. The penalty is the aggregate penalty for one loss, regardless of the number of employees involved in the loss.

Under the *Blanket Position Bond,* the face amount of the bond applies separately to each employee. For this reason, it is called a "multiple-penalty" bond. It permits the insured to collect up to the face of the bond for each employee involved in a collusive loss.

The difference in the application of the penalty of these two bonds can be illustrated by a simple example. Suppose that the insured has a blanket bond with a penalty of $10,000 and suffers a loss in which each of three employees steals $5000. A Primary Commercial Blanket Bond would pay a maximum of $10,000, but a Blanket Position Bond would pay the entire $15,000, since each of the employees is covered up to $10,000.

The discovery period also differs in the two bonds. Under the Primary Commercial Blanket Bond, the discovery period is 1 year; while under the Blanket Position Bond, it is 2 years. This means that losses that occur during the period of the bond must be discovered within 1 year after the bond is terminated under the Primary Commercial Blanket Bond, or there is no coverage. Under the Blanket Position Bond, the insured has 2 years in which to discover such losses.[6]

**Other important provisions in fidelity bonds.**    In addition to the provisions already discussed, there are others of which the student should be aware. One of the most important provisions found in all fidelity bonds is an exclusion of loss caused by any employee after the employer has knowledge of prior dishonesty on the part of that employee.

The salvage clause of the fidelity bonds provides that if the insured sustains a loss which exceeds the amount of coverage under the bond, he is entitled to any recoveries or salvage up to that point at which he has been fully reimbursed for his loss. Any salvage recovered after the insured has been fully reimbursed goes to the surety company.

Finally, fidelity bonds provide that losses which are based on, or can be proven only by, an inventory shortage are not covered.

---

[6] Both the Primary Commercial Blanket Bond and the Blanket Position Bond include a provision called "superseded suretyship" or "loss under prior bond." Subject to certain restrictions, this clause provides that if a bond is replaced by another bond with a different company, the succeeding insurer becomes liable for losses which occurred during the term of the first bond. This provision applies only when there is absolutely no lapse of coverage from the old bond to the new bond and the loss is discovered after the end of the discovery period of the old bond. If the amounts of the bonds differ, the lower penalty will apply. Without such a provision, the insured would be penalized by changing insurers. The superseded suretyship provision may be included in Name Schedule Bonds and Position Schedule Bonds.

### Package Crime Policies

There are a number of dishonesty policies that combine several crime coverages into a single contract. Some of these packages include not only nonemployee dishonesty coverage, but fidelity coverage as well.

**Comprehensive Dishonesty, Disappearance, and Destruction Policy.** The Comprehensive Dishonesty, Disappearance, and Destruction Policy, or as it is called, the "3-D policy," is an excellent example of the package policy approach to crime coverages, including both fidelity and nonemployee and crime coverages. There are five insuring agreements under the contract, and the insured may select any or all of the coverages—none is mandatory. The 3-D policy is a unique package policy, in that the premium is simply a summation of the individual premiums for the separate coverages. Unlike many package policies, there is no discount for the package. The chief benefit derived from packaging is the elimination of conflict regarding which policy should apply in the event of a loss where more than one policy might be applicable. The five insuring agreements of the 3-D policy are:

1. *Employee dishonesty.* There are two options available to the insured. Option A is the Commercial Blanket Bond, in which the penalty applies on a per loss basis, regardless of the number of employees involved. Option B is the Blanket Position Bond, in which the penalty applies per employee.
2. *Broad form money and securities on premises.* As discussed previously, this provides all-risk coverage on money and securities on the insured's premises or in a bank's premises.
3. *Broad form money and securities off premises.* This provides all-risk coverage on money and securities outside the insured's premises while in the custody of an authorized employee, in the custody of an armored car service, or within the living quarters in the home of a messenger.
4. *Money order and counterfeit paper currency.* This provides coverage against loss resulting from acceptance of post office or express money orders, or counterfeit United States or Canadian paper currency.
5. *Depositor's forgery.* This provides protection for losses caused by forgery or alteration of outgoing instruments such as checks, drafts, bills of exchange, or similar promises to pay. Coverage under this section is extended to include the insured's bank, thus eliminating the question of the bank's liability.

The coverages of the package are essentially the same as their individual counterparts. The insured may add open-stock burglary, theft, or paymaster robbery to the 3-D policy by endorsement. As a matter of fact, a total of twelve additional coverages are available as options.[7]

**Blanket Crime Policy.** Another form quite similar to the 3-D policy, the Blanket Crime Policy, provides coverage against the same five basic perils as does the Comprehensive Dishonesty, Disappearance, and Destruction Policy. However, under the Blanket Crime Policy, there is a single limit for all coverages—not a separate limit for each. The fidelity coverage of the Blanket Crime Policy is written on the Commercial Blanket basis, with a single penalty applicable regardless of the number of employees involved in the loss. The coverage of the Blanket Crime Policy may be extended to cover theft of office equipment, but the wide range of coverages available under the 3-D policy may not be added. It is somewhat less expensive than the 3-D policy.

**Storekeeper's Burglary and Robbery Policy.** The Storekeeper's Burglary and Robbery Policy is a package crime policy designed for small mercantile establishments. The insured may select $250, $500, $750, or $1000 in coverage. The maximum amount of coverage that can be purchased is $1000. There are seven distinct insuring agreements, each with a separate limit of liability, although the limits must be the same for all coverages. The seven coverages included are:

1. Premises robbery (same as mercantile robbery)
2. Messenger robbery (or outside robbery)
3. Kidnapping (forcing a messenger to open the premises)
4. Safe burglary
5. Theft from a night depository or residence of a custodian
6. Burglary; robbery of watchman (approximate equivalent of Mercantile Open-Stock Burglary Coverage)
7. Damage to property and premises (caused by burglary or robbery or attempted burglary or robbery)

The coverages afforded under the Storekeeper's Burglary and Robbery Policy are almost identical to those obtained by the purchase of the various individual policies. The coverage is subject to the usual exclusions of employee infidelity, war, and nuclear perils.

---

[7] The optional insuring agreements under the comprehensive 3-D policy are Incoming Check Forgery; Mercantile Open-Stock Burglary; Paymaster Robbery Coverage (inside and outside); Paymaster Broad Form Coverage (inside and outside); Paymaster Broad Form Coverage (inside only); Burglary and Theft Coverage on Merchandise; Warehouse Receipts Forgery; Securities of Lessees of Safe Deposit Box; Burglary Coverage on Office Equipment; Theft Coverage on Office Equipment; Paymaster Robbery Coverage Inside Premises; Credit Card Forgery.

**Broad Form Storekeeper's Burglary and Robbery Policy.** This form is similar to the Storekeeper's Burglary and Robbery Policy discussed above, but adds employee dishonesty coverage, depositor's forgery, and damage caused by vandalism and malicious mischief following burglarious entry into the premises. It is sometimes referred to as a "baby 3-D," because the extent and scope of the coverage is similar. Like the Storekeeper's Burglary and Robbery Policy, it is purchased in increments of $250, up to a maximum of $1000. It provides coverage under the following nine insuring agreements:

1. Employee dishonesty
2. Loss inside the premises (broad form money and securities)
3. Loss outside the premises (broad form money and securities)
4. Merchandise burglary; robbery of a watchman (Mercantile Open-Stock Burglary Coverage)
5. Money orders and counterfeit paper currency
6. Theft from the residence of a messenger.
7. Depositor's forgery
8. Damage by vandalism and malicious mischief
9. Other damage (resulting from an insured crime)

**Office Burglary and Robbery Policy.** The Office Burglary and Robbery form is a package policy similar to the Storekeeper's Burglary and Robbery Policy, except that it is designed for individuals or firms occupying offices. It is intended primarily for professional offices and service businesses. Unlike the storekeeper's forms, there is no coverage for merchandise. The coverage is sold in increments of $250. Unlike the storekeeper's form, which has a maximum of $1000, there is no maximum amount of insurance that may be purchased under the Office Burglary and Robbery Policy. Coverage is afforded under the following six insuring agreements:

1. Robbery inside the premises
2. Theft inside the premises (office equipment only)
3. Safe burglary
4. Robbery outside the premises
5. Theft from a night depository or residence
6. Damage (as a result of an insured crime)

The policy is subject to the normal exclusions of war and nuclear perils. Employee infidelity is also excluded.

## TRANSPORATION COVERAGES

As noted earlier in the chapter, the property forms used to insure business firms do not generally include off-premises coverage as extensive as that of the dwelling or homeowners forms. For this reason, special provision must be made with respect to property owned by business firms while it is away away from the premises. Ocean marine and inland marine forms are designed to provide this coverage.

### Ocean Marine Insurance

As noted earlier, ocean marine is considered to be the oldest form of insurance. Early traders recognized that there were perils involved in the use of the waters of the world as a means of transportation, and the logical result was the institution of loss-sharing and risk-transfer arrangements. In spite of the technological advances in marine transportation, ocean disasters remain an ever-present hazard for those engaged in foreign trade. Through the mechanism of ocean marine insurance, four types of losses, corresponding to the four major classes of ocean marine insurance, are transferred from the individual to professional marine insurers:

1. *Hull insurance.*   Hull insurance is designed to protect the owner of the vessel against loss to the ship itself. This coverage is written on a modified all-risk basis.

2. *Cargo insurance.*   Cargo insurance, which is written separately from the insurance on the ship, protects the owner of the cargo from financial loss which would result if the cargo were lost or destroyed.

3. *Freight insurance.*   Freight insurance is written to protect the owner of the vessel from the loss of the charges made for carrying the goods. If the ship is lost, the income which would have been earned upon the completion of the voyage is also lost. Under the freight insurance coverage, the owner of the ship is reimbursed for the loss of these charges.

4. *Protection and indemnity.*   Protection and indemnity coverage under ocean marine contracts is essentially liability insurance which protects the owner of the ship from the consequences of his negligent acts or the negligent acts of his agents. If the owner should be held legally liable for damage to a third party, the protection and indemnity coverage would provide protection against financial losses by paying those sums which the insured became legally liable to pay.

Ocean marine contracts are written in a strange and antiquated tongue and are governed by principles derived from ancient maritime practice and admiralty law. Ocean marine insurance is a fantastically complicated field, so we will confine ourselves to a brief discussion of a few of the major concepts.

**Perils insured against.**   One of the most interesting aspects of ocean marine policies is that their wording is in language and terms of the past. The perils clause in the Lloyd's policy reads as follows:

TOUCHING The adventures and Perils which we the assurers are contented to bear and to take upon us in this Voyage, they are, of the Seas, Men-of-War, Fire, Enemies, Pirates, Rovers, Thieves, Jettisons, Letters of Mart and Countermart, Surprisals, Taking at Sea, Arrests, Restraints and Detainments of all Kings, Princes and People, of what Nation, Condition, or Quality soever, Barratry of the Master and Mariners, and of all other like Perils, Losses and Misfortunes that have or shall come to the Hurt, Detriment, or Damage of the said Goods and Merchandise and Ship, etc., or any Part thereof.[8]

The clause is an all-risk insuring agreement but with certain limitations. Damage arising from perils "of the seas" is covered, and here the clause is definitely all-risk. Damage could be caused by waves, the ship stranding on reefs or rocks, lightning, collisions, or the ship could sink from any number of causes due to perils of the sea. The list of such perils is almost endless. The clause also provides for coverage for "perils on the seas" specifically listed, including fires, pirates, thieves, jettisons,[9] barratry,[10] and all other *like* perils. The coverage for perils on the seas then does not provide coverage for anything that could happen on the seas, but only loss or damage arising from perils of the same nature as those specifically listed. In addition to the specified perils, marine policies are frequently expanded to include others. A good example is the "Inchmaree clause" which covers bursting of boilers and latent defect in machinery or errors in navigation or management of the vessel by the master or crew.[11]

Certain perils that would otherwise be included in the broad insuring agreement are specifically excluded. The two most important exclusions are the free of capture and seizure (FC&S) clause and the strike, riot, and civil commotion (SR&CC) clause. The FC&S clause excludes war in all its aspects, including collision with a mine or torpedo where there was no hostile act. The policy could be made to include the war peril simply by deleting the FC&S clause, but the common practice is to issue a separate war risk policy to provide coverage for the perils of war. The SR&CC clause excludes loss or

[8]The wording was adopted in 1779 and is still in use. There are, of course, good reasons for the continued utilization of wording so antiquated. Almost every word in the Lloyd's policy has been the subject of a court decision, so while the wording is quaint, there is no doubt about its meaning, and any material change might weaken the legal force of the document.

[9]Jettison is the voluntary act of destruction in which cargo is cast overboard in order to save the ship.

[10]Barratry involves a situation in which the master and/or mariners steal the ship and its cargo, willfully sink or desert the ship, or put the ship in peril by disobeying instructions.

[11]This clause is named after the ship Inchmaree, which suffered loss as a result of breakage of a pump resulting from negligence in maintenance by the crew. The British House of Lords decided that the loss was not covered, since it was not of the same nature as a "peril on the sea." To counteract this decision the Inchmaree clause was added to hull policies.

damage caused by the acts of strikers, rioters, or persons engaged in civil commotion. This exclusion may be deleted if the underwriter is willing to assume the risk.

**Average conditions.** The term "average" is considered by many persons to be the most important single word in the terminology of ocean marine insurance. It is synonomous with "partial loss."[12] "Average" or loss under an ocean marine policy may be a "particular average" or "general average." A "particular average" is defined as a partial loss to the property of a particular interest only. It is borne entirely by the owner of the property involved in the loss. A particular average is contrasted with a general average loss, which is a loss that is borne by all parties to the venture.

**General average losses.** The general average loss is based on ancient maritime law and requires that all persons involved in a venture share in the loss of the goods of one individual that are sacrificed to save the entire venture. The simplest example of a general average loss involves jettison of a part of the cargo to lighten the ship in time of stress. If goods are intentionally jettisoned in an attempt to save the ship, and the attempt is successful, the ship owner and the other cargo owners will share in the loss of the jettisoned cargo with its owner, based on the proportion of the total value of the venture each owned. To illustrate, assume that a ship, valued at $5 million is carrying $5 million in cargo. The cargo is owned by five different parties, with each party's cargo valued at $1 million. In the middle of the voyage, the ship runs into bad weather and is in danger of sinking. To lighten the ship, the goods belonging to X are thrown overboard. The jettison is successful, and the ship reaches port safely. The entire burden of the loss will not fall on X or upon his insurer. He will be forced to bear 10% of the loss, since this was the proportion of the total venture that he owned. If his cargo was insured, his insurer will indemnify him for this 10%. The owner of the ship will bear 50% of the value of the cargo jettisoned, and each of the remaining cargo owners will bear 10%. The other parties become liable to X for their share of the general average loss. Under the terms of the ocean marine policy, the insurance company insuring each of the participants will pay their insured's share of the general average loss. Amounts payable for general average and salvage charges[13] are in addition to the amount payable for loss of the insured's property.

---

[12] "Average" as used in marine insurance comes from the French word *avarie* meaning "damage."

[13] Salvage charges are expenses payable to third parties known as *salvors* for assistance rendered in saving property exposed to loss. Such charges may be incurred under contract, or they may be incurred to parties acting independently of any contractual obligation. For example, the ship owner and cargo owners might be assessed salvage charges if the ship was in danger of sinking and was forced to accept help from another vessel in order to reach port.

**The free of particular average clause.**    The free of particular average (FPA) clause of the ocean marine policy is essentially an exclusion of partial losses. The clause specifies that partial losses resulting from the perils of the sea are recoverable, but only if the vessel has been stranded, sunk, on fire, or in a collision.[14] Partial losses resulting from other causes are not covered. In some cases, the FPA clause applies only to losses that are less than some specified percentage of the insured value. For example, the contract may state that the coverage is "free of particular average under 3%...." In this instance, the clause acts as a franchise deductible—if the loss is less than 3%, it is not covered; if it exceeds 3% of the amount of insurance, it is covered in full.

**Valuation.**    A brief comment concerning valuation in the field of ocean marine insurance seems appropriate at this point. It is important to recall that almost all ocean marine policies are valued contracts. You will recall that in a valued policy, the face amount of the insurance is payable in the event of a total loss. In addition, most ocean marine policies are interpreted as if they contained a 100% coinsurance clause. The policy does not specifically contain the 100% coinsurance clause, but the legal custom of 100% insurance to value has been in existence for so long that legally it is considered to be a condition of the contract.

**Implied warranties.**    In addition to the express warranties stated in the contract, ocean marine contracts involve four warranties that are not stated but, rather, are implied. In making the contract, the parties agree by implication that certain conditions exist and that certain rules will be followed in the conduct of the voyage. The first involves legal conduct, and it is warranted that the venture is not illegal. The second is that the vessel is seaworthy.[15] The third involves prompt attachment of the risk. Since weather conditions may affect the risk involved, the underwriter has a right to assume that insurance purchased on a shipment of goods in May will not be providing protection against loss on a voyage in the middle of January. The final warranty is that of no deviation. Here, it is warranted that the vessel will proceed without deviation by the most direct or customary route. There are excusable deviations, such as deviation arising from stress of weather or an errand of mercy to save life, but inexcusable deviations will void the policy.

---

[14] There are actually two forms of the FPA clause: free of particular average English conditions and free of particular average American conditions. The English conditions merely require that one of the enumerated perils has taken place, without requiring that the damage result from the peril. The American conditions require that the damage must be caused by stranding, sinking, burning, or collision.

[15] The owner of cargo shipped on someone else's vessel probably has little opportunity to verify the seaworthiness of the vessel. Therefore, the cargo policy typically contains a provision in which the seaworthiness of the vessel is admitted.

**The warehouse-to-warehouse clause.** Unless the policy designates to the contrary, coverage is provided only from the time the goods are actually loaded on the transporting vessel. However, since a shipment may originate at a point far from the place of ocean shipment, policies may be endorsed to cover the goods during transportation to the vessel. In these cases, it is customary for the ocean marine insurer to endorse the policy to provide coverage for the entire exposure from the time the goods leave the premises of the shipper until they arrive at the premises of the consignee under the warehouse-to-warehouse clause.

### Inland Marine Insurance

Inland marine insurance is much younger than ocean marine, having developed as an outgrowth of the warehouse-to-warehouse clause. It is designed to provide coverage on property that is exposed to loss as a result of transportation. We divide inland marine coverages into five distinct classes:

1. Transportation forms, which are designed to cover shipments of goods by rail, motor carrier, or air carrier. These include forms which cover the interest or legal liability of the carrier and forms designed to protect the owner of the goods against loss resulting from damage to his goods.
2. Floater policies designed to insure personal property, including business personal property, which by its nature is subject to the perils of transportation. Although coverage may be provided both on and off the premises of the insured, the primary coverage is while away from the premises.
3. Dealer forms, which are designed to cover the stocks of merchandise of certain types of businesses, such as jewelers and furriers. These forms cover the merchandise while it is on the insured's premises and also provide incidental off-premises coverage.
4. The forms designed to cover instrumentalities of transportation and communication. These provide a broad form of all-risk coverage on fixed objects such as bridges, tunnels, pipelines, power transmission lines, radio and television communication equipment, and the like.
5. The bailee forms, which are designed to cover goods which are in the custody of someone other than the owner to whom the goods have been entrusted. These forms may be written to cover the interest of the bailee only, or to cover the interest of the bailor as well.

Here we are concerned primarily with the first three of these classifications; the transportation forms, the floater policies, and the dealers forms. The bailee forms will be discussed in Chapter 22, which deals with liability coverages for business firms. The transportation forms designed to protect common carriers against liability losses arising out of damage to property in their care will also be treated along with the liability coverages.

**Transportation forms.**    Damage to property in transit may cause financial loss to two interests: the owner of the goods and the person or organization to whom the goods have been entrusted for transportation. Inland marine policies are written to protect against both types of losses, and there are transportation forms designed for the owner of the goods, and a trucker's liability form designed for the carrier. The owner's transportation forms are designed to protect the insured against loss or damage of goods in transit, usually by express, railroad freight, public trucking firms, owner's trucks, coastwise and inland steamers, air, or any combination of these.

The owner of goods may ship these goods by common carrier, contract carrier, or his own trucks. A common carrier is one offering scheduled service between designated points. A contract carrier, as the name implies, carries goods under a contract, without scheduled routes, times, or charges. An important distinction between contract and common carriers exists regarding their liability for damage to property in their custody. A contract carrier is legally liable as a bailee, and has an obligation to exercise care with respect to the goods; it may be held liable for any damage arising out of its negligence. The legal liability of a common carrier is much stricter. Only a few causes of loss are considered to be beyond the control of the common carrier, and with the exception of these exclusions, a common carrier is legally liable for any loss or damage to goods it transports.

The common carrier can, and frequently does, limit its liability[16] through the use of a "released bill of lading," under the terms of which the carrier specifices the maximum amount for which it will be held liable. For example, a common carrier may use a bill of lading with the stipulation that its liability will be limited to 0.50 per pound. Under the terms of the Interstate Commerce Act, as amended, a common carrier may limit its liability if it provides for a difference in rates, offering a lower rate to those who are willing to accept this limitation, and charging a higher rate for those who do not accept the released bill of lading.

Even though the legal liability of the common carrier is extremely broad, there are some instances in which the carrier might not be held liable. In addition, it has been noted that carriers frequently make use of the released bill of lading. Both these factors constitute reasons why the owner of the goods being shipped may desire coverage on his goods in addition to that carried by the trucker. In addition to these reasons, the owner of the goods may not want to wait until he can collect from the trucker for the loss. It may be more convenient to collect from his own insurer and then permit the insurer to subrogate against the trucker. For these reasons, many businesses purchase policies to cover their goods while in transit. Since the liability of contract carriers is even more limited than that of common carriers, goods

[16]The liability exposure of the common carrier will be discussed in greater detail in Chapter 22.

shipped by contract carrier must also be insured. Finally, in those instances in which the owner ships goods on his own trucks, the possibility of recovery from another party is slight, and insurance must often be obtained. The decision as to whether goods in transit should be insured depends on the value of such goods, possible concentrations of such values, and the ability of the business to withstand such a loss.

The transportation forms are not controlled, and as a result there are no standard forms. Policies are written to meet the requirements of individual risks. The basic contract used to insure property in transit is the Inland Transit Policy, which may be modified to meet the specific situation of the owner of the goods. There are forms designed to cover property in the custody of railroads and coastwise shipping firms or on trucks used in connection with railroads and steamers, and there is a railway express form for those who ship by truck. In addition, there is an air-cargo form available for those who ship by airplane. These forms cover the property while it is in the hands of common carriers. Other forms provide coverage for goods shipped by contract carrier or on the owner's own trucks.

Coverage is normally on a named peril basis, covering fire and lightning, and the perils of extended coverage (except strike, riot, and civil commotion, which are optional), plus the "perils of transportation," which include flood, collision, overturn of a vehicle, bridge collapse, derailment, earthquake, and landslide. Theft coverage is also available by endorsement. The limit of liability applies on any one truck or at any one place, with a further limit on any one disaster.

There are two standard approaches to insuring goods in transit. Under the "Annual Transit Policy," all shipments during the year are insured. The insured pays a deposit premium at the inception, based on estimated shipments. At the end of the year, an adjustment is made based on actual shipments as disclosed by the insured's records. The "Trip Transit Policy" covers specified lots of goods for a specified trip. The trip transit coverage may be written in a specific policy, or it may be written under a master policy with certificates of insurance for each trip.

Other transportation forms include the "Parcel Post Policy," designed for firms that make frequent parcel post shipments and desire to insure these with a commercial insurer rather than purchase government insurance, and the "Registered Mail Policy," designed for banks and other businesses that ship securities, money, or other valuable property by registered mail or express.

**Business floater policies.**    Merchandise being shipped is not the only business property that is likely to be exposed to damage away from the business premises. There are many classes of business property which are mobile in nature and which may be exposed to such damage. To meet the need for protection of these classes of property, there are a large number of inland marine floater policies. In general, we may divide these business floaters as follows:

1. *Equipment Floaters.* These are designed to cover business property not held for sale or on consignment, that is in the hands of the owner to be used for its intended purpose.
2. *Processing and Storage Floaters.* These are designed to cover property in temporary storage and property undergoing processing outside the owner's premises.
3. *Consignment or Sales Floaters.* These are designed to cover goods being held for sale under consignment, goods being installed, or goods being sold under an installment plan.

A slight indication of the scope of the classes that may be insured under the various business floaters may be gained by the following list of floaters for which the nationwide definition makes provision:

| | |
|---|---|
| Radium Floaters | Installation Floaters |
| Pattern and Die Floaters | Manufacturers Output Policy |
| Theatrical Floaters | Mobile Equipment Floaters |
| Film Floaters | Installment Sales and Leased Property |
| Salesmen's Sample Floaters | Garment Contractor's Floaters |
| Live Animal Floaters | Wool Grower's Floaters |

The coverage of these forms may be written on an all-risk or named peril basis, and the coverage varies under different forms. In some cases, the coverage is all-risk, in other classes it is named peril. In several classes, the insured has a choice between all-risk and named peril coverage. Additionally, the coverage may be written on a scheduled or blanket basis. Once again, a detailed analysis of each form of coverage available is impractical, but a very brief outline of several of them should serve to illustrate the nature of the coverage and some of their more important features and provisions.

*Contractor's Equipment Floater.* This form is designed to cover mobile equipment of practically any nature from hand tools to large machines. It can be written to cover equipment used by a contractor or equipment which may be rented to others. The named peril form covers fire, lightning, explosion, windstorm, flood, collapse of bridges, and docks and, subject to a deductible, theft, collision, upset, and overturning. There is an all-risk form, subject to the normal exclusions, written with a deductible. The coverage is usually written on a schedule basis, with a specific amount of insurance for each item. In some cases, blanket coverage is written, subject to a coinsurance requirement.

*Installation Floater.* This is designed to cover property consisting principally of machinery and equipment which is to be installed, while that property is in transit to the place of installation, and during the period of installation and testing. Building materials may be covered while in transit to the place of installation and after arrival at the place of installation, but coverage terminates when such materials are installed or become a physical part of the building, or when the seller's interest ceases. The perils that may be covered under this form vary from fire and the perils of transportation to all-risk coverage. The form may be written to cover one contract, reporting or nonreporting, or to cover all contracts the insured enters into in the future on a reporting basis.

*Floor Plan Merchandise Form.* This coverage is designed to insure merchandise subject to a floor plan (or similar financing arrangement) while the goods are in the hands of the dealer. Under a floor plan arrangement, the dealer borrows from a financial institution, using the stock of merchandise as security. The form covers the dealer's interest, and may also be written to cover the interest of the lender only, or it may be written to cover the interest of both. Coverage is on an all-risk basis, and attaches to merchandise that is specifically identifiable as encumbered to a bank or lending institution.

*Installment Sales Floater.* This is designed for businesses which sell merchandise (such as household furniture, appliances, etc.) on installment sales arrangements. There are two forms of the coverage available: one covers the insured's interest in the property as measured by the unpaid balance, and the other covers the interest of both the buyer and the seller. Coverage applies from the time the merchandise leaves the seller's shipping room and continues at the purchaser's premises until the indebtedness has been satisfied or until the merchandise is returned to the seller's premises. The coverage may be on a named peril or all-risk basis.

**Dealer's insurance.** Most inland marine policies are designed to cover insured property while it is away from the named insured's premises. The dealer's forms represent an exception to this principle. The merchandise of certain types of dealers may be insured both on and off premises under the inland marine forms. The eligible classes are limited to dealers in jewels, furs, musical instruments, cameras, equipment, and fine art. Essentially, these forms provide coverage on the business personal property of the insured while principally located at the business premises, but with incidental floater coverage away from the premises. Three of the more important of the dealer's forms are discussed briefly below to indicate the general nature of this form of coverage.

*Jeweler's Block Policy.*[17] This is designed to insure the stock of the

---

[17] The term "block" as used in conjunction with the Jeweler's Block and Furrier's Block policies comes from the French *en bloc*, which means "all together." Thus, block policies are intended to cover all the property of the business in a single contract.

jeweler, but covers other property as well. Three different classes of property are covered: stock owned by the jeweler, customers' goods in the custody of the jeweler, and goods of other jewelers that have been entrusted to the insured. Coverage on customers' goods includes both the interest of the insured and the customer, so coverage is provided regardless of whether the jeweler is legally liable for the loss. Coverage on goods belonging to other jewelers includes only the insured's interest, so the policy provides coverage on these goods only if the insured is liable, and then only for the extent of his liability. The coverage is written on an all-risk basis, subject to the normal exclusions.

*Furrier's Block Policy.*    This is quite similar to the Jeweler's Block Policy discussed above. It covers the stock of furs the insured carries for sale on an all-risk basis. It does not, however, cover the furs of customers which are in storage or being worked on.[18]

*Equipment Dealer's Policy.*    This is designed to cover farm implement dealers or heavy machinery dealers for loss or damage to their stock of equipment or customers' property while on their premises, in transit, or elsewhere. The policy provides all-risk coverage, again subject to the normal exclusions. Certain classes of property are also specifically excluded from coverage:

1. Automobiles, motortrucks, motorcycles, aircraft, or watercraft
2. Property sold by or under encumbrance to the insured, or property leased or rented by the insured to others after it leaves the custody of the insured or an employee of the insured
3. Property while in the course of manufacture

### THE SPECIAL MULTI-PERIL PROGRAM

The introduction of the Special Multi-Peril (SMP) program was one of the most significant developments in the multiple-line trend. The SMP is a package policy approach to insurance for commercial risks, which is similar in certain respects to the Homeowners program for residential risks. Like the Homeowners program, the SMP permits the insured to purchase one policy with several insuring agreements. The coverage can be tailored to meet the needs of eligible risks, covering most of the risks previously insured under separate contracts. The only major coverages that cannot be included in the SMP program are workmen's compensation, automobile coverage, and surety bonds. As a result of the packaging, there are fewer gaps in coverage, less overlapping, and premium savings for the insured. The aspect of the SMP that has received by far the greatest attention is the package discount

---

[18] Coverage for customers property is afforded under a Furriers' Customer Policy, discussed in Chapter 22.

the program entails. Depending on the type of business, discounts range from 15% to 20%.

The program has been in effect since late in 1960, when it was originally developed for the service industries. When it was first introduced, it included forms and rates for only one class of business—motels. Since that time, the SMP program has been extended to include hotels, apartment houses, offices, mercantile risks, institutional risks, processing risks, and most recently, manufacturing and industrial risks.

**Eligibility.**   One chief feature of the SMP program is a set of rather strict underwriting rules and eligibility requirements. There are seven separate programs, each with its own set of eligibility rules, designed to provide package protection for over 700 classifications of risks. The seven programs and the business for which they are designed are outlined briefly below.

*Motel–hotel program.*   Under this program, the SMP policy may be written to insure hotels, motor inns, motels, or tourists' courts, including operations incidental or necessary thereto.

*Apartment house program.*   This program includes apartment houses containing three or more units, each of which is equipped with cooking facilities. Rooming or boarding houses, or habitational structures providing facilities for transients are not eligible.

*Office program.*   Under the office program, the SMP policy may be written to provide coverage on buildings and their contents which are used principally for office purposes and which are not located on the premises of a manufacturing plant. The policy may also be written for a tenant whose occupancy is principally for office purposes, located in a building of any general occupancy, except one in which manufacturing operations exceed 25% of the area.

*Mercantile program.*   This program is designed to provide coverage for mercantile establishments and auxiliary warehouses and buildings occupied principally by eligible mercantile establishments. Firms that are engaged in manufacturing at the described premises and certain other classes such as automobile service stations, bars and grills, pawnbrokers, and auctions are not eligible.

*Institutional program.*   The institutional program provides for coverage on educational, religious, sanatory, charitable, government, and nonprofit organizations.

*Processing and service program.*   This program provides for insuring a wide range of processing and service businesses. The definition of eligible businesses includes such firms as bottlers, dry cleaners and laundries, installation services, service and repair businesses, laboratories, printers, warehouses, and certain other miscellaneous businesses.

*Industrial policy.* This policy is intended for manufacturing businesses and certain processing businesses that are not eligible for the processing program. Certain classes of risks are specifically excluded from eligibility: mining; public utilities, fuel, gas, or petroleum; auto repairing and rebuilding.

## The Special Multi-Peril Policy

It would have been needlessly expensive and complicated to provide a separate multiple-line contract for each of the specific groups within the overall commercial class. Instead, the program is built around a single contract, the Special Multi-Peril Policy, which can be modified and adapted to each of the seven individual programs. The policy consists of a jacket with a declarations page, the insuring agreement, and three pages of provisions. In addition, there are over 100 forms and endorsements that may be used to complete and modify the basic contract. The coverages are divided into four sections in the policy:

| | |
|---|---|
| Section I | Property coverage |
| Section II | Liability coverage |
| Section III | Crime coverage |
| Section IV | Boiler and machinery coverage |

The SMP program is a multiple-line program in the fullest sense of the term. Sections I and II are mandatory. The minimum coverages required are fire and extended coverage on the insured's buildings and contents (if they are under common ownership), and premises and operations liability coverage. With this base of coverage as a minimum, there is a wide range of optional coverages, including additional perils on the building and contents, all-risk, replacement cost, time-element, crime, boiler and machinery, glass and neon sign, premises medical payments, products liability, comprehensive general liability, and a vast array of other coverages.

## Questions for Discussion and Review

**1.** Insurance to value is of paramount importance in the operation of the insurance mechanism. Describe the technique used to induce the insured to carry insurance to value in each of the following fields of coverage: (a) fire insurance; (b) extended coverage; (c) reporting forms (fire); (d) blanket insurance (fire); (e) business interruption insurance; (f) extra expense insurance; (g) the open-stock burglary policy; (h) fidelity bonds.

**2.** The Widget Manufacturing Company insures its plant against loss by fire for $900,000, under a policy written with an 80% coinsurance clause. At the time that a $600,000 loss takes place, it is determined that the building is worth $1,250,000. How much will the insurer pay? How much would be paid in the event of a total loss?

**3.** Although it is difficult to compare the insurable exposures of a business firm with those of an individual, there are similarities. Which of the coverages studied in this chapter would a retail clothing store have to buy to have the same types of protection a family enjoys under a Homeowners policy?

**4.** With respect to each type of coverage discussed in the chapter, indicate whether the coverage would probably be considered "essential," "recommended," or "available" in programming insurance for the largest bookstore on or near your campus.

**5.** You have prepared a recommendation with respect to insurance coverage for your father, who runs a small business. He says, "If I buy all the insurance you say I would need to protect against those losses that would bankrupt me, the premiums will bankrupt me. At least if I don't buy the insurance, I will have a chance of surviving." Any comment on your part?

### Suggestions for Additional Reading

*Fire, Casualty and Surety Bulletins,* Casualty and Surety Volume, "Bonds," "Burglary," and "Power Plant" Sections. Cincinnati, Ohio: The National Underwriter Co.

*Fire, Casualty and Surety Bulletins,* Fire and Marine Volume, "Commercial Multi-Peril," "Miscellaneous Fire," "Fire," "Business Interruptions," "Inland Marine," and "Consequential" Sections. Cincinnati, Ohio: The National Underwriter Co.

Gordis, P. *Property and Casualty Insurance,* 17th ed. Indianapolis, Ind.: The Rough Notes Co., 1970, Chaps. 3–9, 11–15, 17, 21, 22, 35.

Klein, H. C. *Business Interruption Insurance.* Indianapolis, Ind.: The Rough Notes Co., 1957.

Kulp, C. A. and Hall, J. *Casualty Insurance,* 4th ed. New York: Ronald Press, 1968, Chaps. 14–16.

Long, J. D. and Gregg, D. W. *Property and Liability Insurance Handbook.* Homewood, Ill.: Richard D. Irwin, 1965, Chaps. 5–10, 19, 23–27, 41 43, 50.

Magee, J. H. and Serbein, O. N. *Property and Liability Insurance,* 4th ed. Homewood, Ill.: Richard D. Irwin, 1967, Chaps. 9–15, 21.

Rodda, W. H. *Inland Marine and Transportation Insurance,* 2nd ed. Englewood Cliffs, N.J.: Prentice-Hall, 1958.

Stevens, W. L. *A Producer's Boiler and Machinery Notebook.* Cincinnati, Ohio: The National Underwriter Co., 1963.

Williams, C. A., Jr. and Heins, R. M. *Risk Management and Insurance,* 2nd ed. New York: McGraw-Hill, 1971, Chap. 17.

Winter, W. D. *Marine Insurance,* 3rd ed. New York: McGraw-Hill, 1952.

*1967 Special Multi-peril Guide.* Indianapolis, Ind.: The Rough Notes Co., 1967.

# 22 Commercial Liability Coverages

*If you have known one, you have known them all.*

—Terence, *Phormio*

The liability exposures that arise in connection with business operations are both numerous and varied, and for the business firm as for the individual, there is virtually no calculable limit to the losses that can arise from legal liability. The number of sources from which liability can result multiplies with the complexity of the business, and as a result the field of commercial liability is a good deal more complicated than the liability coverages for the individual. In this chapter, we will examine the liability exposure of the business firm and some of the insurance contracts available to protect against financial losses resulting from this exposure.

As noted in Chapter 18, liability coverages can be conveniently divided into three classes: employers' liability and workmen's compensation, automobile liability, and general liability. The principles surrounding the liability of an employer to his employees and the modifications of this liability through workmen's compensation laws will be examined in Chapter 23. Here, we are concerned primarily with general liability and automobile liability coverages. In addition, we will discuss the bailee liability coverages and the liability coverages for common carriers.[1]

---

[1] Bailee liability coverages and the liability coverages for common carriers are classed as inland marine coverages and are traditionally treated in connection with the floater policies discussed in Chapter 21. The authors feel that they are more appropriately treated in this section along with the other liability coverages.

## GENERAL LIABILITY EXPOSURES

Before examining the various general liability contracts that are designed to protect the firm against the peril of legal liability, it may be helpful to examine the major areas that these contracts are designed to protect against. In general, these liability forms provide protection against nonautomobile liability which does not involve injuries to employees. Because business firms vary greatly in their activities, their liability exposures also vary considerably, but every business firm is subject to one or a combination of the liability exposures described below.

### Ownership and Maintenance of Premises

The basic exposure the individual faces in connection with the ownership of his home also exists for the business firm. The owner or a tenant of a building may be held legally liable for damages in the event a member of the public is injured, or damage to property of others results from a condition in, or arising out of, the premises. There is almost no end to the list of possible defects that may cause injury—the student's imagination will provide an adequate substitute for a listing of such defects.

### Conduct of Business Operations

In addition to the liability exposures which exist in connection with premises occupied, the individual or firm may be held liable if a member of the public or the property of others is injured by some activity of the owner or an employee, either on or away from the premises. For example, employees of a contractor may injure someone at some place other than the firm's premises. The liability in connection with the ownership and maintenance of the premises and the conduct of business operations both on and away from the premises is covered under the general liability coverage entitled "Premises and Operations Coverage."

### Products

The manufacturer or distributor of a faulty product that injures someone or damages property may be held legally liable. As a matter of fact, any firm that has anything to do with a product that eventually reaches the public faces a risk in this connection, regardless of whether the firm is a manufacturer, wholesaler, or retailer. In general, legal liability in connection with products may arise in one of two ways: on the basis of negligence and on the basis of warranty.

Product liability based on negligence follows from the principles discussed in Chapter 17. If a product is negligently made or improperly designed, or if proper warning is not given to the consumer about dangerous qualities of the product, the manufacturer may be held to have been negligent and can be held responsible for any resulting injury or damage. Liability from the sale of products can also arise under the doctrine of "breach of warranty," and it is becoming much more common to impose liability for breach of warranty than for negligence.

When a product is sold, it is generally warranted that it is fit for the purpose intended. If it should prove defective and injurious in use or consumption, the warranty is breached and liability can result. Breach of warranty is a type of absolute liability. It is immaterial whether due care was exercised in the manufacture. For this reason, injured persons prefer to establish liability on the rather simple basis of breach of warranty rather than on the principle of negligence, in which duty and failure to exercise reasonable care must be proved. The major problem in using breach of warranty as the basis for a claim for injuries is that traditionally there must be privity of contract between the injured party and the person against whom suit is brought. Under common law, the seller or distributor of a product could be liable for breach of warranty only to those with whom he was in privity of contract, i.e., only those with whom he had direct contractural relations. This means that he could be liable only for the injuries to the purchaser and not to any other user of the product. For example, if Mr. Jones purchases a loaf of bread at the local bakery, eats it, and becomes seriously ill because of the ingredients, he could obtain damages under the doctrine of breach of warranty. However, if Jones Jr. eats the bread and becomes ill, the child could not obtain damages under common law on the basis of breach of warranty, because no contractual relationship existed between the child and the bakery. Strict application of the requirement of privity of contract also means that the consumer could not bring action against the manufacturer on the breach of warranty basis, again because there is no privity of contract between the manufacturer and the consumer. This means that under the doctrine of warranty, most claims for breach of warranty would have to be against the immediate seller, such as the retailer, rather than against the manufacturer. However, in an ever-increasing number of cases, the courts are abandoning the requirement of privity of contract and permitting suits based on breach of warranty to be brought against the manufacturer as well as the retailer, and also permitting persons other than the direct purchaser to bring action based on the breach of warranty doctrine.

In most cases, the Premises and Operations Coverage protects against liability arising out of products while they are still on the insured's premises, but this coverage does not apply after the products have been turned over to the customer and he has left the premises. Coverage for liability arising out of products after they have been relinquished to the customer must be obtained under a special coverage designed to protect against liability arising out of products.

### Completed Operations

The completed operations exposure is quite similar to the products exposure and consists of the possibility of liability arising out of work that has been performed by the firm. Completed operations may represent a liability exposure for all firms that do construction or installation work, servicing or repair. Such work is, in a sense, the product of the firm, and any damage arising out of it could result in liability. While the work is being performed, the exposure is an operations exposure, and is covered under the Premises and Operations Coverage. Once the work has been completed, the Premises and Operations Coverage no longer applies. The legal liability in connection with products and completed operations exposures are both covered under the Products and Completed Operations Coverage.

### Contingent Liability

It is possible for an individual or a business to be held legally liable because of work performed by independent contractors. We have seen already that an employer can be held liable for the acts of his employees, but this is based on the principle that the employer has some control over the actions of the employee, and in the case of an independent contractor, very little control is exercised. As a result, the general rule is that the principal is not liable for the negligent acts of independent contractors, but there are important exceptions. First, if the work being performed by the independent contractor is unlawful in itself, the principal may be held liable. In addition, the principal may be held liable because there are certain duties and obligations that cannot be delegated. Also, if the principal exercises any supervision, liability may be imposed on him for injuries. Finally, liability for negligence normally cannot be transferred in those situations in which the work is inherently dangerous. Thus, in many instances, the negligence of the independent contractor may be imputed to the owner of the property who has engaged the contractor. Every firm which may have occasion to engage contractors, or contractors who engage subcontractors, to engage in construction, demolition, alteration, or repair has a contingent liability exposure. This exposure is protected against by the Owners and Contractor Protective Liability Coverage, which is also called Independent Contractors Coverage.

### Contractural Liability

In certain instances, it also is possible that a business firm (or an individual) may, by means of a written or oral contract, become liable for the negligent acts of another. This should not be confused with the vicarious liability situation, in which the principal becomes liable for the acts of the agent. Here, the legal liability for the negligent behavior of someone else is incurred because of a voluntary assumption of that liability through a contractual agreement. For example, it is not unusual in construction contracts to include a provision in which one party agrees to hold the other harmless for all claims for injuries arising out of the performance of the work. In such cases, the "indemnitor" (i.e., the individual who assumes the liability) promises to pay any judgments which might be entered against the other party (the indemnitee) arising out of the work. Some types of contractual liability are covered automatically under the Premises and Operations Liability Coverage, but other contracts must be specifically insured under Contractual Liability Coverage.

### Miscellaneous Exposures

In addition to these major exposures, which are covered under the liability coverages mentioned, there may be certain additional exposures which result from gaps or exclusions in the contracts. For example, most general liability policies contain the same "care, custody, and control" exclusion that we saw in the Comprehensive Personal Liability Policy (CPL), and while this exclusion may be troublesome for the individual, it creates an unbearable burden for the business firm whose primary function involves working on the property of others. In addition, exposures may result from specialized activities in which the firm engages. In many cases, it is possible to eliminate the gaps in coverage under the general liability policies by endorsement, and specialized forms of coverage are available for most businesses with specialized needs.

## GENERAL LIABILITY COVERAGES

The General Liability contracts permit the combination of two or more types of liability insurance in a single policy by means of a policy jacket and coverage parts with provisions unique to each type of liability insurance. The coverage parts are inserted in the policy jacket in various combinations to provide the desired coverage.

### General Provisions

The policy jacket contains the provisions that are applicable to both General Liability and Comprehensive Automobile Liability. Since space does not permit a detailed examination of all these provisions, only a few of the more important ones will be discussed.

**Coverage is on an "occurrence" basis.**   At one time, the insuring agreement of most liability policies restricted coverage to liability of the insured for bodily injury or property damage that was caused by "accident." An accident is defined as a "sudden, unexpected and undesigned event, identifiable as to time and place." As a result, such policies did not include coverage for damage that took place over an extended period of time. In the 1966 revision of the general liability forms, the insuring agreement was changed to cover bodily injury or property damage caused by "occurrence." The term "occurrence" is defined in the policy as an accident, ". . . including injurious exposure to conditions, which results during the policy period, in bodily injury or property damage neither expected nor intended." The extension of the term to include "injurious exposure to conditions" greatly increases the scope of the coverage by providing coverage for losses that are not sudden and not identifiable specifically as to time. For example, coverage would be provided for damage caused by a pile-driving operation to buildings in the vicinity, even though the exact time of the damage could not be fixed.

**Supplementary payments.** Under the supplementary payments section, the company promises to pay, in addition to the limits of liability:

(a) All expenses incurred by the company in defending a suit against the insured and interest on the amount of the judgment from the time it is awarded until it is paid.

(b) premiums on appeal bonds required in such suits, and the cost of bail bonds required of an insured in connection with accidents and traffic law violations involving vehicles which are covered under the policy. The company is not obligated to furnish such bonds.

(c) expenses which are incurred for first aid to others at the time of an accident involving bodily injury to which the policy applies.

(d) other expenses incurred by the insured at the request of the company, including loss of wages up to $25 per day while attending trials or hearings at the company's request.

**Duties of the insured.** In addition to provisions relating to the right of the company to inspect the premises, premium audits, etc., the policy sets forth certain obligations of the insured, the most important of which involve the duties of the insured in the event of loss:

(a) in the event of an occurrence which may give rise to a claim under the policy, the insured must give written notice to the company or its authorized agents as soon as possible.

(b) in the event of a loss the insured is required to take all reasonable steps to prevent other bodily injury or property damage from arising out of the same or a similar condition. These steps are to be taken at the insured's expense, and such expenses are not recoverable under the policy.

(c) if claim is made or suit is brought, the insured must immediately forward to the company every demand, notice, summons, or other process which he receives.

(d) the insured must cooperate with the company and at the company's request, assist in making settlement. The insured must not, except at his own cost, voluntarily make any payment or assume any obligation, other than first aid at the time of the accident.

The requirement that the insured take steps to prevent other bodily injury or property damage from arising out of the same or a similar condition which caused a loss is intended to eliminate coverage for a second accident which results from the same defect in premises or other conditions. If a customer trips on a loose stair tread and is injured, the insured is required by the policy provision to have the stair tread repaired. If he does not do so, the company may maintain that he has violated one of the policy conditions and that a loss involving a second accident from the stair tread is not covered.

### The Coverage Parts

A coverage part identifies the type of insurance for which coverage is provided. Each of the coverage parts contains the basic insuring agreement for bodily injury and property damage and the agreement pertaining to defense, and the exclusions applicable to the respective coverage. Each coverage part also includes a separate schedule for exposures, rates, and premiums applicable to the hazards of the respective coverage. Separate coverage parts are provided for over twenty specialized liability needs; we will examine a few of the more important of them.

**Premises and Operations Coverage.** Coverage for the premises and operations exposure is provided under one of three basic forms: the Owners', Landlords', and Tenants' Coverage Part (OL&T), the Manufacturers' and Contractors' Coverage Part (M&C); or the Comprehensive General Liability Coverage Part. The OL&T and the M&C do not provide coverage for products and completed operations, and there is no provision for including this coverage in either of these forms, so if the insured has an exposure in these areas, the Premises and Operations Coverage must be written under the Comprehensive General Liability Coverage Part,[2] which provides for the inclusion of the products and completed operations coverage. The OL&T is used for risks where the exposure results primarily from property owner-

---

[2] The Comprehensive General Liability Policy will be discussed later in this chapter. In general, however, the premises and operations coverage of that form is essentially the same as that of the OL&T and M&C discussed above.

ship and mercantile operations. It is designed to insure owners and lessees of buildings, vacant land, mercantile establishments of all kinds, and various service businesses of a nonmanufacturing nature. The M&C form is used, as its title indicates, for manufacturing and contracting firms. Both forms provide Premises and Operations Coverage, including coverage on elevators.[3]

The coverage under both forms is divided into Coverage A, which covers bodily injury, and Coverage B, which covers property damage. The basic limits under either policy, which may be increased, are $5000 per person and $10,000 per occurrence for bodily injury, and $5000 per occurrence for property damage.

*Exclusions.* The coverage is, of course, subject to exclusions, and certain of these should be discussed. The first exclusion of both contracts excludes liability assumed under contract, except contracts which the policy defines as "Incidental Written Agreements." The policies afford contractual liability coverage in connection with these Incidental Written Agreements without additional premium. The contracts that are covered under the basic Premises and Operations Coverage include:

1. A lease of premises agreement
2. Easement agreements except in connection with construction or demolition on, or adjacent to, a railroad
3. Agreements required by municipal ordinance except in connection with work for the municipality
4. Railroad sidetrack agreements
5. Elevator maintenance agreements

All other contractual liability is excluded and must be covered under the contractual liability part.

In addition, the policy excludes liability arising out of automobiles or aircraft. However, the various types of equipment used by building and road contractors, such as power cranes, bulldozers, road graders, and the like, are not automobiles. This type of equipment and other vehicles which are not subject to motor vehicle registration are included within the policy definition of "mobile equipment," which is not excluded. In addition to the exclusion of automobiles and aircraft, watercraft is excluded while away from the premises.

Liability arising out of injury to employees of the insured is excluded, as are any benefits payable or required to be paid under any workmen's compensation, unemployment compensation, disability benefits, or similar law. These risks are to be insured under other forms of insurance. In addition,

[3] Prior to November 1969, an additional premium was charged for liability insurance in connection with elevators. It is now included without additional charge in almost all states.

since a separate coverage part is designed to provide protection against liability arising out of the products and completed operations hazard, the Premises and Operations Coverage Parts exclude this exposure.

The "care, custody, and control" exclusion which we have seen on several occasions is also included, providing that there is no coverage for damage to property owned by, rented to, or in the care, custody, or control of, the insured, or property for which the insured is for any purpose exercising physical control. A special exception to this exclusion provides that it does not apply to damage to property in the care, custody, or control of the insured which arises out of the use of elevators at the premises of the insured. This seems only logical. If the property damage coverage on elevators excluded damage to property in the care, custody, or control of the insured, what would it cover?[4]

One of the special problems raised by the "care, custody, and control" exclusion is the lack of coverage for damage to property rented or leased to the firm. For example, because of the exclusion, the tenant of any building becomes exposed to a special risk in connection with damage to the building he rents. If a fire occurs as a result of the negligence of the tenant or one of his employees, action for recovery may be brought by the owner of the building or by his insurance company under the provisions of the subrogation clause in the fire policy. Since the Premises and Operations Coverage excludes damage to property in the care, custody, or control of the insured, it would not provide coverage for the loss. The risk must be insured under the Fire Legal Liability Coverage.[5] As you will recall, Fire Legal Liability Coverage is automatically included in the CPL. In the case of business liability policies, it must be added by endorsement. The coverage may be limited to real property or it may include personal property as well. Although the standard form of the coverage covers liability arising out of fire only,

---

[4]Although the exclusion of damage to property in the care, custody, or control of the insured does not apply to damage caused by elevators, damage to property owned by, or rented to, the insured is still excluded. However, even this damage may be insured. Coverage for damage to the elevator itself and to property owned by, or rented to, the insured may be added through the "Elevator Collision Coverage Part."

[5]Other solutions have been proposed. One is to have the "care, custody, and control" exclusion of the general liability policies removed, but insurers are generally reluctant to do this. As an alternative, a hold-harmless agreement, in which the owner of the building waives right of recovery against the tenant in writing prior to any loss, would provide protection. However, many landlords are reluctant to enter into such agreements, or are willing to waive right of recovery only to the extent that the loss is covered by valid and collectible insurance. Naming the tenant on the landlord's fire policy would serve the same purpose, in that it would protect him from subrogation by the insurance company. The major drawback to both of the last two alternatives is that they protect the tenant from liability only if the owner carries sufficient insurance coverage himself. The tenant would still be liable for any part of a loss which the landlord did not collect under his insurance. The most effective approach remains the Fire Legal Liability Coverage.

it may be written to include other perils such as inherent explosion, the perils of extended coverage, vandalism and malicious mischief, and sprinkler leakage.

Another exclusion creating a need for a specialized coverage is the exclusion of liability arising out of the business of manufacture, sale, or serving of alcoholic beverages, or as the owner or lessor of premises used for such purposes. Liability of this kind has been imposed in a large number of states in the form of "dram shop" or liquor control laws of some kind. These laws provide for a right of action against a seller of alcoholic beverages in the event the purchaser injures a third party. The laws vary greatly in their details and particularly with respect to the number and classes of persons affected. Some are applicable only in cases in which an injury results from selling or serving liquor to a minor or intoxicated person. Others have no such qualification. Some laws provide for liability even to the intoxicated person, while others are applicable only to others injured by the intoxicated person and to such consequential situations as his family's loss of support. If the firm engages in activities which might result in liability under the dram shop law of the state, it must cover this exposure under a Dram Shop Liability Policy, a coverage which is available only in a limited market.

**Completed Operations and Products Liability Coverage Part.** The Completed Operations and Products Liability Coverage Part is used rather infrequently, since most insureds who have a need for this coverage also need Premises and Operations Coverage, and the combination of these coverages must be provided under the Comprehensive General Liability Policy. However, the provisions of this coverage part are applicable to the Completed Operations and Products Coverage when included in the Comprehensive General Liability Policy, so a discussion of the provisions at this point will provide a basis for discussion of the Comprehensive General Liability contract.

The Completed Operations and Products Coverage Part protects the insured against claims arising out of work completed by the insured or products sold. In most instances, the products portion of the coverage applies only after the product has been turned over to the customer and has left the premises. Exceptions to this are certain classes of business (such as restaurants) where the product is consumed on the premises. In these cases, the products coverage applies from the time the product is sold and relinquished to the customer.

The Completed Operations Coverage and Products Coverage apply only to bodily injury or property damage that occur during the policy period. The time at which the product was sold or the work completed does not influence the coverage. For example, if an insured sells a product in 1970, and then purchases products liability coverage in 1971, and during the course of the policy period bodily injury or property damage arises out of a product sold in 1970, the policy in effect in 1971 will cover the loss. The policy that was in effect when the product was manufactured or sold is not applicable.

*Exclusions.*   In addition to the exclusions of contractual liability, liquor liability, workmen's compensation, and injury to employees, the products coverage part contains four exclusions that are frequently troublesome. The first of these is called the "business risk exclusion." It excludes coverage when a product or work fails to perform the function, or serve the purpose intended by the insured in those instances where the failure is due to a mistake or deficiency in design, formula, specification, or the like.

The second exclusion is called the "sistership" or "recall" exclusion. It excludes liability for damage or claims for damages arising out of the withdrawal or repair of products which are defective or which are believed to be defective. If the withdrawal of products from dealers, distributors, or purchasers because of a known or suspected defect results in legal liability, the claims for damages because of the loss of use of the product or costs of withdrawal are not covered.

The final two exclusions are related. The policy states that the products coverage does not apply

(1) to property damage to the named insured's products arising out of such products or any part of such products.
(2) to property damage to work performed by or on behalf of the named insured arising out of the work or any portion thereof, or out of materials, parts or equipment furnished therewith.

The traditional example is that of a tire sold by a service station or garage. If the tire is defective and blows out, there is no coverage for the loss of the tire. If, on the other hand, as a result of the blowout the customer loses control of his automobile and demolishes it, or damages other property, or is injured himself, or injures someone else, everything would be covered except the tire itself. The basic point is that the products coverage is designed to cover damage caused by the product, and not damage to such a product. The case involving work completed sometimes becomes more complicated. The basic principle, however, remains the same. There is no coverage under the completed operations coverage for damage to work which has been performed by the insured or for the insured if that damage arises out of the work itself.

**Contractual Liability Part.**   The Contractual Liability Part of the general liability program may be used as a separate contract, or it may be included as a supplement to the OL&T or the M&C, or to the Comprehensive General Liability contract. It is designed to cover designated contracts only. It is possible to purchase blanket Contractual Liability Coverage, in which all contractual liability is covered, but there is no standard form for this coverage, and it is provided only by certain insurers.

*Exclusions.* The student should recognize that the Contractual Liability Coverage Part contains exclusions just as do the other coverage parts, so that not all liability assumed under contracts is covered. If the contract under which the liability is assumed includes liability which is not covered under the Contractual Liability Coverage, the insured will be forced to bear the loss himself. The exclusions include, among others, the liquor liability exclusion, care, custody, and control exclusion, exclusion of damage to the product or work performed, business risk exclusion, and recall exclusion. One of the more important features of this form is the workmen's compensation exclusion. It applies only to liability imposed on the *insured* under the workmen's compensation law, and does not apply to liability imposed on another party which the insured may have assumed under the designated contract or contracts.

**Owners' and Contractors' Protective Liability Coverage Part.** This coverage protects the insured against vicarious liability which might be imposed on the insured because of work performed for him by an independent contractor.[6] It is relatively simple. The insuring agreement agrees to pay all sums the insured becomes legally obligated to pay for bodily injury or property damage arising out of

> Operations performed for the named insured by the contractor designated in the declarations at the location designated or acts or omissions of the named insured in connection with his general supervision of such operations.

*Exclusions.* The major exclusions under this form include contractual liability (except incidental written contracts), completed operations, care, custody, and control, injury to employees, and workmen's compensation liability. In addition, it excludes liability resulting from any act or omission of the named insured or his employees (except general supervision of the work being performed by the independent contractor), making it clear that

---

[6] There may be situations in which it is difficult to determine if the person performing the work is an employee or an independent contractor. If he is an employee, any liability arising out of his negligent acts will be covered under premises and operations, but if he is an independent contractor, his negligent acts might result in liability which would be covered only under protective liability insurance. Because of the uncertainties in defining some relationships, a special type of liability insurance has been developed, called "principal protective liability insurance," which provides protection in the event that it is held that the individual is an independent contractor rather than an employee. This coverage applies to both liability to the independent contractor and to liability to others which results from actions of the independent contractor.

this coverage is intended to cover vicarious liability, and that liability resulting from acts or omissions of the insured and his employees must be covered under the Premises and Operations Coverage.

**Medical Payments Coverage Part.**   Like the Premises Medical Payments Coverage of the Homeowners policy which was examined in Chapter 16, the Premises Medical Payments Coverage is not a liability coverage. It is designated to pay for injuries of members of the public caused by accident on the premises regardless of the insured's liability or lack of it. The Medical Payments Coverage is quite similar to the medical payments of the Homeowners policies already discussed. The limits of liability under the coverage are $250, $500, or $1000 per person, subject to corresponding aggregate limits of $10,000, $25,000, and $50,000 for all persons injured in one accident.

**The Comprehensive General Liability Policy.**   The Comprehensive General Liability Policy (CGL) is designed to provide liability coverage for all the basic business liability hazards discussed thus far. A single insuring clause is applicable to the various subdivisions. Liability arising from premises–operations, elevators, products, contractual, and owners-and-contractors protective comprises the "package" of coverages in the CGL.

Perhaps the most unique feature of the CGL is that newly developed exposures during the policy period are automatically insured without notice to the insurance company. This feature will probably result in fewer gaps in coverage for an insured than would be true without the CGL. For example, if the insured has purchased a separate OL&T policy, and during the policy period he has acquired ownership or control of premises other than those described in the policy, coverage would exist automatically for the newly acquired premises for a limited period of 30 days. In the CGL, on the other hand, newly developed exposures are automatically covered without the requirement of a 30-day notice to the insurance company.

The premium for the CGL begins with an advance payment determined by applying to each element of existing exposure the rules, classifications, rates, and minimum premiums applicable to that element. At the end of the policy period, an audit is performed to determine what, if any, additional exposures have developed, and an additional charge is made for these.

There is one type of exposure that is not covered automatically under the CGL, and that is contractual liability. Only incidental written agreements are automatically included. Any other assumption of liability is covered under the CGL only if it is designated and endorsed into the policy and the proper premium is paid.

The CGL is an attractive contract for almost any business. In some instances, there is a feeling that it is of little value to a small business because of the limited number of exposures that must be insured. However, even in such instances, new exposures may develop during the policy period, and the automatic coverage could be desirable. In the case of small business, the cost of the CGL would be no greater than the cost of separate coverages, because the premium is paid only on exposures that actually exist.

**Personal Injury Liability Coverage Part.** The bodily injury insuring agreement of the basic general liability policies does not include liability arising out of such torts as libel, slander, or defamation of character. These perils are within the broader classification of "personal injury" which may be added by endorsement to the general liability forms. The Personal Injury Liability Coverage Part, which may be purchased separately, as well as by endorsement to the basic liability policy, covers three groups of hazards:

1. False arrest, detention, imprisonment, or malicious prosecution
2. Libel, slander, defamation, or violation of right of privacy
3. Wrongful entry or eviction, or other invasion of the right of private occupancy

The insured may choose one, two, or all three groups of perils.

*Exclusions.* There are relatively few exclusions under the personal injury coverage. Liability assumed under contract is excluded. In addition, personal injury arising out of the willful violation of a penal statute committed by, or with, the knowledge or consent of the insured is excluded. Also, personal injury sustained by an employee is excluded. Finally, as respects libel, slander, and defamation, there is no coverage if the statements were made by, or at, the direction of the insured with knowledge that they were false, or if such statements were made prior to the inception of the insurance.

## COMMERCIAL AUTOMOBILE INSURANCE

American business moves on wheels, and these wheels are a frequent source of legal liability to business firms. Most businesses own or lease automobiles for their business activities, but even the firm which does not own any automobiles may be exposed to vicarious liability as a result of the use of automobiles by its employees. The policies used to cover commercial automobiles are similar in many respects to those studied in Chapter 19. If the business firm is a proprietorship and the insured is an individual, the automobile may be insured under the Family Automobile Policy, provided the automobile is otherwise eligible. If the firm is a corporation or if for some other reason the vehicle is not eligible for coverage under the Family Automobile Policy or Special Automobile Policy, the automobiles must be insured under one of the other forms available. The most common forms are the Basic Automobile Policy, which has already been examined briefly, and the Comprehensive Automobile Policy.

### Basic Automobile Policy

The basic policy may be written to include all the coverages discussed in Chapter 19, including liability, medical payments, physical damage, and uninsured motorists coverage, which may be added by endorsement. In addition, it may be modified by endorsement to broaden its coverage in several respects. If the insured desires, "drive other car" coverage may be added for an additional premium. Also, coverage for hired cars can be added, and coverage for the liability of the employer arising out of the use of employees' automobiles by the employees in the employer's business may be added.

**Employer's Nonownership Automobile Liability.**    Employer's Nonownership Automobile Liability Coverage provides coverage for an employer for liability arising out of the use of any private passenger automobile not owned, hired, or leased by, loaned to, or registered in the name of the insured, by anyone (employee or nonemployee) in the business of the insured. The endorsement also covers occasional and infrequent use of similarly owned and registered commercial automobiles such as trucks, trailers, or semi-trailers.[7]

If the employee has coverage of his own on his automobile, the employer is automatically included as an insured, with respect to liability arising out of acts of the employee. The danger exists, however, that the limits of liability on the employee's policy may be inadequate. Employer's Nonownership Liability Coverage will provide excess coverage for the interest of the employer. The interest of the employee is not covered. As a matter of fact, if the insurance company pays a claim under the Employer's Nonownership Coverage, the insurance company can subrogate against the employee.

**Hired cars coverage.**    A business that rents or hires motor vehicles is not covered under the Basic Automobile Policy for liability arising out of such vehicles. Even with drive other car coverage, there is no protection, since this provision limits the operation of hired cars to those that are not regularly hired. Coverage for hired cars may be added by endorsement to the Basic Automobile Policy. The coverage may apply to a specified hired car, or it may be written to cover automatically all cars hired by the insured during the policy period. The definition of "hired cars" provides that the coverage does

---

[7]The Employer's Nonownership Coverage may be added to the automobile policy or it may be added by endorsement to the Comprehensive General Liability Policy.

not apply to cars owned by employees who are granted an operating allowance of any sort for the use of their automobiles.

### Comprehensive Automobile Liability Coverage

The most effective means of providing automobile liability coverage for a business firm is through the Comprehensive Automobile Liability Policy (CAL). The policy is designed to provide liability coverage for bodily injury and property damage arising out of the ownership, maintenance or use of *any* automobile, including owned, hired, or nonowned automobiles.

As in the case of the automobile policies already discussed, the definition of persons insured is of particular importance. Basically, coverage is afforded for the named insured, any partner or executive officer of the named insured, and any other person while using an owned or hired automobile with the permission of the named insured.

The rating of the CAL is similar to that of the CGL; there is an advance premium based on the existing hazards at the inception of the policy. New exposures are covered automatically during the policy period, and the premium is adjusted following an audit at the end of the policy period.

The CAL may be combined with the CGL into a single policy. In this way, all exposures, both automobile and general liability, may be covered under a single contract. This combination of the CAL and the CGL into a single contract approaches the practical ideal of insurance coverage for the business firm. There are a number of reasons for combining the two coverages into a single contract, but the primary reason is to eliminate any possible gap that might result from a situation in which it is unclear as to which coverage applies.

### Garage Liability Policy

The Garage Liability Policy is designed to provide comprehensive liability coverage for businesses commonly known as garages, or which are engaged in certain businesses pertaining to motor vehicles. The classes of business that are eligible for this contract include automobile sales agencies, repair shops, service stations, storage garages, public parking places and equipment, and implement dealers.

The basic premium for the policy provides coverage for legal liability arising out of three general classifications of hazards: the Premises and Operations Exposure, the Products and Completed Operations Hazard, and the Automobile Liability Hazard.

The Premises and Operations Coverage is basically the same as that of the OL&T policy. It provides coverage for the ownership, maintenance and use of the premises for the purpose of a garage, and all operations necessary or incidental thereto. The exclusions applicable to the Premises and Operations Coverage are the same as those of the OL&T.

The Products Liability Coverage provides coverage for completed operations and products sold. The exclusions of this coverage are the same as those for the separate Completed Operations and Products Coverage part. The care, custody, and control exclusion causes an inordinate number of problems in this class of business, since it excludes damage to any automobiles belonging to customers which are in the care of the insured.[8]

The automobile coverage provides two options. The insured may elect to cover all automobiles, or only automobiles not owned or hired.[9] The definition of "automobile" is quite comprehensive. It includes land motor vehicles or trailers, other land equipment capable of moving under its own power, equipment for use therewith, and animal-drawn equipment. This definition is broad enough to include private passenger automobiles, trucks, trailers of all kinds, tractors, motor scooters, and self-propelled construction and farm equipment.

## AVIATION INSURANCE

The rapid growth and importance of the aviation industry makes it desirable to include at least a brief discussion of aviation insurance. Aviation insurance is a general classification, embracing all the risks encountered in, or associated with, the ownership, maintenance, or use of aircraft. The most common aviation coverages are aircraft liability insurance and hull insurance.[10]

### Aviation Liability Insurance

Aircraft liability coverages are quite similar to automobile liability coverages with one major difference—bodily injury liability is divided into two coverages:

---

[8] Coverage for some damage to customers' automobiles may be added to the policy under Garage Keepers Legal Liability Coverage, a bailee liability coverage. Bailee coverages are discussed later in this chapter.

[9] As you will recall, the Family Automobile Policy and the Special Automobile Policy contain an exclusion which states that the policy does not apply to the owned automobile while it is being used in the automobile business by any one except the named insured, a resident relative, or a partner of the insured. In addition, nonowned automobiles are excluded while used by any person while such person is employed or otherwise engaged in the automobile business. Either option discussed above provides coverage on customers' cars while being used by the garage.

[10] There are two basic forms of hull coverage: one which provides all-risk coverage both on the ground and in flight, and the other which provides all-risk coverage on the ground with limited coverage in flight. Under the more limited form, coverage in flight is limited to the perils of fire, lightning, and explosion, but not crash or collision.

1. Passenger liability
2. Bodily injury excluding passengers

While the basic limits of aircraft liability insurance are patterned after those of automobile liability, it should be borne in mind that most insureds desire much higher limits of liability to cover adequately the catastrophe exposure involved. It is possible to cover bodily injury excluding passengers, passenger bodily injury liability, and property damage liability with a single limit to cover all three exposures.

**Admitted liability.**    Admitted liability coverage, also known as "Voluntary Settlement Coverage," is available only in conjunction with passenger legal liability. It is written on a per seat limit basis, and promises to pay a certain sum for loss of life, limb, or sight by a passenger. When voluntary settlement is offered, a release of liability against the insured is obtained from the passenger to whom the settlement is paid. Although payment is made regardless of liability, if the injured party refuses to sign a release, the offer of payment is withdrawn. The injured party must then bring suit against the insured, who is then protected by the passenger bodily injury coverage.

**Medical payments.**    The aviation liability coverage may be written to include medical payments coverage. The medical payments coverage is similar to that of the automobile policy, except that the injury must be sustained while in, entering, or alighting from the insured aircraft. Medical payments coverage is available only when the policy is written to include passenger bodily injury liability.

## LIABILITY INSURANCE FOR COMMON CARRIERS

### The Liability of a Common Carrier

As you will recall from the discussion in Chapter 21, a common carrier is one offering scheduled service between designated points, offering to carry goods for the public, and is distinguished from a contract carrier, which operates under contract with individual customers. The legal liability of a common carrier for damage to the goods it carries is quite strict, and goes far beyond liability resulting from negligence. The common carrier is held responsible for any damage to the goods it carries except in cases in which the damage is caused by one of a few specified causes:

1. Acts of God
2. Acts of a public enemy
3. Order of public authority
4. Neglect of the shipper
5. Inherent vice

*Acts of God* are, of course, such things as floods, tornadoes, earthquakes, and the like. Damage caused by *acts of a public enemy* involves war. Damage caused by *order of public authority* might include a wide range of loss situations. For example, a government authority might order a dike to be cut to prevent flooding of a city downstream. Water from the cut dike may damage the goods in the custody of a common carrier, but the carrier would be excused from liability. *Neglect of the shipper* is concerned primarily with faulty packing on the part of the owner and shipper of the goods. *Inherent vice* is a quality in a good that causes it to destroy itself. For example, there will be a normal amount of spoilage of fresh fruit and vegetables that are being shipped by carrier, and the carrier is not held liable for such loss.

It is important to recognize that a common carrier is not absolved absolutely from liability even in these five situations. It is still required to take all precautions possible to prevent loss if disaster threatens. For example, a flood is an act of God, but if a railroad could have moved the freight cars from the path of a flood and failed to do so, its negligence becomes a contributing factor, and it could be held liable for the resulting damage.

### Insurance for Common Carriers

Although railroads, airlines, and trucking firms may all act as common carriers, insurance for common carriers is concerned primarily with trucking firms. For many years, trucking operations were notorious in that many trucking firms were financially irresponsible and many became insolvent the first time a large loss occurred. For these and other reasons, the interstate trucking industry became subject to rigid control by the Interstate Commerce Commission (ICC) under the Motor Carrier Act of 1935. The ICC requires that each trucking company purchase liability insurance that will provide coverage in the event of legal liability of the trucker for loss or damage to the property of the shipper. Originally, the required insurance was $1000 for the contents of any one vehicle and $2000 for aggregate losses at any one time or place. This has been increased to $2500 on the contents of any one vehicle and $5000 for aggregate losses at any one time or place.[11] In actual practice, most trucking firms carry limits of coverage substantially in excess of the prescribed minimum amounts; the limits depend upon the types and values of the merchandise being transported.

**The Motor Truck Cargo Form.**   Truck cargo forms are designed to insure public truckmen against losses resulting from damage to merchandise in their possession. The trucker's form is a liability policy in the true sense of the word; it pays only when the trucker is legally obligated to pay for the damage.

[11] In many states, similar insurance requirements are imposed on the intrastate trucking industry. These states require truckers licensed to operate as common carriers to furnish evidence of their financial ability to pay for damage to customers' goods, which is usually done through the truckers' form of the motor cargo policy.

There are two forms available, both of which are intended to insure the legal liability of public truckmen: a named peril form and an all-risk form. The named peril form covers against damage caused by fire, flood, cyclone, windstorm, tornado, perils of the sea, lakes, rivers, or inland waters while on ferries, collision and overturn of the vehicle, and collapse of bridges.[12] Coverage for loss by theft may, and sometimes is, added by endorsement. When coverage for theft is added, the insurer may require a sizable deductible with the additional requirement that only theft of an entire shipping package is covered, thus excluding loss by pilferage. Coverage applies to cargo while loaded for shipment or in transit, and if coverage is desired while the cargo is off vehicles in terminals or other locations, it must be endorsed onto the policy.

### The Interstate Commerce Commission

Motor truck cargo policies which are issued to comply with the insurance requirements of the ICC must contain a special endorsement prescribed by the commission.[13] This endorsement makes the insurance company responsible for any liability of the insured for damage to property being carried, *regardless of cause,* up to the limits of $2500 per truck and $5000 per occurrence.[14] The policy to which the endorsement is attached includes a "reimbursement clause" which provides that the trucker will reimburse the insurance company for any loss paid by the insurance company for which it is not liable under the terms of the basic policy. Thus, if a loss occurs as a result of a peril not covered under the basic policy, the insurance company is required under the terms of the ICC endorsement to make payment to the owner of the goods, but may then seek reimbursement from the trucker for the amount paid. In actual practice, the trucker usually reports losses to the insurance company only when the loss is covered under the basic policy, and he pays his customers directly for other losses. The insurance company seldom pays a loss under the ICC endorsement and then seeks recovery from the insured. The real risk to the insurance company in connection with the ICC endorsement is that the trucker may reach a point at which he is unable to pay customers for losses that are not covered under the basic policy but which are covered under the ICC endorsement; at this point, the insurer would be forced to pay the customers and could not be reimbursed by the insured.

---

[12] Even though cyclones, windstorm, tornadoes, and floods are acts of God, the carrier may still be held liable for loss resulting from one of these perils if the loss was due in part to the negligence of the carrier or its employees. As a general rule, insurance companies pay these losses caused by acts of God, since it is difficult to determine if the trucker had taken all reasonable steps to avoid the loss.

[13] A similar endorsement may be used by the states in their regulation of intrastate carriers.

[14] This is the limit of the insurance company's liability under the ICC endorsement regardless of the limits of the policy to which it is attached.

**Contract carriers.**   Our discussion to this point has been concerned with the operations and the liability of common carriers and with their insurance coverage. Contract carriers also have a need for insurance coverage because, while their liability might not be as great as that of a common carrier, a liability could still exist for the results of negligent acts. It is also possible that, by contract, the contract carrier could assume a liability equivalent to that of the common carrier. The policy purchased by the contract carrier would be essentially the same as that sold to a common carrier, although the premium rates could be substantially lower, depending upon the circumstances such as the degree of liability assumed.

## BAILEE LIABILITY

### Bailments

A bailment involves the delivery of property by one person, the "bailor," to another, the "bailee," for some specific purpose. The property may be in the care of the bailee to be worked upon, such as the repair of an automobile, or for storage, or for some other purpose. In general, there are three types of bailment, and the degree of care that the bailee must exercise in protecting the property will depend on the nature of the bailment.

The first is a gratuitous bailment for the benefit of the bailor. As an illustration, you may ask your neighbors to take care of your cat while you are on vacation. In this situation, perhaps *slight care* is all that is necessary, since the bailment is gratuitous and is for the benefit of the bailor. The second type of bailment is also gratuitous but exists here for the benefit of the bailee. For example, if you borrow your neighbor's power lawn mower, you must use *ordinary care* to protect the property from loss or damage. The third, and perhaps the most important type of bailment, is a bailment for hire. Here, for example, if you should store your automobile in an overnight parking garage, the operator of the garage must use *reasonable care* to protect the property. He could become legally liable for damage to your car if it should be damaged as a result of his negligence.

The degree of care which a bailee must exercise is less than that of a common carrier. In general, a bailee is required to use the care that a reasonable and prudent individual would exercise under the same or similar circumstances. However, the degree of care which must be exercised will be greater in a bailment for hire than that necessary in a gratuitous bailment.[15]

---

[15]The burden of proof of the exercise of reasonable and prudent care is on the bailee. The courts have held rather extensively that a *prima facie* case of negligence exists by the bailor showing that the property was not returned or that it was returned in a damaged condition.

A bailee may by contract or advertisement extend or limit his liability for the bailed property. He may assume complete responsibility for damage to property of customers, regardless of negligence. This assumption is somewhat common with respect to the storage of fur coats. He may also, by contract, limit his liability. For example, he may specify that his total liability for damage to a single fur coat which he is storing will be $200. Normally, it is legal for a bailee to limit his liability. However, the courts frown on attempts of a bailee to relieve himself of liability completely. The decided trend of modern decisions is against the validity of exculpatory clauses or provisions on behalf of proprietors of parking lots, garages, parcel check rooms, and warehouses, where the proprietors undertake to protect themselves against their own negligence by posting signs or printing limitations on the receipts or identification tokens delivered to the bailor–owner at the time of the bailment.

### Bailee Liability Coverages

The need for specialized coverages to cover the liability of a bailee arises because of the "care, custody, and control" exclusion of the general liability policies. If it were not for this exclusion, sums which the bailee became obligated to pay because of damage to his customers' goods would be covered under the general liability policies. Since these do not cover this exposure, special forms of insurance have been developed, most frequently under inland marine contracts.[16]

The bailee coverages sometimes depart from the other liability coverages we have noted in a very fundamental respect. Under many of the bailee policies, payment is made regardless of whether the bailee is legally liable for the damage. In other words, they cover the interest not only of the bailee, but also of the customer. In this sense, bailee coverages are more than just liability coverage. Under most of the bailee forms, payment is made by the insurance company regardless of the legal liability of the bailee, as long as the cause of the loss is a peril under the policy.[17] This approach is the result of the demand of customers that their property be returned to them in good condition, regardless of the liability of the bailee. A merchant who refused to reimburse a customer for the loss of property because he was not liable under the specific set of circumstances might soon find himself without customers. While some bailee coverage provides for payment

---

[16]The bailor may of course insure his property under all conditions, including the period while it is in the custody of the bailee, but the general principle is that coverage purchased by the bailor shall not benefit the bailee. If the bailor has his property insured and collects from his insurance company, the insurer may then subrogate against the bailee.

[17]For the purpose of comparison, you should recall that the trucker's form of the Motor Truck Cargo Policy provides coverage only if the trucker is legally liable for the loss.

only when the insured is legally liable, these are the exception rather than the rule.

**The Bailee's Customers Policy.**    The Bailee's Customers Policy, which is the basic policy for bailees' customers' insurance, is completed by the attachment of a special form designed for the particular class of risk. Coverage may be afforded under these forms for such businesses as laundries, dyers, and dry cleaners, processors, and service risks. There is a Dyer's and Cleaner's Form of the Bailee's Customers Policy, a Laundry Form, a Tailor's Form, a Rug and Carpet Cleaner's Form, and other forms which are designed for appliance repair stores, radio and television repair stores, and other service industries of a similar nature.

In general, the Bailee's Customers Policy covers all kinds of lawful goods and articles which are the property of customers in the custody of the insured. The normal perils insured against include fire, lightning, windstorm, explosion, riot, earthquake, sprinkler leakage, burglary, and holdup, and confusion of goods caused by any perils while in transit or at the insured's premises.[18] In addition, the usual perils of transportation are covered. The normal exclusions are loss while the goods are in the custody of other processors, unless specifically endorsed onto the policy, loss due to shortage, unless caused by burglary or holdup, loss resulting from delay, misdelivery or mysterious disappearance, infidelity, nuclear energy, and war risk losses.

In addition to the Bailee's Customers Policy, there are more specialized bailee forms for certain business classes. There is a Furrier's Customer Form, a Cold Storage Locker Bailee Floater, Innkeeper's Liability contract, and a special form for garages and firms engaged in the automobile business, Garage Keeper's Legal Liability. Each of these has special policy provisions necessary to tailor the coverage to the unique risks of the businesses involved.

## THE BLANKET CATASTROPHE EXCESS (UMBRELLA) LIABILITY POLICY

The average size of liability claims has increased steadily over time and will undoubtedly continue in this direction in the future. The occasional gigantic liability claims that appear in the newspapers are stark reminders of the catastrophic proportions the liability risk may assume.[19] To provide

[18] Confusion of goods refers to the inability to identify the ownership of the goods even though they are not destroyed, but the confusion must result from an insured peril.

[19] This may be emphasized in a rather dramatic manner by recent reports of the damage claims and lawsuits confronting the Richardson–Merrell Drug firm with respect to its anticholesterol drug, MER-29. The alleged adverse side effects of the drug have produced products liability covers marine liability as well as nonmarine liability.

protection against the catastrophic loss which businesses may suffer in this area, excess liability policies and the blanket catastrophe excess liability policy (frequently call the "umbrella") were developed.[20]

The commercial umbrella liability policy, like the personal umbrella, is a form of excess liability insurance and differs from primary insurance in that the company promises to indemnify the insured for his "ultimate net loss" in excess of some retained limit. The policy is usually written in amounts which are quite high, ranging upward from $1 million. When purchased in conjunction with the other liability policies normally purchased by the business firm, the umbrella serves three functions: First, it applies as excess coverage over the other liability coverage purchased by the insured. It takes over when the limits of the basic policies are inadequate to pay any judgment against the insured. Second, it provides more comprehensive coverage than that afforded by the underlying policies. Certain losses not covered by the underlying insurance are included within the broad scope of the umbrella. In these instances, the umbrella provides protection against loss, subject to a deductible ranging from $10,000 upward. Finally, if the underlying coverage becomes exhausted, as might be the case with respect to the aggregate limit concerning products liability, the umbrella becomes the underlying coverage, subject to the terms and conditions of the underlying contracts.

Like the personal umbrella, the commercial umbrella liability policy is written only for risks that have a broad and substantial program of underlying coverage. Normally, the insurance company requires Comprehensive General Liability and automobile liability with limits of $100,000/$300,000/$100,000. In addition, employers' liability coverage for $25,000 per accident is required, and when the exposures exist, bailee liability and aviation liability coverage are required. The policy conditions call for the maintenance of the underlying coverage, and the liability of the insurer is determined as if the underlying coverage is in force, whether or not it is.

Likewise, the insurers usually require that the amount of the net retention or deductible be substantial. Until recently, most umbrella liability policies were written with a net retention limit on exposures not covered by underlying insurance of $25,000. Recently, it has become possible to obtain policies with a $10,000 retention. It should be pointed out that the deductible or retention applies only in those instances where the loss is not covered by the underlying coverage. In other words, there is no "corridor" deductible on those losses which are covered by the underlying coverage.

---

[20]An excess liability policy covers liability above some specified amount up to the limit of the policy, but only for losses as covered and defined in primary or underlying policies. It is never wider or more comprehensive than the basic coverage. It is distinguished from the umbrella which covers losses not covered by the underlying coverage. A third form, the "bumbershoot," covers marine liability as well as nonmarine liability.

## Coverage under the Umbrella Liability Policy

There is no "standard" form of commercial umbrella liability. Each insurer draws up its own contract, and while most of the contracts are quite similar in nature, there may be substantial differences. These can be identified only by a detailed analysis of the specific contract being considered. The insuring agreements are broad and comprehensive in nature. It is common to provide coverage under three sections:

1. Personal injury
2. Property damage
3. Advertising liability

The *personal injury* coverage includes coverage for bodily injury, mental injury or mental anguish, sickness, disease, disability, false arrest or imprisonment, wrongful eviction, detention, malicious prosecution discrimination, and humiliation, plus libel, slander, defamation of character, and invasion of rights of privacy that are not the result of advertising activity. The *property damage* coverage applies to damage to, or destruction of, all tangible property not owned by the insured. There is no exclusion of damage to property in the care, custody, or control of the insured. *Advertising liability* covers liability arising out of the insured's advertising activities, including libel, slander, defamation, infringement of copyright, title or slogan, piracy or unfair competition, or invasion of right of privacy.

The broadness of the umbrella is evident from the above. A further indication may be made by the following list of perils and hazards covered under most umbrella contracts, which are not normally covered under the underlying contracts:

1. Coverage is on a worldwide basis
2. Contract includes personal injury liability
3. Contract includes blanket contractual liability
4. Coverage is provided on property in the care, custody, or control
5. Malpractice coverage is afforded under some contracts
6. Employer's liability is provided
7. Employees are included as additional insureds
8. Coverage is afforded for nonowned aircraft
9. Coverage is afforded for nonowned watercraft
10. Liquor liability is covered
11. Innkeeper's liability is covered
12. Bailee liability is covered
13. Advertising liability is covered
14. Damage to property rented or occupied by the insured is covered

### Exclusions

While the coverage under the umbrella liability policy is far broader than that of the individual contracts, it is not all-risk. There are exclusions, and many of the exclusions are quite important. Some of the more common exclusions contained in the current umbrella liability contracts are the following:

1. Any liability arising out of any workmen's compensation, unemployment compensation, or disability benefits law. As in the case of the underlying contracts, this exclusion does not apply to liability of others assumed by the insured under contract.
2. Liability arising out of claims against the insured for repairing or replacing any defective products manufactured, sold, or distributed by the insured.
3. Liability arising out of the ownership, maintenance, use, loading, or unloading of any aircraft owned by, or chartered without a pilot by, the insured.
4. Liability of any employee with respect to liability for injury to, or death of, a fellow employee. This exclusion is important because employees are included as insureds under the policy.
5. Many policies also exclude any error or omission, malpractice or mistake of a professional nature committed by, or alleged to have been committed by, or on behalf of, the insured.
6. Many policies contain exclusions relating to watercraft over a certain size (e.g., 75 ft in length).

Since there is no standard form of umbrella liability, contracts sold by various companies may vary considerably in this area of exclusions.

The recent trend has been toward higher and higher liability suits, particularly in the case of the individual versus the corporation. The liability contracts discussed in this chapter represent the major forms of coverage available to businesses to protect against this exposure. The umbrella liability policy is a part of the overall framework of liability protection, and constitutes a critical part of the overall need of many businesses.

### Questions for Discussion and Review

**1.** The liability exposures of a business firm are far more complex than those of an individual. What characteristics of the business firm make this so?

**2.** Products liability coverage applies at the time of the injury rather than at the time the product is produced or sold. Joe Smith has been in the plumbing business as a proprietor for the past 35 years and is now preparing to retire. Would you recommend that he continue to carry products liability coverage?

**3.** The "care, custody, and control" exclusion continues to cause difficulties in the field of liability insurance. Assume that a business firm carries a comprehensive general liability policy. What additional coverages, endorsements, or techniques should it consider to eliminate the loss potential in connection with property in its care, custody, and control.

**4.** Of the liability exposures discussed, which do you suspect are the most frequently overlooked in programming liability insurance for business firms?

**5.** You have just opened a new motel with an attached restaurant and cocktail lounge. What liability coverages will you consider essential in your insurance program?

### Suggestions for Additional Reading

*Fire, Casualty and Surety Bulletins,* Casualty and Surety Volume, "Public Liability" and "Auto" Sections. Cincinnati, Ohio: The National Underwriter Co.

*Fire, Casualty and Surety Bulletins,* Fire and Marine Volume, "Inland Marine" Section. Cincinnati, Ohio: The National Underwriter Co.

Gordis, P. *Property and Casualty Insurance,* 17th ed. Indianapolis, Ind.: The Rough Notes Co., 1970, Chaps. 19, 24, 25.

Kulp, C. A. and Hall, J. *Casualty Insurance,* 4th ed. New York: Ronald Press, 1968, Chap. 6.

Long, J. D. and Gregg, D. W. *Property and Liability Insurance Handbook.* Homewood, Ill.: Richard D. Irwin, 1965, Chaps. 32, 34, 38, 40.

Magee, J. H. and Serbein, O. N. *Property and Liability Insurance,* 4th ed. Homewood, Ill.: Richard D. Irwin, 1967, Chap. 17.

# 23 Compulsory Compensation Programs

*. . . it is impossible for them to find work and useless for them to beg.*

—Karl Marx, *Das Kapital*

In addition to the coverages that the business firm must purchase to protect itself against financial loss, the firm may also have an obligation to procure insurance for the economic security of its employees. Although their origins are quite different, the workmen's compensation and unemployment compensation laws enacted by all the states impose such an obligation. Workmen's compensation and unemployment compensation are social insurance coverages, compulsory by law and designed to provide economic security to those individuals covered under the programs. As you will recall, under the Old-Age, Survivors, Disability, and Health Insurance (OASDHI) program the worker and the employer share the cost of the program. Under the workmen's compensation and unemployment compensation laws, the contributions are made entirely by the employer.

Workmen's compensation benefits are designed to compensate workers for occupational injuries and replace action at common law. Unemployment compensation, on the other hand, is designed to replace part of the worker's income when he is unemployed but is willing and able to work. In addition to these two programs, six jurisdictions (California, Hawaii, New Jersey, New York, Rhode Island, and Puerto Rico) have enacted compulsory temporary disability laws which require insurance coverage against loss of income from nonoccupational disabilities. Our purpose here is to describe the general nature of these programs.

## EMPLOYER'S LIABILITY AND
## WORKMEN'S COMPENSATION

While the areas of workmen's compensation and employer's liability are closely related to the general principles of legal liability that have already been examined, there are differences between the areas which are sufficiently significant to warrant a separate treatment of these important areas. In workmen's compensation, the basic principle of legal liability which maintains that there can be no liability without negligence is modified. Under the workmen's compensation laws that have been passed by the various states, liability to an injured worker is imposed on the employer regardless of the negligence involved.

Workmen's compensation laws have been a result of the industrialization of the economy. As production moved out of the handicraft stage and into the factory, injuries as a result of employment became more prevalent and more serious. It is virtually impossible to estimate accurately the number of industrial accidents which caused death or disability of workers during the latter half of the nineteenth century, but as the industrial revolution progressed and new sources of power were applied to the operation of machinery, the frequency and severity of industrial accidents increased. The estimates of American insurance companies indicate that beginning in 1900 there were 25,000–35,000 deaths annually, and more than 2 million serious injuries occurred as a result of employment each year. It became apparent, especially to the injured workers or the survivors of workers who had been killed by work-connected accidents, that the industrial revolution was something of a mixed blessing. It also became apparent that some modification of the basic principles of legal liability and negligence were necessary to protect the workers and their families from the unfortunate consequences of these industrial accidents.

### Employers' Common Law Obligations

Under English common law (which had developed in a society dominated by handicrafts industries), certain legal principles had been developed which made it difficult, if not impossible, for an injured worker to collect indemnity in the event of an industrial injury. The obligation to behave in the same manner as would a reasonable and prudent individual was imposed on the employer, but the specifications as to what was reasonable and prudent did not favor the employee. Under the English common law, the employer had five obligations:

1. To provide a reasonably safe place to work
2. To provide reasonably safe tools
3. To provide reasonably sane and sober fellow employees

4. To set up safety rules and enforce them
5. To inform the worker of any dangers inherent in the work which the employee could not be expected to know about

Once he had done these five things, the employer was deemed to have complied with the "prudent man" obligation. This made it quite difficult for the employee to prove negligence on the part of the employer. Furthermore, even in the unlikely event that the worker was able to prove negligence on the part of his employer, there were certain defenses which the employer could use which acted to bar the injured employee from recovery. They are known as the "employer's common law defenses."

### Employer's Common Law Defenses

**Contributory negligence.** The doctrine of contributory negligence, which was discussed in Chapter 22, was used by employers to defeat the claims of workers. Under the doctrine of contributory negligence, any negligence on the part of the worker who had been injured, no matter how slight, was normally sufficient to defeat the claim.

**Fellow servant rule.** The fellow servant doctrine simply stated that a fellow servant of the injured worker, whose negligence caused the accident or injury, was not considered to be an agent of the employer. Under such circumstances, i.e., where the injury was caused by a fellow worker, the injured worker was expected to seek damages from that fellow worker and not from the employer.[1]

**The assumption of risk doctrine.** This doctrine was based on the differing degrees of compensation paid for workers engaged in more hazardous employment. The fact that more dangerous work normally carries a higher wage rate was implied to be payment for the risk which the worker assumed in the job. Since he was paid a higher rate for doing hazardous work, the worker should not expect to turn to his employer in the event of an injury; he had already been paid for taking the risk. Furthermore, if a worker continued his employment while knowing, or when he might have been expected to discover, that the premises, tools, or fellow employees were unsafe, he was deemed to have assumed the risks connected with the unsafe conditions.

**Death of the right of claim.** If these three common law defenses were not sufficient to defeat the worker's claim, there was still another principle which

---

[1] This rule appears to be in direct contradiction to the basic principle of *respondeat superior*, i.e., a principal is vicariously liable for the negligent acts of his agent. This modification became firmly established in American law in the case of *Farwell vs. Boston and Wooster Railway* in 1842. Here the court decided that the doctrine of *respondeat superior* did not apply in the case of injury to a fellow employee.

worked against the dependents of a worker. Under the common law doctrines, only the injured worker had the right to bring action against his employer for damages. If the worker died as a result of the accident, the right of claim against the employer died with him.

**Agreement not to sue.** Finally, as if the scales were not already balanced unfavorably against the worker, employers hit upon an additional device to guarantee that they would not become legally liable for damage on account of injury to a worker. As a condition of employment, the worker was required to sign a statement in which he agreed that he would not institute any suit for damages against the employer in the event of occupational injury.

**Modifications.** The harshness of the above principles of employer's liability resulted in a modification of certain of the more severe doctrines. In some states the fellow servant doctrine was modified to the less severe "vice principal doctrine." In essence, the vice principal rule stated that not all employees of the employer came under the "fellow servant doctrine." If, for example, the fellow servant who caused the injury was a foreman, or a worker from another part of the plant, the employer could be held vicariously liable. Shortly after the turn of the century, most of the states enacted legislation permitting the heirs of a deceased worker to file suit for damages, and by 1908, over half the states had declared illegal the contracts in which employees agreed not to sue in the event they were injured at work.

While the modifications of the common law doctrines were helpful to the workers, they did not solve the basic problems inherent in a system of employer's liability based on the principle of negligence. To establish negligence, litigation was necessary. In most cases, the workers did not have the resources to bring suit, and the workers felt the natural reluctance one might expect to testify on the part of a fellow worker who had been injured. Even if the worker was successful in his suit for damages, a substantial portion of the judgment went to the attorney who had accepted the case on a "contingency basis." It was not unusual for the size of the attorney's fee to represent 50–75% of the amount of the judgment.

## WORKMEN'S COMPENSATION LAWS

The unsatisfactory status of the worker and the social and economic consequences of the entire situation under common law finally led to the adoption of a new way of distributing the financial costs of industrial accidents. The workmen's compensation principle is based on the notion that industrial accidents are an inevitable result of the industrialized society. Since the entire society gains as a result of the industrialization, it should bear the burden of these costs. In other words, the workmen's compensation laws made the cost of industrial accidents a part of the cost of production by imposing liability on the employer even if he was not negligent. The first workmen's compensation laws were passed in Germany (1884) and England (1897). In the United States, the first workmen's compensation law was passed by Maryland in 1902. This law was declared unconstitutional. Before the first effective law was passed by Wisconsin, a number of states experimented with workmen's compensation laws. The Wisconsin law, which went into effect May 3, 1911, set a pattern for many of the laws that followed. Workmen's compensation laws now exist in all 50 states.[2] The provisions of the laws all differ somewhat, but the basic intent is the same in all of them. The workmen's compensation laws impose absolute liability on the employer for injury suffered by a covered employee, which arises out of, or in the course of, his employment. The basic purpose of the laws is to avoid litigation, lessen the expense of the claimant, and provide for a speedy and efficient means of compensating injured employees.

### Principles of Workmen's Compensation

While the provisions of the workmen's compensation laws in the various states differ somewhat, there is a good deal of uniformity concerning the operation of these laws. The major differences among the laws of the various states involve the definition of persons covered under the law and the magnitude and duration of benefits.[3] In spite of the differences, certain basic principles still appear to be characteristic of the laws in general. There are five of these basic principles.

**Negligence is no longer a factor in determining liability.** The workmen's compensation laws impose absolute liability on the employer for injury suffered by the employee which arises "out of and in the course of his employment." If the worker is injured, the employer is obligated to pay benefits according to a schedule in the law, regardless of whose negligence caused the injury to occur. The employer is considered liable without any necessary fault on his part, and will be assessed the compensable costs of the job-connected

---

[2] In addition, there is a workmen's compensation law in Puerto Rico and three federal laws, applicable to civilian workers of the federal government, longshoremen and harbor workers, and to nongovernment workers in the District of Columbia, making a total of 54 different laws.

[3] The student should obtain a copy of the workmen's compensation law of his own state or a digest of the law from the office of the industrial commissioner or other authority supervising the administration of the law. For a more complete digest of the provisions of the various laws of the states see *Analysis of Workmen's Compensation Laws* (Chamber of Commerce of the United States: Washington, D.C., 1971) and the *Workmen's Compensation Law Reporter* (New York: Commerce Clearing House, biweekly).

injury not because he is responsible for it, not because he caused it, not because he was negligent, but simply because of social policy.[4]

**The indemnity is partial but final.**    The second basic principle of workmen's compensation involves the amount of the benefit. In general, there is no attempt to provide an injured workman with complete damages. The worker gives up his right to sue the employer in return for a schedule of benefits set forth in the law. The size of these benefits is based on the severity of the injury, the wage of the worker, and in some states, the size of his family. In most cases, the total benefits payable are less than the employee could receive if he were permitted to sue and could establish a case of negligence on the part of the employer, but he is entitled to the benefits as a matter of right, without the necessity of going through the courts.

**Periodic payments.**    The third principle involves the basis of payment of benefits, which is arranged to assure a greater degree of security for the recipients. In most cases, the indemnity is paid on a periodic basis rather than as a lump sum, although under certain circumstances the periodic payments may be commuted to a lump sum. The requirement of periodic rather than a lump sum settlement is designed to protect the recipient against his ineptness and the possibility that the recipient might squander the lump sum.

**The cost of the program is made a cost of production.**    Unlike many other social insurance coverages, the employees cannot be required to contribute to the financing of the workmen's compensation program. The employer must pay the premium for the insurance coverage, or pay the benefits required by law, without any contribution on the part of the workers. The employer can predict the cost of accidents under a workmen's compensation program and build this cost into the cost of his product, thereby passing the cost of industrial accidents on to the consumer. Since it is the consumer that enjoys the benefits of industrialization and mass production, it is only equitable that the consumer should also bear the cost of the injuries that are involved in production.

**Insurance is required.**    In general, the employer is required to purchase and maintain workmen's compensation insurance to protect against the losses covered under the law. Since most employers do not have sufficient resources

[4]The passage of the workmen's compensation laws did not eliminate the employer's liability laws. These laws are still applicable to the employments that are not covered under workmen's compensation. For example, in practically all states an injured farm worker or domestic servant would have a remedy against the employer only under employer's liability laws, which means that the negligence of the employer would have to be the proximate cause of the injury, and the employer would, in most cases, have the right to interpose the common law defenses in a suit against him.

to guarantee indemnities, insurance provides the security which must be built into the program. Most states will permit the employer to self-insure the workmen's compensation exposure, provided he has a sufficiently large number of employees and some protection against catastrophic loss through dispersion.

Insurance plays an essential part in the operation of the workmen's compensation laws. While the laws impose the obligation to provide benefits on the employer, he may transfer this obligation to the insurer. Under the workmen's compensation policy (which we will examine in greater detail later), the insurance company promises to pay all sums that the insured (i.e., the employer) is obligated to pay under the law. In the event of injury to an employee, the insurance company will pay the schedule of benefits which the employer would otherwise have been required to pay.

In 6 states, the insurance must be purchased from a monopolistic state insurance fund. In 12 states the private insurance industry operates side by side with state workmen's compensation insurance funds.[5]

### Persons Covered

None of the state workmen's compensation laws cover all employees in the state. Some laws list the classes of employment that are covered, normally referring to such employments as "hazardous" or "extra-hazardous." The more common approach is to exclude specifically certain groups, and to cover all other employees.[6] The occupations most frequently excluded are agriculture and domestic employees. Only 9 states cover agricultural workers on the same basis as other occupations, and only 2 states provide full cover-coverage on domestic employees. In addition, only 11 states cover casual

---

[5] The 6 states which maintain monopolistic workmen's compensation programs are Nevada, North Dakota, Ohio, Washington, West Virginia, and Wyoming. The 12 states in which the workmen's compensation fund maintained by the state competes with private insurers are Arizona, California, Colorado, Idaho, Maryland, Michigan, Montana, New York, Oklahoma, Oregon, Pennsylvania, and Utah.

[6] First and foremost, the individual must be an employee; there must be an employer–employee relationship. Persons who are independent contractors do not come under the provision of the laws, since they are not employees of the person or persons for whom they are performing the services. An independent contractor is distinguished from an employee by a number of factors, the most important of which seems to be the right of control. The primary test of the employer–employee relationship is the right of an employer to direct the manner in which an employee renders his service, while an independent contractor normally has the right to determine the manner in which he will achieve the ultimate result of his work. In addition, there are certain other circumstances which may indicate that there is an independent contractor relationship rather than an employer–employee one. Among these are the existence of a contract, the right of the contractor to employ and supervise assistants, and the obligation of a contractor to furnish his own tools.

employees (i.e., those whose employment is occasional, incidental, or irregular).[7] In addition, some states have a numerical limitation, providing that if the employer has fewer than some number of employees (ranging from 3 to 15), he is not required to come under the act. Twenty-four states have no such limitation, and require the employer of one or more employees in the covered employments to come under the law.

The laws generally provide that the employer of employees not covered under the law may bring these workers under the law voluntarily if he wishes to do so. This applies in the case of classes of employment which are excluded, nonhazardous occupations in those states where only designated hazardous occupations are covered, and in the case of the employer with fewer than the number of employees specified in the law. A very few states may require that the employee consent.

### Elective and Compulsory Laws

Compensation laws are classified as compulsory or elective.[8] There are 31 compulsory laws and 23 laws that are elective. A compulsory law requires every employer defined by the law to accept the act and pay the compensation specified. In many states, however, the law is elective, which means that either the employer or the employee has the option of accepting or rejecting the act. In most cases, both employers and employees are presumed to accept the provisions of the act, and if either desires to exercise his right of election, a notice of this election must be filed with the administrative agency of the state which supervises the law. If either party rejects the provisions of the law, the right to indemnity and the amount of damages are determined under the principles of employer's liability, but on a modified basis.

The provisions of the elective laws are designed to discourage either party from electing out. If the employer elects not to come under the act, any injury

---

[7]The "casual" employee classification frequently creates problems, for these laws generally require that the employee is excluded only if he is both casual and not engaged in the employer's trade or business. The mere fact that the employment is occasional, incidental, or irregular does not necessarily exclude that employment from coverage. Unless both elements are present in the employment (i.e., casual, meaning occasional, incidental, or irregular, *and* not for the purpose of the employer's trade or business), the workers are not excluded. It should be noted that the courts tend to construe the meaning of "casual" employment against the employer, in order to increase the coverage of the act.

[8]The elective laws are patterned after the early laws which were made elective in order that they would not be declared unconstitutional. The New York law of 1910 was declared unconstitutional on the grounds that it violated the constitution by depriving the employer of liberty and property without due process. The problem of constitutionality was finally settled by the United States Supreme Court in 1917 in the case of *The New York Central Railroad vs. White (243 U.S. 188)*, in which it upheld the right of the state to pass a compulsory law under its police power.

to a worker is presumed to be due to the negligence of the employer, and the burden of proof is shifted from the injured worker to the employer. In attempting to prove the absence of negligence, the employer is not permitted to use the common law defenses of contributory negligence, assumption of risk, or the fellow servant doctrine. On the other hand, if the employee elects out, the employer is permitted to use the common law defenses. The laws make the employee's rejection applicable only to subsequent injuries; therefore, the election must be made before the injury is sustained. Generally, if both the employer and the employee elect not to be covered under the act, the situation is the same as if the employer had rejected the act. Once either party has elected out, the election is binding until the party elects to come under the law. The elective provisions thus make it disadvantageous for either party to elect out. If the employer elects out, he will in all probability be forced to pay damages at common law, for he will lose his right to impose the common law defenses. If the employee elects out, he will probably not be able to collect damages, because the employer will be permitted to use the common law defenses.[9]

### Injuries Covered

The workmen's compensation laws provide that employee injuries are compensable only when connected with the employment, requiring that the injury arise "out of and in the course of employment." In the vast majority of cases there is little problem in determining whether or not the injury is compensable, but problems do arise. The question may arise first as to whether the injured employee was actually "in the course of employment" at the time of the injury in cases where the injury was sustained while coming or going to and from the job or while engaged in social events which may be connected with employment. The greater problem frequently arises when it is clear that the injury occurred in the course of the employment, but there is question as to whether it occurred out of the employment. Generally injuries sustained while at work are considered to arise out of the work, but there are exceptions. Injuries may be noncompensable if they are deliberately self-inflicted or result from intoxication.[10] In addition, there may be difficulties in such cases as heart attacks, mental or nervous disorders, or even suicide. In many cases, the only way these questions can be settled is by means of litigation, and litigation involving these issues has been almost endless. In general, the courts have taken a liberal attitude and have done their best to compensate the injured worker or his dependents.

[9] In some states, if the employer fails to purchase insurance and does not notify the administrative authority that he intends to self-insure, he is deemed to have elected not to come under the law.

[10] Normally, before intoxication is a bar to recovery, the intoxication itself rather than some other factor must be the proximate cause of the injury.

In addition to the traumatic type of injury, all laws provide coverage for occupational diseases. Most of the states provide coverage for all occupational diseases, either under a separate occupational disease law, or by defining injury broadly enough under the workmen's compensation law to include disease. In 19 states only those diseases specifically listed or scheduled in the law are covered, but the trend appears to be toward blanket coverage of occupational disease.

### Benefits

There are generally seven classes of benefits payable to the injured worker or his dependents under the workmen's compensation laws:

1. Medical expenses
2. Total temporary disability
3. Partial temporary disability
4. Total permanent disability
5. Partial permanent disability
6. Survivor's death
7. Rehabilitation benefits

**Medical expense benefits.**   Medical expense benefits account for about one-third of the total benefit payments under workmen's compensation laws. In most jurisdictions, medical expenses involved with employment-connected injuries are covered without limit. Fourteen jurisdictions impose a dollar limit on the medical expenses, but even under these laws there may be provision for exceeding the limitation upon the authorization of the administrative body.

**Total temporary disability.**   There are four classes of disability income benefits under the workmen's compensation laws. The most frequent type of disability is total temporary disability, which exists when the worker is unable to work because of an injury, but it is evident that he will eventually recover and will return to work. All states provide for a waiting period before disability benefits are payable.[11] This waiting period is a deductible and serves the function of eliminating coverage for short periods of disability and reducing the administrative costs. The normal waiting period is 1 week, although some states have waiting periods as short as 3 days. Normally, the waiting period does not apply if the disability lasts beyond some specified number of weeks, usually four.

The amount of the benefit is set by statute, and varies with the worker's wage and in some cases with the number of dependents he has. The most frequently used percentage of the injured worker's wage is $66\frac{2}{3}\%$, subject to a

---

[11] The waiting period applies only to disability benefits. Medical benefits are payable immediately.

maximum and minimum also imposed by the law.[12] Fourteen states provide for a sliding maximum based on the number of dependents. The maximums under the various state laws vary from about $35 to $150 per week. In 10 states these benefits for total temporary disability are payable for the entire period of the disability, but in the remaining jurisdictions there is a time limit (such as 300 weeks) or a total dollar limit to the benefits (such as $20,000), or both.

**Partial temporary disability.**  Many states include a provision in the law which provides disability benefits in the event of partial temporary disability, to cover those cases in which the worker cannot perform the duties of his own occupation, but can engage in some work for remuneration. In these cases, the laws provide for payment of a percentage of the difference between the wages received before the accident and those received afterward. This benefit is also subject to a maximum and a minimum and is usually payable for the same period of time as the total temporary disability benefit.

**Total permanent disability.**  A worker who suffers an industrial injury is defined as totally and permanently disabled when he is unable to obtain any gainful employment as a result of an industrial accident.[13] The emphasis is on "industrial incapacitation," and the actual degree of physical capacity may have little relationship to industrial incapacity. Instances could arise in which an unskilled worker is deemed totally disabled, even though his physical disability was limited. The fact that the injured worker can still find a few odd jobs does not normally reflect on his total disability status.[14] In addition to the inability to obtain gainful employment, most laws specifically provide that the loss of both hands, arms, feet, legs, or eyes, or any combination of two of these constitutes total and permanent disability.

Benefits for total and permanent disability are payable for the entire period of disability under 23 laws. Under the other laws, they are payable for some maximum number of weeks specified by the law (varying from 300 to 1000 weeks) or are subject to a dollar maximum (ranging from $10,000 to $30,000), or both. The amount of the benefit is computed on the same basis as the total temporary disability benefit. Usually, the percentage and the weekly minima and maxima are the same as for total temporary disability, but the limit of

[12] In some states, if the actual wage at the time of the injury is less than the minimum, the actual wage will be the amount of indemnity.

[13] In most states, total permanent disability benefits are payable in the case of any disability which lasts beyond the number of weeks specified for total temporary disability.

[14] For example, an unskilled worker whose disability prevents him from engaging in manual labor and who cannot obtain employment in any other type of occupation could be considered totally disabled. He might, as a matter of fact, be able to do everything except work.

time for which the benefits are payable is longer. Some laws provide for a reduction in the amount of the benefit after a period of time.

**Partial permanent disability.** An injury resulting from an industrial accident may be deemed a partial permanent disability on one of two bases. In one instance, the loss of a member such as an arm or a leg is considered to constitute partial disability. In addition, the disability may consist of a disability of the body in general without the loss of a member. In cases of permanent partial disability of the entire body (e.g., an injured spine) as distinguished from the loss of a limb, the usual procedure is to provide for payment of some percentage of the total permanent disability benefit which is equal to the percentage of disability. For example, if it is determined that the worker is 50% disabled as a result of the injury and the law provides total permanent disability benefits for 500 weeks, he will collect a weekly benefit for 250 weeks.

The compensation for the loss of a member such as an arm or a leg is usually some multiple of the weekly disability benefit, which may be commuted and paid as a lump sum. To illustrate, the Iowa law provides the following schedule of benefits for the loss of members:

| | |
|---|---|
| Loss of thumb | 60 weeks |
| Loss of first finger | 35 weeks |
| Loss of second finger | 30 weeks |
| Loss of third finger | 25 weeks |
| Loss of fourth finger | 20 weeks |
| Loss of hand | 175 weeks |
| Loss of arm | 230 weeks |
| Loss of great toe | 40 weeks |
| Loss of any other toe | 15 weeks |
| Loss of foot | 150 weeks |
| Loss of leg | 200 weeks |
| Loss of eye | 125 weeks |
| Loss of hearing (1 ear) | 50 weeks |
| Loss of hearing (both ears) | 175 weeks |

There are wide variations among the states with respect to the amount of compensation for the various extremities and also with respect to the value of one member as opposed to another.[15]

Under most of the laws, the compensation for scheduled injuries is payable in addition to any benefits otherwise payable to the injured worker under the

[15] For example, benefits for the loss of an arm to the shoulder vary from about $6300 to about $38,000. For the great toe, the range varies from $700 to about $4600. In addition, some states place a greater value on an arm than a leg, while other states value a leg more highly. It would be interesting indeed to discover how the values were determined for the various parts of the body.

total temporary disability benefit. However, 16 states provide for limitations on the total temporary disability benefit when payment is made for a scheduled injury, and 7 states deduct any amount paid under the total temporary disability benefit from the allowance for the scheduled injury.

**The death benefit.**    Benefits may also be payable when a worker is killed. Practically all laws provide two types of death benefits. Under the first, payment is made for the reasonable expenses of burial, but not to exceed some maximum amount, such as $750 or $1000. The second death benefit is a survivor's benefit payable to surviving dependents. Although the definition of dependent varies from state to state, in general the laws provide that a dependent may be a spouse, a child of the deceased worker, or a dependent parent. A child is typically defined as under 18 years of age or physically or mentally incapacitated and receiving support from the worker. The child may be a natural born, adopted, or stepchild of the deceased worker, or even an unborn child, if conceived at the time of the worker's injury.

The survivor's benefit is usually paid as a weekly benefit, subject to determination by the usual formula. Under 11 of the laws it is payable to the surviving spouse for life or until remarriage without limit. Thirty laws provide for a maximum number of weeks, and 43 laws provide dollar limits ranging from $10,000 to $32,000. In 23 states, the survivor's benefit is based on the number of dependents. The majority (35) of the states provide that the death benefit payable to survivors is to be reduced by the amount of any disability benefits the worker might have received before death in connection with the injury causing death. For example, if the law provides survivor's benefits for 500 weeks and the worker received benefits for 200 weeks before dying, the survivors would receive benefits for only 300 weeks rather than the full 500 weeks specified by the law.

**Rehabilitation benefits.**    Thirty-one state workmen's compensation laws contain specific rehabilitation benefit provisions, but even in those states in which the law does not specifically provide for such benefits, rehabilitation benefits are provided. Under the rehabilitation benefit provisions, the injured worker may be entitled to additional compensation during a period of vocational training, transportation and other necessary expenses, artificial limbs and mechanical appliances, and other benefits. The funds for payment of the rehabilitation benefits may or may not come from the employer or his insurance company. In some cases, state funds are used; in other cases, the funds come from a tax imposed on insurance companies operating in the state or on insurance companies in death cases in which no surviving dependents receive benefits. Finally, the Federal Vocational Rehabilitation Act provides for federal funds to aid states in vocational rehabilitation.

### Second Injury Funds

Under most state workmen's compensation laws, the loss of both arms, feet, legs, or eyes, or any two thereof, is defined as total and permanent disability. As a result, situations may arise in which an injury which is partial in nature leaves the worker totally disabled. For example, a worker who has lost an arm or a leg as a result of an industrial accident and who has returned to work would be considered totally disabled if he should lose another arm or leg. Injuries to workers with preexisting disabilities pose something of a dilemma in the application of the compensation principle. Obviously, it would be unfair to hold the new employer responsible for the earlier injury, yet if the worker is compensated for only partial disability when he loses a second limb, the indemnity is tragically inadequate. Second injury funds have been established, to meet the problem of injury to workers with preexisting industrially caused disabilities, in all but four states. When a worker suffers a second injury which makes him permanently and totally disabled and the injury is of a nature that would constitute only partial permanent disability but for the previous injury, the employer is liable only for the benefits payable for the partial disability. The second injury fund pays the difference between the partial permanent benefit and the total permanent benefit. The fund is supported by required contributions from insurance companies operating in the state, either as a percentage tax or payment to the fund in death cases in which there are no dependents.

Second injury funds encourage employment of the physically handicapped. They make certain that an employer who hires a handicapped worker will not, in the event such a worker suffers a subsequent injury on the job, be responsible for a greater indemnity than actually incurred while the worker was in his employ. The existence of the second injury funds helps to overcome any reluctance an employer may have in hiring the physically handicapped because of the possibility of paying such increased compensation.

## WORKMEN'S COMPENSATION INSURANCE

### Insurance Requirements

All states require the employers coming under the workmen's compensation law to insure their obligation, either through commercial insurance companies, a state fund, or by qualification as a self-insurer. In general, the penalties for failure to comply are severe. Thirty-seven states provide that failure to insure is punishable by fines (which vary from state to state, ranging from $50 up to $5000), by imprisonment, or both. Other laws provide that the employer may be enjoined from doing business. Perhaps the most severe penalty, which is used in about two-thirds of the states, is the provision for common law suit by the employee against the employer. When such an action is brought against a noncomplying employer, the employer may be presumed to have been negligent, the burden of conclusively rebutting this presumption of negligence is imposed on the employer, and the employer is deprived of his common law employer's liability defenses. Not only may the employee proceed at common law, but many acts provide that he may elect to institute compensation proceedings and may collect compensation benefits instead of seeking common law recovery. Thus, for the noninsuring employer in these jurisdictions, the worst of two worlds exists. If the injured employee has a good case, he will bring suit at common law. On the other hand, if it appears likely that a common law suit would not be successful in spite of the abrogation of the common law defenses, he will proceed under the workmen's compensation law as if the employer had insured his obligation.

Unfortunately, the need to insure the workmen's compensation exposure is not as widely recognized as one might hope, and as a result, this required coverage is conspicuously absent from the insurance program of many business firms. The reason for this oversight is probably the confusion which exists on the part of employers concerning the distinction between the workmen's compensation act and the unemployment compensation law. In most states, there are no numerical exemptions under the workmen's compensation act, but the unemployment compensation act generally applies only to employers of four or more employees. The employer confuses the two laws and does not insure the compensation exposure. The legal consequences of this misunderstanding can be severe, for as we have seen, the laws impose drastic penalties on employers who fail to insure.

### The Workmen's Compensation Policy

The workmen's compensation policy is one of the simplest contracts in the entire field of insurance. There are two basic insuring agreements, designated Coverage A and Coverage B. Coverage A is the workmen's compensation coverage. Under this insuring agreement, the insurer agrees to pay promptly when due all compensation and other benefits required of the insured under the workmen's compensation law or laws listed in the declarations of the policy. Coverage B, designated "employer's liability," provides for payment on behalf of the insured all sums which the insured becomes legally obligated to pay because of bodily injury or disease by any employee of the insured which arises out of, and in the course of, his employment by the insured. There are only six exclusions in the contract, two which are applicable to the workmen's compensation coverage and four which apply to the employer's liability coverage.

**Workmen's compensation coverage.**   The status of the employee, the employer, and the insurance company which results from the issuance of a workmen's compensation policy is unique from an insurance point of view. The law imposes certain obligations on the employer, requiring an indemnity to injured workers and requiring the employer to secure this obligation through insurance. The workmen's compensation insurance policy assumes the obligation imposed on the employer, but it does so on a virtually unlimited basis. In a legal sense, the workmen's compensation portion of the policy is not a pure insurance contract nor a contract indemnifying the employer. It is a contract providing direct benefits to the employee even though he is not named in the contract. From the point of view of the employee, the workmen's compensation policy is somewhat akin to group disability insurance. The great difference is that the employee does not contribute to the premium payment, and the benefits are fixed by statute rather than by agreement among the private parties.

One of the most unusual conditions to be found in any insurance policy is the "statutory provision" of the workmen's compensation policy. This incorporates the provision of the workmen's compensation law involved into the policy just as if it had been fully written out in the contract. The provision also states that the policy, in addition to protecting the named insured, creates a direct obligation of the insurance company to the injured employee, or in the event of his death, to his dependents. Since the workmen's compensation policy is primarily for the benefit of the employee and his dependents, they have a direct right of action against the insurance company and are in effect insured under the policy as much as if specifically named. For the further protection of the employees, the policy provides that the obligations of the insuring company to the employee shall not be affected by the failure of the employer in any way to comply with the policy requirements. For example, failure of the employer to give notice to the company of a claim as required by the policy does not act to the disadvantage of the employee; neither does failure to disclose operations or locations of the insured. In other words, as respects the workmen's compensation law or laws listed in the policy declarations, it is no defense to a compensation claim under the policy that the coverage is not written broadly enough to cover the activities of the employer. Regardless of the policy provisions or how the employer and the insurer may handle the matter, liability of the insurer to the employee is determined by the compensation law. The only matter to be determined is whether the employer is liable to the claimant for the injury sustained. When a claim is proved, the insurer makes direct payment to the worker or dependents on behalf of the employer. The insurance company may then seek recovery from the employer for amounts paid which would not have been paid except for the unique position of the employee as a direct beneficiary under the policy. While the insurer's liability to the employee is governed by the law, the insurer's liability to the employer is governed by the policy. Even the two exclusions which apply to the workmen's compensation section of the policy do not eliminate coverage where it is required under the law. Exclusion (a) excludes coverage for any operations not listed in the declarations if the insured has other workmen's compensation coverage for such operations. Exclusion (b) refers to domestic workers and farm employees, eliminating coverage on these classes of workers unless it is required by law or described in the declarations. In states in which agricultural workers are covered under the act, the exclusion does not apply. If the employer has elected to bring his agricultural workers under the act, they will be listed in the declarations, and again the exclusion does not apply.

**Employer's liability coverage.**   The employer's liability section of the policy is automatically included with the workmen's compensation coverage, but it is important to recognize that the workmen's compensation coverage and the employer's liability coverage are distinct. The workmen's compensation coverage applies only to obligations payable under the workmen's compensation law, and the employer's liability coverage applies only to suits which are brought against the insured by an employee or someone else because of the injury of an employee. It should be fairly obvious that the employer needs both coverages for complete protection. Even if the employer does not employ workers who are excluded from the workmen's compensation law, he may face a suit from a worker who has elected not to come under the law, or the spouse of a worker who is covered under the law. Although workmen's compensation benefits are an exclusive remedy for the injured worker, some courts have held that the spouse of the injured worker has an independent right of action against the employer. Even in cases in which the chances of collecting on such a suit are slight, there is still the cost of defending such suits. Like most liability policies, the employer's liability coverage provides for the payment of defense costs in connection with the employer's liability coverage.

The four exclusions under the employer's liability coverage are rather simple and straightforward. Exclusion (c) (which, like the other three discussed here, applies only to the employer's liability coverage), excludes liability assumed under contract. Employees hired in violation of the law are excluded under the employer's liability coverage by exclusion (d). Exclusion (e) eliminates coverage under the employer's liability coverage unless proper written claim is made or suit is brought against the insured within 36 months after the end of the policy. Finally, exclusion (f) simply provides that all coverage for the liability of the insured under any and all workmen's compensation laws is confined to Coverage A and no part of any such obligation is insured under Coverage B.

### Possible Gaps in Coverage

Most workmen's compensation laws are extraterritorial, which means that the provisions apply to injuries to employees while in the state and also while traveling outside its boundaries. In addition, the laws have further extraterritorial effect in that they may impose liability on an employer who is located in another state if one of his workers is injured in the state. For example, the employee of an Iowa firm who is injured while working in Nebraska may still bring action for workmen's compensation benefits under the Iowa law. In addition, however, the injured worker may decide to bring action under the law of the state where he was injured, which he might do if the benefits under that law were higher than those of his home state. The worker in our example is entitled to benefits under either the Iowa or the Nebraska law, and the employer is obligated to make payment in either case. A serious gap may develop in this connection. As noted previously, the workmen's compensation insuring agreement provides for payment of benefits required under the workmen's compensation laws of the states listed in the declarations. If the employer becomes liable under the law of a state not listed, the policy will not provide workmen's compensation benefits, and the employer will be obligated to pay them himself.

Initially, the employer should list all the states in which he has employees or in which he feels he might have employees during the policy period, and the "all-states endorsement" may be used to further broaden the coverage. Under the provisions of the all-states endorsement, the policy is extended to cover the liability of the employer under any workmen's compensation law of a state not listed in the declarations where such coverage may be lawfully provided. No coverage is provided under the compensation laws of the states having monopolistic state funds (Nevada, North Dakota, Ohio, Washington, West Virginia, and Wyoming). Employers who are exposed under these laws must purchase their compensation coverage from the state fund. There is usually no specific premium charge for the all-states endorsement, but a premium for any exposure which develops is charged at the end of the policy when the audit is made.

In those states in which the coverage of the workmen's compensation law does not apply to executive officers of corporations, the workmen's compensation policy may be extended to include these persons through the "voluntary compensation endorsement." Under the provisions of this endorsement, the insurance company agrees to offer to such executives the same payment as it would make if the law did apply to them, in return for a release of further liability. In other words, the provision simply brings the executive officers under the law at their option.

### The Future of Workmen's Compensation

The wide variations in coverage and benefits under the various state workmen's compensation laws have brought the entire system under attack. While some states cover virtually all employees, many of the states restrict coverage to certain occupations or eliminate many workers from coverage by exempting employers with a small number of employees. Proponents of the federal approach to social insurance argue that the variations in the state laws result in inequities, that the benefits payable under most of the laws are inadequate, and that a national system would better serve the injured workers. They point out that the mechanism for a national system already exists in the form of the social security system.[16]

In 1970, Congress ordered a study of the state workmen's compensation laws in order to determine their adequacy. Under the provisions of the Occupational Safety and Health Act of 1970, provision was made for the establishment of a National Commission on State Workmen's Compensation Laws, to study and evaluate such laws and report to the president and Congress by July 1, 1972. Prompted by this pressure, many of the state legislatures have moved to improve their laws. It may be anticipated that further improvement will take place in the near future, for there is a growing recognition that unless improvement is made, the compensation of injured workers is likely to pass out of the hands of the states and into a federal system.

## UNEMPLOYMENT INSURANCE

In addition to the hazards of death and disability, the individual faces loss of income from another source. The problem of unemployment has been one of the major problems in our economy in the recent past; it promises to become even more crucial in the future. Commercial insurance companies cannot deal with the peril of unemployment, and because commercial insurers could not, the government has undertaken a system of unemployment compensation to protect members of the society against loss from this source. The unemployment insurance program of the United States is subject to control by both the federal and state governments. This division of control resulted from the reluctance of the states to enact unemployment insurance programs. For a considerable period of time, many authorities, led by the great labor economist John R. Commons, have advocated a system of social insurance designed to protect workers against the peril of unemployment, but until they were forced to do so by federal legislation, only two of the

---

[16] Disability benefits were added to the social security act in 1956, but at that time they applied only to persons over 50 years of age. In 1960 the provision restricting disability benefits to persons over 50 was eliminated and the new qualification requirements discussed in Chapter 13 were instituted. Since 1965, the social security law has contained a provision reducing disability benefits under social security by the amount of any workmen's compensation benefits received, to the point at which the combined benefits do not exceed 80% of the disabled individual's average wage over a 5 year period prior to the date of disability.

states were willing to experiment with the idea. Wisconsin enacted an unemployment compensation act in 1932, and New York had one shortly thereafter, but with these two exceptions there was almost no legislation at the state level in the area of unemployment insurance. Most of the states were reluctant to enact unemployment insurance programs because they feared that it would place the industries in their state at a competitive disadvantage with other states where such legislation had not been enacted.

### The Social Security Act and Unemployment Insurance

The Social Security Act of 1935 induced the several states to enact unemployment insurance plans through the power of the federal government to levy taxes. The Social Security Act imposed a payroll tax of 1% on the total wages of all employers who had eight or more employees in each of 20 weeks during the year and who were not exempted because of occupational classification. After imposing the tax, the law went on to provide that employers would be permitted to offset 90% of the tax through credit for taxes paid to a state unemployment insurance program meeting standards specified in the law. In effect, this meant that any state which did not enact a qualified unemployment compensation law would experience a financial drain which could be avoided by passage of an unemployment compensation system. It is not surprising that all the states elected to enact programs which met the conditions required by the federal law and so qualified for the tax offset.

The Social Security Act provided for a tax on employers in covered occupations who had eight or more employees for at least one day in 20 separate weeks. The number of employees required has since been reduced to four. Occupations excluded were:

1. Agricultural employees
2. Domestic employees
3. Crews of vessels on navigable waters of the U.S.
4. Immediate members of the employer's family
5. Federal government or federal agency employees
6. State and local government or agency employees
7. Employees of nonprofit organizations of a religious, charitable, scientific, literary, or educational nature

Since the enactment of the law, the amount of the tax has been increased several times, but the base rate upon which it is levied was reduced to $3000 in 1939, and it has remained at that point. From the original level of 1%, the tax was increased to 2%, then to 3%, and more recently to 3.1%. When the tax was increased to 3.1%, the federal tax credit remained at 90% of the

3%, or 2.7%.[17] The 0.4% tax on payrolls up to $3000 retained by the federal government is used to cover the administrative costs of the programs.

The conditions required in each state's unemployment compensation program in order to qualify for the 90% tax credit against the federal tax were the following:

1. All unemployment compensation benefits must be paid through state public employment offices
2. All state unemployment taxes must be paid to the Secretary of Treasury for deposit in the Unemployment Trust Fund
3. Withdrawals from the fund are to be used only to pay unemployment compensation benefits
4. Compensation cannot be denied to an individual solely because he refuses to accept a job that is vacant because of a labor dispute; furthermore, a worker cannot be denied benefits for refusing to accept a job if one of the conditions of employment is that he join or not join a union
5. The administrative staff of the program must be selected on a merit basis
6. A fair hearing must be granted to those whose claims are denied
7. Reports must be made available to the federal government

These standards represent the minimum for the state laws, and the states are permitted to enact laws which are more liberal or to include employees not subject to the federal tax. In addition, they are free to impose any additional tax rates they desire.

As a result of the fact that each state has enacted separate legislation and operates a separate program, there are considerable differences among the programs in almost every respect. However, it may serve some purpose to discuss the general nature of the programs.[18]

---

[17] The federal government permits the states to enact "experience-rating" provisions which relate the tax paid by the employer to the benefits which have been paid out to his former workers who were involuntarily terminated. Almost all the states have taken advantage of this option; Alaska is the only state that has not done so. The basic intention of the experience-rating plans is to promote employment stability by rewarding those employers with a low turnover rate by requiring a lower premium from them. In most cases, the rate paid by the employer under an experience-rating plan is based on a ratio of past premiums paid to past benefits paid. The lower the benefits in relation to tax deposits made by the employer, the lower his current tax rate. The federal tax credit remains at 90% of the tax which the employer would have paid without the experience-rating credit.

[18] The student will no doubt want to look at the unemployment compensation act of his own state. One of the most up-to-date compilations of the laws of all the states is *The Unemployment Insurance Reporter*, a loose-leaf reporting service published weekly by the Commerce Clearing House, New York.

### Eligibility for Benefits

The eligibility requirements vary from state to state, but all states require previous employment in a covered occupation and continued attachment to the labor force as a prerequisite for benefits. Some states exceed the minimum standard of the federal act with respect to the definition of employment. Twenty-six states, for example, go beyond the requirements of the federal act and include employers with fewer than four employees. In addition, all states which do not automatically include employers with fewer than four employees permit these exempted employers to elect to cover their employees under the law. Twenty-nine states include employers with employees for fewer than the federally specified 20 weeks. In general, the occupational classifications excluded under the federal law are also excluded under the state laws. For example, only the District of Columbia, Hawaii, and Puerto Rico do not exclude agricultural workers, and only New York covers domestic employees in private homes.

In addition to the requirement of covered employment, which means that a tax must have been paid on behalf of the worker, additional qualification requirements are also imposed. In most states, the worker must also have earned a certain minimum amount of income during the preceding year, referred to as the "base period." Fifteen states require that the worker must have been paid a stated dollar minimum during the base period, and 6 other states require a specified number of weeks of employment with a minimum amount of earnings each week. The remaining states require the employee to have earned some multiple of the weekly benefit amount he will receive (e.g., 30 times).

Continued attachment to the labor force is also required. The basic philosophy of the unemployment compensation program is that only those workers who are legitimate members of the labor force are eligible for benefits. Therefore, unemployment must be involuntary before the worker can collect benefits, which means that the worker must be willing and able to work. This is the principal reason that benefits are payable through the state employment offices. The worker desiring to draw benefits must present himself at the employment office to collect his benefits, and he must be willing to accept suitable employment if it is offered to him.[19] The question of what constitutes "suitable" employment can be an extremely difficult problem, but normally the administrative staff of the state employment

---

[19] For example, students are not available for work while attending school and women who quit their jobs because of pregnancy or to get married are not eligible for benefits. As a note to the student who might be tempted to seek benefits under the law after working in covered employment during the summer, and who is not a bona fide member of the labor force, all state laws contain a provision for recovery of benefits paid because of fraudulent misrepresentation.

office makes the decision as to whether the work is suitable. If the worker feels that he has been unfairly treated, he is entitled to a hearing. Under the same basic philosophy that only those who are involuntarily unemployed are entitled to benefits, most states have provisions in the law which deny or limit benefits to those workers who quit their place of work without sufficient reason, or who are discharged for misconduct.[20]

### Amount and Duration of Benefits

If the worker meets the requirements of previous employment and involuntary unemployment, he is entitled to certain benefits as a matter of right, without the necessity of meeting a needs test. There is no uniformity among the states in terms of the amount of the benefits to which the qualified worker is entitled. The benefits paid in some states are far higher than those paid in other states. Some states have accumulated substantial reserves in their unemployment compensation fund, while other states with more generous benefits constantly face depleted accounts.

In all states, the amount of the benefits to which the worker is entitled is related to his previous earnings. In most states, the method of determining benefits is to take some percentage or fraction of the wages of the worker during the quarter of highest earnings in his base year. One of the most commonly used fractions is 1/26. If the worker was fully employed during the quarter, a 1/26 benefit provides him with a weekly benefit equal to approximately 50% of his normal full-time earnings. This amount is subject to a weekly minimum and maximum prescribed by the law. The maximum under the various laws in mid-1969 ranged from $38 to $72 per week. A few states provide for a sliding maximum, based on the number of dependents the unemployed worker has. The maximum weekly benefit including the allowance for dependents in any state is $105.

In addition, all states provide a maximum period of time for which the benefits are payable. In 41 states the maximum period is 26 weeks and in 9 states it is longer. The maximum in any state is 39 weeks in Oklahoma.[21]

From our short discussion, it is apparent that the unemployment insurance programs of the individual states are essentially short-term programs. They

[20] Benefits may be completely forfeited or only partially. For example, under the Iowa law a worker discharged for misconduct forfeits from 4 to 9 weeks of benefits. A worker who voluntarily quits his job forfeits all the benefits for which he had accumulated benefits in that particular job, but he forfeits benefits accumulated only during the job that was quit.

[21] Although the shortest maximum for which benefits are payable in any state is 26 weeks, the Puerto Rico law provides for a maximum of 15 weeks. The trend is to increase the period for which benefits are paid. A number of states provide for payment of additional benefits during periods of high unemployment to any workers who have exhausted their regular unemployment benefits.

are designed to provide additional income to the worker who is temporarily unemployed—the "between jobs" worker. In addition, the programs may serve to provide income to unemployed workers during periods of cyclical unemployment. The underlying assumption is that the premium tax will be more than sufficient to provide benefits during periods of peak employment, and the excess may be used to meet the additional benefits that are payable during periods of mass short-run unemployment. Although the unemployment compensation program was devised during a period of mass unemployment, it is not designed to cope with large-scale unemployment over an extended period of time. Structural unemployment and technological unemployment must be met through other income redistribution techniques and retraining of workers.

## COMPULSORY TEMPORARY DISABILITY INSURANCE LAWS

Workers who are unable to work because of an injury resulting from an industrial accident are entitled to disability income benefits under the workmen's compensation laws. In addition, persons in covered employment who are able to, and available for, work and who are involuntarily unemployed, are entitled to unemployment compensation benefits. The Old-Age, Survivors, Disability, and Health Insurance (OASDHI) program, as we have seen, provides disability income benefits for covered employees who become totally and permanently disabled. In spite of the broad coverage of these three programs, there exists a risk in connection with income that is not generally protected under the social insurance programs: loss of income resulting from temporary nonoccupational disability. While it is true that many private employers have established plans covering their employees against loss of income due to nonoccupational injuries, only six jurisdictions require such coverage by law: California, Hawaii, New Jersey, New York, Rhode Island, and Puerto Rico. The basic emphasis of these laws differs from both workmen's compensation and unemployment compensation. Workmen's compensation provides protection against job-connected disabilities; unemployment compensation provides benefits for the healthy person who is unemployed. The temporary disability laws of these six jurisdictions provide benefits for loss of income resulting from nonoccupational disabilities.

Rhode Island was the first state to adopt such a law in 1942. California passed its law in 1946, New Jersey in 1948, and New York in 1949. There was no similar legislation until 1968, when Puerto Rico enacted its law. Hawaii enacted its law in 1969.

### Persons Covered

In California, Rhode Island, and New Jersey, the laws cover the same employments as the unemployment compensation law. In New York, any employee who works for an employer of four or more persons on at least 30 days during the year is covered. The laws of Hawaii and Puerto Rico apply to the same classes of employment as the unemployment laws of those jurisdictions, except that coverage is also included on all agricultural workers as well.

### Benefits

All the programs provide weekly income benefits, equal to between one-half and two-thirds of the average weekly wage, subject to a minimum and a maximum. The minima range from $7 to $20 and the maxima range upward to $78. In general, the duration of the benefits follows the duration under the unemployment compensation law, with the typical maximum being 26 weeks. All the programs require a waiting period of 1 week before benefits are payable. The California law also provides hospital benefits on a flat daily basis and eliminates the waiting period for claimants who are hospitalized. Disability is defined as the inability to perform normal duties because of a mental or physical condition. The New York law limits coverage to nonoccupational illness or injury, and no benefits are paid in New York or New Jersey to anyone who is receiving workmen's compensation benefits. In the other states, which include occupational disability, the amount of the benefit is reduced by any workmen's compensation benefit payable. All the jurisdictions disqualify a disabled person who is receiving unemployment compensation benefits.

### Insurance

The Rhode Island program is insured in a monopolistic state fund. In California, New Jersey, and Puerto Rico, coverage is provided automatically from a state fund, using the machinery of the unemployment insurance program, except with respect to employers who elect to provide similar benefits under a private plan. The employer must purchase insurance from the state fund until such time as he has qualified as a self-insurer or purchased insurance from a private insurer. In New York and Hawaii, a competitive state fund or a private insurer may be used. In all the states in which private insurance is permitted, the law requires that the plan must be at least as liberal as the state fund plan, and in California, there is a requirement that the private plan be superior to the state plan in at least one respect.

### Financing

All the programs are financed by a payroll tax. In some cases, this is paid entirely by the employee, while in other cases, the employer may pay part or all of the cost. In Rhode Island, the employee pays the entire tax, which amounts to 1% of the first $3600 of wages. The tax in California is also 1% of the first $3600 of wages, but many employers who have elected private plans pay part or all of the cost. Under the New Jersey plan, the employer and the employee share the cost of the coverage, with the employee paying 0.5% and the employer 0.25% on the first $3000 of wages. Under the New York plan, the employee pays 0.5% on the first $60 of weekly wages, with the employer paying the additional cost, if any. In Hawaii, the tax imposed on the employee is one-half the cost of the program, not to exceed 0.5% of a flexible tax base, which is computed once a year as 120% of the state average annual wage in covered employment. Under the Puerto Rico law, the employer and employee each pay a tax of 0.5% on the first $7800 of wages.

### Questions for Discussion and Review

**1.** Explain the nature of the common law obligations and the common law defenses of employers' liability. Are these obligations and defenses ever used today? Under what circumstances?

**2.** Explain the various classifications of disability under the workmen's compensation law of your state. How do the benefit levels in your state compare with the benefit levels of other states?

**3.** In view of the wide variations in the extent of coverage under the workmen's compensation laws and the differences in benefit levels, do you think it would be a good idea to expand the social security system to provide benefits under social security in lieu of the state workmen's compensation act?

**4.** What occupational classifications or persons are excluded from the provisions of the workmen's compensation law in your state? Why are they excluded? Is the exclusion justifiable?

**5.** Unemployment results in a loss of income regardless of the cause. We ought, therefore, to eliminate the distinction in social insurance programs between unemployment resulting from occupational disability, nonoccupational disability, and unemployment not connected with disability. Do you agree or disagree?

**Suggestions for Additional Reading**

*Analysis of Workmen's Compensation Laws.* Washington, D.C.: Chamber of Commerce of the United States, current.

*Fire, Casualty and Surety Bulletins,* Casualty and Surety Volume, "Workmen's Compensation" Section. Cincinnati, Ohio: The National Underwriter Co.

Gentile, W. J. *The Workmen's Compensation and Employers' Liability Policy.* New York: Insurance Advocate, 1962.

Gordis, P. *Property and Casualty Insurance,* 17th ed. Indianapolis, Ind.: The Rough Notes Co., 1970, Chap. 30.

Kulp, C. A. and Hall, J. *Casualty Insurance,* 4th ed. New York: Ronald Press, 1968, Chaps. 7–9.

Long, J. D. and Gregg, D. W. *Property and Liability Insurance Handbook.* Homewood, Ill.: Richard D. Irwin, 1965, Chaps. 35, 36.

Magee, J. H. and Serbein, O. N. *Property and Liability Insurance,* 4th ed. Homewood, Ill.: Richard D. Irwin, 1967, Chap. 18.

Osborn, G.: *Compulsory Temporary Disability Insurance in the United States.* Homewood, Ill.: Richard D. Irwin, 1958.

Ratcliffe, D. *Workmen's Compensation Insurance Handbook.* Philadelphia: McCombs & Co., 1954.

Somers, H. M., and Somers, A. R. *Workmen's Compensation.* New York: John Wiley & Sons, 1954.

# 24 Surety Bonds and Credit Insurance

*Better is the end of a thing than the beginning thereof.*

—*Old Testament,* Eccles. 7:8

In this chapter, we will discuss surety bonds and credit insurance. Although these two fields might seem completely unrelated, there is a basic similarity: both are designed to protect against financial losses which may result from default by someone upon whom the insured depends.

When a business firm or a government organization hires a contractor to build a building or perform some other work, it is assumed that the building will be built according to plan or that the work will be completed. Such is not always the case. The contractor may become bankrupt and be unable to complete the job. When a business extends credit to one of its customers, it assumes that the customer will eventually pay for the goods; but credit losses do arise. Insofar as these possibilities exist, risk exists, for such failures as the above may be the occasion of serious financial loss.

One approach to dealing with these exposures is, of course, loss prevention. Care in the selection of clients to whom credit is to be granted and investigation of the financial stability of the contractor are steps which may help to avoid loss. Another alternative is assumption, and the individual or business faced with these risks may elect or have no choice but to assume the risk. The coverages discussed in this chapter represent a third alternative—that of transferring the risk to a professional risk bearer.

**604**

## SURETY BONDS

Technically, all bonds are surety bonds, including the fidelity coverages discussed in Chapter 21. However, the term "surety" is generally reserved for the nonfidelity field. Fidelity bonds are more closely related to insurance coverages than they are to suretyship as discussed here.

As we have noted previously, suretyship is the practice of guaranteeing obligations through a three-party contract. Under the provisions of this contract, one party (the surety) agrees to be held responsible to a second party (the obligee), for the obligations of a third party (the principal). Under a surety bond, the surety lends its name and credit to guarantee the obligation of the principal. In other words, the surety guarantees a certain type of conduct on the part of the principal, and if the principal fails to behave in the manner guaranteed, the surety will be responsible to the obligee.

Originally, the surety was a friend or a relative. When doubt existed regarding the ability of a person to perform some task, the individual to whom the obligation was due required a friend or relative to guarantee the performance.[1] Personal suretyship frequently proved to be unsatisfactory, both to the obligee and to the surety, and the natural result was corporate suretyship, which was developed in about 1842 in England.

Surety bonds are used today in situations in which one of the parties insists on a guarantee of indemnity in the event of failure of the second party to perform a specified act. Such a requirement may arise in connection with construction contracts, court procedures, or other situations in which there may be doubt concerning ability to perform.

### Suretyship Distinguished from Insurance

Suretyship differs from insurance in a number of ways. The most frequently stated distinction is that a surety bond is a three-party contract, involving the surety, the principal, and the obligee, while the insurance contract is a two-party contract between the insured and the insurer. The most important distinction, however, is one of basic philosophy regarding losses. In the field of insurance, the insurer generally expects losses to occur. In the surety field, no losses are expected, primarily because the surety will not issue the bond if it appears that a loss is likely. For example, before issuing a bond for the completion of a construction project by a contractor, the surety will examine the financial resources of the contractor, his manner of operation, and past history. If it appears that the contractor has the financial ability and the technical skill required for the completion of the project, the surety

---

[1] One of the earliest forms of suretyship was the hostage. A debtor might offer as security for a debt a hostage who was usually a close relative. When the debt was paid, the hostage was released. If the debt was not paid, the hostage was likely to be in for a hard time.

will issue the bond. This bond is a certificate of character, ability, and financial worth of the principal. In essence the surety says, "We have examined the financial statements and the performance record of this principal, and we are convinced that he has the financial resources and skills to complete the project for which he intends to contract; if we are wrong in our opinion, we will be held responsible." This is an unusually strong guarantee, and a bond will be issued only when the surety has the utmost confidence in the ability of the principal to perform. If there is any question about the ability of the principal to perform, the bond will not be issued. In some cases, the surety may require the principal to put up collateral equal to the amount of the maximum possible loss under the bond. Thus, while actuarial science is the basis for insurance rates, the fee in connection with a surety bond is primarily a payment for the investigation and certification, with only a small element to cover inevitable losses.

It is important to note that although the purchaser of the bond is normally the principal, a surety bond is issued for the benefit of the obligee. The fact that a bond is for the benefit of the obligee and not the principal is illustrated by the fact that in the event of a loss under the bond, the surety has a right to collect from the principal any amount that the surety has been obligated to pay to the obligee. In other words, when a loss is paid by the surety, the surety obtains full rights of recovery against the principal.

The main categories into which surety bonds may be divided are:

1. Contract bonds
2. Court bonds
3. License and permit bonds
4. Public official bonds
5. Miscellaneous bonds

A brief discussion of the more important bonds under each of these classifications should serve to illustrate more fully the nature of suretyship.

### Contract Bonds

The general purpose of the contract bond is to guarantee that the principal, who is normally a contractor or supplier, will fulfill his commitment according to specifications under the contract. For this reason, many of these bonds are designated "Performance Bonds." Performance Bonds provide for indemnification if the principal fails to perform on his contract.

**Construction contract bonds.** This type of bond is designed for use in connection with contracts to build real property. Under a construction bond, the surety agrees to indemnify the obligee in the event that the principal fails to complete the construction according to specifications in the contract.

If the contractor cannot, for some reason or another, finish the agreed construction, it is up to the surety to see that it is done. The construction contract bond may be written to include the terms of a Labor and Materials Bond, which is discussed below.

**Labor and materials bond.**    The labor and materials bond is a form under which the surety guarantees that the principal will pay all bills for labor and material in connection with the contract, thus assuring the obligee that the work completed will be free of all mechanics' or other types of liens. It may be written separately or it may be included in the provisions of a construction contract bond.

**Supply contract bond.**    This bond guarantees faithful performance under a contract to supply goods or materials. The bond guarantees that the principal will furnish the obligee with the goods contracted for in accordance with the specifications in the contract to supply goods.

**Completion bond.**    Here the obligee is normally a lender who has furnished funds to a contractor in connection with construction work. It guarantees the obligee that the principal (who is the borrower) will use the money in accordance with the terms of the contract and will complete the work undertaken.

**Bid bond.**    In many cases, where a contract is being let for public bids, the person or persons letting the contract require all bidders to furnish a bid bond. This is required to establish that the bid is a bona fide bid by the one required to post the bond. It protects against loss resulting from failure of the bidder to accept the bid. If the bidder who is awarded the contract fails to sign the contract, or is unable to provide the required performance bond, the contract may then be awarded to the next lower bidder. The surety on the bid bond then becomes liable for the difference between the bid of its principal and the next lowest bidder. A point of frequent misunderstanding has to do with the obligation of the surety under a bid bond. The surety on a bid bond is not required to furnish its principal with a performance bond if he is awarded the contract; however, if the principal cannot obtain a performance bond, the surety on the bid bond becomes liable.

### Court Bonds

In many proceedings conducted in a court of law, some form of bond may be required by the court. There are two basic forms of court bonds:

1. Fiduciary bonds are required when an individual is appointed by the court to hold, control, or manage the property of others; examples of

persons who are required to post fiduciary bonds are executors and administrators of estates, guardians, and receivers.

2. Litigation bonds are required of a person who wishes to bring action in a court of law or equity; normally, these bonds are required when the person bringing suit wishes to tie up the assets of the other party in the suit or restrain the other party from doing something.

**Fiduciary bonds.**   A fiduciary is a person appointed by the court to hold, control, or manage the property of others. The fiduciary bond guarantees that the fiduciary (who is the principal under the bond) will faithfully perform the duties of his trust. In most cases, the form of the bond is prescribed by the court, and in addition the face amount of the bond (the "penalty") is also set by the court.

To protect itself, the surety frequently asks for joint control of the assets of the estate. Under this arrangement, all the funds of the estate are kept in a joint account, and disbursements from this account are made only with the signature of both the principal and the surety. The major subclassifications of fiduciary bonds are described below.

*Executor's bond.*   This is the bond required of the person named in the will of the deceased to administer the estate.

*Administrator's bond.*   When a person dies without a will, the court appoints an administrator, whose duties are similar to those of an executor. The obligee under both the Executor's Bond and the Administrator's bond is the state or the court for the benefit of the beneficiaries.

*Guardian's bond.*   This is required when it becomes necessary to appoint someone to administer property belonging to a minor. The guardian is normally appointed by the court; the court then requires a bond which guarantees the faithful performance of the guardian. The obligee is the state for the benefit of the minor.

*Bonds in trust estates.*   These are required when the owner of property directs that the property which he owns be held in trust for his heirs, either for a given period of years, or until the death of the heirs. Such a trust may be established by will (Testamentary Trust) or it may be established during the lifetime of the owner of the property (inter-vivos trust). In either case, when a trust is established, the property must be turned over to a trustee who is responsible for its administration. The trustee's bond guarantees the faithful performance of the trustee.

*Committee bonds.*   These are required when a person is not competent to handle his own affairs and the court appoints someone (known as the "committee") to protect his property. A committee bond guarantees the faithful performance of the committee.

*Miscellaneous fiduciary bonds.*   In addition to those already discussed, there are a number of other bonds of similar nature which are required of persons who have custody or control over the property of others. Examples of such bonds are Receiver's Bonds, which are required of a court-appointed receiver in bankruptcy proceedings; Trustee's Bonds, which are also appointed in bankruptcy proceedings; and bonds which are required of conservators or liquidators of business firms or partnerships.

**Litigation bonds.** Litigation bonds are the second major class of court bonds. The bonds in this class are required for the purpose of obtaining some restriction on property of others or releasing property from such restrictions. If a person bringing action seeks to attach property, and the case is finally decided against him, the person whose property was attached might maintain that the action injured him and caused him damages. The bonds that are required in litigation will pay any such damages. In addition, under certain circumstances, the person bringing suit must furnish security to guarantee the payment of court costs. The more common types of litigation bonds are described below.

*Attachment bonds.* These are required when property is attached in advance of the court decision in order to prevent its disposal by the person having custody of it. The bond guarantees reimbursement for damages if the attachment is unjustified.

*Garnishment bonds.* These are required when the plaintiff wishes to attach wages or financial assets in the hands of a third party. It is much the same as an attachment bond, except that the assets distrained are in the hands of a third party.

*Replevin Bonds.* These are similar to attachment bonds, except that the plaintiff is suing to recover specific property. The Replevin Bond guarantees that the property will be returned to the defendant in proper condition if the plaintiff loses the suit.

*Bonds for distraint of rent.* These are required of a landlord who seeks to have the personal property of his tenant seized in an action to recover rent.

*Release of attachment bond.* This enables the defendant, whose goods have been attached, to recover possession of the goods. It guarantees that the goods will be available and will be turned over to the plaintiff in the event that the defendant loses the suit.

*Appeal bonds.* These are required of individuals who have lost in a suit and wish to appeal and suspend execution of the judgment pending the decision of a higher court. The bond guarantees payment of the costs of appeal.

*Removal bonds.* These are required in certain cases when the defendant who is being sued in a state court wishes the suit to be removed to a federal court, or from the court of one state to another state. The bond guarantees the payment of court costs by the principal if it is found that the case was improperly removed to the new court.

*Nonresident cost bonds.* These are sometimes required when a nonresident of a state, city, or county wishes to institute action against a resident. The bond guarantees payment of costs in the event of failure of the suit.

*Injunction bonds.* These are required when the plaintiff alleges that he is being injured by the actions of the defendant and requests the court to restrain the defendant from further action. If an injunction is granted, a bond is required of the plaintiff, which guarantees payment of damages if the injunction proves to be unwarranted.

*Discharge of mechanics lien bond.* The owner of property can obtain removal of a lien before trial by furnishing a bond which promises to indemnify the claimant if the claimant wins the suit.

### License and Permit Bonds

Many state and federal licenses are required for manufacturing, tax, and occupational purposes. In many cases the applicant for a license is required to post a bond, guaranteeing faithful performance of duties or payment of taxes collected. The purpose and intent of these bonds is to protect the state and the public from damages arising out of the manner in which the business is conducted, or to guarantee the payment of taxes collected by the license holder. The major classes of License and Permit Bonds and some of the classes of individuals which require the bonds are:

1. *Federal license bonds for manufacturers*
2. *State tax bonds* are required in connection with the sale of gasoline, cigarettes, liquor taxes, sales taxes, etc; these guarantee that the principal will deliver to the state all taxes collected
3. *Occupational bonds* are required for security salesmen, liquor stores, undertakers, collection agencies, warehousemen, and a vast array of other occupational classifications; these guarantee honest and faithful performance by the principal
4. *License bonds required in connection with placing or construction of materials which might cause injury or inconvenience to the public*—in many cities permit bonds are required in connection with signs and billboards, or street obstructions; these guarantee indemnity to anyone who is injured as a result of the construction or materials

### Public Official Bonds

The law requires that certain persons elected to fill positions of trust must furnish bonds which guarantee their faithful performance of duties. The public officials are generally held to be liable for the faithful accounting for all money they receive. If for any reason the public official cannot turn over to the state all the money he has received, or if he dissipates assets belonging to the government unit he serves, he is personally liable. Public Official Bonds are designed to guarantee payment of funds which the public official has not turned over or which he has dissipated. These bonds are designed to protect against dishonesty, negligence, and even lack of ability.

Most Public Official Bonds are referred to as "statutory," because they are required by law, and most of the forms are also prescribed by law. The surety cannot reduce its liability by inserting provisions in the bond; the provisions spelled out by statute take precedence. These bonds are normally written for the term of the elected or appointed official and are noncancellable during its term. In most instances, the cost of the bond is paid out of public funds.

**Public Employees Bond.**  The Public Employees Bond is closely related to the Public Officials Bond. It is available to cover employees who are not required by law to post a bond, which includes most workers in public service other than tax collectors and treasurers. The minimum amount for which this bond may be written is $2500. The coverage may be written to cover honesty of the public employees, or it may be written to cover "faithful performance." The faithful performance form will pay losses resulting from dishonesty of the bonded person, and in addition will pay for losses resulting from negligence or lack of ability.

### Miscellaneous Bonds

In addition to the bonds discussed above, there are others that do not fall into any of the described categories.

**Lost instrument bonds.**  These bonds, which are also called "lost securities bonds," are required of an individual who has lost or accidentally destroyed securities or other valuable papers and wishes to obtain duplicates. The bond guarantees that the principal will reimburse the issuer of a duplicate instrument if the original security or instrument later turns up and its holder is able to collect on it.

**Workmen's compensation bonds.**  In many states, the workmen's compensation law permits certain employers to self-insure their workmen's compensation exposure. To guarantee that the benefits to which an injured worker is entitled will be paid, the self-insurer is required to post a "self-insurer bond," which guarantees payment of benefits to workers who are injured and entitled to workmen's compensation benefits under the workmen's compensation law.

## CREDIT INSURANCE

Most business firms deal with the risk of financial loss as a result of bad debts and credit losses through loss-prevention techniques and risk assumption. Care is exercised regarding customers to whom credit is to be extended and allowances are made in the budgeting process for normal bad debt losses. In some cases, these approaches may be inadequate, particularly when outstanding credit is a large item in the balance sheet of the firm or when questionable accounts must be carried. In instances where the credit risk is great, the firm may prefer to transfer the risk through credit insurance, which provides protection against abnormal credit losses. Credit insurance, which is sold only to manufacturers and wholesalers, and is not available to retail establishments, protects against loss resulting from the inability to collect accounts due to insolvency of the debtor or the debtor's unwillingness or inability to pay.[2] Policies may be written to cover losses arising out of defaults occurring during the policy term, without regard to the time of the sale, or they may be written to cover losses that arise from sales during the term of the contract, regardless of when the default occurs. Policies which cover losses arising out of defaults during the policy period are referred to as "back coverage policies," while policies which cover losses arising out of sales during the policy period are called "forward coverage policies." Both types are written with a maximum amount of coverage on each account.

Credit insurance is a highly specialized field, and the coverage is written by a limited number of insurers. The bulk of the credit insurance sold in the United States is sold by two companies, the American Credit Indemnity Company and the London Guarantee Company. The American Credit Indemnity Company writes approximately 75% of the coverage sold and the London Guarantee Company writes the bulk of the remainder.

### Types of Policies

In addition to the distinction between forward coverage and back coverage policies already noted, credit policies may also be subdivided according to the accounts covered. In general, there are two types of contracts. The first type, known as "extraordinary coverage" or "specific coverage" covers losses involving specific customers of the insured, and is generally limited to coverage on one or a few accounts. It is used when the outstanding balances of a single customer or a few customers represent a serious exposure to the

---

[2] It is important at the outset of our discussion to clearly distinguish "credit insurance" from "accounts receivable coverage" discussed in Chapter 21. As the reader will recall, the accounts receivable coverage provides indemnification of the insured in the event of a loss resulting from the destruction of accounts receivable records as a result of an insured peril. In the case of credit insurance, the peril insured against is insolvency or default of a debtor to whom credit has been extended.

firm, and it is generally purchased by firms who deal with a limited number of buyers. It is issued only after an investigation of the individual debtors and acceptance of each debtor by the insurer. Under this form of coverage, the insurer is permitted to cancel coverage as to future shipments to any debtor, but must give written notice of such cancellation.

The second type of coverage is known as the "general coverage policy;" it includes coverage on all customers of the insured with a credit rating as specified in the policy. Investigation of the individual customers is not necessary under the general policies, because they describe the amount of coverage and the quality of accounts coverage by reference to mercantile credit ratings such as those published by Dun and Bradstreet, Inc. Each account insured must have a capital and credit rating, which express the net worth of the company and its credit standing. The coverage on each account is determined by a table of mercantile ratings, selected by the insured and incorporated as a part of the contract.[3] Only debtors whose credit rating comes within the limitations of the ratings adopted by the insured are covered. For example, the insured might select coverage on accounts having a general credit rating of "high" or "good," and with a net worth of over $500,000. If he then sells to customers outside these classifications, he does so at his own risk. The total amount of coverage for each debtor is dependent on the rating of that debtor. For example, the policy might specify that the maximum amount of coverage for an account with a Dun and Bradstreet rating of AA-A1 is $50,000, and the maximum for an account with an AA-1 rating is $40,000. If the insured suffers a credit loss of $75,000 on an account with an AA-A1 rating, only $50,000 of that loss will enter into the computation of the amount recoverable.

### Coinsurance and the Normal Loss

Every credit insurance policy provides that the insured shall bear the first portion of each net loss through the application of a coinsurance percentage. This coinsurance percentage operates in essentially the same manner as that of the major medical policy; that is, it provides that the insured bear a specified percentage of each loss. The normal coinsurance percentages are 10% and 20%, but higher percentages may be used when the risk is great, as in the case of a debtor with an inferior credit rating.

In addition to the coinsurance percentage, the policy also includes an annual deductible, known as the "primary loss" or "normal loss." This deductible is equal to the normally expected bad debt write-off that is experienced by most business firms. It is calculated from the previous experience of

---

[3] Normally, the policies are written on Dun and Bradstreet, Inc., ratings, but some other trade mercantile agencies are also acceptable.

the firm insured or as a percentage of the firm's net annual sales from tables which express bad debt ratios for various industries. It is not insurable and is generally adjusted at each renewal. The insurer relies on the coinsurance percentage and the normal loss to induce the insured to exercise care in the extension of credit. Thus, credit insurance is not a substitute for a sound credit policy. As a matter of fact, if the firm does not have a sound credit policy, it will be very difficult for it to obtain credit insurance.

Loss settlement is made on an annual basis, with the coinsurance percentage applied to each loss before the application of the normal loss deductible. In addition, losses in excess of the coverage on individual accounts is excluded prior to loss computation.

To illustrate, assume that the credit insurer limits coverage to $50,000 on each of the accounts receivable with a Dun and Bradstreet rating of AA-A1. If the amount owed by such an account is $50,000, the most that the creditor could lose on this account (over and above the primary loss) would be $5000, assuming a 10% coinsurance provision. If the amount owed were $70,000, the insurance company would admit $50,000 of this account for coverage purposes and assume 90% of that amount. All such losses during the year would then be subject to the normal loss deductible. The loss computation below should serve to further illustrate the process.

|  | Amount of debt | Admitted loss | Less coinsurance |
|---|---|---|---|
| Account with AA-A1 rating | $70,000 | $50,000 | $45,000 |
| Account with AA-1 rating | 50,000 | 40,000 | 36,000 |
|  |  |  | 81,000 |
| Less primary loss |  |  | 10,000 |
| Recoverable from credit insurer |  |  | $71,000 |

## Collection Service

Although not all credit policies include provision for collection of past due accounts by the insurer, many contracts do, and the collection service is one of the most attractive aspects of credit insurance. Contracts differ regarding the provision for collection. In some contracts, the insured is required to turn past due accounts over to the insurer for collection. In other contracts, it is optional. Finally, some contracts make no provision for collection by the insurer. In those instances where the insured is required or permitted to turn past due accounts over to the insurer, accounts which are overdue a stated period (e.g., 60 days) under the original terms of sale, are turned over to the insurer for collection. If the insurer is successful in attempting to collect, a small service charge is made for the collection. If unsuccessful, the account becomes a loss under the policy and payment is made in the usual manner.

### Questions for Discussion and Review

**1.** Joe Smith, who is the insurance buyer for the Widget Manufacturing Company is confused about the difference between credit insurance and the accounts receivable insurance which his firm has purchased. Explain the difference to him.

**2.** Why are retail establishments not generally able to obtain credit insurance?

**3.** The university decides to ask for bids on the construction of a new dormitory. Make a list of all the bonds that might be involved in connection with the construction, indicating who would be the principal, the obligee, and the obligor in each case.

**4.** A property and liability insurance agent is generally authorized to bind coverage. This is not true with respect to surety coverages. Why not?

**5.** Is the treatment of suretyship and credit insurance in the same chapter a logical combination? What is the similarity or dissimilarity in their nature upon which you base your answer?

### Suggestions for Additional Reading

Crist, G. W. *Corporate Suretyship*, 2nd ed. New York: McGraw-Hill, 1950.

Gordis, P. *Property and Casualty Insurance*, 17th ed. Indianapolis, Ind.: The Rough Notes Co., 1970, Chap. 16.

Huebner, S. S., Black, K., and Kline, R. *Property and Liability Insurance*, 5th ed. New York: Appleton-Century-Crofts, 1968, Chaps. 25, 28.

Long, J. D. and Gregg, D. W. *Property and Liability Insurance Handbook*. Homewood, Ill.: Richard D. Irwin, 1965, Chaps. 53, 55.

Magee, J. H. and Serbein, O. N. *Property and Liability Insurance,* 4th ed. Homewood, Ill.: Richard D. Irwin, 1967, Chap. 16.

Morgan, W. D. "The History and Economics of Suretyship." *Cornell Law Quarterly* **XII** (1926–1927).

Phelps, C. W. *Commercial Credit Insurance as a Management Tool*. Baltimore: Commercial Credit Company, 1961.

Riegel, R. and Miller, J. *Insurance Principles and Practices,* 5th ed. Englewood Cliffs, N.J.: Prentice-Hall, 1966, Chaps. 38, 39.

# APPENDICES

# Appendix A

# GLOSSARY

**Abandonment**   The act of surrendering to the insurer all interest in the thing insured; it is generally conceded that property cannot be voluntarily abandoned to the insurance company—one notable exception to this general rule occurs in ocean marine, where abandonment is merely one step in proving a loss

**Acceptance**   agreeing to terms by means of which a bargain is concluded and the parties are bound; the binding of an insurance contract by the insurer

**Accident**   an event or occurrence which is unforeseen and unintended

**Accident insurance**   a form of health insurance against loss by accidental bodily injury

**Accidental bodily injury**   injury to the body of the insured as the *result* of an accident

**Accidental death benefit**   a provision added to an insurance policy for payment of an additional benefit in case of death by accidental means; it is often referred to as "double indemnity"

**Accidental means**   appearing in some policies, the unexpected or undesigned *cause* of an accident; the "means" which caused the mishap must be accidental in order to claim policy benefits

**Acquisition cost**   that portion of an insurance premium which represents the cost of producing the insurance business; it includes the agent's commission, the company field expense, and other related expenses

**Actual cash value**   the limit of indemnification under the Standard Fire Policy and other property contracts; in most cases it is replacement cost minus depreciation

**Actuary**   a person professionally trained in the technical aspects of insurance and related fields, particularly in the mathematics of insurance such as the calculation of premiums, reserves, and other values

**619**

**Additional interest**  one who may claim under, or is protected by, an insurance policy issued to another, as a mortgagee named in a fire policy

**Additional living expense**  insurance paying the extra expense involved in living elsewhere during the period of time it is impossible to remain in a dwelling which has been damaged by fire or another insured peril

**Adjuster**  one who settles insurance claims; may be a salaried employee or an independent operator

**Administrator**  a person authorized to administer the state of a deceased person by the court; his duties are to collect assets of the estate, pay its debts, and distribute the residue to those entitled; he resembles an executor, who is appointed by the will of the deceased—the administrator is appointed by the court and not by the deceased and therefore must give security for the administration of the estate called an *administration bond*

**Admiralty**  involving maritime law; concerning the high seas or navigable waters

**Adverse selection**  the tendency of poorer risks of less desirable insureds to seek or continue insurance to a greater extent than do the better risks

**Agent**  in property and casualty insurance, an individual authorized by an insurance company to create, modify, and terminate contracts of insurance; in life insurance, a sales and service representative who is also called a "life underwriter"

**Aggregate**  the greatest amount recoverable on account of a single loss or during a policy period, or on a single project

**Alien company**  an insurance company organized under the laws of a foreign country

**All-risk**  a term commonly used by insurance people to describe broad forms of coverage; it is misleading because no property or liability insurance policy is truly an all-risk coverage; these policies insure "all risks" of loss subject to the listed exclusions

**Allied lines**  a term that has been adopted to refer to the lines of insurance that are allied with property insurance; these coverages provide protection against perils traditionally written by fire companies, such as sprinkler leakage, water damage, and earthquake

**American agency system**  the term applied to the system of insurance marketing in which the agent is an independent businessman rather than an employee of the company

**Annuitant**  the person during whose life an annuity is payable, usually the person to receive the annuity

**Annuity**  a contract that provides an income for a specified period of time, such as a number of years or for life

**Annuity certain** a contract that provides an income for a specified number of years, regardless of life or death, to the insured if living or to his beneficiary if he has died

**Application** a statement of information made by a person applying for life insurance; it is used by the insurance company to determine the acceptability of the risk and the basis of the policy contract

**Apportionment** a division according to the interests of the various parties therein, as the apportionment clause in a fire policy

**Appraisal** an estimate of value, loss or damage; see Arbitration

**Arbitration** the submitting of a matter in dispute to the judgment of a specified number of disinterested persons called "arbitrators," whose decision, called an "award," is binding upon the parties

**Assault** an intentional, unlawful threat of bodily injury to another by force, or force unlawfully directed toward the person of another, under such circumstances as create well-founded fear of imminent peril, coupled with apparent present ability to execute the attempt; *battery* consists of the actual execution of the act offered in an assault—hence, the placing of the victim in fear (assault) and the actual infliction of the injury (battery) constitute what is commonly referred to as *assault and battery*

**Assessment** a charge sometimes levied against policyholders by certain types of companies

**Assigned risk** an applicant for automobile or workmen's compensation insurance declined by one or more companies; such a risk may be assigned to designated companies as directed by recognized authority—the operation is called an "assigned-risk plan"

**Assignment** the legal transfer of one person's interest in an insurance policy to another person

**Assured** a person who has been insured by an insurance company or underwriter against loss

**Attachment** a statutory legal remedy whereby one party may prevent removal of property belonging to another party, pending determination of a court action

**Attorney-in-fact** one appointed to act for another; the chief administrative officer of a reciprocal insurance group, who uses his power of attorney to commit the members of the group as insurers of each other; also one who executes a surety bond on behalf of the company he represents

**Attractive nuisance** a dangerous place, condition, or object that is particularly attractive to children; in these cases the courts have frequently held that where "attractiveness" exists, the owner is under a duty to take steps to prevent injury to those that may be attracted and the owner may be held liable for failure to do so

**Audit premium**  the additional premium to which the company is entitled or the return premium to which the insured is entitled after an audit and refiguring of the base on which the original or deposit premium was charged

**Automatic premium loan**  a provision in a life insurance policy authorizing the company to pay automatically by means of a policy loan any premium not paid by the end of the grace period

**Average clause**  a coinsurance clause; a clause requiring an insured to purchase insurance for a stipulated portion of the entire value of the thing insured; see General average; Particular average

**Bail**  a deposit or assignment guaranteeing appearance of a defendant for a trial and which is forfeited if the defendant fails to appear at the stipulated time

**Bailee**  one who has possession of property belonging to another; he may be a bailee for the benefit of the bailor, his own benefit, or for their mutual benefit

**Bailment**  a delivery of goods or personal property by one person to another in trust for the execution of a special object upon or in relation to such goods

**Battery**  any unlawful beating or other wrongful physical violence or constraint inflicted upon a human being without his consent; see Assault

**Beneficiary**  one for whose benefit a contract is made; the person to whom a policy of insurance is payable

**Beneficiary, contingent**  the person or persons designated to receive the death benefit if the primary beneficiary dies prior to the death of the insured

**Beneficiary, primary**  the person or persons designated to receive the benefits under the policy

**Betterment**  an improvement rendering property better than mere repairs would do

**Bid**  a proposal or offer

**Binder**  a written agreement (sometimes oral) whereby one party agrees to insure another party pending receipt of, and final action upon, the application

**Blanket**  in property and liability, used to designate insurance which extends to more than one location, or one class of property or one employee

**Blanket medical expense** (accident)  a provision for the payment of actual expense of hospital, nurse, surgical, and medical care subject to an overall maximum for all such expense

**Blue cross**   an independent, nonprofit membership corporation providing protection against the costs of hospital care in a limited geographical area

**Blue shield**   an independent, nonprofit membership corporation providing protection against the costs of surgery and other items of medical care in a limited geographical area

**Bodily injury**   physical injury to a person

**Boiler and machinery insurance**   coverage for loss arising out of the operation of pressure, mechanical, and electrical equipment; it may cover loss suffered by the boiler and machinery itself and may include damage done to other property, as well as business interruption losses

**Bond**   a written agreement of obligation under seal; the person to whom the undertaking is given is called "obligee"; the person liable for the undertaking is called the "obligor" or "principal," if a third party guarantees performance of the agreement, he is called the "surety"

**Breach of contract**   failure to comply with the terms or conditions incorporated in an insurance policy, frequently resulting in a restriction of coverage or a voiding of a policy itself

**Broker**   an individual who arranges and services insurance policies on behalf of the insurance buyer; he is the representative of the insured, although he receives his compensation in the form of a commission from the company

**Bureau**   a cooperative rate-making body, which is supported by member companies; the member companies agree to abide by the rates published by the bureau

**Burglary**   felonious abstraction of property from within premises by persons making felonious entry by force of which there are visible marks on the exterior

**Business interruption**   the name given to insurance covering the loss of earnings resulting from, and occurring after, destruction of property; also called "use and occupancy insurance"

**Business life insurance**   life insurance purchased by a business enterprise on the life of a member of the firm; it is often bought by partnerships to protect the surviving partners against loss caused by the death of a partner, or by a corporation to reimburse it for loss caused by the death of a key employee

**Capital sum**   a lump sum payable for dismemberment and sight losses

**Cash surrender value**   the amount available in cash upon voluntary termination of a policy before it becomes payable by death or maturity

**Catastrophe loss**   a loss of unusual size; a shock loss; a very large loss

**Cession**    the amount of a risk which the insurance company reinsures; the amount passed on to the reinsurer

**Claim**    notification to an insurance company that payment of an amount is due under the terms of a policy

**Coinsurance**    in property and casualty insurance, a clause or provision in an insurance policy requiring a specified amount of insurance based on the value of the property insured; normally, there is a premium reduction for purchasing insurance to some percentage of the value of the property—if the insured fails to comply with the clause, he will suffer a penalty in the event of partial loss; in health insurance, a policy provision requiring the insured to share a given percentage of the loss

**Collusion**    a compact between persons usually to the detriment of other persons or for some improper purpose

**Commercial**    the opposite of personal; of a business nature, usually mercantile or manufacturing

**Commission**    the fee paid by insurance companies to agents for the sale of policies

**Common carrier**    a transportation company such as a railroad or bus line

**Common law**    distinguished from law created by enactment of statutes; common law comprises the body of principles and rules of action, relating to the government and security of persons and property, which derive their authority solely from usages and customs of immemorial antiquity, or from the judgments and decrees of the courts

**Compensation**    wages, salaries, awards, fees, commissions, financial returns of any kind

**Comprehensive**    a loosely used term signifying broad or extensive insurance coverage

**Comprehensive major medical insurance**    a policy designed to give the protection offered by both a basic and major medical health insurance policy; it is characterized by a low "deductible" amount, coinsurance feature, and high maximum benefits—usually $5000–$10,000 or higher

**Comprehensive personal liability insurance**    a type of insurance that reimburses the policyholder if he becomes liable to pay money for damage or injury he has caused to others; this form does not include automobile liability, but does include almost every activity of the policyholder except his business operations

**Concealment**    deliberate failure to reveal material facts, which would affect the validity of a policy of insurance

**Concurrent**    covering the same kind of property at the same location under the same terms and conditions, with the same types of coverage, as two or more insurance policies

**Confining sickness**  that which confines an individual to his home or a hospital (visits to physicians and hospitals are generally considered as not terminating confinement)

**Consequential loss**  loss occurring after, and as a result of, some other loss, as loss of profits resulting from a fire or a loss of frozen foods resulting from electrical failure

**Consideration**  price, token, or other matter used as an inducement for the completion of a contract, as an insurance premium

**Constructive total loss**  a loss of sufficient amount to make the cost of salvaging or repairing the property equal to or greater than the value of the property when repaired

**Contingent**  conditional; depending upon another happening—a contingent beneficiary is one next in line after the first named

**Contribution**  a participation, as two insurance policies in the same loss

**Conversion**  wrongful appropriation to one's own use of property belonging to another

**Convertible term insurance**  term insurance which can be exchanged, at the option of the policyholder and without evidence of insurability, for another plan of insurance

**Cosurety**  a personal or corporate guarantor of a surety obligation on which one or more of the sureties are directly responsible for the same obligation

**Counter signature**  an additional signature required in most states to comply with residence agency laws; applies when a producer in one state controls business located in, or operating in, another state

**Coverage**  the insurance afforded by the policy

**Credit life insurance**  term life insurance issued through a lendor or lending agency to cover repayment of a specific loan, installment purchase, or other obligation in case of the debtor's death

**Crime**  a wrong against public laws or customs punishable by fine, imprisonment, or death after trial in a criminal court

**Crop–hail insurance**  protection for monetary loss resulting from hail damage to growing crops; although hail is the basic peril named in crop–hail policies, a number of other perils are covered as well, depending on the crop and area; crop–hail policies cover fire, lightning, windstorm, aircraft, smoke, and other miscellaneous perils

**Daily report**  a copy of that portion of an insurance contract dealing with the description of the risk and the amount of insurance, which is sent to the home office of the insurance company and retained in the agent's files

**Damages**   the amount claimed or allowed as compensation for injuries sustained or property damaged through the wrongful acts or the negligence of another; an award

**Declarations**   that part of an insurance policy containing the representations of the applicant

**Declination**   the rejection by a life insurance company of an application for life insurance, usually for reasons of the health or occupation of the applicant

**Deductible**   a provision whereby an insured may be required to pay part of a loss, the insurance being excess over the amount of the deductible

**Deferred anuity**   an annuity providing for the income payments to begin at some future date, such as in a specified number of years or at a specified age

**Deferred group annuity**   a type of group annuity providing for the purchase each year of a paid-up deferred annuity for each member of the group, the total amount received by the member at retirement being the sum of these deferred annuities

**Deposit administration**   a type of group annuity providing for the accumulation of contributions in an undivided fund out of which annuities are purchased as the individual members of the group retire

**Deposit premium**   an original premium paid by the insured at the inception date of the policy; estimated premium, subject to later adjustment; see Audit premium

**Depreciation**   the lessening of value through age, deterioration, and obsolescence

**Deviation**   use of a premium rate other than the standard rate filed with the state insurance department

**Direct loss**   loss resulting directly and immediately from the hazard insured against

**Direct writer**   an insurance carrier that deals directly with the insured through a salaried representative, as opposed to those carriers which use agents (also used to refer to carriers which operate through exclusive agents; in reinsurance, the company that originally writes the business

**Disability**   inability to perform all or part of one's occupational duties because of an accident or illness; see Total disability and Partial disability

**Disability benefit**   a provision added to a life insurance policy for waiver of premium, and sometimes payment of monthly income, if the insured becomes totally and permanently disabled

**Discovery period**   the period after termination of an insurance policy or bond, or after the occurrence of a loss, within which the loss must be discovered to be covered

**Dismemberment** accidental loss of limb or sight

**Distress carrier** an insurance company specializing in substandard risks, usually in the field of automobile insurance

**Dividend addition** an amount of paid-up insurance purchased with a policy dividend and added to the face amount of the policy

**Domestic company** a name given to a company in the state of its incorporation, as an Iowa company is domestic in the state of Iowa, foreign as to all other states, and alien as to all other countries

**Double indemnity** a provision under which certain benefits are doubled when accident is due to specified circumstances, such as public conveyance accidents; in a life insurance policy, a provision that the face amount payable on death will be doubled if the death is a result of an accident

**Effective date** the date upon which the policy is put in force; the inception date

**Effective benefit** a benefit payable in lieu of another; e.g., a lump sum benefit may be allowed for specified fractures or dislocations in lieu of weekly indemnity

**Elimination period** see Waiting period

**Endorsement** a written amendment affecting the declarations, insuring agreements, exclusions, or conditions of an insurance policy; a rider

**Endowment insurance** insurance payable to the insured if he is living on the maturity date stated in the policy, or to a beneficiary if the insured dies prior to that date

**Estate** possessions of a deceased person; possessions of a minor or incompetent person; possessions of a bankrupt person or corporation; worldly goods of anyone

**Estoppel** an admission or declaration by which a person is prevented from proving the contrary

**Excess** that which goes beyond, as excess insurance, over and above a primary amount

**Exclusion** that which is expressly eliminated from the coverage of an insurance policy

**Expectation of life** (life expectancy) The average number of years of life remaining for persons of a given age according to a particular mortality table

**Experience rating** the act of computing a premium based on the loss experience of the risk itself

**Expiration**   the date upon which an insurance policy terminates unless continued or renewed by an additional premium

**Extended coverage insurance**   protection for the insured against loss or damage of his property caused by windstorm, hail, smoke, explosion, riot, riot attending a strike, civil commotion, vehicle, and aircraft; this is provided in conjunction with the fire insurance policy

**Extended-term insurance**   a form of insurance available as a nonforfeiture option; it provides the original amount of insurance for a limited period of time

**Face amount**   the amount stated on the face of a life insurance policy that will be paid in case of death or at the maturity of the contract; it does not include dividend additions, or additional amounts payable under accidental death or other special provisions

**Family income policy**   a life insurance policy, combining whole life and decreasing term insurance, under which the beneficiary receives income payments to the end of a specified period if the insured dies prior to the end of the period, and the face amount of the policy either at the end of the period or at the death of the insured

**Family maintenance policy**   life insurance which pays, in addition to the face of the policy, a monthly income for a period commencing with the insured's death and continuing for the number of years specified; the period is most often 10, 15, or 20 years

**Family policy**   a life insurance policy providing insurance on all or several family members in one contract, generally whole life insurance on the husband and smaller amounts of term insurance on the wife and children, including those born after the policy is issued

**Fellow servant**   one who serves and is controlled by the same employer; also those engaged in the same common pursuit under the same general control

**Fellow servant rule**   rule that a master is not liable for injuries to a servant caused by the negligence of a fellow servant engaged in the same general business and where the master has exercised due care in the selection of servants

**Fidelity bond**   a contract of fidelity insurance; a guarantee of personal honesty of the person furnishing indemnity against his defaultation or negligence; a form of insurance or suretyship which protects a party against loss from the dishonesty of his employees

**Fiduciary**   a person or corporation having the duty created by his undertaking to act primarily for another's benefit in matters connected with such undertaking, or an agent handling the business of another when the business he transacts or the money or property he handles is not his own or for his own benefit

**Field supervisor** a salaried employee of an insurance company, whose responsibilities are (a) production of new business through existing agents, (b) the appointment of new agents, (c) general supervision of the company's affairs in his territory

**Financial responsibility law** a statute which requires motorists to show evidence of financial responsibility following an accident which involves bodily injury or property damage in excess of some amount; normally, proof of financial responsibility is given through a valid policy of insurance

**Fire insurance** coverage for losses caused by fire and lightning, as well as the resultant damage caused by smoke and water

**Fleet** a group, as of automobiles

**Floater** a marine or fire policy, the coverage of which follows the movement of the property insured

**General average** in marine insurance, a loss that must be borne partly by someone other than the owner of the goods that were lost or destroyed; for example, if it is necessary to jettison cargo to save a ship, the owners of the ship and the rest of the cargo which is saved will share in the loss of the goods that were intentionally sacrificed

**Graded commission** a reduced commission justified by the size of the premium

**Graded expense** a reduced expense item for the insurance company justified by the size of the premiums

**Gratuitous** made without a consideration, as a gift, requiring nothing in return

**Group annuity** a pension plan providing annuities at retirement to a group of persons under a single master contract, with the individual members of the group holding certificates stating their coverage; it is usually issued to an employer for the benefit of employees—the two basic types are "deferred" and "deposit administration" group annuities

**Group insurance** any insurance plan under which a number of employees and their dependents are insured under a single policy, issued to their employer, with individual certificates given to each insured employee; the most commonly written lines are life and accident and health

**Guaranteed renewable policy** a policy which the insured has the right to continue in force by the timely payment of premiums to a specified age, (usually age 50), during which period the insurer has no right to make unilaterally any change in any provision of the policy while the policy is in force, but may make changes in premium rates by policyholder class

**Hazard** a condition that creates or increases the probability of a loss

**Hazard, moral** the chance that a loss may be caused by, or due to, a lack of character or integrity on the part of the insured

**Hold-harmless agreement**    a contract usually written whereby one party assumes legal liability on behalf of another party

**Hostile fire**    a fire burning where none is intended

**Health insurance**    a generic term applying to all types of insurance indemnifying or reimbursing for expenses or losses caused by bodily accident or sickness or for expenses of medical treatment necessitated by sickness or accidental bodily injury

**Health Insurance Association of America**    a voluntary, nonprofit association of companies organized for the purpose of promoting "the development of voluntary health insurance providing sound protection against loss of income and other financial burdens resulting from sickness or accidental bodily injury"

**Improvements and betterments insurance**    insurance that protects a tenant against loss to improvements made by him to property in which he is a tenant

**Incontestable clause**    a provision that prevents the carrier from challenging the coverage because of alleged misstatements by the insured after a stipulated period has passed, usually 2 or 3 years

**Independent contractor**    one who performs work for another in his own manner and method, and who is not subject to the control or direction of the party for whom the work is performed; he is not an employee of the party for whom the work is performed.

**Indirect**    contingent; that which happens only after something else has occurred

**Individual policy pension trust**    a type of pension plan, frequently used for small groups, administered by trustees who are authorized to purchase individual level premium policies or annuity contracts for each member of the plan; the policies usually provide both life insurance and retirement benefits

**Industrial life insurance**    life insurance issued in small amounts, usually less than $1000 on a single life exclusive of additional benefits, with premiums payable on a monthly or more frequent basis, and generally collected at the insured's home by an agent of the company

**Inherent vice**    a characteristic depreciation such as the fading of ink, a cracking of parchment, the graying of hair

**Inland marine insurance**    a broad type of insurance, generally covering articles that may be transported from one place to another; the essential condition is that the insured property be moveable, though bridges, tunnels, and similar instrumentalities of transportation are also considered inland marine; this form of insurance was developed originally by marine underwriters to cover goods while in transit by other than ocean vessels; it now includes any goods in transit (generally excepting trans-ocean) as well as numerous "floater" policies such as personal effects, personal property, jewelry, furs, fine arts, and others

**Inspection**    an examination by those having authority; right usually reserved by an insurance company with respect to any property it insures

**Insurable interest**    an interest which might be damaged if the peril insured against occurs; the possibility of a financial loss to an individual which can be protected against through insurance

**Insurance**    an economic device whereby the individual substitutes a small certain cost (the premium) for a large uncertain financial loss (the contingency insured against) which would exist if it were not for the insurance contract; an economic device for reducing and eliminating risk through the process of combining a sufficient number of homogeneous exposures into a group in order to make the losses predictable for the group as a whole

**Insured**    in life insurance, the person on whose life an insurance policy is issued; in property and liability insurance, the person to whom or on whose behalf benefits are payable under the policy

**Intestate**    leaving no will at death

**Invitee**    a person having an express or implied invitation to enter a given location

**Joint insured**    one of two or more persons whose names or interests are insured under the same or identical contracts

**Judgment**    the decision of a court or the reason for such decision

**Jumbo risk**    a risk requiring exceptionally high benefit limits

**Key-man insurance**    a life insurance program designed to cover the key employees of an employer; it may be written on a group or individual policy basis

**Lapse**    termination of a policy due to failure by the insured to pay the premium as required

**Lapsed policy**    a policy discontinued for nonpayment of premiums; the term is technically limited to a termination occurring before a life insurance policy has a cash or other nonforfeiture value

**Legal reserve life insurance company**    a life insurance company operating under state insurance laws specifying the minimum basis for the reserves the company must maintain on its policies

**Level premium insurance**    insurance for which the cost is distributed evenly over the premium-paying period; the premium remains constant from year to year, and is more than the actual cost of protection in the earlier years of the policy and less than the actual cost in the later years—the excess paid in the early years accumulates the reserve

**Liability** a debt or responsibility; an obligation which may arise by a contract made or by a tort committed

**Life annuity** a contract that provides an income for the life of the annuitant

**Lifetime disability benefit** a benefit for loss of income payable as long as the insured is totally disabled, even for life

**Limited-payment life insurance** a form of whole life insurance on which premiums are payable for a specified number of years less than the period or protection, or until death if death occurs before the end of the specified period

**Limited policies** those which cover specified accidents or sickness

**Limits** the value or amount of a policy; the greatest amount which can be collected under the policy

**Livery** in automobile insurance, the carrying of passengers for hire

**Lloyd's** a voluntary unincorporated association of individuals organized for the purpose of writing insurance; normally refers to Lloyd's of London, a group of individual underwriters and syndicates that underwrite insurance risks severally, using facilities maintained by the Lloyd's of London Corporation

**Local agent** a producer of insurance whose activities are purely of local extent

**Long-term disability** a generally accepted period of time for more than 2 years—can vary according to company standards

**Loss** the unintentional decline in, or disappearance of, value due to a contingency

**Loss frequency** the number of claims on a policy during a premium period

**Loss ratio** the relationship between premiums collected and losses paid; losses (net) divided by premiums (net)

**Major medical expense insurance** policies especially designed to help offset the heavy medical expenses resulting from catastrophic or prolonged illness or injury; they provide benefit payments for 75–80% of all types of medical treatment by a physician above a certain amount first paid by the insured person and up to the maximum amount provided by the policy—usually $5000, $10,000, or higher

**Manual** a book of rates, rules, and coverages usually available for each kind of insurance

**Marine** pertaining to the sea or to transportation; usually divided as to "ocean marine" and "inland marine"; the insurance covering transportation risks

**Miscellaneous hospital expense**  a provision for the payment on a blanket basis or schedule basis of hospital services (other than room and board, special nursing care, and doctors fees) up to a stipulated maximum amount

**Misrepresentation**  a misstatement; if done with intent to mislead, it may void the policy of insurance

**Morbidity tables**  actuarial statistics showing the incidence and duration of disability

**Mortality table**  a statistical table showing the probable rate of death at each age, usually expressed as so many per thousand

**Mortgage**  a deposit or conditional transfer to secure the performance of some act; the person who makes the transfer is called the "mortgagor," the other party, the "mortgagee"; sometimes an intermediary called a "trustee" is appointed

**Multiple-line insurance**  policies that combine many perils previously covered by individual policies of fire and liability companies; the homeowner's policy is one example; other examples are the commercial property policy, the farmowner's policy, and the special multiperil policy for motels and apartments

**Mutual insurance company**  a nonprofit insurance carrier, without capital stock, which is owned by the policyholders; it may be incorporated or unincorporated

**Mutual life insurance company**  a life insurance company whose legal ownership and control is vested in policyholders whose management is directed by a board elected by the policyholders; mutual companies, in general, issue participating insurance only

**Named insured**  the one named in the policy; see Additional interest

**National Association of Insurance Commissioners**  a national organization of state officials who are charged with the regulation of insurance; although the organization has no official power, it exerts a strong influence through its recommendations

**Net retention**  the final amount of insurance retained by the company after reinsuring such amounts as it did not wish to retain

**Nonadmitted carriers**  an insurer that has not been licensed to write insurance in a given jurisdiction

**Noncancellable or noncancellable and guaranteed renewable policy**  a continuous term health insurance policy which guarantees the insured the right to renew for a stated number of years or to a stated age (usually 60 or 65), with the premium at renewal guaranteed

**Nonconfining sickness**  a sickness that does not confine the insured to his home or a hospital

**Nondisabling injury** an injury which does not cause total or partial disability

**Nonforfeiture option** privilege available to the policyholder based upon his interest in the contract or once cash value has been created

**Nonoccupational policy** one which does not cover loss resulting from accidents or sickness arising out of or in the course of employment or covered under any workmen's compensation law.

**Nonparticipating insurance** policy insurance on which the premium is calculated to cover as closely as possible the anticipated cost of the insurance protection and on which no dividends are payable to the insured

**Not taken** insurance policy issued and delivered to an insured but returned for flat cancellation; see Lapse

**Notary** commonly, a political appointee invested with the right to swear in a person making a statement under oath and to certify his signature

**Obligee** the person in favor of whom some obligation is contracted, whether such obligation be to pay money, or to do, or not do something; the party to whom a bond is given

**Obligor** the person who has engaged to perform some obligation; one who makes a bond; the bonding company

**Occupational disease** a disease or condition of health resulting from performance of an occupation as psittacosis, mercury poisoning, dust collection in the lungs, and the like; in most states occupational disease is now covered as part of the workmen's compensation exposure

**Occurrence** a happening which occupies some length of time, as an individual catching cold after sitting in a draft in a theater all evening; sometimes a series of accidents; see Accident

**Ocean marine insurance** coverage on all types of vessels, including liabilities connected with them, and on their cargoes; the cargo coverage has been expanded to protect the owners from warehouse to warehouse, inclusive of all intermediate transit by rail, truck, or otherwise

**Open form** a continuous policy written on a reporting basis

**Ordinary life insurance** a form of whole life insurance usually issued in amounts of $1000 or more with premiums payable on an annual, semiannual, quarterly, or monthly basis to the death of the insured or to the end of the mortality table employed, whichever occurs first and at which time (benefits) proceeds are due; the term is also used to mean straight life insurance

**Paid-up insurance** insurance on which all required premiums have been paid; the term is frequently used to mean the reduced paid-up insurance available as one of the nonforfeiture options

**Parol evidence**    oral or verbal evidence; that which is given by word of mouth; the ordinary kind of evidence that is given by witnesses in court

**Parol evidence rule**    when the parties to a contract have purported to embody their contract in writing, that writing is the contract and all of the contract; therefore no evidence is admissable to prove any terms of the contract different from, or in addition to, those set forth in writing

**Partial disability**    a provision generally found in accident and occasionally in sickness policies designed to offer some weekly or monthly indemnity benefit if the insured cannot perform all the important daily duties of his occupation

**Participating insurance**    policies which entitle the policyholder to receive dividends reflecting the difference between the premium charged and the actual operating expenses and mortality experience of the company; if expenses and mortality are better than anticipated so that an excess of premium has been collected, a portion of the excess then so available is returned to the insured in the form of dividends—the premium is calculated to provide some margin over the anticipated cost of the insurance protection

**Particular average**    a term meaning an accidental and usually a partial loss suffered by one interest and not chargeable against others; see General average

**Peril**    the event insured against; the cause of possible loss

**Permanent life insurance**    a phrase used to cover any form of life insurance except term; generally insurance, such as whole life or endowment, that accrues cash value

**Permissible loss ratio**    the maximum percentage of premium income which can be expended by the company to pay claims without loss of profit

**Plaintiff**    a party to a law suit who brings charges against another party called the defendant

**Policy**    the written contract of insurance which is issued to the policy holder insured by the company insurer

**Policy dividend**    a refund of part of the premium on a participating life insurance policy reflecting the difference between the premium charged and actual experience

**Policy fee**    an additional charge placed on the initial premium designed to offset a portion of the expense of policy issuance

**Policy loan**    a loan made by an insurance company to a policyholder on the security of the cash value of his policy

**Policy period**    the term for which insurance remains in force, sometimes definite, sometimes not

**Policy reserve**    the amounts that an insurance company allocates specifically for the fulfillment of its policy obligations; reserves are so calculated that, together with future premiums and interest earnings, they will enable the company to pay all future claims

**Pool**    a group of companies, the purpose of which is to undertake something the membership itself could not or would not do individually

**Preexisting condition**    a physical condition that existed prior to the effective date of the policy

**Preauthorized check plan**    a plan by which a policyholder arranges with his bank and insurance company to have his premium payments drawn, usually monthly, from his checking account

**Premium**    the payment, or one of the periodical payments, a policyholder agrees to make for an insurance policy

**Premium loan**    a policy loan needed for the purpose of paying premiums

**Premium period**    the length of time covered by the premium, usually identical with the policy period but frequently not

**Primary**    basic, fundamental; an insurance policy which pays first with respect to other outstanding policies

**Principal**    the applicant for, or subject of, insurance; the one from whom an agent derives his authority

**Principal sum**    a term used to refer to the lump sum amount payable for accidental death, dismemberment, or loss of sight

**Probationary period** (also sometimes called "waiting period")    a period of time from the policy date to a specified date, usually 15–30 days, during which no sickness coverage is effective; it is designed to eliminate a sickness actually contracted before the policy went into effect—occurs only at the inception of a policy

**Producer**    an agent for an insurance company

**Prohibited risks**    those not written by a company because of an unusual occupational exposure or uninsurable physical or moral conditions

**Proof**    the act of substantiating another act, such as a claim for insurance payment

**Proposal**    an application for insurance or the facts contained in it; a recommendation

**Pro rata apportionment**    a division of loss according to the interest of the various companies providing insurance; thus, if Company A has insured the property involved for $10,000 and Company B has insured the property for $20,000, Company A will pay one-third of any loss and Company B will pay two-thirds

**Pro rata cancellation**   cancellation with a return of premium charged for the period of time the policy was in force equal to the ratio of the total premium to the total policy period; see Short rate cancellation

**Pro rata distribution clause**   a clause that provides that the face amount of the insurance will be divided between the objects insured in the proportion that the value of each bears to the value of all

**Prorate clause**   in health insurance, an optional policy provision designed to protect the company when an insured changes to a more hazardous occupation and does not have his policy amended accordingly; the company may pay only such portion of the indemnities provided as the premium paid would have purchased at the higher classification, subject to the maximum limits fixed by the company for such more hazardous occupation; it also protects the insured when he changes to a less hazardous occupation by providing for a return premium

**Provisions**   the terms or conditions of an insurance policy

**Proximate cause**   the immediate or actual cause of loss under an insurance policy

**Rate**   the cost of a unit of insurance

**Rated policy**   an insurance policy issued at a higher than standard premium rate to cover the extra risk involved in certain instances where the insured does not meet the standard underwriting requirements; for example, impaired health or a particularly hazardous occupation

**Realty**   real property; real estate

**Rebate**   the improper return of part or all of a premium to the policyholder

**Reciprocal exchange**   an association of individuals who agree to exchange insurance risks—each member of the association insures each of the other members and in turn is insured by each of the other members; see Attorney-in-fact

**Recurring clause**   a period of time during which a recurrence of a condition is considered as being a continuation of a prior period of disability or hospital confinement

**Reduced paid-up insurance**   a form of insurance available as a nonforfeiture option; it provides for continuation of the original insurance plan, but for a reduced amount

**Regional agent**   a district agent; the grade between local and general agent

**Reimbursement benefits**   those for which the insured is reimbursed on an actual expense incurred basis

**Reinstatement**   the restoration of a lapsed policy

**Reinsurance**   insurance placed by an underwriter in another company to cut down the amount of the risk he has assumed under the original insurance

**Release**   a discharge, as from further liability under an insurance policy

**Renew**   to continue; to replace, as with new policy

**Renewable term insurance**   term insurance which can be renewed at the end of the term, at the option of the policyholder, and without evidence of insurability, for a limited number of successive terms; the rates increase at each renewal as the age of the insured increases

**Rental value insurance**   insurance arranging to pay the reasonable rental value of property which has been rendered untenable by fire or some other peril insured against, for the period of time which would be required to restore the property to tenable condition

**Reporting form**   insurance which depends upon regular reports from the insured to determine the amount of insurance or the premium or both

**Representation**   statements made by an applicant in the application which he represents as being substantially true to the best of his knowledge and belief, but which are not warranted as exact in every detail

**Res ipsa loquitur**   *the thing speaks for itself*   rebuttable presumption that the defendant was negligent; the presumption arises upon proof that the instrumentality causing the injury was in the defendant's exclusive control, and that the accident is one which ordinarily does not happen in the absence of negligence

**Reserve**   liability set up for particular purposes

**Residuary**   the balance remaining, as in an estate after specific bequests and debts have been paid

**Respondeat superior**   *let the master answer*   the principal is liable in certain cases for the wrongful acts of his agent; the doctrine does not apply where the injury occurs while the servant is acting outside the legitimate scope of his authority

**Restoration**   reinstatement, as the amount of coverage after a loss

**Retrocession**   the amount of risk which a reinsurance company reinsures; the amount of a cession which the reinsurer passes on

**Return premium**   an amount due the insured upon cancellation of a policy

**Revival**   the reinstatement of a lapsed policy by the company upon receipt of evidence of insurability and payment of past due premiums with interest

**Rider**   a document which amends the policy; it may increase or decrease benefits, waive a condition or coverage, or in any other way amend the original contract—the terms "rider" and endorsement" are often used interchangeably

**Risk**   in the abstract, used to indicate a condition of the real world in which there is a possibility of loss; also used by insurance practitioners to indicate the property insured or the peril insured against

**Robbery**   the unlawful taking of property by violence or threat of violence

**Salvage**   value recoverable after a loss; that which is recovered by an insurance company after paying a loss; see Subrogation

**Schedule**   a list of coverages or amounts concerning things or persons insured

**Settlement option**   one of the ways, other than immediate payment in a lump sum, in which the policyholder or beneficiary may choose to have the policy proceeds paid

**Short rate cancellation**   cancellation with a less than proportionate return of premium; see Pro rata cancellation

**Short-term disability**   a generally accepted period of time for 2 years or less; can vary according to company standards

**Sickness insurance**   a form of health insurance against loss by illness or disease

**Sprinkler leakage insurance**   insurance against loss from accidental leakage or discharge from a sprinkler system due to some cause other than a hostile fire or certain other specified causes

**Standard provisions** (health insurance)   a set of policy provisions prescribed by law setting forth certain rights and obligations of both the insured and company; these were originally introduced in 1912 and have now been replaced by the Uniform Provisions

**Stock insurance company**   an insurance company owned by stockholders, usually for the purpose of making a profit

**Straight life insurance**   whole life insurance on which premiums are payable for life

**Subrogation**   an assignment or substituting of one person for another by which the rights of one are acquired by another in collecting a debt or a claim, as an insurance company stepping into the rights of a policyholder indemnified by the company

**Substandard** (impaired risk)   risks that have some physical impairment requiring the use of a waiver, a special policy form, or a higher premium charge

**Supplementary contract**   an agreement between a life insurance company and a policyholder or beneficiary by which the company retains the proceeds payable under an insurance policy and makes payments in accordance with the settlement option chosen

**Surety**   a guarantor of a duty or obligation assumed by another

**Surety bond**   an agreement providing for monetary compensation should there be a failure to perform certain specified acts within a stated period;

the surety company, for example, becomes responsible for fulfillment of a contract if the contractor defaults

**Surplus lines law**   a provision in the Insurance Code of certain jurisdictions which permits an agent to place coverage with a nonadmitted carrier if he has exhausted the admitted market and cannot obtain coverage

**Term**   the length of time covered by a policy or a premium

**Term insurance**   insurance payable to a beneficiary at the death of the insured, provided death occurs within a specified period, such as 5 or 10 years, or before a specified age

**Theft**   the unlawful taking of property of another; the term includes such crimes as burglary, larceny, and robbery

**Third party**   someone other than the insured and insuring company

**Tort**   an injury or wrong committed against an individual

**Total disability**   disability which prevents the insured from performing all the duties of his occupation or any occupation; the exact definition varies among policies

**Travel accident policies**   those that are limited to paying for loss arising out of accidents occurring while traveling

**Trust**   transfer of property right to one person called a "trustee" for the benefit of another called a "beneficiary"

**Twisting**   the act of switching insurance policies from one company to another, to the detriment of the insured

**Underwriting**   the process by which an insurance company determines whether or not and on what basis it will accept an application for insurance

**Unearned premium**   that portion of an insurance premium covering the unexpired term of the policy

**Uniform provisions**   statutory policy provisions which specify the rights and obligations of the insured and company

**Valued policy**   an insurance contract in which the value of the thing insured and the amount to be paid in case of total loss is settled at the time of making the policy

**Void**   of no force or effect; null

**Waiting period** (also sometimes called "elimination period" or "probation period")   a provision designed to eliminate disability claims for the first number of days specified for each period of disability; the waiting period may run from 7 days to as long as 1 year; this term is also sometimes used to refer to a period of time after policy issuance during which specified conditions are not covered

**Waiver**  an agreement attached to the policy and accepted by the insured which eliminates a specified preexisting physical condition from the policy

**Waiver of premium**  a provision which waives payment of the premium which becomes due during a period of covered total disability which has lasted for a specified period of time, usually, 3 to 6 months

**Warranty**  a statement concerning the condition of the item to be insured which is made for the purpose of permitting the underwriter to evaluate the risk; if found to be false, it provides the basis for voidance of the policy

**Whole life insurance**  insurance payable to a beneficiary at the death of the insured whenever that occurs; premiums may be payable for a specified number of years (limited-payment life) or for life (straight life)

**Workmen's compensation**  a system of providing for the cost of medical care and weekly payments to injured employees or to dependents of those killed in industry in which absolute liability is imposed on the employer requiring him to pay benefits prescribed by law

# Appendix B

# Whole Life Policy

The                    Insurance Company agrees to pay the face amount to the direct beneficiary upon receipt at its Home Office of due proof of the death of the Insured.

The provisions on the following pages are a part of this contract which was signed at                    , on the date of issue.

*W. B. Minehan*
Secretary

*Donald C. Dichter*
President

Registrar

# SPECIMEN COPY

Provisions may vary slightly in certain States

---

### LIFE POLICY — ANNUAL DIVIDENDS

Face Amount payable at death of Insured.

Premiums payable for stated period unless previously paid-up by dividends.

Schedule of benefits and premiums — page 2.

# POLICY SPECIFICATIONS

Date of Issue **MAY 1, 1963**

| | | | |
|---|---|---|---|
| Insured | JOHN J. DOE | **21 MALE** | Age and Sex |
| Policy Date | MAY 1, 1963 | **0 000 000** | Policy Number |
| Plan | WHOLE LIFE | **$100,000** | Face Amount |

Direct Beneficiary

**JANE M. DOE, WIFE OF THE INSURED**

Owner **JOHN J. DOE, THE INSURED**

## PREMIUM SCHEDULE

A premium is payable on the policy date and every **12** policy months thereafter during the lifetime of the Insured as provided below:

| PLAN AND ADDITIONAL BENEFITS | AMOUNT | PAYABLE FOR |
|---|---|---|
| WHOLE LIFE | $1,574.00 | LIFE—to age 90 |
| DISABILITY PREMIUM WAIVER | 26.00 | 39 YEARS |
| ACCIDENTAL DEATH $100,000 | 80.00 | 49 YEARS |
| ADDITIONAL PURCHASE $10,000 | 13.30 | 19 YEARS |

The first premium of **$1,693.30** has been paid.

## TABLE OF GUARANTEED VALUES — Dollar Values Are Per $1,000 of Face Amount

| End of Policy Year | Cash or Loan Value | Paid-up Insurance | Extended Term Insurance | | End of Policy Year | Cash or Loan Value | Paid-up Insurance | Extended Term Insurance | |
|---|---|---|---|---|---|---|---|---|---|
| | | | Years | Days | | | | Years | Days |
| 01 | $ .00 | $ 0 | 0 | 0 | 13 | $ 154.22 | $ 341 | 28 | 259 |
| 02 | 7.01 | 19 | 2 | 265 | 14 | 167.89 | 364 | 28 | 310 |
| 03 | 19.86 | 53 | 8 | 328 | 15 | 181.81 | 387 | 28 | 332 |
| 04 | 32.95 | 86 | 15 | 36 | 16 | 195.97 | 409 | 28 | 329 |
| 05 | 46.30 | 119 | 19 | 108 | 17 | 210.36 | 430 | 28 | 304 |
| 06 | 59.89 | 151 | 22 | 72 | 18 | 224.94 | 452 | 28 | 261 |
| 07 | 73.74 | 183 | 24 | 102 | 19 | 239.71 | 472 | 28 | 200 |
| 08 | 87.84 | 214 | 25 | 302 | 20 | 254.65 | 492 | 28 | 126 |
| 09 | 102.20 | 244 | 27 | 3 | @55 | 475.97 | 721 | 23 | 101 |
| 10 | 114.81 | 269 | 27 | 237 | @60 | 555.90 | 781 | 20 | 338 |
| 11 | 127.68 | 293 | 28 | 48 | @62 | 587.11 | 802 | 19 | 344 |
| 12 | 140.82 | 317 | 28 | 173 | @65 | 632.61 | 831 | 18 | 164 |

Paid-up additions and dividend accumulations increase the cash values; indebtedness decreases them.

# OWNERSHIP PROVISIONS

## 1. THE OWNER

This policy shall belong to the Owner or to the successor or transferee of the Owner. All policy rights and privileges may be exercised by the Owner without the consent of any beneficiary. Such rights and privileges may be exercised only during the lifetime of the Insured except as provided in the Beneficiary and Settlement Provisions.

## 2. CHANGE OF OWNERSHIP

The Owner may change the ownership of this policy. If ownership is changed, the policy rights and privileges of the Owner may be exercised only if written evidence of change satisfactory to the Company has been filed at its Home Office and this policy endorsed to show the change. The endorsement requirement may be waived by the Company. A change of ownership, of itself, shall not affect the interest of any beneficiary.

# PREMIUM and REINSTATEMENT PROVISIONS

## 1. PREMIUMS

(a) **Payment.** All premiums are payable at the Home Office or to an authorized agent. An official receipt signed by an executive officer of the Company and duly countersigned is available on request.

(b) **Frequency.** Premiums may be paid annually, semi-annually, or quarterly at the published rates for this policy. A change to any such frequency shall be effective upon acceptance by the Company of the premium for the changed frequency. Premiums may be paid on any other frequency approved by the Company.

(c) **Default.** If a premium is not paid on or before its due date, that premium is in default. This policy shall then terminate except as provided in the Grace Period, Extended Term Insurance, and Paid-up Insurance provisions. The date of premium default is the due date of the unpaid premium.

(d) **Grace Period.** A grace period of thirty-one days shall be allowed for payment of a premium in default. This policy shall continue in full force during the grace period. If the Insured dies during such period, the premium in default shall be paid from the proceeds of this policy.

(e) **Premium Refund at Death.** That portion of any premium paid which applies to a period beyond the policy month in which the Insured died shall be refunded as part of the proceeds of this policy.

## 2. REINSTATEMENT

This policy may be reinstated within five years after the date of premium default if it has not been surrendered for its cash value. Reinstatement is subject to:

(a) receipt of evidence of insurability of the Insured satisfactory to the Company;

(b) payment of all overdue premiums with interest from the due date of each at the rate of 5% per annum; and

(c) payment or reinstatement of any indebtedness existing on the date of premium default with interest from that date.

# GENERAL PROVISIONS

## 1. THE CONTRACT

This policy and the application, a copy of which is attached when issued, constitute the entire contract. All statements in the application shall, in the absence of fraud, be deemed representations and not warranties. No statement shall avoid this policy or be used in defense of a claim under it unless contained in the application.

Only an officer or a registrar of the Company is authorized to alter this policy or to waive any of the Company's rights or requirements.

Policy months, years, and anniversaries shall be computed from the policy date.

All payments by the Company under this policy are payable at its Home Office.

## 2. INCONTESTABILITY

This policy shall be incontestable after it has been in force during the lifetime of the Insured for two years from the date of issue.

## 3. SUICIDE

If within two years from the date of issue the Insured shall die by suicide, whether sane or insane, the amount payable by the Company shall be the premiums paid.

## 4. AGE

If the age of the Insured has been misstated, the amount payable shall be such as the premium paid would have purchased at the correct age.

## 5. COLLATERAL ASSIGNMENT

The Owner may assign this policy as collateral security. The interest of any beneficiary and any settlement option elected shall be subordinate to any collateral assignment made either before or after the beneficiary designation or settlement option election.

The Company assumes no responsibility for the validity or effect of any collateral assignment of this policy or any interest in it. The Company shall not be charged with notice of any such assignment unless the assignment is in writing and filed at its Home Office.

A collateral assignee is not an Owner and a collateral assignment is not a change of ownership as these terms are used in this policy.

## 6. CHANGE OF PLAN

The Owner may change this policy to any plan of insurance acceptable to the Company upon payment of such cost, if any, and subject to such conditions as the Company shall determine.

The cost shall not exceed the difference in cash values plus 3½ % of such difference for a change made after the first policy year to a plan having a higher cash value and requiring at least five annual premiums after the change.

## 7. RESERVES AND NET SINGLE PREMIUMS

The Commissioners 1958 Standard Ordinary Mortality Table is used to establish all reserves and net single premiums in this policy except those for the first five years of extended term insurance for which the Commissioners 1958 Extended Term Insurance Table is used. Calculations are based on the net level premium method, continuous functions, and interest at 2¼ % per annum. The reserve on this policy shall be exclusive of any additional benefits.

Page 4

646

# DIVIDEND PROVISIONS

## 1. ANNUAL DIVIDENDS

This policy shall share in the divisible surplus of the Company. Its share shall be determined annually by the Company and credited as a dividend. The first dividend shall be payable in equal parts on each premium due date during the second policy year if the premium then due is paid. Each dividend thereafter shall be payable on the policy anniversary.

## 2. USE OF DIVIDENDS

Dividends credited may be applied under one of the following:

**(a) Paid-up Addition.** Applied to purchase a paid-up addition to this policy. The addition shall share in dividends.

**(b) Dividend Accumulation.** Left to accumulate at interest. Interest shall be credited annually at a rate of at least 2¼% per annum.

**(c) Premium Payment.** Applied toward payment of any premium due within one year if the remainder of such premium is paid in cash or by loan. If such remainder is not so paid, or if this policy is in force as paid-up insurance, the dividend will be applied instead to purchase a paid-up addition.

If none of the foregoing has been elected, dividends shall be paid in cash.

Any paid-up additions and dividend accumulations not required under the Loan, Extended Term Insurance, or Paid-up Insurance Provisions may be surrendered at any time for their then present value which shall not be less than the original cash dividends. Otherwise they are payable as part of the proceeds of this policy.

## 3. DIVIDEND AT DEATH

A dividend shall be paid as part of the proceeds of this policy for the period from the beginning of the policy year in which the Insured died to the end of the policy month of death.

## 4. PAID-UP OR ENDOWMENT PRIVILEGE

The Company will endorse this policy as full paid whenever the cash value shall equal the net single premium at the attained age of the Insured. A written request will be required. Any indebtedness shall remain as a lien against this policy.

The Company will pay as an endowment the cash value less any indebtedness whenever the cash value shall equal the face amount. A written request and surrender of this policy will be required.

# LOAN PROVISIONS

## 1. POLICY LOAN

The Owner may obtain a policy loan from the Company upon satisfactory assignment of this policy. The amount of the loan, together with any other indebtedness, shall not exceed the loan value. A loan cannot be granted if the policy is in force as extended term insurance. The Company may defer making the loan for a period not exceeding six months unless the loan is to be used to pay premiums on policies in the Company.

## 2. AUTOMATIC PREMIUM LOAN

A premium loan shall be automatically granted to pay a premium in default. A premium for any other frequency permitted by this policy shall be loaned whenever the loan value, less any indebtedness, is sufficient for such premium but is insufficient for a loan of the premium in default. A revocation or reinstatement of this provision shall be made by written notice filed at the Home Office.

## 3. LOAN VALUE

The loan value is the largest amount which, with accrued interest, does not exceed the cash value either on the next premium due date or at the end of one year from the date of the loan.

## 4. LOAN INTEREST

Policy and premium loans shall bear interest at the rate of 5% per annum. Interest on policy loans shall accrue from the date of the loan and on premium loans from the premium due date. Interest shall be payable annually. Unpaid interest shall be added to and become part of the loan and shall bear interest on the same terms.

## 5. INDEBTEDNESS

Indebtedness means all outstanding policy and premium loans on this policy including interest accrued and accruing from day to day. Indebtedness may be repaid at any time and if not repaid shall be deducted as a single sum from any settlement.

Whenever indebtedness equals or exceeds the cash value, this policy shall be deemed surrendered and shall terminate thirty-one days after a notice of termination has been mailed to the last known address of the Owner and of any assignee of record at the Home Office.

# CASH VALUE, EXTENDED TERM
## and PAID-UP INSURANCE

### 1. CASH VALUE

The cash value at any time when all premiums due have been paid shall be the reserve on this policy less the deduction described in section 5, plus the reserve on any paid-up additions and the amount of any dividend accumulations.

The cash value within three months after the date of premium default shall be the cash value on that date except as reduced by surrender of paid-up additions or withdrawal of dividend accumulations. The cash value at any time after such three months shall be the reserve on the form of insurance then in force and on any paid-up additions, plus the amount of any dividend accumulations.

If this policy is surrendered within thirty-one days after a policy anniversary, the reserve shall be taken as not less than on that anniversary.

### 2. CASH SURRENDER

The Owner may surrender this policy for its cash value less any indebtedness. The insurance shall terminate upon receipt at the Home Office of this policy and a written surrender of all claims. Receipt of the policy may be waived by the Company.

The Company may defer paying the cash value for a period not exceeding six months from the date of surrender. If payment is deferred thirty days or more, interest at the rate of 2¼% per annum from the date of surrender to the date of payment shall be allowed on the cash value less any indebtedness.

### 3. EXTENDED TERM INSURANCE

If any premium remains unpaid at the end of the grace period, this policy shall be automatically continued in force as nonparticipating extended term insurance. The amount of such insurance shall be the face amount of this policy, plus any paid-up additions and dividend accumulations, less any indebtedness. The term of such insurance shall begin as of the date of premium default and shall be determined by applying the cash value less any indebtedness as a net single premium at the attained age of the Insured. If such term ends on or after attained age 100, paid-up insurance as described in section 4 below will be provided instead.

### 4. PAID-UP INSURANCE

In lieu of extended term insurance this policy may be continued in force as participating paid-up life insurance. The insurance will be for such amount as the cash value will purchase as a net single premium at the attained age of the Insured. Any indebtedness shall remain as a lien against this policy.

Such paid-up insurance may be requested before or within three months after the date of premium default. A request or revocation shall be made by written notice filed at the Home Office.

### 5. TABLE OF VALUES

The values shown on page 3 are for the end of the policy year indicated; allowance shall be made for any portion of a year's premium paid and for the time elapsed in that year. Values for policy years not shown shall be calculated on the same basis as this table and shall be furnished on request. All values are greater than or equal to those required by statute.

These values are based on the assumption that premiums have been paid for the number of years stated and are exclusive of any paid-up additions, dividend accumulations, or indebtedness.

In determining the cash values a deduction has been made from the reserve. During the first policy year, the deduction is $16 for each $1,000 of face amount. The deduction decreases by one-eighth in each succeeding year until there is no deduction in the ninth and subsequent policy years.

648

# BENEFICIARY and SETTLEMENT PROVISIONS

## 1. DESIGNATION AND CHANGE OF BENEFICIARIES

**(a) By Owner.** The Owner may designate and change direct and contingent beneficiaries of death proceeds:

(1) during the lifetime of the Insured.

(2) during the sixty days following the date of death of the Insured if the Insured immediately before his death was not the Owner. Any such designation of direct beneficiary may not be changed. If the Owner elects a settlement option, any such designation of contingent beneficiary may not be changed unless the Owner is the direct beneficiary.

**(b) By Direct Beneficiary.** The direct beneficiary may designate contingent beneficiaries under any of the following conditions subject in each case to any remaining rights of the Owner:

(1) If the Owner is designated as the direct beneficiary of death, endowment, or surrender proceeds.

(2) If the direct beneficiary of death proceeds elects a settlement option after the death of the Insured. In this event, the interest in the share of such direct beneficiary of any other payee designated by the Owner shall terminate.

(3) If, at any time after the death of the Insured, no contingent beneficiary of death proceeds is living.

Any such designation made by the direct beneficiary shall be with the right of change.

## 2. SUCCESSION IN INTEREST OF BENEFICIARIES

The proceeds of this policy whether payable in one sum or under a settlement option shall be payable in equal shares to such direct beneficiaries as survive to receive payment. The share of any direct beneficiary who dies before receiving payments due or to become due shall be payable in equal shares to such direct beneficiaries as survive to receive payment.

At the death of the last surviving direct beneficiary payments due or to become due shall be payable in equal shares to such contingent beneficiaries as survive to receive payment. The share of any contingent beneficiary who dies before receiving payments due or to become due shall be payable in equal shares to such contingent beneficiaries as survive to receive payment.

At the death of the last to survive of the direct and contingent beneficiaries:

(1) if no settlement option is in effect, any remaining proceeds shall be paid to the Owner or to the executors, administrators, successors, or transferees of the Owner; or

(2) if a settlement option is in effect, the withdrawal value of payments due or to become due shall be paid in one sum to the executors or administrators of the last to survive of the direct and contingent beneficiaries.

A direct or contingent beneficiary succeeding to an interest in a settlement option shall continue under such option, subject to its terms as stated in this policy, with the rights of transfer between options and of withdrawal under options as provided in this policy.

## 3. SETTLEMENT OF POLICY PROCEEDS

**(a) Payment.** All of the policy proceeds or each part, if the proceeds are divided into parts, may be paid in one sum or under a settlement option.

So far as permitted by law no amount payable under this policy shall be assigned or pledged or be subject to the claims of creditors of the payee.

**(b) Availability of Options.** The settlement options shall be available for any direct or contingent beneficiary who is a natural person taking benefit in his own right. In addition, Options B and D shall be available to a corporation as direct beneficiary for its own use and benefit and Options C and F shall be similarly available when the installments depend upon the life of the Insured. Otherwise the settlement options shall not be available.

**(c) Minimum Amount.** The Company shall not be required to apply under or transfer to a settlement option or retain under Option A an amount less than $2,000 for any payee. The Company may pay the withdrawal value of any settlement option where payments to any payee are or become less than $20.

**(d) Date of Settlement.** The date of settlement for any part of the proceeds shall be the date of payment in one sum or if settled under one of the options the date settlement becomes effective.

## 4. ELECTION OF OPTIONS

**(a) By Owner.** The Owner may:

(1) elect a settlement option for death proceeds during the lifetime of the Insured. Any such election may be changed during the Insured's lifetime.

(2) revoke any existing election and elect a settlement option for death proceeds during the sixty days following the date of death of the Insured if the Insured immediately before his death was not the Owner. Any such election shall be final.

(3) elect a settlement option for surrender or maturity proceeds. Any such election shall be for the Owner as direct beneficiary.

**(b) By Direct Beneficiary.** A direct beneficiary may make an election of a settlement option if no election is in force when this policy becomes payable. Such election shall be subject to any remaining rights of the Owner.

**(c) By Contingent Beneficiary.** A contingent beneficiary may make an election of a settlement option if the policy proceeds become payable to such contingent beneficiary and if no election is in force. Such election shall be subject to any remaining rights of the Owner.

## 5. INTEREST BEFORE SETTLEMENT

Interest shall accrue on death proceeds from the date of the Insured's death to the date of settlement, but not for more than one year. The rate of such interest shall be at least 2½% per annum. Interest shall be paid in cash on the date of settlement to the payee then entitled to settlement.

## 6. INTEREST OPTION

**Option A:** Proceeds Left at Interest

The Company shall pay interest monthly at the rate of $2.06 per month per $1,000. The first payment shall be due one month after the date of settlement. The payments will be increased by dividends as determined by the Company.

The withdrawal value at any time shall be the proceeds held by the Company.

A contingent beneficiary shall not elect or continue under this option beyond his 30th birthday but shall take the withdrawal value or transfer to another option.

## 7. INSTALLMENT OPTIONS

**Option B:** Installments for a Specified Period

The Company shall pay monthly installments for a specified number of years as stated in the Option B Table. The first installment shall be due on the date of settlement. Subsequent installments will be increased by dividends as determined by the Company.

The withdrawal value at any time shall be the commuted value of any unpaid installments. Commutation shall be on the basis of compound interest at 2½% per annum.

### OPTION B TABLE
**Monthly Installments for Each $1,000 of Net Proceeds**

| Number of Years Specified | Each Monthly Payment | Number of Years Specified | Each Monthly Payment | Number of Years Specified | Each Monthly Payment |
|---|---|---|---|---|---|
| 1 | $84.28 | 11 | $8.64 | 21 | $5.08 |
| 2 | 42.66 | 12 | 8.02 | 22 | 4.90 |
| 3 | 28.79 | 13 | 7.49 | 23 | 4.74 |
| 4 | 21.86 | 14 | 7.03 | 24 | 4.60 |
| 5 | 17.70 | 15 | 6.64 | 25 | 4.46 |
| 6 | 14.93 | 16 | 6.30 | 26 | 4.34 |
| 7 | 12.95 | 17 | 6.00 | 27 | 4.22 |
| 8 | 11.47 | 18 | 5.73 | 28 | 4.12 |
| 9 | 10.32 | 19 | 5.49 | 29 | 4.02 |
| 10 | 9.39 | 20 | 5.27 | 30 | 3.93 |

**Option D:** Installments of a Specified Amount

The Company shall pay from a fund established by the proceeds equal monthly installments of a specified amount not less than $5 per $1,000 of the fund. The fund shall be credited annually with interest at the rate of 2½% per annum on the balance and will be increased by dividends as determined by the Company. The first installment shall be due on the date of settlement. Installments shall continue until the fund is exhausted, the final payment not to exceed the unpaid balance.

The withdrawal value at any time shall be the balance in the fund at such time.

## 8. LIFE INCOME OPTIONS

**(a) Description of Options.**

**Option C:** Life Income with Installments Certain

The Company shall pay monthly installments during the period certain elected and thereafter during the remaining lifetime of the beneficiary upon whose life the installments depend. The period certain elected may be 10 or 20 years or a refund period certain such that the sum of the installments certain shall be equal to the proceeds settled under this option, the final payment not to exceed the unpaid balance.

**Option E:** Joint and Survivor Life Income with Installments Certain

The Company shall pay monthly installments certain for 10 years and thereafter during the joint lifetime of the two direct beneficiaries upon whose lives the installments depend and the remaining lifetime of the survivor. Installments shall be paid jointly and to the survivor. In the event of the death of either of such beneficiaries before the date of settlement, the proceeds shall be payable to the survivor under Option C with installments certain for 10 years.

**(b) Amount of Installments.** The amount payable under the Option C or E Table shall be determined by the sex and adjusted age of any beneficiary upon whose life the installments depend.

Proof of date of birth satisfactory to the Company must be furnished. The first installment shall be due on the date of settlement. Subsequent installments certain will be increased by dividends as determined by the Company.

The withdrawal value under Option C or E, where available, shall be the commuted value of any unpaid installments certain. Commutation shall be on the basis of compound interest at 3% per annum.

**(c) Adjusted Age.** The adjusted age shall be the age at nearest birthday adjusted according to the calendar year in which settlement under Option C or E becomes effective.

This age adjustment shall be as follows:

| Year of Settlement | 1968 or Prior | 1969 thru 1973 | 1974 thru 1978 | 1979 thru 1988 | 1989 thru 1993 | 1994 thru 1998 | 1999 or After |
|---|---|---|---|---|---|---|---|
| Age Adjustment | +3 | +2 | +1 | 0 | −1 | −2 | −3 |

**(d) Annuity Income Privilege.** Instead of the amount of installments for Option C or E determined as provided in (b) and (c) of this section, nonparticipating installments determined in accordance with the terms of Option F, adjusted to provide for the period certain of the option selected, may be elected. The basis for determining the commuted value of unpaid installments certain shall be the same as provided in the Single Premium Refund Immediate Life Annuity issued by the Company on the date of settlement.

# MONTHLY INSTALLMENTS FOR EACH $1,000 OF NET PROCEEDS
## OPTION C TABLE
### Monthly Life Income with Payments Certain
To Determine Adjusted Age See Section 8(c)

| Adjusted Age of Beneficiary | | Installment Refund** | Adjusted Age of Beneficiary | | 10 Years | 20 Years | Installment Refund | Adjusted Age of Beneficiary | | 10 Years | 20 Years | Installment Refund |
|---|---|---|---|---|---|---|---|---|---|---|---|---|
| Male | Female | | Male | Female | | | | Male | Female | | | |
| | 10* | $2.51 | 30 | 35 | $3.07 | $3.05 | $3.02 | 55 | 60 | $4.68 | $4.33 | $4.37 |
| | 11 | 2.52 | 31 | 36 | 3.10 | 3.08 | 3.05 | 56 | 61 | 4.79 | 4.40 | 4.46 |
| | 12 | 2.54 | 32 | 37 | 3.14 | 3.12 | 3.09 | 57 | 62 | 4.91 | 4.46 | 4.56 |
| | 13 | 2.55 | 33 | 38 | 3.18 | 3.15 | 3.12 | 58 | 63 | 5.03 | 4.53 | 4.66 |
| | 14 | 2.57 | 34 | 39 | 3.22 | 3.19 | 3.16 | 59 | 64 | 5.16 | 4.59 | 4.76 |
| 10* | 15 | 2.58 | 35 | 40 | 3.26 | 3.23 | 3.20 | 60 | 65 | 5.30 | 4.65 | 4.87 |
| 11 | 16 | 2.60 | 36 | 41 | 3.30 | 3.27 | 3.23 | 61 | 66 | 5.43 | 4.71 | 4.98 |
| 12 | 17 | 2.61 | 37 | 42 | 3.35 | 3.31 | 3.27 | 62 | 67 | 5.58 | 4.77 | 5.10 |
| 13 | 18 | 2.63 | 38 | 43 | 3.40 | 3.36 | 3.32 | 63 | 68 | 5.72 | 4.82 | 5.22 |
| 14 | 19 | 2.65 | 39 | 44 | 3.45 | 3.40 | 3.36 | 64 | 69 | 5.87 | 4.88 | 5.34 |
| 15 | 20 | 2.66 | 40 | 45 | 3.50 | 3.45 | 3.40 | 65 | 70 | 6.03 | 4.93 | 5.49 |
| 16 | 21 | 2.68 | 41 | 46 | 3.56 | 3.50 | 3.45 | 66 | 71 | 6.19 | 4.97 | 5.63 |
| 17 | 22 | 2.70 | 42 | 47 | 3.61 | 3.55 | 3.50 | 67 | 72 | 6.35 | 5.02 | 5.78 |
| 18 | 23 | 2.72 | 43 | 48 | 3.67 | 3.60 | 3.55 | 68 | 73 | 6.52 | 5.05 | 5.90 |
| 19 | 24 | 2.74 | 44 | 49 | 3.74 | 3.65 | 3.61 | 69 | 74 | 6.69 | 5.09 | 6.03 |
| 20 | 25 | 2.76 | 45 | 50 | 3.80 | 3.71 | 3.66 | 70 | 75 | 6.86 | 5.12 | 6.17 |
| 21 | 26 | 2.78 | 46 | 51 | 3.87 | 3.76 | 3.72 | 71 | 76 | 7.03 | 5.14 | 6.34 |
| 22 | 27 | 2.81 | 47 | 52 | 3.95 | 3.82 | 3.78 | 72 | 77 | 7.20 | 5.17 | 6.50 |
| 23 | 28 | 2.83 | 48 | 53 | 4.02 | 3.88 | 3.84 | 73 | 78 | 7.37 | 5.19 | 6.68 |
| 24 | 29 | 2.86 | 49 | 54 | 4.10 | 3.94 | 3.91 | 74 | 79 | 7.54 | 5.20 | 6.87 |
| 25 | 30 | 2.88 | 50 | 55 | 4.19 | 4.00 | 3.98 | 75 | 80 | 7.69 | 5.22 | 7.05 |
| 26 | 31 | 2.91 | 51 | 56 | 4.28 | 4.07 | 4.05 | 76 | 81 | 7.84 | 5.23 | 7.26 |
| 27 | 32 | 2.93 | 52 | 57 | 4.37 | 4.14 | 4.13 | 77 | 82 | 7.98 | 5.24 | 7.49 |
| 28 | 33 | 2.96 | 53 | 58 | 4.47 | 4.20 | 4.21 | 78 | 83 | 8.13 | 5.25 | 7.69 |
| 29 | 34 | 2.99 | 54 | 59 | 4.57 | 4.26 | 4.29 | 79 | 84 | 8.26 | 5.26 | 7.94 |
| | | | | | | | | 80 | 85† | 8.39 | 5.26 | 8.20 |
| | | | | | | | | 81 | | 8.51 | 5.27 | 8.43 |
| | | | | | | | | 82 | | 8.63 | 5.27 | 8.72 |
| | | | | | | | | 83 | | 8.73 | 5.27 | 9.02 |
| | | | | | | | | 84 | | 8.83 | 5.27 | 9.35 |
| | | | | | | | | 85† | | 8.92 | 5.27 | 9.62 |

\* and under      \*\* rates also apply to 10 and 20 year certain periods      † and over

## OPTION E TABLE
### Monthly Joint and Survivor Life Income with Payments Certain for 10 Years for Beneficiaries of Equal Age
To Determine Adjusted Ages See Section 8(c)

| Adjusted Age of Beneficiary | One Male and One Female | Two Male Lives | Two Female Lives | Adjusted Age of Beneficiary | One Male and One Female | Two Male Lives | Two Female Lives | Adjusted Age of Beneficiary | One Male and One Female | Two Male Lives | Two Female Lives |
|---|---|---|---|---|---|---|---|---|---|---|---|
| 25 | $2.65 | $2.70 | $2.61 | 55 | $3.79 | $4.00 | $3.63 | 65 | $4.73 | $5.11 | $4.46 |
| 30 | 2.75 | 2.81 | 2.70 | 56 | 3.86 | 4.08 | 3.69 | 66 | 4.85 | 5.23 | 4.57 |
| 35 | 2.87 | 2.95 | 2.81 | 57 | 3.93 | 4.16 | 3.76 | 67 | 4.97 | 5.35 | 4.69 |
| 40 | 3.02 | 3.12 | 2.95 | 58 | 4.01 | 4.25 | 3.83 | 68 | 5.11 | 5.49 | 4.82 |
| 45 | 3.22 | 3.35 | 3.12 | 59 | 4.09 | 4.34 | 3.92 | 69 | 5.25 | 5.64 | 4.96 |
| 50 | 3.46 | 3.63 | 3.35 | 60 | 4.18 | 4.46 | 4.00 | 70 | 5.40 | 5.80 | 5.11 |
| 51 | 3.52 | 3.69 | 3.39 | 61 | 4.27 | 4.57 | 4.08 | 71 | 5.53 | 5.95 | 5.23 |
| 52 | 3.57 | 3.76 | 3.44 | 62 | 4.38 | 4.69 | 4.16 | 72 | 5.69 | 6.13 | 5.35 |
| 53 | 3.64 | 3.83 | 3.50 | 63 | 4.48 | 4.82 | 4.25 | 73 | 5.85 | 6.31 | 5.49 |
| 54 | 3.71 | 3.92 | 3.56 | 64 | 4.60 | 4.96 | 4.34 | 74 | 6.01 | 6.49 | 5.64 |
| | | | | | | | | 75 | 6.19 | 6.69 | 5.80 |

The amount of the payments for any other combination of ages will be furnished by the Company on request.
The maximum monthly income per $1,000 shall be $6.69.

## 9. LIFE ANNUITY OPTION
**Option F:** Immediate Life Annuity

The Company shall pay monthly installments during the lifetime of the beneficiary upon whose life the installments depend. The first installment shall be due on the date of settlement. The amount of each installment shall be 104% of the monthly income based upon the Company's Immediate Life Annuity rate at date of settlement and upon the sex and age nearest birthday of the beneficiary upon whose life the installments depend, adjusted to provide for immediate payment of the first installment. This option shall not participate in the surplus of the Company.

## 10. TRANSFER BETWEEN OPTIONS
A direct or contingent beneficiary who is receiving payment under Option A, B, or D may transfer the withdrawal value to Option B, C, D, or F.

## 11. WITHDRAWAL UNDER OPTIONS
A direct or contingent beneficiary may elect to receive the withdrawal value instead of continuing to receive payments under a settlement option; except that under Option C or E any beneficiary upon whose life the installments depend may not elect to receive the withdrawal value.

## 12. POSSESSION OF POLICY
This policy shall remain in the possession of the direct or contingent beneficiaries receiving payments under a settlement option.

## 13. EXERCISE OF RIGHTS
The policy rights stated in these Beneficiary and Settlement Provisions shall be exercised only by a proper request in writing. All requests must be filed at the Home Office and must be endorsed on this policy unless the Company waives endorsement.

The effective date of a request for designation, revocation, or change of beneficiary shall be as of the date the request was signed. The effective date of an election of a settlement option for death proceeds made by the Owner during the Insured's lifetime shall be the date of the Insured's death. All other requests shall be effective when filed at the Home Office and endorsed on this policy.

The Company shall not be prejudiced on account of any payment made or other action taken by it before a request is filed at its Home Office.

## Appendices

# WAIVER OF PREMIUM BENEFIT ON DISABILITY

### 1. THE BENEFIT

The Company will waive the payment of all premiums becoming due during the total disability of the Insured.

The dividends, policy values, and other benefits of this policy shall be the same as if premiums waived had been paid in cash.

### 2. DEFINITION OF TOTAL DISABILITY

Total disability means disability which:

(a) resulted from bodily injury or disease;

(b) began after the issue date of this policy and before the policy anniversary nearest the Insured's 60th birthday;

(c) has existed continuously for at least six months; and

(d) prevents the Insured from engaging for remuneration or profit in an occupation. During the first twenty-four months of disability, occupation means the occupation of the Insured at the time such disability began; thereafter it means any occupation for which he is or becomes reasonably fitted by education, training, or experience.

The total and irrecoverable loss of the sight of both eyes, or of the use of both hands, or of both feet, or of one hand and one foot shall be considered total disability even if the Insured shall engage in an occupation.

### 3. PROOF OF DISABILITY

Before any premium is waived due proof of total disability must be received by the Company at its Home Office:

(a) during the lifetime of the Insured;

(b) during the continuance of total disability; and

(c) not later than one year after the policy anniversary nearest the Insured's 60th birthday.

Premiums will be waived although proof of total disability was not given within the time specified if it is shown that it was given as soon as reasonably possible but not later than one year after recovery.

### 4. PROOF OF CONTINUANCE OF DISABILITY

Due proof of the continuance of total disability may be required once a year. If such proof is not furnished, no further premiums shall be waived.

Any future premiums shall be waived without further proof of continuance of disability if, on the policy anniversary nearest the Insured's 65th birthday, the Insured is then and has been totally and continuously disabled for five or more years since proof of disability was submitted.

### 5. PREMIUMS

Any premium becoming due during disability and before receipt of due proof of total disability is payable and should be paid. Any such premiums paid shall be refunded by the Company upon acceptance of proof of total disability. If such premiums are not paid, this benefit shall be allowed if total disability is shown to have begun before the end of the grace period of the first such premium in default.

While premiums are being waived, the frequency of premium payment shall remain unchanged. This benefit shall not participate in the surplus of the Company.

### 6. TERMINATION

This benefit shall be in effect while this policy is in force but shall terminate on the policy anniversary nearest the Insured's 60th birthday unless the Insured is then totally disabled. It may be terminated upon receipt at the Home Office, within thirty-one days of a premium due date, of the Owner's written request.

# ACCIDENTAL DEATH BENEFIT

### 1. THE BENEFIT

The Company agrees to pay an Accidental Death Benefit upon receipt at its Home Office of due proof that the death of the Insured resulted, directly and independently of all other causes, from accidental bodily injury, provided that death occurred within ninety days after such injury and while this benefit is in effect.

### 2. AMOUNT OF BENEFIT

The amount of this benefit is shown in the Premium Schedule on page 3 of this policy. This Additional Benefit shall be payable as part of the policy proceeds. It shall not participate in the surplus of the Company.

### 3. RISKS NOT ASSUMED

This benefit shall not be payable for death of the Insured resulting from suicide, whether sane or insane, for death resulting from or contributed to by bodily or mental infirmity or disease, or for any other death which, such as the foregoing, did not result, directly and independently of all other causes, from accidental bodily injury.

Even though death resulted directly and independently of all other causes from accidental bodily injury, this benefit shall not be payable if the death of the Insured resulted from:

(a) Any act or incident of war. The word "war" includes any war, declared or undeclared, and armed aggression resisted by the armed forces of any country or combination of countries.

(b) Riding in or descent from any kind of aircraft, if the Insured participated in training or had any duties whatsoever aboard such aircraft or if such aircraft was operated by or for the armed forces.

### 4. TERMINATION

This benefit shall be in effect while this policy is in force other than under the Extended Term Insurance, Paid-up Insurance, or Optional Maturity Date provisions but shall terminate on the policy anniversary nearest the Insured's 70th birthday. It may be terminated upon receipt at the Home Office, within thirty-one days of a premium due date, of the Owner's written request accompanied by this policy for endorsement.

# RIGHT TO PURCHASE ADDITIONAL INSURANCE POLICIES
## (Additional Purchase Benefit)

### 1. THE BENEFIT

The Company agrees to issue an additional policy of insurance on the life of the Insured, without evidence of insurability, as of each Purchase Date.

### 2. PURCHASE DATES

The Purchase Dates shall be each policy anniversary on which the Insured's age nearest birthday is 25, 28, 31, 34, 37, and 40. The right to purchase an additional policy as of any Purchase Date will expire on the 30th day after that date.

### 3. ADVANCE PURCHASE PRIVILEGE

If the Insured is a male, upon his marriage or upon the birth of his child, the right to purchase an additional policy as of the next available Purchase Date may be exercised immediately. The additional policy shall be in lieu of the policy which otherwise might be purchased as of such date. Each such privilege shall expire on the 90th day after it becomes exercisable.

### 4. AUTOMATIC TERM INSURANCE

The Company will automatically provide term insurance on the life of the Insured beginning on the date of a marriage or of a birth which gives the right to purchase a policy under the Advance Purchase Privilege and ending on the day preceding the expiry of such Privilege. However, if an additional policy is purchased under the Advance Purchase Privilege, any proceeds of the term insurance will be payable only if the additional policy is surrendered to the Company without any payment thereunder other than a refund of the premiums paid.

The amount of the term insurance shall be the maximum amount which could be purchased as an additional policy. The term insurance shall be subject to the beneficiary designation and the other terms and conditions of this policy.

### 5. ADDITIONAL POLICY

(a) **Face Amount.** The face amount of each additional policy may not be less than $5,000. It may not be more than $10,000 or the face amount of this policy, whichever is the smaller.

However, in the event of a multiple birth the face amount which may be purchased under the Advance Purchase Privilege will be the amount available from a single birth multiplied by the number of children of such multiple birth.

(b) **Plan.** Each additional policy shall be on any level annual premium life or endowment plan being issued by the Company on the date of purchase of such additional policy.

(c) **Waiver of Premium Benefit on Disability.** If the Waiver of Premium Benefit is a part of this policy at the time an additional policy is issued:

(1) An additional policy on the Whole Life or 65 Life plan may contain the Waiver of Premium Benefit even though premiums are then being waived under this policy. If premiums are being waived under this policy when such additional policy is purchased, premiums will also be waived under the additional policy.

(2) An additional policy on other than the Whole Life or 65 Life plan may contain the Waiver of Premium Benefit only if premiums are not then being waived under this policy. The Waiver of Premium Benefit of such additional policy will apply only if total disability resulted from bodily injury or disease originating after the effective date of such policy.

(d) **Accidental Death Benefit.** Each additional policy may contain the Accidental Death Benefit in an amount equal to its face amount if such benefit is a part of this policy when the additional policy is issued.

(e) **Provisions.** Each additional policy, and any Waiver of Premium Benefit on Disability and Accidental Death Benefit which are a part of it, shall include all such provisions as are regularly included in new policies at the time of purchase of such additional policy including any war and aviation restrictions. The incontestability provision in each additional policy shall be effective from the date of issue of this policy. The suicide provision in each additional policy shall be effective from the date of issue of such additional policy.

(f) **Premiums.** The premium for each additional policy shall be at the standard premium rates of the Company on the date of issue of such policy for the plan and amount of insurance requested at the Insured's then attained age.

### 6. APPLICATION AND EFFECTIVE DATE

Written application and the first premium for an additional policy must be received by the Company during the lifetime of the Insured and not more than sixty days before nor more than thirty days after a Purchase Date. If so received, the additional policy will be dated and effective upon receipt of the application or the first premium, whichever is the later.

Under the Advance Purchase Privilege, written application including proof of marriage or birth, and the first premium must be received by the Company during the lifetime of the Insured and not later than ninety days following the date of such marriage or birth. If so received, the additional policy will be dated and effective upon receipt of the application or the first premium, whichever is the later.

### 7. TERMINATION

This benefit shall be in effect while this policy is in force other than under the Extended Term Insurance or Paid-up Insurance Provisions but shall terminate on the policy anniversary on which the Insured's age nearest birthday is 40 or upon previous exercise of all available purchase privileges. It may be terminated upon receipt at the Home Office, within thirty-one days of a premium due date, of the Owner's written request accompanied by this policy for endorsement.

### 8. GENERAL

An additional policy shall not be issued unless the Owner has an insurable interest in the life of the Insured. This benefit shall not participate in the surplus of the Company.

## ELECTION OF TRUSTEES

The                                    Company is owned
by its Policyowners who exercise control through a Board
of Trustees. Elections to this Board are held each year at
the Home Office,
               on the third Wednesday of July. Policyowners
with insurance in force one year are entitled to vote in
person or by mail in these elections.

## LIFE POLICY — ANNUAL DIVIDENDS

Face Amount payable at death
of Insured. Premiums payable
for stated period unless previously paid-up by dividends.

Schedule of benefits and premiums — page 3.

APRIL 1, 1963

**654**

# Appendix C

# Standard Fire Policy

**No.**

CAPITAL STOCK COMPANY

RENEWAL OF NUMBER

[AUTHENTIC]

SPACE FOR COMPANY NAME, INSIGNIA, AND LOCATION

Insured's Name and Mailing Address

SPACE FOR
PRODUCER'S NAME AND
MAILING ADDRESS

Inception (Mo. Day Yr.)  Expiration (Mo. Day Yr.)   Years

It is important that the written portions of all policies covering the same property read exactly alike. If they do not, they should be made uniform at once.

INSURANCE IS PROVIDED AGAINST ONLY THOSE PERILS AND FOR ONLY THOSE COVERAGES INDICATED BELOW BY A PREMIUM CHARGE AND AGAINST OTHER PERILS AND FOR OTHER COVERAGES ONLY WHEN ENDORSED HEREON OR ADDED HERETO.

| AMOUNT | RATE | PREPAID TERM PREMIUM DUE AT INCEPTION | ANNUAL PAYMENT DUE UNDER DEF. PREM. PAY. PLAN | PERIL(S) Insured Against and Coverage(s) Provided (Insert Name of Each) |
|---|---|---|---|---|
| $ | $ | $ | $ | FIRE AND LIGHTNING |
| x x x x x x x | $ | $ | $ | EXTENDED COVERAGE |
| | $ | $ | $ | |
| | $ | $ | $ | |
| $  TOTAL PREMIUM FOR POLICY TERM UNDER D. P. P. | TOTAL(S) $ | $ | | |

| Item No. | Amount Fire or Fire and Extended Coverage, or Other Peril | Per Cent of Co-Insurance Applicable | DESCRIPTION AND LOCATION OF PROPERTY COVERED Show construction, type of roof and occupancy of building(s) covered or containing the property covered. If occupied as a dwelling state number of families. |
|---|---|---|---|

I. - $

Subject to Form No(s).                    INSERT FORM NUMBER(S) AND EDITION DATE(S)                    **attached hereto.**

**Mortgage Clause:** Subject to the provisions of the mortgage clause attached hereto, loss, if any, on building items, shall be payable to:

INSERT NAME(S) OF MORTGAGEE(S) AND MAILING ADDRESS(ES)

Agency at

Countersignature Date

_____Agent

**IN CONSIDERATION OF THE PROVISIONS AND STIPULATIONS HEREIN OR ADDED HERETO** AND OF the premium above specified, this Company, for the term of years specified above from inception date shown above At Noon (Standard Time) to expiration date shown above At Noon (Standard Time) at location of property involved, to an amount not exceeding the amount(s) above specified, does insure the insured named above and legal representatives, to the extent of the actual cash value of the property at the time of loss, but not exceeding the amount which it would cost to repair or replace the property with material of like kind and quality within a reasonable time after such loss, without allowance for any increased cost of repair or reconstruction by reason of any ordinance or law regulating construction or repair, and without compensation for loss resulting from interruption of business or manufacture, nor in any event for more than the interest of the insured, against all **DIRECT LOSS BY FIRE, LIGHTNING AND BY REMOVAL FROM PREMISES ENDANGERED BY THE PERILS INSURED AGAINST IN THIS POLICY, EXCEPT AS HEREINAFTER PROVIDED,** to the property described herein while located or contained as described in this policy, or pro rata for five days at each proper place to which any of the property shall necessarily be removed for preservation from the perils insured against in this policy, but not elsewhere.

Assignment of this policy shall not be valid except with the written consent of this Company.

This policy is made and accepted subject to the foregoing provisions and stipulations and those hereinafter stated, which are hereby made a part of this policy, together with such other provisions, stipulations and agreements as may be added hereto, as provided in this policy.

**656**

1 **Concealment,** This entire policy shall be void if, whether
2 **fraud.** before or after a loss, the insured has wil-
3 fully concealed or misrepresented any ma-
4 terial fact or circumstance concerning this insurance or the
5 subject thereof, or the interest of the insured therein, or in case
6 of any fraud or false swearing by the insured relating thereto.
7 **Uninsurable** This policy shall not cover accounts, bills,
8 **and** currency, deeds, evidences of debt, money or
9 **excepted property.** securities; nor, unless specifically named
10 herein in writing, bullion or manuscripts.
11 **Perils not** This Company shall not be liable for loss by
12 **included.** fire or other perils insured against in this
13 policy caused, directly or indirectly, by: (a)
14 enemy attack by armed forces, including action taken by mili-
15 tary, naval or air forces in resisting an actual or an immediately
16 impending enemy attack; (b) invasion; (c) insurrection; (d)
17 rebellion; (e) revolution; (f) civil war; (g) usurped power; (h)
18 order of any civil authority except acts of destruction at the time
19 of and for the purpose of preventing the spread of fire, provided
20 that such fire did not originate from any of the perils excluded
21 by this policy; (i) neglect of the insured to use all reasonable
22 means to save and preserve the property at and after a loss, or
23 when the property is endangered by fire in neighboring prem-
24 ises; (j) nor shall this Company be liable for loss by theft.
25 **Other Insurance.** Other insurance may be prohibited or the
26 amount of insurance may be limited by en-
27 dorsement attached hereto.
28 **Conditions suspending or restricting insurance. Unless other-**
29 **wise provided in writing added hereto this Company shall not**
30 **be liable for loss occurring**
31 (a) while the hazard is increased by any means within the con-
32 trol or knowledge of the insured; or
33 (b) while a described building, whether intended for occupancy
34 by owner or tenant, is vacant or unoccupied beyond a period of
35 sixty consecutive days; or
36 (c) as a result of explosion or riot, unless fire ensue, and in
37 that event for loss by fire only.
38 **Other perils** Any other peril to be insured against or sub-
39 **or subjects.** ject of insurance to be covered in this policy
40 shall be by endorsement in writing hereon or
41 added hereto.
42 **Added provisions.** The extent of the application of insurance
43 under this policy and of the contribution to
44 be made by this Company in case of loss, and any other pro-
45 vision or agreement not inconsistent with the provisions of this
46 policy, may be provided for in writing added hereto, but no pro-
47 vision may be waived except such as by the terms of this policy
48 is subject to change.
49 **Waiver** No permission affecting this insurance shall
50 **provisions.** exist, nor waiver of any provision be valid,
51 unless granted herein or expressed in writing
52 added hereto. No provision, stipulation or forfeiture shall be
53 held to be waived by any requirement or proceeding on the part
54 of this Company relating to appraisal or to any examination
55 provided for herein.
56 **Cancellation** This policy shall be cancelled at any time
57 **of policy.** at the request of the insured, in which case
58 this Company shall, upon demand and sur-
59 render of this policy, refund the excess of paid premium above
60 the customary short rates for the expired time. This pol-
61 icy may be cancelled at any time by this Company by giving
62 to the insured a five days' written notice of cancellation with
63 or without tender of the excess of paid premium above the pro
64 rata premium for the expired time, which excess, if not ten-
65 dered, shall be refunded on demand. Notice of cancellation shall
66 state that said excess premium (if not tendered) will be re-
67 funded on demand.
68 **Mortgagee** If loss hereunder is made payable, in whole
69 **interests and** or in part, to a designated mortgagee not
70 **obligations.** named herein as the insured, such interest in
71 this policy may be cancelled by giving to such
72 mortgagee a ten days' written notice of can-
73 cellation.
74 If the insured fails to render proof of loss such mortgagee, upon
75 notice, shall render proof of loss in the form herein specified
76 within sixty (60) days thereafter and shall be subject to the pro-
77 visions hereof relating to appraisal and time of payment and of
78 bringing suit. If this Company shall claim that no liability ex-
79 isted as to the mortgagor or owner, it shall, to the extent of pay-
80 ment of loss to the mortgagee, be subrogated to all the mort-
81 gagee's rights of recovery, but without impairing mortgagee's
82 right to sue; or it may pay off the mortgage debt and require
83 an assignment thereof and of the mortgage. Other provisions

84 relating to the interests and obligations of such mortgagee may
85 be added hereto by agreement in writing.
86 **Pro rata liability.** This Company shall not be liable for a greater
87 proportion of any loss than the amount
88 hereby insured shall bear to the whole insurance covering the
89 property against the peril involved, whether collectible or not.
90 **Requirements in** The insured shall give immediate written
91 **case loss occurs.** notice to this Company of any loss, protect
92 the property from further damage, forthwith
93 separate the damaged and undamaged personal property, put
94 it in the best possible order, furnish a complete inventory of
95 the destroyed, damaged and undamaged property, showing in
96 detail quantities, costs, actual cash value and amount of loss
97 claimed; **and within sixty days after the loss, unless such time**
98 **is extended in writing by this Company, the insured shall render**
99 **to this Company a proof of loss,** signed and sworn to by the
100 insured, stating the knowledge and belief of the insured as to
101 the following: the time and origin of the loss, the interest of the
102 insured and of all others in the property, the actual cash value of
103 each item thereof and the amount of loss thereto, all encum-
104 brances thereon, all other contracts of insurance, whether valid
105 or not, covering any of said property, any changes in the title,
106 use, occupation, location, possession or exposures of said prop-
107 erty since the issuing of this policy, by whom and for what
108 purpose any building herein described and the several parts
109 thereof were occupied at the time of loss and whether or not it
110 then stood on leased ground, and shall furnish a copy of all the
111 descriptions and schedules in all policies and, if required, verified
112 plans and specifications of any building, fixtures or machinery
113 destroyed or damaged. The insured, as often as may be reason-
114 ably required, shall exhibit to any person designated by this
115 Company all that remains of any property herein described, and
116 submit to examinations under oath by any person named by this
117 Company, and subscribe the same; and, as often as may be
118 reasonably required, shall produce for examination all books of
119 account, bills, invoices and other vouchers, or certified copies
120 thereof if originals be lost, at such reasonable time and place as
121 may be designated by this Company or its representative, and
122 shall permit extracts and copies thereof to be made.
123 **Appraisal.** In case the insured and this Company shall
124 fail to agree as to the actual cash value or
125 the amount of loss, then, on the written demand of either, each
126 shall select a competent and disinterested appraiser and notify
127 the other of the appraiser selected within twenty days of such
128 demand. The appraisers shall first select a competent and dis-
129 interested umpire; and failing for fifteen days to agree upon
130 such umpire, then, on request of the insured or this Company,
131 such umpire shall be selected by a judge of a court of record in
132 the state in which the property covered is located. The ap-
133 praisers shall then appraise the loss, stating separately actual
134 cash value and loss to each item; and, failing to agree, shall
135 submit their differences, only, to the umpire. An award in writ-
136 ing, so itemized, of any two when filed with this Company shall
137 determine the amount of actual cash value and loss. Each
138 appraiser shall be paid by the party selecting him and the ex-
139 penses of appraisal and umpire shall be paid by the parties
140 equally.
141 **Company's** It shall be optional with this Company to
142 **options.** take all, or any part, of the property at the
143 agreed or appraised value, and also to re-
144 pair, rebuild or replace the property destroyed or damaged with
145 other of like kind and quality within a reasonable time, on giv-
146 ing notice of its intention so to do within thirty days after the
147 receipt of the proof of loss herein required.
148 **Abandonment.** There can be no abandonment to this Com-
149 pany of any property.
150 **When loss** The amount of loss for which this Company
151 **payable.** may be liable shall be payable sixty days
152 after proof of loss, as herein provided, is
153 received by this Company and ascertainment of the loss is made
154 either by agreement between the insured and this Company ex-
155 pressed in writing or by the filing with this Company of an
156 award as herein provided.
157 **Suit.** No suit or action on this policy for the recov-
158 ery of any claim shall be sustainable in any
159 court of law or equity unless all the requirements of this policy
160 shall have been complied with, and unless commenced within
161 twelve months next after inception of the loss.
162 **Subrogation.** This Company may require from the insured
163 an assignment of all right of recovery against
164 any party for loss to the extent that payment therefor is made
165 by this Company.

IN WITNESS WHEREOF, this Company has executed and attested these presents; but this policy shall not be valid unless countersigned by
the duly authorized Agent of this Company at the agency hereinbefore mentioned.

INSERT SIGNATURES AND
TITLES OF PROPER OFFICERS

# Appendix D

# The Dwelling Building(s) and Contents Form

## DWELLING BUILDING(S) AND CONTENTS FORM
### (SEASONAL PROPERTY SHALL BE SO DESCRIBED IN THIS POLICY)

Insurance attaches only to those items specifically described in this policy for which a specific amount is shown and, unless otherwise provided, all conditions of this form and the provisions of the policy to which it is attached shall apply separately to each item covered.

**WINDSTORM AND HAIL DEDUCTIBLE:** The sum of $50 shall be deducted from the amount of loss to each building or structure resulting from each windstorm or hailstorm. This deductible does not apply to contents nor rental value coverage.

## SECTION I — DESCRIPTION OF COVERAGE

**A. DWELLING COVERAGE:** Unless the occupancy is otherwise described on the first page of this policy, or by endorsement(s) attached thereto, the term "dwelling" shall mean a building occupied for dwelling purposes by the number of families stated in this policy.

When the insurance under this policy covers a dwelling, such insurance shall include additions in contact therewith; also, if the property of the owner of the described dwelling and when not otherwise covered, building equipment, fixtures and outdoor equipment, (but not lawns, trees, shrubs or plants or outdoor radio and television equipment), all pertaining to the service of the described premises and while located thereon; also, materials and supplies located on the described premises or· adjacent thereto, intended for use in construction, alteration or repair of such dwelling or private structures on the described premises.

**B. PRIVATE STRUCTURES COVERAGE:** When the insurance under this policy covers private structure(s) such insurance shall cover private structures (other than the described dwelling and additions in contact therewith) appertaining to the described premises and located thereon, but not structures used in whole or in part for commercial, manufacturing or farming purposes. Structures used exclusively for private garage purposes shall not be deemed to be used for commercial, manufacturing or farming purposes.

**C. CONTENTS COVERAGE:** When the insurance under this policy covers contents, such insurance shall cover all household and personal property usual or incidental to the occupancy of the premises as a dwelling (except animals, birds, fish, aircraft, motor vehicles other than motorized equipment used for maintenance of the premises, and boats other than rowboats and canoes); belonging to the Insured or members of the Insured's family of the same household, or for which the Insured may be liable, or, at the option of the Insured, belonging to a servant or guest of the Insured; all while on the described premises.

**As to "Contents" —**

(1) If, during the term of this policy, such property is removed to another location which is within this state and occupied in whole or in part as the Insured's residence, this policy shall cover such property while at such new location up to the amount applicable to contents and shall cease to cover at the former location, except that during the period of removal this policy shall cover at each location in the proportion that the value of such property at each location bears to the aggregate value at both locations.

(2) Loss shall be adjusted with and made payable to the named Insured unless other payee is specifically named.

## SECTION II — PERILS INSURED AGAINST

This policy insures against all direct loss caused by:

**1. FIRE AND LIGHTNING,** excluding any loss resulting from any electrical injury or disturbance to electrical appliances, devices, fixtures or wiring caused by electrical currents artificially generated unless fire ensues and, if fire does ensue, this Company shall be liable only for its proportion of loss caused by such ensuing fire.

**2. REMOVAL,** meaning loss by removal of the property covered hereunder from premises endangered by the perils insured against, and the amount of insurance applies pro rata for 5 days at each proper place to which such property shall necessarily be removed for preservation from the perils insured against.

**3. INHERENT EXPLOSION,** meaning explosion occurring in the described dwelling or appurtenant private structures or in any structure containing property covered hereunder from hazards inherent therein.

Loss by explosion shall include direct loss resulting from the explosion of accumulated gases or unconsumed fuel within the firebox (or combustion chamber) of any fired vessel or within the flues or passages which conduct the gases of combustion therefrom.

This Company shall not be liable for loss by explosion of steam boilers, steam pipes, steam turbines or steam engines, if owned by, leased by or operated under the control of the Insured.

The following are not explosions within the intent or meaning of these provisions: (a) Electric arcing, (b) Rupture or bursting of rotating or moving parts of machinery caused by centrifugal force or mechanical breakdown, (c) Water hammer, (d) Rupture or bursting of water pipes, (e) Rupture, bursting or operation of pressure relief devices.

*This policy is extended to insure against loss by the following perils as hereinafter provided, only when rate and premium for EXTENDED COVERAGE are inserted in the spaces provided on the first page of this policy or endorsed hereon.*

**4. WINDSTORM AND HAIL,** excluding loss caused directly or indirectly by frost or cold weather, or ice (other than hail), snow or sleet, whether driven by wind or not.

This Company shall not be liable for loss to the interior of the building(s) or the property covered therein caused: (a) by rain, snow, sand or dust, whether driven by wind or not, unless the building(s) covered or containing the property covered shall

(CONTINUED OVER)

**4. Windstorm and Hail—Cont'd.**

first sustain an actual damage to roof or walls by the direct action of wind or hail and then shall be liable for loss to the interior of the building(s) or the property covered therein as may be caused by rain, snow, sand or dust entering the building(s) through openings in the roof or walls made by direct action of wind or hail; or (b) by water from sprinkler equipment or from other piping, unless such equipment or piping be damaged as a direct result of wind or hail.

Unless liability therefor is assumed by endorsement hereon, this Company shall not be liable for damage to the following property: (a) grain, hay, straw or other crops outside of buildings; or (b) windmills, windpumps or their towers; or (c) crop silos (or their contents); or (d) metal smokestacks or, when outside of buildings, awnings, canopies (fabric or slat) including their supports, signs, radio or television antennas including their lead-in wiring, masts or towers; or (e) lawns, trees, shrubs or plants.

**5. EXPLOSION,** including direct loss resulting from the explosion of accumulated gases or unconsumed fuel within the firebox (or combustion chamber) of any fired vessel or within the flues or passages which conduct the gases of combustion therefrom.

This Company shall not be liable for loss by explosion of steam boilers, steam pipes, steam turbines or steam engines, if owned by, leased by or operated under the control of the Insured.

The following are not explosions within the intent or meaning of these provisions:

(a) Shock waves caused by aircraft, generally known as "sonic boom,"

(b) Electric arcing,

(c) Rupture or bursting of rotating or moving parts of machinery caused by centrifugal force or mechanical breakdown,

(d) Water hammer,

(e) Rupture or bursting of water pipes,

(f) Rupture or bursting due to expansion or swelling of the contents of any building or structure, caused by or resulting from water,

(g) Rupture, bursting or operation of pressure relief devices.

*This Explosion provision, when effective, supersedes Inherent Explosion provision 3 herein.*

**6. RIOT, RIOT ATTENDING A STRIKE AND CIVIL COMMOTION,** including direct loss by acts of striking employees of the owner or tenant(s) of the described building(s) while occupied by said striking employees and shall also include direct loss from pillage and looting occurring during and at the immediate place of a riot, riot attending a strike or civil commotion. Unless specifically endorsed hereon, this Company shall not be liable for loss resulting from damage to or destruction of the described property due to change in temperature or humidity or interruption of operations whether or not such loss is covered by this policy as to other perils.

**7. AIRCRAFT AND VEHICLES,** meaning only direct loss resulting from actual physical contact of an aircraft or a vehicle with the property covered hereunder or with the building(s) containing the property covered hereunder, except that loss by aircraft includes direct loss by objects falling therefrom. This Company shall not be liable for loss: (a) by any vehicle owned or operated by an Insured or by any tenant of the described premises; (b) by any vehicle to fences, driveways, walks or lawns, trees, shrubs or plants.

The term "vehicles," means vehicles running on land or tracks but not aircraft. The term "aircraft," shall include self-propelled missiles and spacecraft.

**8. SMOKE,** meaning only smoke due to a sudden, unusual and faulty operation of any heating or cooking unit, only when such unit is connected to a chimney by a smoke pipe or vent pipe, and while in or on the described premises but not smoke from fireplaces.

## SECTION III — EXTENSIONS OF COVERAGE

As respects the following Extensions of Coverage — It is a condition of this policy that in the event the Insured elects to apply the extensions of coverage herein, this Company shall not be liable for a greater proportion of any loss then would have been the case if all policies covering the described property had contained identical provisions and the same election were made under all policies.

A. **PRIVATE STRUCTURES:** The Insured may apply up to 10% of the amount of insurance applicable to the dwelling covered under this policy, not as an additional amount of insurance, to cover loss to private structures as defined in paragraph B of Section I. This extension of coverage shall not apply to structures (other than structures used exclusively for private garage purposes) which are rented or leased in whole or in part, or held for such rental or lease, to other than a tenant of the described dwelling.

B. **RENTAL VALUE:** The Insured may apply up to 10% of the amount of insurance applicable to the dwelling covered under this policy, not as an additional amount of insurance, to cover rental value but not exceeding 1/12 of said 10% for each month the dwelling or appurtenant private structures, or parts thereof, are untenantable.

The term "rental value" shall mean the fair rental value of the building(s) or parts thereof, as furnished and equipped by the owner whether rented or not. Loss of Rental Value shall be computed for the period of time, following damage to or destruction of the building(s) or equipment therein or on the described premises (caused by the peril(s) insured against) which would be required with the exercise of due diligence and dispatch, and not limited by the termination date of this

policy, to restore the property to a tenantable condition, less such charges and expenses as do not continue.

This extension of coverage shall not apply to loss resulting from damage to or destruction of buildings or structures used in whole or in part for commercial, manufacturing or farming purposes, or structures (other than structures used exclusively for private garage purposes) which are rented or leased in whole or in part, or held for such rental or lease, to other than a tenant of the described dwelling.

C. **OFF PREMISES CONTENTS:** The Insured may apply up to 10% of the amount of insurance applicable to the contents covered under this policy, not as an additional amount of insurance, to cover loss to contents, as defined in paragraph C of Section I (except rowboats and canoes), belonging only to the Insured or members of the Insured's family of the same household, while elsewhere than on the described premises but within the limits of that part of Continental North America included within the United States of America and Canada, and in the State of Hawaii. This extension of coverage shall not inure directly or indirectly to the benefit of any carrier or other bailee.

660

**D. IMPROVEMENTS, ALTERATIONS AND ADDITIONS:**
The Insured, if not the owner of the described premises, may apply up to 10% of the amount of insurance applicable to the contents covered under this policy, not as an additional amount of insurance, to cover loss to improvements, alterations and additions to the described dwelling and to private structures as defined in paragraph B of Section I.

**E. DEBRIS REMOVAL:** This insurance covers expense incurred in the removal of debris of the property covered hereunder, which may be occasioned by loss caused by any of the perils insured against in this policy.

The total liability under this policy for both loss to property and debris removal expense shall not exceed the amount of insurance applying under this policy to the property covered.

## SECTION IV — GENERAL EXCLUSIONS

A. **This policy does not insure against loss —**

1. Caused by, resulting from, contributed to or aggravated by any of the following:

(a) flood, surface water, waves, tidal water or tidal wave, overflow of streams or other bodies of water, or spray from any of the foregoing, all whether driven by wind or not;

(b) water which backs up through sewers or drains;

(c) water below the surface of the ground including that which exerts pressure on or flows, seeps or leaks through sidewalks, driveways, foundations, walls, basement or other floors, or through doors, windows or any other openings in such sidewalks, driveways, foundations, walls or floors;

unless loss by fire or explosion as insured against hereunder ensues, and then this Company shall be liable for only such ensuing loss.

2. Caused by or resulting from power, heating or cooling failure, unless such failure results from physical damage to power, heating or cooling equipment situated on premises where the property covered is located, caused by the peril(s) insured against. This Company shall not be liable for any loss specifically excluded under (a) the riot peril in Section II, or (b) the Vandalism and Malicious Mischief Endorsement.

3. Occasioned directly or indirectly by enforcement of any local or state ordinance or law regulating the construction, repair or demolition of building(s) or structure(s).

B. **WAR RISK EXCLUSION CLAUSE** (This clause applies to all perils insured against hereunder except the perils of fire and lightning, which are otherwise provided for in this policy): This Company shall not be liable for loss caused directly or indirectly by (a) hostile or warlike action in time of peace or war, including action in hindering, combating or defending against an actual, impending or expected attack, (1) by any government or sovereign power (de jure or de facto), or by any authority maintaining or using military, naval or air forces; or (2) by military, naval or air forces; or (3) by an agent of any such government, power, authority or forces, it being understood that any discharge, explosion or use of any weapon of war employing nuclear fission or fusion shall be conclusively presumed to be such a hostile or warlike action by such a government, power, authority or forces; (b) insurrection, rebellion, revolution, civil war, usurped power, or action taken by governmental authority in hindering, combating or defending against such an occurrence.

C. **NUCLEAR CLAUSE:** The word "fire" in this policy or endorsements attached hereto is not intended to and does not embrace nuclear reaction or nuclear radiation or radioactive contamination, all whether controlled or uncontrolled, and loss by nuclear reaction or nuclear radiation or radioactive contamination is not intended to be and is not insured against by this policy or said endorsements, whether such loss be direct or indirect, proximate or remote, or be in whole or in part caused by, contributed to, or aggravated by "fire" or any other perils insured against by this policy or said endorsements; however, subject to the foregoing and all provisions of this policy, direct loss by "fire" resulting from nuclear reaction or nuclear radiation or radioactive contamination is insured against by this policy.

D. **NUCLEAR EXCLUSION** (This clause applies to all perils insured against hereunder except the perils of fire and lightning, which are otherwise provided for in the Nuclear Clause above): Loss by nuclear reaction or nuclear radiation or radioactive contamination, all whether controlled or uncontrolled, or due to any act or condition incident to any of the foregoing, is not insured against by this policy, whether such loss be direct or indirect, proximate or remote, or be in whole or in part caused by, contributed to, or aggravated by any of the perils insured against by this policy.

## SECTION V — OTHER PROVISIONS

A. **LOSS CLAUSE:** Any loss hereunder shall not reduce the amount of this policy.

B. **CONTROL OF PROPERTY:** This insurance shall not be prejudiced by any act or neglect of any person (other than the named Insured), when such act or neglect is not within the control of the named Insured.

C. **VACANCY AND UNOCCUPANCY:** Permission granted for vacancy or unoccupancy without limit of time, except as provided in any endorsement attached to this policy.

D. **SUBROGATION:** This insurance shall not be invalidated should the Insured waive in writing prior to a loss any or all right of recovery against any party for loss occurring to the described property.

E. **ALTERATIONS AND REPAIRS:** Permission granted to make alterations, additions and repairs, and to complete structures in course of construction.

In the event of loss hereunder, the Insured is permitted to make reasonable repairs, temporary or permanent, provided such repairs are confined solely to the protection of the property from further damage and provided further that the Insured shall keep an accurate record of such repair expenditures. The cost of any such repairs directly attributable to damage by any peril insured against shall be included in determining the amount of loss hereunder. Nothing herein contained is intended to modify the policy requirements applicable in case loss occurs, and in particular the requirement that the Insured shall protect the property from further damage.

F. **LIBERALIZATION CLAUSE:** If during the period that insurance is in force under this policy, or within 45 days prior to the inception date thereof, on behalf of this Company there be adopted, or filed with and approved or accepted by the insurance supervisory authorities, all in conformity with law, any changes in the form attached to this policy by which this form of insurance could be extended or broadened without increased premium charge by endorsement or substitution of form, then such extended or broadened insurance shall inure to the benefit of the Insured hereunder as though such endorsement or substitution of form had been made.

(CONTINUED OVER)

 Form No. 49 (10-68)

G. **PRO RATA CLAUSE:** If this policy covers on two or more items for which specific amounts are shown, the amount of this policy applies to each item in the proportion that the specific amount shown for each item bears to the sum of all items.

H. **APPORTIONMENT:** This Company shall not be liable for a greater proportion of any loss less the amount of deductible, if any, from any peril or perils insured against in this form than (1) the amount of insurance under this policy bears to the whole amount of fire insurance covering the property, or which would have covered the property except for the existence of this insurance, whether collectible or not, whether or not such other fire insurance insures against the additional peril or perils insured against hereunder, nor (2) for a greater proportion of any loss less the amount of deductible, if any, than the amount hereby insured bears to all insurance whether collectible or not, covering in any manner such loss, or which would have covered such loss except for the existence of this insurance; except if any type of insurance other than fire extended to cover additional perils or windstorm insurance applies to any loss to which this insurance also applies, or would have applied to any such loss except for the existence of this insurance, the limit of liability of each type of insurance for such loss, hereby designated as "joint loss", shall first be determined as if it were the only insurance, and this type of insurance shall be liable for no greater proportion of joint loss than the limit of its liability for such loss bears to the sum of all such limits. The liability of this Company (under this form) for such joint loss shall be limited to its proportionate part of the aggregate limit of this and all other insurance of the same type. The words "joint loss", as used in the foregoing, mean that portion of the loss in excess of the highest deductible, if any, to which this form and other types of insurance above referred to both apply.

I. **DEFERRED PREMIUM PAYMENTS:** If the Insured elects to pay the premium in annual payments as specified on the first page of this policy, the premium for this policy is hereby made so payable; except that in the event of any changes in the rates or premium charges, which are in effect for this Company and applicable to the insurance provided herein after the inception date of this policy, subsequent annual payments shall be calculated from the dates when such payments shall be due at the annual rates or premium charges then in effect. No payment shall be less than the minimum premium applicable.

If the Insured is in default of any such premium payment and this Company elects to cancel this policy, notice of cancellation shall be as required by law.

J. **OCCUPANCY CLAUSE:** In consideration of the rate at which this policy is written, it is a condition of this policy that if the described dwelling is associated with and in proximity to farming operations (1) the agricultural products produced on the land are incidental to the occupancy of the dwelling and are principally for home consumption OR (2) that the occupants of the dwelling and buildings appurtenant thereto are not engaged in the operation of the farm and said buildings are in addition to a complete set of farm buildings on the farm and are not exposed within 200 feet by any farm building.

K. **STANDARD MORTGAGE CLAUSE:** Applies to Building Items only; (but this entire clause is void unless name of mortgagee or trustee is inserted on the first page of this policy in space provided therefor):

Loss or damage, if any, under this policy, shall be payable to the mortgagee [or trustee], named on the first page of this policy, as interest may appear, and this insurance as to the interest of the mortgagee [or trustee] only therein, shall not be invalidated by any act or neglect of the mortgagor or owner of the within described property, nor by any foreclosure or other proceedings or notice of sale relating to the property, nor by any change in the title or ownership of the property, nor by the occupation of the premises for purposes more hazardous than are permitted by this policy; provided, that in case the mortgagor or owner shall neglect to pay any premium due under this policy, the mortgagee [or trustee] shall, on demand, pay the same.

Provided also, that the mortgagee [or trustee] shall notify this Company of any change of ownership or occupancy or increase of hazard which shall come to the knowledge of said mortgagee [or trustee] and, unless permitted by this policy, it shall be noted thereon and the mortgagee [or trustee] shall, on demand, pay the premium for such increased hazard for the term of the use thereof; otherwise this policy shall be null and void.

This Company reserves the right to cancel this policy at any time as provided by its terms, but in such case this policy shall continue in force for the benefit only of the mortgagee [or trustee] for ten days after notice to the mortgagee [or trustee] of such cancellation and shall then cease, and this Company shall have the right, on like notice, to cancel this agreement.

Whenever this Company shall pay the mortgagee [or trustee] any sum for loss or damage under this policy, and shall claim that, as to the mortgagor or owner, no liability therefor existed, this Company shall, to the extent of such payment, be thereupon legally subrogated to all the rights of the party to whom such payment shall be made, under all securities held as collateral to the mortgage debt, or may at its option pay to the mortgagee [or trustee] the whole principal due or to grow due on the mortgage, with interest accrued thereon to the date of such payment, and shall thereupon receive a full assignment and transfer of the mortgage and of all such other securities; but no subrogation shall impair the right of the mortgagee [or trustee] to recover the full amount of his, her or their claim.

**NOTES TO AGENTS:** 1. **NO CHANGE OR ALTERATION IN THIS FORM WILL BE PERMITTED EXCEPT BY ENDORSEMENT, COPY OF WHICH MUST BE SENT TO COMPANY.** 2. **This form is to be used only for covering buildings or contents of buildings defined in the Rule Book as Dwellings and Private Outbuildings in connection therewith; but excluding Farm Property.**

662

# Appendix E

# Homeowners Policy

**No. H** ............................................................

CAPITAL STOCK COMPANY

RENEWAL OF NUMBER

[AUTHENTIC]

SPACE FOR COMPANY NAME, INSIGNIA, AND LOCATION

**DECLARATIONS**

**Named Insured and P.O. Address**   (Number, Street, Town or City, County, State, Zip Code)

SPACE FOR
PRODUCER'S NAME AND
MAILING ADDRESS

**Policy Term:** _____

Years _____ Inception _____ Expiration

The described residence premises covered hereunder is located at the above address, unless otherwise stated herein (No., Street, Town or City, County, State, Zip Code)

Insurance is provided only with respect to the following Coverages for which a limit of liability is specified, subject to all conditions of this policy.

| Coverages and Limit of Liability | Section I | | | | Section II | | |
|---|---|---|---|---|---|---|---|
| | A. Dwelling | B. Appurtenant Structures | C. Unscheduled Personal Property | D. Additional Living Expense | E. Personal Liability (Bodily Injury and Property Damage) Each occurrence | F. Medical Payments to Others | |
| | | | | | | Each person | Each accident |
| | $ | $ | $ | $ | $ | $ | $ 25,000 |

| Premium | Basic Policy Premium | Theft Extension | Additional Premiums | | Total Prepaid Premium | Premium if paid in installments | At Inception (and) Payable: | At each subsequent anniversary |
|---|---|---|---|---|---|---|---|---|
| | $ | $ | $ | $ | $ | $ | $ | $ |

| Premium for Scheduled Personal Property | $ | $ | $ | $ |
|---|---|---|---|---|

Form and Endorsements made part of this Policy at time of issue: Insert Number(s) and Edition Date(s)

Form HO-

Endorsement(s) HO-

| **Combined Premium** | $ | $ | $ | $ |
|---|---|---|---|---|

**DEDUCTIBLE—SECTION I:** Any loss by perils insured against under Section I of this policy is subject to a deductible. Exceptions, if any:

☐ Deductible applicable only to loss caused by the peril of windstorm or hail (Clause No. 1)

☐ Deductible applicable to loss caused by other perils (Clause No. 2)

☐ Deductible not applicable

☐ Special Loss Deductible $ _____ Clause (Amount)

**Special State Provisions:** South Carolina: Valuation Clause (Coverage A) $ _____

New York: Coinsurance Clause Applies ☐ Yes ☐ No

**Section II**—Additional residence premises, if any, located: (No., Street, Town or City, County, State, Zip Code)

Mortgagee(s)

(NAME AND ADDRESS)

Countersignature Date

Agency at

_____ Agent

| Rating Information Only | Dwelling occupied by | | | | Tenant | Deductibles: | All Perils | Clause No. 1 | Clause No. 2 | Zone | Not more than | Not more than |
|---|---|---|---|---|---|---|---|---|---|---|---|---|
| | ☐ 1 ☐ 2 ☐ 3 ☐ 4 families. | | | | ☐ | | $ | $ | $ | | ____ feet from Hydrant | ____ miles from Fire Dept. |
| | Code (1) (3) (7) (7) | | | | (7) | Type Code: | | Size Code: | | Code: | | |

| Construction of dwelling: | Code (1) ☐ Frame | Code (5) ☐ Frame with aluminum or plastic siding | Code (2) ☐ Brick, Stone or Masonry Veneer | Code (3) ☐ Stone or Masonry | Code (4) ☐ Fire Resistive | Roof ☐ Approved ☐ Unapproved | Prot. Cl. ☐ | Code | Premium Group No. |
|---|---|---|---|---|---|---|---|---|---|

Complete when Form HO-4 is made a part of this policy — Southern States — Fire District — Code

| Total Annual Fire and Extended Coverage Rate | Number of Apartments in building | Inside City Limits ☐ | Inside Protected Suburban Area ☐ | Inside Fire District ☐ |
|---|---|---|---|---|

**(a)** The described dwelling is not seasonal; (b) no business pursuits are conducted on the described premises; (c) the described premises is the only premises where the Named Insured or spouse maintains a residence other than business or farm properties; (d) the Insured has no full time residence employee(s); (e) the Insured has no outboard motor(s) or watercraft otherwise excluded under this policy for which coverage is desired. Exception, if any, to (a), (b), (c), (d) or (e)*

*Absence of an entry means "no exceptions".

**In Consideration of the Provisions and Stipulations Herein or Added Hereto and of the Premium Above Specified** (or specified in endorsement(s) made a part hereof), this Company, for the **term shown above** from inception date shown above at noon (Standard Time) to **expiration date shown above** at noon (Standard Time) at location of property involved, to an amount not exceeding the limit of liability above specified, does insure **the Insured named in the Declarations above** and legal representatives, to the extent of the actual cash value of the property at the time of loss, but not exceeding the amount which it would cost to repair or replace the property with material of like kind and quality within a reasonable time after such loss, without allowance for any increased cost of repair or reconstruction by reason of any ordinance or law regulating construction or repair, and without compensation for loss resulting from interruption of business or manufacture, nor in any event for more than the interest of the Insured, against all DIRECT LOSS BY FIRE, LIGHTNING AND OTHER PERILS INSURED AGAINST IN THIS POLICY INCLUDING REMOVAL FROM PREMISES ENDANGERED BY THE PERILS INSURED AGAINST IN THIS POLICY, EXCEPT AS HEREINAFTER PROVIDED, to the property described herein while located or contained as described in this policy, or pro rata for five days at each proper place to which any of the property shall necessarily be removed for preservation from the perils insured against in this policy, but not elsewhere.

Assignment of this policy shall not be valid except with the written consent of this Company.

This policy is made and accepted subject to the foregoing provisions and stipulations and those hereinafter stated, which are hereby made a part of this policy, together with such other provisions, stipulations and agreements as may be added hereto, as provided in this policy.

OKP 1001-1-C (Ed. 10-68 Standard)

**664**

| | | |
|---|---|---|
| 1 **Concealment,** | This entire policy shall be void if, whether | |
| 2 **fraud.** | before or after a loss, the insured has wil- | |
| 3 | fully concealed or misrepresented any ma- | |
| 4 terial fact or circumstance concerning this insurance or the | | |
| 5 subject thereof, or the interest of the insured therein, or in case | | |
| 6 of any fraud or false swearing by the insured relating thereto. | | |

1 **Concealment,**    This entire policy shall be void if, whether
2 **fraud.**    before or after a loss, the insured has wil-
3    fully concealed or misrepresented any ma-
4 terial fact or circumstance concerning this insurance or the
5 subject thereof, or the interest of the insured therein, or in case
6 of any fraud or false swearing by the insured relating thereto.
7 **Uninsurable**    This policy shall not cover accounts, bills,
8 **and**    currency, deeds, evidences of debt, money or
9 **excepted property.**    securities; nor, unless specifically named
10    hereon in writing, bullion or manuscripts.
11 **Perils not**    This Company shall not be liable for loss by
12 **included.**    fire or other perils insured against in this
13    policy caused, directly or indirectly, by: (a)
14 enemy attack by armed forces, including action taken by mili-
15 tary, naval or air forces in resisting an actual or an immediately
16 impending enemy attack; (b) invasion; (c) insurrection; (d)
17 rebellion; (e) revolution; (f) civil war; (g) usurped power; (h)
18 order of any civil authority except acts of destruction at the time
19 of and for the purpose of preventing the spread of fire, provided
20 that such fire did not originate from any of the perils excluded
21 by this policy; (i) neglect of the insured to use all reasonable
22 means to save and preserve the property at and after a loss, or
23 when the property is endangered by fire in neighboring prem-
24 ises; (j) nor shall this Company be liable for loss by theft.
25 **Other Insurance.**    Other insurance may be prohibited or the
26    amount of insurance may be limited by en-
27 dorsement attached hereto.
28 **Conditions suspending or restricting insurance. Unless other-**
29 **wise provided in writing added hereto this Company shall not**
30 **be liable for loss occurring**
31 (a) while the hazard is increased by any means within the con-
32 trol or knowledge of the insured; or
33 (b) while a described building, whether intended for occupancy
34 by owner or tenant, is vacant or unoccupied beyond a period of
35 sixty consecutive days; or
36 (c) as a result of explosion or riot, unless fire ensue, and in
37 that event for loss by fire only.
38 **Other perils**    Any other peril to be insured against or sub-
39 **or subjects.**    ject of insurance to be covered in this policy
40    shall be by endorsement in writing hereon or
41 added hereto.
42 **Added provisions.**    The extent of the application of insurance
43    under this policy and of the contribution to
44 be made by this Company in case of loss, and any other pro-
45 vision or agreement not inconsistent with the provisions of this
46 policy, may be provided for in writing added hereto, but no pro-
47 vision may be waived except such as by the terms of this policy
48 is subject to change.
49 **Waiver**    No permission affecting this insurance shall
50 **provisions.**    exist, or waiver of any provision be valid,
51    unless granted herein or expressed in writing
52 added hereto. No provision, stipulation or forfeiture shall be
53 held to be waived by any requirement or proceeding on the part
54 of this Company relating to appraisal or to any examination
55 provided for herein.
56 **Cancellation**    This policy shall be cancelled at any time
57 **of policy.**    at the request of the insured, in which case
58    this Company shall, upon demand and sur-
59 render of this policy, refund the excess of paid premium above
60 the customary short rates for the expired time. This pol-
61 icy may be cancelled at any time by this Company by giving
62 to the insured a five days' written notice of cancellation with
63 or without tender of the excess of paid premium above the pro
64 rata premium for the expired time, which excess, if not ten-
65 dered, shall be refunded on demand. Notice of cancellation shall
66 state that said excess premium (if not tendered) will be re-
67 funded on demand.
68 **Mortgagee**    If loss hereunder is made payable, in whole
69 **interests and**    or in part, to a designated mortgagee not
70 **obligations.**    named herein as the insured, such interest in
71    this policy may be cancelled by giving to such
72    mortgagee a ten days' written notice of can-
73 cellation.
74 If the insured fails to render proof of loss such mortgagee, upon
75 notice, shall render proof of loss in the form herein specified
76 within sixty (60) days thereafter and shall be subject to the pro-
77 visions hereof relating to appraisal and time of payment and of
78 bringing suit. If this Company shall claim that no liability ex-
79 isted as to the mortgagor or owner, it shall, to the extent of pay-
80 ment of loss to the mortgagee, be subrogated to all the mort-
81 gagee's rights of recovery, but without impairing mortgagee's
82 right to sue; or it may pay off the mortgage debt and require
83 an assignment thereof and of the mortgage. Other provisions

84 relating to the interests and obligations of such mortgagee may
85 be added hereto by agreement in writing.
86 **Pro rata liability.**    This Company shall not be liable for a greater
87    proportion of any loss than the amount
88 hereby insured shall bear to the whole insurance covering the
89 property against the peril involved, whether collectible or not.
90 **Requirements in**    The insured shall give immediate written
91 **case loss occurs.**    notice to this Company of any loss, protect
92    the property from further damage, forthwith
93 separate the damaged and undamaged personal property, put
94 it in the best possible order, furnish a complete inventory of
95 the destroyed, damaged and undamaged property, showing in
96 detail quantities, costs, actual cash value and amount of loss
97 claimed; **and within sixty days after the loss, unless such time**
98 **is extended in writing by this Company, the insured shall render**
99 **to this Company a proof of loss,** signed and sworn to by the
100 insured, stating the knowledge and belief of the insured as to
101 the following: the time and origin of the loss, the interest of the
102 insured and of all others in the property, the actual cash value of
103 each item thereof and the amount of loss thereto, all encum-
104 brances thereon, all other contracts of insurance, whether valid
105 or not, covering any of said property, any changes in the title,
106 use, occupation, location, possession or exposures of said prop-
107 erty since the issuing of this policy, by whom and for what
108 purpose any building herein described and the several parts
109 thereof were occupied at the time of loss and whether or not it
110 then stood on leased ground, and shall furnish a copy of all the
111 descriptions and schedules in all policies and, if required, verified
112 plans and specifications of any building, fixtures or machinery
113 destroyed or damaged. The insured, as often as may be reason-
114 ably required, shall exhibit to any person designated by this
115 Company all that remains of any property herein described, and
116 submit to examinations under oath by any person named by this
117 Company, and subscribe the same; and, as often as may be
118 reasonably required, shall produce for examination all books of
119 account, bills, invoices and other vouchers, or certified copies
120 thereof if originals be lost, at such reasonable time and place as
121 may be designated by this Company or its representative, and
122 shall permit extracts and copies thereof to be made.
123 **Appraisal.**    In case the insured and this Company shall
124    fail to agree as to the actual cash value or
125 the amount of loss, then, on the written demand of either, each
126 shall select a competent and disinterested appraiser and notify
127 the other of the appraiser selected within twenty days of such
128 demand. The appraisers shall first select a competent and dis-
129 interested umpire; and failing for fifteen days to agree upon
130 such umpire, then, on request of the insured or this Company,
131 such umpire shall be selected by a judge of a court of record in
132 the state in which the property covered is located. The ap-
133 praisers shall then appraise the loss, stating separately actual
134 cash value and loss to each item; and, failing to agree, shall
135 submit their differences, only, to the umpire. An award in writ-
136 ing, so itemized, of any two when filed with this Company shall
137 determine the amount of actual cash value and loss. Each
138 appraiser shall be paid by the party selecting him and the ex-
139 penses of appraisal and umpire shall be paid by the parties
140 equally.
141 **Company's**    It shall be optional with this Company to
142 **options.**    take all, or any part, of the property at the
143    agreed or appraised value, and also to re-
144 pair, rebuild or replace the property destroyed or damaged with
145 other of like kind and quality within a reasonable time, on giv-
146 ing notice of its intention so to do within thirty days after the
147 receipt of the proof of loss herein required.
148 **Abandonment.**    There can be no abandonment to this Com-
149    pany of any property.
150 **When loss**    The amount of loss for which this Company
151 **payable.**    may be liable shall be payable sixty days
152    after proof of loss, as herein provided, is
153 received by this Company and ascertainment of the loss is made
154 either by agreement between the insured and this Company ex-
155 pressed in writing or by the filing with this Company of an
156 award as herein provided.
157 **Suit.**    No suit or action on this policy for the recov-
158    ery of any claim shall be sustainable in any
159 court of law or equity unless all the requirements of this policy
160 shall have been complied with, and unless commenced within
161 twelve months next after inception of the loss.
162 **Subrogation.**    This Company may require from the insured
163    an assignment of all right of recovery against
164 any party for loss to the extent that payment therefor is made
165 by this Company.

| | |
|---|---|
| **STATE** **EXCEPTIONS** | **Kansas** — In the numbered line provisions, the words "demand and" in line 58 and "on demand" in lines 65 and 67 are deleted and the words "twelve months" in line 161 are changed to "sixty months". **North Dakota** — The words "twelve months" in line 161 of the numbered line provisions are changed to "thirty-six months". |

**In Witness Whereof,** this Company has executed and attested these presents; but this policy shall not be valid unless countersigned by the duly authorized Agent of this Company at the agency hereinbefore mentioned.

INSERT SIGNATURES AND
TITLES OF PROPER OFFICERS

# GENERAL CONDITIONS

**1. EXCLUSION OF LOSS BY GOVERNMENTAL ACTION:** Under Section I as respects all perils insured against hereunder (except the perils of fire and lightning which are otherwise provided for on page 2 of this policy), and under Section II, this policy shall not apply to loss, bodily injury or property damage caused directly or indirectly by:

a. hostile or warlike action in time of peace or war, including action in hindering, combating or defending against an actual, impending or expected attack, (1) by any government or sovereign power (de jure or de facto), or by any authority maintaining or using military, naval or air forces; or (2) by military, naval or air forces; or (3) by an agent of any such government, power, authority or forces, it being understood that any discharge, explosion or use of any weapon of war employing nuclear fission or fusion shall be conclusively presumed to be such a hostile or warlike action by such government, power, authority or forces;

b. insurrection, rebellion, revolution, civil war, usurped power, or action taken by governmental authority in hindering, combating or defending against such an occurrence; seizure or destruction under quarantine or customs regulations, confiscation by order of any government or public authority; or risks of contraband or illegal transportation or trade.

**2. NUCLEAR CLAUSE—SECTION I — (Not Applicable in New York):** The word "fire" in this policy is not intended to and does not embrace nuclear reaction or nuclear radiation or radioactive contamination, all whether controlled or uncontrolled, and loss by nuclear reaction or nuclear radiation or radioactive contamination is not intended to be and is not insured against by this policy, whether such loss be direct or indirect, proximate or remote, or be in whole or in part caused by, contributed to, or aggravated by "fire" or any other perils insured against by this policy, however, subject to the foregoing and all provisions of this policy, direct loss by "fire" resulting from nuclear reaction or nuclear radiation or radioactive contamination is insured against by this policy.

**3. NUCLEAR EXCLUSION—SECTION I — (Not Applicable in New York):** This policy does not insure against loss by nuclear reaction or nuclear radiation or radioactive contamination, all whether controlled or uncontrolled, or due to any act or condition incident to any of the foregoing, whether such loss be direct or indirect, proximate or remote, or be in whole or in part caused by, contributed to, or aggravated by any of the perils insured against by this policy; and nuclear reaction or nuclear radiation or radioactive contamination, all whether controlled or uncontrolled, is not "explosion" or "smoke". This clause applies to all perils insured against hereunder except the perils of fire and lightning, which are otherwise provided for in the Nuclear Clause contained above.

**4. NUCLEAR EXCLUSION—SECTION II:** This policy does not apply, under Coverage E — Personal Liability, to bodily injury or property damage with respect to which any Insured under this policy is also an Insured under a nuclear energy liability policy issued by Nuclear Energy Liability Insurance Association, Mutual Atomic Energy Liability Underwriters or Nuclear Insurance Association of Canada, or would be an Insured under any such policy but for its termination upon exhaustion of its limit of liability.

**5. MODIFICATION OF TERMS:**

a. The provisions on page 2 of this policy relating to uninsurable and excepted property, the exclusion of loss by theft and suspension of insurance are hereby waived.

b. The provisions on page 2 of this policy, other than those pertaining to waiver, cancellation, concealment and fraud and subrogation do not apply to Section II of this policy.

c. The provisions on page 2 of this policy relating to subrogation are not applicable to Coverage F — Medical Payments to Others and Supplementary Coverages — Damage to Property of Others.

d. The words "five days" in the cancellation provision on page 2 of this policy are deleted and the words "ten days" are substituted therefor.

e. The terms of this policy which are in conflict with the statutes of the state wherein this policy is issued are hereby amended to conform to such statutes.

**6. APPORTIONMENT — SECTION I:**

a. **Loss by fire or other perils not provided for in 6 b. below:**

This Company shall not be liable for a greater proportion of any loss from any peril or perils included in this policy than:

(1) the amount of insurance under this policy bears to the whole amount of fire insurance covering the property, or which would have covered the property except for the existence of this insurance, whether collectible or not, and whether or not such other fire insurance covers against the additional peril or perils insured hereunder; nor

(2) for a greater proportion of any loss than the amount hereby insured bears to all insurance, whether collectible or not, covering in any manner such loss or which would have covered such loss except for the existence of this insurance.

b. **Coverage C — Unscheduled Personal Property — Loss by theft or loss of unscheduled personal property covered on an unspecified peril basis:** Insurance under this policy shall apply as excess insurance over any other valid and collectible insurance which would apply in the absence of this policy.

c. **Deductible:** When loss under this policy is subject to a deductible, this Company shall not be liable for more than its share of such loss in excess of the deductible amount as provided in 6 a. or 6 b. above.

**7. APPORTIONMENT — SECTION II:**

a. Except as provided in 7 b. below if the Insured has other valid and collectible insurance against a loss covered under Coverage E — Personal Liability, this Company shall not be liable under this policy for a greater proportion of such loss than that stated in the applicable following provision:

(1) Contribution by Equal Shares;

If all of such other insurance includes a provision for contribution by equal shares, this Company shall not be liable for a greater proportion of such loss than would be payable if each insurer contributes an equal share until the share of each insurer equals the lowest applicable limit of liability under any one policy or the full amount of the loss is paid. With respect to any amount of loss not so paid the remaining insurers then continue to contribute equal shares of the remaining amount of loss until each such insurer has paid its limit in full or the full amount of the loss is paid.

(2) Contribution by Limits;

If any of such other insurance does not include a provision for contribution by equal shares, this Company shall not be liable for a greater proportion of such loss than the applicable limit of liability under this policy for such loss bears to the total applicable limit of liability of all valid and collectible insurance against such loss.

b. With respect to bodily injury or property damage arising out of the ownership, maintenance, operation, use, loading or unloading of any motor vehicle, recreational motor vehicle or watercraft to which this policy applies, this insurance under Coverage E — Personal Liability, shall be excess insurance over any other valid and collectible insurance available to the Insured.

**8. DEFINITIONS: (Refer to Section II of the Form made a part of this policy for Additional Definitions).**

When used in this policy the following definitions apply:

a. "Insured" means

(1) the Named Insured stated in the Declarations of this policy;

(2) if residents of the Named Insured's household, his spouse, the relatives of either, and any other person under the age of twenty-one in the care of any Insured; and

(3) under Coverage E — Personal Liability and Coverage F — Medical Payments to Others:

(a) with respect to animals or watercraft to which this insurance applies, owned by any Insured, any person or organization legally responsible therefor, except a person or organization using or having custody or possession of any such animal or watercraft in the course of his business or without the permission of the owner; and

(b) with respect to any vehicle to which this insurance applies, any employee of any Insured while engaged in the employment of the Insured.

b. "insured premises" means

(1) the residence premises described in the Declarations of this policy; and

(2) Under Section II only:

(a) any other residence premises specifically named in this policy;

(b) any residence premises acquired by the Named Insured or his spouse during the term of this policy;

(c) any residence premises which are not owned by any Insured but where an Insured may be temporarily residing;

(d) vacant land, other than farm land, owned by or rented to any Insured; and

(e) individual or family cemetery plots or burial vaults.

c. "residence premises" means

(1) a one or two family dwelling building, appurtenant structures, grounds and private approaches thereto; or

(2) that portion of any other building occupied as a residence;

provided that such premises is used as a private residence by the Named Insured or his spouse but excluding any portion of the premises used for business purposes.

d. "business" means

(1) a trade, profession or occupation, including farming, and the use of any premises or portion of residence premises for any such purposes; and

(2) the rental or holding for rental of the whole or any portion of the premises by any Insured;

but business shall not include:

(a) the occasional rental or holding for rental of the residence premises for dwelling purposes;

(b) the rental or holding for rental of a portion of the residence premises for dwelling purposes unless for the accommodation of three or more roomers or boarders;

(c) the rental or holding for rental of a portion of the residence premises for private garage purposes; or

(d) the rental or holding for rental of a portion of the residence premises as an office, school or studio.

**666**

**9. DEATH OF NAMED INSURED:** In the event of death of the Named Insured, the definition of "Insured" is modified as follows:

a. the Named Insured shall mean:

(1) the spouse, if a resident of the household at the time of such death; and

(2) the legal representative but only with respect to the premises and property of the deceased covered under this policy at the time of such death.

b. Insured shall also include:

(1) any member of the deceased's household who was covered under this policy at the time of such death, but only while a resident of the insured premises; and

(2) with respect to the property of the Named Insured, the person having proper temporary custody thereof, but only until the appointment and qualification of the legal representative.

**10. LIBERALIZATION CLAUSE:** If within 45 days prior to the inception of this policy, or during the term hereof, this Company adopts any revision of the forms or endorsements made part of this policy which would broaden coverage presently granted hereunder without additional premium charge, such broadened coverage will automatically apply to this policy.

**11. POLICY TERM:** This policy applies only to loss under Section I or bodily injury or property damage under Section II, which occurs during the policy term.

## CONDITIONS APPLICABLE ONLY TO SECTION I

**1. PERMISSION GRANTED:**

a. for such use of the premises as is usual or incidental to a dwelling;

b. for the premises to be vacant or unoccupied without limit of time, except as otherwise provided in this policy for certain specified perils; however, a building in the course of construction shall not be deemed vacant;

c. for Named Insured to make alterations, additions and repairs, and to complete structures in course of construction;

d. for Insured, in the event of loss hereunder, to make reasonable repairs, temporary or permanent, provided such repairs are confined solely to the protection of the property from further damage and provided further that the Insured shall keep an accurate record of such repair expenditures. The cost of any such repairs directly attributable to damage by any peril insured against shall be included in determining the amount of loss hereunder. Nothing herein contained is intended to modify the policy requirements applicable in case loss occurs, and in particular the requirement that in case loss occurs the Insured shall protect the property from further damage.

**2. OTHER INSURANCE:** Other insurance covering the described dwelling building (except insurance against perils not covered by this policy) is not permitted.

**3. CONTROL OF PROPERTY:** This insurance shall not be prejudiced by any act or neglect of any person, other than an Insured, when such act or neglect is not within the control of any Insured.

**4. SUBROGATION:** This insurance shall not be invalidated should the Named Insured waive in writing prior to a loss any or all right of recovery against any party for loss occurring to the property covered herein.

**5. NO BENEFIT TO BAILEE:** This insurance shall not inure directly or indirectly to the benefit of any carrier or other bailee for hire.

**6. PAIR AND SET CLAUSE:** If there is loss of an article which is part of a pair or set, the measure of loss shall be a reasonable and fair proportion of the total value of the pair or set, giving consideration to the importance of said article, but such loss shall not be construed to mean total loss of the pair or set.

**7. LOSS PAYABLE CLAUSE:** Loss, if any, shall be adjusted with the Named Insured and shall be payable to him unless other payee is specifically named hereunder.

## CONDITIONS APPLICABLE ONLY TO SECTION II

**1. LIMITS OF LIABILITY:**

Regardless of the number of:

a. Insureds under this insurance;

b. persons or organizations who sustain bodily injury or property damage;

c. claims made or suits brought on account of bodily injury or property damage;

this Company's liability is limited as follows:

(1) Coverage E — Personal Liability — The limit of liability stated in the Declarations as applicable to "each occurrence" is the total limit of the Company's liability under Coverage E — Personal Liability for all damages as the result of any one occurrence.

(2) Coverage F — Medical Payments to Others — The limit of liability stated in the Declarations as applicable to "each person" is the limit of the Company's liability under Coverage F — Medical Payments to Others for all medical expense for bodily injury to any one person as the result of any one accident; but subject to the above provision respecting "each person", the total liability of the Company under Coverage F — Medical Payments to Others for all medical expense for bodily injury to two or more persons as the result of any one accident shall not exceed the limit of liability stated in the Declarations as applicable to "each accident".

**2. SEVERABILITY OF INSURANCE:** The insurance afforded under Section II applies separately to each Insured against whom claim is made or suit is brought except with respect to this Company's limit of liability.

**3. INSURED'S DUTIES IN THE EVENT OF ACCIDENT, OCCURRENCE, CLAIM OR SUIT:**

a. Under Coverage E — Personal Liability and Coverage F — Medical Payments to Others:

(1) In the event of an accident or occurrence, written notice containing particulars sufficient to identify the Insured and also reasonably obtainable information with respect to the time, place and circumstances thereof, and the names and addresses of the injured and of available witnesses, shall be given by or for the Insured to this Company or any of its authorized agents as soon as practicable.

(2) If claim is made or suit is brought against the Insured, the Insured shall immediately forward to this Company every demand, notice, summons or other process received by him or his representative.

(3) The Insured shall cooperate with this Company and, upon this Company's request, assist in making settlements, in the conduct of suits and in enforcing any right of contribution or indemnity against any person or organization who may be liable to the Insured because of bodily injury or property damage with respect to which insurance is afforded under this policy; and the Insured shall attend hearings and trials and assist in securing and giving evidence and obtaining the attendance of witnesses. The Insured shall not, except at his own cost, voluntarily make any payment, assume any obligation or incur any expense other than for first aid to others at the time of accident.

b. Under Supplementary Coverages — Damage to Property of Others: When loss occurs, the Insured shall give written notice as soon as practicable to this Company or any of its authorized agents and file sworn proof of loss with this Company within sixty days after the occurrence of loss. The Insured shall exhibit the damaged property, if within his control, and cooperate with this Company in all matters pertaining to the loss or claims with respect thereto.

**4. INJURED PARTY'S DUTY IN CASE OF ACCIDENT — UNDER COVERAGE F — MEDICAL PAYMENTS TO OTHERS:** The injured party or someone on his behalf shall:

a. give this Company written proof of claim, under oath if required, as soon as practicable;

b. execute authorizations enabling this Company to obtain copies of medical reports and records, and the injured party shall submit to physical examination by a physician selected by this Company at such times and as often as this Company may reasonably require.

**5. PAYMENT OF CLAIM — COVERAGE F — MEDICAL PAYMENTS TO OTHERS:** This Company may pay the injured party or any person or organization rendering medical services and the payment shall reduce the amount payable hereunder for such injury. Payment hereunder shall not constitute an admission of any liability by any Insured or this Company.

**6. SUIT AGAINST THIS COMPANY:**

a. No suit or action shall lie against this Company, unless:

(1) as a condition precedent thereto there has been full compliance with all of the provisions and stipulations of this policy, and

(2) the amount of the Insured's obligation to pay has been finally determined:

(a) by judgment against the Insured after actual trial; or

(b) by written agreement of the Insured, the claimant and this Company.

b. Any person or organization or the legal representative thereof who has secured such judgment or written agreement shall thereafter be entitled to recover under this policy to the extent of the insurance afforded under this policy.

c. No person or organization shall have any right under this policy to join the Company as a party to any action against the Insured to determine the Insured's liability. This Company shall not be impleaded.

d. Bankruptcy or insolvency of the Insured or his estate shall not relieve this Company of its obligations under this policy.

667

# Appendix F

# Homeowners
# Special Form

## DESCRIPTION OF PROPERTY AND INTERESTS COVERED

**COVERAGE A — DWELLING**

This policy covers the described dwelling building, including additions in contact therewith, occupied principally as a private residence.

This coverage also includes:

1. if the property of the Insured and when not otherwise covered, building equipment, fixtures and outdoor equipment all pertaining to the service of the premises and while located thereon or temporarily elsewhere; and

2. materials and supplies located on the premises or adjacent thereto, intended for use in construction, alteration or repair of such dwelling.

**COVERAGE B — APPURTENANT STRUCTURES**

This policy covers structures (other than the described dwelling building, including additions in contact therewith) appertaining to the premises and located thereon.

This coverage also includes materials and supplies located on the premises or adjacent thereto, intended for use in construction, alteration or repair of such structures.

This coverage excludes:

1. structures used in whole or in part for business purposes; or

2. structures rented or leased in whole or in part or held for such rental or lease (except structures used exclusively for private garage purposes) to other than a tenant of the described dwelling.

**COVERAGE C — UNSCHEDULED PERSONAL PROPERTY**

This policy covers unscheduled personal property usual or incidental to the occupancy of the premises as a dwelling and owned or used by an Insured, while on the described premises and, at the option of the Named Insured, owned by others while on the portion of the premises occupied exclusively by the Insured.

This coverage also includes such unscheduled personal property while elsewhere than on the described premises, anywhere in the world:

1. owned or used by an Insured; or

2. at the option of the Named Insured,

a. owned by a guest while in a residence occupied by an Insured; or

b. owned by a residence employee while actually engaged in the service of an Insured and while such property is in the physical custody of such residence employee or in a residence occupied by an Insured;

3. but the limit of this Company's liability for the unscheduled personal property away from the premises shall be an additional amount of insurance equal to 10% of the amount specified for Coverage C, but in no event less than $1,000.

This coverage excludes:

1. animals, birds or fish;

2. motorized vehicles, except such vehicles pertaining to the service of the premises and not licensed for road use;

3. aircraft;

4. property of roomers and boarders not related to the Insured;

5. property carried or held as samples or for sale or for delivery after sale;

6. property rented or held for rental to others by the Insured, except property contained in that portion of the described premises customarily occupied exclusively by the Insured and occasionally rented to others or property of the Insured in that portion of the described dwelling occupied by roomers or boarders;

7. business property while away from the described premises;

8. any device or instrument for the recording, reproduction or recording and reproduction of sound which may be operated by power from the electrical system of a motor vehicle, or any tape, wire, record disc or other medium for use with any such device or instrument while any of said property is in or upon a motor vehicle; or

9. property which is separately described and specifically insured in whole or in part by this or any other insurance.

**COVERAGE D — ADDITIONAL LIVING EXPENSE**

If a property loss covered under this policy renders the premises untenantable, this policy covers the necessary increase in living expense incurred by the Named Insured to continue as nearly as practicable the normal standard of living of the Named Insured's household for not exceeding the period of time required:

1. to repair or replace such damaged or destroyed property as soon as possible; or

2. for the Named Insured's household to become settled in permanent quarters; whichever is less.

This coverage also includes:

1. the fair rental value of any portion of the described dwelling or appurtenant structures covered under this policy, as furnished or equipped by the Named Insured, which is rented or held for rental by the Named Insured. The fair rental value shall not include charges and expenses that do not continue during the period of untenantability. Coverage shall be limited to the period of time required to restore, as soon as possible, the rented portion to the same tenantable condition;

2. the period of time, not exceeding two weeks, while access to the premises is prohibited by order of civil authority, as a direct result of damage to neighboring premises by a peril not otherwise excluded.

The periods described above shall not be limited by the expiration of this policy.

This coverage excludes expense due to cancellation of any lease, or any written or oral agreement.

## SUPPLEMENTARY COVERAGES

The following supplementary coverages shall not increase the applicable limit of liability under this policy:

**1. Automatic Removal:** If, during the term of this policy, the Named Insured removes unscheduled personal property covered under Coverage C from the premises to another location within the Continental United States or the State of Hawaii, to be occupied as his principal residence, the limit of liability for Coverage C shall apply at each location in the proportion that the value at each location bears to the total value of all such property covered under Coverage C.

Property in transit shall be subject to the limit of liability for unscheduled personal property away from the premises.

This coverage shall apply only for a period of 30 days from the date removal commences and shall then cease.

**2. Debris Removal:** This policy covers expenses incurred in the removal of all debris of the property covered hereunder, occasioned by loss thereto for which coverage is afforded.

**3. Fire Department Service Charge: (Not applicable in New Mexico)**

This policy covers for an amount not exceeding $250 the Named Insured's liability, assumed by contract or agreement for fire department charges where fire department is called because of a fire in, on or exposing property insured hereunder, while located on the premises described. This coverage does not cover Named Insured's liability, by contract or otherwise, to indemnify either a city, municipality or fire protection district, or any other person, firm or corporation against loss, claim or liability arising by reasons of the movement or functioning of fire apparatus or members of a fire department; or by reason of any accident arising out of the performance of services by any fire department. Coverage afforded under this clause applies only if the property is not located within the limits of the city, municipality or fire protection district furnishing such fire department response.

**4. Cellar and Foundation Clause: (Applicable only in Ohio).** The Named Insured may apply up to 5% of the limit of liability applicable to Coverage A to cover cellar and foundation walls of the described dwelling building insured thereunder.

## DEDUCTIBLE

**Loss Deductible Clause:** With respect to loss covered under this policy, this Company shall be liable only when such loss in each occurrence exceeds $50. When loss is between $50 and $500 this Company shall be liable for 111% of loss in excess of $50 and when loss is $500 or more, this loss deductible clause shall not apply. This loss deductible clause shall not apply to Coverage D—Additional Living Expense or Fire Department Service Charge.

This policy insures under:

**COVERAGE A—DWELLING and COVERAGE B—APPURTENANT STRUCTURES** against all risks of physical loss to the property covered (and under **COVERAGE D, ADDITIONAL LIVING EXPENSE** resulting from such loss), except as otherwise excluded or limited.

**COVERAGE C—UNSCHEDULED PERSONAL PROPERTY** against direct loss to the property covered by the following perils as defined and limited, except as otherwise excluded.

**1. Fire or Lightning.**

**2. Removal,** meaning direct loss by removal of the property covered hereunder from premises endangered by the perils insured against. The applicable limit of liability, had the property not been removed, applies pro rata for 30 days at each proper place to which any of the property shall necessarily be removed for preservation from or for repair of damages caused by the perils insured against.

**3. Windstorm or Hail,** excluding loss:

a. caused directly or indirectly by frost or cold weather or ice (other than hail), snow or sleet, all whether driven by wind or not;

b. caused by rain, snow, sand or dust, all whether driven by wind or not, unless the building containing the property covered shall first sustain an actual damage to roof or walls by the direct force of wind or hail and then this Company shall be liable for loss to the property covered therein caused by rain, snow, sand or dust entering the building through openings in the roof or walls made by direct action of wind or hail; or

c. to watercraft (except rowboats and canoes on premises) including their trailers, furnishings, equipment and outboard motors while such property is not inside fully enclosed buildings.

**4. Explosion.**

**5. Riot or Civil Commotion,** including direct loss from pillage and looting occurring during and at the immediate place of a riot or civil commotion.

**6. Aircraft,** including self-propelled missiles and spacecraft.

**7. Vehicles.**

**8. Sudden and accidental damage from smoke,** other than smoke from agricultural smudging or industrial operations.

**9. Vandalism or Malicious Mischief,** meaning only the wilful and malicious damage to or destruction of the property covered.

**10. Theft,** meaning any act of stealing or attempt thereat, including loss of property from a known place under circumstances when a probability of theft exists.

Unscheduled personal property contained in any bank, trust or safe deposit company, public warehouse or occupied dwelling not owned or occupied by or rented to an Insured in which the property covered has been placed for safekeeping shall be considered as being on the described premises.

Upon knowledge of loss under this peril or of an occurrence which may give rise to a claim for such loss, the Insured shall give immediate notice to this Company or its authorized agents and also to the police.

a. General Theft Exclusions:

This policy does not apply to loss:

(1) if committed by an Insured;

(2) in or to a dwelling under construction or of materials or supplies therefor until completed and occupied;

(3) arising out of or resulting from the theft of any credit card or loss by forgery or alterations of any check, draft, promissory note, bill of exchange, or similar written promise, order or direction to pay a sum certain in money; or

(4) of a precious or semi-precious stone from its setting.

b. Theft Exclusions applicable while the described dwelling is rented to others:

This policy does not apply to loss from the described dwelling while the portion of the described dwelling customarily occupied exclusively by an Insured is rented to others:

(1) of money, bullion, numismatic property or bank notes;

(2) of securities, accounts, bills, deeds, evidences of debt, letters of credit, notes other than bank notes, passports, railroad and other tickets or stamps, including philatelic property;

(3) of jewelry, watches, necklaces, bracelets, gems, precious and semi-precious stones; articles of gold and platinum; or any article of fur or article containing fur which represents its principal value; or

(4) caused by a tenant, his employees or members of his household while renting the portion of the described dwelling customarily occupied exclusively by an Insured.

c. Theft Exclusions applicable to property away from the described premises:

This policy does not apply to loss away from the described premises of:

(1) property while in any dwelling or premises thereof, owned, rented or occupied by an Insured, except while an Insured is temporarily residing therein;

(2) property while unattended in or on any motor vehicle or trailer, other than a public conveyance, unless the loss is the result of forcible entry into such vehicle while all doors, windows or other openings thereof are closed and locked, provided there are visible marks of forcible entry upon the exterior of such vehicle or the loss is the result of the theft of such vehicle which is not recovered within 30 days, but property shall not be considered unattended when the Insured is required to surrender the keys of such vehicle to a bailee;

(3) property while unattended in or on private watercraft unless the loss is the direct result of forcible entry into a securely locked compartment and provided there are visible marks of forcible entry upon the exterior of such compartment;

(4) watercraft, their furnishings, equipment and outboard motors; or

(5) trailers, whether licensed or not.

**11. Falling objects,** but excluding loss to property within a building, unless the building containing the property covered shall first sustain an actual damage to the exterior of the roof or walls by the falling object.

**12. Weight of ice, snow or sleet,** but only with respect to property contained in a building and then only if the weight of ice, snow or sleet results in physical damage to such building.

**13. Collapse of buildings or any part thereof,** but collapse does not include settling, cracking, shrinkage, bulging or expansion.

**14. Sudden and accidental tearing asunder, cracking, burning or bulging of a steam or hot water heating system or of appliances for heating water,** but not including loss caused by or resulting from freezing.

**15. Accidental discharge, leakage or overflow of water or steam** from within a plumbing, heating or air conditioning system or from within a domestic appliance but excluding loss to the appliance from which the water or steam escapes. This peril does not include loss caused by or resulting from freezing.

**16. Freezing of plumbing, heating and air conditioning systems and domestic appliances.**

**17. Sudden and accidental injury from electrical currents artificially generated** to electrical appliances, devices, fixtures and wiring, except tubes, transistors and similar electronic components.

## ADDITIONAL EXCLUSIONS

This policy does not insure against loss:

Under Coverages A, B and C (and under Coverage D—Additional Living Expense resulting from such loss):

1. caused by, resulting from, contributed to or aggravated by any of the following:

a. flood, surface water, waves, tidal water or tidal waves, overflow of streams or other bodies of water, or spray from any of the foregoing, all whether driven by wind or not;

b. water which backs up through sewers or drains; or

c. water below the surface of the ground including that which exerts pressure on or flows, seeps or leaks through sidewalks, driveways, foundations, walls, basement or other floors or through doors, windows

or any other openings in such sidewalks, driveways, foundations, walls, or floors;

unless loss by fire or explosion ensues, and this Company shall then be liable only for such ensuing loss, but these exclusions do not apply to loss by theft;

2. caused by, resulting from, contributed to or aggravated by any earth movement, including but not limited to earthquake, volcanic eruption, landslide, mudflow, earth sinking, rising or shifting; unless loss by fire, explosion or breakage of glass constituting a part of the building(s) covered hereunder, including glass in storm doors and storm windows, ensues, and this Company shall then be liable only for such ensuing loss, but this exclusion does not apply to loss by theft;

**Page 2 HO-3**

670

**3.** to plumbing, heating or air conditioning systems or domestic appliances, or by discharge, leakage or overflow from such systems or appliances, caused by or resulting from freezing while the building covered is vacant or unoccupied unless the Insured shall have exercised due diligence with respect to maintaining heat in the building or unless such systems and appliances had been drained and the water supply shut off during such vacancy or unoccupancy;

**4.** occasioned directly or indirectly by enforcement of any local or state ordinance or law regulating the construction, repair, or demolition of building(s) or structure(s) unless such liability is otherwise specifically assumed by endorsement hereon;

**5.** to fences, pavements, patios, swimming pools, foundations, retaining walls, bulkheads, piers, wharves or docks when such loss is caused by freezing, thawing or by the pressure or weight of ice or water whether driven by wind or not;

**6.** caused by or resulting from power, heating or cooling failure, unless such failure results from physical damage to power, heating or cooling equipment situated on the premises, caused by a peril not otherwise excluded.

**Under Coverages A and B** (and under **Coverage D—Additional Living Expense** resulting from such loss):

  **1.** by wear and tear; marring or scratching; deterioration; inherent vice; latent defect; mechanical breakdown; rust; mold; wet or dry rot; contamination; smog; smoke from agricultural smudging or industrial operations; settling, cracking, shrinkage, bulging or expansion of pavements, patios, foundations, walls, floors, roofs or ceilings; birds, vermin, rodents, insects or domestic animals; unless loss by fire, smoke (other than smoke from agricultural smudging or industrial operations), explosion, collapse of a building, glass breakage or water not otherwise excluded ensues, then this policy shall cover only such ensuing loss. If loss by water not otherwise excluded ensues, this policy shall also cover the cost of tearing out and replacing of any part of the building covered required to effect repairs to the plumbing, heating or air conditioning system or domestic appliance but excluding loss to the system or appliance from which the water escapes;

**2.** by theft in or to a dwelling under construction or of materials or supplies therefor until completed and occupied;

**3.** by vandalism and malicious mischief or glass breakage, if the property covered hereunder had been vacant beyond a period of 30 consecutive days immediately preceding the loss.

**4.** loss caused by continuous or repeated seepage or leakage of water or steam from within a plumbing, heating or air conditioning system or from within a domestic appliance which occurs over a period of weeks, months or years.

671

**1. Replacement Cost — Coverages A and B:**

This condition shall be applicable only to a building structure covered hereunder excluding outdoor radio and television antennas and aerials, carpeting, awnings, domestic appliances and outdoor equipment, all whether attached to the building structure or not.

a. If at the time of loss the whole amount of insurance applicable to said building structure for the peril causing the loss is 80% or more of the full replacement cost of such building structure, the coverage of this policy applicable to such building structure is extended to include the full cost of repair or replacement (without deduction for depreciation).

b. If at the time of loss the whole amount of insurance applicable to said building structure for the peril causing the loss is less than 80% of the full replacement cost of such building structure, this Company's liability for loss under this policy shall not exceed the larger of the following amounts (1) or (2):

(1) the actual cash value of that part of the building structure damaged or destroyed; or

(2) that proportion of the full cost of repair or replacement without deduction for depreciation of that part of the building structure damaged or destroyed, which the whole amount of insurance applicable to said building structure for the peril causing the loss bears to 80% of the full replacement cost of such building structure.

c. This Company's liability for loss under this policy shall not exceed the smallest of the following amounts (1), (2), or (3):

(1) the limit of liability of this policy applicable to the damaged or destroyed building structure;

(2) the replacement cost of the building structure or any part thereof identical with such building structure on the same premises and intended for the same occupancy and use; or

(3) the amount actually and necessarily expended in repairing or replacing said building structure or any part thereof intended for the same occupancy and use.

d. When the full cost of repair or replacement is more than $1,000 or more than 5% of the whole amount of insurance applicable to said building structure for the peril causing the loss, this Company shall not be liable for any loss under paragraph a. or sub-paragraph (2) of paragraph b. of this condition unless and until actual repair or replacement is completed.

e. In determining if the whole amount of insurance applicable to said building structure is 80% or more of the full replacement cost of such building structure, the cost of excavations, underground flues and pipes, underground wiring and drains, and brick, stone and concrete foundations, piers and other supports which are below the under surface of the lowest basement floor, or where there is no basement, which are below the surface of the ground inside the foundation walls, shall be disregarded.

f. The Named Insured may elect to disregard this condition in making claim hereunder, but such election shall not prejudice the Named Insured's right to make further claim within 180 days after loss for any additional liability brought about by this policy condition.

**2. Special Limits of Liability on Certain Property:**

a. This Company shall be liable for loss to trees, shrubs, plants and lawns (except those grown for business purposes) only when the loss is caused by fire, lightning, explosion, riot, civil commotion, vandalism, malicious mischief, theft, aircraft, or vehicles not owned or operated by an occupant of the premises. This Company's liability for loss in any one occurrence under this provision shall not exceed in the aggregate for all such property 5% of the limit of liability of Coverage A, nor more than $250 on any one tree, shrub or plant, including expense incurred for removing debris thereof.

b. Under Coverage C, this Company shall not be liable for loss in any one occurrence with respect to the following property for more than:

(1) $100 in the aggregate on money, bullion, numismatic property and bank notes;

(2) $500 in the aggregate on securities, accounts, bills, deeds, evidences of debt, letters of credit, notes other than bank notes, passports, railroad and other tickets or stamps, including philatelic property;

(3) $1,000 on manuscripts;

(4) $500 in the aggregate for loss by theft of jewelry, watches, necklaces, bracelets, gems, precious and semi-precious stones, gold, platinum and furs including articles containing fur which represents its principal value;

(5) $500 in the aggregate on watercraft, including their trailers (whether licensed or not), furnishings, equipment and outboard motors; or

(6) $500 on trailers, not otherwise provided for, whether licensed or not.

**3. Loss Clause:**

Loss hereunder shall not reduce the applicable limit of liability under this policy.

**4. Mortgage Clause** — Coverages A and B only — (Not Applicable in Minnesota): (This entire clause is void unless name of mortgagee [or trustee] is inserted in the Declarations):

Loss, if any, under this policy, shall be payable to the mortgagee (or trustee), named on the first page of this policy, as interest may appear, under all present or future mortgages upon the property herein described in which the aforesaid may have an interest as mortgagee (or trustee), in order of precedence of said mortgages, and this insurance as to the interest of the mortgagee (or trustee) only therein, shall not be invalidated by any act or neglect of the mortgagor or owner of the within described property, nor by any foreclosure or other proceedings or notice of sale relating to the property, nor by any change in the title or ownership of the property, nor by the occupation of the premises for purposes more hazardous than are permitted by this policy; provided, that in case the mortgagor or owner shall neglect to pay any premium due under this policy, the mortgagee (or trustee) shall, on demand, pay the same.

Provided also, that the mortgagee (or trustee) shall notify this Company of any change of ownership or occupancy or increase of hazard which shall come to the knowledge of said mortgagee (or trustee) and, unless permitted by this policy, it shall be noted thereon and the mortgagee (or trustee) shall, on demand, pay the premium for such increased hazard for the term of the use thereof, otherwise this policy shall be null and void.

This Company reserves the right to cancel this policy at any time as provided by its terms but in such case this policy shall continue in force for the benefit only of the mortgagee (or trustee) for ten days after notice to the mortgagee (or trustee) of such cancellation and shall then cease, and this Company shall have the right, on like notice to cancel this agreement.

Whenever this Company shall pay the mortgagee (or trustee) any sum for loss under this policy, and shall claim that, as to the mortgagor or owner, no liability therefor existed, this Company shall, to the extent of such payment, be thereupon legally subrogated to all the rights of the party to whom such payment shall be made, under all securities held as collateral to the mortgage debt; or may at its option pay to the mortgagee (or trustee) the whole principal due or to grow due on the mortgage, with interest accrued and shall thereupon receive a full assignment and transfer of the mortgage and of all such other securities; but no subrogation shall impair the right of the mortgagee (or trustee) to recover the full amount of said mortgagee's (or trustee's) claim.

**5. Installment Payment** — (Applicable only in Ohio) Not applicable if policy is written on a Continuous Renewal basis: If the Insured elects to pay the premium in equal annual payments as indicated on the first page of this policy the premium for this policy is hereby made so payable.

Default in making any payment shall be construed as a request of the Insured to cancel this policy, in which case this Company shall, upon demand and surrender of this policy, or after ten days written notice to the Insured, comply with the said request.

If this policy is cancelled, either at the request of the Insured or at the election of this Company, this Company shall refund to the Insured only the excess of paid premium over earned premium. In the event the earned premium exceeds the paid premium the Insured shall pay this Company the difference.

**6. Occupancy Clause:** It is a condition of this policy that if the described dwelling is associated with and in proximity to farming operations (1) the agricultural products produced on the land are incidental to the occupancy of the dwelling and are principally for home consumption, or (2) that the occupants of the dwelling and buildings appurtenant thereto are not engaged in the operation of the farm and said buildings are in addition to a complete set of farm buildings on the farm and are not exposed within 200 feet by any farm building.

## SECTION II
## COVERAGES

**COVERAGE E — PERSONAL LIABILITY**

This Company agrees to pay on behalf of the Insured all sums which the Insured shall become legally obligated to pay as damages because of bodily injury or property damage, to which this insurance applies, caused by an occurrence. This Company shall have the right and duty, at its own expense, to defend any suit against the Insured seeking damages on

**(OVER)**

account of such bodily injury or property damage, even if any of the allegations of the suit are groundless, false or fraudulent, but may make such investigation and settlement of any claim or suit as it deems expedient. This Company shall not be obligated to pay any claim or judgment or to defend any suit after the applicable limit of this Company's liability has been exhausted by payment of judgments or settlements.

## COVERAGE F — MEDICAL PAYMENTS TO OTHERS

This Company agrees to pay all reasonable medical expenses, incurred within one year from the date of the accident, to or for each person who sustains bodily injury to which this insurance applies caused by an accident, while such person is:

1. on an insured premises with the permission of any Insured; or
2. elsewhere, if such bodily injury
   a. arises out of a condition in the insured premises or the ways immediately adjoining,
   b. is caused by the activities of any insured, or by a residence employee in the course of his employment by any Insured,
   c. is caused by an animal owned by or in the care of any Insured, or
   d. is sustained by any residence employee and arises out of and in the course of his employment by any Insured.

## EXCLUSIONS

This policy does not apply:

1. **Under Coverage E — Personal Liability and Coverage F — Medical Payments to Others:**
   a. to bodily injury or property damage arising out of the ownership, maintenance, operation, use, loading or unloading of:
      (1) any aircraft; or
      (2) any motor vehicle owned or operated by, or rented or loaned to any Insured; but this subdivision (2) does not apply to bodily injury or property damage occurring on the residence premises if the motor vehicle is not subject to motor vehicle registration because it is used exclusively on the residence premises or kept in dead storage on the residence premises; or
      (3) any recreational motor vehicle owned by any Insured, if the bodily injury or property damage occurs away from the residence premises; but this subdivision (3) does not apply to golf carts while used for golfing purposes.
   This exclusion does not apply to bodily injury to any residence employee arising out of and in the course of his employment by any Insured except while such employee is engaged in the operation or maintenance of aircraft;
   b. to bodily injury or property damage arising out of the ownership, maintenance, operation, use, loading or unloading of any watercraft:
      (1) owned by or rented to any Insured if the watercraft has irboard or inboard-outboard motor power of more than 50 horsepower or is a sailing vessel (with or without auxiliary power) 26 feet or more in overall length; or
      (2) powered by any outboard motor(s), singly or in combination of more than 25 total horsepower, if such outboard motor(s) is owned by any Insured at the inception of this policy and not endorsed hereon, unless the Insured reports in writing to this Company within 45 days after acquisition his intention to insure the outboard motor or combination of outboard motors, ownership of which was acquired prior to the policy term.
   This exclusion does not apply to (a) bodily injury or property damage occurring on the residence premises or (b) bodily injury to any residence employee arising out of and in the course of his employment by any Insured;
   c. to bodily injury or property damage arising out of the rendering of or failing to render professional services;
   d. to bodily injury or property damage arising out of business pursuits of any Insured except activities therein which are ordinarily incident to non-business pursuits;
   e. to bodily injury or property damage arising out of any premises, other than an insured premises, owned, rented or controlled by any Insured; but this exclusion does not apply to bodily injury to any residence employee arising out of and in the course of his employment by any Insured;
   f. to bodily injury or property damage which is either expected or intended from the standpoint of the Insured.

2. **Under Coverage E — Personal Liability**
   a. to liability assumed by the Insured under any contract or agreement not in writing or under any contract or agreement in connection with the Insured's business;
   b. to bodily injury to any person, including a residence employee, if the Insured has a policy providing workmen's compensation or occupational disease benefits for such bodily injury or if benefits for such bodily injury are in whole or in part either payable or required to be provided by the Insured under any workmen's compensation or occupational disease law;
   c. to property damage to property owned by the Insured;
   d. to property damage to property occupied or used by the Insured or rented to or in the care, custody or control of the Insured or as to which the Insured is for any purpose exercising physical control;
   e. to sickness, disease or death resulting therefrom of any residence employee unless written claim is made or suit is brought therefor against the Insured within 36 months after the end of the policy term.

3. **Under Coverage F — Medical Payments to Others**
   a. to bodily injury to any person, including a residence employee; if any person or organization has a policy providing workmen's compensation or occupational disease benefits for such bodily injury or if benefits for such bodily injury are in whole or in part either payable or required to be provided under any workmen's compensation or occupational disease law;
   b. to bodily injury to:
      (1) any Insured under parts (1) and (2) of the definition of "Insured",
      (2) any person, other than a residence employee, regularly residing on any part of the insured premises, or
      (3) any person while on the insured premises because a business is conducted or professional services are rendered thereon.

## 673

**1. Damage to Property of Others:** This Company will, at its option, either pay for the actual cash value of property damaged or destroyed during the policy period by any Insured, or repair or replace such property with other property of like quality and kind, but in no event shall this Company's limit of liability exceed $250 in any one occurrence.

This coverage does not apply to damage to or destruction of property:
a. caused intentionally by any Insured who has attained the age of 13;
b. owned by or rented to any Insured, any tenant of any Insured or any resident of Named Insured's household;
c. arising out of (1) any act or omission in connection with premises (other than the insured premises) owned, rented or controlled by any Insured, (2) business pursuits or professional services or (3) the ownership, maintenance, operation, use, loading or unloading of any land motor vehicle, trailer or semi-trailer, farm machinery or equipment, aircraft or watercraft;
d. if insurance therefor is provided under Section 1 of this policy.

**2. Personal Liability Claim Expenses:** This Company will pay:
a. all expenses incurred by this Company and all costs taxed against the Insured in any suit defended by this Company;
b. all premiums on appeal bonds required in any such suit, premiums on bonds to release attachments in any such suit for an amount not in excess of the applicable limit of liability of this policy, and the cost of bail bonds required of the Insured because of accident or traffic law violation arising out of the use of any vehicle to which this policy applies, not to exceed $250 per bail bond, but this Company shall have no obligation to apply for or furnish any such bonds;
c. all interest on the entire amount of any judgment which accrues after entry of the judgment and before this Company has paid or tendered or deposited in court that part of the judgment which does not exceed the limit of this Company's liability thereon;
d. reasonable expenses incurred by the Insured at this Company's request, including actual loss of earnings (but not loss of other income) not to exceed $25 per day because of his attendance at hearings or trials at such request.

Any expenses incurred by this Company under this provision shall not reduce the applicable limit of liability.

**3. First Aid Expenses:** In addition to this Company's limit of liability, this Company will pay expenses incurred by the Insured for first aid to others at the time of an accident, for bodily injury to which this insurance applies.

**4. Property in Control of the Insured:** Such insurance as is afforded under Coverage E — Personal Liability, applies to property damage to any insured premises and to house furnishings therein if such property damage arises out of fire, explosion, or smoke or smudge caused by sudden, unusual and faulty operation of any heating or cooking unit. Exclusion 2.d. does not apply to this Supplementary Coverage.

**5. Construction of New Residence:** Such insurance as is afforded under Coverage E — Personal Liability, applies to bodily injury and property damage arising out of any vacant land owned by or rented to any Insured on which a one or two family dwelling is being constructed for use by any Insured as a residence. Such insurance as is afforded under Coverage F — Medical Payments to Others, applies to bodily injury sustained by any person while on such vacant land with the permission of any Insured. This coverage does not apply to bodily injury to any employee, other than a residence employee, of any Insured arising out of and in the course of his employment by any Insured. Exclusion 1.e. does not apply to this Supplementary Coverage.

---

## ADDITIONAL DEFINITIONS

The following definitions apply only to coverage afforded under Section II of this policy.

1. "**bodily injury**": means bodily injury, sickness or disease, including care, loss of services and death resulting therefrom.
2. "**medical expenses**": means expenses for necessary medical, surgical, x-ray, dental services, including prosthetic devices, ambulance, hospital, professional nursing and funeral services.
3. "**motor vehicle**": means a land motor vehicle, trailer or semi-trailer designed for travel on public roads (including any machinery or apparatus attached thereto) but does not include, except while being towed by or carried on a motor vehicle, any of the following: utility, boat, camp or home trailer, recreational motor vehicle, crawler or farm type tractor, farm implement or, if not subject to motor vehicle registration, any equipment which is designed for use principally off public roads.

4. "**property damage**": means injury to or destruction of tangible property, including loss of use thereof.
5. "**occurrence**": means an accident, including injurious exposure to conditions, which results, during the policy term, in bodily injury or property damage.
6. "**recreational motor vehicle**": means (1) a golf cart or snowmobile or (2) if not subject to motor vehicle registration, any other land motor vehicle designed for recreational use off public roads.
7. "**residence employee**": means an employee of any Insured whose duties are in connection with the maintenance or use of the insured premises, including the performance of household or domestic services, or who performs elsewhere duties of a similar nature not in connection with any Insured's business.

Page 4 HO-3

674

# Appendix G

## Family Automobile Policy

**No. ACF**

RENEWAL OF NUMBER

CAPITAL STOCK COMPANY

AUTHENTIC

SPACE FOR COMPANY NAME, INSIGNIA, AND LOCATION

**DECLARATIONS**

**Item 1. Named Insured and Address:** (No., Street, Town or City, County, State)

SPACE FOR
PRODUCER'S NAME AND
MAILING ADDRESS

**Item 2. Policy Period:** (Mo. Day Yr.) ( Months)

From                to

12:01 A.M., standard time at the address of the named insured as stated herein.

Occupation of the named insured is IF MARRIED WOMAN, GIVE HUSBAND'S OCCUPATION OR BUSINESS (ENTER BELOW)

**Item 3.** The insurance afforded is only with respect to such of the following coverages as are indicated by specific premium charge or charges. The limit of the company's liability against each such coverage shall be as stated herein, subject to all the terms of this policy having reference thereto.

| CAR 1 | PREMIUMS | CAR 2 | LIMITS OF LIABILITY | | COVERAGES |
|---|---|---|---|---|---|
| $ | | $ | thousand dollars each person / thousand dollars each occurrence | A | Bodily Injury Liability |
| $ | | $ | thousand dollars each occurrence | B | Property Damage Liability |
| $ | | $ | dollars each person | C | Medical Payments |
| | | $ | Actual Cash Value* | D | (1) Comprehensive (excluding Collision) |
| $ | | $ | $ 100 | | (2) Personal Effects |
| $ | | $ | Actual Cash Value less $ deductible | E | Collision |
| $ | | $ | $ | F | Fire, Lightning and Transportation |
| $ | | $ | $ | G | Theft |
| $ | | $ | $ | H | Combined Additional Coverage |
| $ | | $ | $ 25 per disablement | I | Towing and Labor Costs |
| $ | | $ | thousand dollars each person / thousand dollars each accident | J | Uninsured Motorists |
| | | | Form numbers of endorsements attached to policy at issue | | |
| $ | | | | | |
| $ | | $ | Total Car 1 - Car 2 | | |
| $ | Total Premium | | | | |

* STRIKE OUT "ACTUAL CASH VALUE" AND INSERT AMOUNT IF POLICY IS WRITTEN ON STATED AMOUNT BASIS.

**Item 4.** Description of owned automobile or trailer

| | Year of Model | Trade Name | Body Type; Model | Identification Number (I) Serial Number (S) Motor Number (M) | F.O.B. List Price or Delivered Price at Factory | Purchased Month, Year   New or Used | Class & Rating Symbol | Sub-Class (if any) |
|---|---|---|---|---|---|---|---|---|
| Car 1 | | | | | | | | |
| Car 2 | | | | | | | | |

**Item 5.** Loss Payee: Any loss under Part III is payable as interest may appear to the named insured and (NAME AND ADDRESS—ENTER BELOW)

**Item 6.** The owned automobile will be principally garaged in the town or city designated in Item 1 above, unless otherwise stated herein: (ENTER BELOW)

**Item 7.** During the past three years no insurer has canceled insurance, issued to the named insured, similar to that afforded hereunder, unless otherwise stated herein:

Countersigned:

OKP 6013-O-G
(Rev. 1-1-63)

*NOTE: This Policy is subject to the "Sound-Reproducing or Recording Equipment Excluded" Endorsement, "Uninsured Motorists Coverage Amendment (Insolvent Insurer)" Endorsement and "Amendment of Termination Provisions" Endorsement*

By_____

Authorized Representative

**676**

RESERVED FOR YOUR COMPANY'S NAME

(A stock insurance company, herein called the company)

Agrees with the insured, named in the declarations made a part hereof, in consideration of the payment of the premium and in reliance upon the statements in the declarations and subject to all of the terms of this policy:

## PART I — LIABILITY

**Coverage A—Bodily Injury Liability; Coverage B—Property Damage Liability:** To pay on behalf of the insured all sums which the insured shall become legally obligated to pay as damages because of:

A. bodily injury, sickness or disease, including death resulting therefrom, hereinafter called "bodily injury," sustained by any person;

B. injury to or destruction of property, including loss of use thereof, hereinafter called "property damage";

arising out of the ownership, maintenance or use of the owned automobile or any non-owned automobile, and the company shall defend any suit alleging such bodily injury or property damage and seeking damages which are payable under the terms of this policy, even if any of the allegations of the suit are groundless, false or fraudulent; but the company may make such investigation and settlement of any claim or suit as it deems expedient.

**Supplementary Payments:** To pay, in addition to the applicable limits of liability:

(a) all expenses incurred by the company, all costs taxed against the insured in any such suit and all interest on the entire amount of any judgment therein which accrues after entry of the judgment and before the company has paid or tendered or deposited in court that part of the judgment which does not exceed the limit of the company's liability thereon;

(b) premiums on appeal bonds required in any such suit, premiums on bonds to release attachments for an amount not in excess of the applicable limit of liability of this policy, and the cost of bail bonds required of the insured because of accident or traffic law violation arising out of the use of an automobile insured hereunder, not to exceed $100 per bail bond, but without any obligation to apply for or furnish any such bonds;

(c) expenses incurred by the insured for such immediate medical and surgical relief to others as shall be imperative at the time of an accident involving an automobile insured hereunder and not due to war;

(d) all reasonable expenses, other than loss of earnings, incurred by the insured at the company's request.

**Persons Insured:** The following are insureds under Part I:

(a) with respect to the owned automobile,
  (1) the named insured and any resident of the same household,
  (2) any other person using such automobile with the permission of the named insured, provided his actual operation or (if he is not operating) his other actual use thereof is within the scope of such permission, and
  (3) any other person or organization but only with respect to his or its liability because of acts or omissions of an insured under (a) (1) or (2) above;

(b) with respect to a non-owned automobile,
  (1) the named insured,
  (2) any relative, but only with respect to a private passenger automobile or trailer,
  provided his actual operation or (if he is not operating) the other actual use thereof is with the permission, or reasonably believed to be with the permission, of the owner and is within the scope of such permission, and
  (3) any other person or organization not owning or hiring the automobile, but only with respect to his or its liability because of acts or omissions of an insured under (b) (1) or (2) above.

The insurance afforded under Part I applies separately to each insured against whom claim is made or suit is brought, but the inclusion herein of more than one insured shall not operate to increase the limits of the company's liability.

**Definitions:** Under Part I:

**"named insured"** means the individual named in Item 1 of the declarations and also includes his spouse, if a resident of the same household;

**"insured"** means a person or organization described under "Persons Insured";

**"relative"** means a relative of the named insured who is a resident of the same household;

**"owned automobile"** means

(a) a private passenger, farm or utility automobile described in this policy for which a specific premium charge indicates that coverage is afforded,

(b) a trailer owned by the named insured,

(c) a private passenger, farm or utility automobile ownership of which is acquired by the named insured during the policy period, provided
  (1) it replaces an owned automobile as defined in (a) above, or
  (2) the company insures all private passenger, farm and utility automobiles owned by the named insured on the date of such acquisition and the named insured notifies the company during the policy period or within 30 days after the date of such acquisition of his election to make this and no other policy issued by the company applicable to such automobile, or

(d) a temporary substitute automobile;

**"temporary substitute automobile"** means any automobile or trailer, not owned by the named insured, while temporarily used with the permission of the owner as a substitute for the owned automobile or trailer when withdrawn from normal use because of its breakdown, repair, servicing, loss or destruction;

**"non-owned automobile"** means an automobile or trailer not owned by or furnished for the regular use of either the named insured or any relative, other than a temporary substitute automobile;

**"private passenger automobile"** means a four wheel private passenger, station wagon or jeep type automobile;

**"farm automobile"** means an automobile of the truck type with a load capacity of fifteen hundred pounds or less not used for business or commercial purposes other than farming;

**"utility automobile"** means an automobile, other than a farm automobile, with a load capacity of fifteen hundred pounds or less of the pick-up body, sedan delivery or panel truck type not used for business or commercial purposes;

**"trailer"** means a trailer designed for use with a private passenger automobile, if not being used for business or commercial purposes with other than a private passenger, farm or utility automobile, or a farm wagon or farm implement while used with a farm automobile;

**"automobile business"** means the business or occupation of selling, repairing, servicing, storing or parking automobiles;

**"use"** of an automobile includes the loading and unloading thereof;

**"war"** means war, whether or not declared, civil war, insurrection, rebellion or revolution, or any act or condition incident to any of the foregoing.

**Exclusions:** This policy does not apply under Part I:

(a) to any automobile while used as a public or livery conveyance, but this exclusion does not apply to the named insured with respect to bodily injury or property damage which results from the named insured's occupancy of a non-owned automobile other than as the operator thereof;

(b) to bodily injury or property damage caused intentionally by or at the direction of the insured;

(c) to bodily injury or property damage with respect to which an insured under this policy is also an insured under a nuclear energy liability policy issued by Nuclear Energy Liability Insurance Association, Mutual Atomic Energy Liability Underwriters or Nuclear Insurance Association of Canada, or would be an insured under any such policy but for its termination upon exhaustion of its limit of liability;

(d) to bodily injury or property damage arising out of the operation of farm machinery;

(e) to bodily injury to any employee of the insured arising out of and in the course of (1) domestic employment by the insured, if benefits therefor are in whole or in part either payable or required to be provided under any workmen's compensation law, or (2) other employment by the insured;

(f) to bodily injury to any fellow employee of the insured injured in the course of his employment if such injury arises out of the use of an automobile in the business of his employer, but this exclusion does not apply to the named insured with respect to injury sustained by any such fellow employee;

(g) to an owned automobile while used by any person while such person is employed or otherwise engaged in the automobile business, but this exclusion does not apply to the named insured, a resident of the same household as the named insured, a partnership in which the named insured or such resident is a partner, or any partner, agent or employee of the named insured, such resident or partnership;

(h) to a non-owned automobile while maintained or used by any person while such person is employed or otherwise engaged in
  (1) the automobile business of the insured or of any other person or organization,
  (2) any other business or occupation of the insured, but this exclusion (h) (2) does not apply to a private passenger automobile operated or occupied by the named insured or by his private chauffeur or domestic servant or a trailer used therewith or with an owned automobile;

(i) to injury to or destruction of (1) property owned or transported by the insured or (2) property rented to or in charge of the insured other than a residence or private garage;

(j) to the ownership, maintenance, operation, use, loading or unloading of an automobile ownership of which is acquired by the named insured during the policy period or any temporary substitute automobile therefor, if the named insured has purchased other automobile liability insurance applicable to such automobile for which a specific premium charge has been made.

**Financial Responsibility Laws:** When this policy is certified as proof of financial responsibility for the future under the provisions of any motor vehicle financial responsibility law, such insurance as is afforded by this policy for bodily injury liability or for property damage liability shall comply with the provisions of such law to the extent of the coverage and limits of liability required by such law, but in no event in excess of the limits of liability stated in this policy. The insured agrees to reimburse the company for any payment made by the company which it would not have been obligated to make under the terms of this policy except for the agreement contained in this paragraph.

**Limits of Liability:** The limit of bodily injury liability stated in the declarations as applicable to "each person" is the limit of the company's liability for all damages, including damages for care and loss of services, arising out of bodily injury sustained by one person as the result of any one occurrence; the limit of such liability stated in the declarations as applicable to "each occurrence" is, subject to the above provision respecting each person, the total limit of the company's liability for all such damages arising out of bodily injury sustained by two or more persons as the result of any one occurrence.

The limit of property damage liability stated in the declarations as applicable to "each occurrence" is the total limit of the company's liability for all damages arising out of injury to or destruction of all property of one or more persons or organizations, including the loss of use thereof, as the result of any one occurrence.

**Other Insurance:** If the insured has other insurance against a loss covered by Part I of this policy the company shall not be liable under this policy for a greater proportion of such loss than the applicable limit of liability stated in the declarations bears to the total applicable limit of liability of all valid and collectible insurance against such loss; provided, however, the insurance with respect to a temporary substitute automobile or non-owned automobile shall be excess insurance over any other valid and collectible insurance.

## PART II — EXPENSES FOR MEDICAL SERVICES

**Coverage C—Medical Payments:** To pay all reasonable expenses incurred within one year from the date of accident for necessary medical, surgical, X-ray and dental services, including prosthetic devices, and necessary ambulance, hospital, professional nursing and funeral services:

**Division 1.** To or for the named insured and each relative who sustains bodily injury, sickness or disease, including death resulting therefrom, hereinafter called "bodily injury", caused by accident,

(a) while occupying the owned automobile,

(b) while occupying a non-owned automobile, but only if such person has, or reasonably believes he has, the permission of the owner to use the automobile and the use is within the scope of such permission, or

(c) through being struck by an automobile or by a trailer of any type;

**Division 2.** To or for any other person who sustains bodily injury, caused by accident, while occupying

(a) the owned automobile, while being used by the named insured, by any resident of the same household or by any other person with the permission of the named insured; or

(b) a non-owned automobile, if the bodily injury results from
  (1) its operation or occupancy by the named insured or its operation on his behalf by his private chauffeur or domestic servant, or

(2) its operation or occupancy by a relative, provided it is a private passenger automobile or trailer,

but only if such operator or occupant has, or reasonably believes he has, the permission of the owner to use the automobile and the use is within the scope of such permission.

**Definitions:** The definitions under Part I apply to Part II, and under Part II:

**"occupying"** means in or upon or entering into or alighting from.

**Exclusions:** This policy does not apply under Part II to bodily injury:

(a) sustained while occupying (1) an owned automobile while used as a public or livery conveyance, or (2) any vehicle while located for use as a residence or premises;

(b) sustained by the named insured or a relative while occupying or through being struck by (1) a farm type tractor or other equipment designed for use principally off public roads, while not upon public roads, or (2) a vehicle operated on rails or crawler-treads;

(c) sustained by any person other than the named insured or a relative,

(1) while such person is occupying a non-owned automobile while used as a public or livery conveyance, or

(2) resulting from the maintenance or use of a non-owned automobile by such person while employed or otherwise engaged in the automobile business, or

(3) resulting from the maintenance or use of a non-owned automobile by such person while

employed or otherwise engaged in any other business or occupation, unless the bodily injury results from the operation or occupancy of a private passenger automobile by the named insured or by his private chauffeur or domestic servant, or of a trailer used therewith or with an owned automobile;

(d) sustained by any person who is employed in the automobile business, if the accident arises out of the operation thereof and if benefits therefor are in whole or in part either payable or required to be provided under any workmen's compensation law;

(e) due to war.

**Limit of Liability:** The limit of liability for medical payments stated in the declarations as applicable to "each person" is the limit of the company's liability for all expenses incurred by or on behalf of each person who sustains bodily injury as the result of any one accident.

**Other Insurance:** If there is other automobile medical payments insurance against a loss covered by Part II of this policy the company shall not be liable under this policy for a greater proportion of such loss than the applicable limit of liability stated in the declarations bears to the total applicable limit of liability of all valid and collectible automobile medical payments insurance; provided, however, the insurance with respect to a temporary substitute automobile or non-owned automobile shall be excess insurance over any other valid and collectible automobile medical payments insurance.

## PART III — PHYSICAL DAMAGE

**Coverage D (1)—Comprehensive (excluding Collision); (2)—Personal Effects:**

(1) To pay for loss caused other than by collision to the owned automobile or to a non-owned automobile. For the purpose of this coverage, breakage of glass and loss caused by missiles, falling objects, fire, theft or larceny, explosion, earthquake, windstorm, hail, water, flood, malicious mischief or vandalism, riot or civil commotion, or colliding with a bird or animal, shall not be deemed to be loss caused by collision.

(2) To pay for loss caused by fire or lightning to robes, wearing apparel and other personal effects which are the property of the named insured or a relative, while such effects are in or upon the owned automobile.

**Coverage E—Collision:** To pay for loss caused by collision to the owned automobile or to a non-owned automobile but only for the amount of each such loss in excess of the deductible amount stated in the declarations as applicable hereto. The deductible amount shall not apply to loss caused by a collision with another automobile insured by the company.

**Coverage F—Fire, Lightning and Transportation:** To pay for loss to the owned automobile or a non-owned automobile, caused (a) by fire or lightning, (b) by smoke or smudge due to a sudden, unusual and faulty operation of any fixed heating equipment serving the premises in which the automobile is located, or (c) by the stranding, sinking, burning, collision or derailment of any conveyance in or upon which the automobile is being transported.

**Coverage G—Theft:** To pay for loss to the owned automobile or to a non-owned automobile caused by theft or larceny.

**Coverage H—Combined Additional Coverage:** To pay for loss to the owned automobile or a non-owned automobile caused by windstorm, hail, earthquake, explosion, riot or civil commotion, or the forced landing or falling of any aircraft or its parts or equipment, flood or rising waters, malicious mischief or vandalism, external discharge or leakage of water except loss resulting from rain, snow or sleet whether or not wind-driven; provided, with respect to each automobile $25 shall be deducted from each loss caused by malicious mischief or vandalism.

**Coverage I—Towing and Labor Costs:** To pay for towing and labor costs necessitated by the disablement of the owned automobile or of any non-owned automobile, provided the labor is performed at the place of disablement.

**Supplementary Payments:** In addition to the applicable limit of liability:

(a) to reimburse the insured for transportation expenses incurred during the period commencing 48 hours after a theft covered by this policy of the entire automobile has been reported to the company and the police, and terminating when the automobile is returned to use or the company pays for the loss; provided that the company shall not be obligated to pay aggregate expenses in excess of $10 per day or totaling more than $300.

(b) to pay general average and salvage charges for which the insured becomes legally liable, as to the automobile being transported.

**Definitions:** The definitions of "named insured", "relative", "temporary substitute automobile", "private passenger automobile", "farm automobile", "utility automobile", "automobile business", "war", and "owned automobile" in Part I apply to Part III, but "owned automobile" does not include, under Part III, (1) a trailer owned by the named insured on the effective date of this policy and not described herein, or (2) a trailer ownership of which is acquired during the policy period unless the company insures all private passenger, farm and utility automobiles and trailers owned by the named insured on the date of such acquisition and the named insured notifies the company during the policy period or within 30 days after the date of such acquisition of his election to make this and no other policy issued by the company applicable to such trailer.

**"insured"** means

(a) with respect to an owned automobile,

(1) the named insured, and

(2) any person or organization (other than a person or organization employed or otherwise engaged in the automobile business or as a carrier or other bailee for hire) maintaining, using or having custody of said automobile with the permission of the named insured and within the scope of such permission;

(b) with respect to a non-owned automobile, the named insured and any relative while using such automobile, provided his actual operation or (if he is not operating) the other actual use thereof is with the permission, or is reasonably believed to be with the permission, of the owner and is within the scope of such permission;

**"non-owned automobile"** means a private passenger automobile or trailer not owned by or furnished for the regular use of either the named insured or any relative, other than a temporary substitute automobile, while said automobile or trailer is in the possession or custody of the insured or is being operated by him;

**"loss"** means direct and accidental loss of or damage to (a) the automobile, including its equipment, or (b) other insured property;

**"collision"** means collision of an automobile covered by this policy with another object or with a vehicle to which it is attached or by upset of such automobile;

**"trailer"** means a trailer designed for use with a private passenger automobile, if not being used for business or commercial purposes with other than a private passenger, farm or utility automobile, and if not a home, office, store, display or passenger trailer.

**Exclusions:** This policy does not apply under Part III:

(a) to any automobile while used as a public or livery conveyance;

(b) to loss due to war;

(c) to loss to a non-owned automobile arising out of its use by the insured while he is employed or otherwise engaged in the automobile business;

(d) to loss to a private passenger, farm or utility automobile or trailer owned by the named insured and not described in this policy or to any temporary substitute automobile therefor, if the insured has other valid and collectible insurance against such loss;

(e) to damage which is due and confined to wear and tear, freezing, mechanical or electrical breakdown or failure, unless such damage results from a theft covered by this policy;

(f) to tires, unless damaged by fire, malicious mischief or vandalism, or stolen or unless the loss be coincident with and from the same cause as other loss covered by this policy;

(g) to loss due to radioactive contamination;

(h) under coverage E, to breakage of glass if insurance with respect to such breakage is otherwise afforded.

**Limit of Liability:** The limit of the company's liability for loss shall not exceed the actual cash value of the property, or if the loss is of a part thereof the actual cash value of such part, at time of loss, nor what it would then cost to repair or replace the property or such part thereof with other of like kind and quality, nor, with respect to an owned automobile described in this policy, the applicable limit of liability stated in the declarations; provided, however, the limit of the company's liability (a) for loss to personal effects arising out of any one occurrence is $100, and (b) for loss to any trailer not owned by the named insured is $500.

**Other Insurance:** If the insured has other insurance against a loss covered by Part III of this policy, the company shall not be liable under this policy for a greater proportion of such loss than the applicable limit of liability of this policy bears to the total applicable limit of liability of all valid and collectible insurance against such loss; provided, however, the insurance with respect to a temporary substitute automobile or non-owned automobile shall be excess insurance over any other valid and collectible insurance.

**678**

## PART IV — PROTECTION AGAINST UNINSURED MOTORISTS

**Coverage J—Uninsured Motorists (Damages for Bodily Injury):** To pay all sums which the insured or his legal representative shall be legally entitled to recover as damages from the owner or operator of an uninsured automobile because of bodily injury, sickness or disease, including death resulting therefrom, hereinafter called "bodily injury," sustained by the insured, caused by accident and arising out of the ownership, maintenance or use of such uninsured automobile; provided, for the purposes of this coverage, determination as to whether the insured or such representative is legally entitled to recover such damages, and if so the amount thereof, shall be made by agreement between the insured or such representative and the company or, if they fail to agree, by arbitration.

No judgment against any person or organization alleged to be legally responsible for the bodily injury shall be conclusive, as between the insured and the company, of the issues of liability of such person or organization or of the amount of damages to which the insured is legally entitled unless such judgment is entered pursuant to an action prosecuted by the insured with the written consent of the company.

**Definitions:** The definitions under Part I, except the definition of "insured," apply to Part IV, and under Part IV:

**"insured"** means:
(a) the named insured and any relative;
(b) any other person while occupying an insured automobile; and
(c) any person, with respect to damages he is entitled to recover because of bodily injury to which this Part applies sustained by an insured under (a) or (b) above.

The insurance afforded under Part IV applies separately to each insured, but the inclusion herein of more than one insured shall not operate to increase the limits of the company's liability.

**"insured automobile"** means:
(a) an automobile described in the policy for which a specific premium charge indicates that coverage is afforded,
(b) a private passenger, farm or utility automobile, ownership of which is acquired by the named insured during the policy period, provided
 (1) it replaces an insured automobile as defined in (a) above, or
 (2) the company insures under this Coverage all private passenger, farm and utility automobiles owned by the named insured on the date of such acquisition and the named insured notifies the company during the policy period or within 30 days after the date of such acquisition of his election to make the Liability and Uninsured Motorist Coverages under this and no other policy issued by the company applicable to such automobile,
(c) a temporary substitute automobile for an insured automobile as defined in (a) or (b) above, and
(d) a non-owned automobile while being operated by the named insured; and the term "insured automobile" includes a trailer while being used with an automobile described in (a), (b), (c) or (d) above, but shall not include:
 (1) any automobile or trailer owned by a resident of the same household as the named insured,
 (2) any automobile while used as a public or livery conveyance, or
 (3) any automobile while being used without the permission of the owner.

**"uninsured automobile"** includes a trailer of any type and means:
(a) an automobile or trailer with respect to the ownership, maintenance or use of which there is, in at least the amounts specified by the financial responsibility law of the state in which the insured automobile is principally garaged, no bodily injury liability bond or insurance policy applicable at the time of the accident with respect to any person or organization legally responsible for the use of such automobile, or with respect to which there is a bodily injury liability bond or insurance policy applicable at the time of the accident but the company writing the same denies coverage thereunder or
(b) a hit-and-run automobile;
but the term "uninsured automobile" shall not include:
 (1) an insured automobile or an automobile furnished for the regular use of the named insured or a relative,
 (2) an automobile or trailer owned or operated by a self-insurer within the meaning of any motor vehicle financial responsibility law, motor carrier law or any similar law,
 (3) an automobile or trailer owned by the United States of America, Canada, a state, a political subdivision of any such government or an agency of any of the foregoing,
 (4) a land motor vehicle or trailer if operated on rails or crawler-treads or while located for use as a residence or premises and not as a vehicle, or
 (5) a farm type tractor or equipment designed for use principally off public roads, except while actually upon public roads.

**"hit-and-run automobile"** means an automobile which causes bodily injury to an insured arising out of physical contact of such automobile with the insured or with an automobile which the insured is occupying at the time of the accident, provided: (a) there cannot be ascertained the identity of either the operator or the owner of such "hit-and-run automobile"; (b) the insured or someone on his behalf shall have reported the accident within 24 hours to a police, peace or judicial officer or to the Commissioner of Motor Vehicles, and shall have filed with the company within 30 days thereafter a statement under oath that the insured or his legal representative has a cause or causes of action arising out of such accident for damages against a person or persons whose identity is unascertainable, and setting forth the facts in support thereof; and (c) at the company's request, the insured or his legal representative makes available for inspection the automobile which the insured was occupying at the time of the accident.

**"occupying"** means in or upon or entering into or alighting from.

**"state"** includes the District of Columbia, a territory or possession of the United States, and a province of Canada.

**Exclusions:** This policy does not apply under Part IV:
(a) to bodily injury to an insured while occupying an automobile (other than an insured automobile) owned by the named insured or a relative, or through being struck by such an automobile;
(b) to bodily injury to an insured with respect to which such insured, his legal representative or any person entitled to payment under this coverage shall, without written consent of the company, make any settlement with any person or organization who may be legally liable therefor;
(c) so as to inure directly or indirectly to the benefit of any workmen's compensation or disability benefits carrier or any person or organization qualifying as a self-insurer under any workmen's compensation or disability benefits law or any similar law.

**Limits of Liability:**
(a) The limit of liability for uninsured motorists coverage stated in the declarations as applicable to "each person" is the limit of the company's liability for all damages, including damages for care or loss of services, because of bodily injury sustained by one person as the result of any one accident and, subject to the above provision respecting each person, the limit of liability stated in the declarations as applicable to "each accident" is the total limit of the company's liability for all damages, including damages for care or loss of services, because of bodily injury sustained by two or more persons as the result of any one accident.
(b) Any amount payable under the terms of this Part because of bodily injury sustained in an accident by a person who is an insured under this Part shall be reduced by
 (1) all sums paid on account of such bodily injury by or on behalf of (i) the owner or operator of the uninsured automobile and (ii) any other person or organization jointly or severally liable together with such owner or operator for such bodily injury including all sums paid under Coverage A, and
 (2) the amount paid and the present value of all amounts payable on account of such bodily injury under any workmen's compensation law, disability benefits law or any similar law.
(c) Any payment made under this Part to or for any insured shall be applied in reduction of the amount of damages which he may be entitled to recover from any person insured under Coverage A.
(d) The company shall not be obligated to pay under this Coverage that part of the damages which the insured may be entitled to recover from the owner or operator of an uninsured automobile which represents expenses for medical services paid or payable under Part II.

**Other Insurance:** With respect to bodily injury to an insured while occupying an automobile not owned by the named insured, the insurance under Part IV shall apply only as excess insurance over any other similar insurance available to such insured and applicable to such automobile as primary insurance, and this insurance shall then apply only in the amount by which the limit of liability for this coverage exceeds the applicable limit of liability of such other insurance.

Except as provided in the foregoing paragraph, if the insured has other similar insurance available to him and applicable to the accident, the damages shall be deemed not to exceed the higher of the applicable limits of liability of this insurance and such other insurance, and the company shall not be liable for a greater proportion of any loss to which this Coverage applies than the limit of liability hereunder bears to the sum of the applicable limits of liability of this insurance and such other insurance.

**Arbitration:** If any person making claim hereunder and the company do not agree that such person is legally entitled to recover damages from the owner or operator of an uninsured automobile because of bodily injury to the insured, or do not agree as to the amount of payment which may be owing under this Part, then, upon written demand of either, the matter or matters upon which such person and the company do not agree shall be settled by arbitration in accordance with the rules of the American Arbitration Association, and judgment upon the award rendered by the arbitrators may be entered in any court having jurisdiction thereof. Such person and the company each agree to consider itself bound and to be bound by any award made by the arbitrators pursuant to this Part.

**Trust Agreement:** In the event of payment to any person under this Part:
(a) the company shall be entitled to the extent of such payment to the proceeds of any settlement or judgment that may result from the exercise of any rights of recovery of such person against any person or organization legally responsible for the bodily injury because of which such payment is made;
(b) such person shall hold in trust for the benefit of the company all rights of recovery which he shall have against such other person or organization because of the damages which are the subject of claim made under this Part;
(c) such person shall do whatever is proper to secure and shall do nothing after loss to prejudice such rights;
(d) if requested in writing by the company, such person shall take, through any representative designated by the company, such action as may be necessary or appropriate to recover such payment as damages from such other person or organization, such action to be taken in the name of such person; in the event of a recovery, the company shall be reimbursed out of such recovery for expenses, costs and attorneys' fees incurred by it in connection therewith;
(e) such person shall execute and deliver to the company such instruments and papers as may be appropriate to secure the rights and obligations of such person and the company established by this provision.

## CONDITIONS

Conditions 1, 2, 3, 6, 14, 15, 16 and 18 apply to all Parts. Conditions 4 and 5, 7 through 13, and 17 apply only to the Parts noted thereunder.

**1. Policy Period, Territory:** This policy applies only to accidents, occurrences and loss during the policy period while the automobile is within the United States of America, its territories or possessions, or Canada, or is being transported between ports thereof.

**2. Premium:** If the named insured disposes of, acquires ownership of, or replaces a private passenger, farm or utility automobile or, with respect to Part III, a trailer, any premium adjustment necessary shall be made as of the date of such change in accordance with the manuals in use by the company. The named insured shall, upon request, furnish reasonable proof of the number of such automobiles or trailers and a description thereof.

**3. Notice:** In the event of an accident, occurrence or loss, written notice containing particulars sufficient to identify the insured and also reasonably obtainable information with respect to the time, place and circumstances thereof, and the names and addresses of the injured and of available witnesses, shall be given by or for the insured to the company or any of its authorized agents as soon as practicable. In the event of theft the insured shall also promptly notify the police. If claim is made or suit is brought against the insured, he shall immediately forward to the company every demand, notice, summons or other process received by him or his representative.

If, before the company makes payment of loss under Part IV, the insured or his legal representative shall institute any legal action for bodily injury against any person or organization legally responsible for the use of an automobile involved in the accident, a copy of the summons and complaint or other process served in connection with such legal action shall be forwarded immediately to the company by the insured or his legal representative.

**4. Two or More Automobiles—Parts I, II and III:** When two or more automobiles are insured hereunder, the terms of this policy shall apply separately to each, but an automobile and a trailer attached thereto shall be held to be one automobile as respects limits of liability under Part I of this policy, and separate automobiles under Part III of this policy, including any deductible provisions applicable thereto.

**5. Assistance and Cooperation of the Insured—Parts I and III:** The insured shall cooperate with the company and, upon the company's request, assist in making settlements, in the conduct of suits and in enforcing any right of contribution or indemnity against any person or organization who may be liable to the insured because of bodily injury, property damage or loss with respect to which insurance is afforded under this policy; and the insured shall attend hearings and trials and assist in securing and giving evidence and obtaining the attendance of witnesses. The insured shall not, except at his own cost, voluntarily make any payment, assume any obligation or incur any expense other than for such immediate medical and surgical relief to others as shall be imperative at the time of accident.

**Part IV:** After notice of claim under Part IV, the company may require the insured to take such action as may be necessary or appropriate to preserve his right to recover damages from any person or organization alleged to be legally responsible for the bodily injury; and in any action against the company, the company may require the insured to join such person or organization as a party defendant.

**6. Action Against Company—Part I:** No action shall lie against the company unless, as a condition precedent thereto, the insured shall have fully complied with all the terms of this policy, nor until the amount of the insured's obligation to pay shall have been finally determined either by judgment against the insured after actual trial or by written agreement of the insured, the claimant and the company.

Any person or organization or the legal representative thereof who has secured such judgment or written agreement shall thereafter be entitled to recover under this policy to the extent of the insurance afforded by this policy. No person or organization shall have any right under this policy to join the company as a party to any action against the insured to determine the insured's liability, nor shall the company be impleaded by the insured or his legal representative. Bankruptcy or insolvency of the insured or of the insured's estate shall not relieve the company of any of its obligations hereunder.

**Parts II, III and IV:** No action shall lie against the company unless, as a condition precedent thereto, there shall have been full compliance with all the terms of this policy nor, under Part III, until thirty days after proof of loss is filed and the amount of loss is determined as provided in this policy.

**7. Medical Reports; Proof and Payment of Claim—Part II:** As soon as practicable the injured person or someone on his behalf shall give to the company written proof of claim, under oath if required, and shall, after each request from the company, execute authorization to enable the company to obtain medical reports and copies of records. The injured person shall submit to physical examination by physicians selected by the company when and as often as the company may reasonably require.

The company may pay the injured person or any person or organization rendering the services and such payment shall reduce the amount payable hereunder for such injury. Payment hereunder shall not constitute an admission of liability of any person or, except hereunder, of the company.

**8. Insured's Duties in Event of Loss—Part III:** In the event of loss the insured shall:
(a) protect the automobile, whether or not the loss is covered by this policy, and any further loss due to the insured's failure to protect shall not be recoverable under this policy; reasonable expenses incurred in affording such protection shall be deemed incurred at the company's request;
(b) file with the company, within 91 days after loss, his sworn proof of loss in such form and including such information as the company may reasonably require and shall, upon the company's request, exhibit the damaged property and submit to examination under oath.

**9. Proof of Claim; Medical Reports—Part IV:** As soon as practicable, the insured or other person making claim shall give to the company written proof of claim, under oath if required, including full particulars of the nature and extent of the injuries, treatment, and other details entering into the determination of the amount payable. The insured and every other person making claim shall submit to examinations under oath by any person named by the company and subscribe the same, as often as may reasonably be required. Proof of claim shall be made upon forms furnished by the company unless the company shall have failed to furnish such forms within 15 days after receiving notice of claim.

The injured person shall submit to physical examinations by physicians selected by the company when and as often as the company may reasonably require and he, or in the event of his incapacity his legal representative, or in the event of his death his legal representative or the person or persons entitled to sue therefor, shall upon each request from the company execute authorization to enable the company to obtain medical reports and copies of records.

**10. Appraisal—Part III:** If the insured and the company fail to agree as to the amount of loss, either may, within 60 days after proof of loss is filed, demand an appraisal of the loss. In such event the insured and the company shall each select a competent appraiser, and the appraisers shall select a competent and disinterested umpire. The appraisers shall state separately the actual cash value and the amount of loss and failing to agree shall submit their differences to the umpire. An award in writing of any two shall determine the amount of loss. The insured and the company shall each pay his chosen appraiser and shall bear equally the other expenses of the appraisal and umpire.

The company shall not be held to have waived any of its rights by any act relating to appraisal.

**11. Payment of Loss—Part III:** The company may pay for the loss in money; or may repair or replace the damaged or stolen property; or may, at any time before the loss is paid or the property is so replaced, at its expense return any stolen property to the named insured, or at its option to the address shown in the declarations, with payment for any resultant damage thereto; or may take all or such part of the property at the agreed or appraised value but there shall be no abandonment to the company. The company may settle any claim for loss either with the insured or the owner of the property.

**Part IV:** Any amount due is payable (a) to the insured, or (b) if the insured be a minor to his parent or guardian, or (c) if the insured be deceased to his surviving spouse, otherwise (d) to a person authorized by law to receive such payment or to a person legally entitled to recover the damages which the payment represents; provided, the company may at its option pay any amount due in accordance with division (d) hereof.

**12. No Benefit to Bailee—Part III:** The insurance afforded by this policy shall not inure directly or indirectly to the benefit of any carrier or other bailee for hire liable for loss to the automobile.

**13. Subrogation—Parts I and III:** In the event of any payment under this policy, the company shall be subrogated to all the insured's rights of recovery therefor against any person or organization and the insured shall execute and deliver instruments and papers and do whatever else is necessary to secure such rights. The insured shall do nothing after loss to prejudice such rights.

**14. Changes:** Notice to any agent or knowledge possessed by any agent or by any other person shall not effect a waiver or a change in any part of this policy or estop the company from asserting any right under the terms of this policy; nor shall the terms of this policy be waived or changed, except by endorsement issued to form a part of this policy.

**15. Assignment:** Assignment of interest under this policy shall not bind the company until its consent is endorsed hereon; if, however, the insured named in Item 1 of the declarations, or his spouse if a resident of the same household, shall die, this policy shall cover (1) the survivor as named insured, (2) his legal representative as named insured but only while acting within the scope of his duties as such, (3) any person having proper temporary custody of an owned automobile, as an insured, until the appointment and qualification of such legal representative, and (4) under division 1 of Part II any person who was a relative at the time of such death.

**16. Cancelation:** This policy may be canceled by the insured named in Item 1 of the declarations by surrender thereof to the company or any of its authorized agents or by mailing to the company written notice stating when thereafter the cancelation shall be effective. This policy may be canceled by the company by mailing to the insured named in Item 1 of the declarations at the address shown in this policy written notice stating when not less than ten days thereafter such cancelation shall be effective. The mailing of notice as aforesaid shall be sufficient proof of notice. The time of the surrender or the effective date and hour of cancelation stated in the notice shall become the end of the policy period. Delivery of such written notice either by such insured or by the company shall be equivalent to mailing.

If such insured cancels, earned premium shall be computed in accordance with the customary short rate table and procedure. If the company cancels, earned premium shall be computed pro rata. Premium adjustment may be made either at the time cancelation is effected or as soon as practicable after cancelation becomes effective, but payment or tender of unearned premium is not a condition of cancelation.

**17. Cancelation by Company Limited—Part I:** After this policy has been in effect for sixty days or, if the policy is a renewal, effective immediately, the company shall not exercise its right to cancel the insurance afforded under Part I unless:
1. the named insured fails to discharge when due any of his obligations in connection with the payment of premium for this policy or any installment thereof whether payable directly or under any premium finance plan; or
2. the insurance was obtained through fraudulent misrepresentation; or
3. the insured violates any of the terms and conditions of the policy; or
4. the named insured or any other operator, either resident in the same household, or who customarily operates an automobile insured under the policy,
   (a) has had his driver's license suspended or revoked during the policy period, or
   (b) is or becomes subject to epilepsy or heart attacks, and such individual cannot produce a certificate from a physician testifying to his unqualified ability to operate a motor vehicle, or
   (c) is or has been convicted of or forfeits bail, during the 36 months immediately preceding the effective date of the policy or during the policy period, for:
   (1) any felony, or
   (2) criminal negligence resulting in death, homicide or assault, arising out of the operation of a motor vehicle, or
   (3) operating a motor vehicle while in an intoxicated condition or while under the influence of drugs, or
   (4) leaving the scene of an accident without stopping to report, or
   (5) theft of a motor vehicle, or
   (6) making false statements in an application for a driver's license, or
   (7) a third violation, committed within a period of 18 months, of (i) any ordinance or regulation limiting the speed of motor vehicles or (ii) any of the provisions in the motor vehicle laws of any state, the violation of which constitutes a misdemeanor, whether or not the violations were repetitions of the same offense or were different offenses.

**18. Declarations:** By acceptance of this policy, the insured named in Item 1 of the declarations agrees that the statements in the declarations are his agreements and representations, that this policy is issued in reliance upon the truth of such representations and that this policy embodies all agreements existing between himself and the company or any of its agents relating to this insurance.

---

*In Witness Whereof, the company has caused this policy to be executed and attested, but this policy shall not be valid unless countersigned by a duly authorized representative of the company.

Company's language may be substituted as desired.

INSERT SIGNATURES AND
TITLES OF PROPER OFFICERS

AUTOMOBILE                                          A925                                          GU 4208
                      SOUND-REPRODUCING OR RECORDING EQUIPMENT EXCLUDED                         (Ed. 5-70)

This endorsement, effective ........................................................... , forms a part of policy No.
                              (12:01 A.M., standard time)

issued to

by
                              ...................................................................
                                              Authorized Representative

It is agreed that such insurance as is afforded by the policy under the Physical Damage Coverages is subject to the following additional
exclusions:

The insurance does not apply:

(1) to loss of or damage to any device or instrument designed for the recording, reproduction, or recording and reproduction of sound unless
such device or instrument is permanently installed in the automobile;

(2) to loss of or damage to any tape, wire, record disc or other medium for use with any device or instrument designed for the recording, reproduction, or recording and reproduction of sound.

---

AUTOMOBILE                                          A 888                                          AL 8831
                       UNINSURED MOTORISTS COVERAGE AMENDMENT                                    (Ed. 9-67)
                                        (Insolvent Insurer)

This endorsement, effective ........................................................... , forms a part of policy No.
                              (12:01 A. M., standard time)

issued to

by
                              ...................................................................
                                              Authorized Representative

It is agreed that the term "uninsured automobile" includes an automobile with respect to which there is a bodily injury liability insurance
policy applicable at the time of the accident but the company writing the same is or becomes insolvent.

---

AUTOMOBILE                                          A 895                                          GU 8916
                            NAUA No. 231 — Edition, January, 1968                                (Ed. 1-68)
                           AMENDMENT OF TERMINATION PROVISIONS

This endorsement, effective ........................................................... , forms a part of policy No.
                              (12:01 A. M., standard time)

issued to

by
                              ...................................................................
                                              Authorized Representative

It is agreed that:

A. The first paragraph of the "Cancellation" Condition is replaced by the
following:

This policy may be cancelled by the insured named in Item 1 of the
declarations by surrender thereof to the company or any of its authorized agents or by mailing to the company written notice stating when
thereafter the cancellation shall be effective.

This policy may be cancelled by the company by mailing to the insured
named in Item 1 of the declarations at the address shown in this
policy, written notice stating when not less than twenty days thereafter such cancellation shall be effective; provided that,

1. if the named insured fails to discharge when due any of his obligations in connection with the payment of premium for this policy or
any installment thereof, whether payable directly to the company
or its agent or indirectly under any premium finance plan c extension of credit, or

2. if this policy has been in effect less than sixty days at the time
notice of cancellation is mailed and this is not a renewal policy,

this policy may be cancelled by the company by mailing to such insured
written notice stating when not less than ten days thereafter such
cancellation shall be effective.

The mailing of notice as aforesaid shall be sufficient proof of notice.
The time of surrender or the effective date and hour of cancellation
stated in the notice shall become the end of the policy period. Delivery
of such written notice either by such insured or by the company shall
be equivalent to mailing.

B. The following Condition is added or, if the policy contains a Condition
so entitled, such Condition is replaced by the following:

Cancellation by Company Limited
After this policy has been in effect for sixty days or, if this policy is
a renewal, effective immediately, the company shall not exercise its
right to cancel the insurance unless:

1. the named insured fails to discharge when due any of his obligations in connection with the payment of premium for this policy or
any installment thereof, whether payable directly to the company
or its agent or indirectly under any premium finance plan or extension of credit; or

2. the driver's license or motor vehicle registration of the named
insured or of any other operator who either resides in the same
household or customarily operates an automobile insured under
this policy has been under suspension or revocation during the

policy period (or, if this policy is a renewal, during its policy period
or the 180 days immediately preceding its effective date);
provided that the company shall have the right to modify any physical
damage coverage afforded by this policy (except coverage for loss
caused by collision) by inclusion of a deductible not exceeding $100.
This agreement shall apply to each successive policy period for which
the company consents to renew or continue this policy but nothing
herein shall obligate the company to renew or continue this policy
beyond the expiration of any annual period commencing with its original effective date; provided that, if this policy is written without a
fixed expiration date or for a period longer than one year, this
policy may be terminated by the company for any cause effective on
the expiration of any such annual period by mailing to the insured
named in Item 1 of the declarations at the address shown in this
policy, written notice of such termination not less than twenty days
prior to the expiration of such annual period. The mailing of notice as
aforesaid shall be sufficient proof of notice. Delivery of such written
notice by the company shall be equivalent to mailing.

C. The following Condition is added:

Renewal
If this policy is written for a policy period of less than one year, the
company agrees that it will not refuse to renew except as of the expiration of a policy period which coincides with the end of an annual
period commencing with its original effective date.

If the company elects not to renew this policy, it shall mail to the
insured named in Item 1 of the declarations, at the address shown in
this policy, written notice of such nonrenewal not less than twenty
days prior to the expiration date; provided that, notwithstanding the
failure of the company to comply with the foregoing provisions of this
paragraph, this policy shall terminate

1. on such expiration date, if
(a) the named insured has failed to discharge when due any of
his obligations in connection with the payment of premium
for this policy or any installment thereof, whether payable
directly to the company or its agent or indirectly under any
premium finance plan or extension of credit, or
(b) the company has by any means manifested its willingness to
renew to the named insured or his representative, or

2. on the effective date of any other automobile insurance policy,
with respect to any automobile designated in both policies.
The mailing of notice as aforesaid shall be sufficient proof of notice.
Delivery of such written notice by the company shall be equivalent to
mailing.

681

# Author Index

**683**

# Subject Index

Inherent vice, 567, 630
Injunction Bond, 610
Injury, definition in health insurance, 267
Inland marine insurance
   Annual Transit Policy, 542
   Antique Floater Policy, 400
   Camera Dealers Policy, 544
   Camera Floater Policy, 399
   Coin Collection Floater, 401
   Contractors Equipment Floater, 543
   Fine Arts Floater Policy, 400
   Floor Plan Merchandise Form, 544
   Fur Floater Policy, 398
   Furriers Block Policy, 545
   Golfers Equipment Floater, 543
   Installation Floater Policy, 543
   Installment Sales Floater, 544
   Jeweler's Block Policy, 544
   Jewelry Floater Policy, 398
   Motor Truck Cargo Policy, 568
   Musical Instruments Dealers Policy, 544
   Musical Instruments Floater Policy, 401
   Parcel Post Policy, 542
   Personal Property Floater, 401
   Silverware Floater, 399
   Stamp Collection Floater, 401
   Trip Transit Policy, 542
   Wedding Present Floater, 401
Installation Floater, 543
Installment refund annuity, 173
Installment Sales Floater, 544
Institute of Life Insurance, 83
Insurable interest, 631
   as a limit of recovery, 135
   defined, 135
   in life insurance, 136, 161
   in property insurance, 136
   when it must exist, 136
   who has an insurable interest, 137
   why required, 135
Insurable risk, elements of, 36
Insurable value, 138
Insurance
   as a last resort, 57
   basic purposes of social, 39, 292
   channels of distribution, 79
   competition in, 84
   defined from individual's viewpoint, 25
   defined from society's viewpoint, 35
   distinguished from gambling, 39

Insurance (*continued*)
   fields of, 39
   government regulation of, 110
   history of, 65
   private, 39
   reasons for government regulation of, 110
   *See also* Automobile insurance, Consequential loss insurance, Crime insurance, Health insurance, Inland marine insurance, Liability insurance coverages and Property insurance
Insurance agents, *See* Agents
Insurance and gambling, 36
Insurance and risk management, 56
Insurance Buyers of New York, 50
Insurance commissioner, 116
Insurance Company of North America, 67
Insurance contracts
   as aleatory contracts, 146
   as contracts of adhesion, 146
   as contracts of indemnity, 134
   as contracts of utmost good faith, 146
   as personal contracts, 144
   as unilateral contracts, 145
   characteristics of, 111
   competent parties and, 132
   defined, 130
   duty of insured to read, 146
   essentials of, 130
   legal principles underlying, 130
   offer and acceptance, 131
   oral, validity of, 131
   *See also* kinds of coverage, such as Health insurance, Life insurance, etc.
Insurance management, 49
Insurance pricing, problems in, 93
Insurance rate, 93
Insurance versus bonding, 46
Insurers
   accounting, 99
   alien, 115
   assets of, 64
   capital stock, 71
   classification of, 71
   domestic, 115, 627
   financial solvency of, 60
   foreign, 115
   functions of, 89
   investments of, 98
   liabilities of, 100

474